Advancements in Optical Measurement Devices and Technologies

Advancements in Optical Measurement Devices and Technologies

Guest Editors

Michele Norgia

Rahul Kumar

MDPI

Basel • Beijing • Wuhan • Barcelona • Belgrade • Novi Sad • Cluj • Manchester

Guest Editors

Michele Norgia
Dipartimento di Elettronica,
Informazione e Bioingegneria
Politecnico di Milano
Milano
Italy

Rahul Kumar
Department of Engineering
and Computing
University of Chichester
Bognor Regis
UK

Editorial Office
MDPI AG
Grosspeteranlage 5
4052 Basel, Switzerland

This is a reprint of the Special Issue, published open access by the journal *Metrology* (ISSN 2673-8244), freely accessible at: https://www.mdpi.com/journal/metrology/special_issues/01RZT1P1XN.

For citation purposes, cite each article independently as indicated on the article page online and as indicated below:

Lastname, A.A.; Lastname, B.B. Article Title. *Journal Name* **Year**, *Volume Number*, Page Range.

ISBN 978-3-7258-7050-9 (Hbk)
ISBN 978-3-7258-7051-6 (PDF)
https://doi.org/10.3390/books978-3-7258-7051-6

Contents

About the Editors

Michele Norgia

Michele Norgia is a Professor at the Dipartimento di Elettronica, Informazione e Bioingegneria (DEIB), Politecnico di Milano, Italy. His research activities focus on optical measurement systems, laser-based sensing technologies, interferometry, optoelectronic instrumentation, and metrological applications in industrial and scientific environments. He has contributed extensively to the development of advanced optical sensors and measurement techniques, with particular interest in precision displacement and vibration measurements, optical signal processing, and photonic instrumentation. Prof. Dr. Norgia has authored numerous peer-reviewed journal publications and has actively participated in national and international research projects in the field of optical metrology. His academic work supports the advancement of modern measurement technologies for high-accuracy monitoring and quality control applications.

Rahul Kumar

Rahul Kumar is the Academic Lead of Engineering and a Senior Lecturer in Electrical and Electronics Engineering at the University of Chichester, United Kingdom. He holds a PhD in Optics from Northumbria University and has significant experience in applied photonics, optical sensing, and measurement technologies. His research interests include optical fiber sensors, photonic devices, advanced instrumentation, and experimental techniques for precision measurement in engineering applications. Dr. Kumar has been involved in interdisciplinary research and innovation projects, with a strong focus on practical implementation of optical measurement methods for real-world industrial and academic use. He is actively engaged in higher education leadership and international academic collaboration, supporting the development of research-led teaching and impactful engineering research.

metrology

MDPI

Editorial

Closing Editorial: Advancements in Optical Measurement Devices and Technologies

Rahul Kumar [1,*] and Michele Norgia [2,*]

[1] Department of Engineering, Tech Park, Bognor Regis Campus, University of Chichester, Bognor Regis PO21 1HR, UK
[2] Dipartimento di Elettronica, Informazione e Bioingegneria, Politecnico di Milano, Via Ponzio 34/5, 20133 Milano, Italy
* Correspondence: rahul.kumar@chi.ac.uk (R.K.); michele.norgia@polimi.it (M.N.)

1. Introduction

Optical measurement technologies have emerged as indispensable tools in modern metrology, offering precision, noninvasive measurement capabilities, and remarkable versatility across diverse scientific and industrial applications [1,2]. The field of optical metrology encompasses a wide range of techniques, from classical interferometry to quantum-enhanced measurements, each contributing to our ability to measure physical quantities with ever-increasing accuracy [3]. As we enter an era defined by the second quantum revolution, optical measurement devices are at the forefront of technological innovation, enabling breakthroughs in fields ranging from fundamental physics to advanced manufacturing [4,5].

The Special Issue entitled "Advancements in Optical Measurement Devices and Technologies" was conceived to provide a comprehensive platform for disseminating cutting-edge research in this rapidly evolving field. We present the successful conclusion of this Special Issue, which has attracted 12 high-quality research contributions from leading international research groups. These articles collectively address the critical challenges and opportunities in optical metrology, spanning fundamental research to practical applications, which have garnered over 23,000 views in a few months, demonstrating the strong engagement of and relevance to the broader scientific community.

2. An Overview of Published Articles

The contributions to this Special Issue encompass several thematic areas that represent the current state of the art and emerging directions in optical measurement technologies.

2.1. Quantum Metrology and Frequency Standards

The pursuit of high measurement precision has driven the development of quantum-based measurement standards. Quantum metrology exploits quantum mechanical phenomena to surpass classical measurement limits, with optical frequency standards representing some of the most successful applications [6,7]. The democratization of quantum technologies, particularly the development of compact optical frequency standards suitable for medium-sized national metrology institutes, addresses a critical need in global metrology infrastructure. This trend toward accessibility shows promise for expanding participation in the development and use of precision measurements beyond traditional large-scale facilities, fostering broader innovation in quantum-enhanced metrology [8].

 https://doi.org/10.3390/metrology6010014

2.2. Interferometry: Evolution and Innovation

Interferometric techniques have been the cornerstone of precision optical measurements for over a century, yet they continue to evolve through new approaches and refinements [9,10]. The field encompasses both fundamental advances in measurement principles and practical improvements in system design and component quality. Contemporary research has addressed the long-standing challenges in interferometric measurements, including the minimization of systematic errors, enhancement in measurement sensitivity, and extension of measurement ranges. The investigation of gauge-invariant optical scatterers and the analysis of measurement inconsistencies in various interferometer configurations exemplify the ongoing efforts to perfect these essential measurement tools [11].

2.3. Spectroscopy and Molecular Analysis

Spectroscopic methods continue to be revolutionized through advances in optical technologies and computational capabilities [12]. The integration of extensive parallelism in spectroscopic measurements represents a paradigm shift, enabling substantially higher measurement throughput and sensitivity. Modern spectroscopic techniques, including dual-comb spectroscopy and frequency-comb-based methods, have transformed molecular analysis capabilities, opening new possibilities in chemical sensing, environmental monitoring, and biomedical diagnostics [13,14]. The ability to perform rapid, high-resolution spectral measurements across broad wavelength ranges has profound implications for fundamental research and practical applications.

2.4. Photonic Devices and Components

The performance of optical measurement systems fundamentally depends on the quality and characteristics of photonic components [15]. Research in this area has focused on understanding and optimizing the optical losses, reflectivity characteristics, and other performance parameters of photonic devices. Resonant photonic cavities, in particular, play crucial roles in enhancing measurement sensitivity and enabling novel measurement modalities. The development of accurate simulation tools and analytical approaches for predicting device performance directly contributes to the design of more sensitive and efficient optical sensors [16].

2.5. Industrial Metrology and Quality Control

The application of optical measurement technologies in industrial settings addresses critical needs for non-destructive evaluation, in-line quality control, and precision manufacturing [17,18]. As manufacturing processes advance toward smaller features and more complex geometries, the demand for high-resolution, non-contact measurement techniques has intensified. Optical methods offer unique advantages in measuring micro- and nanostructures, characterizing surface properties, and ensuring dimensional accuracy in advanced manufacturing processes. The integration of multiple optical techniques and the development of intelligent measurement strategies have enhanced the robustness and versatility of industrial metrology systems [19].

2.6. Three-Dimensional Metrology

Three-dimensional optical measurement techniques, including fringe projection, structured light, and laser scanning methods, have become essential in numerous applications [20]. These techniques enable the rapid, non-contact, and high-accuracy acquisition of complex surface geometries. Ongoing research is focusing on increasing measurement accuracy, extending measurement ranges, and enhancing system robustness against environmental disturbances. The integration of vision-based characterization with mechanical

https://doi.org/10.3390/metrology6010014

system analysis exemplifies the multidisciplinary approach needed to achieve optimal measurement performance [21].

2.7. Biomedical Applications

Optical measurement technologies have been extensively applied in biomedical research and clinical diagnostics, offering non-invasive methods for tissue characterization, blood flow measurement, and functional imaging [22]. Photoacoustic techniques, in particular, combine the high contrast of optical absorption with the deep penetration of ultrasound, enabling novel measurement capabilities. The investigation of factors affecting measurement accuracy in biomedical applications, such as particle concentration effects in flow measurements, contributes to the development of more reliable diagnostic tools [23].

2.8. Accessible and Cost-Effective Technologies

Recognizing the importance of democratizing the access to precision measurement capabilities, research efforts have focused on developing cost-effective optical measurement devices using readily available components [24]. The integration of smartphones and embedded devices as measurement platforms represents an innovative approach to increasing the accessibility of optical metrology for educational purposes and resource-limited settings. These developments align with broader efforts to ensure that the benefits of advanced measurement technologies reach the wider communities.

3. Impact and Future Directions

The research presented in this Special Issue demonstrates the inherently interdisciplinary nature of optical metrology, with contributions spanning physics, engineering, materials science, and biomedical research. This cross-pollination of ideas and methodologies enriches the field and accelerates innovation. The strong readership engagement, with over 23,000 views, reflects the broad relevance of optical measurement technologies and the importance of the open-access dissemination of research findings.

Looking forward, several key directions emerge for future development in optical metrology:

Quantum-Enhanced Measurements: The continued advancement of quantum technologies promises improvements in measurement precision. The trend toward more compact and accessible quantum systems will democratize these capabilities, enabling broader participation in quantum-enhanced metrology [25].

Artificial Intelligence Integration: The incorporation of machine learning and artificial intelligence techniques for data analysis, system optimization, and real-time adaptive measurements will markedly enhance the capabilities of optical measurement systems [26].

Multimodal and Multiscale Measurements: The integration of optical techniques with complementary measurement modalities and the development of systems capable of operating across multiple length scales will address the increasingly complex measurement challenges in materials science, biology, and nanotechnology [27].

Sustainability and Accessibility: The development of energy-efficient, cost-effective optical measurement solutions will support broader adoption and enable precision metrology in resource-limited settings, contributing to global technological equity [28].

4. Conclusions

This Special Issue entitled "Advancements in Optical Measurement Devices and Technologies" provides a comprehensive overview of the current research frontiers in optical metrology. The published contributions demonstrate the breadth and vitality of this field, from fundamental quantum standards to practical industrial applications. The

https://doi.org/10.3390/metrology6010014

articles collectively showcase the continued evolution of optical measurement techniques and their critical role in advancing science, technology, and industry.

We express our sincere gratitude to all contributing authors for their research, to the reviewers for their thorough and constructive feedback, and to the editorial team of *Metrology* for their professional support throughout this project. We are confident that the research presented in this Special Issue will serve as a valuable resource for the scientific community and inspire continued innovation in precision measurement science.

Conflicts of Interest: The authors declare no conflicts of interest.

List of Contributions: The following is the list of articles published in this Special Issue (they are not cited in the text; the order is alphabetical):

1. Burkert, S.; Schwörer, L.; Schubert, T.; Grundmann, J.; Stein, D.; Heinrich, A. Investigation of the Measurement Systems' Suitability for the Non-Destructive Measurement of Complex Polymer-Based Micro and Nanostructures. *Metrology* **2024**, *4*, 673–694. https://doi.org/10.3390/metrology4040040.
2. Dohmen, M.; Heinrich, A.; Neumann, C. Polar Fitting and Hermite Interpolation for Freeform Droplet Geometry Measurement. *Metrology* **2025**, *5*, 56. https://doi.org/10.3390/metrology5030056.
3. Ferreira, P.H.D.; do Amaral, D.R.; Tribuzi, V.; Marroquin, J.F.R.; Felix, J.F.; Ghiglieno, F. Reflectivity Thresholds and Optical Loss Predictions in Resonant Photonic Cavities. *Metrology* **2024**, *4*, 765–775. https://doi.org/10.3390/metrology4040044.
4. Ito, S.; Yamagishi, T.; Matsumoto, A.; Kamiya, K. Investigation and Improvement of Inconsistency in Surface-Form Measurement Results Due to Difference of Incident Direction of Measuring Light in Abramson-Type Oblique-Incident Interferometer. *Metrology* **2025**, *5*, 34. https://doi.org/10.3390/metrology5020034.
5. Juarez-Salazar, R.; Esquivel-Hernandez, S.; Diaz-Ramirez, V.H. Optical Fringe Projection: A Straightforward Approach to 3D Metrology. *Metrology* **2025**, *5*, 47. https://doi.org/10.3390/metrology5030047.
6. Kaal, J.; Feltin, N.; Lelong, M.; Yin, H.; Glidle, A.; Romieu, K.; Batista, E. Comparison of Measurement Protocols for Internal Channels of Transparent Microfluidic Devices. *Metrology* **2025**, *5*, 4. https://doi.org/10.3390/metrology5010004.
7. Li, J.; Fernandez, R.; Gutierrez, B.; Pedersen, J.; Zhou, Y. Advancing Molecular Spectroscopy Efficiency with Extensive Parallelism. *Metrology* **2024**, *4*, 736–764. https://doi.org/10.3390/metrology4040043.
8. Loose, J.; Hales, S.H.; Kendell, J.; Cutler, I.; Ruth, R.; Redd, J.; Lino, S.; Munro, T. An Inexpensive, 3D-Printable, Arduino- and Blu-Ray-Based Confocal Laser and Fluorescent Scanning Microscope. *Metrology* **2025**, *5*, 2. https://doi.org/10.3390/metrology5010002.
9. Lopez-Medina, F.; Núñez-Lopez, J.A.; Sergiyenko, O.; Molina-Quiroz, D.; Sepulveda-Valdez, C.; Herrera-Garcia, J.R.; Tyrsa, V.; Alaniz-Plata, R. Vision-Based Characterization of Gear Transmission Mechanisms to Improve 3D Laser Scanner Accuracy. *Metrology* **2025**, *5*, 58. https://doi.org/10.3390/metrology5040058.
10. Palos, A.; Caballero, I.; de Mercado, D.; Álvarez, Y.; Peral, D.; Díaz de Aguilar, J. Towards the Development of an Optical Quantum Frequency Standard Feasible for a Medium-Size NMI. *Metrology* **2025**, *5*, 75. https://doi.org/10.3390/metrology5040075.
11. Schwarze, C.R.; Manni, A.D.; Simon, D.S.; Ndao, A.; Sergienko, A.V. Next-Generation Interferometry with Gauge-Invariant Linear Optical Scatterers. *Metrology* **2025**, *5*, 65. https://doi.org/10.3390/metrology5040065.
12. Tsuboi, H.; Kaizuka, T.; Shirai, K. Effect of Dispersed Particle Concentration on Photoacoustic Flowmetry Using Low-Frequency Transducers. *Metrology* **2025**, *5*, 79. https://doi.org/10.3390/metrology5040079.

https://doi.org/10.3390/metrology6010014

References

1. Gao, W.; Kim, S.W.; Bosse, H.; Haitjema, H.; Chen, Y.L.; Lu, X.D.; Knapp, W.; Weckenmann, A.; Estler, W.T.; Kunzmann, H. Measurement technologies for precision positioning. *CIRP Ann.* **2015**, *64*, 773–796. [CrossRef]
2. Hecht, E. *Optics*, 5th ed.; Pearson: London, UK, 2017.
3. Diddams, S.A.; Vahala, K.; Udem, T. Optical frequency combs: Coherently uniting the electromagnetic spectrum. *Science* **2020**, *369*, eaay3676. [CrossRef]
4. Ludlow, A.D.; Boyd, M.M.; Ye, J.; Peik, E.; Schmidt, P.O. Optical atomic clocks. *Rev. Mod. Phys.* **2015**, *87*, 637–701. [CrossRef]
5. Acín, A.; Bloch, I.; Buhrman, H.; Calarco, T.; Eichler, C.; Eisert, J.; Esteve, D.; Gisin, N.; Glaser, S.J.; Jelezko, F.; et al. The quantum technologies roadmap: A European community view. *New J. Phys.* **2018**, *20*, 080201. [CrossRef]
6. Pezzè, L.; Smerzi, A.; Oberthaler, M.K.; Schmied, R.; Treutlein, P. Quantum metrology with nonclassical states of atomic ensembles. *Rev. Mod. Phys.* **2018**, *90*, 035005. [CrossRef]
7. Bothwell, T.; Kennedy, C.J.; Aeppli, A.; Kedar, D.; Robinson, J.M.; Oelker, E.; Staron, A.; Ye, J. Resolving the gravitational redshift across a millimetre-scale atomic sample. *Nature* **2022**, *602*, 420–424. [CrossRef] [PubMed]
8. Riehle, F. Optical clock networks. *Nat. Photonics* **2017**, *11*, 25–31. [CrossRef]
9. Hariharan, P. *Basics of Interferometry*, 2nd ed.; Academic Press: Burlington, MA, USA, 2007.
10. Wyant, J.C. Advances in interferometric optical profiling. *Int. J. Mach. Tools Manuf.* **1998**, *38*, 691–698. [CrossRef]
11. Schmit, J.; Creath, K.; Wyant, J.C. Surface profilers, multiple wavelength, and white light interfer ometry. In *Optical Shop Testing*, 3rd ed.; Malacara, D., Ed.; Wiley: Hoboken, NJ, USA, 2007; pp. 667–755.
12. Picqué, N.; Hänsch, T.W. Frequency comb spectroscopy. *Nat. Photonics* **2019**, *13*, 146–157. [CrossRef]
13. Coddington, I.; Newbury, N.; Swann, W. Dual-comb spectroscopy. *Optica* **2016**, *3*, 414–426. [CrossRef]
14. Fortier, T.; Baumann, E. 20 years of developments in optical frequency comb technology and applications. *Commun. Phys.* **2019**, *2*, 153. [CrossRef]
15. Vahala, K.J. Optical microcavities. *Nature* **2003**, *424*, 839–846. [CrossRef]
16. Bogaerts, W.; Pérez, D.; Capmany, J.; Miller, D.A.B.; Poon, J.; Englund, D.; Morichetti, F.; Melloni, A. Programmable photonic circuits. *Nature* **2020**, *586*, 207–216. [CrossRef]
17. Leach, R. *Optical Measurement of Surface Topography*; Springer: Berlin/Heidelberg, Germany, 2011.
18. Gao, W.; Haitjema, H.; Fang, F.Z.; Leach, R.K.; Cheung, C.F.; Savio, E.; Linares, J.M. On-machine and in-process surface metrology for precision manufacturing. *CIRP Ann.* **2019**, *68*, 843–866. [CrossRef]
19. Fang, F.Z.; Zhang, X.D.; Weckenmann, A.; Zhang, G.X.; Evans, C. Manufacturing and measurement of freeform optics. *CIRP Ann.* **2013**, *62*, 823–846. [CrossRef]
20. Gorthi, S.S.; Rastogi, P. Fringe projection techniques: Whither we are? *Opt. Lasers Eng.* **2010**, *48*, 133–140. [CrossRef]
21. Zhang, S. High-speed 3D shape measurement with structured light methods: A review. *Opt. Lasers Eng.* **2018**, *106*, 119–131. [CrossRef]
22. Wang, L.V.; Hu, S. Photoacoustic tomography: In vivo imaging from organelles to organs. *Science* **2012**, *335*, 1458–1462. [CrossRef]
23. Beard, P. Biomedical photoacoustic imaging. *Interface Focus* **2011**, *1*, 602–631. [CrossRef]
24. Sung, Y.; Campa, F.; Shih, W.C. Open-source do-it-yourself multi-color fluorescence smartphone microscopy. *Biomed. Opt. Express* **2017**, *8*, 5075–5086. [CrossRef] [PubMed]
25. Degen, C.L.; Reinhard, F.; Cappellaro, P. Quantum sensing. *Rev. Mod. Phys.* **2017**, *89*, 035002. [CrossRef]
26. Krenn, M.; Malik, M.; Fickler, R.; Lapkiewicz, R.; Zeilinger, A. Automated search for new quantum experiments. *Phys. Rev. Lett.* **2016**, *116*, 090405. [CrossRef] [PubMed]
27. Leach, R.K.; Boyd, R.; Burke, T.; Danzebrink, H.U.; Dirscherl, K.; Dziomba, T.; Gee, M.; Koenders, L.; Morazzani, V.; Pidduck, A.; et al. The European nanometrology landscape. *Nanotechnology* **2011**, *22*, 062001. [CrossRef] [PubMed]
28. Lloyd, S.; Mohseni, M.; Rebentrost, P. Quantum principal component analysis. *Nat. Phys.* **2014**, *10*, 631–633. [CrossRef]

https://doi.org/10.3390/metrology6010014

metrology

Review

Advancing Molecular Spectroscopy Efficiency with Extensive Parallelism

Jiaqi Li [1,†], Rodrigo Fernandez [2,†], Bernardo Gutierrez [2], Jan Pedersen [1] and Yan Zhou [2,*]

[1] Department of Computer Science, University of Nevada, Las Vegas, NV 89154, USA; lij50@unlv.nevada.edu (J.L.); matt.pedersen@unlv.edu (J.P.)
[2] Department of Physics and Astronomy, University of Nevada, Las Vegas, NV 89154, USA; ferna233@unlv.nevada.edu (R.F.); gutieb3@unlv.nevada.edu (B.G.)
[*] Correspondence: yan.zhou@unlv.edu; Tel.: +1-702-895-3084
[†] These authors contributed equally to this work.

Abstract: Molecular spectroscopy, with a legacy spanning over a century, has profoundly enriched our understanding of the microscopic world, driving major advancements across science and engineering. Over time, this field has steadily advanced, incorporating innovations such as lasers and digital computers to reach new levels of precision and sensitivity. Over the past decade, the integration of high-speed embedded electronic systems and advanced light sources has ushered molecular spectroscopy into a new era, characterized by extensive parallelism and enhanced sensitivity. This review delves into two pioneering technologies that embody recent advancements in molecular spectroscopy: Chirped-Pulse Fourier Transform Microwave (CP-FTMW) spectroscopy and optical frequency comb (OFC) spectroscopy. We provide an overview of the fundamental principles behind these methods, examine their most impactful applications across diverse fields, and discuss their potential to drive future developments in molecular spectroscopy. By highlighting these technologies, we aim to underscore the transformative impact of integrating high-speed digital electronics and advanced light sources with molecular spectroscopy, enabling extensive parallelism and paving the way for groundbreaking discoveries and innovations in this rapidly evolving field.

Keywords: molecular spectroscopy; chirped-pulsed Fourier transform microwave spectroscopy (CP-FTMW); optical frequency comb (OFC) spectroscopy; parallelism

1. Introduction

Molecular spectroscopy, which investigates the interaction between matter and electromagnetic radiation, has a rich history marked by groundbreaking experiments that have profoundly deepened our understanding of the microscopic world. These studies have illuminated the fundamental characteristics and quantum properties of molecules. From the early 20th century, when scientists first analyzed molecular spectra to reveal chemical compositions and molecular structures, to the mid-20th century's introduction of laser spectroscopy—which dramatically enhanced precision—the field has consistently remained at the forefront of scientific innovation. Each technological and methodological advancement has expanded our knowledge of molecular structures and dynamics, playing a pivotal role in the progression of the physical sciences. This continuous evolution reflects the intrinsic curiosity that drives scientific inquiry and underscores the central role of molecular spectroscopy in uncovering the universe's complexities at its most fundamental level.

Over the past few decades, groundbreaking advancements in molecular spectroscopy have significantly expanded the scope of scientific research, particularly by improving spectroscopic accuracy [1–4] and increasing detection sensitivity [5–9]. The field is also experiencing a profound shift toward quantum control of molecular systems [10–14]. This transition from passive observation to active manipulation of molecular behavior is opening up exciting possibilities for uncovering novel physical phenomena. Additional key advancements include (1) the development of rapid data acquisition, facilitating the real-time analysis of complex molecular interactions [15,16]; (2) the integration of Artificial Intelligence (AI), enhancing data interpretation and key information extraction [17,18]; and (3) the progress of portable spectroscopic devices, marking a leap beyond traditional laboratory settings [19,20]. Together, these breakthroughs are expanding the scope of molecular spectroscopy and paving the way for transformative discoveries across a wide range of scientific disciplines.

This review highlights two cutting-edge technologies that have become prominent in molecular spectroscopy: Chirped-Pulse Fourier Transform Microwave (CP-FTMW) spectroscopy and optical frequency comb (OFC) spectroscopy. These innovative techniques leverage broad excitation sources, enabling extensive parallel measurements and marking a substantial shift from the narrowband sources traditionally used in microwave and laser spectroscopy. This multiplexing capability significantly improves experimental efficiency, allowing for more comprehensive data collection in a shorter time frame.

The primary aim of this paper is not to provide a comprehensive history of molecular spectroscopy. Instead, our focus is on highlighting recent frequency synthesis methods that have driven significant advancements in the field. These innovations have catalyzed substantial scientific progress across a range of disciplines, including physics, chemistry, biology, and environmental science.

2. CP-FTMW Spectroscopy

Microwave spectroscopy is a benchmark technique for identifying molecular species and determining molecular structures. With a spectroscopic resolution of approximately 0.1 MHz, it offers a resolution 3–4 orders of magnitude higher than traditional laser spectroscopy, allowing for the precise extraction of essential molecular constants, such as rotational constants, hyperfine splittings, and isotope shifts [21–24]. In addition to high resolution, detection sensitivity and data acquisition speed are crucial factors, which determine the experimental efficiency. Traditional instruments, such as the Balle–Flygare Fourier transform microwave (BF-FTMW) spectrometer, achieve enhanced sensitivity by employing a high-quality (high-Q) resonant cavity, which traps the microwave field, allowing repeated interactions with the sample and thus improving signal strength [25]. However, the narrowband excitation pulse, typically around 1 MHz, limits the speed of spectral acquisition. Capturing a spectrum with multiple rotational transitions requires extensive frequency scanning, often involving thousands of steps, which is time-consuming and susceptible to intensity fluctuations caused by variations in the molecular source or state preparation.

To address the slow data acquisition limitations of traditional BF-FTMW spectrometers, a fast tunable or broadband microwave source is essential. Developed in the 1950s, the backward-wave oscillator (BWO) is a high-power, tunable continuous-wave (CW) microwave source with a broad frequency range, making it suitable for applications requiring stable and precise frequency control, such as microwave spectroscopy and radar [26–29]. Compared to BF-FTMW sources, the BWO offers much faster frequency tuning rates, typically on the order of milliseconds. Recent advancements have extended its operating frequencies into the THz range, achieving continuous tunability of approximately 100 GHz [30]. While the BWO is primarily used in continuous frequency-scanning mode, some experiments have demonstrated its potential for broadband excitation in the time domain, which could further expand its range of applications [31].

At the beginning of the 21st century, advances in high-speed digital electronics led to the development of a transformative technology: the CP-FTMW spectrometer, pioneered by Pate's group at the University of Virginia [32–34]. Unlike the BWO source, which typically operates in CW mode, the CP-FTMW spectrometer generates extremely short pulses, typically in the sub-microsecond range, with a bandwidth exceeding 10 GHz. This broadband excitation allows for the simultaneous recording of multiple molecular transitions, significantly enhancing the data acquisition speed. Moreover, digital frequency synthesis enables the CP-FTMW spectrometer to generate arbitrary frequency patterns with precise phase control, yielding highly accurate phase information. In addition to these advantages, the CP-FTMW spectrometer is significantly lighter and more portable than the bulky, high-power-consuming BWO system, making it ideal for on-site applications in both scientific and industrial settings.

2.1. CP-FTMW Spectrometer

The CP-FTMW spectrometer eliminates the need for frequency stepping, allowing the rapid acquisition of high-resolution broadband spectra. This capability is realized through four key aspects:

- The approach of using rapid frequency sweeps to generate strong polarization was first demonstrated by McGurk, Schmalz, and Flygare in 1974 [35]. At that time, however, technological limitations made it difficult to quickly adjust microwave frequencies. To overcome this, they used a ramped electric field to produce a rapid Stark shift sweep, effectively shifting the relative frequency between the microwave signal and the molecular transitions.
- To achieve broadband excitation, the chirped-pulse (CP) approach replaces ultra-short, Fourier-transform-limited pulses, which typically distribute low power across individual frequency components. In contrast, CPs have longer pulse durations ($\sim$1 μs) and wide bandwidths (>10 GHz), providing broad spectral coverage with a more uniform power distribution. High-speed digital Arbitrary Waveform Generators (AWGs) are now commonly used to efficiently generate CPs.
- Molecules polarized by CPs emit a Free-Induction Decay (FID) signal, which can be captured and digitized in the time domain using a high-speed oscilloscope. This FID signal contains information across the entire bandwidth (>10 GHz) in a single-shot measurement. A frequency-domain spectrum is then obtained by applying a fast Fourier transform (FFT) to the FID signal.
- The devices used for generating the CPs and detecting the FID signals are phase-referenced to an accurate frequency standard. This precise synchronization ensures that the phase-reproducible FID signals are coherently averaged in the time domain, resulting in a linear enhancement of the signal-to-noise ratio (SNR).

Building on these advancements, Pate's group developed the first CP-FTMW spectrometer in 2006 [32,33]. This spectrometer generates a one-microsecond CP that linearly sweeps frequencies from 7.5 to 18.5 GHz. As shown in Figure 1, the setup is organized into three main operational components: (1) the CP synthesizer, (2) the interaction zone, and (3) the FID detector. In the interaction zone, a supersonic molecular beam interacts with the CP within a vacuum chamber, where the pressure is kept below 0.01 torr to minimize collisional broadening to less than 100 kHz.

In the CP-FTMW spectrometer, the initial CP is generated by a 4.2 Gs/s AWG, covering a frequency range of 162.5 to 1537.5 MHz. To broaden the CP's bandwidth, the spectrometer employs a series of frequency multiplication and mixing stages, as illustrated in Figure 2a. First, the initial CP is mixed with a 9.9 GHz single-frequency wave from a Phase-locked Dielectric Resonator Oscillator (PDRO). Second, the resulting signals (sum and difference) pass through a bandpass filter to isolate the desired difference frequency. Third, a frequency quadrupler increases both the frequency and bandwidth by a factor of four, extending the range to 33.45–38.95 GHz. Fourth, a second mixer down-converts the frequency to 13.65–19.15 GHz by mixing it with a 19.8 GHz single-frequency wave, generated by doubling the 9.9 GHz signal from the PDRO. Fifth, a frequency doubler further doubles the frequency and bandwidth, resulting in a CP spanning 27.3–38.3 GHz. Finally, a third mixer down-converts the signal to the final range of 7.5–18.5 GHz by mixing it with an additional 19.8 GHz single-frequency wave.

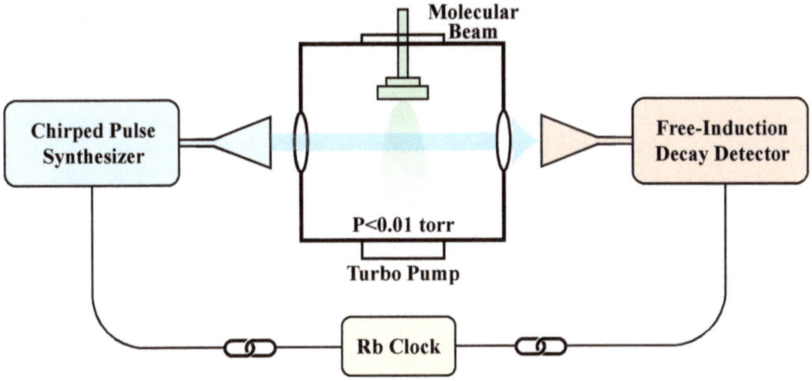

Figure 1. A schematic diagram of the Chirped-Pulse Fourier Transform Microwave (CP-FTMW) spectrometer. Molecules cooled to a few kelvins are generated by a supersonic molecular beam within a vacuum chamber, where the pressure is maintained below 0.01 torr by a turbo pump to minimize collisional broadening. The microwave pulse from the chirped-pulse (CP) synthesizer intersects the molecular beam perpendicularly and is detected by the Free-Induction Decay (FID) detector. Both the CP synthesizer and FID detector are phase-referenced to a rubidium (Rb) clock for phase stability. Teflon lenses are used to seal the vacuum chamber and to collimate the microwave beam.

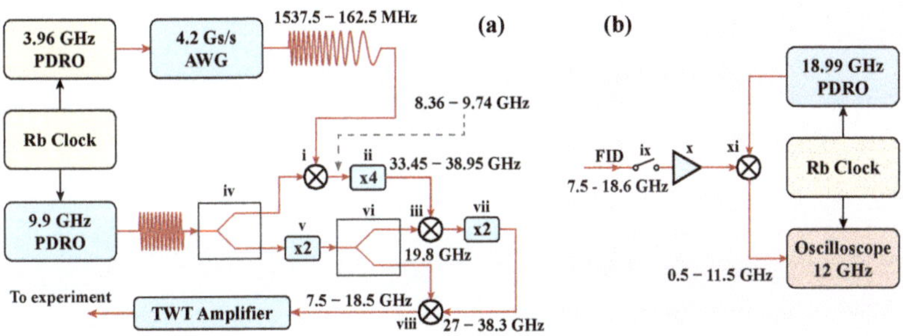

Figure 2. Schematic diagram illustrating (**a**) the synthesis of the chirped pulse (CP) and (**b**) the detection of Free-Induction Decay (FID). Black lines indicate low-frequency radio frequency signals, while red lines represent high-frequency microwave signals transmitted through coaxial cables. AWG: Arbitrary Waveform Generator; TWT: Traveling-Wave Tube; PDRO: Phase-locked Dielectric Resonator Oscillator; i, iii, viii, and xi: frequency mixer; ii: frequency quadrupler; vii and v: frequency doubler; iv and iv: power divider; ix: fast microwave switch; x: power amplifier. Further details are provided in the main text. The figure is adapted from Brown (2006) [32].

Through these processes, the CP's bandwidth expands eightfold, from an initial 1.375 GHz to a final 11 GHz, with sequential mixing steps preserving the bandwidth while shifting the center frequency to approximately 10 GHz. After frequency synthesis, the CP is amplified by a high-power Traveling-Wave Tube (TWT) amplifier, raising its peak power to 2 kW. This amplification is essential for achieving sufficient rotational polarization across the entire 11 GHz frequency range within a one-microsecond window.

To detect the FID signal, a frequency down-conversion circuit is used, as shown in Figure 2b. First, a fast microwave switch eliminates or significantly attenuates the strong CP to prevent the saturation of subsequent components. Second, the FID signal, which follows the CP, is amplified by a low-noise amplifier. Third, the amplified FID signal is down-converted by mixing it with an 18.99 GHz single-frequency wave generated by a PDRO.

Finally, the down-converted signal is digitized using a high-speed oscilloscope with a 12 GHz bandwidth and a sampling rate of 40 Gs/s.

To enable the coherent averaging of FID signals up to several thousand times, all time-critical components—including the AWG, oscilloscope, and PDROs—are phase-referenced to a rubidium clock to ensure precise phase stability. The AWG's versatility is especially valuable, as it supports not only linear frequency sweeps but also complex, arbitrary frequency modulations. This flexibility is essential for tailoring excitation pulses to a wide range of applications beyond spectroscopy, such as coherent quantum control of atoms and molecules [10,36,37].

2.2. Extensions of CP Spectrometers

Since its invention, the CP-FTMW spectrometer, with its unique high-bandwidth capability—four orders of magnitude greater than that of the traditional BF-FTMW spectrometer—has transformed molecular rotational spectroscopy. Over the past decade, substantial technological advancements have been made to extend its applications across diverse scientific fields, including (1) reaching higher frequency ranges and wider bandwidths, (2) developing more cost-effective and compact systems, and (3) hybridizing CP-FTMW and BF-FTMW technologies to improve accuracy and detection sensitivity.

2.2.1. Spectrometers Toward Terahertz Frequencies

In 2011, Field's group at MIT extended CP-FTMW technology into the millimeter-wave domain by leveraging advancements in broadband millimeter-wave amplifiers and heterodyne receivers [38]. This extension is especially beneficial for small molecules with large rotational constants. The Chirped-Pulse millimeter-Wave (CPmmW) spectrometer operates in the 70–102 GHz range, as illustrated in Figure 3.

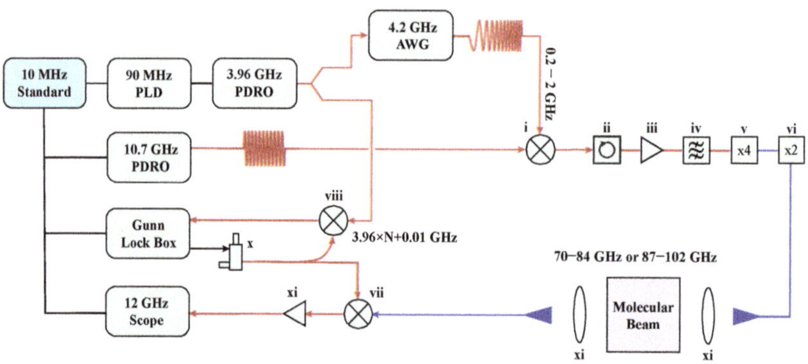

Figure 3. A schematic diagram of the Chirped-Pulse millimeter-Wave (CPmmW) spectrometer. Black lines represent low-frequency radio frequency signals, red lines indicate high-frequency microwave signals in coaxial cables, and blue lines denote high-frequency millimeter-wave signals in waveguides. PLD: Phase-locked Crystal Oscillator; PDRO: Phase-locked Dielectric Resonator Oscillator; i, vii, and viii: frequency mixer; ii: microwave circulator; iii and xi: power amplifier; iv: bandpass filter; v: frequency quadrupler; vi: frequency doubler; x: Gunn diode oscillator; xi: Teflon lens. Further details are provided in the main text. The figure is adapted from Park (2011) [38].

In this configuration, a CP spanning 0.2 to 2 GHz, generated by a 4.2 Gs/s AWG, is mixed with a 10.7 GHz radio frequency (RF) signal from a PDRO in mixer i. This setup retains both the sum (10.9–12.7 GHz) and difference (8.7–10.5 GHz) frequencies. Through an active frequency multiplication chain (v: x4; vi: x2), the CP covers frequencies from 69.6 to 84 GHz and 87.2 to 101.6 GHz, achieving a maximum bandwidth exceeding 28 GHz.

A bandpass filter (iv) allows the selection of a specific frequency range or coverage of the entire bandwidth as needed.

As with its predecessor, the CPmmW spectrometer requires the down-conversion of the detection signal for digitization by an oscilloscope. A Gunn oscillator with a phase-locked loop (PLL) circuit (x), synchronized to a 3.96 GHz PDRO, generates harmonic frequencies of the form 3.96 GHz $\times$ N + 0.01 GHz, where N is an adjustable integer between 18 and 24. For instance, setting N to 20 provides a down-conversion mixer (vii) input at 79.2 GHz, enabling the digitization of frequency components in the ranges of 69.6–84 GHz and 87.2–91.2 GHz using a 12 GHz oscilloscope. To detect higher-frequency components, adjusting N on the Gunn oscillator (e.g., setting N to 23 to obtain 91.08 GHz) allows the detection of frequencies up to 101.6 GHz.

In the coming decade, advancements in high-frequency circuits and opto-electronic hybrid technologies are expected to extend operational frequencies toward, and potentially beyond, one terahertz (THz) [39–43]. This progress could enable the exploration of soft vibrational modes in large polyatomic molecules [44]. Additionally, Chirped-Pulse THz (CP-THz) spectrometers offer substantial potential for improving trace gas sensing due to several key advantages: (1) FID detection is inherently free of background noise, (2) coherent averaging in the time domain linearly improves the SNR, and (3) for small polyatomic molecules, the spectral region around 0.5 THz corresponds closely with the peak of the Boltzmann distribution at room temperature. These attributes make the CP-THz spectrometer especially effective for detecting key atmospheric species, such as nitrous oxide and water vapor, as well as volatile organic compounds like formaldehyde and methanol [34,42,45–47].

2.2.2. Segmented CP Spectrometers

Over the past decade, building on the CP-FTMW technology pioneered by Pate's group, more than a hundred CP spectrometers have been constructed and are actively used for molecular physics research worldwide. However, to broaden its applications—particularly for industrial and on-site research outside of laboratories—the cost of the equipment remains a significant challenge. This is largely due to the expense of the two critical components: the AWG and the oscilloscope, especially those with wider bandwidths. Beyond technical challenges, a fundamental limitation exists in that the polarization amplitude induced by the CP is inversely proportional to the excitation bandwidth [38]. Consequently, for a CP with a bandwidth of 20 GHz or more, the excitation power at each frequency component may be insufficient to polarize the molecules. This issue becomes especially pronounced above 100 GHz, where high-power amplifiers are still limited in both availability and performance.

To advance technology and improve cost efficiency, segmented CP-FTMW spectrometers have been developed using low-cost digital hardware, offering broader frequency coverage at significantly reduced costs [43,48–50]. Instead of generating a single CP with a bandwidth of tens or even hundreds of GHz, this system uses multiple segmented 1 GHz CPs to cover the entire frequency range. The design of the segmented CP-FTMW spectrometer developed in Zhou's group is shown in Figure 4 [49]. This approach achieves substantial cost savings by using low-cost embedded devices, including a Direct Digital Synthesizer (DDS, 0.1–5 GHz), a low-speed AWG (100 MHz), and a moderately fast digitizer (1 GHz) based on Field-Programmable Gate Array (FPGA) technology. Further cost reductions are realized by using the same frequency multiplier chain for both up-conversion and down-conversion processes.

First, a CP with a frequency range f_c = 40–60 MHz, generated by an AWG, is mixed with a tunable f_0 = 3–4 GHz wave from a DDS, producing a signal at $f_i = f_0 \pm f_c$. This signal is then frequency-multiplied by a factor of 24 through an active frequency multiplier chain (ii, iv, and v). The multiplier chain not only up-converts the frequency to the 72–96 GHz range but also expands the CP bandwidth from 40 MHz to approximately 1 GHz, including both the sum and difference frequencies at mixer i. Following the excitation pulse, the

FID radiation is received by a second horn, amplified (x), down-converted via a mixer (xi), and recorded by a fast digitizer with a 1 GHz bandwidth. The DDS frequency can be tuned to adjust the center frequency, which automatically shifts the frequency in the down-conversion arm, keeping the signal within the 1 GHz range of the digitizer. To characterize the frequency of the excitation pulse, the notch filter (iii) can be removed, allowing the detection of beat signals between the CP and the leakage DDS frequency through mixer i.

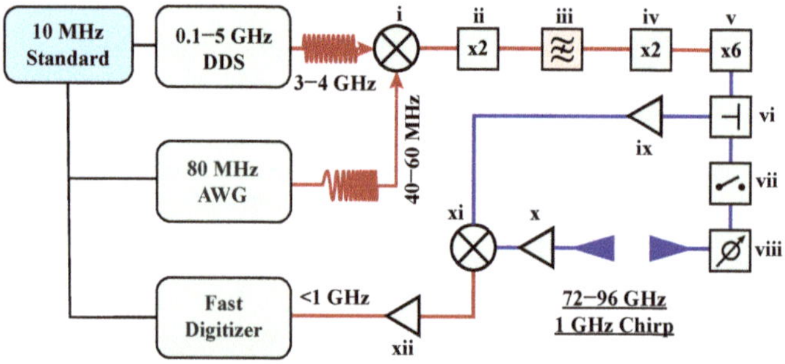

Figure 4. Segmented Chirped-Pulsed millimeter-Wave (CPmmW) spectrometer. Black lines represent low-frequency radio frequency signals, red lines indicate high-frequency microwave signals in coaxial cables, and blue lines denote high-frequency millimeter-wave signals in waveguides. i and xi: frequency mixer; ii and iv: frequency doublers; iii: programmable notch filter; v: frequency sextupler; vi: microwave power divider; vii: fast switch; viii: programmable power attenuator; ix, x, and xii: power amplifiers. DDS: Direct Digital Synthesizer; AWG: Arbitrary Waveform Generator. Further details are provided in the main text.

The complete pulse train, consisting of 24 segments, spans the entire bandwidth from 72 to 96 GHz. While this segmented approach reduces the spectroscopic coverage of a single chirp, it concentrates more power per frequency element, thereby enhancing the strength of the FID signal. Additionally, strategic optimizations—such as adaptive data acquisition, buffered post-data processing, and the use of multiple CPs on a single gas pulse—can improve experimental efficiency. These enhancements have the potential to bring the performance of the segmented spectrometer in line with that of standard CP-FTMW spectrometers while reducing costs by a factor of five to ten. Furthermore, incorporating AI-based algorithms into the data acquisition process could further enhance efficiency by focusing on the most information-rich regions instead of covering the entire bandwidth.

2.2.3. Hybrid of CP-FTMW and BF-FTMW Spectrometers

While the CP-FTMW spectrometer provides a substantial advantage over BF-FTMW spectrometers by capturing spectra across 10 GHz bandwidth, the BF-FTMW approach remains superior in sensitivity for detecting individual transitions, primarily due to its use of high-Q cavities. Moreover, the BF-FTMW spectrometer typically provides higher spectroscopic resolution (several kHz) compared to the CP-FTMW spectrometer (several tens of kHz). This enhanced resolution is also achieved through the high-Q cavity, which traps the coherent microwave field for durations that can exceed the FID decay time. This extended interaction time selectively enhances signals from a subgroup of molecules with longer coherence, partially mitigating inhomogeneous broadening effects such as Doppler broadening and resulting in sharper spectral lines.

While the CP-FTMW spectrometer generally offers slightly lower spectroscopic resolution than the BF-FTMW spectrometer, it remains highly effective for most spectroscopic applications. In cases where exceptionally high frequency accuracy and detection sensitivity are required, McCarthy's group at Harvard University has developed a hybrid method that combines the CP-FTMW spectrometer with the cavity-enhanced BF-FTMW spectrometer [24]. This approach utilizes the broad spectral coverage of CP-FTMW to locate the important regions, followed by the high sensitivity and resolution of the BF-FTMW spectrometer to precisely identify and assign molecular transitions.

Building on the strengths of the hybrid method that combines two spectrometers, McCarthy's group demonstrated a new approach named microwave spectral taxonomy. This method enables rapid, unbiased spectroscopic surveys with substantial potential for discovering new molecules, making it particularly valuable in fields like astrophysics and radical chemistry. By categorizing spectral lines based on their responses to varying experimental conditions—such as applied magnetic fields or changes in gas precursors—McCarthy's group effectively narrows down potential molecular carriers. Follow-up double-resonance experiments are then conducted to link transitions that share common energy levels, further refining the identification process. This semi-automated approach significantly enhances the efficiency and precision of spectroscopic analysis, allowing for more detailed studies of complex molecular mixtures and facilitating the discovery of new species [51,52].

2.3. Applications in Structural Determination

As described in Section 2.1, the multiplexing capabilities of CP-FTMW spectrometers have significantly accelerated spectral acquisition rates, facilitating the study of increasingly complex molecular species. Historically, high-resolution rotational spectroscopy was primarily restricted to molecules with only a few atoms. Recent advancements, however, have expanded its capabilities, enabling the analysis of species with more than ten atoms. [34].

The CP-FTMW spectrometer in the 26.5–40 GHz range has recently been employed to analyze and distinguish two structurally similar organic molecules, N-ethyl maleimide (NEM) and N-ethyl succinimide (NES) [53]. Under cryogenic conditions (<10 K), this technique provides highly precise frequency measurements with sub-100 kHz accuracy and a high signal-to-noise ratio (60–200) across numerous rotational transitions. Such precision allows for the rapid and accurate extraction of molecular constants essential for structural determination, including rotational constants, centrifugal distortion constants, and nuclear quadrupole coupling constants. These constants are obtained by fitting the CP-FTMW spectrum to an effective Hamiltonian model that accounts for rotational energy levels and relevant perturbations. The exceptional agreement between experimental measurements and quantum chemistry calculation—within a 0.15% discrepancy for the A, B, and C rotational constants—demonstrates the power of the CP-FTMW spectrometer in providing detailed structural insights into structurally similar organic molecules.

Another example of structural determination using the CP-FTMW spectrometer is the study of 3′- and 4′-aminoacetophenone [54]. Beyond precise frequency measurements, the technique's ability to capture relative intensity information in a single shot plays a pivotal role. By leveraging the relative intensities of different conformers and assuming thermal equilibrium, the energy difference between the two conformers of aminoacetophenone is determined. This use of intensity data is particularly valuable, as it provides direct insights into conformational stability and energetics, offering a deeper understanding of molecular structure that extends beyond standard frequency measurements.

Chiral molecules are essential to the functionality of many biological systems and are also of significant interest in fundamental physics due to their potential to probe parity violation effects [55–58]. However, while structurally similar molecules can still be differentiated by subtle differences in their molecular constants, enantiomers of chiral molecules share identical constants, making them indistinguishable using traditional microwave spectroscopy. Conventional methods for assessing chirality—such as optical circular birefringence [59,60], circular dichroism [61,62], and Raman optical activity [63,64]—rely on higher-order nonlinear excitation processes. These techniques often produce weaker signals and typically require condensed-phase samples with high molecular concentrations for reliable chirality determination.

The development of CP-FTMW, particularly with advancements in phase information extraction, has introduced a novel approach that combines resonant three-wave mixing with an adiabatically switched DC electric field to tackle the challenge of enantiomer differentiation [23,65–70]. This technique enables the determination of molecular chirality in the gas phase by utilizing linear rotational transitions with large electric dipole moments. Rather than relying on frequency shifts, it distinguishes enantiomers through unique phase signatures, as depicted in Figure 5. The ability to resolve enantiomers of chiral molecules underscores the critical role of phase information extraction in CP-FTMW spectrometers, a capability typically absent in BF-FTMW spectrometers.

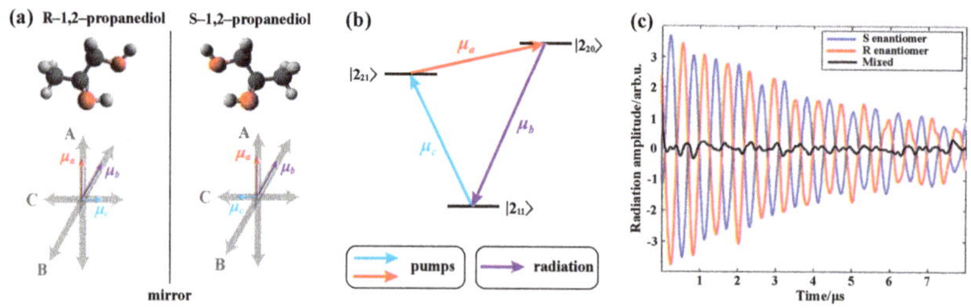

Figure 5. Enantiomer-specific detection of chiral molecules using microwave spectroscopy. (**a**) The two enantiomers of chiral 1,2−propanediol. (**b**) The relevant energy diagram and microwave three-wave mixing scheme. (**c**) Enantiomer-dependent microwave radiation exhibiting distinct phase shifts. The figure is adapted from Patterson (2013) [65].

2.4. Applications in Investigating Dynamics

Beyond molecular structure determination, the CP-FTMW spectrometer has opened new avenues for investigating molecular dynamics. This progress is largely due to its broad bandwidth and rapid time-domain data acquisition, which allow for the precise capture and analysis of intensity information. With this capability, it can directly measure population distributions across a wide range of quantum states. Coupled with high-resolution spectral analysis, the CP-FTMW spectrometer becomes a powerful tool for probing transition states in molecular fragmentation processes [46,71,72]. Furthermore, it is well suited for chemical kinetics studies, enabling the detection and quantification of relative transition intensities among reaction products. This versatility makes it invaluable for extracting detailed information about molecular species, conformers, relative concentrations, vibrational population distributions, and the quantum yields of reaction products [73].

For example, Field's group at MIT utilized intensity data to uncover a previously undetected transition state in the photolysis of CH_2CHCN [46]. Figure 6 illustrates the microwave spectrum of HCN and HNC, the photolysis products of CH_2CHCN. This spectrum highlights the rotational $J = 1 \rightarrow 0$ transitions of both HCN and HNC across various vibrational states within the 86.5–93.0 GHz range, with vibrational quantum numbers assigned based on their corresponding transition frequencies. By analyzing the relative intensities of these $J = 1 \rightarrow 0$ lines, the Vibrational-level Population Distributions (VPDs) of the photolysis products can be precisely determined. These VPDs are critical for understanding the transition state's properties in the parent molecule during fragmentation, offering insights into molecular structures, relative fluxes through different transition state regions, and the post-transition dynamics that drive product formation.

In addition to studying dynamics through key transitions, ultrafast intramolecular dynamics, such as vibrational energy redistribution and isomerization [74], can be captured with sub-nanosecond resolution. Unlike ultrafast pump-probe spectroscopy, which primarily focuses on temporal dynamics, the CP-FTMW spectrometer uniquely provides simultaneous information on both quasi-static molecular structures and dynamics on sub-nanosecond timescales. This integrated approach is critical for identifying the majority of conformers and degrees of freedom involved in the dynamics, effectively bridging the gap between dynamic processes and structural information.

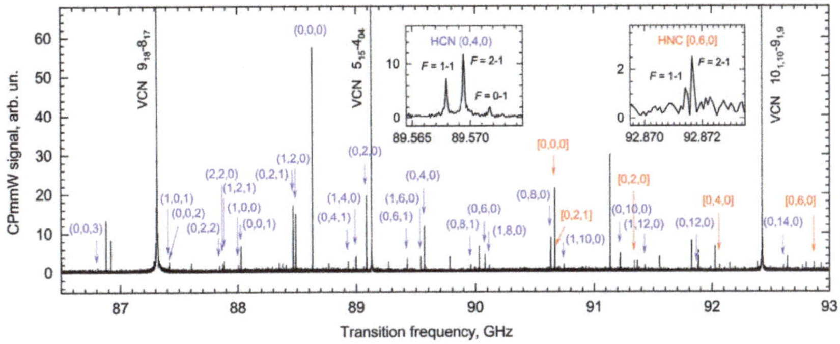

Figure 6. The rotational spectrum of the photolysis products HCN and HNC in the 86.5 to 93.0 GHz region, showing vibrationally assigned $J = 1 \rightarrow 0$ transitions. The vibrational states (v_1: C–H or N–H stretch; v_2: bend; v_3: C–N stretch) of HCN and HNC are indicated in round and square brackets, respectively, near their rotational lines. Two insets illustrate the electric quadrupole hyperfine $(eQq)_N$ structure. The figure is adapted from Prozument (2020) [46].

A milestone study demonstrated the capabilities of the CP-FTMW spectrometer by investigating the nuclear motion dynamics of CPCA ((3α-carbomethoxy-4β-(4-chlorophenyl)-N- methylpiperidine)) molecules, which exhibit two stable conformers, as shown in Figure 7a [75]. In this experiment, CPCA molecules are excited with an infrared laser to energy levels exceeding the threshold of their double-well potential, inducing rapid isomerization between the conformers. In these excited states, the moments of inertia evolve over time. To capture these time-dependent structural changes, multiple rotational transitions spaced several GHz apart are recorded simultaneously. This approach, known as dynamic rotational spectroscopy (DRS), effectively captures time-sensitive dynamics by integrating them into spectral measurements.

To identify the molecular conformers and understand their dynamic behavior, an infrared-microwave two-dimensional (2D) double-resonance spectrum is recorded, as shown in Figure 7b,c. Constructing this 2D spectrum requires collecting about 17,000 rotational spectra while scanning the infrared laser frequency from 2670 to 2850 cm^{-1}. Performing this task with a traditional BF-FT spectrometer would have taken an estimated 27 years. However, the CP-FTMW spectrometer completes the entire dataset in just 52 h.

The ultrafast isomerization dynamics are analyzed using a rotational Bloch model to fit the intensity distribution. The rate of isomerization is extracted from the width of the double-peak fit, with broader peaks indicating faster processes, as illustrated in Figure 7d. The temporal resolution of these dynamics is determined by the Fourier transform limit, which depends on the CP's bandwidth. In this case, the 10 GHz bandwidth enables the detection of dynamics occurring on sub-100-picosecond timescales.

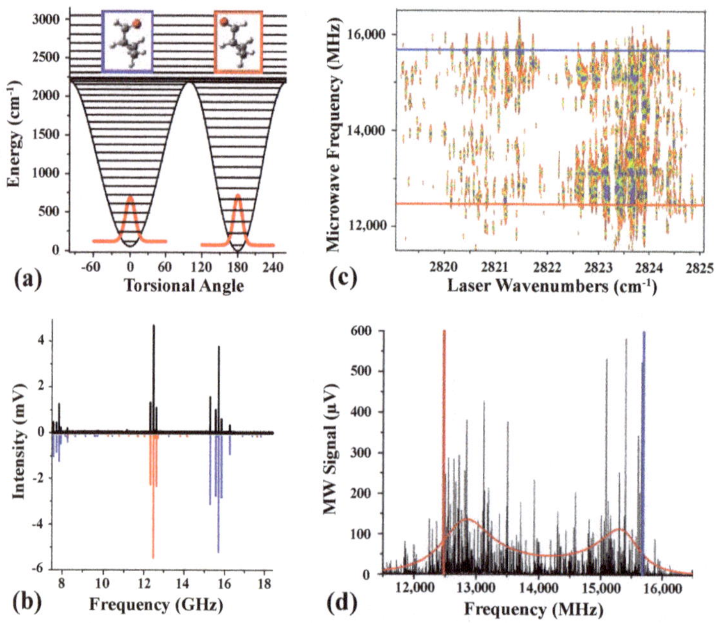

Figure 7. Dynamic rotational spectroscopy (DRS) measurements of CPCA (3α–carbomethoxy–4β–(4–chlorophenyl)–N–methylpiperidine). (**a**) The potential energy surface depicting the conformational isomerization of CPCA. (**b**) The CP-FTMW spectrum of CPCA (positive, black) compared with the calculated spectra for the syn (negative, blue) and anti (negative, red) conformers. (**c**) DRS measurements of CPCA in the 2819 to 2825 cm^{-1} region, presented in a 2D format, with red and blue lines indicating the pure rotational frequencies of the anti and syn transitions, respectively. (**d**) A comparison of the best-fit overall line shape with the DRS measurements in the microwave frequency region, with the smooth line-shape profile from the rotational Bloch model shown in red. The red and blue vertical lines correspond to the horizontal lines shown in (**c**). The figure is adapted from Dian (2008) [75].

2.5. Applications in Rydberg Spectroscopy

In addition to rotational spectroscopy, the CP-FTMW spectrometer has been demonstrated to acquire high-resolution spectra of Rydberg–Rydberg transitions. Rydberg states of atoms or molecules are a class of highly electronically excited states characterized by a loosely bound electron with an orbital radius significantly larger than the Bohr radius [76]. The energies of these states are described by the Rydberg formula: $E = IP - Ry/(n-\delta)^2$, where IP represents the ionization potential, Ry is the Rydberg constant, n is the principal quantum number, and δ is the quantum defect. For states where $n > 30$, Rydberg–Rydberg transitions involving a change in n of one fall within the microwave or millimeter-wave range. Moreover, the wavefunctions associated with a Rydberg series exhibit distinct periodic structures that can be calculated using hydrogenic equations and follow n-dependent scaling rules. Due to the highly nonlinear scaling of many properties with n, Rydberg states have unique features, including transition dipole moments over three orders of magnitude larger than those of the ground state and significantly extended lifetimes.

The study of atomic Rydberg states using microwave radiation began over three decades ago [77]. Recently, interdisciplinary research at the intersection of physics and chemistry has increasingly focused on the control, manipulation, and high-precision spectroscopy of molecular Rydberg states [78–81]. Unlike their atomic counterparts, molecular Rydberg states feature a more complex ion core with additional degrees of freedom, including vibration, rotation, and a permanent electric dipole moment. These characteristics give rise to anisotropic and inelastic interactions between the Rydberg electron and the ion core, involving exchanges of energy and angular momentum [82,83]. Consequently, the Rydberg electron can act as a quantum sensor, utilizing its exceptional sensitivity to probe and reveal the structure of the ion core.

A major challenge in understanding the structure and dynamics of molecular Rydberg states lies in the highly congested spectroscopic data, even for diatomic molecules. For example, in the case of BaF, a typical dataset capturing transitions into $v^+ = 0$ and $l \leq 5$ Rydberg states within an $(n, n + 1)$ energy interval contains about 75 possible electronic-rotational transitions originating from a single initial level with known N ($N \geq 4$) and parity. This complexity arises from the electronic structure, particularly the different values of Λ (orbital angular momentum projection along the inter-nuclear axis) and spin-orbit couplings for each l series. Notably, the energy width of such an interval is only about 3 cm^{-1} for $n = 40$. The introduction of external electric or magnetic fields further complicates the spectrum by lifting the degeneracy of the m-levels, significantly increasing the number of observable transitions.

CP-FTMW spectroscopy provides a powerful experimental approach for capturing a series of Rydberg–Rydberg transitions, uncovering periodic structures across a broad spectral range with high resolution. By analyzing these periodic patterns in Rydberg series, key features of the molecular ion core can be accurately extracted by well-established scaling rules [84,85]. When the transition frequency within the ion core resonates with the Kepler frequency of the Rydberg electron, a resonantly enhanced exchange of energy or momentum occurs between the ion core and the Rydberg electron. This phenomenon, known as "Stroboscopic resonance", arises at specific n values and plays a pivotal role in amplifying and isolating certain interactions within the ion core [86]. Strong interactions manifest as pronounced periodic patterns, while weaker interactions become detectable through the amplification provided by stroboscopic resonances.

Unlike rotational transitions, Rydberg–Rydberg transitions exhibit exceptionally large electric dipole moments, reaching values of several thousand Debyes. This characteristic enables even weak chirped pulses (1 mW, 1 μs, 10 GHz bandwidth) to generate strong FID signals, as demonstrated in Figure 8 [87]. Furthermore, in environments with high densities of Rydberg molecules, the FID signal can experience re-absorption, leading to phase correlations among molecules. Under such conditions, collective dynamics play a significant role in shaping the overall radiative behavior. A striking example of this collective dynamic is superradiance, a quantum many-body phenomenon where coherence among a closely packed ensemble of molecules results in enhanced radiative coupling [88–90]. These interactions provide a compelling platform for investigating quantum optical phenomena.

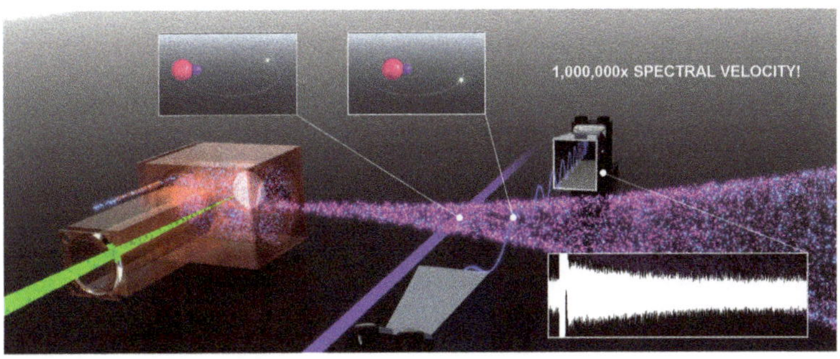

Figure 8. A schematic diagram of Rydberg–Rydberg transitions detected using Chirp-Pulsed millimeter-Wave (CPmmW) spectroscopy. BaF molecules are synthesized, cooled, and directed as a beam from a cryogenic cell. These molecules are subsequently excited to Rydberg states using two lasers. After excitation, a chirp pulse (CP) is applied to polarize the Rydberg molecules, inducing Free-Induction Decay (FID). The resulting FID signals are captured, digitized, and shown in the inset panel. The figure is adapted from Zhou (2015) [87].

2.6. Outlook

The CP-FTMW spectrometer has revolutionized rotational spectroscopy and opened new avenues in Rydberg spectroscopy. Over the next decade, advancements in high-frequency circuits and opto-electronic hybrid technologies are expected to extend operational frequencies beyond one terahertz. In addition to generating linear frequency sweeps, the AWG in the CP-FTMW spectrometer can produce a microwave comb that not only covers a broad spectral range but also enhances detection sensitivity when coupled with a microwave resonant cavity. This approach is analogous to the cavity-enhanced optical frequency comb, which will be discussed in Section 3.2. Furthermore, the evolution of CP-FTMW technology will also benefit from the adoption of FPGA-based embedded hardware systems and AI-driven software, which promise to optimize performance and streamline data processing. Complementing these technological innovations, improvements in molecular sources and sample delivery methods are set to elevate the field of molecular spectroscopy. Developments in supersonic beam technology and cryogenic buffer gas cells, designed to achieve higher molecular densities and lower temperatures, will be instrumental in advancing research [87,91–94]. Together, these advancements will expand the applicability of spectroscopy to a broader range of molecular species, significantly enhancing its impact across diverse scientific disciplines.

3. OFC Spectroscopy

Vibrational spectroscopy, in contrast to rotational spectroscopy—which primarily focuses on determining overall molecular structures—examines the specific vibrations of atoms within molecules. Stronger bonds and lighter atoms typically vibrate at higher frequencies, making vibrational spectroscopy especially effective for accurately identifying chemical bonds. This capability is invaluable for analyzing large molecules by leveraging their distinctive vibrational frequencies. Vibrational spectroscopy has found widespread application across various academic and industrial fields [95–97], including (1) chemical identification and functional group characterization, particularly in large organic molecules; (2) the detection of specific gases and pollutants in environmental matrices, such as air, water, and soil; (3) compound identification, quality assurance, and quantitative analysis of active ingredients in pharmaceuticals; and (4) non-invasive disease diagnostics through the analysis of biological samples like blood or tissue, opening possibilities for early disease detection and monitoring.

Functional groups exhibit distinct absorption signatures at specific frequencies within the infrared (IR) spectrum, typically ranging from 1500 to 3000 cm^{-1} [98]. Traditional Fourier Transform Infrared (FTIR) spectrometers are widely utilized due to their broad spectroscopic range, spanning from 10 to 10,000 cm^{-1} [98]. Equipped with a long-arm scanning Michelson interferometer, these instruments can achieve exceptional resolutions of up to 0.001 cm^{-1}, making them highly effective for detailed vibrational analysis. Despite its many advantages, FTIR spectroscopy faces a significant limitation in its lengthy acquisition time, driven by two key factors: (1) achieving high resolution requires the interferometer arm to scan distances exceeding a meter, and (2) the relatively low brightness of the thermal light source requires a long averaging time to achieve a satisfactory SNR. As a result, there is a growing demand for next-generation IR spectrometers capable of significantly reducing acquisition time. Furthermore, the demand for in situ and real-time sample analysis, particularly in environmental science, underscores the need for instruments that are both highly reliable and portable.

Over the past decade, optical frequency comb (OFC) spectroscopy has emerged as a powerful alternative to traditional FTIR spectrometers [99]. OFCs represent a unique class of light sources that combine ultrafast temporal resolution in the femtosecond range with exceptionally precise phase information, accurate to about 1 part in 10^{19} to 10^{20} over 1000 s [100,101]. Recognized with the Nobel Prize in Physics in 2005 for their transformative role in the development of the world's most accurate atomic clocks, OFCs serve as highly precise optical frequency synthesizers, driving advancements across a wide range of scientific fields [102]. Furthermore, their extensive spectroscopic coverage, ultra-narrow linewidth, and exceptional frequency accuracy have transformed the field of molecular spectroscopy [103]. This paper focuses on the application of OFCs in molecular spectroscopy.

3.1. Fundamental Principles of OFC

The origins of OFCs can be traced back to the well-established field of ultrafast optics, particularly the development of mode-locked lasers (MLLs) [104–107]. This section provides a brief overview of the operational principles of MLLs and highlights a key distinction that sets OFCs apart: phase stability.

By placing a gain medium within a highly frequency-selective optical cavity, a laser can be configured to operate in a single frequency mode, where only one longitudinal mode is amplified, resulting in a narrow and stable output spectrum. In contrast, MLLs utilize a less stringent frequency selectivity, allowing gain media with broader emission spectra to support multiple frequency modes simultaneously, as shown in Figure 9a. The resulting output of an MLL is a coherent superposition of the electric fields from all the excited modes within the cavity:

$$E = E_0 \sum_{q=-(N-1)/2}^{+(N-1)/2} e^{i(2\pi f_0 + q(2\pi f_r))t + i\phi_q}, \tag{1}$$

where f_0 represents the central frequency of the MLL, f_r is the free spectral range (FSR) of the laser cavity, q is an integer identifying each cavity mode, N denotes the total number of modes excited in the cavity, and ϕ_q represents the initial phase associated with each mode. Equation (1) sums over all active lasing modes. The intensity (I) of the laser's output is directly proportional to the square of the electric field, expressed as $I \propto |E|^2$. When the initial phases of the modes are independent, the laser output intensity exhibits random temporal fluctuations, as illustrated in the top panel of Figure 9b. If the initial phases of all lasing modes are identical, the phase component can be factored out of the summation in Equation (1):

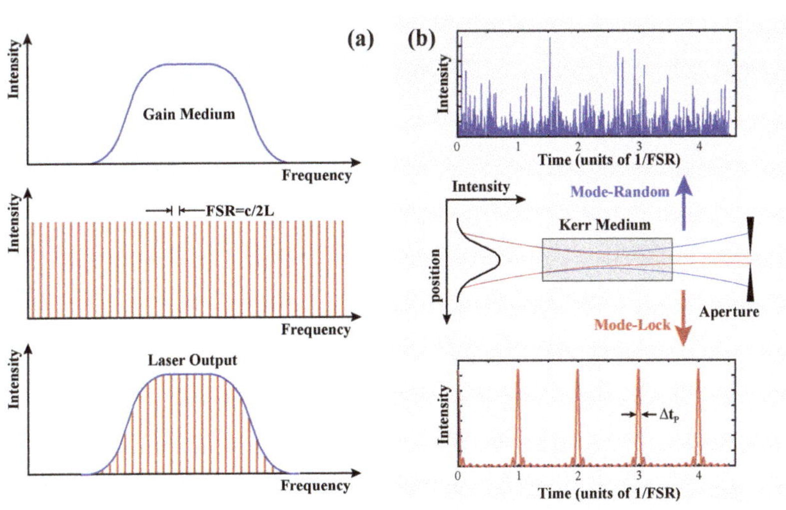

Figure 9. Principles of mode-locked lasers (MLLs). (**a**) Multiple longitudinal modes within the laser cavity are simultaneously excited. c: Speed of light; L: cavity length; FSR: free spectral range. (**b**) The Kerr medium in the laser cavity (middle panel) imposes much higher losses on continuous-wave light (top panel) than on pulsed light (bottom panel).

$$E = E_0 e^{i2\pi f_0 t + i\phi} \sum_{q=-(N-1)/2}^{+(N-1)/2} e^{iq(2\pi f_r)t} = E_0 e^{i2\pi f_0 t + i\phi} \frac{\sin N2\pi f_r t/2}{\sin 2\pi f_r t/2}, \tag{2}$$

$$I = I_0 \left(\frac{\sin N2\pi f_r t/2}{\sin 2\pi f_r t/2} \right)^2. \tag{3}$$

The bottom panel of Figure 9b illustrates the time-dependent intensity of the laser output, characterized by distinct, regularly spaced sharp peaks, as described by Equation (3). In the time domain, the interval between consecutive pulses is determined by the length of the laser cavity, corresponding to a separation of $2L/c$, where L is the cavity length, and c is the speed of light. Furthermore, the width of these pulses depends on the number of modes excited simultaneously; a larger number of active modes results in narrower laser pulses:

$$\Delta t_p \approx \frac{1}{N f_r}. \tag{4}$$

In a standard Ti:Sapphire MLL with a ring cavity design, the cavity length (L) is approximately 1 m, and the optical bandwidth ($\Delta\lambda$) is around 20 nm. This configuration enables the activation of roughly 670,000 lasing modes (N), resulting in the generation of laser pulses with durations as short as 100 femtoseconds. The generation of these ultrashort pulses relies on maintaining a coherent phase relationship among all lasing modes. Over the past four decades, various phase-locking techniques have been developed to achieve this. Two prominent approaches are (1) active mode-locking, which utilizes components such as an electro-optic modulator (EOM) [104,108], acousto-optical modulator (AOM) [109,110], or synchronous pumping [111] within the laser cavity, and (2) passive mode-locking, which employs a saturable absorber [112–115] or nonlinear medium, such as a Kerr lens [106,116–118].

Among these methods, passive mode-locking using a Kerr lens has become the most effective and widely adopted approach for generating stable, ultrashort laser pulses. Unlike a standard optical medium with a fixed refractive index, a Kerr medium exhibits a refractive index that varies with light intensity, described by $n = n_0 + n_2 I$, where I is the light intensity, n_0 is the intensity-independent refraction index, and n_2 represents the medium's nonlinear response to intensity. Since the total optical energy within the laser cavity is conserved, the pulsed mode achieves significantly higher peak intensities by concentrating energy into shorter time intervals. This enhanced peak intensity causes the pulsed beam to bend more strongly when passing through the Kerr medium, as illustrated in the middle panel of Figure 9b. An optical aperture placed within the cavity selectively transmits the pulsed mode while attenuating the continuous-wave mode. This preferential transmission, combined with the stimulated emission cascade within the laser gain medium, enables the pulsed mode to dominate, effectively suppressing the continuous-wave mode.

Femtosecond pulses generated by MLLs are indispensable for probing ultrafast dynamics in the time domain. Furthermore, the precisely defined pulse-to-pulse interval has been a cornerstone of frequency metrology since the late 1980s [119]. Through Fourier transformation, a sequence of time-domain pulses is mapped into the frequency domain, resulting in a comb of discrete frequencies. The spacing between consecutive modes, f_r, is determined by the laser cavity FSR, $2L/c$, and typically lies within the RF spectrum, ranging from 20 MHz to 20 GHz. By precisely measuring the optical frequency of a single lasing mode and calibrating f_r against an RF standard, the frequencies of all other modes can be determined using the relationship $f = f_c + \hat{N} f_r$, where f_c is the known frequency of a reference mode, and $\hat{N}$ identifies the mode index relative to f_c. This technique effectively extends the precision of a single frequency measurement to cover millions of other frequencies.

Accurately determining the absolute frequency hinges critically on f_c. If the discrete frequencies extrapolated to the lowest end were precisely zero, the optical frequency could be directly synthesized as $f = \tilde{N} f_r$, where $\tilde{N}$ is referenced to zero frequency rather than

f_c. However, this ideal scenario is complicated by the presence of a carrier-envelope offset (ceo) offset—a phase mismatch between the oscillation of the carrier wave and the pulse envelope, as illustrated in the inset panel of Figure 10. In the time domain, this phase offset cannot be directly measured with an intensity detector. In the frequency domain, it manifests as a frequency shift affecting all modes, particularly pronounced near the origin of the frequency axis, as depicted in Figure 10. Precisely measuring or effectively eliminating f_{ceo} is essential for establishing an absolute optical frequency, transforming the MLL into an OFC.

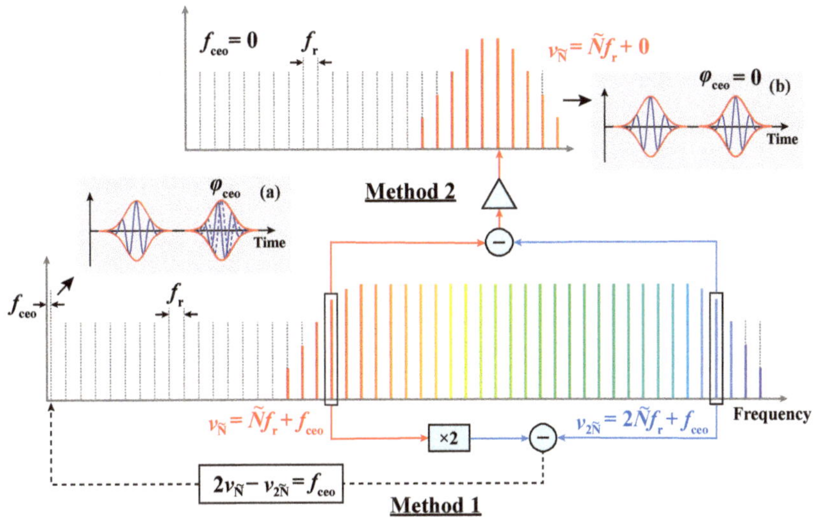

Figure 10. Two methods for determining absolute frequency. f_{ceo}: carrier-envelope frequency offset; ϕ_{ceo}: carrier-envelope phase offset; f_r: repetition rate. $\tilde{N}$ represents the mode index relative to zero frequency. Inset: carrier-envelope phase offset visualized in the time domain. Further details are provided in the main text.

Figure 10 illustrates two widely used methods for determining f_{ceo}. Both approaches start by broadening the OFC's wavelength spectrum to span more than an octave, typically achieved using frequency mixing in a highly nonlinear optical fiber. After spectral broadening, two lasing modes are selected with frequencies nearly a factor of two apart, denoted by $\nu_{\tilde{N}} = \tilde{N}f_r + f_{ceo}$ and $\nu_{2\tilde{N}} = 2\tilde{N}f_r + f_{ceo}$. The first method employs second-harmonic generation (SHG) to double the frequency of the lower mode, $\nu_{\tilde{N}}$, producing $\nu_d = 2\tilde{N}f_r + 2f_{ceo}$. By interfering with ν_d and $\nu_{2\tilde{N}}$ and extracting the resulting RF beat frequency, f_{ceo} can be determined as $f_{ceo} = \nu_d - \nu_{2\tilde{N}}$. This offset frequency is then stabilized using a negative feedback loop to the pump laser [120,121]. The second method, developed by TOPTICA Photonics, utilizes difference frequency generation (DFG) to directly combine light from $\nu_{\tilde{N}}$ and $\nu_{2\tilde{N}}$, effectively canceling f_{ceo} [122,123]. This process yields $\nu = \nu_{2\tilde{N}} - \nu_{\tilde{N}} = \tilde{N}f_r$, which depends solely on f_r. After DFG, the OFC light, now free of f_{ceo}, is amplified to a usable power level.

While CE-DFCS leverages the millions of frequency elements provided by the OFC, it encounters the specific challenge of spectrally resolving individual comb teeth. Two prominent techniques for addressing this challenge are the Virtually Imaged Phase Array (VIPA) etalon and the Michelson interferometer. A VIPA etalon combined with a reflection grating is particularly effective for dispersing OFC light into a two-dimensional array, enabling single-shot capture by a camera [124,125]. However, extending this method to the mid- and far-IR spectral regions is limited by the diffraction constraints of optical components and the resolution of available cameras. The Michelson interferometer, a cornerstone of FTIR spectroscopy, provides broad spectral coverage in the infrared region and sufficient resolution to distinguish individual comb teeth. Despite its advantages, the mechanical scanning required by this approach is inherently slow and can undermine system stability, posing challenges for applications requiring high-speed data acquisition.

A promising alternative is the dual-comb configuration, which leverages the interference between OFC light and an additional phase-referenced OFC beam. This approach has the potential to surpass both the VIPA etalon and the Michelson interferometer in terms of efficiency and resolution, as will be further explored in Section 3.3.

3.2. Direct Frequency Comb Spectroscopy

As described above, the absolute frequencies of all comb teeth can be precisely determined using either an RF source or an optical frequency reference. When comb light interacts with a molecular sample, it facilitates the simultaneous acquisition of a broadband absorption spectrum encompassing the frequencies of all comb teeth. This technique, known as Direct Frequency Comb Spectroscopy (DFCS), has revolutionized molecular spectroscopy by leveraging massive parallelism. With millions of comb teeth probing the sample in parallel, DFCS achieves data acquisition speeds that are up to six orders of magnitude faster than those of traditional laser-scanning spectrometers [126,127].

Compared to FTIR spectrometers, which also utilize broadband light sources, DFCS delivers a substantial enhancement in spectroscopic resolution, often exceeding that of FTIR systems by several orders of magnitude. In FTIR spectrometry, the maximum resolution is determined by the translation distance of the interferometer arm, which defines the achievable optical path difference and, consequently, the ability to resolve fine spectral details. For a double-pass interferometer arm with a one-meter travel distance, the resolution is 150 MHz. In contrast, the resolution in DFCS depends on the stability of the OFC and the interrogation time. With an interrogation time of approximately 100 μs, the Fourier transform limit yields a resolution on the order of a few kilohertz—four to five orders of magnitude finer than that of an FTIR spectrometer [126].

Furthermore, the evenly spaced frequency intervals of the OFC light source enable resonant coupling with high-finesse optical cavities that exhibit a matching frequency structure. The enhanced cavity significantly extends the interaction time between the light and the sample. This approach, known as Cavity-Enhanced Direct Frequency Comb Spectroscopy (CE-DFCS) [124,125], can amplify the absorption signal by up to three orders of magnitude. Such an enhancement allows for the highly sensitive and precise detection of trace amounts of low-concentration toxic or indicator gases [128,129].

Since its inception, the CE-DFCS spectrometer has been a transformative tool in decoding the complexities of molecular structures, leveraging its broad spectral coverage, exceptional resolution, and remarkable sensitivity. One of its most notable achievements is its application in the high-resolution spectroscopy of large polyatomic molecules, such as adamantane ($C_{10}H_{16}$) and fullerene (C_{60}) [130,131]. By integrating buffer gas cooling technology, which significantly reduces the number of molecular degrees of freedom, with the advanced capabilities of CE-DFCS to enhance parallelism, the rovibrational transitions of adamantane and C_{60} have been successfully recorded and meticulously characterized, as shown in Figure 11.

Another notable application of CE-DFCS is its use in recording the high-resolution spectra of molecular ions in a plasma tube, facilitated by velocity modulation. While neutral molecules can often be produced with high number densities in molecular beams, ion beams typically have much lower densities due to strong Coulomb repulsion. Generating ions within plasma provides a sufficiently dense sample for absorption detection. However, the presence of background noise, especially from neutral molecules, can obscure the signals of target ions. To overcome this limitation, velocity modulation combined with lock-in detection is employed, effectively isolating the Doppler-shifted signals of ions. Figure 12 illustrates the experimental setup and high-resolution spectroscopy of HfF^+ [132], which has enabled the most precise measurement of the electron's electric dipole moment (eEDM) to date, imposing stringent constraints on the Standard Model of particle physics [133,134].

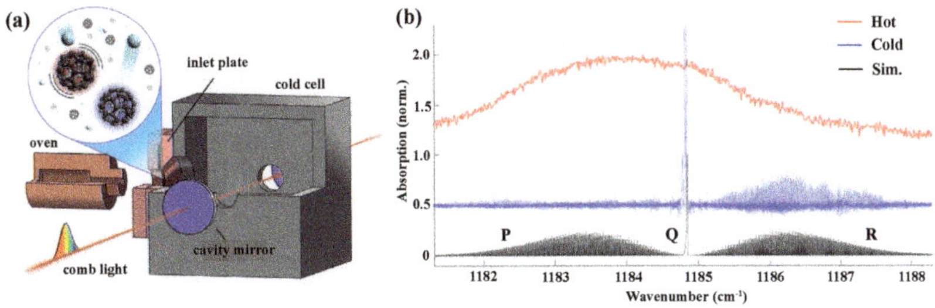

Figure 11. Cavity-Enhanced Direct Frequency Comb Spectroscopy (CE-DFCS) of C_{60}. (**a**) A schematic of the experimental setup integrating CE-DFCS with a cryogenic buffer gas cell. (**b**) High-resolution rovibrational spectra of C_{60} recorded at room temperature and cryogenic temperature. The figure is adapted from Changala (2019) [131].

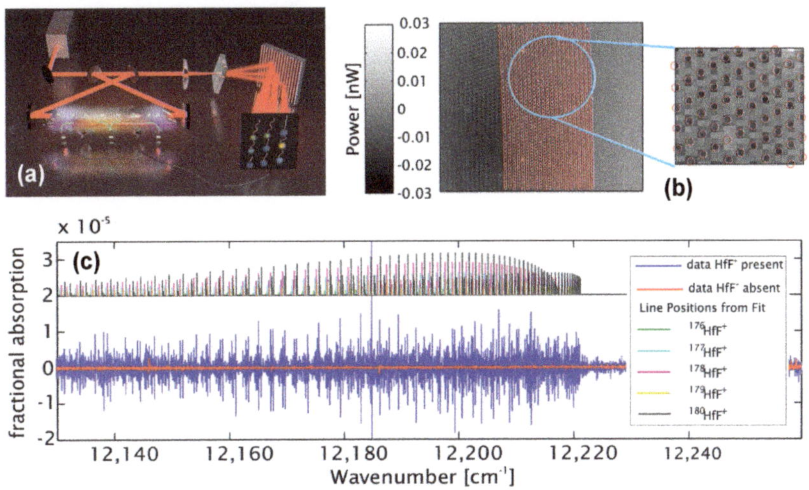

Figure 12. Cavity-Enhanced Direct Frequency Comb Spectroscopy (CE-DFCS) of velocity-modulated HfF^+. (**a**) A schematic of the experimental setup featuring a VIPA etalon and a grating for resolving individual comb teeth. (**b**) Visualization of the resolved comb teeth. (**c**) High-resolution spectrum of HfF^+, including five isotopes with assigned rotational band structures. The figure is adapted from Sinclair (2011) [132].

Beyond its contributions to fundamental research, the extensive spectroscopic capabilities of CE-DFCS—enabling simultaneous analysis of multiple molecular species in a single experiment—have proven invaluable in fields such as environmental science, industrial process monitoring, and the life sciences. One notable application emerged in 2008 with the development of a CE-DFCS-based breathalyzer [135]. Human breath, which contains over 1000 distinct trace molecules serving as biomarkers for various health conditions, presents a highly complex sample matrix. The precise identification of these trace molecules using CE-DFCS is critical for accurate chemical and biological diagnostics, offering a non-invasive yet powerful tool for health monitoring and disease detection.

Over the past decade, the sensitivity of the CE-DFCS breathalyzer has improved by a factor of 1000, largely due to the transition from near-IR to mid-IR wavelengths, where breath molecules exhibit stronger rovibrational absorption features. This shift has significantly enhanced the instrument's ability to detect and quantify molecular concentrations. Furthermore, advancements in data acquisition and analysis have become increasingly important, particularly for biological systems where simple models may not apply. Machine learning has emerged as a transformative tool in this domain, enabling the analysis of complex datasets from breath samples to create predictive models for disease diagnosis. By detecting subtle changes in molecular concentrations associated with specific health conditions, machine learning algorithms identify patterns and establish robust diagnostic criteria. A compelling demonstration of this approach was the detection of SARS-CoV-2 infection in a cohort of 170 volunteers, where the CE-DFCS breathalyzer achieved an impressive accuracy rate of 84.9%, as illustrated in Figure 13 [136]. This underscores the potential of integrating advanced spectroscopy with machine learning to revolutionize non-invasive diagnostics and disease monitoring.

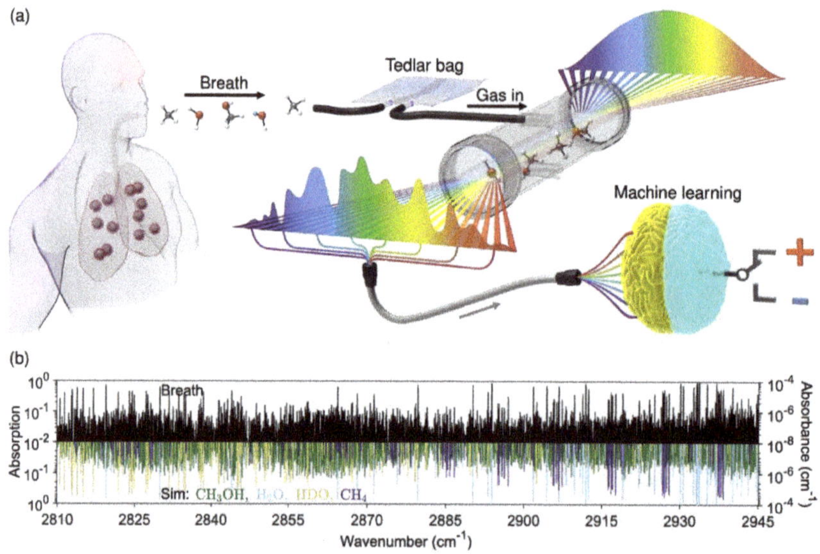

Figure 13. A Cavity-Enhanced Direct Frequency Comb Spectroscopy (CE-DFCS) breathalyzer. (**a**) A schematic diagram illustrating the working principle. Exhaled human breath was collected in a Tedlar bag and introduced into an analysis chamber surrounded by high-reflectivity optical mirrors. A mid-infrared frequency comb laser interacted with the sample, generating a broadband molecular absorption spectrum. This spectroscopy data were then analyzed using supervised machine learning to classify the research subject's condition as either positive or negative. (**b**) A sample absorption spectrum obtained from a research subject's breath (black line). Inverted and displayed in different colors are the fitted contributions from four dominant species (CH_3OH, H_2O, HDO, and CH_4) responsible for the most significant absorption features. Figure is adapted from Liang (2023) [136].

In addition to capturing static information, the broad spectroscopic coverage of CE-DFCS, combined with its rapid data acquisition and ability to perform extended coherent averaging, enables the study of chemical reaction kinetics on microsecond timescales [137–139]. This capability is particularly advantageous for tracking the evolution of multiple transient intermediate compounds within a reaction sequence. A notable application of this technique is its time-resolved implementation to investigate the pressure-dependent kinetics of the OH + CO → HOCO → H + CO_2 reaction [140], a critical pathway in the atmospheric degradation of OH radicals. These studies highlight CE-DFCS's ability to provide detailed insights into dynamic chemical processes with precision and speed.

3.3. Dual-Comb Spectroscopy

While OFC light sources have been successfully extended into the mid- and far-infrared regions, implementing CE-DFCS in these spectral ranges remains challenging, primarily due to the limitations of existing detection techniques. The VIPA etalon method is constrained by significant diffraction at long wavelengths and its reliance on high-performance infrared imaging detectors, whereas the Michelson interferometer is hindered by slow scanning rates and stability issues. To overcome these obstacles, researchers have developed an innovative technique: employing a second OFC beam that is phase-coherent with the original to decode spectral information through precise interference measurements. This method, known as dual-comb spectroscopy (DCS), offers a highly efficient and promising solution for extracting and analyzing spectral data in the challenging mid- and far-infrared regions [99,141–143].

DCS utilizes the first OFC beam to interact with the sample and a second, phase-coherent OFC beam to down-convert optical frequencies—too high for direct digitization—into RF frequencies, as depicted in Figure 14. Only the first OFC, operating at a repetition rate f_r, is coupled to an enhancement cavity, where it directly interacts with the sample. The second OFC, with a slightly offset repetition rate of $f_r + \Delta f_r$, is combined and interferes with the first OFC beam after its interaction with the sample. The resulting heterodyne RF signals are captured by a single photodetector, generating an RF comb with a spacing of Δf_r that can be directly digitized. Typically, f_r ranges from tens of MHz to tens of GHz, and Δf_r falls within 100 Hz to tens of kHz. By applying a Fourier transform to the heterodyne RF signals, the sample's absorption or emission spectrum can be reconstructed with exceptional spectroscopic resolution and precision.

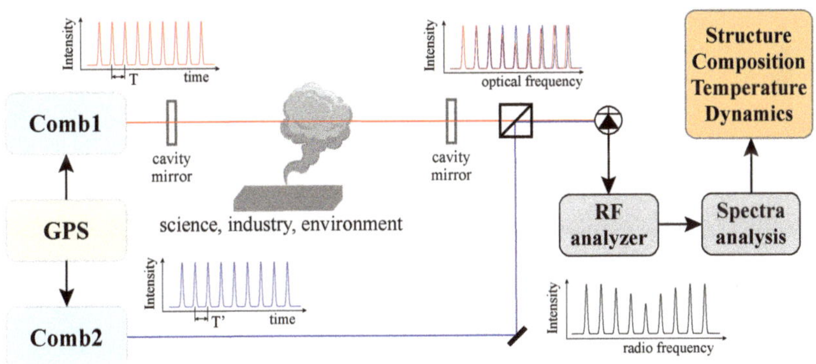

Figure 14. Working principle of dual-comb spectroscopy (DCS), with optional cavity mirrors for enhanced sensitivity.

DCS retains the advantages of DFCS while significantly streamlining detection processes and broadening its spectroscopic capabilities. Like FTIR spectroscopy, DCS utilizes a single-point detector, eliminating the need for a high-resolution infrared camera. Moreover, unlike FTIR, DCS bypasses the mechanically moving Michelson interferometer, enabling much faster data acquisition and enhanced system stability. DCS also offers a high SNR and a consistent baseline, achieved through extended coherent averaging, time-multiplexed signal and reference measurements, and sequential acquisition of subbands to mitigate detector nonlinearity. Additionally, incorporating a high-finesse optical cavity into the path of the first comb beam to enhance detection sensitivity aligns closely with the CE-DFCS approach.

Over the past decade, DCS has emerged as a transformative tool, particularly in environmental science and atmospheric chemistry. One of its most groundbreaking advancements is real-time, high-resolution atmospheric gas analysis, enabling precise and rapid monitoring of pollutants and greenhouse gases [129,144–146]. A remarkable example is shown in Figure 15, where DCS was deployed over a 113 km horizontal open-air path. Using two synchronized OFCs, DCS provided direct measurements of spectral features without the need for moving parts or scanning lasers. This innovative setup, incorporating a bistatic configuration and advanced time–frequency dissemination, facilitated broadband, high-speed measurements of greenhouse gases such as CO_2 over a long distance. The experiment achieved a CO_2 sensing precision of less than 2 parts per million (ppm) within 5 min, further improving to below 0.6 ppm over 36 min—an unprecedented level of accuracy for long-distance, open-air measurements. Moreover, this advancement paves the way for deploying DCS in satellite-based systems, offering the potential for real-time, global environmental monitoring.

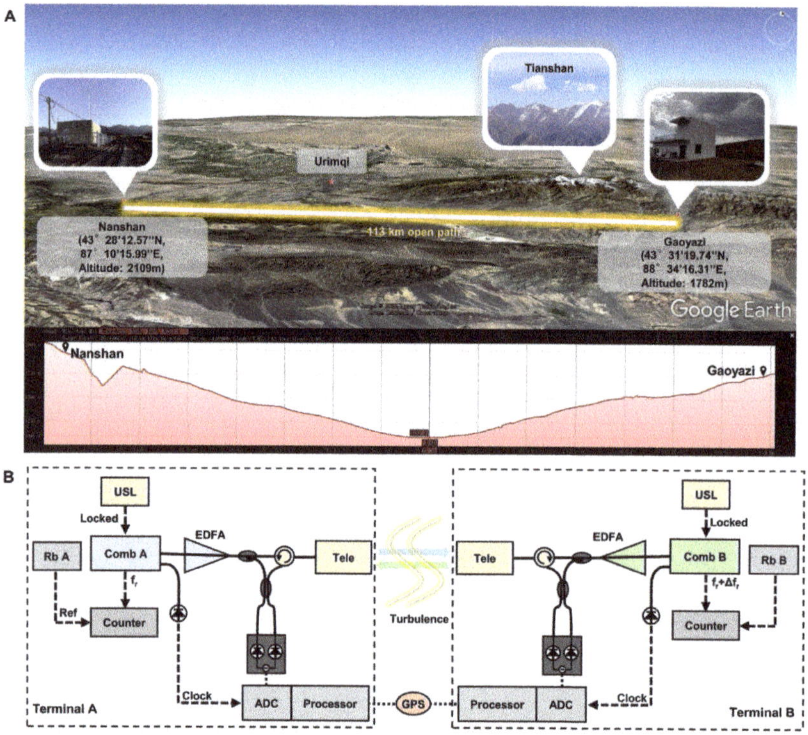

Figure 15. Dual-comb spectroscopy (DCS) over a 100 km open-air path. (**A**) An overview of the 113 km DCS. (**B**) The main configuration and setup at each terminal. Rb: rubidium clock; USL: ultrastable laser; EDFA: Erbium-doped fiber amplifier; Tele: telescope; ADC: Analog-to-Digital Converter; GPS: global positioning system. Figure is adapted from Han (2023) [146].

To advance DCS for field applications and potential satellite-based deployments, the development of compact optical devices is essential to enhance portability and reliability. Recent breakthroughs in photonic technologies have led to the creation of on-chip DCSs [147–150]. The on-chip DCSs leverage microresonators to generate two stable OFCs, enabling high-precision, broadband spectroscopic measurements in a compact form factor. Microresonators, typically designed as ring or disk structures, are fabricated from high-quality materials like silicon nitride or silicon dioxide, which facilitate low-loss light propagation. When a continuous-wave (CW) laser is coupled to these microresonators, nonlinear optical processes such as four-wave mixing produce a series of equally spaced comb lines, forming an OFC. The spacing between these comb lines, known as the FSR, is determined by the geometry of the microresonator. The compact, power-efficient architecture significantly reduces the size and complexity of DCS systems, making them well suited for portable and field-deployable devices.

In addition to the MLL-based OFC generation discussed in Section 3.1, a novel approach utilizing EOMs has emerged and developed rapidly in recent years [139,151–153]. In this configuration, a CW laser is passed through one or more EOMs, which impose periodic phase modulation on the light. When the modulation amplitude is sufficiently large, multiple rounds of sideband generation occur, significantly extending the spectral coverage of the OFC. By precisely controlling the modulation frequency and amplitude with advanced, high-speed digital devices, such as Arbitrary Waveform Generators (AWGs), a series of equally spaced spectral lines can be generated, forming a highly tunable and stable OFC. Figure 16 illustrates the use of an EOM-based OFC to perform nanosecond time-resolved absorption spectroscopy on a supersonic jet.

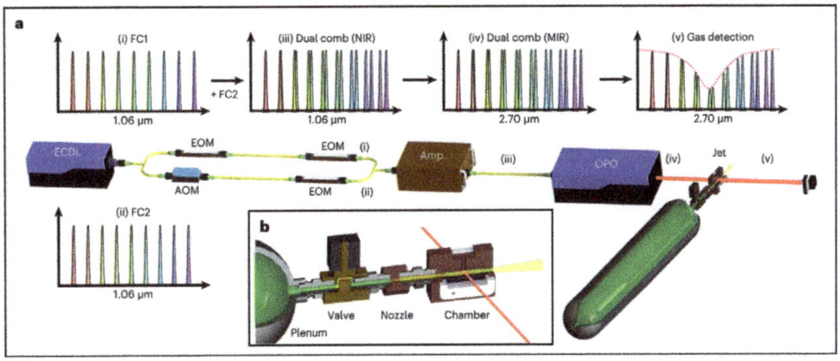

Figure 16. A schematic of the electro-optic modulator (EOM)-based, mid-infrared dual-comb spectrometer (DCS) used to interrogate a supersonic pulsed jet. (**a**) A near-infrared external cavity diode laser (ECDL) serves as the common source for two optical frequency combs generated using EOMs with slightly different repetition rates. To enhance the modulation depth, the two EOMs in the upper path are driven by identical waveforms. An acousto-optic modulator (AOM) in the lower beam path shifts the beat frequencies between the two optical frequency combs away from DC. The two OFCs are then combined and converted to mid-infrared wavelengths using an amplifier and a singly resonant CW optical parametric oscillator (OPO). The idler beam passes through the supersonic jet and is detected with a photodiode. All couplings shown in yellow indicate fiber connections. (**b**) A machine drawing of the supersonic pulsed jet, illustrating the plenum, a normally closed solenoid valve, a convergent–divergent (CD) nozzle, and the optical test chamber. The figure is adapted from Long (2023) [139].

One of the primary advantages of the EOM-based OFC is its simplicity and compactness. Unlike MLLs, which require complex cavity designs, EOM-based OFCs can be seamlessly integrated with a single CW laser and are highly amenable to miniaturization, making them ideal for portable applications. The digital electronics driving the EOMs are compact and robust, resulting in a system that is inherently more stable and less susceptible to environmental disturbances, such as temperature fluctuations, which can affect traditional OFC sources. Moreover, the comb line spacing in an EOM-based system is governed by the electronic modulation frequency, which can be precisely controlled and easily adjusted. This flexibility allows for the fine-tuning of the comb spacing to meet the resolution and bandwidth requirements of specific spectroscopic applications. Another notable advantage of EOM-based OFCs is their low power consumption. While MLLs typically require significant power to maintain stable comb operation, EOM-based systems achieve comb generation with substantially lower power demands. This efficiency makes EOM-based DCS particularly well suited for remote sensing and field-deployable applications, where power resources are often limited.

3.4. Outlook

Over the next decade, DCS is anticipated to increasingly supplant DFCS, particularly in the mid-IR and far-IR spectral regions. However, transitioning to high-repetition, high-precision DCS poses significant technical challenges. These challenges arise from the need to generate two highly correlated OFCs, where even femtosecond-scale temporal discrepancies or phase variations can distort interference patterns and introduce anomalies that are difficult to correct during post-processing [154,155]. While this level of precision has been largely achieved in the near-IR spectrum, extending such accuracy to the mid-IR and far-IR regions remains a key focus of ongoing research [156].

In parallel, extending the operational wavelength into the ultraviolet (UV) and extreme UV (XUV) regimes has already unlocked new applications, leveraging the high peak power of short pulses. This advancement has facilitated studies of rare isotope atomic ions, highly charged ions, and even nuclear transitions, with further breakthroughs anticipated in these domains [127,157–159].

Simultaneously, the integration of advanced digital technologies, such as embedded systems and FPGAs, into both DFCS and DCS systems holds great potential for enhancing efficiency and performance. Embedded systems can streamline control sequences, minimize downtime, and improve the experimental duty cycle [160]. Meanwhile, FPGAs, with their capabilities for high-speed data processing and reconfigurability, can manage the substantial data throughput inherent in these techniques. This enables real-time data acquisition and processing, improved coherence averaging efficiency, faster data acquisition rates, and enhanced temporal resolution—critical for investigating transient phenomena.

4. Conclusions

The development of innovative spectroscopic technologies, such as CP-FTMW and OFC spectroscopy, has revolutionized the field of molecular spectroscopy by dramatically improving precision, sensitivity, and efficiency. These advancements, driven by rapid progress in fast digital electronics and parallel processing, have broadened the horizons of molecular spectroscopy, enabling transformative applications across a wide range of scientific domains, including nuclear physics, environmental science, and astrophysics. As these technologies continue to advance, particularly with the integration of embedded systems and FPGAs, their capabilities are expected to reach unprecedented levels.

Looking forward, the transition to advanced techniques such as CE-DCS is anticipated to overcome existing challenges in mid-IR and far-IR spectroscopy, opening new frontiers for molecular analysis. The integration of cutting-edge digital technologies and the development of novel experimental designs will be critical to pushing the boundaries of these methodologies. These advancements promise to make complex, high-resolution spectroscopic measurements more accessible, versatile, and efficient, unlocking new possibilities for both discovery and practical applications. Such efforts will not only deepen our understanding of molecular dynamics and structures but also drive groundbreaking discoveries across a broad spectrum of scientific disciplines.

Author Contributions: Conceptualization, Y.Z. and J.P.; writing—original draft preparation, J.L. and R.F.; writing—review and editing, B.G. All authors have read and agreed to the published version of the manuscript.

Funding: This work is financially supported by the NSF RII Track-4 (Grant No. 2327247), HDRFS Nevada grant (70524459), NASA Space Grant Consortium (70524408), and UNLV TTDGRA program.

Acknowledgments: Y. Zhou thanks the host of the Ion Storage Group, NIST, Boulder.

Conflicts of Interest: The authors declare no conflicts of interest.

References

1. Quack, M.; Merkt, F. *Handbook of High-Resolution Spectroscopy*; Wiley: Hoboken, NJ, USA, 2011. [CrossRef]
2. Riyadh, S.M.S.; Telfah, H.; Jones, I.W.; Bersson, J.S.; Cheng, C.F.; Hu, S.M.; Foote, D.B.; Liu, J. Mid-infrared Doppler-free saturation absorption spectroscopy of the Q branch of CH_4 ν_3=1 band using a rapid-scanning continuous-wave optical parametric oscillator. *Opt. Lett.* **2024**, *49*, 4230–4233. [CrossRef] [PubMed]
3. Liu, Q.H.; Tan, Y.; Cheng, C.F.; Hu, S.M. Precision spectroscopy of molecular hydrogen. *Phys. Chem. Chem. Phys.* **2023**, *25*, 27914–27925. [CrossRef] [PubMed]
4. Wieman, C.; Hansch, T.W. Doppler-free laser polarization spectroscopy. *Phys. Rev. Lett.* **1976**, *36*, 1170–1173. [CrossRef]
5. Zalicki, P.; Zare, R.N. Cavity ring-down spectroscopy for quantitative absorption measurements. *J. Chem. Phys.* **1995**, *102*, 2708–2717. [CrossRef]
6. Berden, G.; Peeters, R.; Meijer, G. Cavity ring-down spectroscopy: Experimental schemes and applications. *Int. Rev. Phys. Chem.* **2000**, *19*, 565–607. [CrossRef]
7. Scherer, J.J.; Paul, J.B.; O'keefe, A.; Saykally, R.J. Cavity ringdown laser absorption spectroscopy: History, development, and application to pulsed molecular beams. *Chem. Rev.* **1997**, *97*, 25–52. [CrossRef]
8. Fiedler, S.E.; Hese, A.; Ruth, A.A. Incoherent broad-band cavity-enhanced absorption spectroscopy. *Chem. Phys. Lett.* **2003**, *371*, 284–294. [CrossRef]
9. Engeln, R.; Berden, G.; Peeters, R.; Meijer, G. Cavity enhanced absorption and cavity enhanced magnetic rotation spectroscopy. *Rev. Sci. Instrum.* **1998**, *69*, 3763–3769. [CrossRef]
10. Schindewolf, A.; Bause, R.; Chen, X.Y.; Duda, M.; Karman, T.; Bloch, I.; Luo, X.Y. Evaporation of microwave-shielded polar molecules to quantum degeneracy. *Nature* **2022**, *607*, 677–681. [CrossRef]
11. Bigagli, N.; Yuan, W.; Zhang, S.; Bulatovic, B.; Karman, T.; Stevenson, I.; Will, S. Observation of Bose–Einstein condensation of dipolar molecules. *Nature* **2024**, *631*, 289–293. [CrossRef]
12. Vilas, N.B.; Hallas, C.; Anderegg, L.; Robichaud, P.; Winnicki, A.; Mitra, D.; Doyle, J.M. Magneto-optical trapping and sub-Doppler cooling of a polyatomic molecule. *Nature* **2022**, *606*, 70–74. [CrossRef] [PubMed]
13. Jin, D.S.; Ye, J. Introduction to ultracold molecules: New frontiers in quantum and chemical physics. *Chem. Rev.* **2012**, *112*, 4801–4802. [CrossRef] [PubMed]
14. Tobias, W.G.; Matsuda, K.; Li, J.R.; Miller, C.; Carroll, A.N.; Bilitewski, T.; Rey, A.M.; Ye, J. Reactions between layer-resolved molecules mediated by dipolar spin exchange. *Science* **2022**, *375*, 1299–1303. [CrossRef] [PubMed]
15. Xia, J.; Enemali, G.; Zhang, R.; Fu, Y.; McCann, H.; Zhou, B.; Liu, C. FPGA-accelerated distributed sensing system for real-time industrial laser absorption spectroscopy tomography at kilo-hertz. *IEEE Trans. Ind. Inform.* **2024**, *20*, 2529–2539. [CrossRef]
16. Davies, V.; Wandy, J.; Weidt, S.; Hooft, J.J.V.D.; Miller, A.; Daly, R.; Rogers, S. Rapid development of improved data-dependent acquisition strategies. *Anal. Chem.* **2021**, *93*, 5676–5683. [CrossRef]
17. Manu, V.S.; Olivieri, C.; Veglia, G. AI-designed NMR spectroscopy RF pulses for fast acquisition at high and ultra-high magnetic fields. *Nat. Commun.* **2023**, *14*, 4144. [CrossRef]
18. Angulo, A.; Yang, L.; Aydil, E.S.; Modestino, M.A. Machine learning enhanced spectroscopic analysis: towards autonomous chemical mixture characterization for rapid process optimization†. *Digit. Discov.* **2022**, *1*, 35–44. [CrossRef]
19. Crocombe, R.A. Portable spectroscopy. *Appl. Spectrosc.* **2018**, *72*, 1701–1751. [CrossRef]
20. Yu, H.; Tan, Y.; Cunningham, B.T. Smartphone fluorescence spectroscopy. *Anal. Chem.* **2014**, *86*, 8805–8813. [CrossRef]
21. Townes, C.; Schawlow, A. *Microwave Spectroscopy*; Dover books on physics; Dover Publications: Mineola, NY, USA, 2013.
22. Schwarting, M.; Seifert, N.A.; Davis, M.J.; Blaiszik, B.; Foster, I.; Prozument, K. Twins in rotational spectroscopy: Does a rotational spectrum uniquely identify a molecule? *arXiv* **2024**, arXiv:2404.04225. [CrossRef]
23. Patterson, D.; Schnell, M.; Doyle, J.M. Enantiomer-specific detection of chiral molecules via microwave spectroscopy. *Nature* **2013**, *497*, 475–477. [CrossRef] [PubMed]
24. Crabtree, K.N.; Martin-Drumel, M.A.; Brown, G.G.; Gaster, S.A.; Hall, T.M.; McCarthy, M.C. Microwave spectral taxonomy: A semi-automated combination of chirped-pulse and cavity Fourier-transform microwave spectroscopy. *J. Chem. Phys.* **2016**, *144*, 124201. [CrossRef] [PubMed]
25. Balle, T.J.; Flygare, W.H. Fabry-Perot cavity pulsed Fourier transform microwave spectrometer with a pulsed nozzle particle source. *Rev. Sci. Instrum.* **1981**, *52*, 33–45. [CrossRef]
26. Johnson, H.R. Backward-Wave Oscillators. *Proc. IRE* **1955**, *43*, 684–697. [CrossRef]
27. Goebel, D.M.; Butler, J.M.; Schumacher, R.W.; Santoru, J.; Eisenhart, R.L. High-power microwave source based on an unmagnetized backward-wave oscillator. *IEEE Trans. Plasma Sci.* **1994**, *22*, 547 – 553. [CrossRef]
28. Chen, C.; Liu, G.; Huang, W.; Song, Z.; Fan, J.; Wang, H. A repetitive X-band relativistic backward-wave oscillator. *IEEE Trans. Plasma Sci.* **2002**, *30*, 1108–1111. [CrossRef]
29. Nusinovich, G.S.; Member, S.; Carmel, Y.; Antonsen, T.M.; Goebel, D.M.; Santoru, J. Recent progress in the development of plasma-filled traveling-wave tubes and backward-wave oscillators. *IEEE Trans. Plasma Sci.* **1998**, *26*, 151. [CrossRef]
30. Hummelt, J.S.; Lewis, S.M.; Shapiro, M.A.; Temkin, R.J. Design of a metamaterial-based backward-wave oscillator. *IEEE Trans. Plasma Sci.* **2014**, *42*, 930–936. [CrossRef]
31. Khodos, V.V.; Ryndyk, D.A.; Vaks, V.L. Fast-passage microwave molecular spectroscopy with frequency sweeping. *Eur. Phys. J. Appl. Phys.* **2004**, *25*, 203–208. [CrossRef]

32. Brown, G.G.; Dian, B.C.; Douglass, K.O.; Geyer, S.M.; Pate, B.H. The rotational spectrum of epifluorohydrin measured by chirped-pulse Fourier transform microwave spectroscopy. *J. Mol. Spectrosc.* **2006**, *238*, 200–212. [CrossRef]
33. Brown, G.G.; Dian, B.C.; Douglass, K.O.; Geyer, S.M.; Shipman, S.T.; Pate, B.H. A broadband Fourier transform microwave spectrometer based on chirped pulse excitation. *Rev. Sci. Instrum.* **2008**, *79*, 053103. [CrossRef] [PubMed]
34. Park, G.B.; Field, R.W. Perspective: The first ten years of broadband chirped pulse Fourier transform microwave spectroscopy. *J. Chem. Phys.* **2016**, *144*, 200901. [CrossRef] [PubMed]
35. McGurk, J.C.; Schmalz, T.G.; Flygare, W.H. Fast passage in rotational spectroscopy: Theory and experiment. *J. Chem. Phys.* **1974**, *60*, 4181–4188. [CrossRef]
36. Anderegg, L.; Burchesky, S.; Bao, Y.; Yu, S.S.; Karman, T.; Chae, E.; Ni, K.K.; Ketterle, W.; Doyle, J.M. Observation of microwave shielding of ultracold molecules. *Science* **2021**, *373*, 779–782. [CrossRef] [PubMed]
37. Wright, S.C.; Wall, T.E.; Tarbutt, M.R. Microwave trap for atoms and molecules. *Phys. Rev. Res.* **2019**, *1*, 033035. [CrossRef]
38. Park, G.B.; Steeves, A.H.; Kuyanov-Prozument, K.; Neill, J.L.; Field, R.W. Design and evaluation of a pulsed-jet chirped-pulse millimeter-wave spectrometer for the 70–102 GHz region. *J. Chem. Phys.* **2011**, *135*, 024202. [CrossRef]
39. Lauzin, C.; Schmutz, H.; Agner, J.A.; Merkt, F. Chirped-pulse millimetre-wave spectrometer for the 140–180 GHz region. *Mol. Phys.* **2018**, *116*, 3656–3665. [CrossRef]
40. Gerecht, E.; Douglass, K.O.; Plusquellic, D.F. Chirped-pulse terahertz spectroscopy for broadband trace gas sensing. *Opt. Express* **2011**, *19*, 8973–8984. [CrossRef]
41. Steber, A.L.; Harris, B.J.; Neill, J.L.; Pate, B.H. An arbitrary waveform generator based chirped pulse Fourier transform spectrometer operating from 260 to 295 GHz. *J. Mol. Spectrosc.* **2012**, *280*, 3–10. [CrossRef]
42. Stroud, J.R.; Plusquellic, D.F. Difference-frequency chirped-pulse dual-comb generation in the THz region: Temporal magnification of the quantum dynamics of water vapor lines by >60,000. *J. Chem. Phys.* **2022**, *156*, 044302. [CrossRef]
43. Neill, J.L.; Harris, B.J.; Steber, A.L.; Douglass, K.O.; Plusquellic, D.F.; Pate, B.H. Segmented chirped-pulse Fourier transform submillimeter spectroscopy for broadband gas analysis. *Opt. Express* **2013**, *21*, 19743–19749. [CrossRef] [PubMed]
44. Barnum, T.J.; Lee, K.L.K.; McGuire, B.A. Chirped-Pulse Fourier transform millimeter-wave spectroscopy of Furan, isotopologues, and vibrational excited states. *ACS Earth Space Chem.* **2021**, *5*, 2986–2994. [CrossRef]
45. Sironneau, V.; Chelin, P.; Tchana, F.K.; Kleiner, I.; Pirali, O.; Roy, P.; Guillemin, J.C.; Orphal, J.; Marguls, L.; Motiyenko, R.A.; et al. Reinvestigation of the microwave and new high resolution far-infrared spectra of cis-methyl nitrite, CH3ONO: Rotational study of the two first torsional states. *J. Mol. Spectrosc.* **2011**, *267*, 92–99. [CrossRef]
46. Prozument, K.; Baraban, J.H.; Changala, P.B.; Park, G.B.; Shaver, R.G.; Muenter, J.S.; Klippenstein, S.J.; Chernyak, V.Y.; Field, R.W. Photodissociation transition states characterized by chirped pulse millimeter wave spectroscopy. *Proc. Natl. Acad. Sci. USA* **2020**, *117*, 146–151. [CrossRef] [PubMed]
47. Fritz, S.M.; Mishra, P.; Wullenkord, J.; Fugazzi, P.G.; Kohse-Höinghaus, K.; Zwier, T.S.; Hansen, N. Detecting combustion intermediates via broadband chirped-pulse microwave spectroscopy. *Proc. Combust. Inst.* **2021**, *38*, 1761–1769. [CrossRef]
48. Zou, L.; Motiyenko, R.A.; Margulès, L.; Alekseev, E.A. Millimeter-wave emission spectrometer based on direct digital synthesis. *Rev. Sci. Instrum.* **2020**, *91*, 063104. [CrossRef]
49. Li, J.; Ojeda, J.M.; Letourneau, S.; Zhou, Y. Cost-effective segmented CP-FTMW spectrometers. Department of Physics and Astronomy, University of Nevada, Las Vegas, NV 89154, USA, 2024. *In preparation*.
50. Fatima, M.; Pérez, C.; Arenas, B.E.; Schnell, M.; Steber, A.L. Benchmarking a new segmented K-band chirped-pulse microwave spectrometer and its application to the conformationally rich amino alcohol isoleucinol. *Phys. Chem. Chem. Phys.* **2020**, *22*, 17042–17051. [CrossRef]
51. McCarthy, M.C.; Zou, L.; Martin-Drumel, M.A. To kink or not: A search for long-chain cumulenones using microwave spectral taxonomy. *J. Chem. Phys.* **2017**, *146*, 154301. [CrossRef]
52. McGuire, B.A.; Martin-Drumel, M.A.; Lee, K.L.K.; Stanton, J.F.; Gottlieb, C.A.; McCarthy, M.C. Vibrational satellites of C2S, C3S, and C4S: Microwave spectral taxonomy as a stepping stone to the millimeter-wave band. *Phys. Chem. Chem. Phys.* **2018**, *20*, 13870–13889. [CrossRef]
53. York, L.; Sorrells, C.; Dim, C.A.; Crabtree, K.N.; Hernandez-Castillo, A.O. A Tale of Two Tails: Rotational Spectroscopy of N-Ethyl Maleimide and N-Ethyl Succinimide. *J. Phys. Chem. A* **2024**, *128*, 5541–5547. [CrossRef]
54. Salvitti, G.; Sigismondi, S.; Melandri, S.; López, J.C.; Blanco, S.; Maris, A. Structure and dynamics of 3′-aminoacetophenone and 4′-aminoacetophenone from rotational spectroscopy. *Phys. Chem. Chem. Phys.* **2024**, *26*, 1881–1890. [CrossRef] [PubMed]
55. Landau, A.; Eduardus; Behar, D.; Wallach, E.R.; Pašteka, L.F.; Faraji, S.; Borschevsky, A.; Shagam, Y. Chiral molecule candidates for trapped ion spectroscopy by ab initio calculations: From state preparation to parity violation. *J. Chem. Phys.* **2023**, *159*, 114307. [CrossRef] [PubMed]
56. Fiechter, M.R.; Haase, P.A.; Saleh, N.; Soulard, P.; Tremblay, B.; Havenith, R.W.; Timmermans, R.G.; Schwerdtfeger, P.; Crassous, J.; Darquié, B.; et al. Toward detection of the molecular parity violation in Chiral Ru(acac)$_3$ and Os(acac)$_3$. *J. Phys. Chem. Lett.* **2022**, *13*, 10011–10017. [CrossRef] [PubMed]
57. Quack, M. On the measurement of the parity violating energy difference between enantiomers. *Chem. Phys. Lett.* **1986**, *132*, 147–153. [CrossRef]
58. Quack, M.; Seyfang, G.; Wichmann, G. Perspectives on parity violation in chiral molecules: theory, spectroscopic experiment and biomolecular homochirality. *Chem. Sci.* **2022**, *13*, 10598–10643. [CrossRef]

59. Berry, M.V.; Dennis, M.R. The optical singularities of birefringent dichroic chiral crystals. *Proc. R. Soc. London. Ser. A Math. Phys. Eng. Sci.* **2003**, *459*, 1261–1292. [CrossRef]
60. Hodgkinson, I.; Wu, Q.h. Inorganic Chiral Optical Materials. *Adv. Mater.* **2001**, *13*, 889–897. [CrossRef]
61. Govorov, A.O.; Fan, Z.; Hernandez, P.; Slocik, J.M.; Naik, R.R. Theory of Circular Dichroism of Nanomaterials Comprising Chiral Molecules and Nanocrystals: Plasmon Enhancement, Dipole Interactions, and Dielectric Effects. *Nano Lett.* **2010**, *10*, 1374–1382. [CrossRef]
62. Freedman, T.B.; Cao, X.; Dukor, R.K.; Nafie, L.A. Absolute configuration determination of chiral molecules in the solution state using vibrational circular dichroism. *Chirality* **2003**, *15*, 743–758. [CrossRef]
63. Barron, L.D.; Lutz Hecht, I.H.M.; Blanch, E.W. Raman optical activity comes of age. *Mol. Phys.* **2004**, *102*, 731–744. [CrossRef]
64. He, Y.; Bo, W.; Dukor, R.K.; Nafie, L.A. Determination of absolute configuration of chiral molecules using vibrational optical activity: a review. *Appl. Spectrosc.* **2011**, *65*, 699–723. [CrossRef] [PubMed]
65. Patterson, D.; Doyle, J.M. Sensitive chiral analysis via microwave three-wave mixing. *Phys. Rev. Lett.* **2013**, *111*, 023008. [CrossRef] [PubMed]
66. Lee, J.H.; Bischoff, J.; Hernandez-Castillo, A.O.; Abdiha, E.; Sartakov, B.G.; Meijer, G.; Eibenberger-Arias, S. The influence of microwave pulse conditions on enantiomer-specific state transfer. *New J. Phys.* **2024**, *26*, 033015. [CrossRef]
67. Lee, J.; Abdiha, E.; Sartakov, B.G.; Meijier, G.; Eibenberger-Arias, S. Near-complete chiral selection in rotational quantum states. *Nat. Commun.* **2024**, *15*, 7441. [CrossRef] [PubMed]
68. Singh, H.; Berggötz, F.E.; Sun, W.; Schnell, M. Chiral control of gas-phase molecules using microwave pulses. *Angew. Chem. Int. Ed.* **2023**, *62*, e202219045. [CrossRef]
69. Sun, W.; Schnell, M. Microwave three-wave mixing spectroscopy of chiral molecules in weakly bound complexes. *J. Phys. Chem. Lett.* **2023**, *14*, 7389–7394. [CrossRef]
70. Domingos, S.R.; Pérez, C.; Schnell, M. Sensing Chirality with Rotational Spectroscopy. *Annu. Rev. Phys. Chem.* **2018**, *69*, 499–519. [CrossRef]
71. Prozument, K.; Shaver, R.G.; Ciuba, M.; Muenter, J.S.; Park, G.B.; Stanton, J.F.; Guo, H.; Wong, B.M.; Perry, D.S.; Field, R.W. A new approach toward transition state spectroscopy. *Faraday Discuss.* **2013**, *163*, 33–57. [CrossRef]
72. Prozument, K.; Park, G.B.; Shaver, R.G.; Vasiliou, A.K.; Oldham, J.M.; David, D.E.; Muenter, J.S.; Stanton, J.F.; Suits, A.G.; Ellison, G.B.; et al. Chirped-pulse millimeter-wave spectroscopy for dynamics and kinetics studies of pyrolysis reactions. *Phys. Chem. Chem. Phys.* **2014**, *16*, 15739–15751. [CrossRef]
73. Zaleski, D.P.; Harding, L.B.; Klippenstein, S.J.; Ruscic, B.; Prozument, K. Time-resolved kinetic chirped-pulse rotational spectroscopy in a room-temperature flow reactor. *J. Phys. Chem. Lett.* **2017**, *8*, 6180–6188. [CrossRef]
74. Schnell, M. Broadband rotational spectroscopy for molecular structure and dynamics studies. *Z. Fur Phys. Chem.* **2013**, *227*, 1–21. [CrossRef]
75. Dian, B.C.; Brown, G.G.; Douglass, K.O.; Pate, B.H. Measuring picosecond isomerization kinetics via broadband microwave spectroscopy. *Science* **2008**, *320*, 924–928. [CrossRef] [PubMed]
76. Gallagher, T.F. Rydberg atoms. *Rep. Prog. Phys.* **1988**, *51*, 143. [CrossRef]
77. Gentile, T.; Hughey, B.; Kleppner, D.; Ducas, T. Microwave spectroscopy of calcium Rydberg states. *Phys. Rev. A* **1990**, *42*, 440. [CrossRef]
78. Merkt, F. Molecules in high Rydberg states. *Annu. Rev. Phys. Chem.* **1997**, *48*, 675–709. [CrossRef]
79. Hogan, S.; Seiler, C.; Merkt, F. Rydberg-state-enabled deceleration and trapping of cold molecules. *Phys. Rev. Lett.* **2009**, *103*, 123001. [CrossRef]
80. Seiler, C.; Hogan, S.D.; Merkt, F. Dynamical processes in Rydberg-Stark deceleration and trapping of atoms and molecules. *Chimia* **2012**, *66*, 208. [CrossRef]
81. Hogan, S.D. Rydberg-Stark deceleration of atoms and molecules. *EPJ Tech. Instrum.* **2016**, *3*, 2. [CrossRef]
82. Jakubek, Z.J.; Field, R.W. Core-penetrating Rydberg series of BaF: $s \sim p \sim d \sim f$ supercomplexes. *Phys. Rev. Lett.* **1994**, *72*, 2167. [CrossRef]
83. Kay, J.J.; Coy, S.L.; Petrović, V.S.; Wong, B.M.; Field, R.W. Separation of long-range and short-range interactions in Rydberg states of diatomic molecules. *J. Chem. Phys.* **2008**, *128*, 194301. [CrossRef]
84. Altunata, S.N.; Coy, S.L.; Field, R.W. Properties of nearly one-electron molecules. II. Application to the Rydberg spectrum of CaF. *J. Chem. Phys.* **2005**, *123*, 084319. [CrossRef] [PubMed]
85. Coy, S.L.; Grimes, D.D.; Zhou, Y.; Field, R.W.; Wong, B.M. Electric potential invariants and ions-in-molecules effective potentials for molecular Rydberg states. *J. Chem. Phys.* **2016**, *145*, 234301. [CrossRef] [PubMed]
86. Kay, J.J.; Altunata, S.N.; Coy, S.L.; Field, R.W. Resonance between electronic and rotational motions in Rydberg states of CaF. *Mol. Phys.* **2007**, *105*, 1661–1673. [CrossRef]
87. Zhou, Y.; Grimes, D.D.; Barnum, T.J.; Patterson, D.; Coy, S.L.; Klein, E.; Muenter, J.S.; Field, R.W. Direct detection of Rydberg-Rydberg millimeter-wave transitions in a buffer gas cooled molecular beam. *Chem. Phys. Lett.* **2015**, *640*, 124–136. [CrossRef]
88. Wang, T.; Yelin, S.F.; Côté, R.; Eyler, E.E.; Farooqi, S.M.; Gould, P.L.; Koštrun, M.; Tong, D.; Vrinceanu, D. Superradiance in ultracold Rydberg gases. *Phys. Rev. A* **2007**, *75*, 033802. [CrossRef]
89. Zhou, Y. Cooperative effects in a dense Rydberg gas. *Mol. Phys.* **2012**, *110*, 1909–1915. [CrossRef]

90. Grimes, D.D.; Coy, S.L.; Barnum, T.J.; Zhou, Y.; Yelin, S.F.; Field, R.W. Direct single-shot observation of millimeter-wave superradiance in Rydberg-Rydberg transitions. *Phys. Rev. A* **2017**, *95*, 043818. [CrossRef]
91. Hutzler, N.R.; Lu, H.I.; Doyle, J.M. The buffer gas beam: An intense, cold, and slow source for atoms and molecules. *Chem. Rev.* **2012**, *112*, 4803–4827. [CrossRef]
92. Wright, S.C.; Doppelbauer, M.; Hofsäss, S.; Schewe, H.C.; Sartakov, B.; Meijer, G.; Truppe, S. Cryogenic buffer gas beams of AlF, CaF, MgF, YbF, Al, Ca, Yb and NO - a comparison. *Mol. Phys.* **2023**, *121*, 2146541. [CrossRef]
93. Patterson, D.; Doyle, J.M. Bright, guided molecular beam with hydrodynamic enhancement. *J. Chem. Phys.* **2007**, *126*, 154307. [CrossRef]
94. Lu, H.I.; Rasmussen, J.; Wright, M.J.; Patterson, D.; Doyle, J.M. A cold and slow molecular beam. *Phys. Chem. Chem. Phys. PCCP* **2011**, *13*, 18986–18990. [CrossRef] [PubMed]
95. Baiz, C.R.; Błasiak, B.; Bredenbeck, J.; Cho, M.; Choi, J.H.; Corcelli, S.A.; Dijkstra, A.G.; Feng, C.J.; Garrett-Roe, S.; Ge, N.H.; et al. Vibrational spectroscopic map, vibrational spectroscopy, and intermolecular interaction. *Chem. Rev.* **2020**, *120*, 7152–7218. [CrossRef] [PubMed]
96. Perakis, F.; Marco, L.D.; Shalit, A.; Tang, F.; Kann, Z.R.; Kühne, T.D.; Torre, R.; Bonn, M.; Nagata, Y. Vibrational spectroscopy and dynamics of water. *Chem. Rev.* **2016**, *116*, 7590–7607. [CrossRef] [PubMed]
97. Cheng, J.X.; Xie, X.S. Vibrational spectroscopic imaging of living systems: An emerging platform for biology and medicine. *Science* **2015**, *350*, 6264. [CrossRef] [PubMed]
98. Berthomieu, C.; Hienerwadel, R. Fourier transform infrared (FTIR) spectroscopy. *Photosynth. Res.* **2009**, *101*, 157–170. [CrossRef]
99. Coddington, I.; Newbury, N.; Swann, W. Dual-comb spectroscopy. *Optica* **2016**, *3*, 414–426. [CrossRef]
100. Available online: https://www.menlosystems.com/products/optical-frequency-combs/fc1500-250-uln-plus/ (accessed on 15 November 2024).
101. Available online: https://www.toptica.com/frequency-combs (accessed on 15 November 2024).
102. Hall, J.L. Nobel Lecture: Defining and measuring optical frequencies. *Rev. Mod. Phys.* **2006**, *78*, 1279. [CrossRef]
103. Picqué, N.; Hänsch, T.W. Frequency comb spectroscopy. *Nat. Photonics* **2019**, *13*, 146–157. [CrossRef]
104. Hargrove, L.E.; Fork, R.L.; Pollack, M.A. Locking of hene laser modes induced by synchronous intracavity modulation. *Appl. Phys. Lett.* **1964**, *5*, 4–5. [CrossRef]
105. Kuizenga, D.J.; Siegman, A.E. FM and AM mode locking of the homogeneous laser-Part I: Theory. *IEEE J. Quaktum Electron.* **1970**, *6* , 694–708. [CrossRef]
106. Brabec, T.; Spielmann, C.; Curley, P.F.; Krausz, F. Kerr lens mode locking. *Opt. Lett.* **1992**, *17*, 1292–1294. [CrossRef]
107. Haus, H.A. Mode-Locking of Lasers. *Ieee J. Sel. Top. Quantum Electron.* **2000**, *6*, 1173–1185. [CrossRef]
108. Hudson, D.D.; Holman, K.W.; Jones, R.J.; Cundiff, S.T.; Ye, J.; Jones, D.J. Mode-locked fiber laser frequency-controlled with an intracavity electro-optic modulator. *Opt. Lett.* **2005**, *30*, 2948–2950. [CrossRef] [PubMed]
109. Haus, H. A theory of forced mode locking. *IEEE J. Quantum Electron.* **1975**, *11*, 323–330. [CrossRef]
110. Revin, D.G.; Hemingway, M.; Wang, Y.; Cockburn, J.W.; Belyanin, A. Active mode locking of quantum cascade lasers in an external ring cavity. *Nat. Commun.* **2016**, *7*, 11440. [CrossRef]
111. Mollenauer, L.F.; Vieira, N.D.; Szeto, L. Mode locking by synchronous pumping using a gain medium with microsecond decay times. *Opt. Lett.* **1982**, *7*, 414–416. [CrossRef]
112. Demaria, A.J.; Stetser, D.A.; Heynau, H. Self mode-locking of lasers with saturable absorbers. *Appl. Phys. Lett.* **1966**, *8*, 174–176. [CrossRef]
113. Paschotta, R.; Keller, U. Passive mode locking with slow saturable absorbers. *Appl. Phys. B Lasers Opt.* **2001**, *73*, 653–662. [CrossRef]
114. Kärtner, F.X.; Jung, I.D.; Keller, U. Soliton Mode-Locking with Saturable Absorbers. *Ieee J. Sel. Top. Quantum Electron.* **1996**, *2*, 540–556. [CrossRef]
115. Haus, H.A. Theory of mode locking with a fast saturable absorber. *J. Appl. Phys.* **1975**, *46*, 3049–3058. [CrossRef]
116. Herrmann, J. Theory of Kerr-lens mode locking: Role of self-focusing and radially varying gain. *JOSA b* **1994**, *11*, 498–512. [CrossRef]
117. Cerullo, G.; Silvestri, S.D.; Magni, V. Self-starting Kerr-lens mode locking of a Ti:sapphire laser. *Opt. Lett.* **1994**, *19*, 1040–1042. [CrossRef] [PubMed]
118. Morgner, U.; Cho, S.H.; Chen, Y.; Haus, H.A.; Fujimoto, J.G.; Ippen, E.P.; Scheuer, V.; Angelow, G.; Tschudi, T. Sub-two-cycle pulses from a Kerr-lens mode-locked Ti : Sapphire laser. *Opt. Lett.* **1999**, *24*, 411–413. [CrossRef] [PubMed]
119. Udem, T.; Holzwarth, R.; Hansch, T.W. Optical frequency metrology. *Nature* **2002**, *416*, 233–237. [CrossRef]
120. Telle, H.R.; Steinmeyer, G.; Dunlop, A.E.; Stenger, J.; Sutter, D.H.; Keller, U. Carrier-envelope offset phase control: A novel concept for absolute optical frequency measurement and ultrashort pulse generation. *Appl. Phys. B* **1999**, *69*, 327–332. [CrossRef]
121. Keller, U. Ultrafast solid-state laser oscillators: A success story for the last 20 years with no end in sight. *Appl. Phys. B Lasers Opt.* **2010**, *100*, 15–28. [CrossRef]
122. Krauss, G.; Fehrenbacher, D.; Brida, D.; Riek, C.; Sell, A.; Huber, R.; Leitenstorfer, A. All-passive phase locking of a compact Er:fiber laser system. *Opt. Lett.* **2011**, *36*, 540–542. [CrossRef]
123. Puppe, T.; Sell, A.; Kliese, R.; Hoghooghi, N.; Zach, A.; Kaenders, W. Characterization of a DFG comb showing quadratic scaling of the phase noise with frequency. *Opt. Lett.* **2016**, *41*, 1877–1880. [CrossRef]

124. Thorpe, M.J.; Ye, J. Cavity-enhanced direct frequency comb spectroscopy. *Appl. Phys. B* **2008**, *91*, 397–414. [CrossRef]
125. Adler, F.; Thorpe, M.J.; Cossel, K.C.; Ye, J. Cavity-enhanced direct frequency comb spectroscopy: Technology and applications. *Annu. Rev. Anal. Chem.* **2010**, *3*, 175–205. [CrossRef]
126. Stowe, M.C.; Thorpe, M.J.; Pe'er, A.; Ye, J.; Stalnaker, J.E.; Gerginov, V.; Diddams, S.A. Direct frequency comb spectroscopy. *Adv. At. Mol. Opt. Phys.* **2008**, *55*, 1–60. [CrossRef]
127. Cingoz, A.; Yost, D.C.; Allison, T.K.; Ruehl, A.; Fermann, M.E.; Hartl, I.; Ye, J. Direct frequency comb spectroscopy in the extreme ultraviolet. *Nature* **2012**, *482*, 68–71. [CrossRef] [PubMed]
128. Cossel, K.C.; Adler, F.; Bertness, K.A.; Thorpe, M.J.; Feng, J.; Raynor, M.W.; Ye, J. Analysis of trace impurities in semiconductor gas via cavity-enhanced direct frequency comb spectroscopy. *Appl. Phys. B* **2010**, *100*, 917–924. [CrossRef]
129. Coburn, S.; Alden, C.B.; Wright, R.; Cossel, K.; Baumann, E.; Truong, G.W.; Giorgetta, F.; Sweeney, C.; Newbury, N.R.; Prasad, K.; et al. Regional trace-gas source attribution using a field-deployed dual frequency comb spectrometer. *Optica* **2018**, *5*, 320–327. [CrossRef]
130. Weichman, M.L.; Changala, P.B.; Ye, J.; Chen, Z.; Yan, M.; Picqué, N. Broadband molecular spectroscopy with optical frequency combs. *J. Mol. Spectrosc.* **2019**, *355*, 66–78. [CrossRef]
131. Changala, P.B.; Weichman, M.L.; Lee, K.F.; Fermann, M.E.; Ye, J. Rovibrational quantum state resolution of the C_{60} fullerene. *Science* **2019**, *363*, 49–54. [CrossRef]
132. Sinclair, L.C.; Cossel, K.C.; Coffey, T.; Ye, J.; Cornell, E.A. Frequency comb velocity-modulation spectroscopy. *Phys. Rev. Lett.* **2011**, *107*, 093002. [CrossRef]
133. Cairncross, W.B.; Gresh, D.N.; Grau, M.; Cossel, K.C.; Roussy, T.S.; Ni, Y.; Zhou, Y.; Ye, J.; Cornell, E.A. Precision measurement of the electron's electric Dipole moment using trapped molecular ions. *Phys. Rev. Lett.* **2017**, *119*, 153001. [CrossRef]
134. Roussy, T.S.; Caldwell, L.; Wright, T.; Cairncross, W.B.; Shagam, Y.; Ng, K.B.; Schlossberger, N.; Park, S.Y.; Wang, A.; Ye, J.; et al. An improved bound on the electron's electric dipole moment. *Science* **2023**, *381*, 46–50. [CrossRef]
135. Thorpe, M.J.; Balslev-Clausen, D.; Kirchner, M.S.; Ye, J. Cavity-enhanced optical frequency comb spectroscopy: Application to human breath analysis. *Opt. Express* **2008**, *16*, 2387–2397. [CrossRef]
136. Liang, Q.; Chan, Y.C.; Toscano, J.; Bjorkman, K.K.; Leinwand, L.A.; Parker, R.; Nozik, E.S.; Nesbitt, D.J.; Ye, J. Breath analysis by ultra-sensitive broadband laser spectroscopy detects SARS-CoV-2 infection. *J. Breath Res.* **2023**, *17*, 036001. [CrossRef] [PubMed]
137. Asahara, A.; Minoshima, K. Development of ultrafast time-resolved dual-comb spectroscopy. *APL Photonics* **2017**, *2*, 041301. [CrossRef]
138. Fleisher, A.J.; Bjork, B.J.; Bui, T.Q.; Cossel, K.C.; Okumura, M.; Ye, J. Mid-infrared time-resolved frequency comb spectroscopy of transient free radicals. *J. Phys. Chem. Lett.* **2014**, *5*, 2241–2246. [CrossRef] [PubMed]
139. Long, D.A.; Cich, M.J.; Mathurin, C.; Heiniger, A.T.; Mathews, G.C.; Frymire, A.; Rieker, G.B. Nanosecond time-resolved dual-comb absorption spectroscopy. *Nat. Photonics* **2024**, *18*, 127–131. [CrossRef]
140. Bjork, B.J.; Bui, T.Q.; Heckl, O.H.; Changala, P.B.; Spaun, B.; Heu, P.; Follman, D.; Deutsch, C.; Cole, G.D.; Aspelmeyer, M.; et al. Direct frequency comb measurement of OD + CO→DOCO kinetics. *Science* **2016**, *354*, 444–448. [CrossRef]
141. Makowiecki, A.S.; Herman, D.I.; Hoghooghi, N.; Strong, E.F.; Cole, R.K.; Ycas, G.; Giorgetta, F.R.; Lapointe, C.B.; Glusman, J.F.; Daily, J.W.; et al. Mid-infrared dual frequency comb spectroscopy for combustion analysis from 2.8 to 5 μm. *Proc. Combust. Inst.* **2021**, *38*, 1627–1635. [CrossRef]
142. Hu, G.; Mizuguchi, T.; Oe, R.; Nitta, K.; Zhao, X.; Minamikawa, T.; Li, T.; Zheng, Z.; Yasui, T. Dual terahertz comb spectroscopy with a single free-running fibre laser. *Sci. Rep.* **2018**, *8*, 11155. [CrossRef]
143. Fu, H.; Jiang, X.; Wu, J.; Qiu, L.; Yuan, Y.; Guo, X.; Zhu, Y. Terahertz dual-comb spectroscopy: A comparison between time- and frequency-domain operation modes. *Infrared Phys. Technol.* **2021**, *115*, 103699. [CrossRef]
144. Giorgetta, F.R.; Peischl, J.; Herman, D.I.; Ycas, G.; Coddington, I.; Newbury, N.R.; Cossel, K.C. Open-path dual-comb spectroscopy for multispecies trace gas detection in the 4.5–5 μm spectral region. *Laser Photonics Rev.* **2021**, *15*, 2000583. [CrossRef]
145. Malarich, N.A.; Washburn, B.R.; Cossel, K.C.; Mead, G.J.; Giorgetta, F.R.; Herman, D.I.; Newbury, N.R.; Coddington, I. Validation of open-path dual-comb spectroscopy against an O_2 background. *Opt. Express* **2023**, *31*, 5042–5055. [CrossRef]
146. Han, J.J.; Zhong, W.; Zhao, R.C.; Zeng, T.; Li, M.; Lu, J.; Peng, X.X.; Shi, X.P.; Yin, Q.; Wang, Y.; et al. Dual-comb spectroscopy over 100km open-air path. *arXiv* **2023**, arxiv:2310.19294.
147. Dutt, A.; Joshi, C.; Ji, X.; Cardenas, J.; Okawachi, Y.; Luke, K.; Gaeta, A.L.; Lipson, M. On-chip dual-comb source for spectroscopy. *Sci. Adv.* **2018**, *4*, e1701858. [CrossRef]
148. Gaeta, A.L.; Lipson, M.; Kippenberg, T.J. Photonic-chip-based frequency combs. *Nat. Photonics* **2019**, *13*, 158–169. [CrossRef]
149. Yu, M.; Okawachi, Y.; Griffith, A.G.; Picqué, N.; Lipson, M.; Gaeta, A.L. Silicon-chip-based mid-infrared dual-comb spectroscopy. *Nat. Commun.* **2018**, *9*, 1869. [CrossRef] [PubMed]
150. Suh, M.G.; Yang, Q.F.; Yang, K.Y.; Yi, X.; Vahala, K.J. Microresonator soliton dual-comb spectroscopy. *Science* **2016**, *354*, 600–603. [CrossRef]
151. Rueda, A.; Sedlmeir, F.; Kumari, M.; Leuchs, G.; Schwefel, H.G. Resonant electro-optic frequency comb. *Nature* **2019**, *568*, 378–381. [CrossRef]
152. Long, D.A.; Bresler, S.M.; Bao, Y.; Reschovsky, B.J.; Hodges, J.T.; Lawall, J.R.; LeBrun, T.W.; Gorman, J.J. Single-modulator, direct frequency comb spectroscopy via serrodyne modulation. *Opt. Lett.* **2023**, *48*, 892–895. [CrossRef]
153. Parriaux, A.; Hammani, K.; Millot, G. Electro-optic frequency combs. *Adv. Opt. Photon.* **2020**, *12*, 223–287. [CrossRef]

154. Coddington, I.; Swann, W.C.; Newbury, N.R. Coherent dual-comb spectroscopy at high signal-to-noise ratio. *Phys. Rev. A* **2010**, *82*, 043817. [CrossRef]
155. Phillips, C.R.; Willenberg, B.; Nussbaum-Lapping, A.; Callegari, F.; Camenzind, S.L.; Pupeikis, J.; Keller, U. Coherently averaged dual-comb spectroscopy with a low-noise and high-power free-running gigahertz dual-comb laser. *Opt. Express* **2023**, *31*, 7103–7119. [CrossRef]
156. Chen, Z.; Hänsch, T.W.; Picqué, N. Mid-infrared feed-forward dual-comb spectroscopy. *Proc. Natl. Acad. Sci. USA* **2019**, *116*, 3454–3459. [CrossRef] [PubMed]
157. Zhang, C.; Ooi, T.; Higgins, J.S.; Doyle, J.F.; von der Wense, L.; Beeks, K.; Leitner, A.; Kazakov, G.A.; Li, P.; Thirolf, P.G.; et al. Frequency ratio of the 229mTh nuclear isomeric transition and the 87Sr atomic clock. *Nature* **2024**, *633*, 63–70. [CrossRef] [PubMed]
158. Ozawa, A.; Davila-Rodriguez, J.; Bounds, J.R.; Schuessler, H.A.; Hänsch, T.W.; Udem, T. Single ion fluorescence excited with a single mode of an UV frequency comb. *Nat. Commun.* **2017**, *8*, 44. [CrossRef] [PubMed]
159. Nauta, J.; Borodin, A.; Ledwa, H.B.; Stark, J.; Schwarz, M.; Schmöger, L.; Micke, P.; López-Urrutia, J.R.C.; Pfeifer, T. Towards precision measurements on highly charged ions using a high harmonic generation frequency comb. *Nucl. Instrum. Methods Phys. Res. Sect. B Beam Interact. Mater. At.* **2017**, *408*, 285–288. [CrossRef]
160. Kameyama, R.; Takizawa, S.; Hiramatsu, K.; Goda, K. Dual-comb coherent Raman spectroscopy with near 100% duty cycle. *ACS Photonics* **2021**, *8*, 975–981. [CrossRef]

metrology

MDPI

Review

Optical Fringe Projection: A Straightforward Approach to 3D Metrology

Rigoberto Juarez-Salazar [1,*], Sofia Esquivel-Hernandez [2] and Victor H. Diaz-Ramirez [2]

1 SECIHTI—Instituto Politécnico Nacional, CITEDI, Av. Instituto Politécnico Nacional 1310, Nueva Tijuana, Tijuana 22435, B.C., Mexico
2 Instituto Politécnico Nacional, CITEDI, Av. Instituto Politécnico Nacional 1310, Nueva Tijuana, Tijuana 22435, B.C., Mexico
* Correspondence: rjuarezsa@secihti.mx

Abstract: Optical fringe projection is an outstanding technology that significantly enhances three-dimensional (3D) metrology in numerous applications in science and engineering. Although the complexity of fringe projection systems may be overwhelming, current scientific advances bring improved models and methods that simplify the design and calibration of these systems, making 3D metrology less complicated. This paper provides an overview of the fundamentals of fringe projection profilometry, including imaging, stereo systems, phase demodulation, triangulation, and calibration. Some applications are described to highlight the usefulness and accuracy of modern optical fringe projection profilometers, impacting 3D metrology in different fields of science and engineering.

Keywords: optical metrology; fringe projection; 3D reconstruction; triangulation; calibration

1. Introduction

Optical fringe projection is an essential technology driving important applications in science, engineering, medicine, entertainment, and many other fields [1–3]. The effectiveness of this technology stems from several valuable features, including contactless operation, high accuracy, high resolution, and easy-to-operate equipment [4,5]. Moreover, modern digital cameras, projectors, and high-performance embedded computers enable fringe projection systems to operate at high rates [6,7], allowing the sensing of fast shape changes in dynamic phenomena [8,9]. The development of portable profilometers [10,11] has expanded the usefulness of fringe projection systems for in situ studies in archaeological [12] and forensic applications [13].

Despite progress in hardware and theoretical models, fringe projection profilometry remains an active research area within the scientific community worldwide [14,15]. Researchers are working to overcome new challenges in fringe projection technology [16]. Current investigations include miniaturization of electronic devices [17], multi-dimensional information sensing [18], multimodal imaging [19,20], self-calibration [21–23], motion-induced error suppression [24–27], setup optimization for full-view object reconstruction [28–31], dynamic range improvement for reconstructing reflective objects [32,33], and enabling automatic and adaptive operation [34–36]. For this reason, the specialization of students and professionals in this research area is crucial.

The research on fringe projection profilometry has produced extensive results in optical designs, mathematical models, data processing algorithms, and calibration methods [37–39]. Inexperienced readers may feel overwhelmed by the abundance of specialized literature in books and scientific articles available today [40–43]. Frustrating months of reading literature could pass without acquiring enough background to construct and operate an optical fringe projection profilometer. Given this situation, this paper aims to provide the fundamental knowledge for setting up and operating a fringe projection system, offering practical learning for engaging effectively with specialized literature and research projects.

In this paper, a concise overview of representative optical fringe projection techniques for 3D metrology is provided in Section 2. Then, the five constituent blocks comprising a fringe projection system are examined in Section 3. Next, essential concepts and helpful insights into the working principles of optical fringe projection are presented in Sections 4–6. Illustrative applications where this technology has been implemented are described in Section 7. The concluding remarks for this review are provided in Section 8. This study offers a concise guide through the fundamentals of fringe projection profilometry, making this technology a straightforward tool for driving 3D metrology toward new frontiers.

2. Fringe Projection Profilometry

Fringe projection profilometry has evolved from optical testing techniques that utilize lasers and other light sources [44,45], along with gratings and other reference masks [46,47], designed to capture the topography of surfaces and optical wavefronts [48,49]. Currently, *fringe projection* refers to numerous 3D reconstruction techniques that have emerged from diverse fringe-pattern analysis methods and the numerous options available for producing high-quality gratings, as outlined below.

A typical fringe projection profilometer is an apparatus comprising three elements: a camera, a projector, and a computer, as shown in Figure 1a. The operation of a fringe projection profilometer can be described in simple terms as follows. First, the projector illuminates the object being tested with straight fringes, as shown in Figure 1b. The shape of the object alters the straightness of the displayed fringes. Then, the camera captures one or more images of the deformed fringes, as shown in Figure 1c. Finally, the computer analyzes the captured fringe patterns to determine the object's shape and returns a 3D point cloud, as shown in Figure 1d. The fringe patterns used for shape extraction are two-dimensional sinusoidal signals characterized by the following [50,51]:

- A bias term (background light);
- Fringe amplitude;
- A fringe phase map.

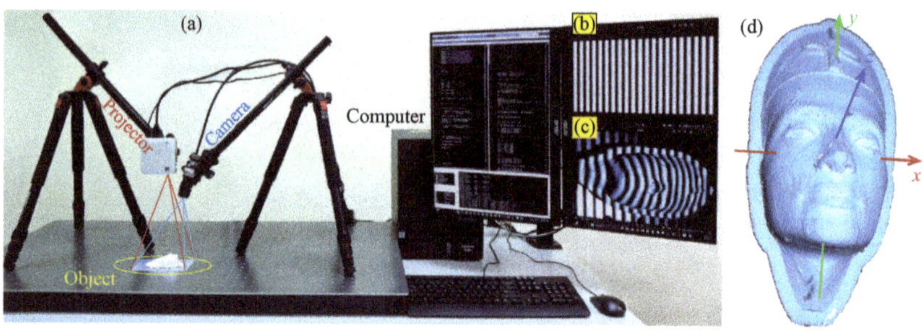

Figure 1. (**a**) Typical fringe projection profilometer setup. (**b**) Grating with straight fringes sent to the projector as a slide to illuminate the object being tested. (**c**) Fringe pattern captured by the camera, observing fringes deformed by the object. (**d**) Resulting 3D point cloud reconstruction.

The deformation from straight to curved fringes corresponds to an alteration in the fringe phase. Therefore, shape extraction is performed through a phase-demodulation process [52]. It is worth mentioning that typical noise sources (e.g., variations in object color and ambient light) affect the bias and amplitude of fringe patterns but have a negligible effect on the phase (curvature of the fringes). Consequently, the phase-based shape extraction approach makes fringe projection profilometry a robust and accurate tool for optical 3D metrology.

Moiré topography (MT) is considered a predecessor of modern fringe projection profilometry techniques [53]. MT produces fringe patterns that are directly related to depth/height contour maps [54,55], as depicted in Figure 2a,b. However, depressions and elevations (hills and valleys) cannot be distinguished [56], as shown in Figure 2c–f. In contrast, Fourier transform profilometry (FTP) employs a carrier frequency to automatically distinguish between surface depressions and elevations [57], as shown in Figure 2g–i. This technique enables real-time applications by requiring only a single fringe pattern for phase demodulation using the Fourier transform method [58]. However, its usability depends on satisfying the continuous surface condition (object surfaces without holes or steps). Unlike FTP, which carries out a filtering process in the frequency domain, alternative techniques such as spatial phase detection (SPD) [59], phase-locked loop profilometry [60], and regularized filters [61] apply the filtering process in the spatial domain [62]. However, the performance of the FTP and SPD techniques depends significantly on the user's ability to design and tune the filters correctly [63].

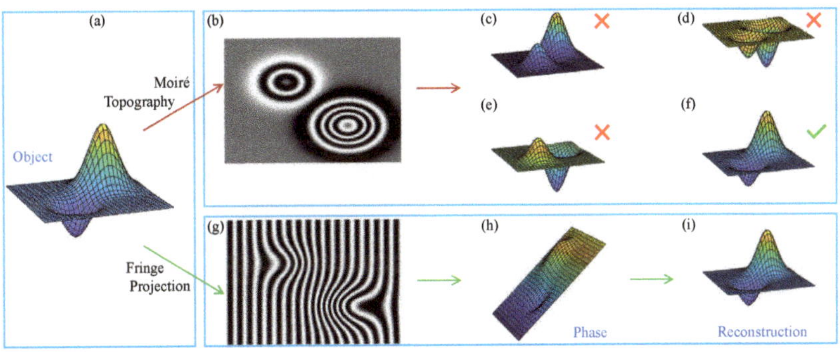

Figure 2. Object reconstruction using Moiré topography and Fourier transform profilometry. (**a**) Object to be recovered. (**b**) Moiré pattern. (**c–f**) Possible reconstructions from the given Moiré pattern. (**g**) Fourier fringe pattern. (**h**) Demodulated phase with carrier. (**i**) Reconstructed object.

Phase-shifting profilometry (PSP) successfully avoids the surface continuity constraint [64,65]. Moreover, this technique achieves maximum spatial resolution and robustness by processing multiple fringe patterns using the phase-shifting method [66]. However, the need for multiple fringe patterns makes PSP challenging to implement in real-time applications. Several approaches have been proposed to combine the advantages of FTP and PSP, such as π-shifted FTP [67] and multi-demodulation phase-shifting [68]. However, a trade-off must be established between the advantages of FTP and PSP for each specific application. Other approaches have been developed to enhance the original FTP and PSP techniques, including windowed FTP [69], fringe-normalized FTP [70], two-step phase-shifting [71,72], and phase-differencing profilometry [73]. However, their implementation is more complex and requires greater computational resources [74].

Alternatively, modulation measurement profilometry (MMP) differs from the previous methods in that the object shape is obtained from the fringe amplitude rather than the phase [75]. This technique exploits the defocus that occurs when observed points move away from the focal plane. The defocus level is estimated through the fringe amplitude, which decreases as the defocus increases. Then, the depth/height is quantified as a function of the defocus. An additional advantage of MMP is that shadows and occlusions are absent because the camera and projector are arranged to share the same optical axis [76]. However, MMP (amplitude-based) is more sensitive to external noise sources than FTP and PSP (phase-based) techniques.

Fringe projection techniques also differ in the hardware and methods used to generate straight fringes for illuminating the test object [77,78], as well as the implemented fringe analysis approach [79,80], which is discussed in Section 3. Complementary surveys about the different fringe projection techniques can be found in [81–83]. For a more comprehensive study of fringe projection profilometry, the reader is referred to [84–86]. The rest of this paper reviews the fundamental concepts of setting up and operating a fringe projection profilometer.

3. Fringe Projection System

The operation of an optical fringe projection profilometer can be analyzed through its five main components, as depicted in Figure 3. The following subsections provide a brief description of each of these components.

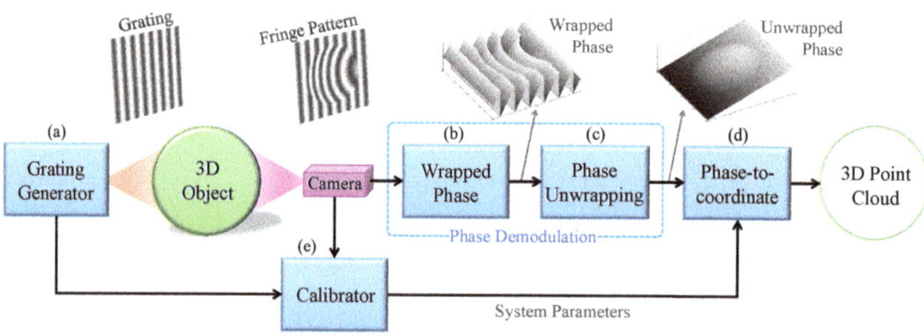

Figure 3. Main components of an optical fringe projection system: (**a**) grating generator, (**b**) wrapped phase extraction, (**c**) phase unwrapping, (**d**) phase-to-coordinate conversion, and (**e**) calibrator.

3.1. Grating Generator

The primary component of an optical fringe projection system is the grating generator [87], as shown in Figure 3a. This component illuminates the object being examined with two-dimensional (2D) cosine signals called *gratings*. The grating generator can control the properties of gratings, such as the phase shift, frequency, and angle [88,89], as well as the properties of the light source, including the wavelength (color) [90–92], intensity [93], and polarization [94]. As a result, the camera captures one or more 2D cosine signals known as *fringe patterns*, which are deformed by the shape of the object being examined.

A grating generator can be constructed using interferometric techniques [95–97]. Although interferometers produce high-quality gratings [98], the equipment is expensive, difficult to use, and sensitive to environmental perturbations [99,100]. Other alternatives to set up grating generators are the Moiré effect [101,102], defocused rulings [103–105], pulse-width modulation (PWM) [106], colored PWM [107], color-encoded projection [108,109], binary dithering [110], filled binary sinusoidal patterns [111], linear light-emitting diode array [112], and rotating slides [113–115]. The advent of digital projectors has simplified the grating generator component to a compact electronic unit [116]. Digital projectors allow easy and precise control of important grating properties such as the phase shift, frequency, and color. Additionally, the polarized light emitted by liquid crystal display-based projectors can be exploited to reconstruct shiny objects such as metallic workpieces and ceramic pottery [117,118]. As discussed in a recent study, the optical fringe projection technique that uses a computer-controlled projector is known as *digital fringe projection* [119].

3.2. Wrapped Phase Extraction

Optical fringe projection systems encode 3D shapes in the phase of the captured fringe patterns. For this reason, the phase recovery process, known as *phase demodulation*, is essential [52]. In practice, phase demodulation is performed through two components: wrapped phase extraction and phase unwrapping. Wrapped phase extraction requires one or more fringe patterns and returns a wrapped phase map, as shown in Figure 3b. Depending on the number of fringe patterns available, wrapped phase extraction can be performed using either the spatial or temporal approach [120].

3.2.1. Spatial Wrapped Phase Extraction and Fourier Fringe Analysis

Spatial wrapped phase extraction methods operate with a single fringe pattern [121]. In general terms, the phase at any pixel of the fringe pattern is computed based on the information from neighboring pixels, as depicted in Figure 4a. The most common approach consists of applying the Fourier transform to the given fringe pattern and exploiting the fact that the spectrum of the encoded phase is isolated around the carrier frequency, distinguishing it from other spectra in the Fourier domain [58]. A filter is used to isolate the spectrum of interest, and the required phase is recovered by applying the inverse Fourier transform [122]. This approach is known as *Fourier fringe analysis* [123]. Other spatial methods include the windowed Fourier transform [69], wavelet transform [124,125], Hilbert transform [126,127], and S-transform [128].

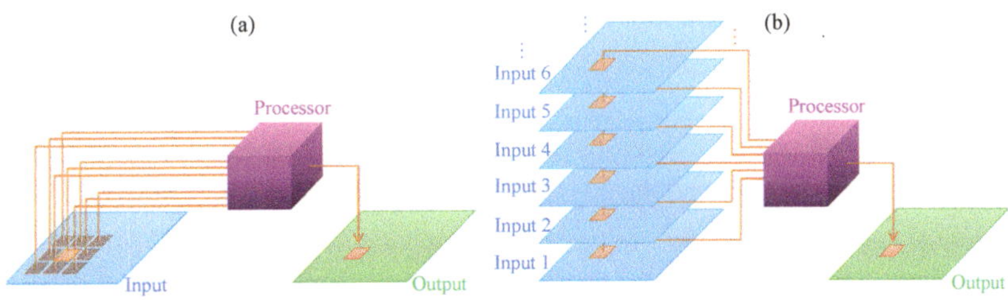

Figure 4. (**a**) Spatial processing approach. (**b**) Temporal processing approach.

The primary advantage of Fourier fringe analysis is the requirement of a single fringe pattern, allowing straightforward implementation in real-time applications [129,130]. However, the fringe pattern must meet certain restrictive conditions for effective spectrum isolation, namely a high carrier frequency and continuity of the encoded phase [131]. Additionally, spatial methods can be computationally demanding [132], and the filtering might yield unsatisfactory results if the fringe pattern is affected by shadows from objects with intricate shapes.

3.2.2. Temporal Wrapped Phase Extraction (Phase-Shifting)

In contrast to using a single fringe pattern with a high carrier frequency, temporal wrapped phase extraction uses three or more fringe patterns with different phase shifts [133]. This approach, known as *phase-shifting*, computes the phase at each pixel by processing that pixel across all the available fringe patterns, as depicted in Figure 4b. Initially, this approach was difficult to implement due to the need for precise phase-shift control [134,135]. Digital projectors have mitigated the challenges of phase-shift control, leading to the widespread implementation of phase-shifting algorithms.

Several phase-shifting algorithms have been proposed, differing mainly in whether the phase shifts are known or unknown and how the phase shifts are distributed [136]. For instance, generalized phase-shifting algorithms are useful when the phase-shift values are unknown because they include a phase-shift estimation module [137–139]. If the phase shifts are known but their distribution is irregular, then the phase-shift least-squares algorithm can be applied [140,141]. Furthermore, if the phase shifts are distributed homogeneously, the so-called *n-step method* can be applied, which is computationally efficient [66].

3.3. Phase Unwrapping

The phase-unwrapping component receives one or more wrapped phase maps and returns the resulting unwrapped phase, as shown in Figure 3c. This component aims to remove the discontinuities caused by the periodicity of trigonometric functions and restore the continuity associated with the object shape [142,143]. Like the previous component, phase unwrapping can be performed using either the spatial or temporal approach.

3.3.1. Spatial Phase Unwrapping

In essence, spatial phase-unwrapping algorithms work by applying an identity operation. Specifically, the wrapped phase map is derived and then integrated, returning the initial phase without discontinuities [144–146]. Depending on how the integration is carried out, spatial phase-unwrapping algorithms are classified as either *path-following* or *path-independent*. Since wrapped phase maps are 2D functions, there are infinite paths that the integration process can follow. Accordingly, path-following algorithms are designed to identify the best integration path by detecting and avoiding noisy pixels [147–149]. Although path-following algorithms are simple to implement and computationally efficient, they can be quite sensitive to noise [150]. Alternatively, path-independent phase-unwrapping algorithms perform the integration by solving a global optimization problem [151–153], removing the need to specify a particular integration path. Although path-independent algorithms are robust to noise, they consume more computational resources. The requirement for a single wrapped phase map is convenient for real-time applications. However, the implementation of spatial algorithms in optical fringe projection is limited because they cannot preserve discontinuities in the object shape [154]. Nevertheless, spatial phase unwrapping is helpful for applications involving objects with continuous surfaces.

3.3.2. Temporal Phase Unwrapping and Multi-Frequency Approach

Instead of processing a single wrapped phase map, temporal phase unwrapping uses complementary images such as gray-coded binary sequences (intensity-based) [155–158] or additional wrapped phase maps (phase-based) [159–161]. Since typical noise sources have a greater impact on image intensity than on the phase of fringe patterns, phase-based temporal phase-unwrapping methods are generally preferred. In particular, the *multi-frequency approach* uses two or more wrapped phase maps obtained by projecting gratings with different frequencies. This approach relies on the fact that low-frequency wrapped phase maps have fewer synthetic discontinuities [162,163]. This observation forms the basis of the so-called *heterodyne* [164–166] and *hierarchical* [167–169] techniques. Heterodyne multi-frequency phase unwrapping exploits the beat phenomenon, which produces a low-frequency wave by superposing two high-frequency waves. Thus, heterodyne techniques can work exclusively with high-frequency wrapped phase maps. This feature is useful when the grating generator is an interferometer, as low-frequency gratings can be difficult to control. However, the unwrapped phase may contain distortion due to the phase synthesis process. On the other hand, hierarchical multi-frequency phase unwrapping uses both low-

and high-frequency wrapped phase maps, overcoming the distortion issues encountered in the phase synthesis process [170].

3.4. Phase-to-Coordinate Conversion

Although the demodulated phase is closely related to the object topography, the phase (in radians) must be converted to spatial information (in length units) [171], as shown in Figure 3d. Earlier proposals were designed assuming particular configurations [172]; for instance, parallel optical axes [173] or orthographic illumination/capture using telecentric lenses [174]. In these systems, the phase encodes only the object's height (z-coordinate), thus leading to the development of *phase-to-height* conversion methods [175–178]. However, in more versatile profilometers, the phase also contains information about the coordinates (x, y) [179,180]; for instance, when the camera and projector are arranged arbitrarily [181,182], divergent illumination/capture is used [183], and the lenses introduce nonlinear distortion [184–186]. These flexible systems require the implementation of generalized *phase-to-coordinate* conversion methods [187,188].

Simple phase-to-coordinate algorithms can be developed by alleviating system parameter requirements through specific setup designs [57,189]. For instance, closed-form expressions can be derived assuming the optical elements are aligned on-axis [190], are parallel [191], or use a camera/projector with telecentric lenses [174,192,193]. Furthermore, knowing one or more points on the object can substitute for some of the system parameters [194]. However, the resulting phase-to-coordinate algorithms impose strict operating conditions, limiting their practical application. Alternatively, when the system parameters are available, generalized phase-to-coordinate algorithms can be designed using the triangulation principle [195]. Triangulation-based algorithms support multiple devices, even if they are misaligned or have lens distortion.

3.5. System Calibration

Since the calibrator component is inactive during a 3D reconstruction experiment [196], it is often underestimated and even excluded. Nonetheless, the contribution of this component is essential for producing metric object reconstructions [197–199], as shown in Figure 3e. The process by which a fringe projection system registers 3D shapes involves a complicated phase-encoding mechanism regulated by system parameters [200]. However, even with the complexity of the phase encoding, clever strategies can be employed to obtain the system parameters in a practical manner [201–203]. Assuming the fringe projection system consists of a camera–projector pair [204–206], the camera and projector can be calibrated independently [207]. Although this approach is simple, the experimental work is time-consuming and inaccurate. In contrast, with the advent of modern camera–projector calibration methods [208–210], experimental work has been substantially simplified, resulting in higher accuracy levels [211–213].

3.6. Miscellaneous

The performance of fringe projection techniques depends significantly on the assumption that gratings and fringe patterns have ideal cosine profiles [214–216]. However, consumer cameras and projectors often exhibit a nonlinear intensity response [217–219], resulting in gamma distortion [220–223], as illustrated in Figure 5. To address this issue, advanced methods have been proposed for processing distorted fringe patterns [224–229]. Moreover, a recommended approach involves preventing distortion by complementing the calibrator component with a gamma value estimator and pre-distorting the generated gratings accordingly [230,231].

Color cameras and projectors also exhibit crosstalk and grayscale imbalance issues [232,233]. These imperfections reduce the accuracy of fringe projection systems that use color multiplexing [234]. Special attention is essential for high-quality reconstructions with color-based profilometer systems [235–238]. It is important to note that the projector's brightness and the camera's exposure time are also important parameters when working with shiny objects [239]. For these challenging applications, particular strategies must be implemented to avoid saturated or underexposed fringe patterns [240,241].

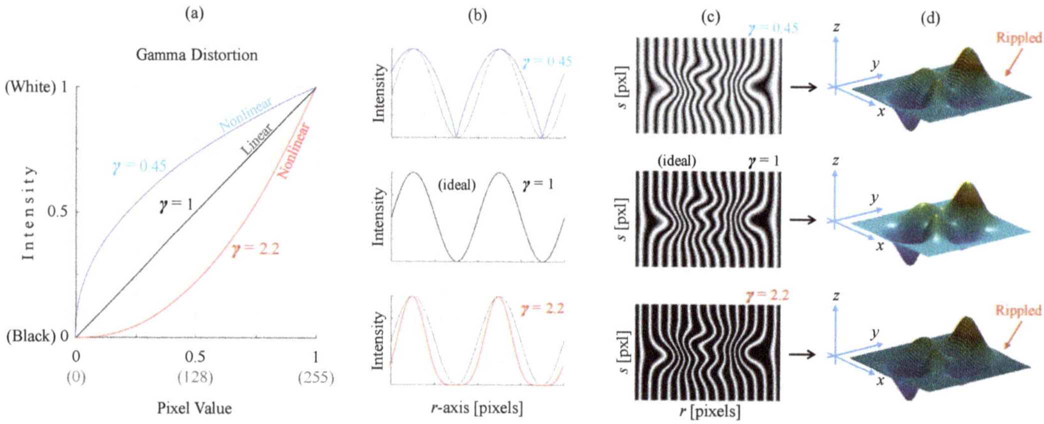

Figure 5. (**a**) Intensity response of cameras or projectors for different gamma values. (**b**) Sine profiles generated using three gamma values. (**c**) Fringe patterns simulated using three values of gamma. (**d**) Effect of gamma distortion on the reconstructed object.

3.7. Hierarchical Multi-Frequency Phase-Shifting Fringe Projection

This section concludes by highlighting the abundant literature on fringe projection systems available nowadays [242–245]. This review aims to be more panoramic than exhaustive, serving as a starting point for readers interested in studying optical fringe projection systems [246–248]. To this end, we provide valuable insights and tools, offering the reader elemental knowledge to construct and operate an optical fringe projection profilometer. This learning-by-doing approach utilizes a simple yet powerful system in which a digital projector serves as the grating generator, phase-shifting and hierarchical multi-frequency methods are implemented for phase demodulation, a triangulation-based algorithm is employed for phase-to-coordinate conversion, and the system parameters are estimated using the camera–projector calibration method. The following sections provide a comprehensive analysis of the recommended hierarchical multi-frequency phase-shifting fringe projection system.

4. Theoretical Preliminaries

4.1. Camera Imaging

A digital camera is a sophisticated device consisting mainly of a compound lens and a photosensitive sensor [249]. Cameras are designed to collect light rays traveling from the 3D space and record their intensities. The resulting intensity map is the camera output, known as the *image*. Although the physical imaging process is a complicated phenomenon, it can be modeled with good approximation using the pinhole model [250,251]. Let $\boldsymbol{p}$ be the vector of a point in the 3D space, and let $\boldsymbol{\mu}$ be the pixel where $\boldsymbol{p}$ was registered by the camera, as shown in Figure 6a. Considering the pinhole model, the vectors $\boldsymbol{p}$ and $\boldsymbol{\mu}$ are related as follows:

$$\boldsymbol{\mu} = \mathcal{H}^{-1}[C\mathcal{H}[\boldsymbol{p}]], \tag{1}$$

where $\mathcal{H}$ is the homogeneous coordinate operator [252], $[\cdot]^{-1}$ denotes the inverse, and

$$C = K[R^T, -R^T\boldsymbol{t}] \tag{2}$$

is a 3×4 matrix, known as the *camera matrix*. K is the intrinsic parameter matrix (non-singular upper triangular), R is a rotation matrix defining the camera orientation, $[\cdot]^T$ denotes the transpose, and $\boldsymbol{t}$ is a translation vector specifying the camera position.

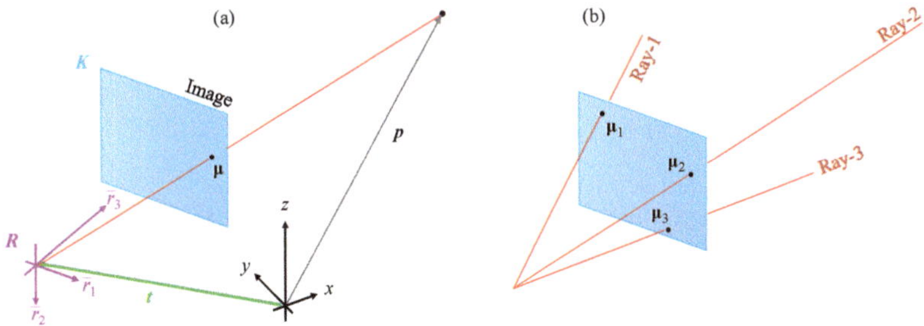

Figure 6. (**a**) Camera pinhole model with the intrinsic parameters given by the upper-triangular matrix K and the extrinsic parameters (pose) consisting of the rotation matrix R and the translation vector $\boldsymbol{t}$. (**b**) Every image pixel is associated with a light ray from the 3D space with a unique direction.

4.2. Cameras as Direction Sensors

Although digital cameras are well-known for their ability to capture photographs, optical fringe projection systems employ cameras for an additional purpose. Note that a digital image is an array of pixels, and each pixel detects a light ray coming from the 3D space in a specific direction, as shown in Figure 6b. Thus, every pixel is associated with a particular light ray with a unique direction. In this context, a helpful insight is that cameras are *direction sensors* [187]. A more formal analysis is performed by reversing the imaging process to return a space point $\boldsymbol{p}$ when the pixel $\boldsymbol{\mu}$ is given. For this, Equations (1) and (2) can be rewritten as

$$\lambda\mathcal{H}[\boldsymbol{\mu}] = K[R^T, -R^T\boldsymbol{t}]\begin{bmatrix}\boldsymbol{p}\\1\end{bmatrix}, \tag{3}$$

where $\lambda \neq 0$ is an arbitrary real-valued variable. After a few algebraic manipulations of Equation (3), the following equation is reached:

$$\boldsymbol{p} = \boldsymbol{t} + \lambda\boldsymbol{d}, \tag{4}$$

which describes a line in the 3D space passing through the camera position $\boldsymbol{t}$, with the direction determined by the pixel $\boldsymbol{\mu}$ as

$$\boldsymbol{d} = RK^{-1}\mathcal{H}[\boldsymbol{\mu}]. \tag{5}$$

4.3. Stereo Camera Systems and Triangulation

How can direction sensors be employed for 3D metrology? Consider two cameras forming a stereo system capturing an object from two different viewpoints, as shown in Figure 7a. Let us assume that the parameters of both cameras are known, say K_1, R_1, and $\boldsymbol{t}_1$ for the first camera, and K_2, R_2, and $\boldsymbol{t}_2$ for the second camera. Let $\boldsymbol{p}$ be a point on the object surface captured by the two cameras at the pixels $\boldsymbol{\mu}_1$ and $\boldsymbol{\mu}_2$, respectively. The lines representing the captured light rays can be reproduced using the available camera parameters and the given pixel points, as shown in Figure 7b, namely

$$\boldsymbol{p} = \boldsymbol{t}_1 + \lambda_1 \boldsymbol{d}_1, \quad \text{(Line-1)}, \tag{6}$$
$$\boldsymbol{p} = \boldsymbol{t}_2 + \lambda_2 \boldsymbol{d}_2, \quad \text{(Line-2)}. \tag{7}$$

This reasoning leads to computing the captured point $\boldsymbol{p}$ as the intersection of Line-1 and Line-2. This computation is generically known as *triangulation*, although more general constructions for determining points are also possible, such as the intersection of multiple lines, planes, and other geometrical objects, even in combinations [195].

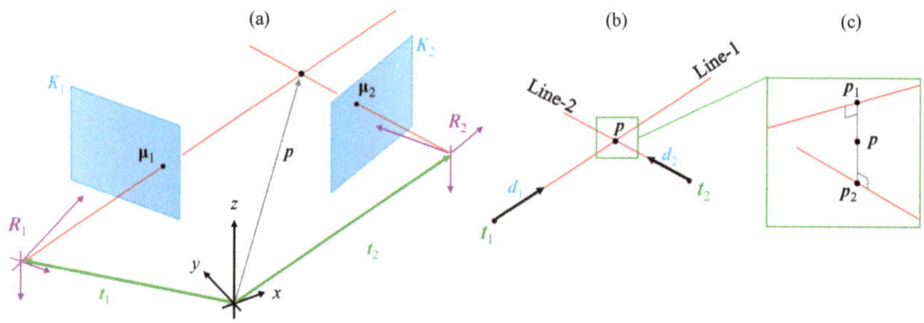

Figure 7. (**a**) Two cameras capturing a point $\boldsymbol{p}$ from different viewpoints. (**b**) The captured point is determined as the intersection of the lines defined by $\boldsymbol{\mu}_1$ and $\boldsymbol{\mu}_2$. (**c**) Experimental noise may cause skewed lines; therefore, $\boldsymbol{p}$ is determined as the mean point between the solution points $\boldsymbol{p}_1$ and $\boldsymbol{p}_2$.

In particular, triangulation in a stereo system can be performed as follows. Since $\boldsymbol{p}$ represents a common point of the intersecting lines, then Equations (6) and (7) can be equated as $\boldsymbol{t}_1 + \lambda_1 \boldsymbol{d}_1 = \boldsymbol{t}_2 + \lambda_2 \boldsymbol{d}_2$, which can be solved for the unknowns λ_1 and λ_2 using the least-squares method as

$$\begin{bmatrix} \lambda_1 \\ \lambda_2 \end{bmatrix} = (D^T D)^{-1} D^T (\boldsymbol{t}_2 - \boldsymbol{t}_1), \tag{8}$$

where $D = [\boldsymbol{d}_1, -\boldsymbol{d}_2]$ is the regression matrix. The computed values of λ_1 and λ_2 allow determining the vector of the captured point $\boldsymbol{p}_1$ using Equation (6) or $\boldsymbol{p}_2$ using Equation (7). Ideally, $\boldsymbol{p}_1$ and $\boldsymbol{p}_2$ are equal due to the intersection assumption. Nevertheless, slight deviations caused by experimental errors may result in skewed lines, as shown in Figure 7c. For this reason, the vector $\boldsymbol{p}$ is defined as the average $(\boldsymbol{p}_1 + \boldsymbol{p}_2)/2$, i.e.,

$$\boldsymbol{p} = \frac{1}{2}(\boldsymbol{t}_1 + \boldsymbol{t}_2) + \frac{1}{2}\begin{bmatrix} \boldsymbol{d}_1, & \boldsymbol{d}_2 \end{bmatrix} \begin{bmatrix} \lambda_1 \\ \lambda_2 \end{bmatrix}. \tag{9}$$

4.4. The Corresponding Point Problem

It is noteworthy that a 3D reconstruction requires the pair of pixels $\boldsymbol{\mu}_1$ and $\boldsymbol{\mu}_2$ where the captured point $\boldsymbol{p}$ was imaged (see Figure 7). The pixels $\boldsymbol{\mu}_1$ and $\boldsymbol{\mu}_2$, related by a common point $\boldsymbol{p}$, are known as a *corresponding point pair*, which is denoted by

$$\boldsymbol{\mu}_1 \leftrightarrow \boldsymbol{\mu}_2. \tag{10}$$

Obtaining corresponding points is a challenging task because it depends on the object's texture [253,254]. For example, no corresponding points can be established from a white object on a white background under homogeneous illumination because of the lack of feature points [255]. Even for objects with abundant texture, such as the human face in biometric applications, the resolution is low because more than one pixel is required to detect a feature, and not all image regions contain reliable features. As a result, stereo camera systems tend to produce low-resolution 3D reconstructions, and their accuracy depends on the texture of the object under study.

4.5. Equivalence Between Cameras and Projectors

Physically, the difference between a camera and a projector is that the light rays propagate in opposite directions, as shown in Figure 8. While a camera captures light rays traveling from space to its image pixels, a projector emits light rays from its slide pixels to space. However, if the sign of the direction vector of the light rays is omitted, cameras and projectors are identical. For this reason, cameras and projectors are mathematically equivalent, and both can be described by the pinhole model given in Equation (1). Therefore, in addition to cameras being direction sensors, another valuable insight is that projectors are *direction-controlled ray generators*.

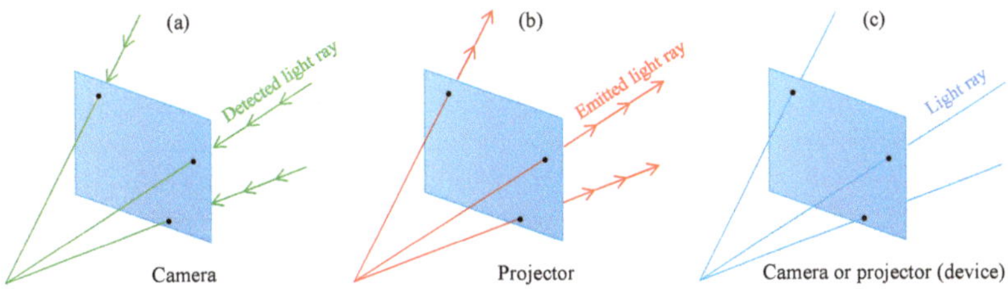

Figure 8. Cameras and projectors differ only in that light rays travel in opposite directions. (**a**) Camera capturing light rays from space. (**b**) Projector emitting light rays towards space. (**c**) If the sign of the light direction vectors is omitted, cameras and projectors are mathematically equivalent (referred to generically as *devices*).

4.6. Camera–Projector Systems

The equivalence between cameras and projectors can be exploited to modify a stereo camera system by replacing one of the cameras with a projector. The resulting camera–projector system has the advantage of not having the corresponding point problem. This advantage is inferred from the following simplified description of the operation of a camera–projector system.

A computer-generated slide controls the brightness of every pixel of the projector. A black slide will turn off all the projector pixels. Suppose this slide is modified by setting the pixel μ_2 to white; then, a light ray will be emitted to 3D space, illuminating the object at point $\mathbf{p}$, as shown in Figure 9. In the absence of additional light sources, the camera would capture a dark image, except for a bright point at the image pixel μ_1. In this way, the corresponding point $\mu_1 \leftrightarrow \mu_2$ is known by simply reading the coordinates of the bright image pixel μ_1 and taking the coordinates of the white slide pixel μ_2. Therefore, sophisticated algorithms that search for corresponding points are unnecessary. For this reason, camera–projector systems can even reconstruct objects without texture, achieving high accuracy and resolution.

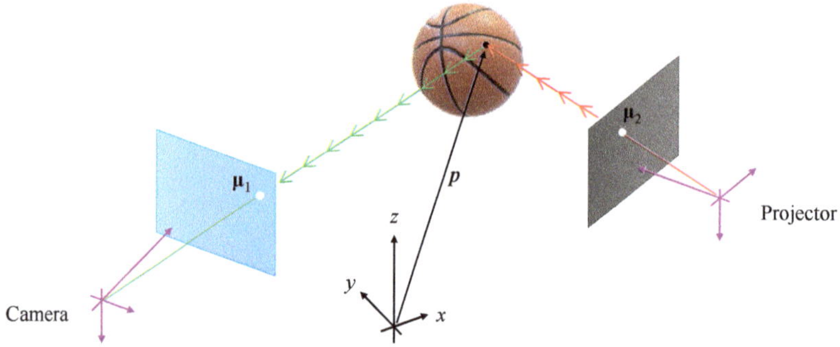

Figure 9. Camera–projector systems lack the corresponding point problem because μ_1 is directly identified as the image's bright pixel, and μ_2 is known from the slide design.

Although illustrative, the described working principle is impractical because one image is required to obtain only one corresponding point. Since modern digital projectors have millions of pixels, millions of images would be required for a single 3D reconstruction. Fortunately, efficient illumination techniques have been proposed to significantly reduce the number of required images.

4.7. Structured Illumination

The primary advantage of camera–projector systems is the absence of the corresponding point problem. Instead, slides are designed to "mark" the projector pixels such that they are recognized by the camera and paired with the image pixels, producing corresponding points. The different techniques for marking and recognizing projector pixels are known generically as *structured illumination* [78].

Typical structured illumination techniques include projecting dots, stripes, grids, codewords, rainbows, and fringes. These techniques can even be combined to produce hybrid structured illumination techniques. Each technique has different advantages and disadvantages in terms of accuracy, resolution, number of images, noise robustness, object color sensitivity, and other criteria. Depending on the application, one technique may be more appropriate. In particular, the fringe projection technique is recommended for applications requiring higher accuracy and resolution.

4.8. Fringe Projection

The "mark-based" approach helps to explain the different structured illumination techniques more intuitively. Alternatively, a powerful insight can be gained by considering a camera–projector setup as a telecommunication system. Remember that the projector-slide coordinates (u, v) must be registered on the camera image plane (r, s) to produce the corresponding points. In this context, the projector is considered a transmitter emitting the signals u and v, while the camera is a receiver detecting u and v to produce the corresponding points.

The projector-slide coordinates can be transmitted using phase modulation. For example, let us encode the values of u as the phase of a 2D cosine signal, known as a *grating*, of the form

$$G_k(u, v) = \frac{1}{2} + \frac{1}{2}\cos(\omega u + \delta_k), \quad \text{for} \quad k = 1, 2, \cdots, n, \tag{11}$$

where ω is the grating spatial frequency, δ_k is a reference phase known as a *phase shift* or *grating displacement*, and n is the number of images required to perform phase demodulation.

Figure 10 shows two gratings, with low and high frequencies, respectively, and four phase shifts. When the grating $G_k(u,v)$ is used as a slide, the object under study is illuminated with fringes, as shown in Figure 11. Consequently, this particular structured illumination technique is known as *fringe projection*. The image captured by the camera is known as a *fringe pattern*, which is modeled as

$$I_k(r,s) = a(r,s) + b(r,s)\cos(\phi(r,s) + \delta_k), \tag{12}$$

where $a(r,s)$ is the background light, $b(r,s)$ is the fringe amplitude, and $\phi(r,s)$ is the phase containing the encoded signal u. Indeed, by comparing the arguments of the cosine functions in Equations (11) and (12), the slide projector coordinate u is read in the camera image plane from the demodulated phase as

$$u(r,s) = \frac{1}{\omega}\phi(r,s). \tag{13}$$

The fringe projection process can be repeated for the projector axis v. Specifically, assuming that the gratings were created using the angular frequency w and that the recovered phase was $\varphi(r,s)$, the projector-slide coordinate v is available in the camera image plane as

$$v(r,s) = \frac{1}{w}\varphi(r,s). \tag{14}$$

As a result, for every camera image pixel (r,s), the corresponding projector-slide coordinates $(u(r,s), v(r,s))$ are determined.

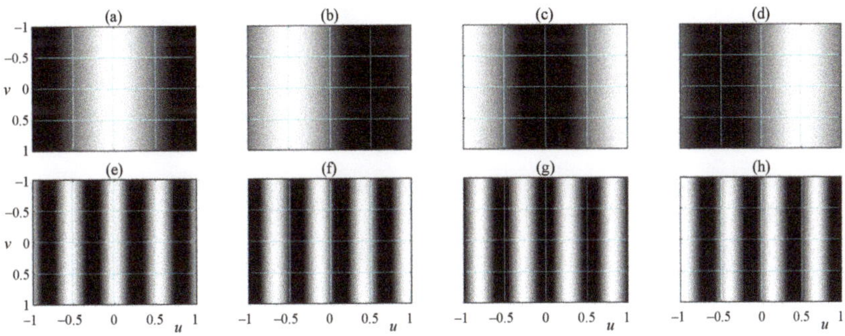

Figure 10. **(a–d)** A grating $G_k(u,v)$ with the frequency $\omega = \pi$ (one fringe) and four phase shifts. **(e–h)** A grating with a higher frequency, $\omega = 3.7\pi$, and four phase shifts.

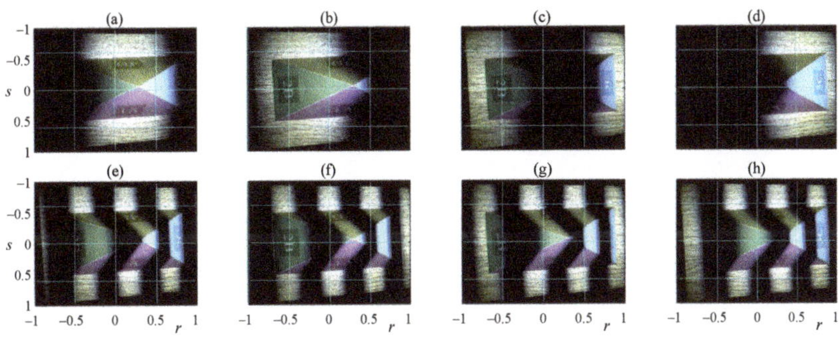

Figure 11. **(a–d)** Fringe patterns $I_k(r,s)$ obtained by illuminating a 3D object with the low-frequency gratings shown in Figure 10a–d. **(e–h)** Fringe patterns obtained using the higher-frequency gratings shown in Figure 10e–h.

The phase retrieval algorithms used in fringe projection systems are inherited from optical metrology. Some adaptations are included considering the convenience of using digital camera–projector systems. For instance, the frequency of the gratings and the phase shifts are controlled precisely by the computer. Section 5 presents a phase retrieval algorithm suitable for fringe projection 3D metrology systems.

4.9. Phase and Object Profile Misconception

It is worth remarking on the frequent confusion occurring when the phase extracted from a fringe projection experiment is plotted, as shown in Figure 12. Since the phase looks like the object profile, inexperienced practitioners may conclude that elementary transformations on the phase, such as rotation and scaling, are sufficient to achieve metric 3D object reconstruction. Unfortunately, this misconception leads to the formulation of a transformation that, in addition to being excessively complicated, is unnecessary. It is important to remember that the phase simply provides the projector-slide coordinates required to establish corresponding points. Subsequently, the corresponding points are used to perform object reconstruction by triangulation.

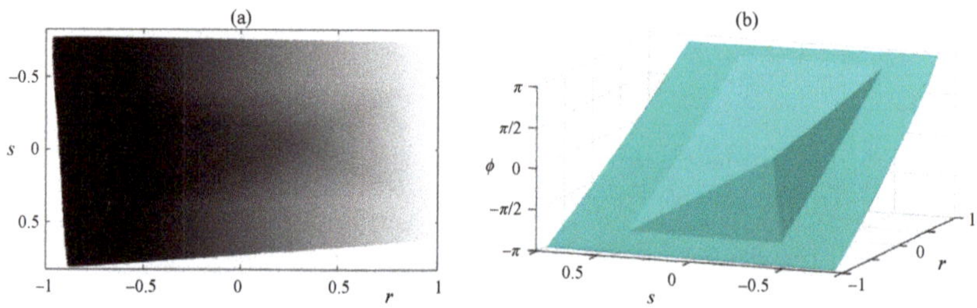

Figure 12. (**a**) Phase $\phi(r,s)$ demodulated from the fringe patterns shown in Figure 11. (**b**) 3D plot of the phase shown in (**a**). It is worth emphasizing that the phase provides the projector-slide coordinates, and direct association with the object profile must be avoided.

5. Phase-Demodulation Fringe-Pattern Processing

The optical metrology community has developed a wide variety of fringe-pattern processing methods for different applications and requirements [52,256]. For instance, Fourier fringe analysis allows phase recovery from a single fringe pattern [58], but the intrinsic spectrum filtering limits the spatial resolution. On the other hand, the phase-shifting method achieves the highest (pixel-wise) spatial resolution [257], but multiple fringe patterns with prefixed phase shifts are required.

Nowadays, digital computer-controlled cameras and projectors allow the capture of multiple fringe patterns at high speed and precise control of the grating frequency and phase shift [84]. For this reason, phase demodulation through phase-shifting and multi-frequency phase unwrapping is the preferred choice for fringe projection profilometry [133].

5.1. Phase-Shifting Wrapped Phase Extraction

The design of phase-shifting algorithms depends mainly on the distribution of the phase shifts and whether they are known or unknown. Exploiting the fact that phase shifts can be controlled with high precision, they are required to be

$$\delta_k = \frac{2\pi}{n}(k-1). \quad (15)$$

For this particular case, the set of n fringe patterns given by Equation (12) can be processed to estimate the background light, the fringe amplitude, and the encoded phase using the Bruning method [66,257] as follows:

$$a(r,s) = \frac{1}{n}\sum_{k=1}^{n} I_k(r,s), \tag{16}$$

$$b(r,s) = \frac{2}{n}\sqrt{J_1^2(r,s) + J_2^2(r,s)}, \tag{17}$$

$$\psi(r,s) = -\tan^{-1}(J_1(r,s)/J_2(r,s)), \tag{18}$$

where $\tan^{-1}$ represents the four-quadrant arctangent function, with the auxiliary functions defined as

$$J_1(r,s) = \sum_{k=1}^{n} I_k(r,s)\sin\delta_k, \quad \text{and} \tag{19}$$

$$J_2(r,s) = \sum_{k=1}^{n} I_k(r,s)\cos\delta_k. \tag{20}$$

As an illustration, the fringe patterns shown in Figure 11e–h were processed using Equations (16)–(18), obtaining the results presented in Figure 13. It is worth noting that the retrieved phase is $\psi(r,s)$, as shown in Figure 13c, and the required phase is $\phi(r,s)$, as shown in Figure 13d. These phases are displayed using 3D plots in Figure 13e,f for better visualization. The function $\psi(r,s)$ is known as the *wrapped phase* due to its distinctive sawtooth-like shape. The phases $\phi(r,s)$ and $\psi(r,s)$ are equivalent since

$$\cos\phi(r,s) = \cos\psi(r,s). \tag{21}$$

Unfortunately, $\phi \in (-\infty,\infty)$ can take any real value, whereas $\psi \in (-\pi,\pi]$ is always constrained to the left-open interval known as *principal values*. Adding any multiple of 2π to the wrapped phase still yields a value equivalent to $\phi(r,s)$, i.e.,

$$\cos\phi(r,s) = \cos[\psi(r,s) + 2\pi h(r,s)], \tag{22}$$

which leads to the general relationship between $\phi(r,s)$ and $\psi(r,s)$ as

$$\phi(r,s) = \psi(r,s) + 2\pi h(r,s), \tag{23}$$

where $h(r,s)$ is an integer-valued function, known as a *fringe order*. Obtaining the actual phase $\phi(r,s)$ from the available wrapped phase $\psi(r,s)$ is a process known as *phase unwrapping*.

5.2. Hierarchical Multi-Frequency Phase Unwrapping

Since the wrapping phenomenon appears when the encoded phase exceeds the principal values, the straightforward way to recover the required phase is by preventing it from exceeding the principal values. For this, the frequency of the grating should be chosen appropriately. For instance, assuming that the projector-slide axis u is normalized in the interval $(-1,1]$, the angular frequency

$$\omega_1 = \pi \tag{24}$$

will limit the fringe-pattern phase $\phi_1 = \omega_1 u$ within the principal values. Therefore, the required phase will coincide with that retrieved using Equation (18), i.e.,

$$\phi_1(r,s) = \omega_1 u(r,s) = \psi_1(r,s). \tag{25}$$

Note that the frequency ω_1 is so low that only one fringe is displayed, as shown in Figure 11a–d. However, low-frequency gratings cannot underline the fine details of the object. On the other hand, high-frequency gratings highlight shape details, as shown in Figure 11e–h, but the wrapping phenomenon appears.

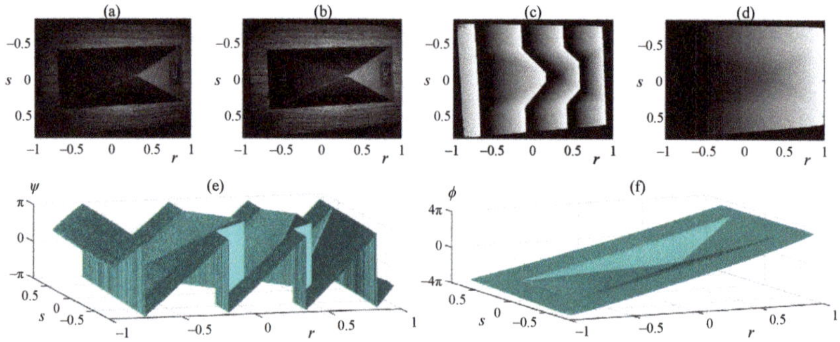

Figure 13. Results of processing the fringe patterns shown in Figure 11e–h. (**a**) Background light. (**b**) Fringe amplitude. (**c**) Extracted wrapped phase, $\psi(r,s)$. (**d**) Required phase, $\phi(r,s)$. (**e**,**f**) 3D plots of the phases shown in (**c**) and (**d**), respectively.

Hierarchical multi-frequency phase unwrapping employs both low- and high-frequency gratings. The phase retrieved from low-frequency gratings assists in solving the wrapping problem, while the phase from high-frequency gratings permits achieving high fidelity. For example, let us consider a second grating with a frequency ω_2 higher than ω_1:

$$\omega_2 > \omega_1. \tag{26}$$

Since the encoded phase exceeds the principal values, the required phase ϕ and the retrieved phase ψ are related as in Equation (23), namely

$$\phi_2(r,s) = \omega_2 u(r,s) = \psi_2(r,s) + 2\pi h_2(r,s). \tag{27}$$

The unknown function $h_2(r,s)$ can be determined using the previous phase $\phi_1(r,s)$, as given by Equation (25). Specifically, substituting $u = \phi_1/\omega_1$ in Equation (27), we obtain

$$\frac{\omega_2}{\omega_1}\phi_1(r,s) = \psi_2(r,s) + 2\pi h_2(r,s), \tag{28}$$

which leads to

$$h_2(r,s) = \left\lfloor \frac{(\omega_2/\omega_1)\phi_1(r,s) - \psi_2(r,s)}{2\pi} \right\rceil, \tag{29}$$

where $\lfloor\cdot\rceil$ is the round operator ensuring that h_2 takes integer values. This process can be repeated for a third frequency $\omega_3 > \omega_2$, and so on, until the desired resolution is reached.

In general, the k-th retrieved phase $\psi_k(r,s)$ can be unwrapped using a previous phase $\phi_{k-1}(r,s)$ as follows:

$$\phi_k(r,s) = \psi_k(r,s) + 2\pi h_k(r,s), \tag{30}$$

$$h_k(r,s) = \left\lfloor \frac{\alpha_k \phi_{k-1}(r,s) - \psi_k(r,s)}{2\pi} \right\rceil, \tag{31}$$

where α_k is the amplification between the adjacent phases ϕ_{k-1} and ϕ_k, defined as

$$\alpha_k = \omega_k / \omega_{k-1}. \tag{32}$$

This phase-unwrapping method is a recursive process that works hierarchically. It starts with the lowest (single-fringe) grating frequency and ends with the highest grating frequency supported by the projector.

5.3. Choosing Grating Frequencies

The operation of the hierarchical phase-unwrapping method depends on how many frequencies can be used. Ideally, two frequencies, the lowest and highest, should be sufficient to attain a high-fidelity phase. However, in practice, using two frequencies often fails due to the excessive difference between the phases, as illustrated in Figure 14a. For this reason, intermediate frequencies are employed to produce phases with less drastic changes, as shown in Figure 14b–i.

Although any set of increasing frequencies can be chosen, using the same amplification between adjacent phases is recommended [187], i.e.,

$$\alpha_1 = \alpha_2 = \cdots = \alpha_m = \alpha, \tag{33}$$

where m is the number of frequencies to be used. The grating frequencies fulfilling the constant amplification requirement are

$$\begin{aligned} \omega_1 &= \pi, \\ \omega_2 &= \pi\alpha, \\ &\vdots \\ \omega_m &= \pi\alpha^{m-1}. \end{aligned} \tag{34}$$

The amplification coefficient α is determined based on the projector resolution, which limits the supported maximum grating frequency. For instance, assuming that the projector has N pixels along the u-axis, the amplification coefficient is given as

$$\alpha = \left(\frac{N}{\xi}\right)^{1/(m-1)}, \tag{35}$$

where ξ is the number of pixels per fringe at maximum frequency (usually between 10 and 20 pixels). The frequencies for the gratings that encode the v-axis of the projector are determined analogously.

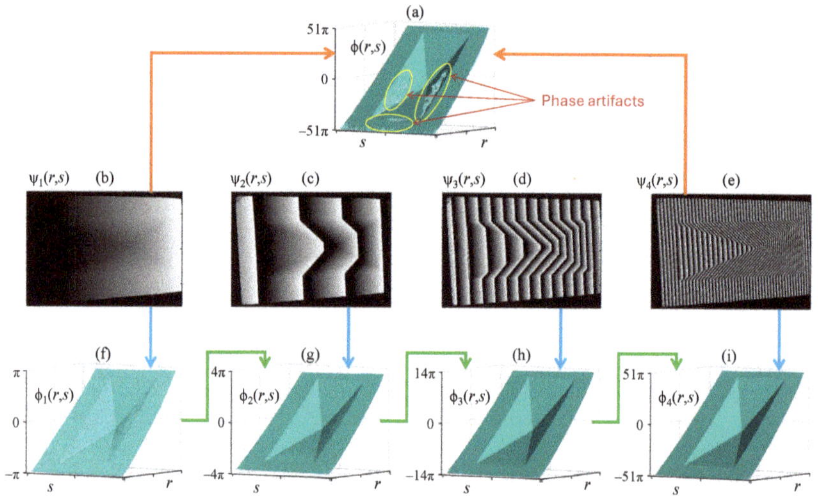

Figure 14. (**a**) Phase obtained using only the lowest and highest wrapped phases (**b**,**e**). The phase artifacts are avoided by including the wrapped phases (**c**,**d**) with intermediate frequencies. (**f**–**i**) Unwrapped phases obtained recursively using the hierarchical multi-frequency method.

6. System Calibration

In the theoretical preliminaries presented in Section 4, the camera and projector parameters were assumed to be known. In practice, these parameters need to be estimated through a process known as *system calibration*. Earlier methods used to calibrate a camera and a projector together employed cumbersome procedures. Nowadays, more practical alternatives are available to calibrate a camera–projector pair. In this section, a simple and flexible camera–projector calibration method is presented. First, the calibration of a single camera is explained to provide background. Then, the methodology is extended to projectors by exploiting the equivalence between cameras and projectors. Finally, the procedure for simultaneous camera and projector calibration is described.

6.1. Camera Calibration

Consider the pinhole model given by Equation (1), rewritten here as

$$\boldsymbol{\mu} = \mathcal{H}^{-1}\left[K\begin{bmatrix} \bar{\boldsymbol{r}}_1, & \bar{\boldsymbol{r}}_2, & \bar{\boldsymbol{r}}_3, & -R^T\boldsymbol{t} \end{bmatrix} \begin{bmatrix} x \\ y \\ z \\ 1 \end{bmatrix} \right], \tag{36}$$

where the rotation matrix was row-partitioned as $R^T = [\bar{\boldsymbol{r}}_1, \bar{\boldsymbol{r}}_2, \bar{\boldsymbol{r}}_3]$. The camera can be seen as a black box that receives a point $\boldsymbol{p} = [x, y, z]^T$ as input and returns an image pixel point $\boldsymbol{\mu}$ as output. Therefore, a 3D target can be used to obtain a set of input–output pairs, as shown in Figure 15a, and estimate the camera matrix C by minimizing the output error [250], as shown in Figure 15c. The parameters K, R, and $\boldsymbol{t}$, can be extracted from C through triangular-orthogonal matrix decomposition. Nonetheless, despite the single-shot calibration feature, this approach is impractical because high-precision multi-point 3D targets are bulky and expensive.

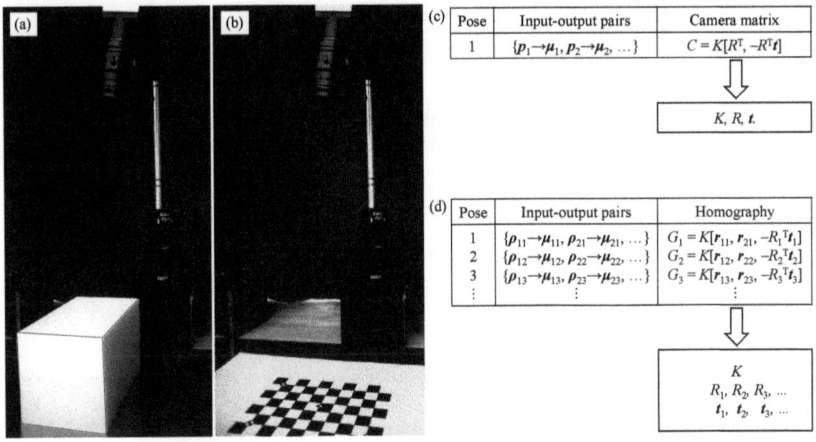

Figure 15. (**a**) Camera calibration using a single image of a 3D target. (**b**) Camera calibration using multiple images of a 2D target captured from different viewpoints. (**c**) A set of 3D input–output pairs is processed to estimate C and extract the camera parameters through matrix decomposition. (**d**) Multiple sets of 2D input–output pairs are processed for homography estimation and further extraction of the camera parameters by exploiting the shape of K and the orthogonality of rotation matrices.

Alternatively, instead of capturing a single image of a 3D target, the camera can be calibrated using multiple images of a 2D target [258], as shown in Figure 15b. We refer to the plane where the calibration target is located as the *reference plane*. Without loss of generality, the reference plane is assumed to be the xy-plane. Therefore, since z is always zero, the third entry of $\boldsymbol{p}$ and the vector $\bar{\boldsymbol{r}}_3$ in Equation (36) can be removed, simplifying the imaging process to

$$\mu = \mathcal{H}^{-1}[G\mathcal{H}[\rho]]. \tag{37}$$

where $\rho = [x, y]^T$ represents the points on the calibration target and G is a 3×3 non-singular matrix known as a *homography*, which is defined as

$$G = K\Big[\bar{\boldsymbol{r}}_1, \quad \bar{\boldsymbol{r}}_2, \quad -R^T\boldsymbol{t}\Big]. \tag{38}$$

An image of the 2D calibration target establishes a set of input–output pairs, allowing a homography to be estimated by minimizing the output error, as shown in Figure 15d. Although a single homography is insufficient for camera calibration, multiple homographies provide enough information to recover the required intrinsic and extrinsic parameters. For this, the upper-triangular shape of K and the orthogonality property of rotation matrices are exploited.

6.2. Projector Calibration

The data required for homography-based calibration are input–output pairs consisting of points from the reference plane matched with points from the device plane. This requirement is independent of whether the device to be calibrated is a camera or a projector due to their mathematical equivalence. Accordingly, the method for calibrating a camera or a projector is the same [259]; they differ only in how the required input–output pairs are acquired.

For camera calibration, input–output pairs are acquired by placing the calibration target on the reference plane and capturing photographs, as shown in Figure 15b. The target provides known points on the reference plane, while the images provide the corresponding pixel points using automatic feature point detection [260]. Note that this input–output acquisition strategy is not suitable for projectors because they cannot take photographs of the reference plane.

For projector calibration, input–output pairs are acquired by placing the calibration target on the device plane as a slide and illuminating the reference plane, as shown in Figure 16a. The target provides known points on the projector plane, and the corresponding points are measured on the reference plane, for instance, using grid-ruled paper. Unlike camera calibration, where the input–output acquisition is automatic using dedicated image processing routines, projector calibration requires a manual measurement of feature point coordinates on the reference plane.

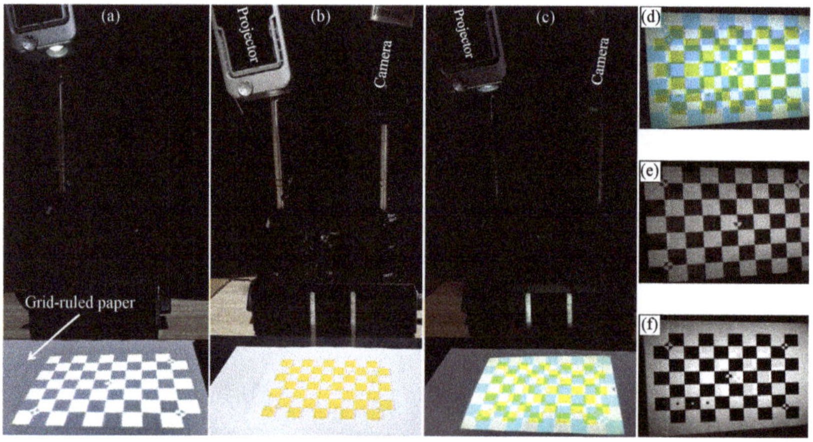

Figure 16. (**a**) Projector calibration by displaying a 2D target on the reference plane covered with grid-ruled paper for manual feature point coordinate measurement. (**b**) Yellow target on the reference plane for camera calibration. (**c**) Camera–projector calibration by displaying a cyan 2D target on the reference-plane yellow target. (**d**) Color image captured by the camera. The captured image provides the displayed and reference calibration targets through its red (**e**) and blue (**f**) channels.

6.3. Camera–Projector Calibration

Calibrating a fringe projection system requires estimating the parameters of a camera and a projector that are working together. Although cameras and projectors can be calibrated independently, simultaneous calibration is advantageous because the camera assists the projector calibration process.

Remember that a physical target on the reference plane is required for camera calibration. In addition, a virtual target on the slide plane is necessary for projector calibration. Although both targets are superposed with each other on the reference plane, they can be distinguished using targets of different colors [208,261]; for instance, a yellow target on the reference plane (see Figure 16b), and a cyan target on the projector plane (see Figure 16c). In this manner, the two superposed targets are retrieved separately from the captured image through its red and blue channels, as shown in Figure 16d–f.

The image of the physical and virtual targets on the camera plane is opportune because manual measurements on the reference plane are avoided. First, the image of the physical target is used to estimate the camera homography G_c from the relation

$$\mu_p = \mathcal{H}^{-1}\big[G_c\mathcal{H}[\rho_p]\big], \tag{39}$$

where ρ_p is a feature point of the physical target (yellow) and μ_p is the corresponding point on the image (blue channel). In addition to using G_c for camera calibration, this homography avoids manually measuring points on the reference plane for projector calibration. Specifically, let μ_v be an image point of the captured virtual target (red channel). The corresponding point ρ_v on the reference plane (cyan) can be computed using the inverse of G_c as follows:

$$\rho_v = \mathcal{H}^{-1}\left[G_c^{-1}\mathcal{H}[\mu_v]\right]. \quad (40)$$

As a result, since the feature points μ_s on the projector-slide plane are known because it contains the virtual calibration target, the projector homography G_p can be estimated from the relation

$$\mu_s = \mathcal{H}^{-1}\left[G_p\mathcal{H}[\rho_v]\right]. \quad (41)$$

This procedure is repeated for three or more poses, either by repositioning the devices or by moving the reference plane freely. Finally, the camera and projector parameters are estimated from the estimated homographies. This methodology, known as *camera–projector calibration*, remains valid even when more advanced imaging models are employed [185,251].

It is worth noting that the developed analysis was simplified using the pinhole model. However, the camera and projector may introduce significant lens distortion in practice. Even under these conditions, the fundamental principles remain valid using a lens distortion correction method [262,263].

For illustration purposes, the camera–projector calibration method was employed to calibrate the experimental system shown in Figure 17a using the software available in [259]. Then, the 50 × 100 × 50 millimeter pyramid on the reference plane was reconstructed. Figures 11 and 14i show some of the captured fringe patterns and the demodulated phase encoding the projector u-axis, respectively. Additional fringe patterns were captured to demodulate the phase encoding the v-axis. Equations (13) and (14) were used to obtain the projector-slide coordinates $u(r,s)$ and $v(r,s)$ from the demodulated phase. Finally, Equation (9) was used to compute an object point for each established corresponding point, resulting in the 3D reconstruction shown in Figure 17b.

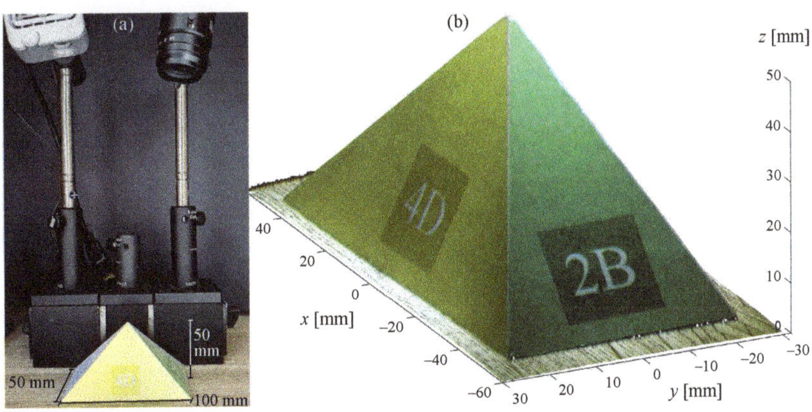

Figure 17. (**a**) Calibrated camera–projector system and an object on the reference plane. (**b**) Metric object reconstruction using fringe projection profilometry.

7. Optical 3D Metrology

Nowadays, fringe projection profilometry has been successfully implemented in several fields, ranging from science and engineering [200,264] to artwork inspection [265] and disease diagnosis [266]. Its valuable features, such as accuracy and high resolution, make it an outstanding 3D metrology tool. This section describes a few illustrative applications in which optical fringe projection has been employed.

Non-contact and high-accuracy features have motivated the implementation of fringe projection profilometry in medical applications [267]. Some representative applications include measurement of human respiration rates [268], diagnosis of tympanic membrane and middle-ear disease [269], skin assessment for research and evaluation of anti-aging products [270], tympanic membrane characterization [271], dynamic body measurement for guided radiotherapy [272], 3D imaging for assistance in laparoscopic surgery procedures [273], optical biomechanical studies for cardiovascular disease research [274], and intraoral measurement for orthodontic treatment [275]. As an example, Figure 18 shows a dental model reconstruction illustrating an intraoral measurement.

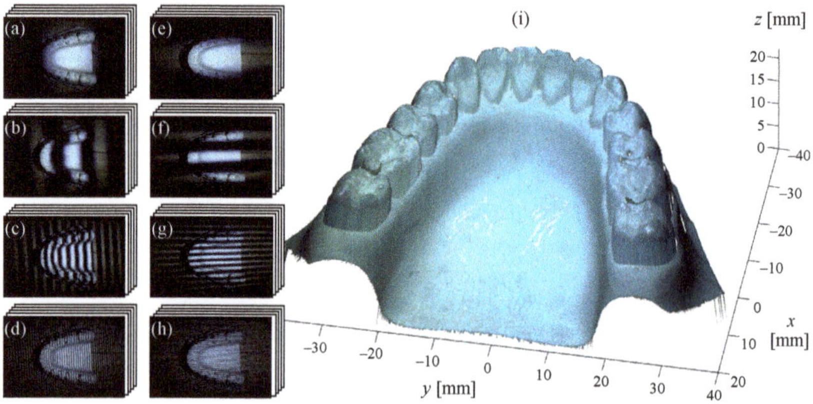

Figure 18. Reconstruction of a dental model using the calibrated camera–projector system shown in Figure 17. **(a–d)** Fringe patterns of four gratings with eight phase shifts encoding the projector's u-axis. **(e–h)** Fringe patterns encoding the projector's v-axis. **(i)** 3D object reconstruction.

Automatic and uninterrupted inspection of items on production lines is essential to ensure high-quality products [276]. For this purpose, fringe projection profilometry is a valuable tool because of its capacity for visual inspection [277]. Other tasks for which fringe projection profilometry is useful include metal corrosion monitoring [278], crack recognition assistance [279], welding surface inspection [280], micro-scale component testing [276], turbine blade wear and damage characterization [281], aircraft surface defect detection [282], and electrical overload fault detection [19]. As an example, Figure 19 shows a visible–thermal profilometer for multimodal 3D reconstruction, detecting a heat source caused by a simulated fault.

Conventional biometric-based security systems employ grayscale images to perform user authentication [283]. However, these systems lose valuable information by omitting important human biometric features such as the color and 3D shape of faces, palms, and fingers [284]. Fringe projection profilometry has been employed in security systems for face recognition [285], 3D palmprint and hand imaging [286,287], 3D fingerprint imaging [288], and ear recognition [289].

Other recent applications using fringe projection profilometry include robot vision for object detection and navigation [290], footwear and tire impression analysis in forensic science [13], shape and strain measurements for mechanical studies [291], plant phenotyping and leafy green evaluation in agriculture [292], high-precision panel telescope alignment [293], whole-body scanning for animation and entertainment [294], airbag inflation analysis for car safety studies [114,295], ancient coin and sculpture imaging for heritage preservation [296,297], fast prototyping and reverse engineering [298], three-dimensional color mural capture for cultural heritage documentation [299], animal body measurement for growth and health studies [300], 3D sensing for autonomous robot construction activities [301], local defect detection for quality inspection [302], wheel tread profile reconstruction for railway inspection [303], and many others.

This section is not intended to be exhaustive, but rather to describe motivating application examples. This paper aims to provide an elementary background for constructing and operating a fringe projection profilometer. Readers are encouraged to contribute innovative ideas, models, techniques, and applications to drive 3D metrology with even more efficient, accurate, practical, affordable, and valuable optical profilometers.

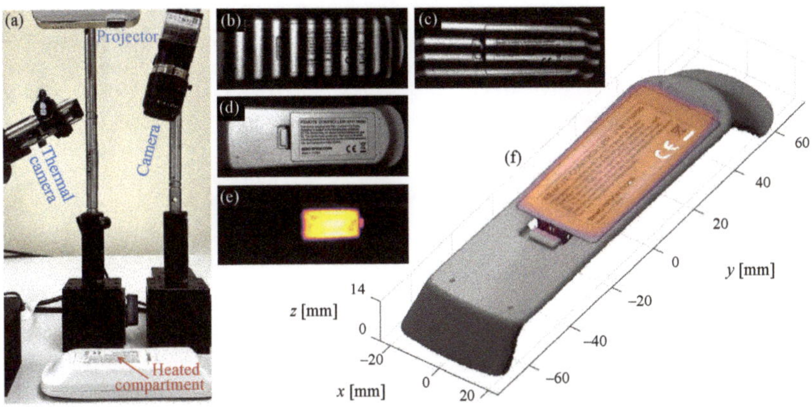

Figure 19. (**a**) Visible–thermal fringe projection profilometry reconstructing a remote controller with a heated battery compartment simulating a failure [19]. (**b**,**c**) Two of the forty-eight fringe patterns used for 3D reconstruction. (**d**,**e**) Visible and thermal images providing multimodal texture on the object surface. (**f**) Multimodal (visible–thermal) 3D object reconstruction.

8. Conclusions

The theoretical and experimental fundamentals of fringe projection profilometry have been reviewed. Helpful insights explaining challenging and confusing concepts were provided, making this technology a straightforward tool. Simple yet powerful methods for fringe-pattern processing, triangulation, and calibration were presented. The studied methods provide the reader with an adequate background to understand and operate a fringe projection profilometer. Some applications were described to expand the reader's scope and stimulate research on further developments, driving 3D metrology toward new frontiers.

Author Contributions: Conceptualization, R.J.-S.; methodology, R.J.-S.; software, R.J.-S.; visualization, R.J.-S.; validation, R.J.-S. and V.H.D.-R.; formal analysis, V.H.D.-R.; investigation, S.E.-H.; data curation, R.J.-S.; writing—original draft preparation, R.J.-S.; writing—review and editing, S.E.-H. and V.H.D.-R.; visualization, R.J.-S. All authors have read and agreed to the published version of the manuscript.

Funding: This research was funded by Secretaría de Ciencia, Humanidades, Tecnología e Innovación (Cátedras CONACYT 880).

Institutional Review Board Statement: Not applicable.

Informed Consent Statement: Not applicable.

Conflicts of Interest: The authors declare no conflicts of interest.

References

1. Zhang, M.; Chen, C.; Xie, L.; Zhang, C. Accurate measurement of high-reflective surface based on adaptive fringe projection technique. *Opt. Lasers Eng.* **2024**, *172*, 107820. [CrossRef]
2. Grambow, N.; Hinz, L.; Bonk, C.; Krüger, J.; Reithmeier, E. Creepage Distance Estimation of Hairpin Stators Using 3D Feature Extraction. *Metrology* **2023**, *3*, 169–185. [CrossRef]
3. Chen, F.; Brown, G.M.; Song, M. Overview of 3-D shape measurement using optical methods. *Opt. Eng.* **2000**, *39*, 10–22.
4. Zhang, S. (Ed.) *Handbook of 3D Machine Vision: Optical Metrology and Imaging*; Series in Optics and Optoelectronics; CRC Press: Boca Raton, FL, USA, 2013.
5. Leach, R. (Ed.) *Advances in Optical Form and Coordinate Metrology*; Emerging Technologies in Optics and Photonics; IOP Publishing Ltd.: Bristol, UK, 2020.
6. Wang, Z. Review of real-time three-dimensional shape measurement techniques. *Measurement* **2020**, *156*, 107624. [CrossRef]
7. Zhang, Q.; Su, X. High-speed optical measurement for the drumhead vibration. *Opt. Express* **2005**, *13*, 3110–3116. [CrossRef]
8. Su, X.; Zhang, Q. Dynamic 3-D shape measurement method: A review. *Opt. Lasers Eng.* **2010**, *48*, 191–204. [CrossRef]
9. Zhang, S. High-speed 3D shape measurement with structured light methods: A review. *Opt. Lasers Eng.* **2018**, *106*, 119–131. [CrossRef]
10. Chen, L.C.; Huang, C.C. Miniaturized 3D surface profilometer using digital fringe projection. *Meas. Sci. Technol.* **2005**, *16*, 1061. [CrossRef]
11. Munkelt, C.; Schmidt, I.; Brauer-Burchardt, C.; Kuhmstedt, P.; Notni, G. Cordless portable multi-view fringe projection system for 3D reconstruction. In Proceedings of the IEEE Conference on Computer Vision and Pattern Recognition, Minneapolis, MN, USA, 17–22 June 2007; pp. 1–2.
12. Zaman, T.; Jonker, P.; Lenseigne, B.; Dik, J. Simultaneous capture of the color and topography of paintings using fringe encoded stereo vision. *Herit. Sci.* **2014**, *2*, 23. [CrossRef]
13. Liao, Y.H.; Hyun, J.S.; Feller, M.; Bell, T.; Bortins, I.; Wolfe, J.; Baldwin, D.; Zhang, S. Portable high-resolution automated 3D imaging for footwear and tire impression capture. *J. Forensic Sci.* **2021**, *66*, 112–128. [CrossRef]
14. Kulkarni, R.; Rastogi, P. Optical measurement techniques—A push for digitization. *Opt. Lasers Eng.* **2016**, *87*, 1–17. [CrossRef]
15. Xing, H.; She, S.; Wang, J.; Guo, J.; Liu, Q.; Wei, C.; Yang, L.; Peng, R.; Yue, H.; Liu, Y. High-frame rate, large-depth-range structured light projector based on the step-designed LED chips array. *Opt. Express* **2024**, *32*, 24117–24127. [CrossRef]
16. Xu, J.; Zhang, S. Status, challenges, and future perspectives of fringe projection profilometry. *Opt. Lasers Eng.* **2020**, *135*, 106193. [CrossRef]
17. Peng, R.; Zhou, G.; Zhang, C.; Wei, C.; Wang, X.; Chen, X.; Yang, L.; Yue, H.; Liu, Y. Ultra-small, low-cost, and simple-to-control PSP projector based on SLCD technology. *Opt. Express* **2024**, *32*, 1878–1889. [CrossRef] [PubMed]
18. Chen, Z.; Li, X.; Wang, H.; Chen, Z.; Zhang, Q.; Wu, Z. Multi-dimensional information sensing of complex surfaces based on fringe projection profilometry. *Opt. Express* **2023**, *31*, 41374–41390. [CrossRef] [PubMed]
19. Juarez-Salazar, R.; Benjumea, E.; Marrugo, A.G.; Diaz-Ramirez, V.H. Three-dimensional object texturing for visible-thermal fringe projection profilometers. In Proceedings of the Optics and Photonics for Information Processing XVIII, San Diego, CA, USA, 18–23 August 2024; Volume 13136, p. 131360E.
20. Benjumea, E.; Vargas, R.; Juarez-Salazar, R.; Marrugo, A.G. Toward a target-free calibration of a multimodal structured light and thermal imaging system. In Proceedings of the Dimensional Optical Metrology and Inspection for Practical Applications XIII, National Harbor, MD, USA, 21–26 April 2024; Volume 13038, p. 1303808.
21. Feng, S.; Zuo, C.; Zhang, L.; Tao, T.; Hu, Y.; Yin, W.; Qian, J.; Chen, Q. Calibration of fringe projection profilometry: A comparative review. *Opt. Lasers Eng.* **2021**, *143*, 106622. [CrossRef]
22. Chen, R.; Xu, J.; Zhang, S.; Chen, H.; Guan, Y.; Chen, K. A self-recalibration method based on scale-invariant registration for structured light measurement systems. *Opt. Lasers Eng.* **2017**, *88*, 75–81. [CrossRef]
23. Xiao, Y.L.; Xue, J.; Su, X. Robust self-calibration three-dimensional shape measurement in fringe-projection photogrammetry. *Opt. Lett.* **2013**, *38*, 694–696. [CrossRef]
24. Wu, G.; Yang, T.; Liu, F.; Qian, K. Suppressing motion-induced phase error by using equal-step phase-shifting algorithms in fringe projection profilometry. *Opt. Express* **2022**, *30*, 17980–17998. [CrossRef]
25. Jeon, S.; Geon Lee, H.; Sung Lee, J.; Min Kang, B.; Wook Jeon, B.; Young Yoon, J.; Hyun, J.S. Motion-Induced Error Reduction for Motorized Digital Fringe Projection System. *IEEE Trans. Instrum. Meas.* **2024**, *73*, 1–13. [CrossRef]
26. Guo, W.; Wu, Z.; Zhang, Q.; Hou, Y.; Wang, Y.; Liu, Y. Generalized Phase Shift Deviation Estimation Method for Accurate 3-D Shape Measurement in Phase-Shifting Profilometry. *IEEE Trans. Instrum. Meas.* **2025**, *74*, 1–11. [CrossRef]

27. He, Q.; Ning, J.; Liu, X.; Li, Q. Phase-shifting profilometry for 3D shape measurement of moving objects on production lines. *Precis. Eng.* **2025**, *92*, 30–38. [CrossRef]
28. Juarez-Salazar, R. Flat mirrors, virtual rear-view cameras, and camera-mirror calibration. *Optik* **2024**, *317*, 172067. [CrossRef]
29. Almaraz-Cabral, C.C.; Gonzalez-Barbosa, J.J.; Villa, J.; Hurtado-Ramos, J.B.; Ornelas-Rodriguez, F.J.; Córdova-Esparza, D.M. Fringe projection profilometry for panoramic 3D reconstruction. *Opt. Lasers Eng.* **2016**, *78*, 106–112. [CrossRef]
30. Flores, V.; Casaletto, L.; Genovese, K.; Martinez, A.; Montes, A.; Rayas, J. A Panoramic Fringe Projection system. *Opt. Lasers Eng.* **2014**, *58*, 80–84. [CrossRef]
31. Wang, Y.; Wu, X.; Hou, B.; Wang, B. Three-dimensional panoramic measurement based on fringe projection assisted by double-plane mirrors. *Opt. Eng.* **2024**, *63*, 114103. [CrossRef]
32. Zhang, S.; Yang, Y.; Shi, W.; Feng, L.; Jiao, L. 3D shape measurement method for high-reflection surface based on fringe projection. *Appl. Opt.* **2021**, *60*, 10555–10563. [CrossRef]
33. Feng, S.; Zhang, L.; Zuo, C.; Tao, T.; Chen, Q.; Gu, G. High dynamic range 3D measurements with fringe projection profilometry: A review. *Meas. Sci. Technol.* **2018**, *29*, 122001. [CrossRef]
34. Zhang, S. Rapid and automatic optimal exposure control for digital fringe projection technique. *Opt. Lasers Eng.* **2020**, *128*, 106029. [CrossRef]
35. Duan, M.; Jin, Y.; Chen, H.; Zheng, J.; Zhu, C.; Chen, E. Automatic 3-D Measurement Method for Nonuniform Moving Objects. *IEEE Trans. Instrum. Meas.* **2021**, *70*, 5015011. [CrossRef]
36. Chen, R.; Xu, J.; Zhang, S. Digital fringe projection profilometry . In *Advances in Optical Form and Coordinate Metrology*; IOP Publishing: Bristol, UK , 2020; pp. 1–28.
37. Zappa, E.; Busca, G. Static and dynamic features of Fourier transform profilometry: A review. *Opt. Lasers Eng.* **2012**, *50*, 1140–1151. [CrossRef]
38. Keller, W.; Girard, J.; Goldberg, M.W.; Zhang, S. Precise calibration for error detection and correction in material extrusion additive manufacturing using digital fringe projection. *Meas. Sci. Technol.* **2025**, *36*, 025203. [CrossRef]
39. Huang, H.; Niu, B.; Cheng, S.; Zhang, F. High-precision calibration and phase compensation method for structured light 3D imaging system. *Opt. Lasers Eng.* **2025**, *186*, 108788. [CrossRef]
40. Yoshizawa, T. (Ed.) *Handbook of Optical Metrology: Principles and Applications*, 2nd ed.; CRC Press: Boca Raton, FL, USA, 2015.
41. Rastogi, P.K. (Ed.) *Digital Optical Measurement Techniques and Applications*; Artech House Applied Photonics Series; Artech House: London, UK, 2015.
42. Lv, S.; Tang, D.; Zhang, X.; Yang, D.; Deng, W.; Kemao, Q. Fringe projection profilometry method with high efficiency, precision, and convenience: Theoretical analysis and development. *Opt. Express* **2022**, *30*, 33515–33537. [CrossRef]
43. Engel, T. 3D optical measurement techniques. *Meas. Sci. Technol.* **2023**, *34*, 032002. [CrossRef]
44. Rowe, S.H.; Welford, W.T. Surface Topography of Non-optical Surfaces by Projected Interference Fringes. *Nature* **1967**, *216*, 786–787. [CrossRef]
45. Wygant, R.W.; Almeida, S.P.; Soares, O.D.D. Surface inspection via projection interferometry. *Appl. Opt.* **1988**, *27*, 4626–4630. [CrossRef] [PubMed]
46. Ronchi, V. Forty Years of History of a Grating Interferometer. *Appl. Opt.* **1964**, *3*, 437–451. [CrossRef]
47. Murty, M.V.R.K.; Shoemaker, A.H. Theory of Concentric Circular Grid. *Appl. Opt.* **1966**, *5*, 323–326. [CrossRef]
48. Case, S.K.; Jalkio, J.A.; Kim, R.C. 3-D Vision System Analysis and Design. In *Three-Dimensional Machine Vision*; Kanade, T., Ed.; Springer: Boston, MA, USA, 1987; pp. 63–95.
49. Malacara, D. (Ed.) *Optical Shop Testing*, 3rd ed.; John Wiley & Sons, Inc.: Hoboken, NJ, USA, 2007.
50. Juarez-Salazar, R.; Robledo-Sanchez, C.; Guerrero-Sanchez, F.; Barcelata-Pinzon, A.; Gonzalez-Garcia, J.; Santiago-Alvarado, A. Intensity normalization of additive and multiplicative spatially multiplexed patterns with n encoded phases. *Opt. Lasers Eng.* **2016**, *77*, 225–229. [CrossRef]
51. Juarez-Salazar, R.; Diaz-Ramirez, V.H. Estimation of amplitude and standard deviation of noisy sinusoidal signals. *Opt. Eng.* **2017**, *56*, 013109. [CrossRef]
52. Servin, M.; Quiroga, J.A.; Padilla, M. *Fringe Pattern Analysis for Optical Metrology: Theory, Algorithms, and Applications*; Wiley: Hoboken, NJ, USA, 2014.
53. Takasaki, H. Moiré Topography. *Appl. Opt.* **1970**, *9*, 1467–1472. [CrossRef]
54. Meadows, D.M.; Johnson, W.O.; Allen, J.B. Generation of Surface Contours by Moiré Patterns. *Appl. Opt.* **1970**, *9*, 942–947. [CrossRef] [PubMed]
55. Li, C.; Cao, Y.; Chen, C.; Wan, Y.; Fu, G.; Wang, Y. Computer-generated moiré profilometry. *Opt. Express* **2017**, *25*, 26815–26824. [CrossRef] [PubMed]
56. Takasaki, H. Moiré Topography. *Appl. Opt.* **1973**, *12*, 845–850. [CrossRef]

57. Takeda, M.; Mutoh, K. Fourier transform profilometry for the automatic measurement of 3-D object shapes. *Appl. Opt.* **1983**, *22*, 3977–3982. [CrossRef]
58. Takeda, M.; Ina, H.; Kobayashi, S. Fourier-transform method of fringe-pattern analysis for computer-based topography and interferometry. *J. Opt. Soc. Am.* **1982**, *72*, 156–160. [CrossRef]
59. Toyooka, S.; Iwaasa, Y. Automatic profilometry of 3-D diffuse objects by spatial phase detection. *Appl. Opt.* **1986**, *25*, 1630–1633. [CrossRef]
60. Rodriguez-Vera, R.; Servin, M. Phase locked loop profilometry. *Opt. Laser Technol.* **1994**, *26*, 393–398. [CrossRef]
61. Villa, J.; Servin, M.; Castillo, L. Profilometry for the measurement of 3-D object shapes based on regularized filters. *Opt. Commun.* **1999**, *161*, 13–18. [CrossRef]
62. Sajan, M.R.; Tay, C.J.; Shang, H.M.; Asundi, A. Improved spatial phase detection for profilometry using a TDI imager. *Opt. Commun.* **1998**, *150*, 66–70. [CrossRef]
63. Berryman, F.; Pynsent, P.; Cubillo, J. A theoretical comparison of three fringe analysis methods for determining the three-dimensional shape of an object in the presence of noise. *Opt. Lasers Eng.* **2003**, *39*, 35–50. [CrossRef]
64. Srinivasan, V.; Liu, H.C.; Halioua, M. Automated phase-measuring profilometry of 3-D diffuse objects. *Appl. Opt.* **1984**, *23*, 3105–3108. [CrossRef] [PubMed]
65. Reich, C.; Ritter, R.; Thesing, J. 3-D shape measurement of complex objects by combining photogrammetry and fringe projection. *Opt. Eng.* **2000**, *39*, 224–231. [CrossRef]
66. Bruning, J.H.; Herriott, D.R.; Gallagher, J.E.; Rosenfeld, D.P.; White, A.D.; Brangaccio, D.J. Digital Wavefront Measuring Interferometer for Testing Optical Surfaces and Lenses. *Appl. Opt.* **1974**, *13*, 2693–2703. [CrossRef] [PubMed]
67. Li, J.; Su, X.; Guo, L. Improved Fourier transform profilometry for the automatic measurement of three-dimensional object shapes. *Opt. Eng.* **1990**, *29*, 1439–1444.
68. Juarez-Salazar, R.; Martinez-Laguna, J.; Diaz-Ramirez, V.H. Multi-demodulation phase-shifting and intensity pattern projection profilometry. *Opt. Lasers Eng.* **2020**, *129*, 106085. [CrossRef]
69. Kemao, Q. Two-dimensional windowed Fourier transform for fringe pattern analysis: Principles, applications and implementations. *Opt. Lasers Eng.* **2007**, *45*, 304–317. [CrossRef]
70. Casco-Vasquez, J.F.; Juarez-Salazar, R.; Robledo-Sanchez, C.; Rodriguez-Zurita, G.; Sanchez, F.G.; Arévalo Aguilar, L.M.; Meneses-Fabian, C. Fourier normalized-fringe analysis by zero-order spectrum suppression using a parameter estimation approach. *Opt. Eng.* **2013**, *52*, 074109. [CrossRef]
71. Liu, Y.; Du, G.; Zhang, C.; Zhou, C.; Si, S.; Lei, Z. An improved two-step phase-shifting profilometry. *Opt.—Int. J. Light Electron Opt.* **2016**, *127*, 288–291. [CrossRef]
72. Juarez-Salazar, R.; Robledo-Sanchez, C.; Meneses-Fabian, C.; Guerrero-Sanchez, F.; Aguilar, L.A. Generalized phase-shifting interferometry by parameter estimation with the least squares method. *Opt. Lasers Eng.* **2013**, *51*, 626–632. [CrossRef]
73. Wei, Z.; Cao, Y.; Wu, H.; Xu, C.; Ruan, G.; Wu, F.; Li, C. Dynamic phase-differencing profilometry with number-theoretical phase unwrapping and interleaved projection. *Opt. Express* **2024**, *32*, 19578–19593. [CrossRef]
74. Juarez-Salazar, R.; Guerrero-Sanchez, F.; Robledo-Sanchez, C. Theory and algorithms of an efficient fringe analysis technology for automatic measurement applications. *Appl. Opt.* **2015**, *54*, 5364–5374. [CrossRef]
75. Su, X.; Su, L.; Li, W.; Xiang, L. New 3D profilometry based on modulation measurement. In *Proceedings of the Automated Optical Inspection for Industry: Theory, Technology, and Applications II, Beijing, China, 16–19 September 1998*; Ye, S., Ed.; SPIE: Bellingham, WA, USA, 1998; Volume 3558, pp. 1–7.
76. Su, L.; Su, X.; Li, W.; Xiang, L. Application of modulation measurement profilometry to objects with surface holes. *Appl. Opt.* **1999**, *38*, 1153–1158. [CrossRef] [PubMed]
77. Fang, Q.; Zheng, S. Linearly coded profilometry. *Appl. Opt.* **1997**, *36*, 2401–2407. [CrossRef] [PubMed]
78. Geng, J. Structured-light 3D surface imaging: A tutorial. *Adv. Opt. Photon.* **2011**, *3*, 128–160. [CrossRef]
79. Deng, J.; Li, J.; Feng, H.; Ding, S.; Xiao, Y.; Han, W.; Zeng, Z. Efficient intensity-based fringe projection profilometry method resistant to global illumination. *Opt. Express* **2020**, *28*, 36346–36360. [CrossRef]
80. An, H.; Cao, Y.; Wu, H.; Yang, N.; Xu, C.; Li, H. Spatial-temporal phase unwrapping algorithm for fringe projection profilometry. *Opt. Express* **2021**, *29*, 20657–20672. [CrossRef]
81. Marrugo, A.G.; Gao, F.; Zhang, S. State-of-the-art active optical techniques for three-dimensional surface metrology: A review [Invited]. *J. Opt. Soc. Am. A* **2020**, *37*, B60–B77. [CrossRef]
82. Gorthi, S.S.; Rastogi, P.K. Fringe projection techniques: Whither we are? *Opt. Lasers Eng.* **2010**, *48*, 133–140. [CrossRef]
83. Zuo, C.; Qian, J.; Feng, S.; Yin, W.; Li, Y.; Fan, P.; Han, J.; Qian, K.; Chen, Q. Deep learning in optical metrology: A review. *Light. Sci. Appl.* **2022**, *11*, 39. [CrossRef] [PubMed]
84. Zhang, S. *High-Speed 3D Imaging with Digital Fringe Projection Techniques*; CRC Press: Boca Raton, FL, USA, 2016 .

85. Harding, K. (Ed.) *Handbook of Optical Dimensional Metrology;* Series in Optics and Optoelectronics; CRC Press: Boca Raton, FL, USA, 2013.
86. Jiang, C.; Li, Y.; Feng, S.; Hu, Y.; Yin, W.; Qian, J.; Zuo, C.; Liang, J. Fringe Projection Profilometry. In *Coded Optical Imaging*; Springer International Publishing: Cham, Switzerland, 2024; Chapter 14, pp. 241–286.
87. Yang, T.; Gu, F. Overview of modulation techniques for spatially structured-light 3D imaging. *Opt. Laser Technol.* **2024**, *169*, 110037. [CrossRef]
88. Li, E.B.; Peng, X.; Xi, J.; Chicharo, J.F.; Yao, J.Q.; Zhang, D.W. Multi-frequency and multiple phase-shift sinusoidal fringe projection for 3D profilometry. *Opt. Express* **2005**, *13*, 1561–1569. [CrossRef] [PubMed]
89. Wang, Y.; Zhang, S. Optimal fringe angle selection for digital fringe projection technique. *Appl. Opt.* **2013**, *52*, 7094–7098. [CrossRef] [PubMed]
90. Geng, Z.J. Rainbow three-dimensional camera: New concept of high-speed three-dimensional vision systems. *Opt. Eng.* **1996**, *35*, 376–383. [CrossRef]
91. Pan, J.; Huang, P.S.; Chiang, F.P. Color-coded binary fringe projection technique for 3-D shape measurement. *Opt. Eng.* **2005**, *44*, 023606. [CrossRef]
92. Su, W.H. Color-encoded fringe projection for 3D shape measurements. *Opt. Express* **2007**, *15*, 13167–13181. [CrossRef]
93. Waddington, C.; Kofman, J. Saturation avoidance by adaptive fringe projection in phase-shifting 3D surface-shape measurement. In Proceedings of the International Symposium on Optomechatronic Technologies, Toronto, ON, Canada, 25–27 October 2010; pp. 1–4.
94. Salahieh, B.; Chen, Z.; Rodriguez, J.J.; Liang, R. Multi-polarization fringe projection imaging for high dynamic range objects. *Opt. Express* **2014**, *22*, 10064–10071. [CrossRef]
95. Lagarde, J.M.; Rouvrais, C.; Black, D.; Diridollou, S.; Gall, Y. Skin topography measurement by interference fringe projection: A technical validation. *Skin Res. Technol.* **2001**, *7*, 112–121. [CrossRef]
96. Wu, F.; Zhang, H.; Lalor, M.J.; Burton, D.R. A novel design for fiber optic interferometric fringe projection phase-shifting 3-D profilometry. *Opt. Commun.* **2001**, *187*, 347–357. [CrossRef]
97. Sánchez, J.R.; Martínez-García, A.; Rayas, J.A.; León-Rodríguez, M. LED source interferometer for microscopic fringe projection profilometry using a Gates' interferometer configuration. *Opt. Lasers Eng.* **2022**, *149*, 106822. [CrossRef]
98. Schaffer, M.; Große, M.; Harendt, B.; Kowarschik, R. Coherent two-beam interference fringe projection for highspeed three-dimensional shape measurements. *Appl. Opt.* **2013**, *52*, 2306–2311. [CrossRef] [PubMed]
99. Sicardi-Segade, A.; Martinez-Garcia, A.; Toto-Arellano, N.I.; Rayas, J.A. Analysis of the fringes visibility generated by a lateral cyclic shear interferometer in the retrieval of the three-dimensional surface information of an object. *Opt.—Int. J. Light Electron Opt.* **2014**, *125*, 1320–1324. [CrossRef]
100. Robledo-Sanchez, C.; Juarez-Salazar, R.; Meneses-Fabian, C.; Guerrero-Sánchez, F.; Aguilar, L.M.A.; Rodriguez-Zurita, G.; Ixba-Santos, V. Phase-shifting interferometry based on the lateral displacement of the light source. *Opt. Express* **2013**, *21*, 17228–17233. [CrossRef] [PubMed]
101. Creath, K.; Schmit, J.; Wyant, J.C. Optical metrology of diffuse surfaces. In *Optical Shop Testing*, 3rd ed.; Malacara, D., Ed.; John Wiley & Sons, Inc.: Hoboken, NJ, USA, 2007; pp. 756–807.
102. Wang, L.; Cao, Y.; Li, C.; Wang, Y.; Wan, Y.; Fu, G.; Li, H.; Xu, C. Orthogonal modulated computer-generated moiré profilometry. *Opt. Commun.* **2020**, *455*, 124565. [CrossRef]
103. Su, X.Y.; Zhou, W.S.; von Bally, G.; Vukicevic, D. Automated phase-measuring profilometry using defocused projection of a Ronchi grating. *Opt. Commun.* **1992**, *94*, 561–573. [CrossRef]
104. Lei, S.; Zhang, S. Flexible 3-D shape measurement using projector defocusing. *Opt. Lett.* **2009**, *34*, 3080–3082. [CrossRef]
105. Lei, S.; Zhang, S. Digital sinusoidal fringe pattern generation: Defocusing binary patterns VS focusing sinusoidal patterns. *Opt. Lasers Eng.* **2010**, *48*, 561–569. [CrossRef]
106. Ayubi, G.A.; Ayubi, J.A.; Martino, J.M.D.; Ferrari, J.A. Pulse-width modulation in defocused three-dimensional fringe projection. *Opt. Lett.* **2010**, *35*, 3682–3684. [CrossRef]
107. Silva, A.; Flores, J.L.; Muñoz, A.M.; Ayubi, G.A.; Ferrari, J.A. Three-dimensional shape profiling by out-of-focus projection of colored pulse width modulation fringe patterns. *Appl. Opt.* **2017**, *56*, 5198–5203. [CrossRef]
108. Huang, P.S.; Hu, Q.; Jin, F.; Chiang, F.P. Color-encoded digital fringe projection technique for high-speed 3-D surface contouring. *Opt. Eng.* **1999**, *38*, 1065–1071. [CrossRef]
109. Liu, W.; Wang, Z.; Mu, G.; Fang, Z. Color-coded projection grating method for shape measurement with a single exposure. *Appl. Opt.* **2000**, *39*, 3504–3508. [CrossRef] [PubMed]
110. Wang, Y.; Zhang, S. Three-dimensional shape measurement with binary dithered patterns. *Appl. Opt.* **2012**, *51*, 6631–6636. [CrossRef] [PubMed]

111. Peng, R.; Tian, M.; Xu, L.; Yang, L.; Yue, H. A novel method of generating phase-shifting sinusoidal fringes for 3D shape measurement. *Opt. Lasers Eng.* **2021**, *137*, 106401. [CrossRef]
112. Fujigaki, M.; Oura, Y.; Asai, D.; Murata, Y. High-speed height measurement by a light-source-stepping method using a linear LED array. *Opt. Express* **2013**, *21*, 23169–23180. [CrossRef]
113. Wissmann, P.; Forster, F.; Schmitt, R. Fast and low-cost structured light pattern sequence projection. *Opt. Express* **2011**, *19*, 24657–24671. [CrossRef]
114. Heist, S.; Lutzke, P.; Schmidt, I.; Dietrich, P.; Kühmstedt, P.; Tünnermann, A.; Notni, G. High-speed three-dimensional shape measurement using GOBO projection. *Opt. Lasers Eng.* **2016**, *87*, 90–96. [CrossRef]
115. Liu, Y.; Zhang, Q.; Liu, Y.; Yu, X.; Hou, Y.; Chen, W. High-speed 3D shape measurement using a rotary mechanical projector. *Opt. Express* **2021**, *29*, 7885–7903. [CrossRef]
116. Huang, P.S.; Zhang, C.; Chiang, F.P. High-speed 3-D shape measurement based on digital fringe projection. *Opt. Eng.* **2003**, *42*, 163–168. [CrossRef]
117. Zhu, Z.; You, D.; Zhou, F.; Wang, S.; Xie, Y. Rapid 3D reconstruction method based on the polarization-enhanced fringe pattern of an HDR object. *Opt. Express* **2021**, *29*, 2162–2171. [CrossRef]
118. Zhu, H.; Guo, H. Surface profile measurement of metal objects by use of a fringe projection system with polarized dual projectors. *Appl. Opt.* **2024**, *63*, 7883–7892. [CrossRef]
119. Zhang, S.; Weide, D.V.D.; Oliver, J. Superfast phase-shifting method for 3-D shape measurement. *Opt. Express* **2010**, *18*, 9684–9689. [CrossRef] [PubMed]
120. Zendejas-Hernández, E.; Trujillo-Schiaffino, G.; Anguiano-Morales, M.; Salas-Peimbert, D.P.; Corral-Martínez, L.F.; Tornero-Martínez, N. Spatial and temporal methods for fringe pattern analysis: A review. *J. Opt.* **2023**, *52*, 888–899. [CrossRef]
121. Zhang, Z. Review of single-shot 3D shape measurement by phase calculation-based fringe projection techniques. *Opt. Lasers Eng.* **2012**, *50*, 1097–1106. [CrossRef]
122. Su, X.; Chen, W. Fourier transform profilometry: A review. *Opt. Lasers Eng.* **2001**, *35*, 263–284. [CrossRef]
123. Takeda, M. Fourier fringe analysis and its application to metrology of extreme physical phenomena: A review [Invited]. *Appl. Opt.* **2013**, *52*, 20–29. [CrossRef]
124. Sandoz, P. Wavelet transform as a processing tool in white-light interferometry. *Opt. Lett.* **1997**, *22*, 1065–1067. [CrossRef]
125. Zhong, J.; Weng, J. Spatial carrier-fringe pattern analysis by means of wavelet transform: Wavelet transform profilometry. *Appl. Opt.* **2004**, *43*, 4993–4998. [CrossRef]
126. Xu, P.; Liu, J.; Zhang, W.; Shan, S.; Wang, J.; Shao, M.; Deng, Z. Few-fringe-based phase-shifting profilometry employing hilbert transform. *Precis. Eng.* **2023**, *83*, 1–11. [CrossRef]
127. Ferrari, J.A.; Flores, J.L.; Fernandez Lakatos, M.; Ayubi, G.A.; Perciante, C.D.; Frins, E. Hilbert's and Takeda's single-shot interferometry with a linear-carrier: A comparison. *Meas. Sci. Technol.* **2024**, *35*, 055006. [CrossRef]
128. Jiang, M.; Chen, W.; Zheng, Z.; Zhong, M. Fringe pattern analysis by S-transform. *Opt. Commun.* **2012**, *285*, 209–217. [CrossRef]
129. Massig, J.H.; Heppner, J. Fringe-Pattern Analysis with High Accuracy by Use of the Fourier-Transform Method: Theory and Experimental Tests. *Appl. Opt.* **2001**, *40*, 2081–2088. [CrossRef]
130. Quan, C.; Chen, W.; Tay, C. Phase-retrieval techniques in fringe-projection profilometry. *Opt. Lasers Eng.* **2010**, *48*, 235–243. [CrossRef]
131. Villa, J.; Luis Flores, J.; Garcia-Torales, G.; Montes-Flores, M. Fourier transform digital moiré interferometry. *Meas. Sci. Technol.* **2025**, *36*, 035208. [CrossRef]
132. Zhang, Z.; Jing, Z.; Wang, Z.; Kuang, D. Comparison of Fourier transform, windowed Fourier transform, and wavelet transform methods for phase calculation at discontinuities in fringe projection profilometry. *Opt. Lasers Eng.* **2012**, *50*, 1152–1160. [CrossRef]
133. Zuo, C.; Feng, S.; Huang, L.; Tao, T.; Yin, W.; Chen, Q. Phase shifting algorithms for fringe projection profilometry: A review. *Opt. Lasers Eng.* **2018**, *109*, 23–59. [CrossRef]
134. Creath, K. V Phase-Measurement Interferometry Techniques. In *Progress in Optics*; Wolf, E., Ed.; Elsevier: Amsterdam, The Netherlands, 1988; Volume 26, pp. 349–393.
135. Hariharan, P.; Oreb, B.F.; Eiju, T. Digital phase-shifting interferometry: A simple error-compensating phase calculation algorithm. *Appl. Opt.* **1987**, *26*, 2504–2506. [CrossRef] [PubMed]
136. Malacara, D.; Servin, M.; Malacara, Z. *Interferogram Analysis for Optical Testing*, 2nd ed.; Taylor & Francis Group: Abingdon, UK, 2010.
137. Carré, P. Installation et utilisation du comparateur photoélectrique et interférentiel du Bureau International des Poids et Mesures. *Metrologia* **1966**, *2*, 13. [CrossRef]
138. Juarez-Salazar, R.; Robledo-Sanchez, C.; Guerrero-Sanchez, F.; Rangel-Huerta, A. Generalized phase-shifting algorithm for inhomogeneous phase shift and spatio-temporal fringe visibility variation. *Opt. Express* **2014**, *22*, 4738–4750. [CrossRef]

139. Meneses-Fabian, C.; Lara-Cortes, F.A. Phase retrieval by Euclidean distance in self-calibrating generalized phase-shifting interferometry of three steps. *Opt. Express* **2015**, *23*, 13589–13604. [CrossRef]
140. Greivenkamp, J.E. Generalized data reduction for heterodyne interferometry. *Opt. Eng.* **1984**, *23*, 234350–234352. [CrossRef]
141. Morgan, C.J. Least-squares estimation in phase-measurement interferometry. *Opt. Lett.* **1982**, *7*, 368–370. [CrossRef] [PubMed]
142. Ghiglia, D.C.; Pritt, M.D. *Two-Dimensional Phase Unwrapping: Theory, Algorithms, and Software*; John Wiley & Sons, Inc.: New York, NY, USA, 1998.
143. Zappa, E.; Busca, G. Comparison of eight unwrapping algorithms applied to Fourier-transform profilometry. *Opt. Lasers Eng.* **2008**, *46*, 106–116. [CrossRef]
144. Itoh, K. Analysis of the phase unwrapping algorithm. *Appl. Opt.* **1982**, *21*, 2470. [CrossRef]
145. Ghiglia, D.C.; Romero, L.A. Robust two-dimensional weighted and unweighted phase unwrapping that uses fast transforms and iterative methods. *J. Opt. Soc. Am. A* **1994**, *11*, 107–117. [CrossRef]
146. Schofield, M.A.; Zhu, Y. Fast phase unwrapping algorithm for interferometric applications. *Opt. Lett.* **2003**, *28*, 1194–1196. [CrossRef]
147. Goldstein, R.M.; Zebker, H.A.; Werner, C.L. Satellite radar interferometry: Two-dimensional phase unwrapping. *Radio Sci.* **1988**, *23*, 713–720. [CrossRef]
148. Flynn, T. Consistent 2-D phase unwrapping guided by a quality map. In Proceedings of the International Geoscience and Remote Sensing Symposium, Lincoln, NE, USA, 31 May 1996; Volume 4, pp. 2057–2059.
149. Su, X.; Chen, W. Reliability-guided phase unwrapping algorithm: A review. *Opt. Lasers Eng.* **2004**, *42*, 245–261. [CrossRef]
150. Zhao, M.; Huang, L.; Zhang, Q.; Su, X.; Asundi, A.; Kemao, Q. Quality-guided phase unwrapping technique: Comparison of quality maps and guiding strategies. *Appl. Opt.* **2011**, *50*, 6214–6224. [CrossRef]
151. Ghiglia, D.C.; Romero, L.A. Minimum Lp-norm two-dimensional phase unwrapping. *J. Opt. Soc. Am. A* **1996**, *13*, 1999–2013. [CrossRef]
152. Flynn, T.J. Two-dimensional phase unwrapping with minimum weighted discontinuity. *J. Opt. Soc. Am. A* **1997**, *14*, 2692–2701. [CrossRef]
153. Costantini, M. A novel phase unwrapping method based on network programming. *Geosci. Remote Sens. IEEE Trans.* **1998**, *36*, 813–821. [CrossRef]
154. Juarez-Salazar, R.; Robledo-Sanchez, C.; Guerrero-Sanchez, F. Phase-unwrapping algorithm by a rounding-least-squares approach. *Opt. Eng.* **2014**, *53*, 024102. [CrossRef]
155. Sansoni, G.; Corini, S.; Lazzari, S.; Rodella, R.; Docchio, F. Three-dimensional imaging based on Gray-code light projection: Characterization of the measuring algorithm and development of a measuring system for industrial applications. *Appl. Opt.* **1997**, *36*, 4463–4472. [CrossRef] [PubMed]
156. Sansoni, G.; Carocci, M.; Rodella, R. Three-Dimensional Vision Based on a Combination of Gray-Code and Phase-Shift Light Projection: Analysis and Compensation of the Systematic Errors. *Appl. Opt.* **1999**, *38*, 6565–6573. [CrossRef]
157. Wu, Z.; Zuo, C.; Guo, W.; Tao, T.; Zhang, Q. High-speed three-dimensional shape measurement based on cyclic complementary Gray-code light. *Opt. Express* **2019**, *27*, 1283–1297. [CrossRef] [PubMed]
158. He, X.; Zheng, D.; Kemao, Q.; Christopoulos, G. Quaternary gray-code phase unwrapping for binary fringe projection profilometry. *Opt. Lasers Eng.* **2019**, *121*, 358–368. [CrossRef]
159. Tian, J.; Peng, X.; Zhao, X. A generalized temporal phase unwrapping algorithm for three-dimensional profilometry. *Opt. Lasers Eng.* **2008**, *46*, 336–342. [CrossRef]
160. Zuo, C.; Huang, L.; Zhang, M.; Chen, Q.; Asundi, A. Temporal phase unwrapping algorithms for fringe projection profilometry: A comparative review. *Opt. Lasers Eng.* **2016**, *85*, 84–103. [CrossRef]
161. Villa, J.; Rodríguez-Reveles, G.A.; Moreno, G.; de la Rosa, I. Temporal phase-unwrapping in fringe projection profilometry: Increasing the accuracy with equidistant long time-steps sampling. *Opt. Lasers Eng.* **2023**, *167*, 107591. [CrossRef]
162. Zhang, S. Absolute phase retrieval methods for digital fringe projection profilometry: A review. *Opt. Lasers Eng.* **2018**, *107*, 28–37. [CrossRef]
163. Wu, Z.; Guo, W.; Zhang, Q. Two-frequency phase-shifting method vs. Gray-coded-based method in dynamic fringe projection profilometry: A comparative review. *Opt. Lasers Eng.* **2022**, *153*, 106995. [CrossRef]
164. Cheng, Y.Y.; Wyant, J.C. Two-wavelength phase shifting interferometry. *Appl. Opt.* **1984**, *23*, 4539–4543. [CrossRef] [PubMed]
165. Towers, C.E.; Towers, D.P.; Jones, J.D.C. Generalized frequency selection in multifrequency interferometry. *Opt. Lett.* **2004**, *29*, 1348–1350. [CrossRef] [PubMed]
166. Zhang, Z.; Towers, C.E.; Towers, D.P. Time efficient color fringe projection system for 3D shape and color using optimum 3-frequency Selection. *Opt. Express* **2006**, *14*, 6444–6455. [CrossRef] [PubMed]

167. Huntley, J.M.; Saldner, H. Temporal phase-unwrapping algorithm for automated interferogram analysis. *Appl. Opt.* **1993**, *32*, 3047–3052. [CrossRef]
168. Saldner, H.O.; Huntley, J.M. Temporal phase unwrapping: Application to surface profiling of discontinuous objects. *Appl. Opt.* **1997**, *36*, 2770–2775. [CrossRef]
169. He, X.; Kemao, Q. A comparative study on temporal phase unwrapping methods in high-speed fringe projection profilometry. *Opt. Lasers Eng.* **2021**, *142*, 106613. [CrossRef]
170. Zhang, M.; Chen, Q.; Tao, T.; Feng, S.; Hu, Y.; Li, H.; Zuo, C. Robust and efficient multi-frequency temporal phase unwrapping: Optimal fringe frequency and pattern sequence selection. *Opt. Express* **2017**, *25*, 20381–20400. [CrossRef]
171. Su, X.; Song, W.; Cao, Y.; Xiang, L. Phase-height mapping and coordinate calibration simultaneously in phase-measuring profilometry. *Opt. Eng.* **2004**, *43*, 708–712.
172. Zhou, W.S.; Su, X.Y. A Direct Mapping Algorithm for Phase-measuring Profilometry. *J. Mod. Opt.* **1994**, *41*, 89–94. [CrossRef]
173. Zhang, J.; Luo, B.; Su, X.; Li, L.; Li, B.; Zhang, S.; Wang, Y. A convenient 3D reconstruction model based on parallel-axis structured light system. *Opt. Lasers Eng.* **2021**, *138*, 106366. [CrossRef]
174. Liu, H.; Lin, H.; Yao, L. Calibration method for projector-camera-based telecentric fringe projection profilometry system. *Opt. Express* **2017**, *25*, 31492–31508. [CrossRef]
175. Zhao, W.; Su, X.; Chen, W. Discussion on accurate phase-height mapping in fringe projection profilometry. *Opt. Eng.* **2017**, *56*, 104109. [CrossRef]
176. Lu, J.; Mo, R.; Sun, H.; Chang, Z. Flexible calibration of phase-to-height conversion in fringe projection profilometry. *Appl. Opt.* **2016**, *55*, 6381–6388. [CrossRef] [PubMed]
177. Xiao, Y.; Cao, Y.; Wu, Y. Improved algorithm for phase-to-height mapping in phase measuring profilometry. *Appl. Opt.* **2012**, *51*, 1149–1155. [CrossRef]
178. Wang, Z.; Du, H.; Bi, H. Out-of-plane shape determination in generalized fringe projection profilometry. *Opt. Express* **2006**, *14*, 12122–12133. [CrossRef]
179. Villa, J.; Araiza, M.; Alaniz, D.; Ivanov, R.; Ortiz, M. Transformation of phase to (x,y,z)-coordinates for the calibration of a fringe projection profilometer. *Opt. Lasers Eng.* **2012**, *50*, 256–261. [CrossRef]
180. Cai, Z.; Liu, X.; Li, A.; Tang, Q.; Peng, X.; Gao, B.Z. Phase-3D mapping method developed from back-projection stereovision model for fringe projection profilometry. *Opt. Express* **2017**, *25*, 1262–1277. [CrossRef]
181. Chen, L.; Quan, C. Fringe projection profilometry with nonparallel illumination: A least-squares approach. *Opt. Lett.* **2005**, *30*, 2101–2103. [CrossRef]
182. Du, H.; Wang, Z. Three-dimensional shape measurement with an arbitrarily arranged fringe projection profilometry system. *Opt. Lett.* **2007**, *32*, 2438–2440. [CrossRef] [PubMed]
183. Martinez, A.; Rayas, J.A.; Puga, H.J.; Genovese, K. Iterative estimation of the topography measurement by fringe-projection method with divergent illumination by considering the pitch variation along the x and z directions. *Opt. Lasers Eng.* **2010**, *48*, 877–881. [CrossRef]
184. Huang, L.; Chua, P.S.K.; Asundi, A. Least-squares calibration method for fringe projection profilometry considering camera lens distortion. *Appl. Opt.* **2010**, *49*, 1539–1548. [CrossRef] [PubMed]
185. Juarez-Salazar, R.; Diaz-Ramirez, V.H. Distorted pinhole camera model for tangential distortion. *Proc. SPIE* **2021**, *11841*, 118410D.
186. Yang, S.; Liu, M.; Song, J.; Yin, S.; Ren, Y.; Zhu, J.; Chen, S. Projector distortion residual compensation in fringe projection system. *Opt. Lasers Eng.* **2019**, *114*, 104–110. [CrossRef]
187. Juarez-Salazar, R.; Giron, A.; Zheng, J.; Diaz-Ramirez, V.H. Key concepts for phase-to-coordinate conversion in fringe projection systems. *Appl. Opt.* **2019**, *58*, 4828–4834. [CrossRef]
188. Pei, X.; Liu, J.; Yang, Y.; Ren, M.; Zhu, L. Phase-to-Coordinates Calibration for Fringe Projection Profilometry Using Gaussian Process Regression. *IEEE Trans. Instrum. Meas.* **2022**, *71*, 5008112. [CrossRef]
189. Li, J.; Ding, S.; Zeng, Z.; Deng, J. Dual-biprism-based coaxial fringe projection system. *Appl. Opt.* **2022**, *61*, 3957–3964. [CrossRef]
190. Sicardi-Segade, A.; Estrada, J.; Martínez-García, A.; Garnica, G. On axis fringe projection: A new method for shape measurement. *Opt. Lasers Eng.* **2015**, *69*, 29–34. [CrossRef]
191. Weng, W.; Chang, M.; Zeng, L.; Zhou, J.; Zhang, L.; Yu, X.; Liu, H. A novel and calibration-simple structured light 3D reconstruction system based on parallel-axis-display system. *Opt. Commun.* **2025**, *579*, 131580. [CrossRef]
192. Li, D.; Liu, C.; Tian, J. Telecentric 3D profilometry based on phase-shifting fringe projection. *Opt. Express* **2014**, *22*, 31826–31835. [CrossRef] [PubMed]
193. Hu, Y.; Chen, Q.; Feng, S.; Tao, T.; Asundi, A.; Zuo, C. A new microscopic telecentric stereo vision system—Calibration, rectification, and three-dimensional reconstruction. *Opt. Lasers Eng.* **2019**, *113*, 14–22. [CrossRef]

194. Zhang, S.; Yau, S.T. High-resolution, real-time 3D absolute coordinate measurement based on a phase-shifting method. *Opt. Express* **2006**, *14*, 2644–2649. [CrossRef] [PubMed]
195. Juarez-Salazar, R.; Rodriguez-Reveles, G.A.; Esquivel-Hernandez, S.; Diaz-Ramirez, V.H. Three-dimensional spatial point computation in fringe projection profilometry. *Opt. Lasers Eng.* **2023**, *164*, 107482. [CrossRef]
196. Wang, Z.; Nguyen, D.A.; Barnes, J.C. Some practical considerations in fringe projection profilometry. *Opt. Lasers Eng.* **2010**, *48*, 218–225. [CrossRef]
197. Yin, Y.; Peng, X.; Li, A.; Liu, X.; Gao, B.Z. Calibration of fringe projection profilometry with bundle adjustment strategy. *Opt. Lett.* **2012**, *37*, 542–544. [CrossRef]
198. Rao, L.; Da, F.; Kong, W.; Huang, H. Flexible calibration method for telecentric fringe projection profilometry systems. *Opt. Express* **2016**, *24*, 1222–1237. [CrossRef]
199. Zhang, S. Flexible and accurate phase-to-coordinate calibration method. In *Proceedings of the Dimensional Optical Metrology and Inspection for Practical Applications XI, Orlando, FL, USA, 3 April–13 June 2022*; Harding, K.G., Zhang, S., Hyun, J.S., Li, B., Eds.; SPIE: Bellingham, WA, USA, 2022; Volume 12098, p. 1209802.
200. Bai, Y.; Zhang, Z.; Fu, S.; Zhao, H.; Ni, Y.; Gao, N.; Meng, Z.; Yang, Z.; Zhang, G.; Yin, W. Recent Progress of Full-Field Three-Dimensional Shape Measurement Based on Phase Information. *Nanomanuf. Metrol.* **2024**, *7*, 9. [CrossRef]
201. Vargas, R.; Romero, L.A.; Zhang, S.; Marrugo, A.G. Calibration method based on virtual phase-to-coordinate mapping with linear correction function for structured light system. *Opt. Lasers Eng.* **2024**, *183*, 108496. [CrossRef]
202. Moreno, D.; Taubin, G. Simple, Accurate, and Robust Projector-Camera Calibration. In Proceedings of the 2012 Second International Conference on 3D Imaging, Modeling, Processing, Visualization Transmission, Zurich, Switzerland, 13–15 October 2012; pp. 464–471.
203. Li, Z.; Shi, Y.; Wang, C.; Wang, Y. Accurate calibration method for a structured light system. *Opt. Eng.* **2008**, *47*, 053604. [CrossRef]
204. Yu, J.; Gao, N.; Meng, Z.; Zhang, Z. High-accuracy projector calibration method for fringe projection profilometry considering perspective transformation. *Opt. Express* **2021**, *29*, 15053–15066. [CrossRef] [PubMed]
205. Salvi, J.; Fernandez, S.; Pribanic, T.; Llado, X. A state of the art in structured light patterns for surface profilometry. *Pattern Recognit.* **2010**, *43*, 2666–2680. [CrossRef]
206. Legarda-Sáenz, R.; Bothe, T.; Jüptner, W.P. Accurate procedure for the calibration of a structured light system. *Opt. Eng.* **2004**, *43*, 464–471. [CrossRef]
207. Kimura, M.; Mochimaru, M.; Kanade, T. Projector Calibration using Arbitrary Planes and Calibrated Camera. In Proceedings of the IEEE Conference on Computer Vision and Pattern Recognition, Minneapolis, MN, USA, 17–22 June 2007; pp. 1–2.
208. Juarez-Salazar, R.; Diaz-Ramirez, V.H. Flexible camera-projector calibration using superposed color checkerboards. *Opt. Lasers Eng.* **2019**, *120*, 59–65. [CrossRef]
209. Wang, J.; Zhang, Z.; Lu, W.; Jiang, X.J. High-Accuracy Calibration of High-Speed Fringe Projection Profilometry Using a Checkerboard. *IEEE/ASME Trans. Mechatronics* **2022**, *27*, 4199–4204. [CrossRef]
210. Zhang, S.; Huang, P.S. Novel method for structured light system calibration. *Opt. Eng.* **2006**, *45*, 083601. [CrossRef]
211. Zhang, C.; Zhu, D.; Shi, W.; Wang, L.; Li, J. Improved calibration and 3D reconstruction for micro fringe projection profilometry. *Opt. Express* **2025**, *33*, 13455–13471. [CrossRef]
212. Huang, B.; Tang, Y.; Ozdemir, S.; Ling, H. A Fast and Flexible Projector-Camera Calibration System. *IEEE Trans. Autom. Sci. Eng.* **2021**, *18*, 1049–1063. [CrossRef]
213. Schreiber, W.; Notni, G. Theory and arrangements of self-calibrating whole-body 3-D-measurement systems using fringe projection technique. *Opt. Eng.* **2000**, *39*, 159–169. [CrossRef]
214. Juarez-Salazar, R.; Diaz-Ramirez, V.H.; Robledo-Sanchez, C.; Diaz-Gonzalez, G. On the use of video projectors for three-dimensional scanning. *Proc. SPIE* **2017**, *10395*, 103950C.
215. Jiang, C.; Xing, S.; Guo, H. Fringe harmonics elimination in multi-frequency phase-shifting fringe projection profilometry. *Opt. Express* **2020**, *28*, 2838–2856. [CrossRef]
216. Sun, X.; Zhang, Y.; Kong, L.; Peng, X.; Luo, Z.; Shi, J.; Tian, L. Multi-Color Channel Gamma Correction in Fringe Projection Profilometry. *Photonics* **2025**, *12*, 74. [CrossRef]
217. Poynton, C.A. "Gamma" and its Disguises: The Nonlinear Mappings of Intensity in Perception, CRTs, Film, and Video. *SMPTE J.* **1993**, *102*, 1099–1108. [CrossRef]
218. Ayubi, G.A.; Martino, J.M.D.; Alonso, J.R.; Fernández, A.; Perciante, C.D.; Ferrari, J.A. Three-dimensional profiling with binary fringes using phase-shifting interferometry algorithms. *Appl. Opt.* **2011**, *50*, 147–154. [CrossRef] [PubMed]
219. Son, S.J.; An, Y.; Hyun, J.S. Fringe projection profilometry using model-free distorted patterns. *Opt. Express* **2025**, *33*, 17527–17543. [CrossRef]
220. Guo, H.; He, H.; Chen, M. Gamma correction for digital fringe projection profilometry. *Appl. Opt.* **2004**, *43*, 2906–2914. [CrossRef]

221. Liu, K.; Wang, Y.; Lau, D.L.; Hao, Q.; Hassebrook, L.G. Gamma model and its analysis for phase measuring profilometry. *J. Opt. Soc. Am. A* **2010**, *27*, 553–562. [CrossRef] [PubMed]
222. Zhang, X.; Zhu, L.; Li, Y.; Tu, D. Generic nonsinusoidal fringe model and gamma calibration in phase measuring profilometry. *J. Opt. Soc. Am. A* **2012**, *29*, 1047–1058. [CrossRef]
223. Wang, Y.; Cai, J.; Zhang, D.; Chen, X.; Wang, Y. Nonlinear Correction for Fringe Projection Profilometry with Shifted-Phase Histogram Equalization. *IEEE Trans. Instrum. Meas.* **2022**, *71*, 5005509. [CrossRef]
224. Hoang, T.; Pan, B.; Nguyen, D.; Wang, Z. Generic gamma correction for accuracy enhancement in fringe-projection profilometry. *Opt. Lett.* **2010**, *35*, 1992–1994. [CrossRef]
225. Yatabe, K.; Ishikawa, K.; Oikawa, Y. Compensation of fringe distortion for phase-shifting three-dimensional shape measurement by inverse map estimation. *Appl. Opt.* **2016**, *55*, 6017–6024. [CrossRef] [PubMed]
226. Yu, X.; Liu, Y.; Liu, N.; Fan, M.; Su, X. Flexible gamma calculation algorithm based on probability distribution function in digital fringe projection system. *Opt. Express* **2019**, *27*, 32047–32057. [CrossRef] [PubMed]
227. García-Isáis, C.A.; Ochoa, N.A.; Cruz-Salgado, J. Simultaneous one-shot profilometry and gamma correction. *Opt. Eng.* **2019**, *58*, 034104. [CrossRef]
228. Munoz, A.; Flores, J.L.; Parra-Escamilla, G.; Morales, L.A.; Ordones, S.; Servin, M. Least-squares gamma estimation in fringe projection profilometry. *Appl. Opt.* **2021**, *60*, 1137–1142. [CrossRef]
229. Li, L.; Xu, X.; Pang, J.; Wu, J. Study on gamma correction for three-dimensional fringe projection measurement based on attention U-Net network. *Opt. Eng.* **2024**, *63*, 053103. [CrossRef]
230. Zhang, S. Comparative study on passive and active projector nonlinear gamma calibration. *Appl. Opt.* **2015**, *54*, 3834–3841. [CrossRef]
231. Gai, S.; Da, F. A novel fringe adaptation method for digital projector. *Opt. Lasers Eng.* **2011**, *49*, 547–552. [CrossRef]
232. Yuan, L.; Kang, J.; Feng, L.; Chen, Y.; Wu, B. Accurate calibration for crosstalk coefficient based on orthogonal color phase-shifting pattern. *Opt. Express* **2023**, *31*, 23115–23126. [CrossRef]
233. Zhu, Q.; Zhao, H.; Zhao, Z. Research on iterative decoupling algorithm in color fringe projection profilometry. *Opt. Laser Technol.* **2023**, *164*, 109541. [CrossRef]
234. Huang, P.S.; Hu, Q.; Jin, F.; Chiang, F.P. Color-encoded fringe projection and phase shifting for 3D surface contouring. *Proc. SPIE* **1998**, *3407*, 477–482.
235. Hu, J.; Mai, S.; Jiang, Y.; Xu, Y. A high-precision crosstalk coefficient calibration method based on maximum distance rotating fringes and noise suppression by spatial matching filtering. *Opt. Laser Technol.* **2025**, *183*, 112301. [CrossRef]
236. Liu, B.; Wang, C.; Wang, S.; Wu, G. Color crosstalk compensation method for color phase-shifting fringe projection profilometry based on the phase correction matrix. *Opt. Express* **2024**, *32*, 5793–5808. [CrossRef] [PubMed]
237. Zhu, L.; Cao, Y.; He, D.; Chen, C. Grayscale imbalance correction in real-time phase measuring profilometry. *Opt. Commun.* **2016**, *376*, 72–80. [CrossRef]
238. Pan, J.; Huang, P.S.; Chiang, F.P. Color-encoded digital fringe projection technique for high-speed 3-D shape measurement: Color coupling and imbalance compensation. In Proceedings of the Two- and Three-Dimensional Vision Systems for Inspection, Control, and Metrology, Philadelphia, PA, USA, 25–28 October 2004; Batchelor, B.G., Hugli, H., Eds.; Volume 5265, pp. 205–212.
239. Zhao, X.; Yu, T.; Liang, D.; He, Z. A review on 3D measurement of highly reflective objects using structured light projection. *Int. J. Adv. Manuf. Technol.* **2024**, *132*, 4205–4222. [CrossRef]
240. Juarez-Salazar, R.; Vega, F.; Esquivel-Hernandez, S.; Diaz-Ramirez, V.H.; Marrugo, A.G. Phase feedback fringe projection profilometry for shiny objects. *Opt. Lasers Eng.* **2025**, *191*, 109013. [CrossRef]
241. Feng, L.; Sun, Z.; Chen, Y.; Li, H.; Chen, Y.; Liu, H.; Liu, R.; Zhao, Z.; Liang, J.; Zhang, Z.; et al. Rapid in-situ accuracy evaluation and exposure optimization method for fringe projection profilometry. *Opt. Laser Technol.* **2025**, *181*, 111844. [CrossRef]
242. Zhang, S. Recent progresses on real-time 3D shape measurement using digital fringe projection techniques. *Opt. Lasers Eng.* **2010**, *48*, 149–158. [CrossRef]
243. Yin, W.; Chen, Q.; Feng, S.; Tao, T.; Huang, L.; Trusiak, M.; Asundi, A.; Zuo, C. Temporal phase unwrapping using deep learning. *Sci. Rep.* **2019**, *9*, 20175. [CrossRef]
244. Wang, K.; Kemao, Q.; Di, J.; Zhao, J. Deep learning spatial phase unwrapping: A comparative review. *Adv. Photonics Nexus* **2022**, *1*, 014001. [CrossRef]
245. Lv, S.; Kemao, Q. Modeling the measurement precision of Fringe Projection Profilometry. *Light. Sci. Appl.* **2023**, *12*, 257. [CrossRef]
246. Shang, H.; Liu, C.; Wang, R. Measurement methods of 3D shape of large-scale complex surfaces based on computer vision: A review. *Measurement* **2022**, *197*, 111302. [CrossRef]
247. An, H.; Cao, Y.; Li, H.; Zhang, H. Temporal Phase Unwrapping Based on Unequal Phase-Shifting Code. *IEEE Trans. Image Process.* **2023**, *32*, 1432–1441. [CrossRef] [PubMed]

248. Wu, H.; Cao, Y.; Dai, Y.; Qin, J. Spatial-Temporal 3-D Directional Binary Coding Method for Fringe Projection Profilometry. *IEEE Trans. Instrum. Meas.* **2025**, *74*, 1009211. [CrossRef]
249. Ray, S. *Applied Photographic Optics*, 3rd ed.; Taylor & Francis: Abingdon, UK, 2002.
250. Hartley, R.; Zisserman, A. *Multiple View Geometry in Computer Vision*, 2nd ed.; Cambridge University Press: Cambridge, UK, 2003.
251. Juarez-Salazar, R.; Zheng, J.; Diaz-Ramirez, V.H. Distorted pinhole camera modeling and calibration. *Appl. Opt.* **2020**, *59*, 11310–11318. [CrossRef]
252. Juarez-Salazar, R.; Diaz-Ramirez, V.H. Operator-based homogeneous coordinates: Application in camera document scanning. *Opt. Eng.* **2017**, *56*, 070801. [CrossRef]
253. Maciel, J.; Costeira, J. A global solution to sparse correspondence problems. *IEEE Trans. Pattern Anal. Mach. Intell.* **2003**, *25*, 187–199. [CrossRef]
254. Mouaddib, E.; Batlle, J.; Salvi, J. Recent progress in structured light in order to solve the correspondence problem in stereovision. In Proceedings of the International Conference on Robotics and Automation, Albuquerque, NM, USA, 25 April 1997; Volume 1, pp. 130–136.
255. Juarez-Salazar, R.; Rios-Orellana, O.I.; Diaz-Ramirez, V.H. Stereo-phase rectification for metric profilometry with two calibrated cameras and one uncalibrated projector. *Appl. Opt.* **2022**, *61*, 6097–6109. [CrossRef]
256. Rastogi, P.; Hack, E. *Phase Estimation in Optical Interferometry*; Taylor & Francis: Abingdon, UK, 2014.
257. Juarez-Salazar, R.; Mendoza-Rodriguez, C.; Hernandez-Beltran, J.E.; Robledo-Sanchez, C. How do phase-shifting algorithms work? *Eur. J. Phys.* **2018**, *39*, 065302. [CrossRef]
258. Zhang, Z. A flexible new technique for camera calibration. *IEEE Trans. Pattern Anal. Mach. Intell.* **2000**, *22*, 1330–1334. [CrossRef]
259. Juarez-Salazar, R.; Esquivel-Hernandez, S.; Diaz-Ramirez, V.H. Are camera, projector, and camera-projector calibrations different? *Appl. Opt.* **2023**, *62*, 5999–6006. [CrossRef]
260. Geiger, A.; Moosmann, F.; Car, O.; Schuster, B. Automatic camera and range sensor calibration using a single shot. In Proceedings of the IEEE International Conference on Robotics and Automation, Saint Paul, MN, USA, 14–18 May 2012; pp. 3936–3943.
261. Juarez-Salazar, R.; Zheng, J.; Giron, A.; Diaz-Ramirez, V.H. Calibration of camera-projector fringe projection systems for three-dimensional scanning. *Proc. SPIE* **2019**, *11136*, 111360D.
262. Xu, L.; Cao, Y.; Yu, Y.; Wang, J.; Zhou, L. Projector undistortion for high-accuracy fringe projection profilometry. *Meas. Sci. Technol.* **2021**, *32*, 105009. [CrossRef]
263. Liu, S.; Zhang, G.; Lau, D.L.; Zhang, B.; Xu, B.; Liu, K. Jointly correcting lens distortion of structured light systems. *J. Opt.* **2024**, *27*, 015702. [CrossRef]
264. Rivera-Ortega, U.; Dirckx, J.; Meneses-Fabian, C. Fully automated low-cost setup for fringe projection profilometry. *Appl. Opt.* **2015**, *54*, 1350–1353. [CrossRef]
265. Spagnolo, G.S.; Guattari, G.; Sapia, C.; Ambrosini, D.; Paoletti, D.; Accardo, G. Three-dimensional optical profilometry for artwork inspection. *J. Opt. A Pure Appl. Opt.* **2000**, *2*, 353. [CrossRef]
266. Vairavan, R.; Retnasamy, V.; Shahimin, M.M.; Sauli, Z.; Leng, L.S.; Norhaimi, W.M.W.; Marimuthu, R.; Abdullah, O.; Kirtsaeng, S. 3D mapping of breast surface using digital fringe projection. *Proc. SPIE* **2017**, *10043*, 1004315.
267. Norouzi, M.; Shirin, M.B. Investigating the precision of 3D scanner systems based on digital fringe projection method for biomedical engineering applications. In Proceedings of the 28th National and 6th International Iranian Conference on Biomedical Engineering, Tehran, Iran, 25–26 November 2021; pp. 58–64.
268. Lorenz, A.L.; Zhang, S. Human Respiration Rate Measurement with High-Speed Digital Fringe Projection Technique. *Sensors* **2023**, *23*, 9000. [CrossRef]
269. Muyshondt, P.G.; Van der Jeught, S.; Dirckx, J.J. A calibrated 3D dual-barrel otoendoscope based on fringe-projection profilometry. *Opt. Lasers Eng.* **2022**, *149*, 106795. [CrossRef]
270. Bielfeldt, S.; Springmann, G.; Seise, M.; Wilhelm, K.P.; Callaghan, T. An updated review of clinical methods in the assessment of ageing skin—New perspectives and evaluation for claims support. *Int. J. Cosmet. Sci.* **2018**, *40*, 348–355. [CrossRef]
271. Liang, J.; Luo, H.; Yokell, Z.; Nakmali, D.U.; Gan, R.Z.; Lu, H. Characterization of the nonlinear elastic behavior of chinchilla tympanic membrane using micro-fringe projection. *Hear. Res.* **2016**, *339*, 1–11. [CrossRef]
272. Price, G.J.; Parkhurst, J.M.; Sharrock, P.J.; Moore, C.J. Real-time optical measurement of the dynamic body surface for use in guided radiotherapy. *Phys. Med. Biol.* **2011**, *57*, 415. [CrossRef]
273. Le, H.N.D.; Nguyen, H.; Wang, Z.; Opfermann, J.; Leonard, S.; Krieger, A.; Kang, J.U. Demonstration of a laparoscopic structured-illumination three-dimensional imaging system for guiding reconstructive bowel anastomosis. *J. Biomed. Opt.* **2018**, *23*, 056009. [CrossRef]
274. Genovese, K.; Humphrey, J.D. Multimodal optical measurement in vitro of surface deformations and wall thickness of the pressurized aortic arch. *J. Biomed. Opt.* **2015**, *20*, 046005. [CrossRef]

275. Chen, S. Intraoral 3-D Measurement by Means of Group Coding Combined with Consistent Enhancement for Fringe Projection Pattern. *IEEE Trans. Instrum. Meas.* **2022**, *71*, 5018512. [CrossRef]
276. Hu, Y.; Chen, Q.; Feng, S.; Zuo, C. Microscopic fringe projection profilometry: A review. *Opt. Lasers Eng.* **2020**, *135*, 106192. [CrossRef]
277. Qian, J.; Feng, S.; Xu, M.; Tao, T.; Shang, Y.; Chen, Q.; Zuo, C. High-resolution real-time 360° 3D surface defect inspection with fringe projection profilometry. *Opt. Lasers Eng.* **2021**, *137*, 106382. [CrossRef]
278. Casavola, C.; Pappalardi, P.; Pappalettera, G.; Renna, G. A Fringe Projection Based Approach for Corrosion Monitoring in Metals. *Exp. Tech.* **2018**, *42*, 291–297. [CrossRef]
279. Ma, H.; Wang, J.; Shao, M. Crack recognition approach assisted by three-dimensional measurement technique. *J. Opt.* **2024**, *53*, 4981–4987. [CrossRef]
280. Li, B.; Xu, Z.; Gao, F.; Cao, Y.; Dong, Q. 3D Reconstruction of High Reflective Welding Surface Based on Binocular Structured Light Stereo Vision. *Machines* **2022**, *10*, 159. [CrossRef]
281. Schlobohm, J.; Bruchwald, O.; Frąckowiak, W.; Li, Y.; Kästner, M.; Pösch, A.; Reimche, W.; Maier, H.J.; Reithmeier, E. Advanced Characterization Techniques for Turbine Blade Wear and Damage. *Procedia CIRP* **2017**, *59*, 83–88. [CrossRef]
282. Xia, R.; Zhao, J.; Zhang, T.; Su, R.; Chen, Y.; Fu, S. Detection method of manufacturing defects on aircraft surface based on fringe projection. *Optik* **2020**, *208*, 164332. [CrossRef]
283. Zhang, D.; Lu, G.; Li, W.; Zhang, L.; Luo, N. Palmprint Recognition Using 3-D Information. *IEEE Trans. Syst. Man Cybern. Part C (Appl. Rev.)* **2009**, *39*, 505–519. [CrossRef]
284. Ou, P.; Li, B.; Wang, Y.; Zhang, S. Flexible real-time natural 2D color and 3D shape measurement. *Opt. Express* **2013**, *21*, 16736–16741. [CrossRef] [PubMed]
285. Guo, H.; Huang, P.S. Face recognition based on fringe pattern analysis. *Opt. Eng.* **2010**, *49*, 037201. [CrossRef]
286. Zhang, Z.; Huang, S.; Xu, Y.; Chen, C.; Zhao, Y.; Gao, N.; Xiao, Y. 3D palmprint and hand imaging system based on full-field composite color sinusoidal fringe projection technique. *Appl. Opt.* **2013**, *52*, 6138–6145. [CrossRef]
287. Bai, X.; Gao, N.; Zhang, Z.; Zhang, D. Person Recognition Using 3-D Palmprint Data Based on Full-Field Sinusoidal Fringe Projection. *IEEE Trans. Instrum. Meas.* **2019**, *68*, 3287–3298. [CrossRef]
288. Huang, S.; Zhang, Z.; Zhao, Y.; Dai, J.; Chen, C.; Xu, Y.; Zhang, E.; Xie, L. 3D fingerprint imaging system based on full-field fringe projection profilometry. *Opt. Lasers Eng.* **2014**, *52*, 123–130. [CrossRef]
289. Chatterjee, A.; Singh, P.; Bhatia, V.; Prakash, S. Ear biometrics recognition using laser biospeckled fringe projection profilometry. *Opt. Laser Technol.* **2019**, *112*, 368–378. [CrossRef]
290. Zhang, H.; Lee, S. Robot Bionic Vision Technologies: A Review. *Appl. Sci.* **2022**, *12*, 7970. [CrossRef]
291. de Jesus Ortiz-Gonzalez, A.; Martinez-Garcia, A.; Pascual-Francisco, J.B.; Rayas-Alvarez, J.A.; de Jesus Flores-Garcia, A. 3D shape and strain measurement of a thin-walled elastic cylinder using fringe projection profilometry. *Appl. Opt.* **2021**, *60*, 1349–1356. [CrossRef]
292. Balasubramaniam, B.; Li, J.; Liu, L.; Li, B. 3D Imaging with Fringe Projection for Food and Agricultural Applications—A Tutorial. *Electronics* **2023**, *12*, 859. [CrossRef]
293. Berkson, J.; Hyatt, J.; Julicher, N.; Jeong, B.; Pimienta, I.; Ball, R.; Ellis, W.; Voris, J.; Torres-Barajas, D.; Kim, D. Systematic Radio Telescope Alignment Using Portable Fringe Projection Profilometry. *Nanomanuf. Metrol.* **2024**, *7*, 6. [CrossRef]
294. Liberadzki, P.; Adamczyk, M.; Witkowski, M.; Sitnik, R. Structured-Light-Based System for Shape Measurement of the Human Body in Motion. *Sensors* **2018**, *18*, 2827. [CrossRef] [PubMed]
295. Heist, S.; Dietrich, P.; Landmann, M.; Kühmstedt, P.; Notni, G.; Tünnermann, A. GOBO projection for 3D measurements at highest frame rates: A performance analysis. *Light. Sci. Appl.* **2018**, *7*, 71. [CrossRef] [PubMed]
296. Spagnolo, G.; Ambrosini, D.; Paoletti, D. Low-cost optoelectronic system for three-dimensional artwork texture measurement. *IEEE Trans. Image Process.* **2004**, *13*, 390–396. [CrossRef]
297. Sansoni, G.; Docchio, F. 3-D optical measurements in the field of cultural heritage: The case of the Vittoria Alata of Brescia. *IEEE Trans. Instrum. Meas.* **2005**, *54*, 359–368. [CrossRef]
298. Burke, J.; Bothe, T.; Osten, W.; Hess, C.F. Reverse engineering by fringe projection. In *Proceedings of the Interferometry XI: Applications, Seattle, WA, USA, 7–11 July 2002*; Osten, W., Ed.; SPIE: Bellingham, WA, USA, 2002; Volume 4778, pp. 312–324.
299. Hu, C.; Wang, Y.; Xia, G.; Han, Y.; Ma, X.; Jing, G. The generation method of orthophoto expansion map of arched dome mural based on three-dimensional fine color model. *Herit. Sci.* **2024**, *12*, 408. [CrossRef]
300. Xu, F.; Zhang, Y.; Zhang, Z.; Geng, N. A Non-Contact Measurement of Animal Body Size Based on Structured Light. *Appl. Sci.* **2024**, *14*, 903. [CrossRef]

301. Hyun, J.S.; Carmichael, M.G.; Tran, A.; Zhang, S.; Liu, D. Evaluation of Fast, High-detail Projected Light 3D Sensing for Robots in Construction. In Proceedings of the 2019 14th IEEE Conference on Industrial Electronics and Applications (ICIEA), Xi'an, China, 19–21 June 2019; pp. 1262–1267.
302. Nogales, S.O.; Servin, M.; Padilla, M.; Choque, I.; Nuñez, J.L.F.; Muñoz, A. Shape defect measurement by fringe projection profilometry and phase-shifting algorithms. *Opt. Eng.* **2020**, *59*, 014107. [CrossRef]
303. Ma, R.; Li, J.; He, K.; Tang, T.; Zhang, Y.; Gao, X. Application of Moire Profilometry in Three-Dimensional Profile Reconstruction of Key Parts in Railway. *Sensors* **2022**, *22*, 2498. [CrossRef]

metrology

MDPI

Review

Next-Generation Interferometry with Gauge-Invariant Linear Optical Scatterers

Christopher R. Schwarze [1,*], Anthony D. Manni [1], David S. Simon [1,2], Abdoulaye Ndao [3] and Alexander V. Sergienko [1,4,*]

[1] Department of Electrical and Computer Engineering & Photonics Center, Boston University, 8 Saint Mary's St., Boston, MA 02215, USA; admanni@bu.edu (A.D.M.); simond@bu.edu (D.S.S.)
[2] Department of Physics and Astronomy, Stonehill College, 320 Washington Street, Easton, MA 02357, USA
[3] Department of Electrical and Computer Engineering, University of California, San Diego, CA 92093, USA; a1ndao@ucsd.edu
[4] Department of Physics, Boston University, 590 Commonwealth Avenue, Boston, MA 02215, USA
* Correspondence: crs2@bu.edu (C.R.S.); alexserg@bu.edu (A.V.S.)

Abstract

Measurement technology employing optical interference phenomena such as a fringe pattern or frequency shift has been evolving for more than a century. Systems are being designed better, and their components are being built better. However, the major components themselves hardly change. Most modern interferometers rely on the same conventional set of components to separate the electromagnetic field into multiple beams, such as plate optics and beam splitters. This naturally limits the design scope and thus the potential applicability and performance. However, recent investigations suggest that incorporating novel, higher-dimensional linear optical splitters in interferometer design can lead to several improvements. In this work, we review the underlying theory of these novel optical scatterers and some demonstrated configurations with enhanced resolution. The basic principles of optical interference and optical phase sensing are discussed in tandem. Emphasis is placed on both familiar and unfamiliar scatterers, such as the maximally symmetric Grover multiport, whose actions are left unchanged by certain gauge transformations. These higher-dimensional, gauge-invariant multiports embody a new class of building blocks that can tailor optical interference to metrology in unconventional ways.

Keywords: optical phase; linear optics; interferometry; multiport; Grover coin; gauge symmetry

1. Introduction

Optical systems have long been a popular choice for high-precision measurement and sensing. Their general use and advancements over the last century have been derived from several factors. First, the intrinsic sensitivity of any wave interference is typically a small fraction of the wavelength, which, for visible light, is on the order of a micron. Technological achievements in lasing and detection at even the single-photon level continue to grow, all while the once room-filling tabletop optical systems are being scaled down to integrated photonic chips.

Another core aspect of any optical system, beyond the optical sources and detectors, is the materials used to manipulate the light. Without matter, generated beams are tautologically only able to propagate through a vacuum. Materials are needed to both control the characteristics of light reflecting from or transmitting through them and impart signatures of physical phenomena on the light for the sake of inference. Common components include beam splitters [1,2], which divide and combine beams, as well as devices to modify the orientation of the electric field [3]. Optical system building blocks like these have been optimized through decades of scientific research and engineering. Tolerances have improved, losses have decreased, and components have become more widely available and customizable, through both traditional component suppliers and chip foundries supporting nanophotonic fabrication processes [4,5].

While undoubtedly novel and sophisticated optical systems have since been proposed and demonstrated for metrological purposes, such as metamaterials and spatial light modulators, these tools are often still used in conjunction with familiar components like the beam splitter and/or are used in unconventional sensing configurations. Meanwhile, the available building blocks for use in traditional interferometers have largely remained the same.

Several alternative elementary linear scatterers have recently been studied and demonstrated for use in optical interferometry. These devices are called higher-dimensional multiports since they actively employ more optical modes than their traditional counterparts [6–10]. The most general class of these multiports admits strong coherent backreflections, which has been demonstrated in a few cases recently [11–13]. One important example in this class is the four-port Grover coin. (This device is named for the diffusion operator used in the quantum search algorithm of L. Grover [14], while the term "coin" is used to describe generic N-port scattering operators, especially in the study of quantum walks, since they behave like a hypothetical N-sided coin. The general form of an N-port Grover coin is specified in Section 2). Another is the symmetric Y-coupler, which is schematically compared to a traditional 50:50 beam splitter in Figure 1. All three of these devices are interrelated and possess certain symmetries, which will be discussed later in the text. These higher-dimensional, backscattering or "directionally unbiased" devices have recently been shown to offer various enhancements to interferometric sensing systems, such as increased resolution, the synchronous readout of several quantities, and a reduced resource count. These devices and the basic interferometric configurations that they improve will form the main subject of this review. Some of the interferometric configurations to be discussed further are depicted in Figure 2. In conjunction with this, we will also present the basic principles of linear optical scatterers and interferometers, emphasizing a practical mathematical framework for identifying the symmetries that these devices possess.

Beyond the devices capable of dividing and recombining light, which typically entails interfacing different materials, yet another crucial building block of an optical system is ordinary transparent matter. Bulk transparent matter imparts a phase to the electromagnetic wave propagating within it. This acquired phase differs from the phase that the wave would normally acquire in empty space. For a transparent region of length d, source wavelength λ (in vacuum), and refractive index n, the phase ϕ acquired is

$$\phi = \frac{2\pi n d}{\lambda}. \tag{1}$$

This simple formula is of fundamental importance in optical phase metrology, since it illustrates precisely which quantities can alter the phase and thus ultimately be inferred from a phase-sensing instrument. The wavelength dependence makes it clear that different colors naturally acquire different phases while propagating through *any* medium, even a vacuum. The refractive index n is a dimensionless quantity that indicates the speed of light propagating through the material or, equivalently, the change in the apparent wavelength. It is entirely responsible for the difference in phase acquired inside and outside the material. Inside a material, its value is intrinsic to its composition of matter and thus varies in a considerable number of ways. These different variations underlie much of optical metrology, enabling many physical quantities to impart an optical phase shift that can be detected.

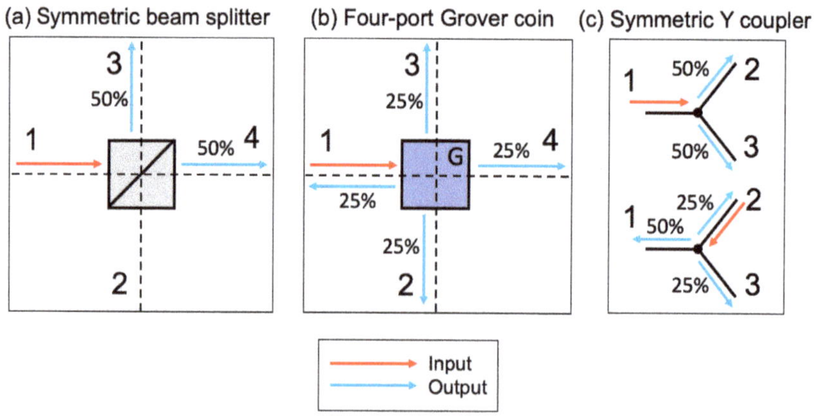

Figure 1. Comparison of some common symmetric multiports. The balanced beam splitter (**a**) produces *two* transmitting beams of equal 50% intensity for any single input, while the four-port Grover coin (**b**) produces *four outgoing beams* of 25% intensity, with one of these being a backreflection. The symmetric Y-coupler (**c**) produces two equally intense beams when input to port 1, with no backreflection. However, when input to port 2, a 25% backreflection occurs, while 50% of the energy returns to port 1 and 25% scattering to port 3. Due to the underlying symmetry, input to port 3 is the same as input to port 2. Symmetry, in this context, is not just in the sense of having equal probabilities. The full mathematical description of the symmetries that a scattering device can possess is given in Section 2.3. These higher-dimensional devices generalize traditional interferometric configurations; some of the examples to be discussed in detail later are shown in Figure 2.

In the next section, we present a general mathematical framework to describe how fixed distributions of optical materials scatter light. This framework abstracts away the underlying physical dynamics, treating the action on an input field energy distribution as a linear transformation enacted by the scatterer. It allows the possessed symmetries of linear optical scatterers to be identified in relation to certain field transformations, which merely represent a change in gauge and therefore do not affect any measurable quantity. Certain symmetric scatterers such as the ones shown in Figure 1 emerge when their parent space is restricted to sets that remain invariant under such transformations. Thereafter, in Section 3, interferometers are defined as *phase-tunable* scatterers, formed from graphs. The nodes of these graphs are scatterers of the static type, and each edge connecting two scatterers is associated with an optical phase parameter. There, we review the operating principles of traditional phase-sensing interferometers. This provides a baseline for contrasting the modern proposals that employ higher-dimensional multiport building blocks. After discussing these systems and their advantages, general conclusions are summarized in Section 4.

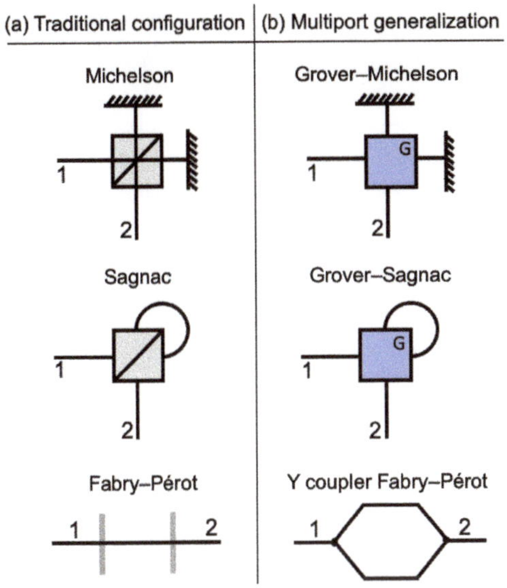

Figure 2. Examples of traditional interferometers (**a**) and their corresponding multiport generalizations (**b**). The beam splitters in the Michelson and Sagnac configurations are replaced with the higher-dimensional Grover coin, while the two-dimensional plate optics forming the Fabry–Pérot interferometer are replaced with three-dimensional Y-couplers. In each of the multiport interferometers in (**b**), the increased dimensionality combined with backscattering behavior creates a new pair of coupled resonators. All of the pictured systems, along with other multiport interferometers, will be presented in detail in Section 3.

2. Optical Interference and Linear Optical Scatterers

2.1. Background

The phenomenon of interference is fundamentally the result of superimposing, or adding together, different waves that exist in space. The goal of this section is to provide a mathematical description of this superposition in optical scattering devices. The optical states will be represented as a vector with complex-valued entries. The complex-number representation allows both the phase and magnitude (total energy) to be encoded in each entry. Meanwhile, the scatterers, which distribute the optical energy according to a linear transformation, will be represented by a matrix, which acts on these vectors.

Generally, any wave or periodic phenomenon can be expressed or decomposed into a basis of orthogonal modes, such as the m-indexed functions $\sin(mx)$ and $\cos(mx)$ that underlie Fourier series expansions. In optics, the fields comprising the electromagnetic waves produced by a given source can be expanded in a modal basis, which depends on the refractive index distribution considered. In a homogeneous medium, such as a vacuum, these are the familiar plane wave functions of the form $E_0 e^{i\mathbf{k}\cdot\mathbf{r}-\omega t}$, where $|\mathbf{k}| = 2\pi n/\lambda$, the optical frequency ω is $2\pi c/\lambda$, c is the vacuum speed of light, n is the material refractive index, and λ is the vacuum wavelength. E_0 is the complex-valued mode amplitude. The problem of finding the modal functions in general involves solving a complicated boundary value problem, which often must be done numerically. However, it is not completely necessary to provide a useful description of optical interferometers. The present approach is one of many other prevalent matrix methods employed in optical calculations [15,16].

2.2. Matrix Formalism of Linear Optical Scattering

We will adopt the quantum optical notation since it generalizes to the two-photon states employed in a later section and encompasses all possible input states. We use the operator $a_j^\dagger(\omega, \boldsymbol{\varepsilon})$ to denote the creation of a photon of fixed frequency ω and polarization vector $\boldsymbol{\varepsilon}$ in spatial mode j. Hereafter, the scope will be confined to a single frequency and polarization, so the explicit dependence of the frequency and polarization of $a_j^\dagger$ can be omitted. The spatial mode index is also implicitly tied to some definite wave vector $\mathbf{k}_j$ (plane wave model). This dependence can also be omitted without loss of generality, as long as the propagation direction is specified with an additional subscript whenever counterpropagating excitations are present within the same spatial mode.

With this notation, a state corresponding to a single photon propagating within this mode would be denoted as $|\psi\rangle = a_j^\dagger|0\rangle = |j\rangle$. These single-photon basis states are orthogonal: $\langle k|j\rangle = 1$ for $k = j$ and 0 otherwise. The general superposition of a photon across d spatial modes is then denoted as

$$|\psi\rangle = \sum_{j=1}^{d} c_j|j\rangle. \tag{2}$$

The coefficients c_j are the photon's complex-valued probability amplitudes. The real number $|c_j|^2 = c_j^* c_j$ is then the probability of measuring the photon in mode j. The state is assumed normalized, so that $\sum_{j=1}^{d} |c_j|^2 = 1$.

By identifying the modal basis vectors $|j\rangle$ with the standard basis vector $\mathbf{e_j}$, whose kth element is 1 for $k = j$ and 0 otherwise, the state in the preceding equation can be placed into a state vector

$$\sum_{j=1}^{d} c_j|j\rangle \longrightarrow \sum_{j=1}^{d} c_j\mathbf{e_j} = \begin{pmatrix} c_1 \\ c_2 \\ \vdots \\ c_d \end{pmatrix}. \tag{3}$$

This representation makes it clear that the total number of modes d is a measure of dimension. Optical qubit states employ two modes. States involving coherent superpositions of d modes are sometimes known as qudits.

The classical equivalent of a state in the form of Equation (2) is found by replacing the creation operator with the classical field mode function. This rescales all of the amplitudes by the square root of the total power in the beam, converting the probabilities into optical power or a proportionally related quantity. Hence, the probability distribution $|c_j|^2$ vs. j is effectively a normalized distribution of optical energy in the state $|\psi\rangle$. Besides this rescaling, in terms of the algebraic formalism, it only shifts what is being tied to the standard basis $\{\mathbf{e_1}, \ldots, \mathbf{e_d}\}$. This has no impact on the description of the scattering devices and thus the resulting interference that they induce. Any distinction made between single-photon states and classical coherent states in the context of linear interferometry is largely inconsequential other than an overall normalization factor. Ref. [17] contains further commentary on this.

A linear scatterer will act on the incident state $|\psi_{\text{in}}\rangle$ according to a $d \times d$ matrix transformation U, producing the state $|\psi_{\text{out}}\rangle = U|\psi_{\text{in}}\rangle$. This implicitly reverses the direction of all modes, as depicted by the general scattering situation in Figure 3. U is known as the scattering matrix. When a photon located entirely in mode j enters the corresponding port of U, the state produced, in the form of Equation (3), is simply column j of U. This implies that the element U_{ij} is the probability amplitude for a photon entering port j of the scattering device to emerge at port i. Thus, $|U_{jj}|^2$ is the probability for a photon entering port j to reflect directly backwards. The corresponding amplitudes for this backscattering lie on the diagonal of U.

When a photon impinges on port j, the requirement for energy or probability conservation entails that $\langle\psi_{\text{out}}|\psi_{\text{out}}\rangle = \sum_{i=1}^{d} |U_{ij}|^2 = 1$, which must then hold for all j. Maintaining orthogonality at the output, across different single-photon inputs, similarly requires that $\sum_{j=1}^{d} U_{ij}U_{jk}^* = 0$ whenever $i \neq k$. These restrictions, when combined, imply that $U^\dagger U = I$, where $U^\dagger$ is the Hermitian conjugate or complex transpose of U, $U^\dagger = (U^T)^*$. This condition is equivalent to the columns of U forming an orthonormal basis of $\mathbb{C}^n$. In other words, energy-conserving linear optical scatterers are represented by unitary matrices. This subset of matrices forms a group, known as the unitary group in d-dimensions, and will be denoted as $U(d)$.

For a general input superposition, the scattering matrix U redistributes the inputted energy into a new outgoing superposition. This redistribution of energy is the harbinger of general interference, allowing energy from separate beams to be combined into one. The net outcome of this redistribution will be a function of both the scattering matrix U and the initial state amplitudes and, in particular, the relative phases of these state amplitudes.

This discussion pertains to an arbitrary but fixed frequency and polarization, making U a constant. Nonetheless, the scattering behavior of photons of different frequencies and/or polarizations will generally vary due to the variation in a material's optical response with respect to changes in these quantities. This in turn causes $U = U(\omega, \varepsilon)$ to be a matrix-valued function. In fact, since the material scattering response will generally be affected by any change in the refractive index distribution of the material comprising the scatterer, U will as well. Optical scattering devices are often engineered to resist this variation.

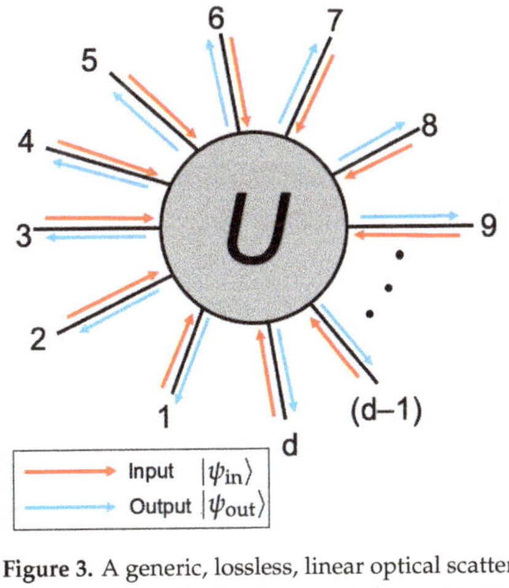

Figure 3. A generic, lossless, linear optical scattering device. This d-port device is mathematically represented by a $d \times d$ unitary scattering matrix U. Port j is identified with two spatial modes, one for each direction of propagation. The scatterer converts an input optical state $|\psi_{\text{in}}\rangle$ to the output state $|\psi_{\text{out}}\rangle = U|\psi_{\text{in}}\rangle$. This scattering action redistributes the optical energy in the input state. The arrows represent the flow of the associated state amplitudes. For clarity, the counterpropagating arrows at the same port are drawn spatially separated, but, in reality, the counterpropagating energy flow is perfectly collinear in each spatial mode. Scattering devices like U can be viewed as nodes of a general graph. Depictions like the above and more traditional nodal depictions such as those in Figure 4 will be used interchangeably. A graph of scattering devices is generally called an interferometer.

Enforcing symmetries by requiring that U remains invariant under a certain field transformation can impose constraints on U [18]. An example is reciprocity, which originates in name from the Lorentz reciprocity theorem. This result pertains to a transformation that interchanges the sources and fields in an enclosed region. A reciprocal scatterer is defined as being invariant to the interchange of the source and detector. Recalling that U_{ij} is the probability of detecting a single photon at port i when it enters port j, we see that reciprocity stipulates that $U_{ij} = U_{ji}$ or that U is a symmetric matrix: $U = U^T$ [19].

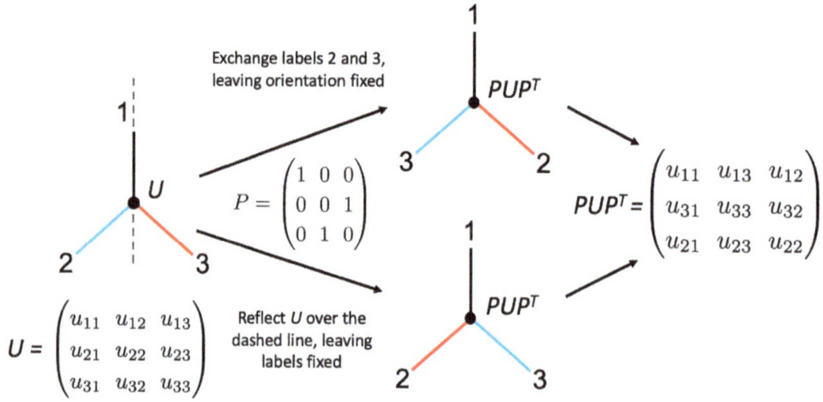

Figure 4. Geometric gauge transformations involve relabeling the field modes identified with the ports of a scattering device U. The indices j of the mode operators undergo a permutation transformation $p(j)$, which transforms the scattering matrix U to PUP^T, where P is the permutation matrix associated with the permutation function p. Permuting the port labels is also equivalent to applying geometric transformations to the scattering device while leaving the labels themselves fixed. Any example is shown here for a generic three-port scattering device, where the exchange of two labels equates to reflection about the line between them. The edge colors at the red and blue ports are used to signify the orientation of this pointlike scatterer U. General permutations P in higher dimensions will enact reflections and/or rotations in higher-dimensional spaces.

Non-reciprocal scattering devices are far less common than reciprocal ones. They often are formed by locally breaking the time reversal symmetry, such as with a Faraday rotator. A global rotation of the system can also produce a non-reciprocal phase accumulation, via the Sagnac effect [20]. In these devices, forward-propagating light will acquire a phase that differs from that of backward-propagating light in the same mode. Transmission can also be non-reciprocal. For instance, a circulator provides the non-reciprocal routing of light. An ideal three-port circulator can be prescribed a scattering matrix

$$U = \begin{pmatrix} 0 & 0 & 1 \\ 1 & 0 & 0 \\ 0 & 1 & 0 \end{pmatrix} \neq U^T. \tag{4}$$

A physical device with this scattering matrix would be able to perfectly convert counterpropagating excitations in one spatial mode into identical excitations that populate separate spatial modes, and vice versa. However, circulators in practice tend to experience both losses and crosstalk. Circulators are readily defined in higher dimensions and can be obtained by chaining together low-dimensional ones.

2.3. Scattering Process Gauge Symmetries

Maxwell's equations are known to possess a certain property known as gauge invariance. This property allows the underlying field potentials to be redefined in a certain way without changing the physical situation. This principle has since been extensively generalized and utilized in other areas of physics. Generally speaking, the transformations between different choices of gauge form a symmetry group. In the following subsections, we describe analogous transformations to the optical states and/or scattering devices. These are reminiscent of the gauge transforms employed in general field theories, mainly in the sense that they do not physically alter the underlying process's description. Any given gauge can be used freely for the sake of convenience. The particular forms of the transformation are different, so, while they might be referred to more precisely as a scattering center symmetry or generalized gauge transformation, we will use the generic terminology "gauge transformation" as shorthand. The first set of scattering gauge transformations considered also forms a group of its own, the symmetric group S_d.

For radiation of a fixed frequency and polarization expanded into a basis of orthogonal spatial modes, as in Equation (2), there are two basic transformations that do not change the physical situation [21]. These each provide a formal equivalence relation, which can be used to relate scattering matrices. Scattering devices within the same equivalence class will not be measurably distinguishable but can appear as completely different scattering matrices. The different scattering matrices can be viewed as the same underlying physical action but expressed in a different gauge.

First, the physical description of any optical scattering process would be unchanged if the numerical labels used to identify the field modes were modified, as these labels are completely arbitrary. Formally, the relabeling process enacts a permutation p on the creation operator indices: $a_j^\dagger \to a_{p(j)}^\dagger$. This is equivalent to relabeling the ports of a given scattering device, such as that shown with its labels in Figure 3. This variant of transformation will be discussed in Section 2.3.1.

The second transformation is the application of a phase shift to each field mode. In a general state of the form of Equation (2), this will enact the change $c_j \to e^{i\phi_j} c_j$. Since $(e^{i\phi_j} c_j)^* (e^{i\phi_j} c_j) = |c_j|^2$, this transformation does not affect the distribution of detection probabilities, which is the physical observable. This transformation can be applied locally to any given scattering device in a general network. Further discussion of this class of transformations is deferred to Section 2.3.2. After presenting an overview of the two interrelated transformations and their general implications, the subsequent sections discuss specific consequences and examples for the scattering groups $U(2)$, $U(3)$, and $U(4)$.

2.3.1. Geometric Scattering Transformations

A permutation or relabeling of d objects can be defined by a bijective function p, which maps the set of original labels $\{1, \ldots, d\}$ onto itself. There are generally $d!$ such maps, and each can be represented by a $d \times d$ matrix P, which acts on a column vector of labels. Throughout this work, we will always denote the permutation function and its corresponding matrix by an upper and lowercase pair of the same symbol. Each permutation P has a well-defined inverse given by P^T, which "undoes" the permutation enacted by P. A full treatment of permutations can be found in any standard algebra text, such as Ref. [22].

For a general d-mode optical scattering state, the permutation of the mode labels acts in the following way:

$$|\psi\rangle = \sum_{j=1}^{d} c_j |j\rangle \to |\psi'\rangle = \sum_{j=1}^{d} c_j |p(j)\rangle \tag{5}$$

The energy distribution encoded by this state is unchanged. It is merely being rewritten in a new basis provided by P. Conversely, had we simultaneously permuted the c_j to $c_{h(j)}$ for a permutation h, which may or may not equal p, then the spatial energy distribution would have been measurably different before and after the permutation. This is why only the labels and not the coefficients are permuted.

Element U_{ij} of a general scattering matrix is the probability amplitude for an incident photon at port j to scatter to port i. Permuting the mode labels affixed to each port maps $U_{ij} \to U_{p(i)p(j)}$. This permutes both the rows and columns by the same permutation p.

It can be shown that the pre-multiplication of U by the associated permutation matrix P will permute the rows of U. Then, post-multiplying U by P^T will enact the permutation p on the columns of U, which can be deduced by expressing $UP^T = (PU^T)^T$. Combining the two results, we see that the aggregate affect of mode or port relabeling on a scattering matrix U is the similarity transformation

$$U \to PUP^T. \tag{6}$$

This is the general form of the geometric gauge transformation—that is, it describes how to transform the matrix U written in one gauge into a different gauge. Being a conjugation transformation, it allows any given U to be associated with the equivalence class $\{PUP^T : P \text{ is a permutation matrix}\}$. Any members common to the same equivalence class will not be physically distinguishable, despite the general possibility that the form of their scattering matrices will differ. In accordance with this, the equivalence of two scattering matrices U_1 and U_2 will be written as $U_1 \sim U_2$.

The gauge freedom provided by this transformation is the ability to label the ports or modes in a way that produces the form that is most convenient to work with. In tandem, it provides a means to show that *two apparently different scatterers are in fact the same*. Beyond this, though, it naturally leads to the notion of a symmetric scatterer. These so-called gauge-invariant devices are left unchanged by a specific permutation. This implies that $U = PUP^T$. After post-multiplying by P and rearranging, this is equivalent to

$$UP - PU := [U, P] = 0. \tag{7}$$

Scattering matrix families can be defined by this condition with a certain P in mind, greatly reducing the number of free parameters that they possess. Specific examples of this will be provided later in this section. In essence, the gauge invariance corresponds to certain subsets of ports behaving identically when excited by the same input state. This can be connected to physical symmetries of the scattering process, such as mirror reflection symmetry and/or rotational symmetry. This is because *permutation operations, such as exchanging or cyclically permuting subsets of the mode labels, are equivalent to reflecting or rotating the physical device while leaving the original labels fixed.* An example illustrating this equivalence notion with a generic three-port device is illustrated in Figure 4.

Like any other scattering matrix, a gauge-invariant device can only be physically specified up to its equivalence class. Applying different gauges to a specific gauge-invariant device will not change the fact that it commutes with some permutation matrix, but the commuting matrix itself can change. It is straightforward to show that, for U_0, which is gauge-invariant with respect to P_0, after expressing U_0 as U in some new gauge Q, the corresponding invariance-inducing permutation is transformed to $P_0 \to QP_0Q^T = P$. This leads to the concept of equivalent permutation classes, which are the conjugacy classes $\{QPQ^T : Q, P \text{ are permutation matrices}\}$. Members of the same class generate the same kind of gauge-invariant scattering device. An intuitive picture of these permutation classes can be built with the equivalence of Figure 4 in mind. First, a gauge-invariant scatterer is viewed as a device that is left unchanged by a geometrical transformation acting on it while its port labels stay fixed. This geometric transformation is tied to an underlying permutation P. Then, the equivalent permutations of P are merely re-expressions of the original port labels that are used to label U before and after the geometrical transformation. Clearly, this relabeling has no effect on the geometrical transformation encoded by P.

The transformation enacted by Equation (6) possesses several basic algebraic properties, which all reflect the fact that it cannot change the physical description of the scattering process that U represents. The gauge transformation will always preserve the reciprocity and unitarity of U. Another important example concerns the spectrum of U as a gauge transformation is made. In this case, the eigenvalues are unchanged while the eigenvectors corresponding to these eigenvalues are permuted by P.

Permutation invariance can also be applied to optical states. Since the phases of the state amplitudes are immaterial when the state undergoes detection, these can be discarded. Then, a symmetric scattering state is defined by having an energy distribution that is left unchanged by some gauge transformation P. This is the type of symmetry usually associated with balanced scatterers that produce beams of equal intensity when a single beam impinges on them. The gauge invariance of the scattering device alone is generally unrelated to the creation of symmetric states.

2.3.2. External Phase Shifts

In addition to relabeling the field mode indices, which are directly tied to a scattering device's port labels, external phase shifts placed around a scattering device will have no affect on its measured energy distribution when a photon enters one of its ports. External phases translate the total phase acquired by the photon in each mode j by some constant ϕ_j. However, the input excitations have no absolute reference phase, so this translation will not be measurable, due to a lack of knowledge of the starting point. (A non-reciprocal phase is a relative entity, shared between the counterpropagating directions of the same spatial mode. Therefore, an external non-reciprocal phase is able to have a measurable effect on scattering systems in general. For example, consider a standard Mach–Zehnder interferometer, where a tunable phase shift ϕ in one arm is used to produce an interferogram. An external phase shift placed in this arm will naturally add with ϕ. If it is reciprocal, this simply translates ϕ and the interferogram that it produces, which has no absolute starting point in any case. However, an external non-reciprocal phase will generate measurable non-reciprocal transmission in a device comprising entirely reciprocal scattering devices.).

The general action of a set of externally placed phase shifts is mapping the input state coefficients $c_j \to c_j e^{i\phi_j}$, which can be encoded as a pre-multiplication by the diagonal matrix $D = \text{diag}(e^{i\phi_1}, \ldots, e^{i\phi_d})$. This means that, when scattering through the device with the external phases, $|\psi_{\text{in}}\rangle \to DUD|\psi_{\text{in}}\rangle$, or, equivalently,

$$U \to DUD. \tag{8}$$

This induces another equivalence notion between different scattering matrices. Two scattering matrices U_1 and U_2 are equivalent in this sense whenever a suitable selection of external reciprocal phases converts one scattering matrix into the other. In other words, this gauge freedom allows the arbitrary selection of desired reciprocal external phases to recast U into the different but equivalent form DUD. It is readily verified that changing the gauge in this form will neither affect unitarity nor reciprocity.

All elements U in the equivalence class $\{DUD : \text{diag}(e^{i\phi_1}, \ldots, e^{i\phi_d}), \phi_1, \ldots, \phi_d \in \mathbb{R}\}$ necessarily have the same probability matrix, formed by taking the elementwise modulus square of U. In some special cases, the probabilities will be zero, allowing the corresponding phases to be chosen freely. This can enable some more non-trivial equivalences. On the other hand, the notion of gauge invariance has little use here, since it would require $DUD = U$. This is generally only valid when the external phases are brought to zero, so that $D = I$. This case is omitted, as it was for $P = I$ in the previous section, since all U are equivalent to a matrix that is gauge-invariant in this sense. For this reason, the term "gauge-invariant" is only used in the context of non-trivial (i.e., $P \neq I$) geometric gauge transformations throughout this work.

Although this phase gauge freedom can be invoked in conjunction with the geometric gauge freedom, the effects of these two gauge freedoms are not completely separate. Scattering devices that are gauge-invariant in the geometric sense will lie in the same phase–gauge equivalence classes as devices that are not, since these phases are easily reselected to break any given geometric symmetry. External phases also will generally change the eigenvectors of the scattering device that they surround. Notwithstanding, considering the two gauge freedoms together allows fairly non-trivial equivalences to be made. Establishing such an equivalence in turn implies that interferometers formed by substituting one scatterer for its equivalent counterpart will produce the same interferometer, up to global translations of its parameter space.

Besides writing the external phase gauge transformation as $U \to DUD$ for a diagonal phase matrix D, the map $U_{ij} \to U_{ij}e^{i\phi_i + i\phi_j}$ admits another useful form. Let $e^{i\phi_i + i\phi_j} = e^{i\phi_i}e^{i\phi_j} = v_i v_j$ be written as the outer product vv^T. When external phases are selected for a scattering matrix U, U is elementwise multiplied by the corresponding matrix vv^T, denoted as $U \odot vv^T$.

This form, $U \to U \odot vv^T$ for $v_j = e^{i\phi_j}$, can be more practical than the first one; it provides an algorithm to quickly determine whether two scatterers are equivalent or not and, if they are, which phases are required to construct the explicit gauge transformation between them. Let U_1 and U_2 be scattering matrices with the same classical probability matrix. Express $U_1 = |U| \odot Q_1$ and $U_2 = |U| \odot Q_2$, where $|U|$ is the matrix formed by taking the magnitude of each element of U_1 and U_2. Next, define $Q = Q_1 \odot Q_2^{\circ -1}$, where $Q_2^{\circ -1}$ is found by taking the scalar inverse of each element of Q_2. The matrices Q_1 and Q_2 will be entirely phase factors, so this inverse is always well defined. Since U_1 and U_2 have the same underlying probability matrix, $Q = U_1 \odot U_2^{\circ -1}$. By the above, if Q is expressible as an outer product, then $U_1 \sim U_2$, and Q directly prescribes the gauge transformation as $U_2 \odot Q = U_1$.

For an outer product matrix, each column must be a scalar multiple of the first column. This is easy to check, can be done in parallel, and can be halted upon any column's failure to meet the condition. If Q meets the condition, the outer product factorization $vw^T = Q$ is found during the assessment stage, since v will form the first column of Q, while the very factors that scale this column to generate each other column will form w. A global scale factor $1 = e^{i\theta - i\theta}$ can then be used to exchange the phase between v and w to symmetrize the outer product into the form vv^T.

2.4. Directionally Biased and Unbiased Devices

Now that the background theory for the two scattering gauge freedoms has been established, specific systems can be considered in detail. When an input scattering state $|\psi_{\text{in}}\rangle$ is directed toward a gauge-transformed $U' = PUP^T$, the output state is $|\psi_{\text{out}}\rangle = PUP^T|\psi_{\text{in}}\rangle$. This product can be intuitively described in the following steps: first, the input state is transformed by $P^T = P^{-1}$ to undo the permutation; then, it experiences the scattering action of the original U; then, it is placed back into the correct labeling with P.

When these permutations are applied to the indices of the scattering state's mode operators, it has been implicitly assumed that the input modes and output modes are the same. This is a direction-free or directionally unbiased convention. Strictly speaking, the incident state basis is different from that of the scattered state leaving the device, since the modes corresponding to counterpropagating optical excitations in a given spatial mode are distinct. It is often unambiguous to disregard this distinction, but, in instances where counterpropagating excitations populate the same spatial mode, the direction needs to be specified. For instance, $a_{jF}^\dagger$ can represent forward propagation, while $a_{jB}^\dagger$ represents backward propagation. This would effectively double the dimensions of all matrices involved: the operator basis would change from $\{a_1^\dagger, \ldots, a_d^\dagger\}$ to $\{a_{1F}^\dagger, \ldots, a_{dF}^\dagger, a_{1B}^\dagger, \ldots, a_{dB}^\dagger\}$, where F represents ingoing and B represents outgoing.

By definition, the only scattering that occurs is cross-coupling between the ingoing and outgoing modes. This means that any scattering or permutation matrix A expressed in the direction-free basis would become a block matrix

$$A \to \begin{pmatrix} 0 & A^* \\ A & 0 \end{pmatrix} \tag{9}$$

in the direction-specific basis. The conjugate is needed to express the coupling going backwards, or from outgoing to ingoing, in order to maintain time reversal symmetry. The dimensionality is not changed in either representation: the block $2d$ system has dimensionality d, so, for the sake of convenience, the compact $d \times d$ notation is used.

The sparse notation in the preceding equation can be viewed as a feedforward or feedthrough system, where the scattering device routes all of the energy in one set of modes through to another disjoint set of modes. An analogous reduction in dimensionality can occur once again, in the direction-free picture, under the assumption of the following gauge symmetry. Let d be an even number and U be a $d \times d$ scattering device (expressed in the compact notation). Assume that U commutes with the gauge transform operator P, where

$$P = \begin{pmatrix} 0 & I \\ I & 0 \end{pmatrix} \tag{10}$$

and I is the $d/2$ identity matrix. Expressing U in the block form

$$U = \begin{pmatrix} A & B \\ C & D \end{pmatrix} \tag{11}$$

and enforcing $PUP^T = U$ leads to the conditions $A = D$ and $B = C$, so that U can be written as

$$U = \begin{pmatrix} A & B \\ B & A \end{pmatrix}. \tag{12}$$

This is the general form of a scattering device endowed with the gauge symmetry P. A *block feedforward* scattering device additionally satisfies the condition $A = 0$. This produces the matrix

$$U = \begin{pmatrix} 0 & B \\ B & 0 \end{pmatrix}. \tag{13}$$

Thus, a block feedforward matrix scatters all light in the set of modes $\{a_1^\dagger, \ldots, a_{d/2}^\dagger\}$ into the disjoint set $\{a_{d/2+1}^\dagger, \ldots, a_d^\dagger\}$, mimicking the form of Equation (9). Sometimes, these scattering devices are called *directionally biased*, since they admit a unidirectional sense of energy flow, which is illustrated in Figure 5. These block feedforward devices are a special case of the general non-reflecting or feedforward scattering device, which is defined by the condition that its diagonal values are all zero. The resemblance to Equation (9) is even closer when the transformation is reciprocal, as this allows U to be written as

$$U = \begin{pmatrix} 0 & B^T \\ B & 0 \end{pmatrix}. \tag{14}$$

Reciprocal block feedforward devices are ubiquitous. They allow the $d \times d$ matrix U to be represented by an even further compactified *transmission matrix* B. B inherits the unitarity of U, so block feedforward scatterers can be viewed as the embedding of a lower-dimensional unitary group in a higher-dimensional space. This change in the effective dimensionality is tied to the underlying gauge symmetry, which itself results from the system possessing a mirror symmetry with respect to the entire sets of input and output modes.

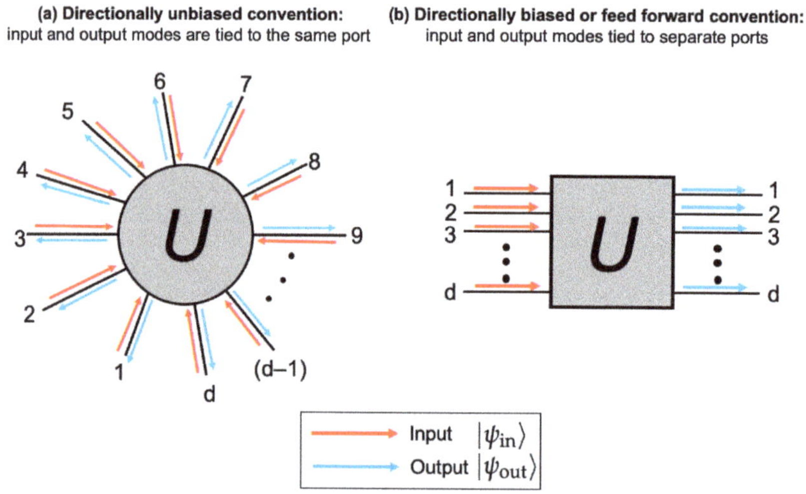

Figure 5. Two equivalent scattering matrix conventions. In convention (**a**), the ingoing and outgoing modes are associated with the same port, producing a $d \times d$ matrix U. In convention (**b**), these sets of modes are kept distinct and assigned to different ports. This produces the $2d \times 2d$ block matrix form in Equation (9). The ports are abstract entities, so their identification with a single mode or pair of counterpropagating modes is immaterial. Nevertheless, certain, so-called block feedforward scattering matrices expressed in the unbiased convention mimic the block form and can be compactified further, as in Equation (13).

Even if U is reciprocal, the block B itself does not need to satisfy $B = B^T$. This allows block feedforward devices to produce effectively non-reciprocal mathematical operations. The aforementioned gauge freedoms also may be applied to B. In fact, the condition $B = B^T$ can be tied to another gauge invariance, corresponding to block mirror symmetry between the input and output sets of modes.

Block feedforward scattering devices include the standard beam splitter, the waveguide coupler, and the Reck and Clements beam splitter meshes [23,24]. Multimode waveguide interferometers and $d \times d$ waveguide couplers such as a fiber tritter also realize this form [25]. The Hadamard convention beam splitter transmission matrix H is

$$H = \frac{1}{\sqrt{2}}\begin{pmatrix} 1 & 1 \\ 1 & -1 \end{pmatrix} \tag{15}$$

whereas its regular scattering matrix is

$$\begin{pmatrix} 0 & H \\ H & 0 \end{pmatrix}. \tag{16}$$

The three-port optical circulator introduced in Equation (4) serves as the physical link between the feedforward and unbiased forms of any given scattering device. Placing a circulator at each port of an unbiased device will produce the equivalent block feedforward one. To convert a block feedforward device into an unbiased one, each input/output pair needs to be connected to a common three-port circulator.

2.5. U(1) Scattering Processes

A $U(1)$ scattering process is simply a backreflection that acquires some necessarily reciprocal constant phase $e^{i\phi}$. This phase can always be gauged away using the external phase shift freedom. The only permutation available is the trivial identity permutation, so no interesting geometric gauge invariants exist in this space. Overall, this scattering space is trivial, containing only the identity equivalence class.

2.6. U(2) Scattering Processes

For a generic $U(2)$ scattering device U with external phase shifts ϕ_j at port j, light entering either port can either transmit through or reflect back. The general form of this transformation (for $\phi_1 = \phi_2 = 0$) is thus

$$U = \begin{pmatrix} r_1 e^{i\delta_1} & t_2 e^{i\gamma_2} \\ t_1 e^{i\gamma_1} & r_2 e^{i\delta_2} \end{pmatrix}. \tag{17}$$

The numbers r_1, r_2, t_1, t_2 are the magnitudes that lie in the range $[0, 1]$, while $\delta_1, \delta_2, \gamma_1$, and γ_2 are the corresponding real-valued phases. Due to unitarity, we have normalization conditions $r_1^2 + t_1^2 = r_2^2 + t_2^2 = 1$, as well as orthogonality, manifesting as

$$r_1 t_1 e^{-i\delta_1 + i\gamma_1} + r_2 t_2 e^{i\delta_2 - i\gamma_2} = 0. \tag{18}$$

This can be rewritten as

$$r_1(1 - r_1^2)^{1/2} + r_2(1 - r_2^2)^{1/2} e^{i\phi} = 0, \tag{19}$$

where $\phi = \delta_1 + \delta_2 + \gamma_1 - \gamma_2$. Both $r_1(1 - r_1^2)^{1/2}$ and $r_2(1 - r_2^2)^{1/2}$ are positive real numbers, implying that the variable ϕ must be selected such that $e^{i\phi} = -1$, yielding

$$r_1(1 - r_1^2)^{1/2} = r_2(1 - r_2^2)^{1/2}. \tag{20}$$

This can only be satisfied for $r_1 = r_2$ (meaning $t_1 = t_2$) as well. Thus, a two-dimensional unitary scattering device *cannot have non-reciprocal transmission*. The phase constraint is that

$$\phi = \delta_1 + \delta_2 - \gamma_1 - \gamma_2 = 2\pi m + \pi \tag{21}$$

for any integer m. This constraint is unchanged when external phases are included, but including them allows us to set $\phi_1 = -(\gamma_1 + \gamma_2 - \delta_2)/2$ and $\phi_2 = -\delta_2/2$, so that $\phi_1 + \phi_2 = -(\gamma_1 + \gamma_2 - \delta_2)/2 - \delta_2/2 = -(\gamma_1 + \gamma_2)/2$, resulting in

$$\begin{pmatrix} -r & (1-r^2)^{1/2}e^{i(\gamma_2-\gamma_1)/2} \\ (1-r^2)^{1/2}e^{-i(\gamma_2-\gamma_1)/2} & r \end{pmatrix} = \begin{pmatrix} -r & (1-r^2)^{1/2}e^{i\Delta} \\ (1-r^2)^{1/2}e^{-i\Delta} & r \end{pmatrix}, \quad (22)$$

where $2\Delta = \gamma_2 - \gamma_1$. This analysis has reduced a generic two-dimensional unitary optical scatterer to its minimum number of measurable parameters—two. r controls the energy division and Δ determines the degree of non-reciprocity. If the device is reciprocal, $\Delta = 0$, and the only measurable parameter is the splitting ratio. In fact, for this two-dimensional case, enforcing U to be gauge-invariant with respect to the swap of labels $1 \leftrightarrow 2$ in turn implies that U is a reciprocal matrix. Consequently, in two dimensions, reciprocity and the only non-trivial gauge symmetry imply one another. This is intuitively rooted in the fact that reciprocity asserts invariance under permutation of the source and detector, and the gauge symmetry P, which permutes the only two ports, effectively asserts the same fact.

Returning to Equation (22) and setting $\Delta \to 0$, we arrive at the reciprocal two-port splitter with reflection probability r^2:

$$U = \begin{pmatrix} -r & (1-r^2)^{1/2} \\ (1-r^2)^{1/2} & r \end{pmatrix}. \quad (23)$$

This matrix is realized by a plate optic excited at normal incidence, with r governed by the interface's refractive indices through the Fresnel equations. The device generates symmetric states when r is set to $1/\sqrt{2}$ artificially; no gauge symmetry can induce this naturally. If another external phase gauge transformation is made, different sign conventions are obtained. For instance, to obtain a geometrically gauge-invariant form of this matrix, add additional external phases $\phi_1' = 3\pi/4$ and $\phi_2' = 5\pi/4$, producing

$$U' = \begin{pmatrix} -re^{i3\pi/2} & (1-r^2)^{1/2}e^{i8\pi/4} \\ (1-r^2)^{1/2}e^{i8\pi/4} & re^{i5\pi/2} \end{pmatrix} = \begin{pmatrix} ir & (1-r^2)^{1/2} \\ (1-r^2)^{1/2} & ir \end{pmatrix} \sim U. \quad (24)$$

2.7. *Gauge-Invariant U(3) Scatterers*

In the two-dimensional case, there was only one gauge-invariant transformation to consider, which was generated by swapping labels 1 and 2. In three dimensions, there are $3! = 6$ permutations comprising two non-trivial classes. These two classes are shown in Figure 6. In this section, we present these gauge-invariant classes, highlighting how the gauge freedoms reduce the number of free variables in the scattering process description.

2.7.1. Generalized Three-Port Circulators

In addition to the permutations that correspond to exchanging the labels of any given pair of modes, there are now distinct cyclic permutations, $(1,2,3) \to (3,1,2)$, with the associated permutation matrix

$$P = \begin{pmatrix} 0 & 0 & 1 \\ 1 & 0 & 0 \\ 0 & 1 & 0 \end{pmatrix}, \quad (25)$$

and $(1,2,3) \to (2,3,1)$, which is similarly associated with P^T.

The general result of imposing a gauge symmetry on a scattering device U will set various elements of U equal to one another, reflecting the fact that input to some ports behaves no differently than the same input to others. For

$$U = \begin{pmatrix} u_{11} & u_{12} & u_{13} \\ u_{21} & u_{22} & u_{23} \\ u_{31} & u_{23} & u_{33} \end{pmatrix} \tag{26}$$

enforcing $PUP^T = U$ generates the constraints $u_{11} = u_{22} = u_{33} := a$, $u_{21} = u_{13} = u_{32} := b$, and $u_{23} = u_{31} = u_{12} := c$, reducing U into the form

$$U = \begin{pmatrix} a & c & b \\ b & a & c \\ c & b & a \end{pmatrix}. \tag{27}$$

Each column of U is a cyclic permutation of its neighbor. Matrices with this general property are known as circulant. The same form can alternatively be derived by assuming *two* reflection symmetries: two exchanges is equivalent to a cyclic permutation in this space. For instance, $(1,2,3) \to (1,3,2)$ after one exchange and then, after the second, $(1,3,2) \to (3,1,2)$ or $(1,3,2) \to (2,3,1)$. The net transformation in either case is a cyclic permutation of $(1,2,3)$.

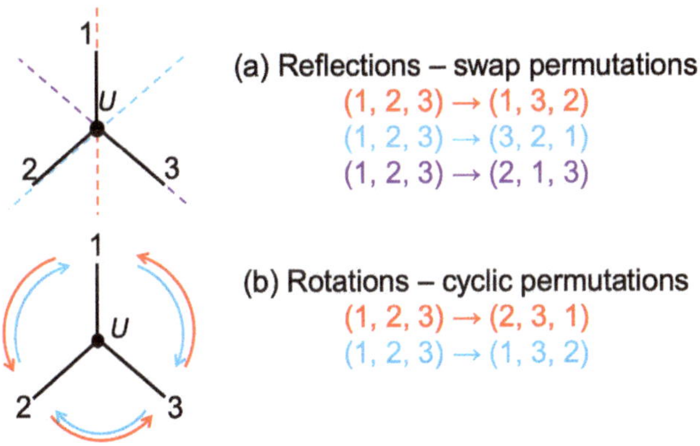

Figure 6. A generic three-dimensional scattering matrix U can be equipped with two distinct gauge symmetries: one corresponding to a reflection symmetry (**a**) and one corresponding to rotation (**b**).

When $a = 0$, exactly one of either b or c must also be zero, and then the system (27) reduces to the circulator, Equation (4), or a matrix that is equivalent to it. This example illustrates that, unlike in the two-dimensional case, a geometric gauge symmetry does not always induce reciprocal symmetry. Imposing reciprocity on U in addition to its rotational symmetry would set $b = c$.

2.7.2. Y-Couplers

The reflection symmetry derived from the exchange of labels 2 and 3 produces a permutation matrix

$$P = \begin{pmatrix} 1 & 0 & 0 \\ 0 & 0 & 1 \\ 0 & 1 & 0 \end{pmatrix}. \tag{28}$$

Imposing this symmetry on the general U of Equation (26) constrains U to be of the form

$$U = \begin{pmatrix} a & c & c \\ b & d & h \\ b & h & d \end{pmatrix}. \tag{29}$$

This is the general form of a non-reciprocal Y-coupler or Y-branch. The $\mathbb{C}$-valued a, b, c, d and h would produce ten unconstrained degrees of freedom, but unitarity reduces this. Normalization lowers the count to eight; then, the orthogonality conditions lower this count to five. Finally, the symmetry-preserving external phases ϕ_1 and $\phi_2 = \phi_3$ can remove two more degrees of freedom, making the final count three.

If this gauge symmetry is also assumed with reciprocity, the added condition $b = c$ removes two more degrees of freedom, leaving just one parameter left. This case was studied in Appendix I of Ref. [26]. The device, which was a backreflecting symmetric Y-branch, was found to have the scattering matrix

$$Y = \begin{pmatrix} r & \sqrt{(1-r^2)/2} & \sqrt{(1-r^2)/2} \\ \sqrt{(1-r^2)/2} & -(1+r)/2 & (1-r)/2 \\ \sqrt{(1-r^2)/2} & (1-r)/2 & -(1+r)/2 \end{pmatrix}, \tag{30}$$

where r can freely be chosen in the set $(-1, 1)$. The different scattering states produced by this device, for a single-photon input on precisely one of its ports, is shown in Figure 7. For any value of r, the output state produced when a single photon enters port 1 will have a symmetric energy distribution under the same symmetry operator, P. Moreover, although the mirror symmetry ensures that the behavior for light entering port 2 is the same as when it enters for port 3, the output state produced when one of these ports is excited is not necessarily symmetric in its energy distribution. This only occurs when r is brought to zero, so that the matrix becomes

$$Y = \begin{pmatrix} 0 & 1/\sqrt{2} & 1/\sqrt{2} \\ 1/\sqrt{2} & -1/2 & 1/2 \\ 1/\sqrt{2} & 1/2 & -1/2 \end{pmatrix}. \tag{31}$$

This matrix, which originated from a nine-parameter unitary space, is uniquely specified by its various symmetries. This is often the intended scattering matrix when an otherwise unspecified Y-branch is discussed. It is conventionally used as a compact beam splitter to realize the transformation $a_1^\dagger \to (a_2^\dagger + a_3^\dagger)/\sqrt{2}$. The device is a hybrid in that it is feedforward for input to port 1 but backreflecting for its other inputs. The general behavior of this symmetric version of the Y-coupler is shown in Figure 1c. This hybrid behavior can only occur in dimensions $d \geq 3$. The complete family of reciprocal, hybrid scattering devices in $U(3)$ is also derived in Appendix I of Ref. [26].

Y-couplers in practice can exhibit losses, violating the assumption of unitarity. This is especially common in integrated photonic implementations, where the light tends to radiate out of the device rather than backreflect at ports 2 and 3. This is *not* due to an inferior design methodology or fabrication quality. Instead, the devices are only designed for the forward transformation. Optimizing the design for the reverse transformation while imposing the reflection gauge symmetry on the device structure would produce a Y-coupler that is more similar to that of Equation (31). It would also automatically produce the forward transformation via reciprocity. For some applications, the backreflections are viewed as an unwanted nuisance, so employing only the forward transform is useful in these cases. Nevertheless, to obtain an ideal Y-coupler, a simple decomposition with a beam splitter can be used. This is shown in Figure 8 and can be employed in any platform, e.g., free-space optics, fiber optics, and integrated photonic waveguides.

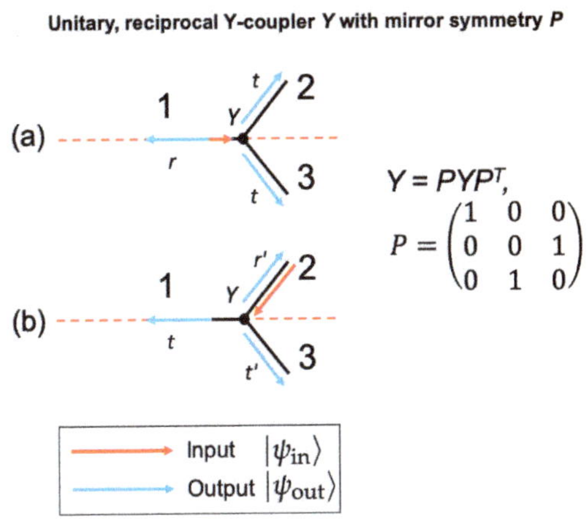

Figure 7. A Y-coupler or Y-branch is a three-port scattering device with a mirror symmetry, such as P shown above. If the device is also reciprocal, its scattering matrix can only have a single degree of freedom r, taking on the form in Equation (30). As shown in diagram (**a**), this device always produces a mirror-symmetric distribution of energy when a photon enters port 1. The transmission coefficient $t = \sqrt{1-r^2}/2$. However, diagram (**b**) illustrates that input to port 2 or 3 generally does not produce another symmetric output state, as $r' = -(1+r)/2$ and $t' = (1-r)/2$. However, when r is brought to zero, these amplitudes become $-1/2$ and $1/2$, respectively, so that their probabilities are equal, and the output state is symmetric. This form of the Y-coupler exhibits added symmetry and is uniquely specified by the scattering matrix (31).

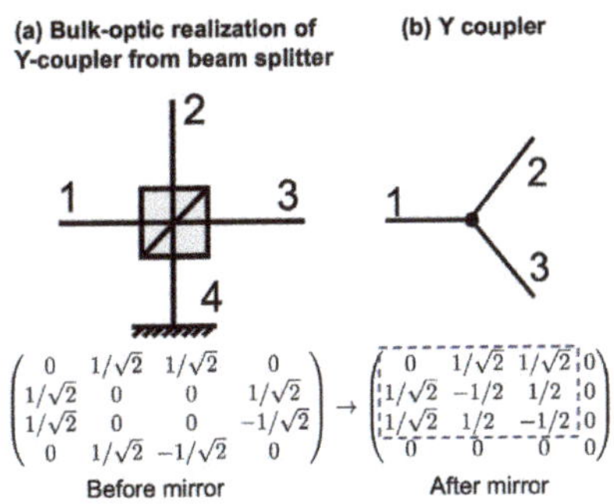

Figure 8. An ideal 50:50 beam splitter and mirror (**a**) can produce an ideal symmetric Y-coupler (**b**). By labeling the beam splitter as shown, its scattering matrix takes on the form below. The first row and column already match those for the intended Y-coupler. However, light entering port 2 or 3 loses energy to port 4. Placing the mirror there redirects the energy back into the beam splitter, splitting the beam a second time. This ultimately produces the Y-coupler matrix. The phase acquired between the mirror and beam splitter is immaterial, since external phases can always be used to equivalently adjust its value.

2.8. Gauge-Invariant U(4) Scatterers

2.8.1. Beam Splitters

The general definition of an ideal beam splitter is a $U(4)$ scattering device that possesses the block feedforward gauge symmetry described above. In this case, the relevant block feedforward permutation invariance is with respect to the swap of the *ordered pairs* $(1,2) \longleftrightarrow (3,4)$. This is associated with a diagonal reflection symmetry in traditional schematics of beam splitters, as shown by the red dashed line in Figure 9. The assumed symmetry produces the beam splitter scattering matrix

$$B = \begin{pmatrix} 0 & 0 & r_1 & t_2 \\ 0 & 0 & t_1 & r_2 \\ r_1 & t_2 & 0 & 0 \\ t_1 & r_2 & 0 & 0 \end{pmatrix} \tag{32}$$

reducing the device to an embedding of a $U(2)$ scattering device in a four-dimensional space. Therefore, in essence, everything pertaining to the four-port optical beam splitter is described in Section 2.6 for two-dimensional scattering devices.

The matrix B in Equation (32) is not necessarily reciprocal. However, in this system, reciprocity is tied to a second reflection symmetry, over the anti-diagonal line in Figure 9. The underlying permutation matrix is

$$P = \begin{pmatrix} \sigma & 0 \\ 0 & \sigma \end{pmatrix}, \tag{33}$$

where σ represents the swap operator for two modes. Once the block feedforward symmetry is assumed, this symmetry P is both a necessary and sufficient condition for reciprocity. If B is reciprocal, adding external phases allows it to be put into the form

$$B = \begin{pmatrix} 0 & 0 & r & t \\ 0 & 0 & t & r \\ r & t & 0 & 0 \\ t & r & 0 & 0 \end{pmatrix}. \tag{34}$$

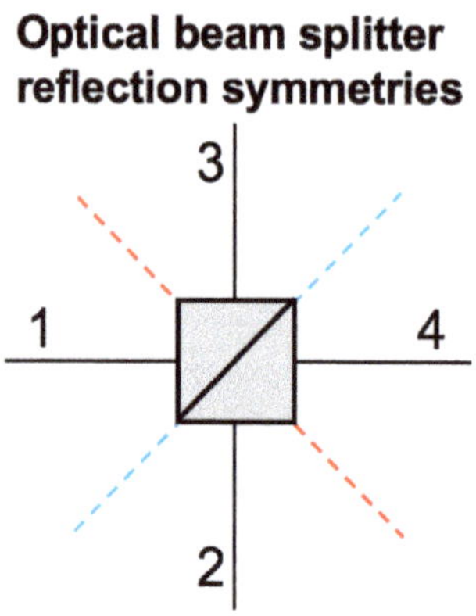

Figure 9. An optical beam splitter is defined as any four-port scattering device that satisfies the following conditions. First, it exhibits zero coupling between (1, 2) and itself, as well as (3, 4) and itself. Second, it possesses the red line mirror symmetry, induced by scattering matrix invariance to the permutation of label pairs $(1,2) \longleftrightarrow (3,4)$. The symmetry over the blue axis is induced by invariance to the simultaneous swap of the mode labels $1 \leftrightarrow 2$ and $3 \leftrightarrow 4$. After the original (red) symmetry constraint is enforced, the second (blue) one becomes a necessary and sufficient condition for reciprocity.

Loopless graphs composed solely of beam splitters will generally produce higher-dimensional scattering devices that also possess block feedforward gauge symmetry. These *decompositions*, which represent a higher-dimensional scattering device as a graph of lower-dimensional ones, can be made to span the full unitary group. Two well-known decompositions with the underlying reflection symmetry of all input and output modes are due to Reck and Clements et al. [23,24,27,28]. These both require $\mathcal{O}(d^2)$ beam splitters and controllable phase shifts to span $U(d)$. These meshes are versatile, but, in practice, they suffer from error accumulation and non-trivial reprogramming procedures. This has limited their size d to about a few dozen modes today [29,30]. A non-reciprocal phase placed inside one of these meshes would break the input/output mirror symmetry, leading to an overall non-reciprocal U. In terms of Equation (11), this scattering matrix would have $A = D = 0$ but $B \neq C$.

2.8.2. Grover Four-Ports

Although a reciprocal, balanced beam splitter commutes with the block feedforward gauge symmetry operator, there are a number of other potential gauge symmetries that it lacks. However, the Grover four-port

$$G = \frac{1}{2}\begin{pmatrix} -1 & 1 & 1 & 1 \\ 1 & -1 & 1 & 1 \\ 1 & 1 & -1 & 1 \\ 1 & 1 & 1 & -1 \end{pmatrix} \tag{35}$$

is unchanged by all possible permutations of its labels and thus commutes with any gauge symmetry operator. Beyond this, it produces a fully uniform, symmetric energy distribution when any one of its ports is excited. It is precisely the uniform energy distribution that is invariant to any permutation of mode labels.

The matrix originally appeared as a quantum logic gate in the Grover search algorithm [14]. It has since been employed as a general scattering coin for quantum walks [31] and more recently as an optical scattering device. Having the same number of ports as a beam splitter allows the Grover coin to replace the latter in any system, effectively boosting the underlying dimensionality. These two devices are compared in Figure 1.

A general d-dimensional Grover coin can be defined by first enforcing reciprocity, a reflection symmetry, and a rotational symmetry, producing a reciprocal, circulant matrix, and then by minimizing the reflection probability [26]. This produces a reflection amplitude $r = 2/d - 1$ with a transmission amplitude $t = 2/d$. In general, Grover coins in one dimension can easily be converted to those in the other dimensions by either closing off ports with a mirror or by connecting two coins together [32]. General circulant matrices have been studied for quantum walks [33].

The realization of a four-port Grover coin is important for interferometric applications, which are discussed in the next section. Although a static, single-element Grover coin has yet to be experimentally realized, a Grover coin can and has been obtained using the decomposition of two Y-couplers [13,26]. The Y-couplers themselves can be decomposed with a beam splitter and a mirror, as shown in Figure 8. The Grover decomposition is shown in Figure 10. It is formed by connecting the feedforward ports of two symmetric Y-couplers to each other. This is a slightly more general decomposition, due to the bridge phase ϕ. ϕ parametrizes a family of uniform-probability $U(4)$ scattering devices. The various static devices produced are generally not gauge-equivalent to one another in the external phase sense. The standard Grover coin occurs for $\phi = 0$.

Y-coupler decomposed generalized Grover coin

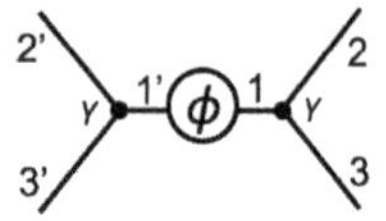

$$G(\phi) = \frac{1}{2}\begin{pmatrix} -1 & 1 & e^{i\phi} & e^{i\phi} \\ 1 & -1 & e^{i\phi} & e^{i\phi} \\ e^{i\phi} & e^{i\phi} & -1 & 1 \\ e^{i\phi} & e^{i\phi} & 1 & -1 \end{pmatrix}$$

Figure 10. Forming a generalized four-port Grover coin using two symmetric Y-couplers. The standard Grover coin is obtained when $\phi = 0$.

3. Optical Interferometry

The previous section dealt entirely with static or passive scattering devices. These are, by definition, presumed to be fixed for excitations of a given frequency and polarization mode. Static scatterers are generally represented as a graphical node, like the Y-coupler shown in Figure 7.

The present section will consider ways in which multiple passive nodes can form a graph, called an optical *interferometer*, which is commonly used as a central element in optical sensors. This graph will generally be a function of both the scattering matrices forming it and the phases acquired on the edges between connected nodes. Controllable phase shifters could also be equivalently affixed to an unweighted graph as block feedforward nodes of their own. In either case, when multiple scattering devices are treated as part of the same system but are left unconnected, a block-diagonal aggregate scattering matrix is obtained. Adding connections couples energy between the constituent scattering nodes, breaking the block-diagonal structure. Any remaining unconnected edges allow light to couple in and out of the network. Thus, the interferometer itself is another scattering device that is tunable or active.

A photon entering an open or unconnected port of a general interferometer can be viewed as conducting a random walk on its graph. This variant of the random walk is known as a quantum walk, since the paths that it traverses are able to coherently interfere; this distinction is embodied in the use of a unitary time evolution operator instead of the traditional probability matrix used in studies of Markov chains. The study of quantum walks in general forms a subdomain of general quantum information processing. It has been shown that universal computation and efficient search on a graph can be achieved with quantum walks [34–38]. For an introduction to the field, consult Ref. [31].

For each set of input phases and constituent scattering devices, the action of any interferometer can be computed by finding the steady-state distribution of the walk, which is the outputted scattering state in the limit of long time. This can be found numerically using a finite element assembly approach. This involves using the graph interconnect information to construct a global time evolution operator for the walk, enforcing boundary conditions pertaining to the unconnected ports, and finally computing its action in the long-time limit. This is effectively accomplished by finding the eigenspectrum of the time evolution operator, either directly or through a matrix inversion problem. The general approach is described in Ref. [39]. For the special case of a chain of two-dimensional scattering devices, this finite element method has been shown to reduce to the Redheffer star product, which is extensively used to compute the aggregate scattering matrices of two or more coupled optical thin films [40].

The quantum walk model of an interferometer typically begins with the assumption that the input single-photon state is perfectly coherent, which is akin to assuming that the source is perfectly monochromatic. This in turn permits the summation of paths with arbitrarily large optical path length differences to obtain the output after interference. For a real source, interference will only be observed among paths whose corresponding path lengths are smaller than the coherence length of the source. The other paths will only appear in the output as an incoherent background. The adoption of a very narrow linewidth source can extend the coherence length to several kilometers or more, making this assumption valid to an excellent approximation. This discussion holds in an analogous way for non-planar sources with finite spatial coherence. To obtain the most ideal behavior, a high degree of collimation and alignment is necessary.

The general methodology of the quantum walk finite element approach can also be followed algebraically, for the sake of finding an interferometer's scattering matrix as a function of its parameters. A common obstruction, however, is arriving at a closed-form expression for the inverse or eigenspectrum of the constructed $d \times d$ matrix function. However, this can often be accomplished in low-dimensional systems; many examples will be discussed in the sections to follow. We will first review the operating principles of several traditional interferometers. Then, by substituting their components for higher-dimensional gauge-symmetric scattering devices, we show that these devices gain access to new degrees of freedom. These in turn lead to various enhancements of the phase readout, thus resulting in a substantial improvement in the resolution of optical sensors.

3.1. Interferometric Gauge Freedoms

The gauge freedoms of passive scatterers naturally generalize to active ones. External phases can be applied to open ports in the same way as before, and phase shifts can also be applied to the ports of the internal nodes. This shifts the total phase acquired between the scattering nodes by a constant. Because the true global value of these phases is indeterminate, translation by another constant will not change the physical situation either. It can be freely absorbed into or removed from the definition of the acquired phase between two nodes. Therefore, two interferometers are considered equivalent in this sense if a suitable translation of each internal and external phase of either system produces the other system, for all values of the internal phases. In other words, it is obtained when the parameter spaces of the two networks coalesce when the input parameters are shifted by appropriate constants.

This definition is employed so that changes in the external phase convention of the internal scattering nodes (such as Hadamard vs. symmetric beam splitters) do not affect the equivalence class of the overall network. It is a different comparison regarding that for two static scattering devices, where only external phases can be placed. To highlight the distinction in an example, consider the generalized Grover coin decomposition in Figure 8 and let the scattering matrix of the network be denoted by $G_1(\phi)$. The standard Grover coin is obtained as a static device when ϕ is fixed at the value 0. For $\phi \neq 0$, the static device produced is, in general, not equivalent to the standard Grover coin. However, now, form a copy of this device, G_2, and add a second phase in the bridge, ϕ_b. ϕ_b may or may not be coming from external phases placed at port 1 and/or port $1'$, since this distinction is immaterial. Nevertheless, the total bridge phase is now $\phi + \phi_b$. Clearly, for non-zero ϕ_b, the static devices produced for fixed values of ϕ and ϕ_b, $G_1(\phi)$ and $G_2(\phi + \phi_b)$ will not be equivalent. However, ϕ cannot be defined up to an absolute, so it can be shifted freely. Redefining the phase $\phi \to \phi - \phi_b$ in G_2 causes G_1 and G_2 to be equal for all values of ϕ, signifying the equivalence of the two networks. This example is trivial because the compared networks have the same graph topology. In some more interesting cases, equivalence in this sense can be established between different graphs.

The geometric gauge symmetry of a scattering node is also able to produce a symmetrical scattering graph, assuming that the graph itself preserves the symmetry in its interconnect configuration. Since the external port relabeling of the graph is equivalent to a geometric transformation enacted on it, the entire graph can remain invariant to such a transformation if the underlying vertices and phase parameters maintain the symmetry. One practical use of interferometric gauge symmetry is to simplify the computation of the network output: if symmetry implies that certain sets of input ports all scatter light in the same way, only one input case has to be studied, and then the rest follow by suitable permutations of the graph parameters. Gauge-invariant interferometric graphs are readily constructed in general. First, form a graph that is invariant to some permutation to any subset of its nodes. This can correspond to a global symmetry of the overall network topology, such as invariance to rotations of the whole graph by a fixed angle. Then, assign the same scattering matrix to each relevant node, providing them with the same vertex label or color.

Two well-known interferometric configurations, the Michelson and Mach–Zehnder interferometers, are shown in Figure 11. As functions of their internal phases ϕ_1 and ϕ_2, these interferometers tunably produce the complete space of reciprocal $U(2)$ and $U(4)$ scattering devices. They inherit the symmetries from the reciprocal beam splitters that form them. In the case of the Michelson one (Figure 11a), the exchange of labels $1 \leftrightarrow 2$ of the external ports and the phase parameters leaves the scattering response unchanged. Thus, the computed output corresponding to an input excitation at port 1 can be converted to the output corresponding to input at port 2 simply by exchanging the output mode labels and exchanging the phase parameter labels. The Mach–Zehnder interferometer shown in Figure 11b can be generated by mirroring the Michelson device about the blue dashed line. This preserves the symmetry defined by the red dashed line. The blue dashed line symmetry represents the gauge invariance tied to the block feedforward symmetry $(1,2) \longleftrightarrow (3,4)$ of the configuration. Together, these two symmetry lines allow the full device output to be found immediately from just one calculation corresponding to input at any single port.

The general output calculation entails starting with an initial state that is a single photon impinging on a given port, such as $|\psi_{\text{in}}\rangle = a_j^\dagger|0\rangle$. Then, the scattering matrices are used to sequentially propagate the state though the graph until every state component has reached the output. This is equivalent to finding all the possible paths that the photon can travel from an input j to each output port i. Each individual path is first weighed by the product of all the scattering amplitudes that it encounters moving from port j to i. The final scattering matrix element is found from the sum of these weighted paths, corresponding to the coherent interference of all paths. The general problem of path counting can become complicated, especially as resonant structures are introduced to the graph, causing the number of possible paths to grow indefinitely. Some cases can be explicitly summed, but, at other times, an automated path-counting and summing algorithm is needed, which is what Ref. [39] accomplishes.

For both of the devices in Figure 11, there are always only two possible paths: one for each arm j containing the phase ϕ_j. Their only difference in output is a meaningless global phase shift of π, originating from the common convention of adding a π phase shift to the state when it reflects at a mirror. Whether this phase can be observed physically or not, it can be lumped into the definition of ϕ_1 and ϕ_2. This causes the device outputs to be identical. We will consider a photon inputted to port 1 of either device and assume, without loss of generality, that the beam splitters take on the Hadamard convention of Equations (15) and (16). Then, there is an initial splitting into two state components, one in each arm. These each acquire a phase ϕ_j and then are reintroduced to a beam splitter in some way, splitting a second time. The possible paths from port 1 to port 1 (3) are double reflection with phase ϕ_1 and double transmission with phase ϕ_2. The corresponding path amplitudes are $(1/\sqrt{2})(e^{i\phi_1})(1/\sqrt{2}) = e^{i\phi_1}/2$ and similarly $e^{i\phi_2}/2$. The aggregate reflection amplitude for the device is then $r(\phi_1, \phi_2) = (e^{i\phi_1} + e^{i\phi_2})/2$. The transmission amplitude is similarly $t(\phi_1, \phi_2) = (e^{i\phi_1} - e^{i\phi_2})/2$, where the minus sign is incurred from the back-side beam splitter reflection when using the Hadamard beam splitter convention.

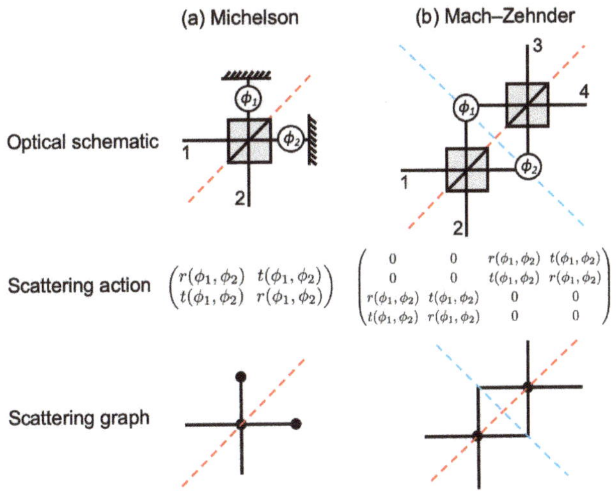

Figure 11. Two common interferometric configurations, due to Michelson (**a**) and Mach and Zehnder (**b**). Like static scattering devices, the open ports of interferometric graphs can also be freely relabeled, naturally extending the notion of geometric gauge symmetry to scattering graphs. Assuming that the underlying 50:50 beam splitters and phase shifters are reciprocal, the devices will possess the reflection symmetry indicated by the red dashed line. This symmetry implies that input to any port on one side of the line will behave in the same way as input to its mirrored counterpart, so long as ϕ_1 and ϕ_2 are exchanged. The Mach–Zehnder interferometer can be viewed as constructed by mirroring the Michelson interferometer over the blue dashed line. This line corresponds to the device's block feedforward symmetry. Since these devices inherit the symmetries and overall dimensionality of their lower-dimensional counterparts (cf. Figure 9), they are often viewed as tunable versions of them. That is, a Michelson interferometer can be viewed as a phase-tunable plate splitter, while the Mach–Zehnder interferometer can be viewed as a tunable beam splitter. These active building blocks can replace their passive equivalents in any larger interferometric graph. The phase gauge freedom also allows the placement of external phases at ports 1 and 2 and the translation of the values of ϕ_1 and ϕ_2 by arbitrary fixed constants. These can be used to put the overall scattering matrix for each device in the form shown beneath its schematic. Here, the correspondence between nodes and local scattering matrices is clear, since the associated optical schematic is shown with it. In general, the nodes of a scattering graph need to be clearly associated with a specific scattering matrix, e.g., through a vertex label or color.

Thus, the aggregate scattering matrix for any lossless Michelson interferometer is equivalent to

$$U_{\mathrm{MI}}(\phi_1, \phi_2) = \begin{pmatrix} r(\phi_1, \phi_2) & t(\phi_1, \phi_2) \\ t(\phi_1, \phi_2) & r(\phi_1, \phi_2) \end{pmatrix} \tag{36}$$

while that for a Mach–Zehnder is equivalent to, in block form,

$$U_{\mathrm{MZI}}(\phi_1, \phi_2) = \begin{pmatrix} 0 & U_{\mathrm{MI}}(\phi_1, \phi_2) \\ U_{\mathrm{MI}}(\phi_1, \phi_2) & 0 \end{pmatrix}. \tag{37}$$

The underlying scattering amplitudes are

$$r(\phi_1, \phi_2) = \frac{e^{i\phi_1} + e^{i\phi_2}}{2} = e^{i\phi_1/2 + i\phi_2/2}\cos(\phi_1/2 - \phi_2/2), \tag{38a}$$

$$t(\phi_1, \phi_2) = \frac{e^{i\phi_1} - e^{i\phi_2}}{2} = e^{i\phi_1/2 + i\phi_2/2} i \sin(\phi_1/2 - \phi_2/2). \tag{38b}$$

From these forms, it is easy to see that the scattering probability for reflection is $R = |r|^2 = \cos^2((\phi_1 - \phi_2)/2)$, while, for transmission, it is $T = |t|^2 = \sin^2((\phi_1 - \phi_2)/2)$. This sinusoidal modulation, which is only sensitive to the optical phase difference $(\phi_1 - \phi_2)$, is characteristic of the two-beam superposition accomplished by devices such as these. A plot of either scattering probability P versus either phase ϕ is known as an interferogram. ϕ itself could be viewed as a phase difference $\Delta\phi = \phi - \phi_g$ for an indeterminable global phase ϕ_g. The typical sinusoidal interferogram for two-beam interference is shown in Figure 12. The system can act as a basic phase sensor: for small changes in the input phase about some bias point ϕ_0, the output change in probability ΔP is given by the product of the input phase change and the slope at the bias point. A bias point with a larger slope will then have heightened sensitivity.

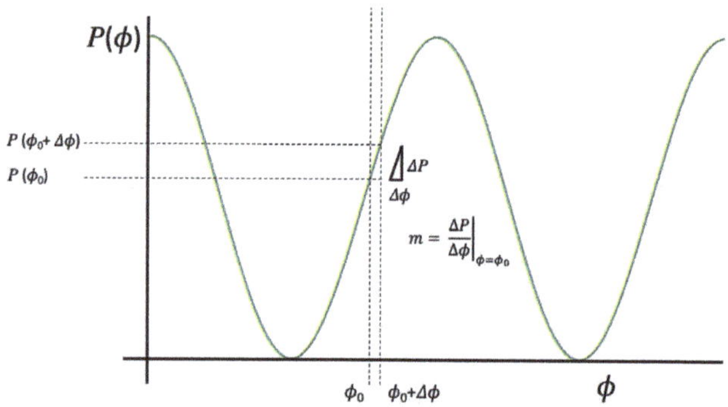

Figure 12. Sinusoidal interferogram produced by two-beam interference, such as with a Michelson or Mach–Zehnder interferometer. This basic interferometric configuration can be used as a phase readout. First, the system is placed at a bias point ϕ_0, verified by measuring the corresponding probability $P(\phi_0)$. Then, a small change in phase $\Delta\phi$ induces a change in probability ΔP given by the product of $\Delta\phi$ and the slope of the probability at the bias point. A larger slope $dP/d\phi$ at ϕ_0 naturally produces a more sensitive response to phase changes, allowing smaller phase changes to be detected.

3.2. *Traditional Interferometric Sensing Systems*

Three two-port interferometers are shown in Figure 13. In case (a), we show the Michelson configuration, which was discussed in the previous section. It is the most simple phase sensor of *reciprocal* phase shifts. Even if ϕ_1 or ϕ_2 were non-reciprocal, meaning that the phase acquired depended on the propagation direction, this could not be observed in a Michelson interferometer. This is because the double pass through each arm gives the summed phase for each direction as a single phase shift: $\phi_j = \phi_{jF} + \phi_{jB}$.

The configuration in Figure 13b is the Sagnac interferometer, which is the simplest configuration for *non-reciprocal* phase inference. By converting the two spatially separated arms of a Michelson interferometer into a loop, any non-reciprocal difference in phase acquired moving clockwise around the common-path loop versus counterclockwise will be evident. Let the total clockwise phase be $\phi + \delta$ and the total counterclockwise phase be $\phi - \delta$. Since this configuration is essentially the same two-beam interference present in a Michelson or Mach–Zehnder interferometer, the same results can be applied here, but with these phases. The corresponding transmission probability is then

$$T = |t|^2 = \sin^2(\phi_1/2 - \phi_2/2) = \sin^2((\phi+\delta)/2 - (\phi-\delta)/2) = \sin^2(\delta). \tag{39}$$

Thus, the transmission probability is zero for a fully reciprocal phase ($\delta = 0$) and increases as the non-reciprocal component δ increases. However, the effect can be challenging to observe due to the intrinsic weakness of non-reciprocal phase sources, combined with this weak $\mathcal{O}(\delta^2)$ response for small δ. Nevertheless, it allows the non-reciprocal portion of a phase shift to be naturally isolated from the reciprocal one and extracted from a direct measurement. The configuration is named for Georges Sagnac, who established the existence of a physical effect by which the rotation of a looped optical path induces a non-reciprocal phase shift [20]. The non-reciprocal phase shift δ is proportional to the product of the loop area and angular velocity and inversely proportional to the optical wavelength. It is the fundamental operating principle of optical gyroscopes and was famously used in 1925 by Michelson and Gale to measure the rotation rate of the Earth [41]. The last century has seen a number of applications and generalizations to the Sagnac effect proposed [42–45].

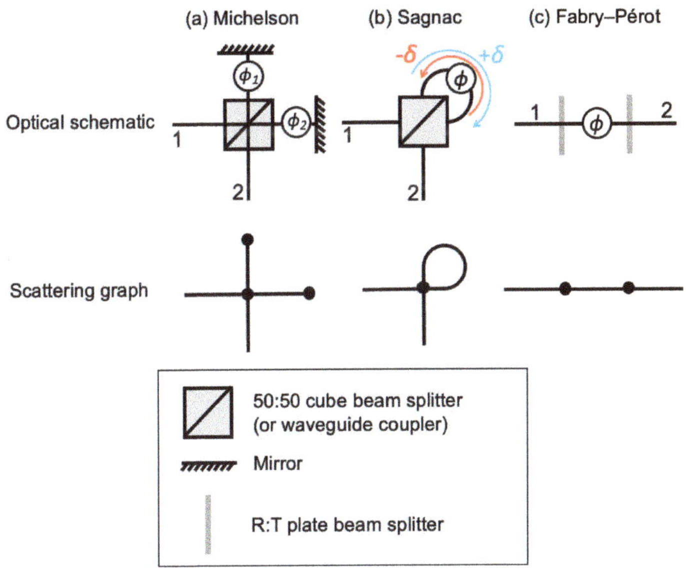

Figure 13. Traditional low-dimensional interferometric configurations. The optical schematic is shown above the associated scattering graph. The Michelson one (**a**) is a common tool for the inference of reciprocal phases, while the Sagnac device (**b**) is used to infer non-reciprocal ones. The Fabry–Pérot interferometer (**c**) is a simple resonant cavity typically employed as a narrowband filter of light.

The third device, in Figure 13c, is the parallel-plate Fabry–Pérot interferometer. (If the plates are movable so that the central phase shift ϕ can be tuned, the device is traditionally called an interferometer, whereas, if the plates are fixed, it is known as an etalon.) The multipass structure allows ϕ to accumulate many times, sharpening the phase response around certain values of ϕ. This translates directly to a sharpened frequency or narrowband wavelength dependence about certain wavelength centers.

The normally incident transmission amplitude of the Fabry–Pérot interferometer is readily calculated by summing the different paths from input to output. For an input to port 1, each path is indexed by the number of bounces that it takes before exiting at port 2. The principle beam transmits directly through both plates, acquiring an amplitude $t_1 e^{i\phi} t_2$, where t_j is the transmission coefficient of plate j and ϕ is the phase acquired between the plates. The plates are assumed to be reciprocal $U(2)$ scattering devices. This allows the reflection coefficients to be written as $r_j = i\sqrt{R_j}$, where R_j is the plate reflection probability. Then, $t_j = \sqrt{1-R_j}$.

The nth beam transmits through the first plate up to the second plate, acquiring $t_1 e^{i\phi}$, and then makes n bounces between the two plates, acquiring $(r_1 r_2 e^{2i\phi})^n$, and finally passes through the last plate with amplitude t_2. The net amplitude for the path conducting n bounces before transmitting is thus $t_1 t_2 e^{i\phi}(r_1 r_2)^n e^{(2i\phi)n}$. Summing these paths produces the Fabry–Pérot transmission amplitude, t, given by

$$t = t_1 t_2 e^{i\phi}\left(1 + \sum_{n=1}^{\infty}(r_1 r_2 e^{i2\phi})^n\right) = t_1 t_2 e^{i\phi}\left(1 + \sum_{n=0}^{\infty}(r_1 r_2 e^{i2\phi})^n - 1\right). \tag{40}$$

Evidently, this amplitude and the associated transmission probability $|t|^2$ can be decomposed into a product of the output that would have resulted without path interference, $|t_1|^2|t_2|^2$, and an interference factor in parentheses. Its sum can be evaluated as a geometric series, which converges whenever the product of plate reflections $|r_1 r_2| = |r_1||r_2|$ is less than 1. This fails to occur only if either plate is fully reflecting, in which case no light will transmit. Otherwise,

$$t(\phi) = t_1 t_2 e^{i\phi}\left(\sum_{n=0}^{\infty}(r_1 r_2 e^{i2\phi})^n\right) = \frac{t_1 t_2 e^{i\phi}}{1 - r_1 r_2 e^{i2\phi}}. \tag{41}$$

Using the fact that $r_j = i\sqrt{R_j}$ and $T_j = |t_j|^2 = 1 - R_j$, the transmission probability $T = |t|^2$ can be written as

$$T(\phi) = \frac{(1-R_1)(1-R_2)}{1 + R_1 R_2 - 2\sqrt{R_1 R_2}\cos(2\phi)}. \tag{42}$$

Now, if the optical plates are symmetric, $R_1 = R_2 = R$, T can be simplified using the fact that $\cos 2\phi = 1 - 2\sin^2\phi$. Substituting this into the denominator yields

$$1 + R^2 - 2R\cos(2\phi) = 1 + R^2 - 2R(1 - 2\sin^2(\phi)) = (1-R)^2 + 4R\sin^2(\phi), \tag{43}$$

so that

$$T(\phi) = \frac{1}{1 + F\sin^2(\phi)}, \tag{44}$$

where the coefficient of finesse is

$$F = \frac{4R}{(1-R)^2}. \tag{45}$$

The transmission probability T is a composition of $f(\phi) = \sqrt{F}\sin\phi$ with the Lorentzian function $L(x) = 1/(1+x^2)$. Several examples of this transmission probability are shown in Figure 14a. The finesse parameter is strictly increasing with R in the range $(0,1)$ and ultimately determines the sharpness of the resonance. The larger the reflection R, the more round trips can occur, on average, before the photon transmits out of the plates. This in turn corresponds to higher phase sensitivity.

Using the fact that $\phi = 2\pi nd/\lambda$ allows the Fabry–Pérot interferometer wavelength response to be investigated. Plots of T vs. λ are shown in Figure 14b for the case where $d = 10^{-4}$ meters. The mirror reflection R is assumed to be constant with respect to the wavelength. The narrowband response around certain wavelengths makes this device an excellent tool for filtering out a specific wavelength or frequency. Perhaps the most intriguing physical aspect of this configuration is that the act of aligning two highly reflective plates perpendicular to one another enables certain colors to pass through with perfect transmission. This is a result of the interference altering the effective transmission and reflection coefficients of the combined system.

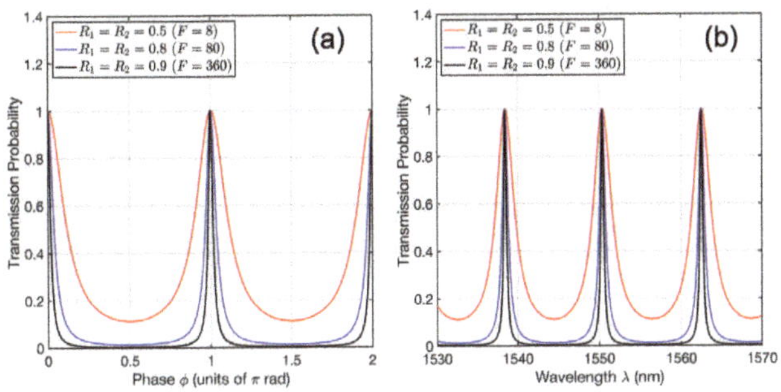

Figure 14. Transmission response of a symmetric Fabry–Pérot interferometer (Figure 13c) vs. the half-round-trip phase ϕ (**a**) and wavelength (**b**).

3.3. Novel Higher-Dimensional Interferometric Sensors

The conventional two-port interferometric configurations shown in Figure 13 employ low-dimensional linear scatterers, namely beam splitters and plate splitters, in simple graphical configurations. The Sagnac and Michelson devices superimposed two beams, producing a sinusoidal interference pattern. This interferogram was ultimately only sensitive to one parameter in either case, despite the general presence of two. In the Michelson one, this was the phase difference $\phi_d = \phi_1 - \phi_2$, and, for the Sagnac case, this was the non-reciprocal portion of the loop δ, which is also a relative phase. Meanwhile, the Fabry–Pérot configuration sums an infinite number of paths in a geometric series, resulting in resonances whose width is a function of the plate reflectivities, which are generally fixed.

In this section, we introduce a basic generalization to each of these interferometric configurations. We shall see how the generalization to higher dimensions results in each system gaining a parametric degree of freedom. For each case, the constituent scattering devices are replaced with a gauge-symmetric, higher-dimensional equivalent. These configurations are pictured in Figure 15. The Grover–Michelson and Grover–Sagnac configurations are formed by replacing the central beam splitter of each conventional configuration with the four-port Grover coin, while a higher-dimensional Fabry–Pérot interferometer is formed by replacing the two-port plate splitter with the three-port, symmetric Y-coupler. The replaced scatterers are directionally unbiased, allowing light to backscatter. As a result, the single-pass arms of the Michelson device are converted to a pair of optical resonators. These cavities are coupled to one other by the Grover coin. The Grover–Sagnac configuration is essentially the same; the two resonators share a common path inside the loop, corresponding to the two counterpropagating modes of the loop. Because it is a common path configuration, phase differences are only acquired through a non-reciprocal phase δ. The Y-coupler system similarly converts the single-cavity Fabry–Pérot into a coupled cavity version.

All of these graphical configurations are highly symmetric. The cavity cross-coupling and out-coupling are equal in each case. Beyond this, each device possesses reflection symmetry with respect to the exchange of its external ports. The Y-coupler device also has reflection symmetry about the line through these two ports, implying that the response is unchanged when ϕ_1 and ϕ_2 are exchanged. The same parametric exchange symmetry is found in the Grover–Michelson case with ϕ_1 and ϕ_2, as well as the Grover–Sagnac one, which occurs when the sign of the non-reciprocal phase port δ is flipped.

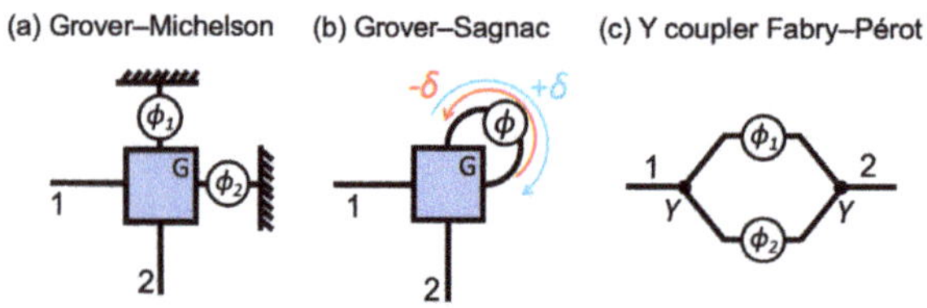

Figure 15. Higher-dimensional analogues of the systems in Figure 13. The Grover–Michelson (**a**) and Grover–Sagnac (**b**) configurations replace the traditional beam splitter with the Grover four-port. In configuration (**c**), three-port Y-couplers replace the $U(2)$ plate beam splitters of the conventional Fabry–Pérot system. The Grover coin, being fully permutation-invariant, does not need to have a specified orientation, but the Y-coupler's feedforward port must be specified. Here, we assume that this port is the external, unconnected one for each side. In all three of these systems, a pair of coupled optical resonators is formed from the backreflecting response of the constituent scattering device. This increase in dimensionality provides access to new degrees of freedom in the system output.

3.3.1. Experimental Demonstration of the Grover–Michelson Interferometer

The Grover–Michelson system was originally considered in Ref. [32]. In that work, the output amplitudes were found by studying the normal-mode evolution of the superposition states $a_{c1}^{\dagger} \pm a_{c2}^{\dagger}$, where $a_{cj}^{\dagger}$ is the creation operator for a photon propagating within arm j. Defining

$$B := \frac{1}{2}(e^{i\phi_1} + e^{i\phi_2}), \tag{46}$$

$$C := \frac{1}{2}(e^{i\phi_1} - e^{i\phi_2}), \tag{47}$$

which are precisely the traditional Michelson scattering amplitudes from Equation (36), the reflection r and transmission t scattering coefficients of the device were found to be

$$r = \left(\frac{C^2}{2B-2} - \frac{B}{2} - \frac{1}{2}\right), \tag{48}$$

$$t = \left(\frac{C^2}{2B-2} - \frac{B}{2} + \frac{1}{2}\right). \tag{49}$$

This can be rewritten as

$$r = \frac{1}{2}(e^{i\gamma_{\mathrm{GMI}}} - 1) = e^{i\gamma_{\mathrm{GMI}}/2} i \sin(\gamma_{\mathrm{GMI}}/2) \tag{50}$$

$$t = \frac{1}{2}(e^{i\gamma_{\mathrm{GMI}}} + 1) = e^{i\gamma_{\mathrm{GMI}}/2} \cos(\gamma_{\mathrm{GMI}}/2) \tag{51}$$

where

$$\gamma_{\text{GMI}}(\phi_1, \phi_2) = \arctan\left(\frac{\sin(\phi_1 + \phi_2) - \sin\phi_1 - \sin\phi_2}{\cos(\phi_1 + \phi_2) - \cos\phi_1 - \cos\phi_2 + (1 + \cos(\phi_1 - \phi_2))/2)}\right). \quad (52)$$

Thus, replacing the beam splitter with a Grover coin can be viewed as a phase transformation of the linear response $(\phi_1 - \phi_2)$ to a synthetic non-linear one $\gamma_{\text{GMI}}(\phi_1, \phi_2)$. This is essentially a reparametrization of the general interferometric graph's phase response. Example plots of the Grover–Michelson transmission probability are shown in Figure 16. The probability is plotted with respect to ϕ_1 for different fixed values of ϕ_2. The red curve is the traditional Michelson response, for $\phi_2 = 0$. Changing ϕ_2 merely translates this curve. However, in the Grover–Michelson interferometer, sweeping ϕ_2 continuously deforms the curves. Being the normal sinusoid but composed of the synthetic phase, the deformation does not affect the visibility, given by $\mathcal{V} = (\max_{\phi_1} T - \min_{\phi_1} T)/(\max_{\phi_1} T + \min_{\phi_1} T)$, which remains fixed at the value of 1 for any ϕ_2. The position of the transmission peak in ϕ_1 is given by $2\pi - \phi_2$. As this peak moves towards the value 0 mod 2π, the peak narrows, leading to a heightened phase response in this region. The slope $\partial T/\partial\phi_1$ grows much larger than in the traditional Michelson case, suggesting much higher phase sensitivity at the appropriate bias point.

The decomposition of the Grover coin into two Y-couplers (Figure 10) and the Y-coupler into a beam splitter and mirror (Figure 8) enables the experimental implementation of the Grover coin with a relatively small number of common tabletop optics. As a proof of principle, a Grover coin was experimentally assembled in this way in bulk and used to form a Grover–Michelson interferometer [13]. The arm phases ϕ_1 and ϕ_2 were controlled by modifying their corresponding optical path lengths, which was accomplished by a piezoelectrically actuated translation stage. The source was a quasi-monochromatic, continuous-wave diode laser with an operating wavelength of 633 nm and coherence length exceeding a kilometer. The input power was in the microwatt range; there was no need to reduce the power to the single-photon level since the output obtained was directly proportional to the output probability in this case. Nevertheless, the genuine single-photon implementation would have presented some differences. As the output power is reduced and approaches the single-photon level, rather than observing a continuous decrease in registered power as the classical wave picture predicts, the quantized nature of the individual photon energies will eventually manifest as a discrete sequence of clicks, corresponding to the detection of single photons. More experimental details of the setup can be found in Ref. [13].

The assembled Grover–Michelson system exhibited curve tunability with high visibility. One example of this, measured from the reflection signal, is overlaid with the measured response of a reference Michelson interferometer. This comparison is shown in Figure 17. The phase response for the same input phase was notably improved, as loosely depicted by the blue lines. In this case, where $\Delta\phi_1 \approx 145$ mrad, the corresponding intensity modulation is about 14 times larger for the Grover–Michelson interferometer than for its traditional counterpart. This might be further improved by reducing the losses. Other modifications to the system could also be considered, as in Ref. [46].

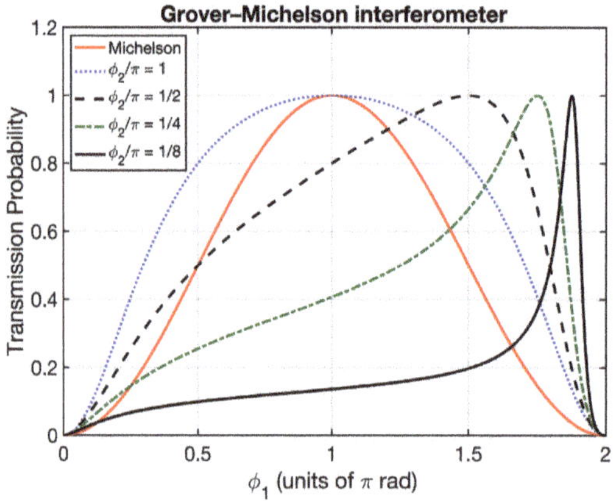

Figure 16. Transmission probability for the Grover–Michelson interferometer. The device is now a function of two parameters, so that the transmission curve generated by sweeping one parameter can be continuously deformed by changing the value of the other parameter. The response can be tuned to exhibit a substantially large slope, which heightens the phase sensitivity. Figure adopted from Ref. [32].

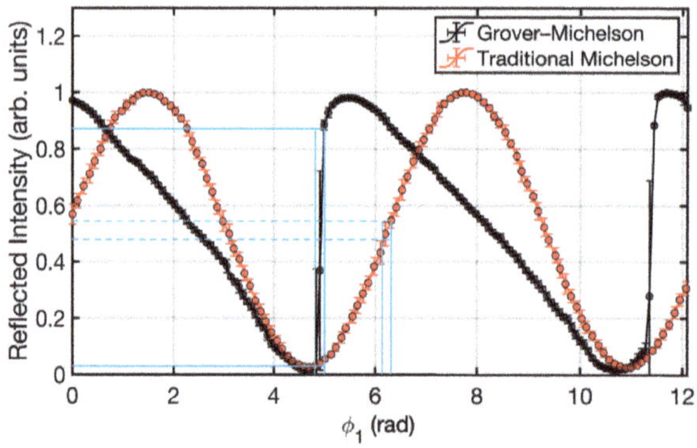

Figure 17. Measured interferogram comparison of a traditional Michelson interferometer (red) and a Grover–Michelson one (black). The blue bars loosely depict the difference in intensity modulation for the same input phase modulation of about 145 mrad. The Grover–Michelson system exhibited a roughly 14× higher intensity change, with visibility of 97%. Figure adopted from Ref. [13].

3.3.2. Grover–Sagnac Interferometer

A similar analysis has been applied to the Sagnac configuration [47]. Instead of γ_{GMI}, the phase function

$$\gamma_{\text{GSI}}(\phi, \delta) = \phi - \arctan\left(\frac{\sin\phi \sin^2\delta}{2\cos\delta - \cos\phi(1 + \cos^2\delta)}\right) \tag{53}$$

is obtained. Plots of the associated transmission are shown in Figure 18. When $\delta = 0$, $\gamma_{\text{GSI}} = \phi$. Thus, the reflection and transmission probabilities depend on the reciprocal part of the loop phase, ϕ, and can take on any output value. This is not the case in a traditional Sagnac interferometer, where the lack of non-reciprocal phase forces the transmission to be zero regardless of the reciprocal loop phase. Moreover, the resonance—or pole in the phase response—occurs around the point $\delta = 0$. This means that small values of δ create a sharp dip in the transmission of full-width 2δ. Scanning ϕ around the origin provides a direct readout for this in the interferogram. This signature is linear in δ for any δ, whereas the traditional Sagnac interferometer's transmission is given by δ^2 for small δ, placing constraints on the detector resolution. The full-modulation dip is easy to detect but requires inducing a change in phase ϕ to be significantly lower than δ in order to resolve δ with high precision.

3.3.3. Higher-Dimensional Fabry–Pérot Interferometer

The output of the Y-coupler Fabry–Pérot device pictured in Figure 15 and also can be expressed in terms of that of a regular Michelson interferometer [26]. The output is given by

$$r = -\frac{C^2}{1 - B^2}, \tag{54a}$$

$$t = B(1 - r). \tag{54b}$$

The traditional Fabry–Pérot system only has one phase parameter, which, for symmetric plates, traced a Lorentzian-like function whose sharpness was determined by the finesse F. F is a function of the plate reflectivity, which is typically a quantity fixed by material properties. In the higher-dimensional Y-coupler version, there are now two phases. The additional degree of freedom allows the tuning of the effective out-coupling between the cavity and the output ports. Thus, the effective finesse is tunable through interference. This allows the widths and heights of certain spectral regions to be controlled with considerable flexibility. A basic example is shown in Figure 19. The arms are each assumed to be $1.55 \cdot 10^{-4}$ meters with a refractive index of 1. By perturbing the index of one relative to the other, a phase difference is created between the two arms. Increasing this index perturbation completely reconfigures the filter characteristics, allowing transmission bands to be converted to reflection bands. Overall, the device acts as a tunable dichroic.

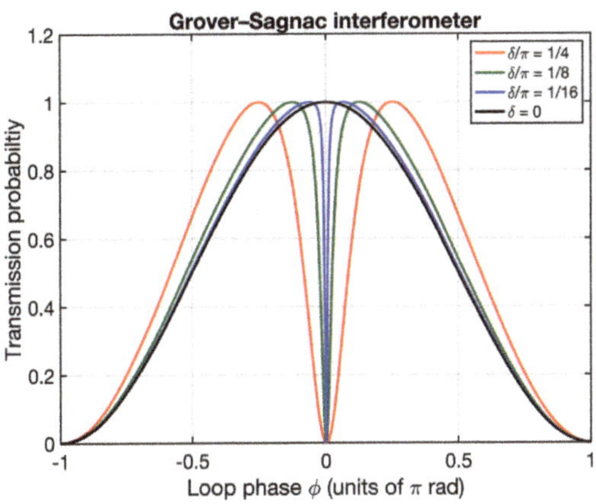

Figure 18. Transmission probability of the Grover–Sagnac interferometer. Unlike in the traditional Sagnac interferometer, the probability is a continuous function of both ϕ and δ. For $\delta = 0$, the curve is sinusoidal in ϕ but exhibits resonance whenever $\delta \neq 0$. This leads to the formation of a sharp dip about the origin $\phi = 0$. The full width of this dip is 2δ, enabling a high-contrast, direct readout of δ. Figure adopted from Ref. [47].

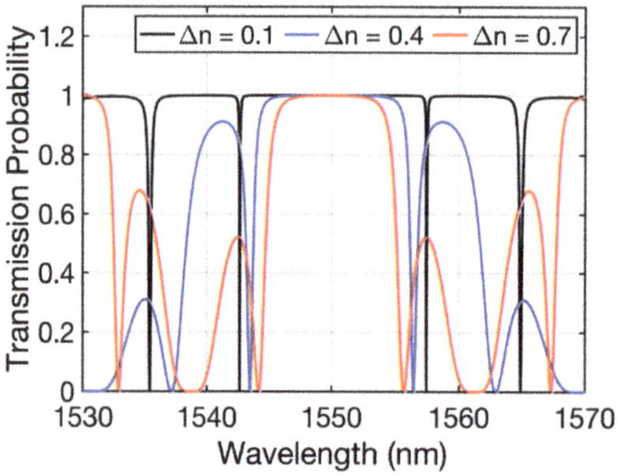

Figure 19. Example output curves for the Y-coupler Fabry–Pérot interferometer. The phase was modulated by perturbing the refractive index in one arm relative to the other. The arms were each assumed to be 155 μm long. Changing the relative phase acquired by each arm can bring certain bands from high transmission to high reflection, acting as a tunable dichroic.

3.4. *Hong–Ou–Mandel Two-Photon Interference*

Up to this point, all of the input states have been single-photon states, which only exhibit classical interference. In this section, we consider two-photon states entering separate ports of an optical scattering device, which are of the form $|\psi_{\text{in}}\rangle = a_1^\dagger a_2^\dagger|0\rangle$. The resulting two-photon interference can be measured with multiple detectors placed at the output ports that count the photons that arrive simultaneously. Perfect destructive interference of the underlying coincident amplitude leads to the famous Hong–Ou–Mandel (HOM) dip in the rate of coincidences [48,49]. This situation is shown in Figure 20a. Two identical photons impinge on separate ports of a generic unitary beam splitter of the form in Equation (32). Each individual photon sees its normal scattering action, resulting in the transformation

$$a_1^\dagger a_2^\dagger|0\rangle \to (r_1 a_3^\dagger + t_1 a_4^\dagger)(r_2 a_4^\dagger + t_2 a_3^\dagger)|0\rangle. \tag{55}$$

The coincident amplitude, which leads to the $a_3^\dagger a_4^\dagger$ term, is then $r_1 r_2 + t_1 t_2$. From the structure of the beam splitter, we recall that the amplitudes r_1, r_2, t_1 and t_2 originate from a two-dimensional unitary transformation, which can be written in the form of Equation (17), in which the coefficients are rewritten as separated magnitudes and phases. A consequence of unitarity in two dimensions is the phase constraint of Equation (21), which states that the difference between the summed phases of the r_j and the summed phases of the t_j has to be π. This is precisely the relative phase between the two terms comprising the coincident term. After dropping the irrelevant global phase, this coincident term can be rewritten as $|r_1||r_2| - |t_1||t_2|$. Accordingly, if and only if the unitary beam splitter has a 50:50 splitting ratio, the coincident term vanishes. This is the origin of the HOM effect, producing an output state $(a_3^{2\dagger} + a_4^{2\dagger})|0\rangle$. The produced state is of two *clustered* photon amplitudes. The clusters each populate a single mode. There is an equal probability of measuring a cluster in either of the two modes.

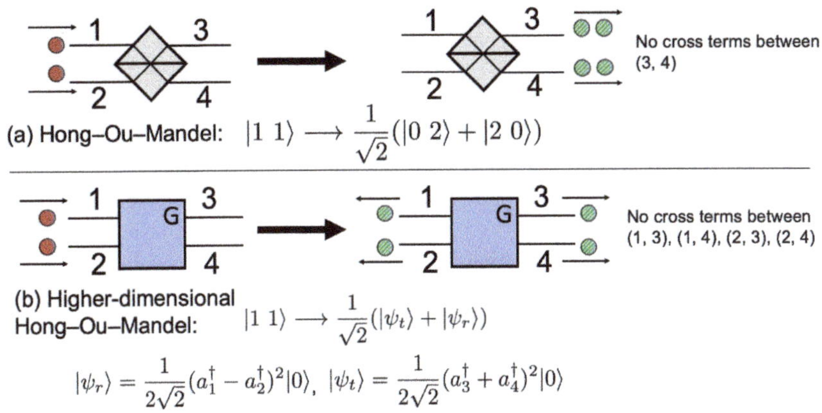

Figure 20. (**a**) The traditional Hong–Ou–Mandel effect. When a pair of identical photons enter different ports of a balanced unitary beam splitter, the coincident amplitude corresponding to one photon populating each of the two output modes destructively interferes. The output state is then composed of two clusters of two photons each. Each cluster occupies a single mode. (**b**) Higher-dimensional Hong–Ou–Mandel effect. When the two photons impinge on a Grover coin, clusters form again, with destructive interference occurring across four pairs of output modes. The resulting clusters are each distributed over two modes instead of the usual one. This increase in dimensionality enables the energy in each cluster to be routed into one of two different output modes.

A higher-dimensional generalization to this occurs when two photons impinge on two ports of a Grover coin [50]. This situation is depicted in Figure 20b. The state produced is

$$a_1^\dagger a_2^\dagger \to \frac{1}{4}(-a_1^\dagger + a_2^\dagger + a_3^\dagger + a_4^\dagger)(a_1^\dagger - a_2^\dagger + a_3^\dagger + a_4^\dagger)|0\rangle. \tag{56}$$

Another cancellation of cross-terms occurs, since $(-a_1^\dagger + a_2^\dagger + a_3^\dagger + a_4^\dagger)(a_1^\dagger - a_2^\dagger + a_3^\dagger + a_4^\dagger) = (a_1^\dagger - a_2^\dagger)^2 + (a_3^\dagger + a_4^\dagger)^2 + (a_3^\dagger + a_4^\dagger)(a_1^\dagger - a_2^\dagger) - (a_3^\dagger + a_4^\dagger)(a_1^\dagger - a_2^\dagger)$. The final state is also clustered into two components,

$$|\psi\rangle = \frac{1}{\sqrt{2}}(|\psi_r\rangle + |\psi_t\rangle). \tag{57}$$

The reflected component is $|\psi_r\rangle = (1/2\sqrt{2})(a_1^\dagger - a_2^\dagger)^2|0\rangle$ whereas the transmitted component is $|\psi_t\rangle = (1/2\sqrt{2})(a_3^\dagger + a_4^\dagger)^2|0\rangle$. These symmetric state components are two-photon eigenstates of the Grover coin: $G|\psi_t\rangle = |\psi_t\rangle$, while $G|\psi_r\rangle = -|\psi_r\rangle$.

The output state (57) encapsulates the simultaneous destructive interference of coincident amplitudes over four mode pairs: $(1,3), (1,4), (2,3)$, and $(2,4)$. These are the pairs on opposite sides of the Grover coin shown in Figure 20. The clustered components are also now distributed over two modes instead of the usual one. This readily enables the energy spread across each cluster to be concentrated into a single mode. There are two routing options for each of the two clusters, allowing the emergent two-photon amplitudes to take on the same form as the traditional Hong–Ou–Mandel effect but with four different switchable options. This effect has since been shown to enable the complete routing of entangled states in a general quantum network [50,51].

If the two photons in either Hong–Ou–Mandel configuration enter the device with a time delay between them, the delay introduces temporal distinguishability, which diminishes the perfect destructive interference [49,52]. Varying the delay allows the degree of distinguishability to be tuned, inducing a change in the coincident rate. As the delay passes through the zero point, perfect destructive interference occurs in a sharp dip, which can be used to measure small time delays or the degree of indistinguishability of the source. *Because of the fourfold cancellation of cross-terms in the higher-dimensional Hong–Ou–Mandel configuration, four simultaneous dips will occur.* The relative positions of each dip and peak will be given by the difference in phase acquired after the photons exit the Grover coin. When the phases are equal, the dips will overlap, allowing the simultaneous determination of the three relative phases. These are defined across a given port and the other three relative to this. Sensing multiple phase shifts is a general benefit of multimode interference systems. Another example will be considered in the next section.

3.5. Two-Photon Grover–Mach–Zehnder Interferometry

A double-rail generalization of the Mach–Zehnder interferometer (shown in Figure 11) can be obtained by replacing the two beam splitters with Grover coins and linking the two unconnected ports to obtain the configuration in Figure 21a. The circulators in red are used to inject two photons into the first Grover coin, G. The emergent state is of the form (57). After it emerges from G_1, the state acquires the phases ϕ_0, ϕ_1 and ϕ_2; scatters from a second Grover coin G_2; and then exits the system with another set of circulators. The state is detected across four detectors, labeled A, B, C and D. (Since the circulators are only used to separate input from output, the same configuration could be achieved without them if block feedforward Grover coins were used. This feedforward Grover matrix is equivalent to the system pictured in Figure 5 of Ref. [53]).

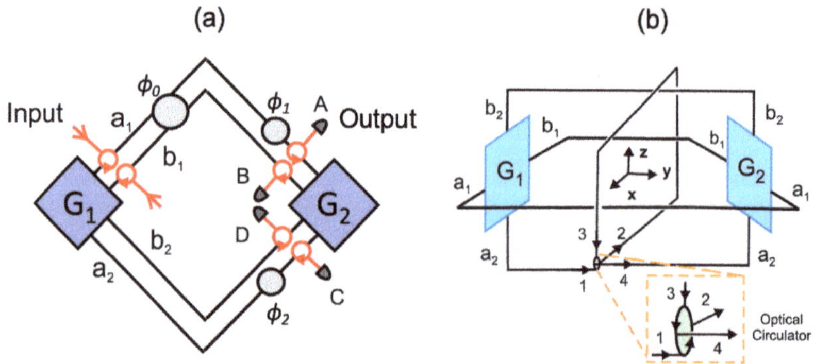

Figure 21. (**a**) Dual-rail Grover–Mach–Zehnder configuration. Two photons are injected at the input via circulators, scatter off a Grover coin G_1, and acquire the phases ϕ_0, ϕ_1, and ϕ_2 while traversing the two double-rail arms. After this, the optical state scatters off another Grover coin G_2 and then is out-coupled to detectors A, B, C, D with circulators. By recording the coincidences of each detector pair, the three phases can be determined simultaneously. (**b**) By introducing a circulator into the dual-rail arms and placing the arms in different planes, the acquired phases can made to depend on the rotation rates of the different axes, as described by Equation (61). This allows the system to simultaneously detect rotations about three axes. Figure adopted from Ref. [54].

The coincidence rates of each detector pair are readily extracted from the output state amplitudes [54]. For i, j in $\{A, B, C, D\}$, denote the coincidence rate between detectors i and j as R_{ij}. These rates can be related to the phases ϕ_0, ϕ_1, and ϕ_2:

$$\frac{R_{AC}+R_{AD}}{2R_0} = \sin^2\phi_1 + \sin^2\phi_2 \tag{58a}$$
$$\frac{R_{AD}+R_{AC}}{2R_0} = 2\sin\phi_1\sin\phi_2\cos(2\phi_0+\phi_1-\phi_2) \tag{58b}$$
$$\frac{R_{AB}+R_{CD}}{2R_0} = (1+\cos^2\phi_1)+(1+\cos^2\phi_2)+2\cos(2\phi_0+\phi_1-\phi_2)(1+\cos\phi_1\cos\phi_2) \tag{58c}$$
$$\frac{R_{AB}+R_{CD}}{2R_0} = 2(\cos\phi_1+\cos\phi_2)(1+\cos(2\phi_0+\phi_1-\phi_2)). \tag{58d}$$

This set of four independent equations allows the three phases and the constant R_0 to be obtained simultaneously. In the case of two independent phase shifts, i.e., $\phi_1 = \phi_2$, the inversion of the above equations becomes direct as, in this case,

$$\cos 2\phi_0 = \Lambda_1 \tag{59a}$$
$$\cos\phi_1 = \frac{1 \pm \sqrt{1-\Lambda_1^2}}{\Lambda_2} \tag{59b}$$

where

$$\Lambda_1 = \frac{R_{AD}-R_{AC}}{R_{AD}+R_{AC}} \tag{60a}$$
$$\Lambda_2 = \frac{R_{AB}-R_{CD}}{R_{AB}+R_{CD}}. \tag{60b}$$

The parameters ϕ_0, ϕ_1, and ϕ_2 are general phase shifts. If the system were rotated, these phases could be shifted in conjunction with the Sagnac effect. Placing the arms in different planes allows rotations about different axes to affect the different phase shift parameters. By adding a circulator to the loops, as shown in Figure 21b, a third loop can be obtained, which allows all three phases to be tied to a rotation direction. With the circulator added, the path from G_1 to G_2 exiting a_1 or b_1 comprises a half-loop about the z axis, the path leaving b_2 comprises a half-loop about the x axis, and each path leaving a_2 comprises both a full loop about y and a half-loop about x. This allows the phase shifts ϕ_0, ϕ_1, and ϕ_2 above to be expressed in terms of the phase shifts induced by rotations about the x, y, and z axes as follows:

$$\phi_0 = (\phi_x - \phi_z)/2, \tag{61a}$$
$$\phi_1 = \phi_z, \tag{61b}$$
$$\phi_2 = \phi_x + \phi_y. \tag{61c}$$

Given the measurement of ϕ_0, ϕ_1, and ϕ_2, the above equations are readily inverted to obtain the rotation phases,

$$\phi_x = 2\phi_0 + \phi_1 \tag{62a}$$
$$\phi_y = -2\phi_0 - (\phi_1 + \phi_2) \tag{62b}$$
$$\phi_z = \phi_1. \tag{62c}$$

Thus, the system offers the simultaneous determination of three rotations about different axes.

4. Discussion

In this review, we have discussed the design principles of novel gauge-invariant optical devices capable of providing a substantial boost in resolution for interferometric sensors. A general approach for identifying physically equivalent scatterers has been presented, which provides a basis on which to recognize or enforce certain symmetries in a scattering transformation. An emphasis is placed on the gauge-invariant, higher-dimensional Y-coupler and Grover coins due to their roles in interferometry. The general matrix theory for optical scattering has several other extensions and applications, such as unitary control [55–57]. Certain assumed global symmetries can also be used to bound the elements of a scattering matrix [58,59]. Although the Grover coin and Y-coupler were constructed through a beam splitter decomposition, there has yet to be a demonstration of a passive, single-element implementation of these devices in any platform. Such an implementation would be valuable to reduce the number of resources used in larger systems. A variety of beam splitters have been realized using metasurface technology, making this a potential candidate for realizing higher-dimensional unbiased multiports in the future [60–64]. Other possible approaches include integrated multimode interference (MMI) devices [65–70] and nanophotonic inverse design [71–73]. These approaches all involve reducing the scale of the optical device. This would be advantageous in situations where the coherence length of the source is no longer large enough to be approximately ignored. When the coherence length becomes finite, as in the case of a pulsed or broadband white light source, the interference of field amplitudes will no longer occur when the difference in the optical path lengths becomes greater than the coherence length. Even if the individual path components are short, devices involving multiple bounces with low loss can obtain a large path length in effect. Here, this potential problem was avoided with perfect coherence, which was provided by an assumed monochromatic source. Nevertheless, this configuration is only employed in some optical interferometric systems, so it remains to be seen how other sources with lower coherence may be employed for unbiased multiport interferometry, as well as the effects of different system scales on the output.

All systems reviewed were also assumed to be unitary. However, non-unitary systems with loss are a practical reality, stemming from artifacts such as absorption or undesired radiation out of the system under consideration. Although a non-unitary system can always be cast into a higher-dimensional unitary space to account for inaccessible "lossy modes", non-unitary systems themselves have become an increasingly popular area of research. This is because, in general, a non-unitary system is not bound to the same limits as a unitary scatterer, which enables other new effects to be observed [74–79].

Interferometers were defined as graphs of static scattering devices, producing a scatterer that is a function of tunable parameters such as the induced phase shifts. After discussing traditional interferometric systems, higher-dimensional systems built around the Grover coin and Y-coupler were presented. These scatterers utilize more field modes per scattering event, exhibiting rich interference effects that directly translated into practical improvements for interferometric phase sensors. These improvements included higher resolution, more control freedom, and the ability to measure several phases simultaneously. Naturally, systems employing coupled resonances, such as the Grover–Michelson interferometer, will tend to exhibit a smaller range where the slope is increased. This local narrowing of the response range requires an active phase controller to bias the system at the sensitive point. Other applications that may benefit from the increased sensitivity exhibited in these systems include optical switches and modulators, phase contrast microscopes, and optical filters.

The enhancements resulted directly from the replacement of a lower-dimensional scattering device with a higher-dimensional one in the same graphical configuration. It remains to be seen which effects other configurations and inputted optical states may produce in these symmetric interferometers.

Author Contributions: Conceptualization, C.R.S., A.D.M., D.S.S., A.N. and A.V.S.; writing—original draft preparation, C.R.S.; writing—review and editing, C.R.S., A.D.M., D.S.S., A.N. and A.V.S.; supervision, A.V.S.; funding acquisition, A.V.S. All authors have read and agreed to the published version of the manuscript.

Funding: This research was funded by the Air Force Office of Scientific Research MURI award number FA9550-22-1-0312.

Data Availability Statement: No new data were created or analyzed in this study.

Conflicts of Interest: The authors declare no conflicts of interest.

References

1. Fearn, H.; Loudon, R. Quantum theory of the lossless beam splitter. *Opt. Commun.* **1987**, *64*, 485–490. [CrossRef]
2. Campos, R.A.; Saleh, B.E.A.; Teich, M.C. Quantum-mechanical lossless beam splitter: SU(2) symmetry and photon statistics. *Phys. Rev. A* **1989**, *40*, 1371–1384. [CrossRef] [PubMed]
3. Rubano, A.; Cardano, F.; Piccirillo, B.; Marrucci, L. Q-plate technology: A progress review [Invited]. *J. Opt. Soc. Am. B* **2019**, *36*, D70–D87. [CrossRef]
4. Lim, A.E.J.; Song, J.; Fang, Q.; Li, C.; Tu, X.; Duan, N.; Chen, K.K.; Tern, R.P.C.; Liow, T.Y. Review of Silicon Photonics Foundry Efforts. *IEEE J. Sel. Top. Quantum Electron.* **2014**, *20*, 405–416. [CrossRef]
5. Smith, J.A.; Francis, H.; Navickaite, G.; Strain, M.J. SiN foundry platform for high performance visible light integrated photonics. *Opt. Mater. Express* **2023**, *13*, 458–468. [CrossRef]
6. Simon, D.S.; Fitzpatrick, C.A.; Sergienko, A.V. Group transformations and entangled-state quantum gates with directionally unbiased linear-optical multiports. *Phys. Rev. A* **2016**, *93*, 043845. [CrossRef]
7. Weihs, G.; Reck, M.; Weinfurter, H.; Zeilinger, A. All-fiber three-path Mach–Zehnder interferometer. *Opt. Lett.* **1996**, *21*, 302–304. [CrossRef]
8. Saleh, A.; Kogelnik, H. Reflective single-mode fiber-optic passive star couplers. *J. Light. Technol.* **1988**, *6*, 392–398. [CrossRef]
9. Metcalf, B.J.; Thomas-Peter, N.; Spring, J.B.; Kundys, D.; Broome, M.A.; Humphreys, P.C.; Jin, X.M.; Barbieri, M.; Steven Kolthammer, W.; Gates, J.C.; et al. Multiphoton quantum interference in a multiport integrated photonic device. *Nat. Commun.* **2013**, *4*, 1356. [CrossRef] [PubMed]
10. Spagnolo, N.; Vitelli, C.; Aparo, L.; Mataloni, P.; Sciarrino, F.; Crespi, A.; Ramponi, R.; Osellame, R. Three-photon bosonic coalescence in an integrated tritter. *Nat. Commun.* **2013**, *4*, 1606. [CrossRef]
11. Osawa, S.; Simon, D.S.; Sergienko, A.V. Experimental demonstration of a directionally-unbiased linear-optical multiport. *Opt. Express* **2018**, *26*, 27201–27211. [CrossRef]
12. Kim, I.; Lee, D.; Hong, S.; Cho, Y.W.; Lee, K.J.; Kim, Y.S.; Lim, H.T. Implementation of a 3 x 3 directionally-unbiased linear optical multiport. *Opt. Express* **2021**, *29*, 29527–29540. [CrossRef]
13. Schwarze, C.R.; Simon, D.S.; Manni, A.D.; Ndao, A.; Sergienko, A.V. Experimental demonstration of a Grover-Michelson interferometer. *Opt. Express* **2024**, *32*, 34116–34127. [CrossRef]
14. Grover, L.K. Quantum Mechanics Helps in Searching for a Needle in a Haystack. *Phys. Rev. Lett.* **1997**, *79*, 325–328. [CrossRef]
15. Gerrard, A.; Burch, J. *Introduction to Matrix Methods in Optics*; Dover Books on Physics: Dover, UK, 1994.
16. Kim, H.; Park, J.; Lee, B. *Fourier Modal Method and Its Applications in Computational Nanophotonics*; Taylor & Francis: Abingdon, UK, 2012.
17. Barnett, S.M. On single-photon and classical interference. *Phys. Scr.* **2022**, *97*, 114004. [CrossRef]
18. Guo, C.; Zhao, Z.; Fan, S. Internal transformations and internal symmetries in linear photonic systems. *Phys. Rev. A* **2022**, *105*, 023509. [CrossRef]
19. Deák, L.; Fülöp, T. Reciprocity in quantum, electromagnetic and other wave scattering. *Ann. Phys.* **2012**, *327*, 1050–1077. [CrossRef]
20. Post, E.J. Sagnac Effect. *Rev. Mod. Phys.* **1967**, *39*, 475–493. [CrossRef]

21. Törmä, P.; Stenholm, S.; Jex, I. Hamiltonian theory of symmetric optical network transforms. *Phys. Rev. A* **1995**, *52*, 4853–4860. [CrossRef] [PubMed]
22. Pinter, C. *A Book of Abstract Algebra*; International series in pure and applied mathematics; McGraw-Hill: Columbus, OH, USA, 1990.
23. Reck, M.; Zeilinger, A.; Bernstein, H.J.; Bertani, P. Experimental realization of any discrete unitary operator. *Phys. Rev. Lett.* **1994**, *73*, 58–61. [CrossRef] [PubMed]
24. Clements, W.R.; Humphreys, P.C.; Metcalf, B.J.; Kolthammer, W.S.; Walmsley, I.A. Optimal design for universal multiport interferometers. *Optica* **2016**, *3*, 1460–1465. [CrossRef]
25. Suzuki, K.; Sharma, V.; Fujimoto, J.G.; Ippen, E.P.; Nasu, Y. Characterization of symmetric 3 x 3 directional couplers fabricated by direct writing with a femtosecond laser oscillator. *Opt. Express* **2006**, *14*, 2335–2343. [CrossRef]
26. Schwarze, C.R.; Manni, A.D.; Simon, D.S.; Sergienko, A.V. Single-photon description of the lossless optical Y coupler. *Phys. Rev. A* **2024**, *110*, 023527. [CrossRef]
27. Kumar, S.P.; Dhand, I. Unitary matrix decompositions for optimal and modular linear optics architectures. *J. Phys. Math. Theor.* **2021**, *54*, 045301. [CrossRef]
28. Yasir, P.A.A.; van Loock, P. Compactifying linear optical unitaries using multiport beamsplitters. *arXiv* **2025**, arXiv:2505.11371. [CrossRef]
29. Taballione, C.; Anguita, M.C.; de Goede, M.; Venderbosch, P.; Kassenberg, B.; Snijders, H.; Kannan, N.; Vleeshouwers, W.L.; Smith, D.; Epping, J.P.; et al. 20-Mode Universal Quantum Photonic Processor. *Quantum* **2023**, *7*, 1071. [CrossRef]
30. Maring, N.; Fyrillas, A.; Pont, M.; Ivanov, E.; Stepanov, P.; Margaria, N.; Hease, W.; Pishchagin, A.; Lemaître, A.; Sagnes, I.; et al. A versatile single-photon-based quantum computing platform. *Nat. Photonics* **2024**, *18*, 603–609. [CrossRef]
31. Kempe, J. Quantum random walks: An introductory overview. *Contemp. Phys.* **2003**, *44*, 307–327. [CrossRef]
32. Schwarze, C.R.; Simon, D.S.; Sergienko, A.V. Enhanced-sensitivity interferometry with phase-sensitive unbiased multiports. *Phys. Rev. A* **2023**, *107*, 052615. [CrossRef]
33. Mizutani, Y.; Horikiri, T.; Matsuoka, L.; Higuchi, Y.; Segawa, E. Implementation of a discrete-time quantum walk with a circulant matrix on a graph by optical polarizing elements. *Phys. Rev. A* **2022**, *106*, 022402. [CrossRef]
34. Childs, A.M. Universal Computation by Quantum Walk. *Phys. Rev. Lett.* **2009**, *102*, 180501. [CrossRef] [PubMed]
35. Lovett, N.B.; Cooper, S.; Everitt, M.; Trevers, M.; Kendon, V. Universal quantum computation using the discrete-time quantum walk. *Phys. Rev.* **2010**, *81*, 042330. [CrossRef]
36. Childs, A.M.; Goldstone, J. Spatial search by quantum walk. *Phys. Rev. A* **2004**, *70*, 022314. [CrossRef]
37. Apers, S.; Chakraborty, S.; Novo, L.; Roland, J. Quadratic Speedup for Spatial Search by Continuous-Time Quantum Walk. *Phys. Rev. Lett.* **2022**, *129*, 160502. [CrossRef]
38. Kendon, V.; Maloyer, O. Optimal computation with non-unitary quantum walks. *Theor. Comput. Sci.* **2008**, *394*, 187–196. [CrossRef]
39. Schwarze, C.R.; Simon, D.S.; Manni, A.D.; Ndao, A.; Sergienko, A.V. Finite-element assembly approach of optical quantum walk networks. *J. Opt. Soc. Am. B* **2024**, *41*, 1304–1316. [CrossRef]
40. Redheffer, R. On the Relation of Transmission-Line Theory to Scattering and Transfer. *J. Math. Phys.* **1962**, *41*, 1–41. [CrossRef]
41. Michelson, A.A.; Gale, H.G. The Effect of the Earth's Rotation on the Velocity of Light. *Nature* **1925**, *115*, 566–566. [CrossRef]
42. Chow, W.W.; Gea-Banacloche, J.; Pedrotti, L.M.; Sanders, V.E.; Schleich, W.; Scully, M.O. The ring laser gyro. *Rev. Mod. Phys.* **1985**, *57*, 61–104. [CrossRef]
43. Ashtekar, A.; Magnon, A. The Sagnac effect in general relativity. *J. Math. Phys.* **1975**, *16*, 341–344. [CrossRef]
44. Wang, R.; Zheng, Y.; Yao, A. Generalized Sagnac Effect. *Phys. Rev. Lett.* **2004**, *93*, 143901. [CrossRef]
45. Shanavas, T.; Krueper, G.; Zhu, J.; Park, W.; Gopinath, J.T. Nonlinear Symmetry Breaking to Enhance the Sagnac Effect in a Microresonator Gyroscope. *arXiv* **2025**, arXiv:2508.09132. [CrossRef]
46. Wei, C.P.; Xu, C.G.; Liu, Q. Phase sensitivity of a modified Grover-Michelson interferometer. *Opt. Contin.* **2025**, *4*, 1266–1278. [CrossRef]
47. Schwarze, C.R.; Manni, A.D.; Simon, D.S.; Ndao, A.; Sergienko, A.V. Grover-Sagnac interferometer. *J. Opt. Soc. Am. A* **2025**, *42*, 290–297. [CrossRef] [PubMed]
48. Hong, C.K.; Ou, Z.Y.; Mandel, L. Measurement of subpicosecond time intervals between two photons by interference. *Phys. Rev. Lett.* **1987**, *59*, 2044–2046. [CrossRef] [PubMed]
49. Drago, C.; Brańczyk, A.M. Hong–Ou–Mandel interference: A spectral–temporal analysis. *Can. J. Phys.* **2024**, *102*, 411–421. [CrossRef]
50. Osawa, S.; Simon, D.S.; Sergienko, A.V. Higher-dimensional Hong-Ou-Mandel effect and state redistribution with linear-optical multiports. *Phys. Rev. A* **2020**, *102*, 063712. [CrossRef]

51. Osawa, S.; Simon, D.S.; Malinovsky, V.S.; Sergienko, A.V. Controllable entangled-state distribution in a dual-rail reconfigurable optical network. *Phys. Rev. A* **2021**, *104*, 012617. [CrossRef]
52. Meany, T.; Delanty, M.; Gross, S.; Marshall, G.D.; Steel, M.J.; Withford, M.J. Non-classical interference in integrated 3D multiports. *Opt. Express* **2012**, *20*, 26895–26905. [CrossRef]
53. Tabia, G.N.M. Recursive multiport schemes for implementing quantum algorithms with photonic integrated circuits. *Phys. Rev. A* **2016**, *93*, 012323. [CrossRef]
54. Simon, D.S.; Schwarze, C.R.; Sergienko, A.V. Interferometry and higher-dimensional phase measurements using directionally unbiased linear optics. *Phys. Rev. A* **2022**, *106*, 033706. [CrossRef]
55. Guo, C.; Miller, D.A.B.; Fan, S. Unitary control of multiport wave transmission. *Phys. Rev. A* **2025**, *111*, 023507. [CrossRef]
56. Guo, C.; Fan, S. Unitary control of partially coherent waves. I. Absorption. *Phys. Rev. B* **2024**, *110*, 035430. [CrossRef]
57. Guo, C.; Fan, S. Unitary control of partially coherent waves. II. Transmission or reflection. *Phys. Rev. B* **2024**, *110*, 035431. [CrossRef]
58. Ma, W.; Pestourie, R.; Johnson, S.G. Time-reversal-symmetry bounds on electromagnetic fields. *Phys. Rev. A* **2025**, *111*, 063518. [CrossRef]
59. Guo, C.; Fan, S. Reciprocity Constraints on Reflection. *Phys. Rev. Lett.* **2022**, *128*, 256101. [CrossRef] [PubMed]
60. Wu, Y.; Chen, J.; Wang, Y.; Yuan, Z.; Huang, C.; Sun, J.; Feng, C.; Li, M.; Qiu, K.; Zhu, S.; et al. Tbps wide-field parallel optical wireless communications based on a metasurface beam splitter. *Nat. Commun.* **2024**, *15*, 7744. [CrossRef] [PubMed]
61. Hemayat, S.; Hsu, L.; Ha, J.; Ndao, A. Near-unity uniformity and efficiency broadband meta-beam-splitter/combiner. *Opt. Express* **2023**, *31*, 3984–3997. [CrossRef]
62. Shen, Z.; Huang, D. A Review on Metasurface Beam Splitters. *Nanomanufacturing* **2022**, *2*, 194–228. [CrossRef]
63. Pei, X.Z.; Bao, L.; Wang, Q.H.; Wu, B.; Fu, P.; Zhou, H.J.; Deng, J.; Ni, P.N.; Kan, Q.; Chen, P.P.; et al. On-chip Integration of Metasurface-Based Beam Splitter with Variable Split Ratio. *Laser Photonics Rev.* **2025**, *19*, 2500140. [CrossRef]
64. Park, J.; Yang, Y.; Park, Y.; Kang, H.; Shin, J.; Keawmuang, H.; Kim, W.S.; Badloe, T.; Kim, Y.K.; Rho, J. Electrically Tunable Metasurfaces for Broadband Beam Splitting Across the Visible Spectrum. *Adv. Opt. Mater.* **2025**, *13*, 2403413. [CrossRef]
65. Soldano, L.; Pennings, E. Optical multi-mode interference devices based on self-imaging: Principles and applications. *J. Light. Technol.* **1995**, *13*, 615–627. [CrossRef]
66. Heaton, J.; Jenkins, R. General matrix theory of self-imaging in multimode interference (MMI) couplers. *IEEE Photonics Technol. Lett.* **1999**, *11*, 212–214. [CrossRef]
67. Pennings, E.; van Roijen, R.; van Stralen, M.; de Waard, P.; Koumans, R.; Verbeck, B. Reflection properties of multimode interference devices. *IEEE Photonics Technol. Lett.* **1994**, *6*, 715–718. [CrossRef]
68. Maese-Novo, A.; Halir, R.; Romero-García, S.; Pérez-Galacho, D.; Zavargo-Peche, L.; Ortega-Moñux, A.; Molina-Fernández, I.; Wangüemert-Pérez, J.G.; Cheben, P. Wavelength independent multimode interference coupler. *Opt. Express* **2013**, *21*, 7033–7040. [CrossRef]
69. Bachmann, M.; Besse, P.A.; Melchior, H. General self-imaging properties in N × N multimode interference couplers including phase relations. *Appl. Opt.* **1994**, *33*, 3905–3911. [CrossRef] [PubMed]
70. Cooney, K.; Peters, F.H. Analysis of multimode interferometers. *Opt. Express* **2016**, *24*, 22481–22515. [CrossRef] [PubMed]
71. Molesky, S.; Lin, Z.; Piggott, A.Y.; Jin, W.; Vucković, J.; Rodriguez, A.W. Inverse design in nanophotonics. *Nat. Photonics* **2018**, *12*, 659–670. [CrossRef]
72. Kang, C.; Park, C.; Lee, M.; Kang, J.; Jang, M.S.; Chung, H. Large-scale photonic inverse design: Computational challenges and breakthroughs. *Nanophotonics* **2024**, *13*, 3765–3792. [CrossRef]
73. Huang, S.Y.; Kumar, S.; Huster, J.; Augenstein, Y.; Rockstuhl, C.; Barz, S. Multiphoton Quantum Interference at Ultracompact Inverse-Designed Multiport Beam Splitter. *arXiv* **2025**, arXiv:2504.00114. [CrossRef]
74. De Carlo, M.; De Leonardis, F.; Soref, R.A.; Colatorti, L.; Passaro, V.M.N. Non-Hermitian Sensing in Photonics and Electronics: A Review. *Sensors* **2022**, *22*, 3977. [CrossRef]
75. Zhu, X.; Wang, H.; Gupta, S.K.; Zhang, H.; Xie, B.; Lu, M.; Chen, Y. Photonic non-Hermitian skin effect and non-Bloch bulk-boundary correspondence. *Phys. Rev. Res.* **2020**, *2*, 013280. [CrossRef]
76. Yan, Q.; Zhao, B.; Zhou, R.; Ma, R.; Lyu, Q.; Chu, S.; Hu, X.; Gong, Q. Advances and applications on non-Hermitian topological photonics. *Nanophotonics* **2023**, *12*, 2247–2271. [CrossRef]
77. Parto, M.; Liu, Y.G.N.; Bahari, B.; Khajavikhan, M.; Christodoulides, D.N. Non-Hermitian and topological photonics: Optics at an exceptional point. *Nanophotonics* **2021**, *10*, 403–423. [CrossRef]
78. Longhi, S.; Gatti, D.; Valle, G.D. Robust light transport in non-Hermitian photonic lattices. *Sci. Rep.* **2015**, *5*, 13376. [CrossRef] [PubMed]

79. Li, A.; Wei, H.; Cotrufo, M.; Chen, W.; Mann, S.; Ni, X.; Xu, B.; Chen, J.; Wang, J.; Fan, S.; et al. Exceptional points and non-Hermitian photonics at the nanoscale. *Nat. Nanotechnol.* **2023**, *18*, 706–720. [CrossRef] [PubMed]

metrology

Article

Investigation of the Measurement Systems' Suitability for the Non-Destructive Measurement of Complex Polymer-Based Micro and Nanostructures

Selina Burkert [1,*], Lukas Schwörer [1], Tim Schubert [2], Jana Grundmann [3], David Stein [4] and Andreas Heinrich [1]

[1] Aalen School of Applied Photonics, Aalen University of Applied Science, 73430 Aalen, Germany; lukas.schwoerer@hs-aalen.de (L.S.); andreas.heinrich@hs-aalen.de (A.H.)
[2] Institute for Materials Research, Aalen University of Applied Science, 73430 Aalen, Germany; tim.schubert@hs-aalen.de
[3] Physikalisch-Technische Bundesanstalt, 38116 Braunschweig, Germany; jana.grundmann@ptb.de
[4] Institute of Physics, University of Augsburg, 86150 Augsburg, Germany; david.stein@uni-a.de
* Correspondence: selina.burkert@hs-aalen.de

Abstract: In the fabrication of optical polymer-based components, such as diffractive gratings and waveguides, high throughput and high precision are required. The non-destructive evaluation of these complex polymer-based structures is a significant challenge. Different measurement techniques can measure the structure geometry directly or via its functionality indirectly. This study investigates various measurement techniques aimed at assessing these structures from 200 nm up to 20 µm. Environmental scanning electron microscopy (ESEM), white light interferometry (WLI), atomic force microscopy (AFM), micro computed tomography (µCT), optical coherence tomography (OCT), phase contrast microscopy (PCM), and Mueller matrix ellipsometry (MME) are investigated for their practical limits of lateral resolution and aspect ratio. The impact of the specimens' complexity factors, including structure width and aspect ratio, on measurement quality is discussed. A particular focus of this study is on the suitability of different measurement systems for evaluating undercuts and enclosed structures while considering structure size, slant angle, and cover thickness. The aim is to discuss the specific advantages of the individual measurement systems and their application areas in order to be able to quickly select suitable measurement systems for a non-destructive evaluation of polymer-based micro and nanostructures.

Keywords: measurement analysis; scanning electron microscopy; white light interferometry; atomic force microscopy; micro computed tomography; optical coherence tomography; phase contrast microscopy; Mueller matrix ellipsometry; polymer structures; nanostructures

1. Introduction

In micro and nanofabrication, polymer-based structures are used to maximize the functionalization of the smallest possible devices [1]. In optics, for example, diffractive gratings are used for light coupling and decoupling, as well as structures for light guiding (waveguides) [2–4] or intended phase shifting (holograms) [5,6]. Typical structure sizes here are in the sub-wavelength range from 200 nm to a single-digit micrometer range. The complexity of these structures increases when the gratings are slanted and overhangs are generated [7]. The quality of diffractive and refractive elements directly influences light transmission and imaging efficiency [8–10]. There are other applications that are based on polymer structures that are larger than those of a single-digit micrometer range, such as biofluidic devices. For example, small channels and filter elements are manufactured for lab-on-chip devices and rapid diagnostics [11,12]. The size of the structure varies from rather small channels with a width of 3 µm [13] to 8 µm [14] up to larger channels of 200 µm [15]. Therefore, precise manufacturing of the chips is a prerequisite for precise diagnostics [16,17].

As already outlined, the precision of micro and nanofabrication is very important with respect to the given examples of optical and biofluidic systems. In order to be able to assess the fabrication processes, measurements and evaluation of the functionalized structures are required. Measurements can be made directly through optical [18] or tactile [19] measurement of the geometry or indirectly through the structure function. The more complex the structures are, the more difficult it is to make a reliable assessment.

A complexity factor is the geometry of the structure. As structures become smaller, microscopic imaging becomes increasingly difficult [20]. Especially if the measuring systems are limited by diffraction, the structures of diffractive gratings are sometimes smaller than the resolution limit of a microscope objective [21]. Another complexity factor is the ratio of structure height and width, the so-called aspect ratio. The greater the aspect ratio, the more difficult it is to detect the interior of the structure, both optically and in a tactile way. A high numerical aperture is required for optical detection [22] and the smallest possible tip for tactile detection [23]. The complexity factor is also increased as soon as structures with overhangs or enclosed structures within a polymer solid are to be measured and evaluated. For this purpose, the measurement system must be able to penetrate the polymer solid [24] and to visualize the undercuts and cavities or derive information about the geometric quality via the optical function of the structures [8,25]. In summary, complex polymer structures are those that are very small (<1 μm), have a large aspect ratio (>1), have overhangs, or are enclosed.

Different measurement techniques have their strengths and weaknesses that can be utilized in the evaluation of complex polymer structures without damaging the structure during measurement. In this study, we investigate different measurement techniques such as environmental scanning electron microscope (ESEM), white light interferometer (WLI), atomic force microscope (AFM), micro computed tomography (μCT), optical coherence tomography (OCT), phase contrast microscope (PCM), and Mueller matrix ellipsometer (MME). First, the limits of lateral resolution and maximum aspect ratio are examined using pillar structures. These pillar structures were written into a commercial acrylate-based resin using two-photon polymerization (2PP) [26]. It will be discussed for which measurement systems the complexity factors, structure width from 200 nm up to 20 μm and aspect ratio 0.1 up to 2.86, have a definable influence on the measurement quality. Furthermore, it will be investigated which measurement systems are suitable for the measurement of undercuts and enclosed structures and where the limits are by taking the structure size and the covering layer height into account. The specific advantages of the individual measuring systems and their application areas are discussed in order to be able to quickly select a suitable measurement system for a given polymer structure.

2. Measurement Systems and Methods

A WLI, AFM, OCT, ESEM, μCT, PCM, and MME were used to investigate polymer-based micro and nanostructures. The applied systems and the respective main settings are summarized in Table 1. For a better understanding, the measurement principle of the used systems and, if necessary, the post-processing method for data acquisition are described below.

Table 1. Used measurement systems and their main settings in the investigation using polymer-based structures.

System	Name	Manufacturer	Dimensions	Main Settings
WLI	NewView8300	Zygo, Weiterstadt, Germany	3d	50×, NA 0.5, 1024 × 1024 px
AFM	EDU-AFM1/M	Thorlabs, New Jersey, Vereinigte Staaten	3d	250 × 250 px, 200 px/s, different magnifications
OCT	Spectral domain OCT according to VDI/VDE 5565	non-commercial	3d	50×, NA 0.8, FOV 0.1 (factor)

Table 1. *Cont.*

System	Name	Manufacturer	Dimensions	Main Settings
ESEM	Prisma ESEM	Thermo Fisher Scientific, Massachusetts, Vereinigte Staaten	2d	LDV, 5 kV, 50 Pa, different magnifications
µCT	Xradia Versa 610	Zeiss, Oberkochen, Germany	3d	40×, 80 kV, 10 W, different magnifications
PCM	BZ-X800	Keyence, Ōsaka, Japan	2d	40×, 960 × 720 px
MME	Imaging Mueller matrix ellipsometry, Accurion EP4	Park Systems, Suwon, Korea	2d	50×, incidence angle 40°, 500 nm

2.1. White Light Interferometer

The used WLI is based on the measuring principle of a Mirau interferometer with a broadband light source (spectral width 120 nm) and a 50× Mirau objective. During the WLI measurement, the Mirau objective is moved by a piezo actuator along the optical axis. The interference signal is processed in a frequency domain analysis (FDA [27,28]) and a three-dimensional profile is reconstructed as shown in Figure 3a. WLI measurements are particularly suitable for flat structures in the sub-micrometer range [18].

2.2. Atomic Force Microscope

In an AFM measurement, a measuring tip scans the sample. The individual AFM techniques differ in how the sample is scanned by the tip and which measurement variables are gained. Using frequency-modulated AFMs, the tip oscillates and the oscillation amplitude or the phase shift of the tip oscillation is acquired with or without contact to the sample [29–32]. In the case of scanning tunneling AFM, an additional reference voltage is applied between the tip and the sample and the tunnel current is measured to reconstruct the height [29,33]. Using the constant force measurement mode, the mechanical deflection of the tip (ContAl-G-10, BudgetSensors, Sofia, Bulgaria, tip radius approx. 10 nm) on the sample's surface is detected by a laser triangulation and compensated by a piezo actuator. The voltage of the piezo actuator, that is needed to compensate for the tip deflection in order to keep the force constant, is recorded [32,34]. The recorded voltage values of the piezo actors are reconstructed to a metric height profile as shown in Figure 3b using a calibration factor. An AFM can be used to resolve structure sizes below the microscopic diffraction limit [19,35].

2.3. Optical Coherence Tomograph

The used spectral domain OCT is based on a broadband point light source, which is directed onto the measurement object and a reference mirror via a beam splitter. The reflection from the mirror and the measurement object is guided back into a spectrometer via the same beam splitter. In the spectral domain analysis, the metric distances of the reflection layers at a certain point of the sample are reconstructed [36]. The sample is scanned laterally with a scanning unit, and a three-dimensional data stack of the reflection layers is generated. Figure 3c shows the recorded surface of the sample based on the summed stack of all vertically recorded reflection intensities. The height data need to be calibrated for an absolute measurement. OCT is particularly suitable for material examinations, as it can detect material layers [24] or defects [37] below the polymer surface based on refraction differences.

2.4. Environmental Scanning Electron Microscope

In the ESEM measurement, the sample is scanned by an electron beam. Atoms in the sample react by emitting secondary electrons (SE), among other things. The SE are captured by a SE-detector. Non-conductive materials, such as polymers, charge up particularly quickly with the primary electrons. To avoid charging defects during an

ESEM measurement, the chamber vacuum is set as low as possible (e.g., 50 Pa) or water is actively introduced into the vacuum chamber to discharge the sample surface. Using the ESEM, structures below the usual light microscopic resolution can be captured in two dimensions [38,39]. Cross-sections of the structures are often recorded to image undercuts [7,40]. An exemplary ESEM measurement is shown in Figure 3d. The gray values represent the detected SE at the respective position in the scan field and no information about the structure height can be gained. Since the structure edges have a significantly higher SE dose as illustrated in Figure 1a and in the respective top view (b), the position of the edges can be used to determine the structure width by binarizing the ESEM image as shown (c). The edges are detected (1) or the entire structure of the pillar is detected (2).

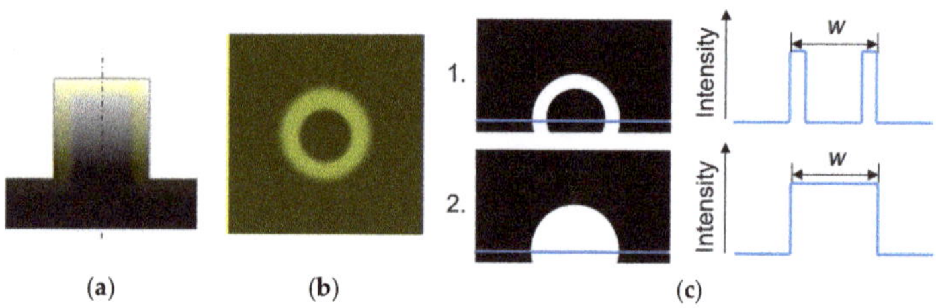

Figure 1. The shot with primary electrons causes secondary electrons to be emitted at the sample surface (**a**). During the scan of the sample surface, the dose of emitted secondary electrons is significantly higher at the structure edges than at the surface areas (**b**). In order to determine the width of the structure, the ESEM images are binarized to identify the edges of the structure. The width of the structure w is equal to the distance between the outer edges (1) or to the diameter of the circular surface (2) (**c**).

2.5. Mirco Computed Thomograph

In a conventional µCT measurement, the object is rotated in an X-ray beam, and the transmitted X-rays are captured by a detector. The single detector images at different rotation angles are combined to form a three-dimensional data stack. For a better resolution down to the sub-micrometer range, magnification lenses are placed in front of the detector of the utilized µCT as standard [41]. Figure 3e shows an image from the top view. Similarly to OCT, µCT is also suitable for sub-surface material analysis of polymers as demonstrated in [42,43].

2.6. Phase Contrast Microscope

The PCM is based on a conventional bright-field microscope. In addition, it has a phase ring for phase shifting by a quarter wavelength ($\lambda/4$) and a ring aperture between the light source and condenser lens. This allows phase shifts to be visualized as intensity differences, as shown in Figure 3f, for example. Thus, the phase shift $\Delta\varphi$ is caused by a change in the propagation time through the sample as visualized in Figure 2a. If the focus is well set, the structure can be well identified in the top view (b). Similarly, to the ESEM images, the PCM images are binarized to detect the edges and calculate the diameters of the structures (c). The visualization of phase shifts can be used in the material analysis of polymers and blends, as demonstrated in [44,45].

2.7. Imaging Mueller Matrix Ellipsometer

The imaging MME system combines conventional ellipsometry and bright-field microscopy. The main measurement parameter is the Mueller matrix M. The 4×4 Mueller matrix describes the change of an electromagnetic wave after interaction with a sample based on the change in the initial Stokes parameters S_i and final Stokes parameters S_f, as can be described by [46]:

$$S_f = M\, S_i \tag{1}$$

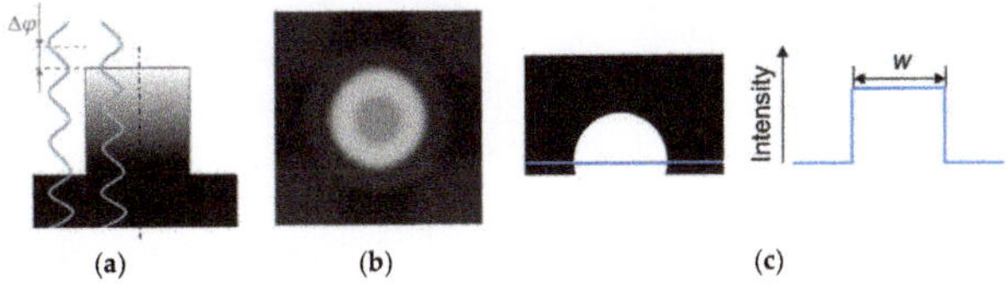

Figure 2. The phase difference in the propagation through the sample $\Delta\varphi$ (**a**) is visible in the intensity image of the top view (**b**). After binarization, the structure width w is equal to the diameter of the white circle (**c**).

Instead of averaging the sample's polarization behavior at the entire illumination spot of the ellipsometer, the Mueller matrix values are calculated for each pixel of the camera image using the imaging MME. Due to the calculation of the local polarization behavior, non-periodic structures and structures that are smaller than the illumination spot can be evaluated [47]. Figure 3f shows the sample's microscope image and the respective normalized value M_{32} of the 4×4 Mueller matrix for example. A change in geometry can be detected indirectly by a shift in the local polarization behavior of the structure. Comparable indirect measurement techniques for polymer nanostructures are scatterometry [10] or diffraction tests [35].

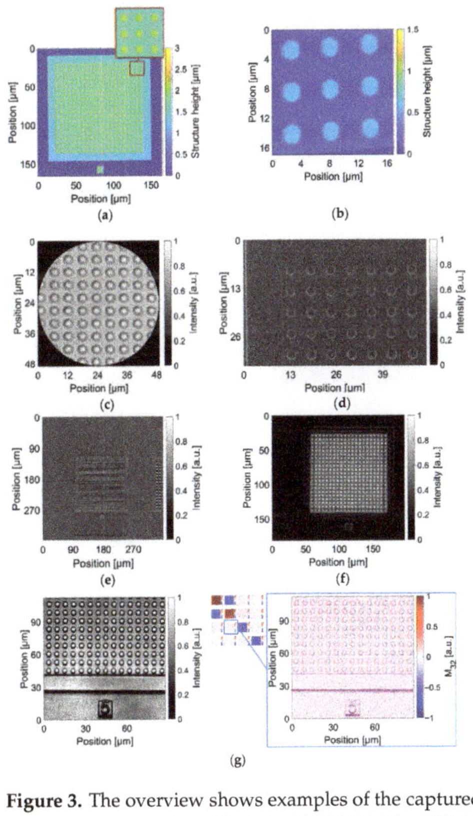

Figure 3. The overview shows examples of the captured images of the investigated measurement systems WLI (**a**), AFM (**b**), OCT (**c**), ESEM (**d**), μCT (**e**), PCM (**f**), and MME (**g**). The respective measurement characteristics such as measurement outputs and the field of view are compared using selected pillars. All images show pillars with a width of 2.8 μm and a height of 0.5 μm. The scaling of the height was adapted to the individual measurement in order to clearly display the measurement characteristics.

3. Polymer-Based Test Patterns

3.1. Pillar Arrays

In the investigation of the practical limits of the lateral resolution and the aspect ratio, a pillar test pattern is used, as shown in Figure 4. A pillar as given in (a) has a diameter of width w and a height h that ranges from the base to the top of the pillar. The base width corresponds to twice the pillar width $2w$ and the base height b is 1.5 μm for all pillar arrays. The pillars are rotationally symmetric as shown in (b). A pillar array consists of integer multiples of a pillar from (b) within a field of 120 μm, as illustrated in (c). To check the directional dependence of the measurement systems, a distinction is made between horizontal slices in the x-direction (blue) and vertical slices in the y-direction (orange).

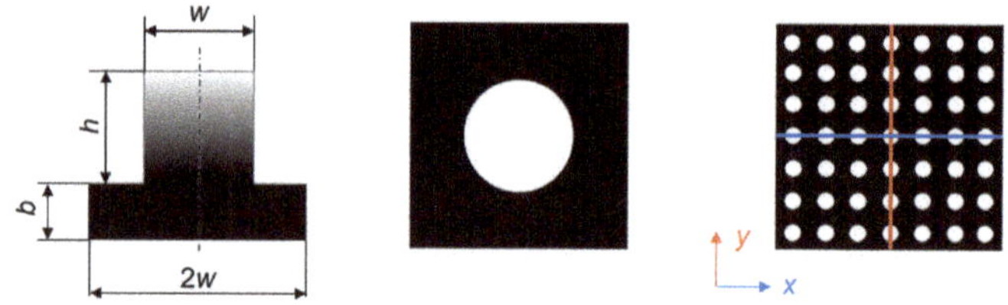

(a) (b) (c)

Figure 4. A polymer-based pillar array is used to investigate the practical limits of the lateral resolution and aspect ratio. The pillar width w varies from 0.2 μm to 20 μm and the height h from 0.5 μm to 4 μm. The base layer height b of 1.5 μm is constant (**a**). The pillars are rotationally symmetrical and measured in the horizontal (blue) and vertical (orange) directions (**b**,**c**). An integer multiple of pillars is arranged in a square array of 120 μm (**c**).

The pillar arrays illustrated in Figure 4 were realized using two-photon polymerization (2PP, introduced in [26,48]). In the manufacturing process, the pillars were written with a 2PP system (QuantumX, Nanoscribe, Karlsruhe, Germany) in a 2PP polymer (IP-Dip, Nanoscribe, refractive index n 1.55 @ 590 nm [49]) on a 2″ borosilicate wafer (MicroChemicals, Ulm, Germany, refractive index n 1.52 @ 590 nm). To improve the adhesion of the 2PP polymer to the borosilicate wafers, the wafers were pretreated with oxygen plasma (Zepto BLS-W6, Electronic Diener, Ebhausen, Germany) and a silanizing adhesion promoter (Primer20, MicroResist, Berlin, Germany). In Table 2, the chosen pillar widths w and heights h are defined concerning the manufacturing process. To achieve the maximum resolution, the pillars are a multiple of the smallest voxel width of 200 nm of the 2PP system. Examining eight different pillar widths ranging from 0.2 μm to 20 μm with an exponential step size ($w = 0.1\ e^{0.66\ n}$), n = [1:8]) ensures a comprehensive investigation, even below the resolution limit of diffraction-limited systems. When varying the height h from 0.5 μm to 4 μm, the aspect ratio a of h/w results in 0.1 to 5. In the design of the experiment, 26 pillar arrays were manufactured and their respective indexes are written in brackets in Table 2.

Table 2. Pillar geometry.

		Width w [μm]							
		0.2	**0.4**	**0.8**	**1.4**	**2.8**	**5.0**	**10.0**	**20.0**
Height h [μm]	**0.5**	2.50 (1)	1.25 (2)	0.63 (3)	0.36 (4)	0.18 (5)	0.10 (6)		
	1.0	5.00 (7)	2.50 (8)	1.25 (9)	0.71 (10)	0.36 (11)	0.20 (12)	0.10 (13)	
	2.0		5.00 (14)	2.50 (15)	1.43 (16)	0.71 (17)	0.40 (18)	0.20 (19)	0.10 (20)
	4.0			5.00 (21)	2.86 (22)	1.43 (23)	0.80 (24)	0.40 (25)	0.20 (26)

A laser scanning microscope image of the realized pillar test structure is shown in Figure 5. According to this figure, arrays with an aspect ratio of 5 (like the arrays 7, 14, and

21) are defectively manufactured in the selected 2PP polymer. Therefore, the test range is restricted to aspect ratios of 0.1 to 2.86.

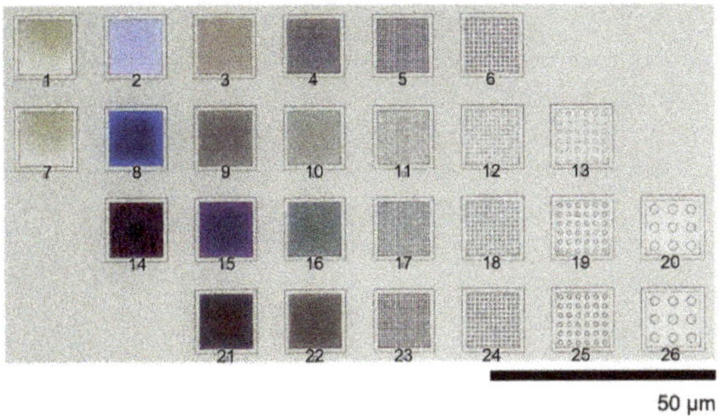

Figure 5. The 2PP pillar test structure captured by a laser scanning microscope consists of 26 pillar arrays. Structures with an aspect ratio of 5 (array 7, 14, and 21) are excluded from the investigation due to their defects.

3.2. *Slanted Test Pattern*

Test patterns with slanted gratings are used to analyze the measurability of the undercuts. The slanted test pattern in Figure 6a is used to investigate the lower limit at which undercuts can be detected with respect to the size of the structure w and the slanted angle α. The structure width w and the height h are always equal. Hence, the aspect ratio always remains one. Structures with a height h of 1, 2, and 3 µm as well as 10, 20, and 30 µm (factor 10 larger) are tested. The slant angle α is varied in steps of 0° to 40° in 10°. A slanted grating element is 12 µm or 120 µm in the y direction with respect to (b). Three slanted grating elements were placed in the x direction. A captured overview of the realized structures is provided in (c). The slanted polymer structure was produced as already described in the manufacturing process of the pillar test structure using the 2PP technique. In the analysis, the slanted test samples are captured from the top, and a slice in the x direction is used for evaluation.

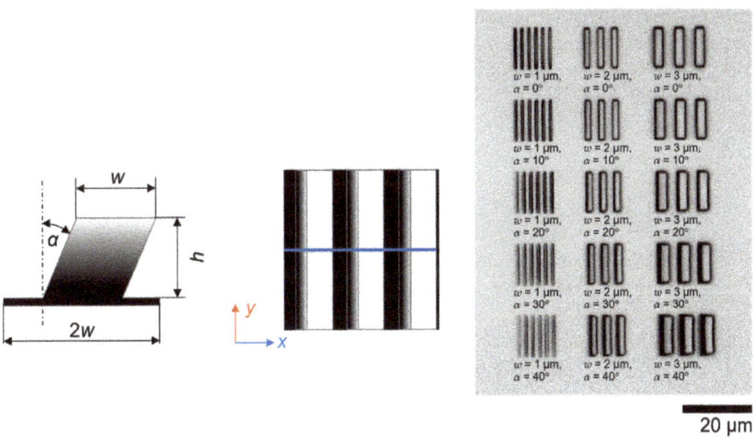

(a) (b) (c)

Figure 6. The slanted gratings vary in height h (=width w) between 1 µm and 30 µm. The slant angle is in the range of 0° to 40° (**a**). At least three elements are investigated based on the top and the cross-section view in the x-direction (blue line) (**b**). The microscope image of the slanted gratings shows the arrangement of the sample (**c**).

3.3. Covered Pillar Test Pattern

Covered pillars are used to assess the possible penetration depths of measurement systems through a polymer layer (IP-Dip, n = 1.55). The design of the covered pillars is visualized in Figure 7. As shown in (a), the pillars are hollow and have a constant width w and height h of 4 µm. The covering layer thickness h_c varies from 0.5 µm to 2 µm in 0.5 µm increments. The 2PP structure is connected to the substrate via base pillars in order to be able to rinse the cavities underneath the covering layer. The base pillars also have a height h_b and a diameter of 4 µm. They are offset symmetrically to the structure pillars as shown in (b) and (c). The pillars fill a square of 80 µm and the different cover heights are tagged on the top side as displayed in (c). For a better understanding, a three-dimensional representation of the designed structure is given in (d).

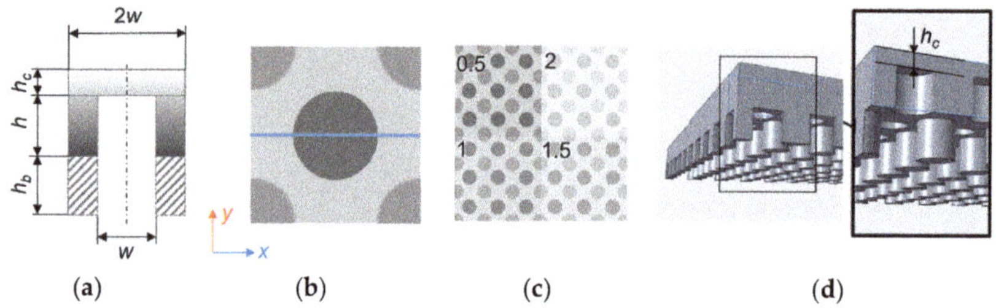

Figure 7. The coved pillar structure is based on hollow pillars (width w = 4 µm, height h = 4 µm) and a varying cover thickness h_c. The cover thickness h_c ranges from 0.5 µm to 2 µm. To be able to flush the hollow pillars free during the 2PP manufacturing process, the structure is supported by base pillars (height h_b = 4 µm) (**a**). The pillars are symmetrically offset (**b**,**c**). The covered pillars are distributed over an area of 80 µm × 80 µm and the quadrants have the given cover thicknesses h_c (**c**). The three-dimensional slice shows how the hollow and base pillars are arranged in relation to each other and where the cover thickness h_c is measured (**d**).

4. Results and Discussion

4.1. Pillar Analysis: Investigation of the Lateral Resolution and Aspect Ratio Limits

For an assessment of the limits with respect to the lateral resolution and the aspect ratio, the pillars' test range and all successful measurements of the measurement systems (WLI, AFM, OCT, ESEM, µCT, PCM, MME) are plotted in Figure 8. The measurements were classified as successful if the pillars were identifiable based on the diameter at half height (FWHM) or at half intensity (using the described image processing methods such as binarization). According to the comparison in Figure 8, the smallest structures from a width of 0.4 µm can be measured with the ESEM. The AFM and OCT measure structures starting at 0.8 µm. The WLI, µCT, PCM, and MME detect structures with a width of at least 1.4 µm. Pillars with a maximum aspect ratio of 2.86 can be visualized using the WLI, OCT, ESEM, PCM, and MME. Due to the end of the test range, it is possible that higher aspect ratios can be measured. This can be investigated by further tests with higher aspect ratios.

At this point, the µCT measurement is remarkable in contrast to other systems' measurements. The smallest pillar array that could be measured by the µCT was the fourth array with a width of 1.4 µm and a height of 0.5 µm. The corresponding µCT images are shown in Figure 9a and the respective slice in (b). The biggest challenge of the µCT measurements is the low contrast of the 2PP polymer. An attempt was made to compensate for this using a long exposure time, power optimization (loss of contrast at high power), and measuring 'in phase'. In the end, long exposure times must be selected that exceed 48 h per pillar array so that the contrast is sufficient and the pillars can be reconstructed. Another way to improve the contrast of the polymer would be to enrich the polymer with high atomic number elements, e.g., barium or silver, and increase its absorption [50].

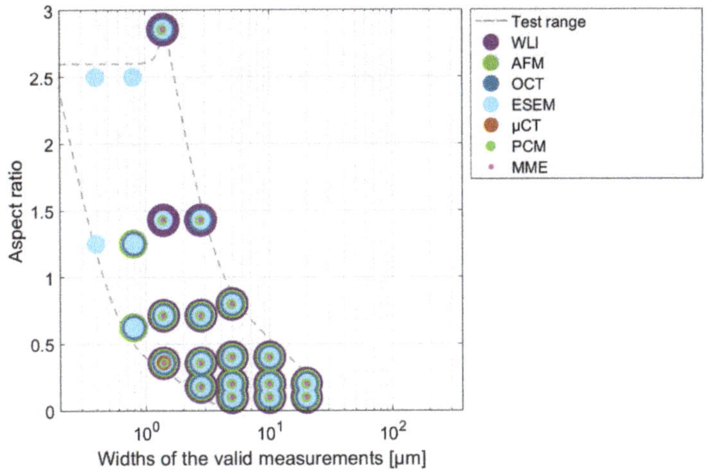

Figure 8. In the pillar analysis, the plotted pillar dimensions could be measured by the referenced measurement systems.

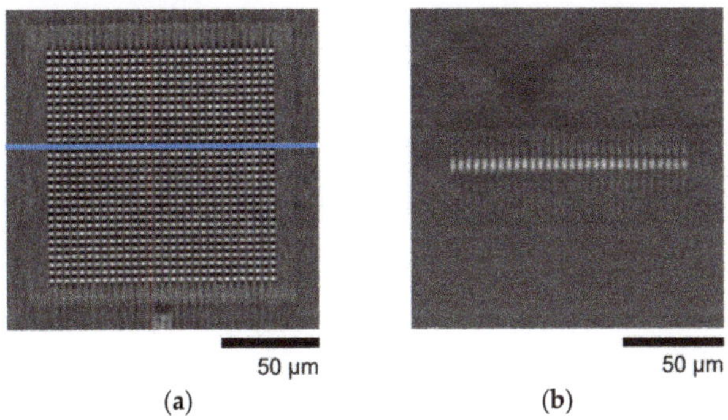

Figure 9. The µCT images of the pillar with a width of 1.4 and a height of 0.5 µm are shown. The individual pillars are visible in the top view (**a**). The cross-section at the blue line is shown in (**b**). There are slight diffraction effects.

Figure 8 shows that several measurement systems are suitable, especially for larger structure widths (>1.4 µm). However, the measurement quality of the measurement systems differs. In order to be able to select the most suitable measurement system for a certain measurements task, the measurement quality is investigated. In the following, the deviation from the expected value (residuals) and the measurement repeatability (standard deviation) of all measurement systems (except MME) are examined as a function of the structure width in Figure 10. Horizontal (▶) and vertical (▲) measurements are separated by their symbols.

The percentage residuals as a function of the structure width for each comparable measurement system are shown in Figure 10. The respective aspect ratio of the measurement can be assigned via the color and the legend of the measurement. The higher the aspect ratio, the lighter the respective color. Analyzing the AFM and ESEM measurements, it is noticeable that the horizontal and vertical measured values including the standard deviation do not overlap. The difference is significant and is examined in more detail. The AFM and ESEM measurement images and the respective statistical evaluation of the third array (w = 0.8 µm, a = 0.63) are shown in Figure 11a,b. These measurements of the same structure clarify that the 2PP pillars are not ideally round. In the analysis of the 0.8 μm pillars, the vertical diameter is 20% (0.16 μm of w = 0.8 μm) smaller than the horizontal diameter. Theoretically, this would be 40% for the 0.4 μm pillars (0.16 μm of w = 0.4 μm). This is confirmed exactly in the ESEM analysis. Therefore, in the measuring range below 1.4 μm, statements can only be made about the repeatability based on the standard deviation. It is assumed that the absolute deviation of 160 nm affects every pillar due to the 2PP manufacturing. However, this deviation is marginal for pillar widths of 1.4 μm and wider, as it is 10% of the total width or less. In that case, it cannot be distinguished from the measurement inaccuracy due to the scattering of the measured values. From a pillar width of 1.4 μm, both the residuals and the standard deviation can be used for evaluation.

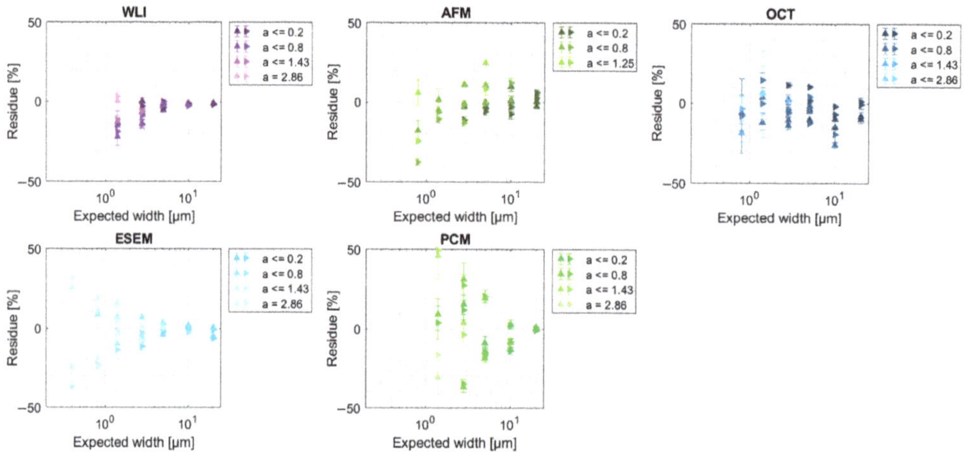

Figure 10. The measurement deviation corresponding to the structure width of comparable geometrical-based systems (WLI, AFM, OCT, ESEM, PCM) is shown to evaluate the measurement quality. Horizontal (▶) and vertical (▲) measurements are plotted separately. The aspect ratio *a* of the measured pillars can be classified using the color bar.

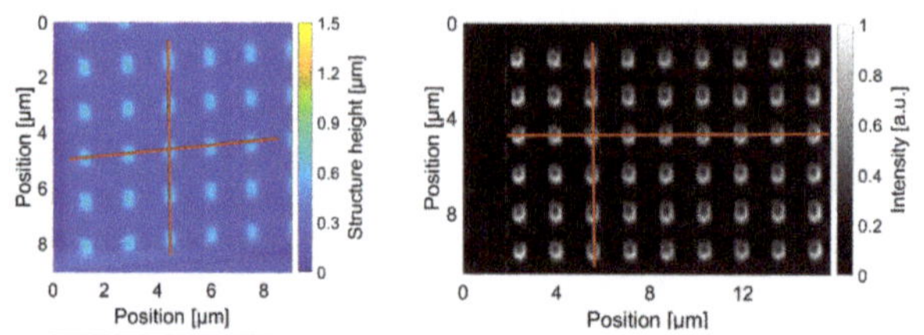

Slice	Width w [μm]
Hor.	0.50 ± 0.02
Ver.	0.66 ± 0.05

(a)

Slice	Width w [μm]
Hor.	0.62 ± 0.01
Ver.	0.87 ± 0.04

(b)

Figure 11. The WLI image (**a**) and the ESEM image (**b**) show pillars with an expected width of 0.8 μm and a height of 0.5 μm. The measurment lines are marked in red. The offset between the horizontal and vertical diameters is 20% of the expected structure width of 0.8 μm.

In the measurement range up to 1.4 μm, the standard deviation of the OCT is the largest reaching more than 20% (e.g., w = 0.8 μm: 23%, w = 1.4 μm: 27%). Compared to the other measuring systems, this is more than twice as large as the maximum deviation of WLI, AFM, and ESEM. Therefore, it is recommended to use OCT for a width of 2.8 μm at least. At a structure size of 1.4 μm, the measured values of all measurement systems overlap within their standard deviation, and the measurement quality does not differ significantly. In the measurement range from a structure width of 5 µm and wider, the measured values of the WLI and the ESEM are the most stable. The deviation from the expected value is less than 10%. The standard deviation is less than 5% and is negligible. From a structure width of 20 µm, the residuals of the PCM are less than 10% as well. In contrast, the AFM and OCT measurements have residuals of up to 25% (w = 5 µm) and −26% (w = 10 µm) in this range. Consequently, the use of WLI and ESEM is recommended for structure widths equal to or greater than 5 µm and the PCM for structures equal to or greater than 20 µm.

Analyzing the residuals and the standard deviation as a function of the structure width, the impact of the aspect ratio has been neglected. Therefore, the impact of the aspect ratio on the reproducibility (standard deviation) is displayed in Figure 12. Up to an aspect ratio of 0.2, the standard deviation of all measuring systems is less than 5%. Subsequently, this deviation can be neglected. In addition, this means that there is no difference between the measurement systems in terms of their repeatability up to an aspect ratio of 0.2. The standard deviation increases on average as the aspect ratio of the measurement system increases according to the dashed trend lines. The measurements of the AFM (slope m = 2.4) and OCT (slope m = 10) are most influenced by an increasing aspect ratio. A linear relationship between aspect ratio and standard deviation could not be demonstrated for any measurement system. The deviation of the measurement points from the trend line is too large, and the coefficient of determination R^2 does not reach a minimum target value of 0.95. In order to improve the measurement accuracy, it is proposed to measure with a maximum of 10% standard deviation. Accordingly, OCT and PCM would be suitable for structures with an aspect ratio up to 0.4.

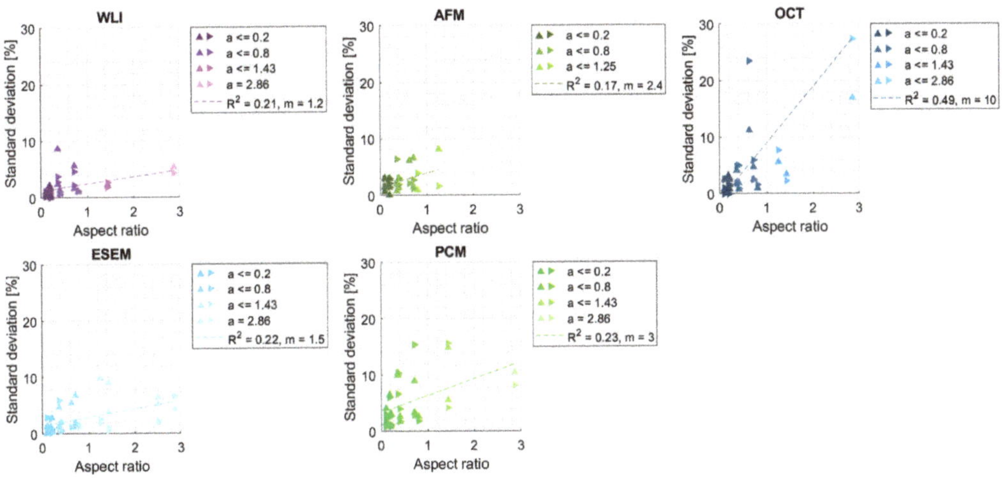

Figure 12. The influence of the aspect ratio is evaluated on the basis of the repeatability (standard deviation) of the measurements. The greater the gradient m of the trend line, the greater the impact of the aspect ratio on the measurement quality.

The limitations and recommendations resulting from the investigation of the measurement quality based on the measurement deviation and repeatability are applied below to the valid measurements map in Figure 13. In addition, application areas are defined. An application area extends from the lower resolution limit (left limit) via the maximum aspect ratio (upper limit) to the maximum measurable structure size (right limit). It is assumed that the maximum structure width is equal to the edge length of the field of view of the measurement system measuring the maximum aspect ratio. Restrictions limit the application areas based on the investigation of the measurement quality. With respect to Figure 13, the smallest structures with a width less than 1.4 µm can be measured by

ESEM and AFM. Medium-sized structures can be measured with OCT. If the structure widths of a sample vary greatly in width, the WLI, µCT, and PCM are suitable because they cover a large structure size range. Structures with high aspect ratios greater than two can preferably be examined with the ESEM, WLI, and MME.

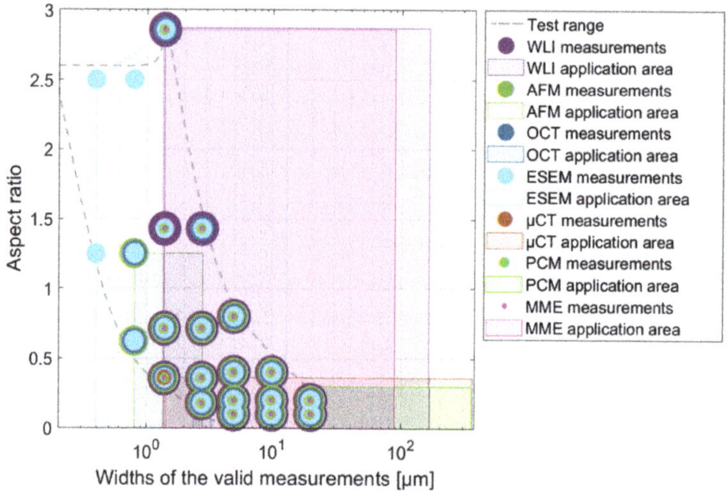

Figure 13. In the map of the application areas, the colored dots indicate valid measurements of the respective measurement systems. The application areas were defined taking into account the quality of the measurement. The application areas range from the lower resolution limit (left limit) to the maximum aspect ratio (upper limit) to the maximum structure width (right limit).

4.2. Undercut and Enclosed Structure Analysis: Evaluation of the Minimum Structure Size and Maximum Cover Heights

4.2.1. White Light Interferometer

The WLI measurements of the chosen slanted gratings and the covered pillars are shown in Figure 14. In (a), the 40° inclined structures with a structure size of 1 µm, 2 µm, and 3 µm are captured from the top view. The respective slice is shown below. In the slice, the ground plane and structure plateaus are connected via less isolated measuring points. These isolated measurement points indicate that the measurement resolution is not sufficient to reconstruct the slanted edge or undercuts for these structure sizes. The larger slanted edges with a height of 10 µm, 20 µm, and 30 µm with a 40° angle in (b) can be reconstructed. Based on the measurements of the larger slanted gratings in (b) and the enclosed structures with different cover heights h_c (0.5 µm–2 µm) in each quadrant in (c), it is clear that the WLI used can only look at a structure from the top and not into or through the structure. This is due to the signal recording of the measurement system. In the specific frequency domain analysis, only the interference signal of the sample's surface is used to calculate the height values [28]. Therefore, the underlying surface cannot be reconstructed.

The reconstruction quality of the WLI depends on the slant angle of the gratings as shown in Figure 15. The density of the measurement points is only sufficient to reconstruct the edges from a slant angle of at least 30°. The reflected light at the edges must be captured by the WLI objective (ZeGage, Zygo, Weiterstadt, Germany, NA 0.5) to enable the reconstruction of slanted edges. Using a high numerical aperture (NA) objective, smaller slant angles can be captured and reconstructed. The exact slant limit could be tested using a sinusoidal structure since it has a continuous change in inclination as demonstrated in [51].

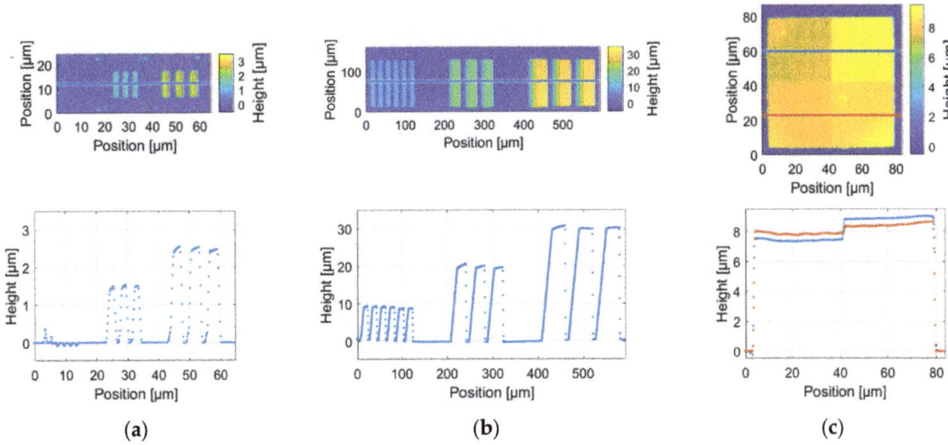

Figure 14. The slices of the 1 µm to 3 µm slanted structures with a 40° slant angle show that the edges cannot be reconstructed sufficiently since only a few measurement points are detected (**a**). The comparable structures with a 10 µm to 30 µm height have reliably measured edges on the top sides (**b**). The undercuts could not be captured. This also becomes clear in the image of the covered pillars (**c**), as no undercuts can be captured below a transparent surface. The steps in the slice view of (**c**) are due to the different cover heights h_c on top of the quadrants ranging from 0.5 µm to 2 µm.

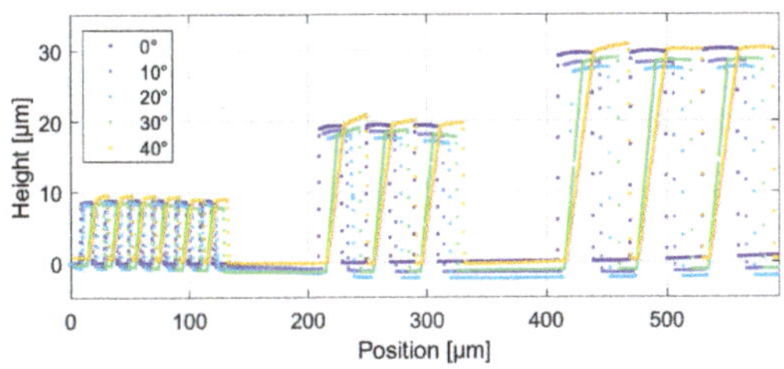

Figure 15. The structures 10 µm to 30 µm are compared with respect to their slant angles. From a slant angle of 30° the edges are captured sufficiently. The minimum slant angle depends on the maximum angle of incidence (numerical aperture) of the WLI objective.

4.2.2. Atomic Force Microscope

The AFM measurements of the slanted gratings and the covered pillars are shown in Figure 16. Only the smaller slanted structures with a size of 1 µm in (a), 2 µm in (b), 3 µm in (c) could be scanned. For example, the measurement of the samples with a 40° slant angle are displayed in Figure 16. The scanned edges in (a) to (c) are blurred and partially distorted, which indicates that the tip is stuck during movement. The standard tip (Tap300Al-G, BudgetSensors, Sofia, Bulgaria, tip height: 17 µm, half cone angles 20°–30°, radius 10 nm) is limited by its geometry. In measurements of larger structures, the tip would have remained stuck in the structures until it broke. According to Figure 16b,c, two tip behaviors can be distinguished. In the first, the tip touches the edges of the structure with its side surfaces, and the edges vanish as shown in (b) and (c) in red-lined area 1. In the scan lines below, there are tip displacements similar to tip contamination artifacts [52,53]. In the second behavior, the tip jumps over the edges as given in (b) and (c) in area 2. The structures look as if they have broken off, although the structures are defect-free. The phenomena are comparable to known misinterpretations by tip-sample convolution [52]. Since measurement defects cannot be sufficiently distinguished from slanted edges, a standard AFM is not recommended for slanted structures, even in the smaller measurement range below 3 µm. However, there are special AFMs with individual tips that are designed for high aspect ratios [23] as well as undercuts and sidewalls [54,55]. The covered pillars of Figure 16d cannot be measured using a basic tactile measurement technique. One possibility would be to measure these covered pillars with contact resonance atomic force microscopy as presented in [56]. The ripples in the slices are caused by the 2PP manufacturing of the cover layer and can also be found in the measurement of the WLI in Figure 14c (different scaling).

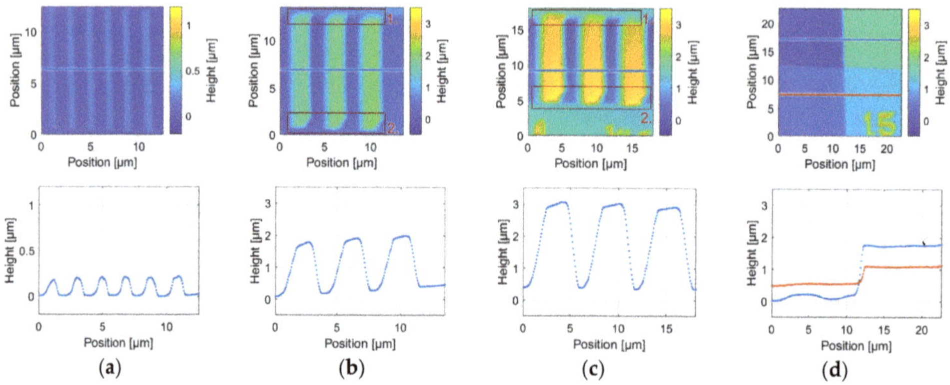

Figure 16. The AFM measurements and the respective slices of the 40° slanted gratings with a structure size of 1 µm (**a**), 2 µm (**b**), and 3 µm (**c**) demonstrate the challenge of a tactile measurement. The AFM tip either sticks with its flange (red area 1) or jumps from the structure top to ground level (red area 2). The measurement of the covered pillars (**d**) shows that no enclosed structures can be detected, but the vertical resolution is very high and small height deviations (<100 nm) can be detected. In (**a**), the height scaling has been changed in order to improve the analysis of the structures.

4.2.3. Optical Coherence Tomograph

The slanted gratings with a size of 10 µm, 20 µm, and 30 µm could be captured by the OCT as shown based on the 40° structures in Figure 17a–c. Smaller slanted structures (1 µm–3 µm) could not be imaged. Especially in the processed slices of the OCT images, the structures appear several times with low intensity (2). These artifacts are caused by the autocorrelation signal which leads to double interpretations. They do not influence the dominant measurement signal (1). Therefore, only the measurement signal (1) is analyzed. The reflection strength at the slanted edges decreases compared to horizontal interfaces, as the reflection cannot be completely captured by the objective. Similarly, to the WLI, the measurability of the edges depends on the NA of the objective. Compared to the WLI, however, undercuts and covered structures can also be measured. In the slice of Figure 17d, the interfaces of the covered structures are visible. At this point, it is important to mention that the scaling of the height refers to air. The average pillar width is 3.7 ± 0.2 µm, measured in the horizontal direction along the blue slice line. In this measurement, the measured pillar widths are independent of the cover thickness h_c (left side: 0.5 µm, right side: 2 µm). It was proven that the measurement with the OCT through a 2 µm thick polymer is successful. It is assumed that much thicker layers than 2 µm can be penetrated since the system has a limiting scan depth of 600 µm and comparable systems (Fourier Domain OCTs) have been shown to penetrate much thicker layers than the tested 2 µm ([57], crack in 1500 µm depth; [58], 50 µm film thickness). A measurement can be carried out without any difficulties as long as the refraction effects along the structure edges still allow for a reliable measurement of the enclosed structure.

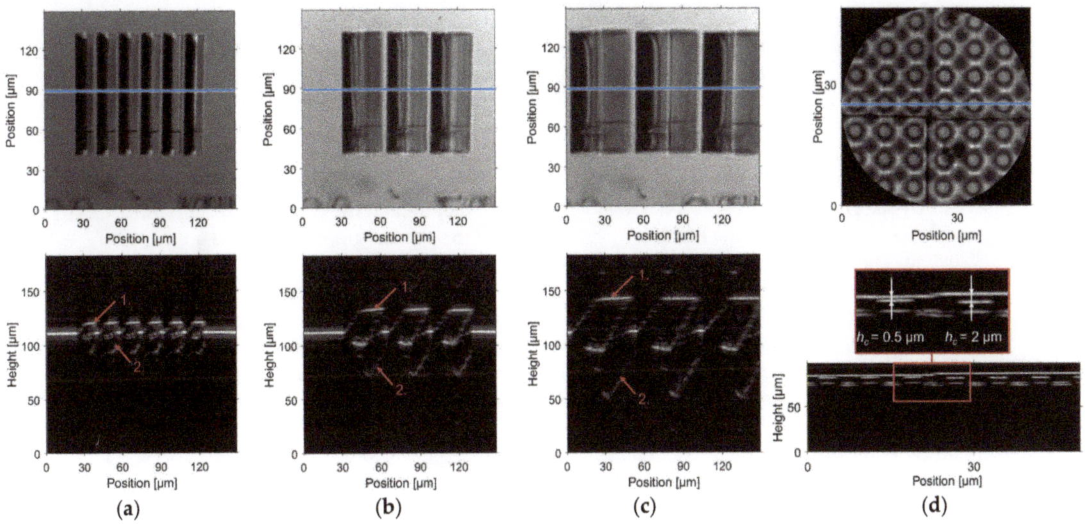

Figure 17. The top view of the OCT measurements and their cross-sections of the 10 µm (**a**), 20 µm, (**b**) and 30 µm (**c**) structures show that the undercuts of the slanted structures can be captured by OCT. The enclosed pillars (**d**) have a cover thickness of 0.5 to 2 µm. In this measurement range, no significant impact of the cover thickness on the measurement accuracy could be proven.

4.2.4. Environmental Scanning Electron Microscope

Using the ESEM, the samples are tilted by 30° in order to detect undercuts based on their lateral profile. The captured ESEM images of the 1 µm, 2 µm, and 3 µm structures as well as the 30 µm structure with a slant angle of 40° are shown in Figure 18a,b. The profile can be reconstructed using the measured distances and recalculating the vertical scale with the factor of the tilt angle. A reconstruction or measurement of the undercuts in the middle of the structure is impossible using the intensity image. Cavity structures such as the covered pillars in Figure 18c cannot be detected unless the cover layer is thin enough that its charge density differs from the surrounding surface areas. At a cover thickness of 0.5 µm (top left), different intensities can be seen at the location of the hollow pillars. It is assumed that the difference in intensity is due to the waviness of the cover layer, which was also seen in the WLI (Figure 14c) and AFM images (Figure 16d).

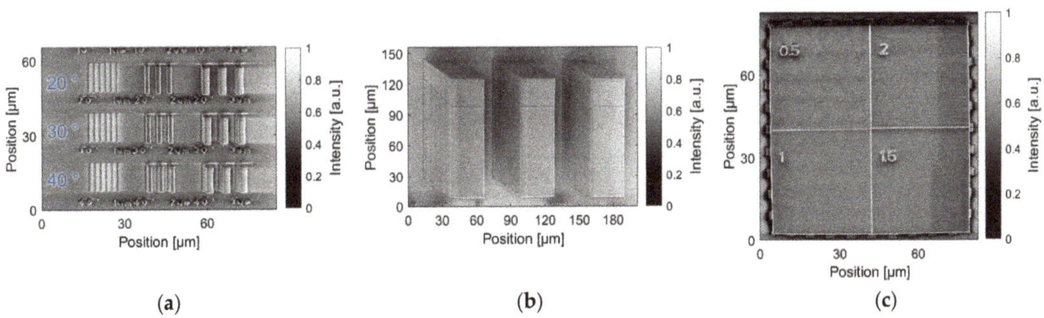

Figure 18. The ESEM images show small structures (1 µm, 2 µm, and 3 µm) with different tilt angles in (**a**) and a large structure (30 µm, 40°) in (**b**). In the ESEM images of (**a**,**b**), the sample was tilted by 30°. The covered pillars in (**c**) are captured from the top view. In the two right-hand quadrants (top: h_c = 2 µm, bottom: h_c = 1.5 µm), a difference in charge density can be seen on the structure's surface. This charge difference was caused by ESEM scans of the left side taken shortly before.

4.2.5. Phase Contrast Microscope

The PCM could capture all slanted structures from 1 µm to 30 µm. The slanted gratings from 1 µm to 3 µm with a slant angle of 20°–40° and the 30 µm structure with 40° slant are shown in Figure 19a,b. The smaller structures in (a) suffer under diffraction effects at the edges. Since the PCM measurement is based on transmitted light, the measurements are susceptible to diffraction effects, which lead to vanished structure edges, especially of slanted structures, as can also be seen in (a). The greater the angle of inclination, the less clearly the geometry is displayed. Due to the refraction of light at the structure's edges and the phase shift filters of the PCM, only the left side of the slanted grating elements appears bright. The right side with the undercut appears dark. As a result, the PCM light image of (b) implies that the structure is tilted to the left, although it is tilted to the right as indicated by the red reference line in the image. Consequently, slanted gratings cannot be captured reliably with the PCM. In contrast, the covered pillars are reliably recognizable in the PCM images in (c). Depending on the focus position, the hollow pillars or the base pillars appear sharp. In (c), the focus was set on the hollow pillars. The intensity slice through the top view image does not contain any helpful information; therefore, it is not shown. Using the image in the top view, an average pillar width of 3.6 ± 0.2 µm could be measured. This is consistent with the OCT measurements (3.7 ± 0.2 µm). The possible penetration depth of the PCM depends on the transmission properties of the polymer. The limit of the PCM's penetration depth could not be identified using a maximum cover layer of 2 µm.

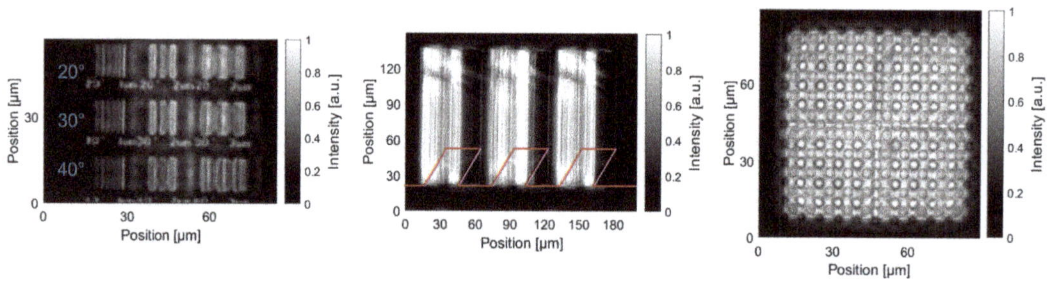

(a) (b) (c)

Figure 19. The PCM image of the small structures (1 µm, 2 µm, and 3 µm) shows increased diffraction effects while increasing the slant angle (**a**). According to the image of the large structure (30 µm, 40°), it seems like the slanted structure is tilted to the left, although it is tilted to the right. A reference slice has been drawn in red corresponding to the position of the PCM image's slanted gratings (**b**). In contrast, the covered pillars are recognizable. When testing a 2 µm cover height (top right), the maximum penetration depth of the PCM has not yet been reached (**c**).

4.2.6. Imagining Mueller Matrix Ellipsometer

The imaging MME enables an analysis of the polarization properties of the slanted gratings as shown for the smaller structures of 1 µm–3 µm and a slant angle of 10°–40° in Figure 20a and the corresponding Mueller matrix in (b). In this case, the Mueller matrix element M_{32} was selected due to its high contrast to determine the influence of the slanted edges on the structure's polarization properties. The different slanted gratings (0°–40°) of the first slanted grating image (SG1) in (b) show in the Mueller matrix element M_{32} that all 1 µm slanted gratings (left column) do not differ in their polarization properties. To confirm this statement, two additional 2PP slanted gratings SG2 in (c) and SG3 in (d) were printed and measured. Consequently, it is assumed that the geometry of 1 µm gratings with slant angles from 0° to 40° does not differ significantly. However, the polarization properties of the 2 µm and 3 µm structures change with an increasing slant angle and an increasing structure width. For example, as the slant angle increases, the areas with higher Mueller matrix values become larger, and more red pixels (especially at the gratings' edges) can be observed in more detail in (b). If the polarization property of a reference structure (same structure, same material) is known, the shape fidelity and the polarization property of the test structure can be compared using the Mueller matrices. In addition, a simulation of the polarization behavior can be applied for a more reliable structural evaluation in order to be independent of system-induced influences [47].

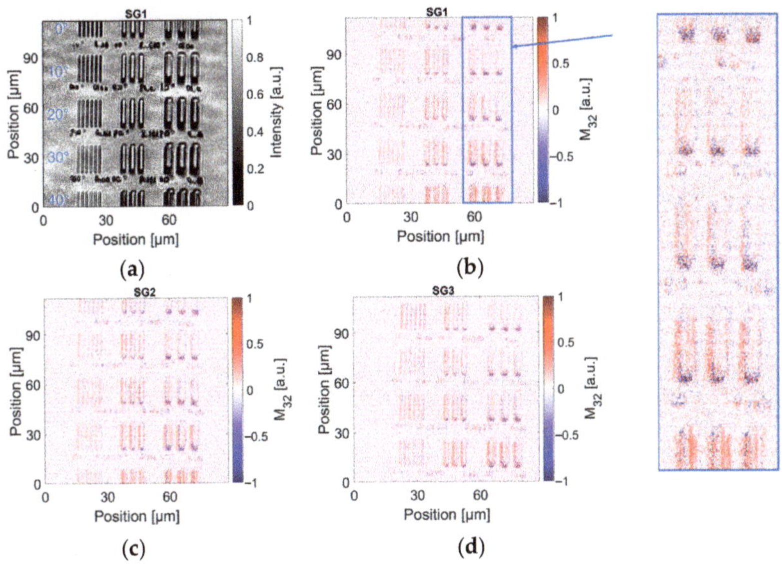

Figure 20. The intensity image in (**a**) shows the 1 µm, 2 µm, and 3 µm structures (left to right) with slant angles from 0° to 40° (top to bottom). The respective polarization property is displayed by the local M_{32} values of the Mueller matrix in (**b**). In comparison, two additional samples SG2 (**c**) and SG3 (**d**) were measured. They show the same polarization behavior as SG1. This proves that the polarization behavior can be measured with imaging MME from a structure width of 1 µm, even with slanted gratings.

As before, the covered pillars were also measured with the imaging MME to investigate the influence of the cover thickness. According to the covered pillars in Figure 21a and the corresponding Mueller matrix elements M_{33} and M_{34} in (b) and (c), the values fluctuate over the entire structure area and no significant difference can be seen in the quadrants with different cover heights. That implies that the polarization properties of the hollow pillars differ over the entire test structure independently from the cover height. Thus, it could be shown that the MME is not significantly influenced by the thickness of the cover in a range of 0.5 µm to 2 µm. The difference between the basic pillar probe of Figure 3g and the covered pillar probe in the polarization property can be seen at the edges of the pillars. In comparison, the edges of the covered pillars are not captured, only the position of the pillar can be estimated due to the dominant polarization change in the middle of the pillar. It is assumed that this difference is due to the inverse geometry (hollow instead of filled pillars), the additional base pillars, and the wet development process of the 2PP structure. If the cavities cannot be completely rinsed out during the wet development process, the propagation and the polarization behavior are changed.

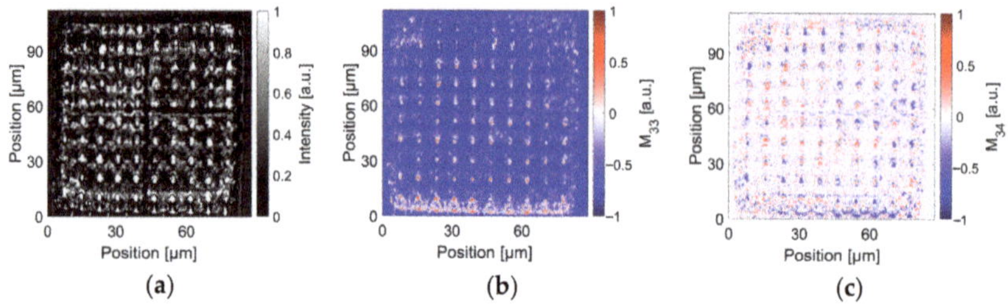

Figure 21. The polarization properties of the covered pillar structure in (**a**) are represented by the Mueller matrix elements M_{33} and M_{34} in (**b**,**c**) using the imaging MME. The polarization properties of the covered pillars vary across the entire structure surface, regardless of the cover height of 0.5 μm to 2 μm. Consequently, it has been demonstrated that the MME is not significantly affected by the cover thickness.

4.2.7. Interim Summary of the Undercut and Enclosed Structure Analysis

The investigations of complex polymer structures with slant angles of 0° to 40° and structure heights of 1 μm to 30 μm show that the application areas of the individual measurement systems differ as summarized in Figure 22. Accordingly, ESEM and MME measurements are suitable for evaluating small slanted structures with a height of less than 10 μm. The slanted edges of structures larger than 10 μm and slant angles equal to and greater than 30° can be reliably captured by WLI and OCT. The suitability of WLI and OCT to detect slanted edges depends on the numerical aperture of their objectives. It is assumed that the μCT can also reliably reconstruct slanted edges from a structure size of 10 μm since its resolution is comparable to the WLI's and OCT's (with respect to the pillar analysis in Figure 8). Due to the sample rotation during the measurement, it should be possible to record the edges regardless of their angles. The AFM and PCM are not suitable for evaluating slanted structures.

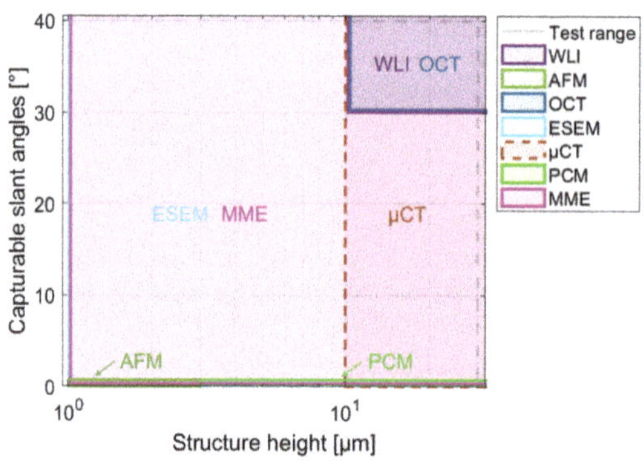

Figure 22. The map shows the application areas of WLI, AFM, OCT, ESEM, μCT, PCM, and MME with respect to their suitability to capture slanted edges in a specific structure size range. The dashed measurement range of the μCT is based on the assumption that structures of 1.4 μm and larger can be resolved and that the slant angle does not influence the measurement quality due to the rotation during the measurement.

The investigation results of covered structures with a cover height of 0.5 μm to 2 μm are illustrated in Figure 23. It could be shown that the tested cover height is not a challenge for the OCT, PCM, and MME and that the limit of penetration was not reached. OCT and μCT in particular are suitable for penetrating deeper polymers. Comparable OCT systems were able to detect objects in thicker polymers of 50 μm [58] and 1500 μm [57]. The used μCT penetrates through a 500 μm thick borosilicate waver (n = 1.52 @ 590 nm, not X-ray related) and a 1.5 µm polymer layer (IP-Dip, n = 1.55 @ 590 nm, not X-ray related) during the measurement of the basic pillars. Comparable µCT systems penetrate polymers based on bisphenylglycidyl dimethacrylate (Bis-GMA) and triethylene glycol dimethacrylate (TEGDMA) with thicknesses of 1000 µm [59] and more than 5000 µm [60]. If necessary, for the µCT measurement, the polymer must be enriched with particles that support X-ray absorption [50,60]. The WLI, AFM, and ESEM only measure the surfaces and are not suitable for measuring structures below the surface. At this point it is important to note that the measurement capability in terms of penetration always depends on the sample's material. We used a standard acrylate (IP-Dip) and in principle the results are transferable to all materials that have similar absorption and scattering properties at the measurement system's specific wavelength.

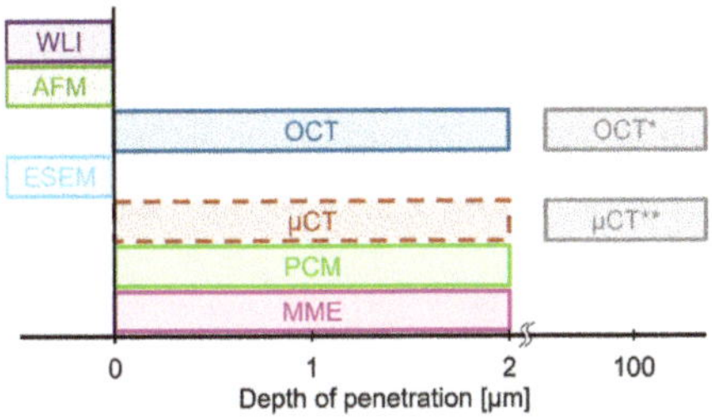

Figure 23. The OCT, µCT, PCM, and imaging MME can penetrate polymer layers of 2 µm without a significant loss of measurement accuracy. OCT and µCT in particular are suitable for deep penetration of polymer layers according to the literature * [57,58] ** [59,60]. The WLI, AFM, and ESEM are only suitable for measuring structures on surfaces.

5. Conclusions

In the investigations, WLI, AFM, OCT, ESEM, PCM, and imaging MME are utilized for the non-destructive evaluation of complex polymer-based micro and nanostructures. According to the pillar analysis, the practical limits of the lateral resolution and aspect ratio were identified for each measurement system, and application areas were defined with respect to the measurement quality. The ESEM and AFM were suitable for measuring the smallest structures down to 0.4 µm, while the WLI, OCT, µCT, PCM, and MME were effective for larger structures starting in the single-digit micrometer range. The WLI, µCT, and PCM in particular cover a wide range of structural width variance. Furthermore, some analysis results of slanted and enclosed structures should be highlighted. According to the analysis, the ESEM (with a tilted sample) and the MME are suitable for measuring slanted edges from 0° to 40° on small structures that are equal or larger than 1 µm. The OCT, µCT, PCM, and imaging MME are reliably suitable for penetrating materials with similar absorption and scattering properties as the standard acrylate (IP-Dip) used, up to a thickness of 2 µm. The OCT and µCT are especially suitable measurement systems for measuring in thicker polymer layers up to the millimeter range. On the basis of the defined application areas, suitable non-destructive measurement systems can be quickly selected to reliably measure polymer structures depending on their specific geometry.

Author Contributions: Conceptualization, S.B. and A.H.; methodology, S.B., L.S., T.S., D.S. and J.G.; validation, S.B.; writing—original draft preparation, S.B.; writing—review and editing, A.H. All authors have read and agreed to the published version of the manuscript.

Funding: This work was supported by German Federal Ministry of Education and Research (BMBF FH Kooperativ grant no. 13FH080KX1 and KMU Innovativ grant no. 01IS20080C). The publication is funded by Aalen University of Applied Sciences.

Data Availability Statement: Data are contained within the article.

Conflicts of Interest: The authors declare no conflicts of interest.

References

1. Yang, L.; Wei, J.; Ma, Z.; Song, P.; Ma, J.; Zhao, Y.; Huang, Z.; Zhang, M.; Yang, F.; Wang, X. The Fabrication of Micro/Nano Structures by Laser Machining. *Nanomaterials* **2019**, *9*, 1789. [CrossRef] [PubMed]
2. Panusa, G.; Pu, Y.; Wang, J.; Moser, C.; Psaltis, D. Fabrication of Sub-Micron Polymer Waveguides through Two-Photon Polymerization in Polydimethylsiloxane. *Polymers* **2020**, *12*, 2485. [CrossRef] [PubMed]
3. Mattelin, M.-A.; Radosavljevic, A.; Missinne, J.; Cuypers, D.; Kommeren, S.; Vandael, J.; ter Meulen, J.M.; Verduyckt, L.; van Steenberge, G. Fabrication and replication of high efficiency blazed gratings with grayscale electron beam lithography and UV nanoimprint lithography. In Proceedings of the Advanced Fabrication Technologies for Micro/Nano Optics and Photonics XIII, San Francisco, CA, USA, 2–5 February 2020. [CrossRef]
4. Lee, K.D.; Ahn, S.W.; Kim, S.H.; Lee, S.H.; Park, J.D.; Yoon, P.W.; Kim, D.H.; Lee, S.S. Nanoimprint technology for nano-structured optical devices. *Curr. Appl. Phys.* **2006**, *6*, e149–e153. [CrossRef]
5. Jang, C.; Mercier, O.; Bang, K.; Li, G.; Zhao, Y.; Lanman, D. Design and fabrication of freeform holographic optical elements. *ACM Trans. Graph.* **2020**, *39*, 1–15. [CrossRef]
6. Lu, W.-G.; Xiao, R.; Liu, J.; Wang, L.; Zhong, H.; Wang, Y. Large-area rainbow holographic diffraction gratings on a curved surface using transferred photopolymer films. *Opt. Lett.* **2018**, *43*, 675–678. [CrossRef]
7. Levola, T.; Laakkonen, P. Replicated slanted gratings with a high refractive index material for in and outcoupling of light. *Opt. Express* **2007**, *15*, 2067–2074. [CrossRef]
8. Jin, G.; Liu, W.; Ye, Z.; Jia, W.; Xie, Y.; Zhou, C. High Efficiency Polarization-Independent Slanted Grating for RGB Bands. *IEEE Photonics J.* **2021**, *13*, 5100108. [CrossRef]
9. Li, H.; Peng, X.; Guan, C.; Hu, H. Ultra-Precision Cutting and Characterization of Reflective Convex Spherical Blazed Grating Elements. *Micromachines* **2022**, *13*, 1115. [CrossRef]
10. Al-Assaad, R.M. Physical characterization of nanoimprinted polymer nanostructures using visible light angular scatterometry. *J. Micro/Nanolith. MEMS MOEMS* **2008**, *7*, 13008. [CrossRef]
11. Varshney, M.; Li, Y.; Srinivasan, B.; Tung, S.; Erf, G.; Slavik, M.F.; Ying, Y.; Fang, W. A Microfluidic Filter Biochip-Based Chemiluminescence Biosensing Method for Detection of Escherichia coli O157:H7. *Trans. ASABE* **2006**, *49*, 2061–2068. [CrossRef]
12. Wengenmayr, R. Zellen unter Druck. *Max Planck Forsch.* **2021**.
13. Tsai, C.-H.D.; Tanaka, J.; Kaneko, M.; Horade, M.; Ito, H.; Taniguchi, T.; Ohtani, T.; Sakata, Y. An On-Chip RBC Deformability Checker Significantly Improves Velocity-Deformation Correlation. *Micromachines* **2016**, *7*, 176. [CrossRef] [PubMed]
14. Keshavarz Motamed, P.; Abouali, H.; Poudineh, M.; Maftoon, N. Experimental measurement and numerical modeling of deformation behavior of breast cancer cells passing through constricted microfluidic channels. *Microsyst. Nanoeng.* **2024**, *10*, 7. [CrossRef] [PubMed]
15. Hongbin, Y.; Guangya, Z.; Siong, C.F.; Shouhua, W.; Feiwen, L. Novel polydimethylsiloxane (PDMS) based microchannel fabrication method for lab-on-a-chip application. *Sens. Actuators B Chem.* **2009**, *137*, 754–761. [CrossRef]
16. An, L.; Ji, F.; Zhao, E.; Liu, Y.; Liu, Y. Measuring cell deformation by microfluidics. *Front. Bioeng. Biotechnol.* **2023**, *11*, 1214544. [CrossRef]
17. Kim, D.S.; Lee, S.H.; Ahn, C.H.; Lee, J.Y.; Kwon, T.H. Disposable integrated microfluidic biochip for blood typing by plastic microinjection moulding. *Lab Chip* **2006**, *6*, 794–802. [CrossRef]
18. Memon, I.; Shen, Y.; Khan, A.; Woidt, C.; Hillmer, H. Highly uniform residual layers for arrays of 3D nanoimprinted cavities in Fabry–Pérot-filter-array-based nanospectrometers. *Appl. Nanosci.* **2016**, *6*, 599–606. [CrossRef]
19. Peter Amalathas, A.; Alkaisi, M.M. Efficient light trapping nanopyramid structures for solar cells patterned using UV nanoimprint lithography. *Mater. Sci. Semicond. Process.* **2017**, *57*, 54–58. [CrossRef]
20. Köhler, H. On Abbe's Theory of Image Formation in the Microscope. *Opt. Acta Int. J. Opt.* **1981**, *28*, 1691–1701. [CrossRef]
21. Kim, J.U.; Lee, S.; Kim, T. Recent Advances in Unconventional Lithography for Challenging 3D Hierarchical Structures and Their Applications. *J. Nanomater.* **2016**, *2016*, 7602395. [CrossRef]
22. Lehmann, P.; Niehues, J.; Tereschenko, S. 3-D Optical Interference Microscopy at the Lateral Resolution. *Int. J. Optomechatron.* **2014**, *8*, 231–241. [CrossRef]
23. Morimoto, T.; Kuroda, H.; Minomoto, Y.; Nagano, Y.; Kembo, Y.; Hosaka, S. Atomic Force Microscopy for High Aspect Ratio Structure Metrology. *Jpn. J. Appl. Phys.* **2002**, *41*, 4238–4241. [CrossRef]
24. Meemon, P.; Yao, J.; Lee, K.-S.; Thompson, K.P.; Ponting, M.; Baer, E.; Rolland, J.P. Optical Coherence Tomography Enabling Non Destructive Metrology of Layered Polymeric GRIN Material. *Sci. Rep.* **2013**, *3*, 1709. [CrossRef]
25. Lu, J.C.; Liu, Q.; Huang, S. Research on slanted trapezoidal surface relief grating. In *Proceedings of the Holography, Diffractive Optics, and Applications IX, Hangzhou, China, 20–23 October 2019*; Zhou, C., Sheng, Y., Cao, L., Eds.; SPIE: Bellingham, WA, USA, 2019; p. 81. ISBN 9781510630932.
26. Wang, H.; Zhang, W.; Ladika, D.; Yu, H.; Gailevičius, D.; Wang, H.; Pan, C.-F.; Nair, P.N.S.; Ke, Y.; Mori, T.; et al. Two-Photon Polymerization Lithography for Optics and Photonics: Fundamentals, Materials, Technologies, and Applications. *Adv. Funct. Mater.* **2023**, *33*, 2214211. [CrossRef]
27. de Groot, P. Method and Apparatus for Surface Topography Measurement by Spatial-Frequency Analysis of Interferograms. U.S. Patent 5,398,113, 14 March 1995. Available online: https://patents.google.com/patent/US5398113A/en (accessed on 5 June 2024).

28. de Groot, P.; Colonna de Lega, X.; Kramer, J.; Turzhitsky, M. Determination of fringe order in white-light interference microscopy. *Appl. Opt.* **2002**, *41*, 4571–4578. [CrossRef]
29. Sugimoto, Y.; Nakajima, Y.; Sawada, D.; Morita, K.; Abe, M.; Morita, S. Simultaneous AFM and STM measurements on the Si(111)−(7 × 7) surface. *Phys. Rev. B* **2010**, *81*, 245322. [CrossRef]
30. Cerreta, A.; Vobornik, D.; Di Santo, G.; Tobenas, S.; Alonso-Sarduy, L.; Adamcik, J.; Dietler, G. FM-AFM constant height imaging and force curves: High resolution study of DNA-tip interactions. *J. Mol. Recognit.* **2012**, *25*, 486–493. [CrossRef]
31. Albrecht, F.; Bischoff, F.; Auwärter, W.; Barth, J.V.; Repp, J. Direct Identification and Determination of Conformational Response in Adsorbed Individual Nonplanar Molecular Species Using Noncontact Atomic Force Microscopy. *Nano Lett.* **2016**, *16*, 7703–7709. [CrossRef]
32. Dufrêne, Y.F.; Ando, T.; Garcia, R.; Alsteens, D.; Martinez-Martin, D.; Engel, A.; Gerber, C.; Müller, D.J. Imaging modes of atomic force microscopy for application in molecular and cell biology. *Nat. Nanotechnol.* **2017**, *12*, 295–307. [CrossRef]
33. Bryant, P.J.; Miller, R.G.; Yang, R. Scanning tunneling and atomic force microscopy combined. *Appl. Phys. Lett.* **1988**, *52*, 2233–2235. [CrossRef]
34. Thorlabs, Inc. EDU-AFM1/M Manual English. Available online: https://www.thorlabs.com/thorproduct.cfm?partnumber=EDU-AFM1/M (accessed on 9 June 2024).
35. Hasko, D.; Kovác, J.; Satka, A.; Drzík, M.; Uherek, F.; Hubbard, G.; Allsopp, D.W.E. Structural and optical characterization of photonics structures prepared by nanoimprint technology. In *Proceedings of the Photonics, Devices, and Systems IV, Prague, Czech Republic, 27–29 September 2008*; Tománek, P., Senderáková, D., Hrabovský, M., Eds.; SPIE: Bellingham, WA, USA, 2008; p. 713824.
36. *VDI/VDE 5565*; Optical Coherence Tomography (OCT): Process Descriptions. Verein Deutscher Ingenieure e.V.: Düsseldorf, Germany, 2023.
37. Stifter, D.; Wiesauer, K.; Wurm, M.; Schlotthauer, E.; Kastner, J.; Pircher, M.; Götzinger, E.; Hitzenberger, C.K. Investigation of polymer and polymer/fibre composite materials with optical coherence tomography. *Meas. Sci. Technol.* **2008**, *19*, 74011. [CrossRef]
38. Osari, K.; Unno, N.; Taniguchi, J.; Machinaga, K.; Ohsaki, T.; Sakai, N. Evaluation of filling behavior on UV nanoimprint lithography using release coating. *Microelectron. Eng.* **2010**, *87*, 918–921. [CrossRef]
39. Schleunitz, A.; Spreu, C.; Vogler, M.; Atasoy, H.; Schift, H. Combining nanoimprint lithography and a molecular weight selective thermal reflow for the generation of mixed 3D structures. *J. Vac. Sci. Technol. B Nanotechnol. Microelectron. Mater. Process. Meas. Phenom.* **2011**, *29*, 06FC01. [CrossRef]
40. LaFratta, C.N.; Li, L.; Fourkas, J.T. Soft-lithographic replication of 3D microstructures with closed loops. *Proc. Natl. Acad. Sci. USA* **2006**, *103*, 8589–8594. [CrossRef]
41. Carl Zeiss Microscopy GmbH. Extend the Limits of Your Exploration: ZEISS Xradia 610 and 620 Versa. Product Brochure. 2024. Available online: https://www.zeiss.com/microscopy/de/produkte/roentgenmikroskopie/xradia-versa.html#accordionItem-818906634 (accessed on 5 June 2024).
42. Szewczykowski, P.P.; Skarzynski, L. Application of the X-ray micro-computed tomography to the analysis of the structure of polymeric materials. *Polimery* **2019**, *64*, 12–22. [CrossRef]
43. Cangül, S.; Adıgüzel, Ö.; Sağmak, S.; Evran, B. A micro-computed tomography evaluation of the change in volume of different bulk-fill composite materials caused by polymerization shrinkage. *Int. Dent. Res.* **2021**, *11*, 75–82. [CrossRef]
44. Xie, X.-M.; Kong, X.-M.; Xiao, T.-J.; Yang, Y.; Gao, N.; Tanioka, A. Interface-Induced Coarsening Process in Polymer Blends. *J. Colloid Interface Sci.* **2001**, *234*, 24–27. [CrossRef]
45. Xu, X.; Zhu, T.; Yan, X.; Zhang, C. Temporal evolution of phase morphology of polypropylene/poly(ethylene octene) elastomer binary polymer blends by phase contrast microscope. *J. Appl. Polym. Sci.* **2007**, *104*, 2778–2784. [CrossRef]
46. Azzam, R.M. Photopolarimetric measurement of the Mueller matrix by Fourier analysis of a single detected signal. *Opt. Lett.* **1978**, *2*, 148. [CrossRef]
47. Käseberg, T.; Grundmann, J.; Siefke, T.; Klapetek, P.; Valtr, M.; Kroker, S.; Bodermann, B. Mueller Matrix Ellipsometric Approach on the Imaging of Sub-Wavelength Nanostructures. *Front. Phys.* **2022**, *9*, 814559. [CrossRef]
48. Cumpston, B.H.; Ananthavel, S.P.; Barlow, S.; Dyer, D.L.; Ehrlich, J.E.; Erskine, L.L.; Heikal, A.A.; Kuebler, S.M.; Lee, I.-Y.S.; McCord-Maughon, D.; et al. Two-photon polymerization initiators for three-dimensional optical data storage and microfabrication. *Nature* **1999**, *398*, 51–54. [CrossRef]
49. Schmid, M.; Ludescher, D.; Giessen, H. Optical properties of photoresists for femtosecond 3D printing: Refractive index, extinction, luminescence-dose dependence, aging, heat treatment and comparison between 1-photon and 2-photon exposure. *Opt. Mater. Express* **2019**, *9*, 4564. [CrossRef]
50. Crica, L.E.; Wengenroth, J.; Tiainen, H.; Ionita, M.; Haugen, H.J. Enhanced X-ray absorption for micro-CT analysis of low density polymers. *J. Biomater. Sci. Polym. Ed.* **2016**, *27*, 805–823. [CrossRef] [PubMed]
51. Gao, F.; Leach, R.K.; Petzing, J.; Coupland, J.M. Surface measurement errors using commercial scanning white light interferometers. *Meas. Sci. Technol.* **2008**, *19*, 15303. [CrossRef]
52. Gołek, F.; Mazur, P.; Ryszka, Z.; Zuber, S. AFM image artifacts. *Appl. Surf. Sci.* **2014**, *304*, 11–19. [CrossRef]
53. Nie, H.Y.; McIntyre, N.S. Unstable amplitude and noisy image induced by tip contamination in dynamic force mode atomic force microscopy. *Rev. Sci. Instrum.* **2007**, *78*, 23701. [CrossRef]

54. Cho, S.-J.; Ahn, B.-W.; Kim, J.; Lee, J.-M.; Hua, Y.; Yoo, Y.K.; Park, S. Three-dimensional imaging of undercut and sidewall structures by atomic force microscopy. *Rev. Sci. Instrum.* **2011**, *82*, 23707. [CrossRef]
55. Murayama, K.; Gonda, S.; Koyanagi, H.; Terasawa, T.; Hosaka, S. Side-Wall Measurement using Tilt-Scanning Method in Atomic Force Microscope. *Jpn. J. Appl. Phys.* **2006**, *45*, 5423. [CrossRef]
56. Wang, W.; Ma, C.; Chen, Y. Measurement of undercut etching by contact resonance atomic force microscopy. *Appl. Phys. Lett.* **2020**, *117*, 023103. [CrossRef]
57. Liu, P.; Groves, R.M.; Benedictus, R. Optical Coherence Tomography for the Study of Polymer and Polymer Matrix Composites. *Strain* **2014**, *50*, 436–443. [CrossRef]
58. Yao, J.; Rolland, J.P. *Optical Coherence Tomography for Polymer Film Evaluation;* IntechOpen: London, UK, 2020. [CrossRef]
59. Sun, J.; Lin-Gibson, S. X-ray microcomputed tomography for measuring polymerization shrinkage of polymeric dental composites. *Dent. Mater.* **2008**, *24*, 228–234. [CrossRef]
60. Cho, E.; Sadr, A.; Inai, N.; Tagami, J. Evaluation of resin composite polymerization by three dimensional micro-CT imaging and nanoindentation. *Dent. Mater.* **2011**, *27*, 1070–1078. [CrossRef]

metrology

Article

Reflectivity Thresholds and Optical Loss Predictions in Resonant Photonic Cavities

Paulo Henrique Dias Ferreira [1,2,*], Douglas Ramos do Amaral [2], Vinicius Tribuzi [1,2], John Fredy Ricardo Marroquin [3], Jorlandio Francisco Felix [3] and Filippo Ghiglieno [1,2,3]

1 Physics Department, Federal University of São Carlos (UFSCar), São Carlos 13565-905, SP, Brazil; tribuzi@ufscar.br (V.T.); filippo.ghiglieno@df.ufscar.br (F.G.)
2 Labóratorio de Óptica, LAser e Fotônica (ÓLAF) Physics Department, Federal University of São Carlos (UFSCar), São Carlos 13565-905, SP, Brazil; douglas.r.a@df.ufscar.br
3 Instituto de Física, Universidade de Brasília (UnB), Brasilia 70910-900, DF, Brazil; johnf1030@hotmail.com (J.F.R.M.); jorlandio@unb.br (J.F.F.)
* Correspondence: paulohdf@df.ufscar.br

Abstract: Minimizing optical losses in resonant cavities is crucial for improving photonic device performance. This study focuses on the development of a simulation tool to analyze scattering losses in Fabry–Pérot interferometers (FPIs), offering precise modeling of waveguide dynamics and contributing to accurate loss predictions across various platforms. Optical cavities often suffer from scattering losses due to surface roughness and material defects. Our approach integrates theoretical models and simulations to quantify these losses, utilizing the FPI as a model system. We identified upper and lower reflectivity thresholds, beyond which accurate measurement of losses becomes unreliable. For reflectivity below a certain threshold, measurement errors arise, while excessively high reflectivity can reduce fringe visibility and introduce detector sensitivity issues. Simulations were used to validate the model's ability to predict reflectivity and attenuation in waveguides with varying loss levels. The software's flexibility to adjust transmission parameters for different cavity configurations enhances its utility for a broad range of photonic systems. Our study offers a novel methodology for optical loss analysis, with practical applications in optimizing photonic devices. By providing a reliable tool for precise loss measurement, this work supports advancements in optical technologies, enabling the design of more efficient, high-performance devices across various applications.

Keywords: optical loss measurement; Fabry–Pérot interferometers; waveguide reflectivity; scattering losses; photonic device optimization

1. Introduction

Integrated photonics leverages light for transporting information and enabling diverse applications on several substrates. The goal is to miniaturize and integrate optical functions and devices into a unified platform, akin to how electronic circuits are incorporated into a microchip [1,2]. The primary advantage of integrated optics lies in its capability to manipulate and control light signals on a microscopic scale, resulting in compact and highly efficient optical systems. By embedding various optical components into a single chip, it becomes feasible to execute complex optical tasks, such as signal generation, modulation, amplification, routing, and detection, using a small and stable platform [3].

Silicon photonics, a dominant technology in this field, allows for seamless integration and fabrication within standard electronics foundries [4–6]. On the other hand, advances in glass waveguide fabrication technologies, such as femtosecond laser writing, offer promising alternatives. This technique employs ultrafast laser pulses to inscribe waveguides directly into glass substrates, providing precise control over the waveguide's geometry and properties [7–9]. By utilizing femtosecond laser writing, it is possible to create complex, three-dimensional photonic circuits that can be used in various applications, enhancing the versatility and performance of photonic devices. Numerous platforms exist for fabricating waveguides, including polymers, crystals, and others, each offering distinct characteristics that make them suitable for specific applications. Polymers, for example, are known for their flexibility and ease of processing, making them ideal for applications requiring large-scale or flexible photonic devices [10]. Crystals, conversely, often provide superior optical properties such as low loss and high nonlinearity, which are crucial for high-precision applications like nonlinear optics and high-power lasers [11]. Each material platform comes with its own set of advantages and disadvantages, necessitating careful selection based on the specific requirements and constraints of the intended application [2,12].

Independent of the technology, waveguides that confine and direct guided modes are central to the functionality of photonic devices. From a platform-based photonic design perspective, the propagation loss coefficient is essential in balancing device performance and physical footprint. Accurate measurement of these losses is, therefore, critical [13–16]. Consequently, developing a comprehensive model to describe the losses occurring in waveguides, regardless of the platform, is essential for the targeted and efficient design of integrated photonic devices. Several established methods for waveguide loss measurements exist [17], including the cut-back method, scattering microscopy, optical time domain reflectometry (OTDR), and integrating sphere techniques. Each of these approaches has specific advantages and limitations. For instance, the cut-back method is simple but destructive, while scattering microscopy provides localized information but lacks a holistic characterization of losses along the waveguide. Transmission-based techniques, such as FPI, offer non-destructive and rapid results but depend heavily on precise facet reflectivity calibration [18,19]. Our proposed methodology builds upon the Fabry–Pérot (FP) approach, addressing challenges in low-reflectivity systems by integrating high-reflectivity coatings and advanced simulations. This enables accurate loss measurements across diverse materials, overcoming the limitations of conventional methods and enhancing the design and optimization of photonic devices. This approach embeds both material absorption and scattering due to surface roughness into a single loss factor. By forming an optical cavity with the waveguide, it allows for the encapsulation of all loss mechanisms within the cavity's behavior. Understanding this combined loss factor enables engineers and researchers to optimize waveguide geometries and material choices, thereby enhancing device performance. Moreover, an accurate loss model is crucial for predicting the overall efficiency and reliability of photonic circuits, facilitating the integration of complex optical functions on a single chip. This predictive capability is indispensable for advancing photonic technologies and expanding their applications in communications, sensing, and computation.

Previous studies have suggested that measuring waveguide losses in glass is challenging due to its very low reflectivity, which impedes reliable loss assessment [20]. However, in a prior work, we demonstrated that this limitation can be overcome by applying a removable highly reflective coating (~0.40 reflectivity) to the waveguide facets [7]. This innovation enabled accurate loss measurements in glass waveguides using the FP technique, and our results showed a strong agreement with theoretical predictions. Building upon these results, the current study introduces advanced simulations developed using our purpose-built software. The simulations are designed to estimate propagation losses based on facet reflectivity, allowing us to explore waveguide performance across different material platforms, including low-, medium-, and high-reflectivity materials. By adjusting the reflectivity, we demonstrate how varying loss factors impact waveguide efficiency and functionality.

Our findings indicate that with appropriate modifications, such as the application of reflective coatings, accurate loss measurements can be achieved across a range of materials. This work not only validates the feasibility of loss measurements in glass but also extends the methodology to other platforms, providing a versatile tool for the design and optimization of integrated photonic devices.

2. Losses in a Waveguide

Waveguide losses can be categorized into three primary components [21]. Firstly, absorption losses arise from the intrinsic properties of the waveguide material itself, where the material absorbs some of the propagating light. Secondly, the finite number of bound modes in the waveguide allows for the existence of a continuum of radiative modes. Surface roughness acts as a perturbative element that couples these guided modes with radiative modes, leading to scattering losses. This scattering effect occurs due to imperfections on the waveguide surface, causing some of the light to scatter out of the guided modes into radiative modes. Thirdly, surface roughness can also induce backscattering within the guided mode, where the light is scattered in the reverse direction. However, material absorption losses are generally smaller compared to scattering losses caused by surface roughness, and, consequently, they are frequently regarded as negligible in many practical scenarios [19,22].

In our FP technique-based method, all contributions to propagation losses are encapsulated into a single factor (attenuation coefficient). This approach simplifies the loss characterization process while enhancing the robustness and accuracy of our simulations. By integrating these loss mechanisms into a unified model, we can more effectively predict and optimize waveguide performance across various platforms. This not only streamlines the design process but also enhances the capability to simulate and mitigate losses in integrated photonic devices.

3. The Fabry–Pérot Technique

Waveguide low-loss evaluation can be effectively performed using the FP technique, which was initially applied to lithium niobate ($Li:NbO_3$) systems [23,24]. This technique offers significant advantages, such as independence from optical coupling and the ability to produce rapid results without altering the physical properties of the sample during testing. The simplicity and non-destructive nature of this method make it particularly appealing for practical applications. However, the accuracy of this method is constrained by the precision with which the modal facet reflectivity is known, as this parameter is critical for accurate measurements [25].

The planar phase front of a guided mode allows the transmission characteristics of a waveguide to be treated similarly to those of an FP resonator under plane–wave approximation [26]. This hypothesis simplifies the analysis, enabling the use of established resonator theory to evaluate waveguide performance. Specifically, in a single-mode waveguide with a monochromatic input, the transmission can be described by the Airy function, which characterizes the resonant behavior of the waveguide, providing a clear framework for understanding and quantifying losses:

$$T_{FP} = \eta \frac{T^2 e^{-\alpha L}}{(1-R')^2 + 4R' sin^2\left(\frac{\phi}{2}\right)}, \tag{1}$$

where η is the coupling efficiency, L the waveguide length, α the modal attenuation coefficient, $R(T)$ the reflectivity (transmission) of the two facets (supposed to be equal), and $R' = R\, e^{(-\alpha L)}$ the combined loss–reflection factor. As in [26], T_{FP} is a periodic function of the round-trip dephasing $\phi = 2k_0 n_{eff} L + \phi_0$, with k_0 being the free-space wave vector and n_{eff} the mode effective index. In practical scenarios, the finite bandwidth of the light source can influence fringe visibility and, consequently, the accuracy of attenuation coefficient calculations, resulting in a slight increase in measurement uncertainty [27]. By adjusting the input wavelength or altering the effective index (such as through changes in sample temperature), the transmission T_{FP} oscillates between its maximum (T_{max}) and minimum (T_{min}) values, which are solely dependent on the reflectivity R'. This variation in transmission can be observed by measuring the contrast of the transmission fringes as

$$K = \frac{(T_{max} - T_{min})}{(T_{max} + T_{min})}, \tag{2}$$

The reflectivity R' can be determined using the following relation:

$$R' = \frac{1}{K}\left(1 - \sqrt{1 - K^2}\right), \tag{3}$$

Given the known modal reflectivity R of the facet, the attenuation coefficient can be computed using the following formula:

$$K = \frac{(T_{max} - T_{min})}{(T_{max} + T_{min})}, \tag{4}$$

For single-mode, weakly confining waveguides (such as, for example, $Ti : LiNbO_3$, or annealed $H^+ : LiNbO_3$ waveguides), the Fresnel formula provides a good approximation for the reflectivity R as

$$R = \left(\frac{n_{eff} - 1}{n_{eff} + 1}\right)^2, \tag{5}$$

due to the guided mode's small numerical aperture. This method typically achieves high accuracy in measuring the attenuation coefficient, often better than 0.1 dB/cm.

Reflectivity R can be modified by applying high-reflectivity coatings (HRCs) or anti-reflection (ARCs) coatings to the end facets. Using HRCs at the waveguide's end facets reduces interference from additional FP cavities in the measurement setup. This interference can introduce modulations in the measured T_{FP} across the wavelength range, complicating the determination of the contrast K from the sample being tested, as shown in [7].

4. Simulation Framework and Experimental Setup

As mentioned before, different systems employ a variety of techniques to measure optical losses, and in cases such as transparent polymers with low reflectivity, the method presented in this study could offer substantial advantages. However, prior to applying the HRCs to the facets of these materials, it is crucial to determine the minimum reflectivity required for accurate attenuation coefficient measurements.

To address this, we developed a Python-based simulator that integrates scientific and graphical packages to model the required reflectivity, based on typical material losses. The simulator is based on the transfer–matrix method (TMM) in optical cavities; it is analytical and scalable [28]. This tool facilitates precise simulations, allowing us to identify the optimal reflectivity necessary for accurate loss measurements. This approach not only improves the reliability of the measurement process but also broadens its applicability across a wider range of material systems. The TMM is inherently flexible and can be adapted to other resonant photonic cavities, such as ring resonators or photonic crystal cavities. However, the effectiveness of the method depends on the specific geometry and refractive index profile of the structure being analyzed. For example, while FP systems are well suited to planar waveguides, additional considerations such as bending losses and mode coupling may arise in ring resonators. This adaptability demonstrates the potential of the proposed methodology to extend beyond glass waveguides, addressing a wide range of photonic platforms. Additionally, the TMM assumes a separation between the transverse (XY) and longitudinal (Z) components of light propagation, enabling an efficient analysis of waveguide behavior. This simplification makes the method particularly suitable for systems dominated by the fundamental mode, which exhibits symmetric field profiles and lower loss characteristics. However, in multimode systems, where higher-order modes exhibit more complex patterns and intermodal coupling, the TMM may provide averaged results rather than mode-specific details. Extensions of the method to account for such complexities are possible but require additional computational frameworks [29].

The Python-based simulation tool (see Supplementary Materials) leverages the TMM to model FP fringes with high accuracy. The methodology accounts for various key parameters, including facet reflectivity, waveguide loss levels, and external cavity interference, systematically varying these factors to replicate experimental conditions for glass waveguides and other materials. This enables the identification of reflectivity thresholds and the precise evaluation of attenuation coefficients. Additionally, the influence of external factors, such as interference from unintended cavities, is integrated into the analysis to ensure robust predictions of fringe visibility and measurement precision.

In a typical characterization setup, the primary components include a fiber at the injection side (see Figure 1a), with the sample positioned centrally (see Figure 1b), and either a fiber or a lens at the collection side (see Figure 1c,d). Utilizing a lens for light collection enhances the efficiency of the characterization process, particularly when dealing with multiple waveguides on the same sample. Switching between waveguides is facilitated by transitioning to visible light and verifying alignment on a whiteboard after the lens, which ensures accurate light injection. This setup involves four interfaces and three optical cavities.

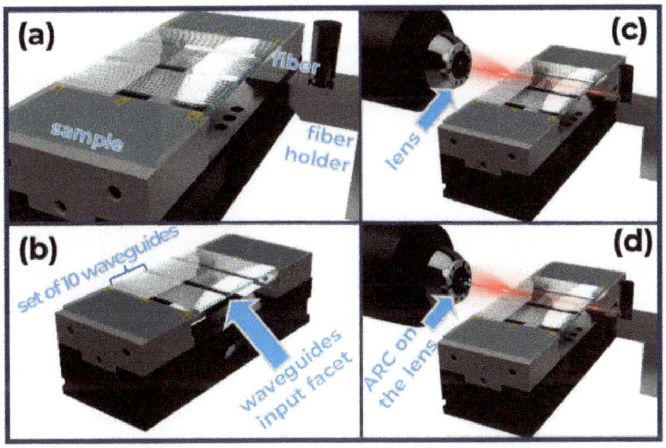

Figure 1. (**a**) The fiber (right) in front of the sample, a waveguide in a glass matrix; (**b**) the sample, 30 waveguides directly written on a glass matrix with femtosecond pulsed laser; (**c**) the characterization setup, the fiber, the sample, and the collecting lens; (**d**) the characterization setup, the fiber, the sample, and the collecting lens with antireflection coating (ARC).

5. Data Analysis

In the subsequent simulation, we analyze the overall transmission across four scenarios where the sample is inscribed within a glass matrix using a femtosecond laser. Figure 2 depicts scenarios with a single cavity (the sample, 2.24 cm in length and 5% reflectivity at both facets, black line), two cavities (the cleaved injection fiber with a micro-scale focal distance, 5% reflectivity, and the sample, blue line), and three cavities (the fiber, the sample, and a BK7 lens with a 1.8 cm focal length) both without (red line) and with waveguide losses ($\alpha_2 = 0.35$ cm^{-1}, magenta line).

The third cavity, formed between the back facet of the sample and the collecting lens, significantly affects the observed fringe pattern. This additional interference distorts the visibility of the fringes, introducing unwanted modulations in the measurement spectrum, which reduce the contrast necessary to accurately assess the waveguide's performance. As a result, the visibility of the fringes is compromised, and it becomes increasingly difficult to obtain a precise estimate of the optical losses within the waveguide. This interference can obscure important details about the attenuation, making it challenging to isolate the FP fringes associated with the sample from those introduced by the external cavity. Such disturbances lead to inaccuracies in loss measurement, particularly when trying to apply standard methods for determining the attenuation coefficient. Therefore, minimizing or mitigating the effects of this third cavity is crucial to ensuring the reliability and precision of the loss measurements.

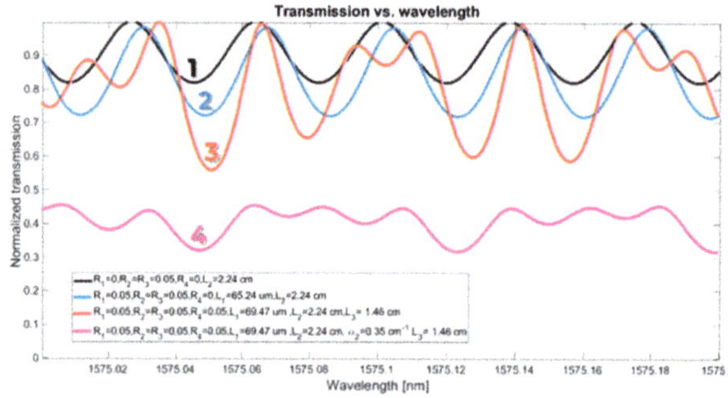

Figure 2. (1) The FP fringes in transmission when we study the waveguide only (setup configuration in Figure 1b); (2) the FP fringes in transmission when we study the waveguide with the coupling fiber (setup configuration in Figure 1a); (3) the FP fringes in transmission when we study the waveguide with the coupling fiber and the collecting lens without losses in the sample (setup configuration in Figure 1c); (4) the FP fringes in transmission when we study the waveguide with the coupling fiber and the collecting lens with losses in the sample (setup configuration in Figure 1c).

Technological advancements in the optical component market now offer solutions to mitigate these issues. To maintain the described setup configuration, it is possible to purchase lenses with anti-reflection coatings (see Figure 1d), which could significantly reduce the influence of the third cavity [30].

Figure 3, line 2 (blue line) demonstrates how the previous configuration (fiber, sample, and lens) with a lossy waveguide could benefit from applying an anti-reflection coating (ARC) to the collecting lens. Despite this, the fringe pattern remains affected by interference between the second and third cavities, which complicates the accurate estimation of visibility—a crucial factor for calculating sample losses, as detailed in the previous paragraph.

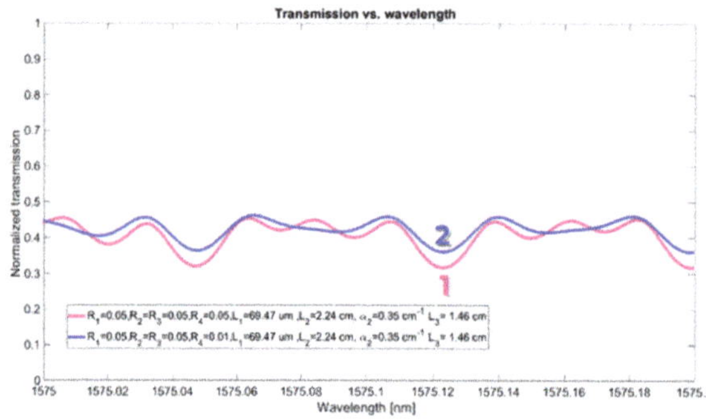

Figure 3. The FP fringes in transmission of lossy waveguides (1) without coating (Figure 1c); and (2) with an anti-reflection coating (ARC) on the collecting lens interface (Figure 1d).

To enhance visibility for a more precise loss estimation in the waveguide, we proposed an additional technological step. By using our simulation software, we provide a method to determine the optimal minimal high-reflectivity coating (HRC) to be deposited on the sample's end facets. This approach strengthens the contribution of the second cavity, effectively amplifying its role in the interference pattern and, as a result, improving the overall accuracy of the measurement.

The results from the simulations are summarized in Figure 4. As shown, we present the outcomes for two different loss levels—0.3 cm^{-1} and 0.5 cm^{-1}—depicted in panels (a) and (b), respectively, as a function of the reflectivity of the device faces. The simulation indicates that higher losses correspond, as expected, to reduced visibility, as observed in the color map.

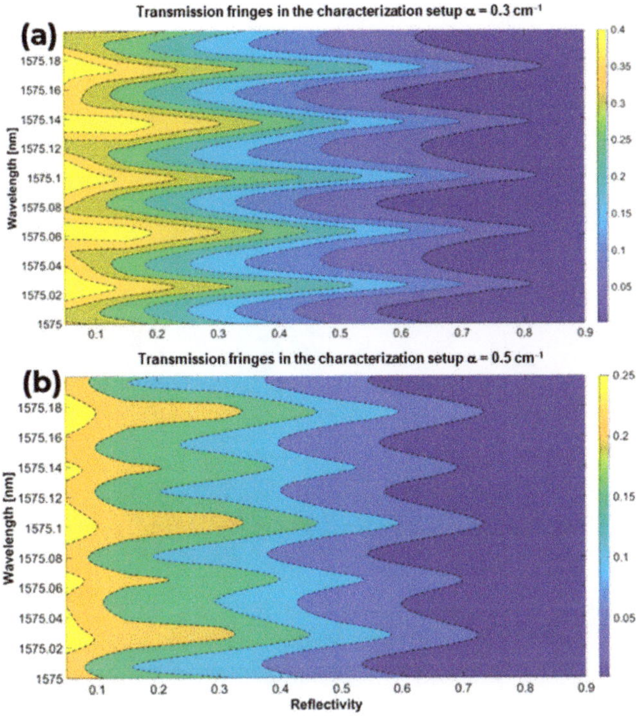

Figure 4. Transmission fringes as function of the wavelength and reflectivity for a waveguide with (**a**) 0.3 cm^{-1} and (**b**) 0.5 cm^{-1} losses.

6. Discussion

As the losses increase, the constraints on the HRC that can be applied to the device also become more stringent. While it might seem logical to assume that increasing HRC would consistently improve the accuracy of attenuation coefficient measurements in waveguides—especially when aiming for nearly perfect reflectivity values such as 99.99%—our simulations revealed a more complex reality. We found that there is a critical threshold to the HRC that can be effectively applied, beyond which further increases in reflectivity not only fail to enhance accuracy but can hinder the measurement process. This threshold becomes particularly important in high-loss systems, where exceeding the optimal reflectivity point results in a significant reduction in fringe visibility. Thus, instead of achieving better precision, excessive reflectivity creates conditions where the measurement's reliability is compromised by detector limitations and noise, ultimately degrading the quality of the data. These findings suggest the importance of carefully balancing HRC values to match the specific loss characteristics of the waveguide material being tested, rather than assuming that higher reflectivity universally leads to better outcomes. For instance, as shown in Figure 4, visibility for waveguides with losses of 0.3 cm^{-1} drops significantly beyond 90% HRC, while for waveguides with losses of 0.5 cm^{-1}, visibility declines sharply after 75% HRC.

Additionally, our findings indicate a lower threshold for the HRC, which is also intricately linked to the inherent losses within the waveguide. This emphasizes the importance of finding the right balance between achieving the desired reflectivity and managing the associated uncertainty. Previous studies, such as that of Hofstetter et al. [31], although providing a foundational analysis of FP resonators, focused on the use of Fourier analysis for loss measurements in high-finesse laser systems. In contrast, this work extends the methodology to include practical limitations such as detector sensitivity and interference from external cavities, providing validated experimental results for materials like glass waveguides. This highlights the applicability of the proposed approach to integrated photonic systems with diverse material platforms. Figure 5a,b illustrate the optimal trade-off between loss measurement and uncertainty, revealing that this balance is highly dependent on the specific loss characteristics of the waveguide. For waveguides with lower losses, convergence occurs more rapidly as the HRC increases, resulting in a corresponding decrease in measurement uncertainty. Conversely, waveguides with higher losses also show convergence as the HRC increases, but at a slightly slower rate and with greater uncertainty.

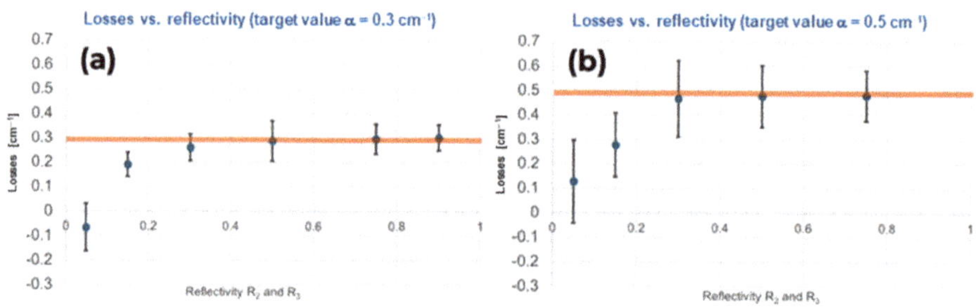

Figure 5. Calculated losses with the FP technique for a waveguide with 0.3 cm^{-1} (**a**) and 0.5 cm^{-1} (**b**) losses as function of the HRC at the sample end facets.

With both sets of results at hand, we present a more comprehensive analysis of the trends depicted in Figures 4 and 5, offering deeper insights into the implications of the simulation outcomes. These figures illustrate the trade-offs associated with high-reflectivity coatings (HRCs). For example, while HRCs improve fringe visibility and measurement accuracy, excessive reflectivity can introduce fringe distortion and achieve detector limitations, particularly in high-loss systems. Figure 5 further demonstrates the critical balance required between reflectivity and loss characteristics, highlighting that the ideal HRC level depends on the material properties and specific experimental conditions. These findings underscore the practical implications of reflectivity optimization and validate the versatility of our approach across different material platforms.

This relationship highlights that while increasing the HRC generally improves measurement accuracy by reducing uncertainty, the extent of this benefit varies depending on the initial loss characteristics of the waveguide. To validate our approach, we conducted a detailed study on a waveguide with 0.1 cm^{-1} loss (Figure 6).

In this scenario, the visibility of the interference fringes can be detected with an HRC of up to 99%. For a loss level value of 0.1 cm^{-1}, the convergence is faster compared to cases with higher losses, such as 0.3 cm^{-1} and 0.5 cm^{-1}. However, it is only when the HRC reaches 60% that the uncertainty is reduced to 20% of the target value, reinforcing the importance of optimizing the HRC to achieve precise measurements. This optimization is essential to minimize measurement uncertainty and ensure precise loss estimation, as shown in the results of Figure 5.

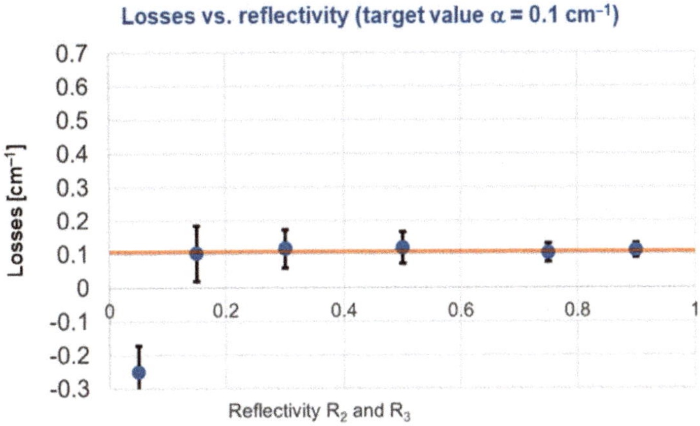

Figure 6. Calculated losses with the FP technique for a waveguide with 0.3 cm^{-1} (**a**) and 0.5 cm^{-1} (**b**) losses as function of the HRC at the sample ad facets.

Additionally, during our study, we observed that for reflectivity below a certain threshold (specifically around 5%), the simulations began to yield negative loss values (particularly for target losses of 0.1 cm^{-1} and 0.3 cm^{-1}), clearly indicating that such low reflectivity values make it impossible to accurately measure waveguide losses. This is a critical insight, as it shows that for reflectivity below this threshold, the interference fringes lack the necessary visibility to produce reliable attenuation measurements. Beyond this observation, our simulations further demonstrate that there is a minimum reflectivity limit which is directly tied to the level of loss in the waveguide. This lower limit is crucial, as it highlights that attempting to measure losses with reflectivity below this value leads not only to unreliable data but also to substantial uncertainty in the results. As waveguide losses increase, the reflectivity threshold required to obtain meaningful measurements also rises. This observation stresses the importance of carefully selecting appropriate reflectivity values based on the specific loss characteristics of the material being tested, ensuring that the measurement process remains both accurate and consistent. These findings underscore that while higher reflectivity helps reduce uncertainty, striking the optimal balance between HRC and waveguide loss characteristics is essential for accurate measurements.

7. Conclusions

In conclusion, our study provides valuable insights into optimizing waveguide loss measurements by carefully tuning the high-reflectivity coatings (HRCs). While earlier studies suggested limitations in measuring losses for low-reflectivity materials, we successfully demonstrated that by applying HRCs and using targeted simulations, it is possible to achieve accurate attenuation coefficient measurements even in challenging systems such as glass or transparent polymer waveguides. Through simulations, we established both upper and lower reflectivity thresholds, ensuring optimal visibility and minimized uncertainty across a range of loss values.

Our findings underscore the importance of balancing HRC to suit the specific loss characteristics of the waveguide. Higher reflectivity does not always guarantee better precision, as there are critical thresholds beyond which further increases in HRC introduce more challenges, such as detector sensitivity issues. At the same time, a lower reflectivity bound is essential to avoid excessive measurement uncertainty. The flexibility of our approach extends beyond glass waveguides, showing promise for use with other platforms like polymers and medium-reflectivity materials.

The methodology developed here not only addresses the critical limitations of existing loss measurement techniques but also introduces a systematic framework for optimizing reflectivity thresholds. This ensures accurate characterization even in low-reflectivity materials, which are essential for the advancement of integrated photonics. Ultimately, this work presents a practical framework for improving the precision and applicability of loss measurements in integrated photonic devices, contributing to advancements in optical communications, sensing technologies, and photonic system optimization. The potential to apply this method across diverse material platforms makes it a relevant tool for future developments in the field.

Supplementary Materials: The following supporting information can be downloaded at: https://www.mdpi.com/article/10.3390/metrology4040044/s1, Figure S1: Graphical user interface (GUI) for simulating waveguide loss measurements using the Fabry-Pérot technique, displaying input parameters and real-time transmittance visualization.

Author Contributions: Conceptualization, P.H.D.F. and F.G.; methodology, P.H.D.F. and F.G.; software, D.R.d.A. and F.G.; validation, D.R.d.A., F.G. and P.H.D.F.; formal analysis, P.H.D.F. and F.G.; investigation, P.H.D.F. and F.G.; resources, P.H.D.F.; data curation, P.H.D.F.; writing—original draft preparation, P.H.D.F. and F.G.; writing—review and editing, P.H.D.F., F.G., V.T., J.F.R.M. and J.F.F.; visualization, J.F.R.M., P.H.D.F. and F.G.; supervision, P.H.D.F. and F.G. All authors have read and agreed to the published version of the manuscript.

Funding: This research was funded by FAPESP, project n° 16/21322-4 (PDE) and n° 13/21569-1 (AUXPE).

Data Availability Statement: The data supporting the findings of this study are available upon request. Interested researchers can contact the corresponding author for access to the datasets generated or analyzed during the study. All data will be provided in accordance with ethical and privacy considerations.

Acknowledgments: The authors would like to express their gratitude to the Physics Department at the Federal University of São Carlos and the Instituto de Física at the Universidade de Brasília (UnB) for their valuable support and resources, which were instrumental in the successful completion of this research.

Conflicts of Interest: The authors declare no conflicts of interest.

References

1. Eldada, L.; Shacklette, L.W. Advances in polymer integrated optics. *IEEE J. Sel. Top. Quantum Electron.* **2000**, *6*, 54–68. [CrossRef]
2. Butt, M.A. Integrated Optics: Platforms and Fabrication Methods. *Encyclopedia* **2023**, *3*, 824–838. [CrossRef]
3. Minzioni, P.; Lacava, C.; Tanabe, T.; Dong, J.; Hu, X.; Csaba, G.; Porod, W.; Singh, G.; Willner, A.E.; Almaiman, A.; et al. Roadmap on all-optical processing. *J. Opt.* **2019**, *21*, 063001. [CrossRef]
4. Stojanović, V.; Ram, R.J.; Popović, M.; Lin, S.; Moazeni, S.; Wade, M.; Sun, C.; Alloatti, L.; Atabaki, A.; Pavanello, F.; et al. Monolithic silicon-photonic platforms in state-of-the-art CMOS SOI processes. *Opt. Express* **2018**, *26*, 13106–13121. [CrossRef]
5. Chrostowski, L.; Hochberg, M. *Silicon Photonics Design: From Devices to Systems*; Cambridge University Press: Cambridge, UK, 2015.
6. Luan, E.; Shoman, H.; Ratner, D.M.; Cheung, K.C.; Chrostowski, L. Silicon Photonic Biosensors Using Label-Free Detection. *Sensors* **2018**, *18*, 3519. [CrossRef] [PubMed]
7. Ferreira, P.H.D.; Tribuzi, V.; Osellame, R.; Ghiglieno, F. Improvement in measuring losses by interferometric technique for glass waveguides produced by femtosecond laser writing. *Opt. Commun.* **2023**, *530*, 129132. [CrossRef]
8. Sugioka, K.; Cheng, Y. Fabrication of 3D microfluidic structures inside glass by femtosecond laser micromachining. *Appl. Phys. A* **2014**, *114*, 215–221. [CrossRef]
9. Blanc, W.; Choi, Y.G.; Zhang, X.; Nalin, M.; Richardson, K.A.; Righini, G.C.; Ferrari, M.; Jha, A.; Massera, J.; Jiang, S.; et al. The past, present and future of photonic glasses: A review in homage to the United Nations International Year of glass 2022. *Prog. Mater. Sci.* **2023**, *134*, 101084.
10. Park, S.; Shou, W.; Makatura, L.; Matusik, W.; Fu, K.K. 3D printing of polymer composites: Materials, processes, and applications. *Matter* **2022**, *5*, 43–76. [CrossRef]
11. Boyd, R.W. *Nonlinear Optics*, 3rd ed.; Academic Press: Cambridge, MA, USA, 2007.
12. DeCorby, R. Glasses for Photonic Integration. In *Springer Handbook of Electronic and Photonic Materials*; Kasap, S., Capper, P., Eds.; Springer: New York, NY, USA, 2007; pp. 1041–1061.
13. Moresco, M.; Romagnoli, M.; Boscolo, S.; Midrio, M.; Cherchi, M.; Hosseini, E.S.; Coolbaugh, D.; Watts, M.R.; Dutt, B. Method for characterization of Si waveguide propagation loss. *Opt. Express* **2013**, *21*, 5391–5400. [CrossRef]

14. Okamura, Y.; Yoshinaka, S.; Yamamoto, S. Measuring mode propagation losses of integrated optical waveguides: A simple method. *Appl. Opt.* **1983**, *22*, 3892–3894. [CrossRef] [PubMed]
15. Tran, M.A.; Komljenovic, T.; Hulme, J.C.; Davenport, M.L.; Bowers, J.E. A robust method for characterization of optical waveguides and couplers. *IEEE Photonics Technol. Lett.* **2016**, *28*, 1517–1520. [CrossRef]
16. Reja, M.I.; Akhtar, J.; Malik, M.N.; Ahmed, S.; Islam, J.; Iqbal, A. A comparative analysis of the characterization methods for submicron silicon waveguide propagation loss. In Proceedings of the 2015 2nd International Conference on Electrical Information and Communication Technologies (EICT), Khulna, Bangladesh, 10–12 December 2015; pp. 347–352.
17. Hunsperger, R.G. Losses in optical waveguides. In *Integrated Optics: Theory and Technology*; Springer: New York, NY, USA, 2009.
18. Selvaraja, S.K.; Sethi, P. Review on Optical Waveguides. In *Emerging Waveguide Technology*; You, K.Y., Ed.; IntechOpen: London, UK, 2018.
19. Melati, D.; Melloni, A.; Morichetti, F. Real photonic waveguides: Guiding light through imperfections. *Adv. Opt. Photon.* **2014**, *6*, 156–224. [CrossRef]
20. He, Y.; Lu, D.; Zhao, L. Reflection Airy distribution of a Fabry-Pérot resonator and its application in waveguide loss measurement. *Opt. Express* **2019**, *27*, 17876–17886. [CrossRef] [PubMed]
21. Hörmann, S.M.; Hinum-Wagner, J.W.; Bergmann, A.; Initio, A.A.; Coherent, F. Semi-Analytical Model of Surface-Roughness-Induced Scattering. *J. Light. Technol.* **2023**, *41*, 1503–1510. [CrossRef]
22. Payne, F.P.; Lacey, J.P.R. A theoretical analysis of scattering loss from planar optical waveguides. *Opt. Quantum Electron.* **1994**, *26*, 977–986. [CrossRef]
23. Regener, R.; Sohler, W. Loss in low-finesse Ti:LiNbO3 optical waveguide resonators. *Appl. Phys. B* **1985**, *36*, 143–147. [CrossRef]
24. De Rossi, A.; Ortiz, V.; Calligaro, M.; Lanco, L.; Ducci, S.; Berger, V.; Sagnes, I. Measuring propagation loss in a multimode semiconductor waveguide. *J. Appl. Phys.* **2005**, *97*, 073105. [CrossRef]
25. Tittelbach, G.; Richter, B.; Karthe, W. Comparison of three transmission methods for integrated optical waveguide propagation loss measurement. *Pure Appl. Opt.* **1993**, *2*, 683. [CrossRef]
26. The Fabry-Perot Interferometer: History, Theory, Practice and Applications. Available online: https://www.routledge.com/The-Fabry-Perot-Interferometer-History-Theory-Practice-and-Applications/Vaughan/p/book/9780852741382 (accessed on 30 August 2024).
27. Yu, B.; Wang, A.; Pickrell, G.R. Analysis of Fiber Fabry–Pérot Interferometric Sensors Using Low-Coherence Light Sources. *J. Light. Technol.* **2006**, *24*, 1758–1767.
28. van de Stadt, H.; Muller, J.M. Multimirror Fabry–Perot interferometers. *J. Opt. Soc. Am. A* **1985**, *2*, 1363–1370. [CrossRef]
29. Li, Z.-Y.; Lin, L.-L.; Ho, K.-M. Light coupling with multimode photonic crystal waveguides. *Appl. Phys. Lett.* **2004**, *84*, 4699–4701. [CrossRef]
30. C280TMD-C-Mounted Aspheric Lens, f = 18.4 mm, NA = 0.15, WD = 15.6 mm, ARC: 1050–1700 nm. Available online: https://www.thorlabs.com/ (accessed on 30 August 2024).
31. Hofstetter, D.; Thornton, R.L. Theory of loss measurements of Fabry–Perot resonators by Fourier analysis of the transmission spectra. *Opt. Lett.* **1997**, *22*, 1831–1833. [CrossRef] [PubMed]

metrology

MDPI

Article

An Inexpensive, 3D-Printable, Arduino- and Blu-Ray-Based Confocal Laser and Fluorescent Scanning Microscope

Justin Loose [1], Samuel H. Hales [1,2], Jonah Kendell [1], Isaac Cutler [1], Ryan Ruth [1], Jacob Redd [1], Samuel Lino [1] and Troy Munro [1,*]

[1] Department of Mechanical Engineering, Brigham Young University, Provo, UT 84602, USA; jsloose@student.byu.edu (J.L.); samuel.hales@utah.edu (S.H.H.)
[2] Department of Mechanical Engineering, University of Utah, Salt Lake City, UT 84112, USA
* Correspondence: troy.munro@byu.edu

Abstract: There is a growing field that is devoted to developing inexpensive microscopes and measurement devices by leveraging low-cost commercial parts that can be controlled using smartphones or embedded devices, such as Arduino and Raspbery Pi. Examples include the use of Blu-ray optical heads like the PHR-803T to perform cytometry, spinning disc microscopy, and lensless holographic microscopy. The modular or disposable nature of these devices means that they can also be used in contaminating and degrading environments, including radioactive environments, where replacement of device elements can be expensive. This paper presents the development and operation of a confocal microscope that uses the PHR-803T optical device in a Blu-ray reader for both imaging and detection of temperature variations with between 1.5 and 15 μm resolution. The benefits of using a PHR-803T confocal system include its relatively inexpensive design and the accessibility of the components that are used in its construction. The design of this scanning confocal thermal microscope (SCoT) was optimized based on cost, modularity, portability, spatial resolution, and ease of manufacturability using common tools (e.g., drill press, 3D printer). This paper demonstrated the ability to resolve microscale features such as synthetic spider silk and measure thermal waves in stainless steel using a system requiring <USD 1000 in material costs.

Keywords: commercial off-the-shelf (COTS); confocal microscopy; blu-ray; thermal characterization

1. Introduction

In the study of nuclear materials, post-irradiation examination (PIE) is a critical part of understanding the impact that radiation damage has had on the material performance [1]. The process is broken up into different stages (Figure 1) based on the size and radioactivity of the sample [2]. The materials of interest are pulled from the reactor core and allowed to cool in a pool, after which they are moved into a hot cell, where handling of materials can only be accomplished with "requester–responder" manipulators [3]. The sample preparation process begins with dismantling the assembly and ends with samples being cut into the appropriately sized specimens for further analysis [2] within a hot cell. The current paper presents the development of an inexpensive microscope (the scanning confocal thermal (SCoT) microscope) that has the potential to be used in these post-irradiation examination (PIE) processes.

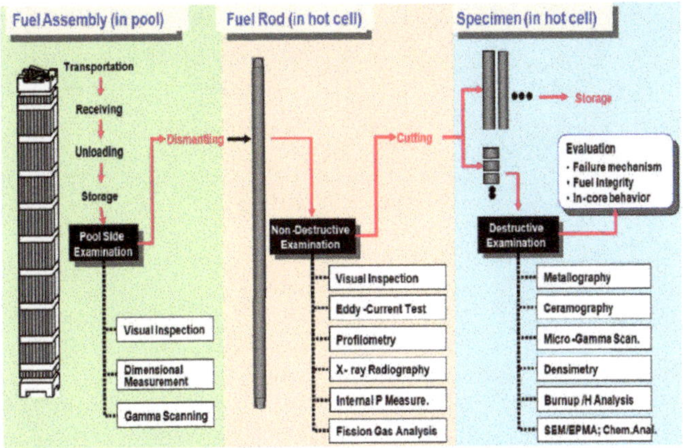

Figure 1. Overview of post-irradiation examination (PIE) process [2].

Prior to more expensive testing, which often involves electron or X-ray microscopy, metallography or ceramography is performed within the hot cell using optical microscopes to understand the macroscopic nature of the material [4]. This allows the 2D morphology of the material to be measured at the µm to mm scale, with a focus on the detection of grains, porosity, bubbles, and cracking [5]. Recent developments in thermal characterization microscopy [6] have also allowed measurements of the spatial distribution of the material's thermal properties to be taken [7]. Confocal microscopy, where either reflected or emitted light is collected from a single optical plane of the sample, has been used to recreate the fracture behavior of ferritic/martensitic steel by measuring the surface topology of the fracture surface [8]. It has also been used to understand the erosion of plasma-facing components in fusion tokamaks [9] by again measuring the topography of the irradiated sample. A microscope that can observe both thermal and topological changes [10] within the material would be a valuable tool.

Confocal microscopy [11] involves the use of an illumination or excitation light source that is focused through a pinhole (or iris) onto a sample that is capable of fluorescing and the collection of the emitted light through a pinhole (Figure 2). The locations of the pinholes are such that only light emitted from the sample at a particular plane is collected into the detector, as opposed to standard microscopy, where light from multiple planes is collected by the detector. This allows for higher-contrast images, while movement of the sample along the focal axis allows "slices" of the sample at different depths to be imaged to understand the topography of the material [12].

As the devices in the hot cell are in a radioactive environment, expensive radiation-resistant materials have to be used to prevent browning of the optical components (i.e., going opaque) and to shield any electrical equipment to ensure the device continues to operate [13]. For imaging, the standard approach is to buy a single, expensive, custom-made radiation-hardened camera from companies such as Optique Peter. A second approach is to buy a commercial off-the-shelf (COTS) webcam, fully expecting it to have a short lifespan. The latter "disposable" model has been implemented successfully at the hot cell in Pacific Northwest National Laboratory [14], but this approach has not yet been applied to other imaging or measurement systems. This paper presents the proof-of-concept of a dual-purpose microscope based on COTS devices and low-cost, modular electronics that is meant to perform optical (confocal in particular) and thermal measurements.

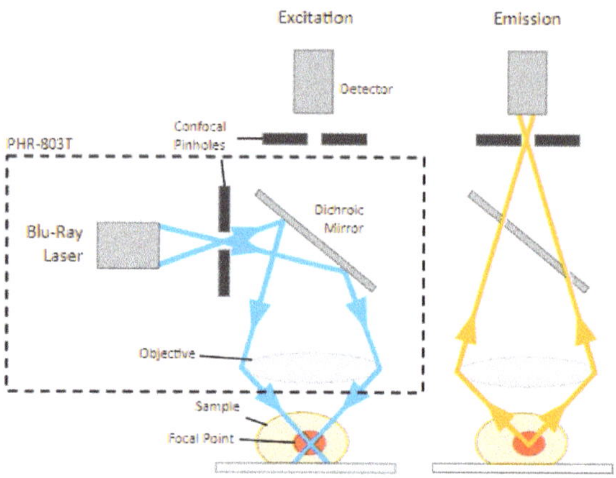

Figure 2. A diagram of the device optics, showing the light paths for both excitation and emission that are required for performing confocal microscopy.

In order to develop inexpensive do-it-yourself (DIY) confocal microscopes, researchers have leveraged a variety of low-cost, commercially available equipment, such as by modifying existing epifluorescence or total internal reflection fluorescence microscopes [15]. As an example, Gong [16] developed a simple LED-powered, camera-imaged, partially 3D-printed, and non-automated confocal microscope for USD 5188, while commercial devices cost between USD 10 k and USD 100 k. Further developments of cheap microscopes involved a scanning point fluorescence microscope that imaged biological samples rapidly by using the disc drive and PHR-803T optical head of a Blu-ray player [17]. An optical head is the part of an optical disc reader that contains the laser diodes, optical components (mirrors, filers, lenses), and detectors to measure light on the optical disc. Another researcher used the Blu-ray PHR-803T optical head to determine impurities in crystals at cryogenic temperatures [18].

In further support of this low-cost, COTS, and expendable approach to instrumentation, there is a surprisingly large, and growing, body of work in the literature on the use of the Arduino platform in the development of measurement systems. The applications of this are varied, including allowing for remote health monitoring [19], remote measurements on UAVs [20], small satellites [21], high-altitude prototypes [22], and educational tools to train students for internet of things [23] or laboratory systems [24]. The Arduino platform has also been used to control fluorescent microscopes using the PHR-803T, a low-cost, compact optical system [25,26].

The PHR-803T is the optical component that is used to read disc data in Blu-ray and HD-DVD players and is often used in many DIY projects by hobbyists and academic researchers [27]. This has ensured that there is a large amount of existing software and hardware to make the optical head function. This is because the optical head is relatively cheap (USD 15) and contains 405 nm, 660 nm, and 785 nm lasers in a small, pre-engineered package [27]. This hacking has been useful in biosensing with bioassays on the Blu-ray disc [27], high-contrast label-free imaging of cells [28], optical tweezers in microfluidic devices controlled by an Arduino [29], atomic force microscope imaging [30], digital lenseless holographic microscopy [31], and as a Blu-ray scanning microscope [17]. Another DIY microscope (not laser scanning) was able to be constructed from an open-source series of modules based on Rasperry Pi and Arduino systems [32]. Our previous research [26] used the PHR-803T in a stationary fluorescent scanning thermal microscope to provide optical illumination, focusing, and optical transmission to a separate photodiode. However, it could not scan the surface of the sample to determine its surface characteristics.

This paper presents the design and operation of a modular, low-cost, confocal laser scanning microscope using the PHR-803T and controlled by an Arduino that would fit within this "disposable" model for hot cell usage to characterize nuclear materials. The ability of the SCoT microscope to measure in reflection mode, confocal fluorescent mode, and temperature-sensitive mode will be demonstrated. The final spatial resolution of the SCoT microscope is 12.5 μm in the horizontal and 1.5 μm in the vertical directions.

2. Device Overview

This section provides an overview of the SCoT microscope (Figure 3), including its basic features, such as the optical system (including the PHR-803T Toshiba PHR-803T, Tokyo, Japan), the positioning system, and the electronics. The design has been guided by constraints on cost, modularity, portability, spatial resolution, and ease of manufacturability using common tools (e.g., drill press, 3D printer).

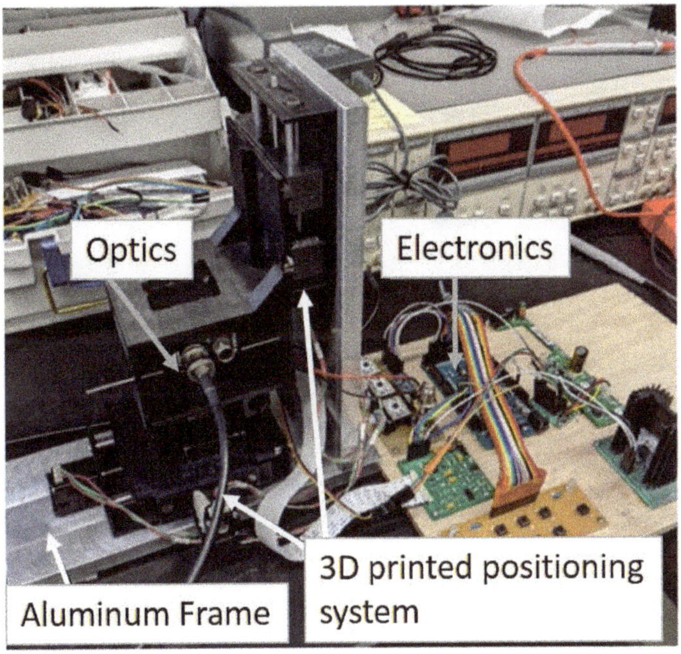

Figure 3. Overview of the entire microscope system, showing the microscope with motors, optics, and sensors on the **left** and the COTS electronics and hardware on the **right**.

2.1. Hardware—Structural Frame

Most of the physical components making up the housing of the device were 3D-printed using fused deposition modeling to supply the diversity of structural frame shapes involved in the design. Having a printable design also allows for easy construction of the device for diverse academic or development purposes, not just those with manufacturing capabilities. A 3D-printed housing contains the optics, motors, and linear bearings for 3D positioning, while the device skeleton consists of two thick (0.5″) plates of aluminum that are joined in an L-shape to provide rigidity to the system, as Figure 3.

2.2. Hardware—Optics and Lasers

The optics of the device include several more expensive components (e.g., <USD 600) that make up the majority of the cost. These components have been mounted into a structural system as shown in Figure 4 and will be discussed in detail below.

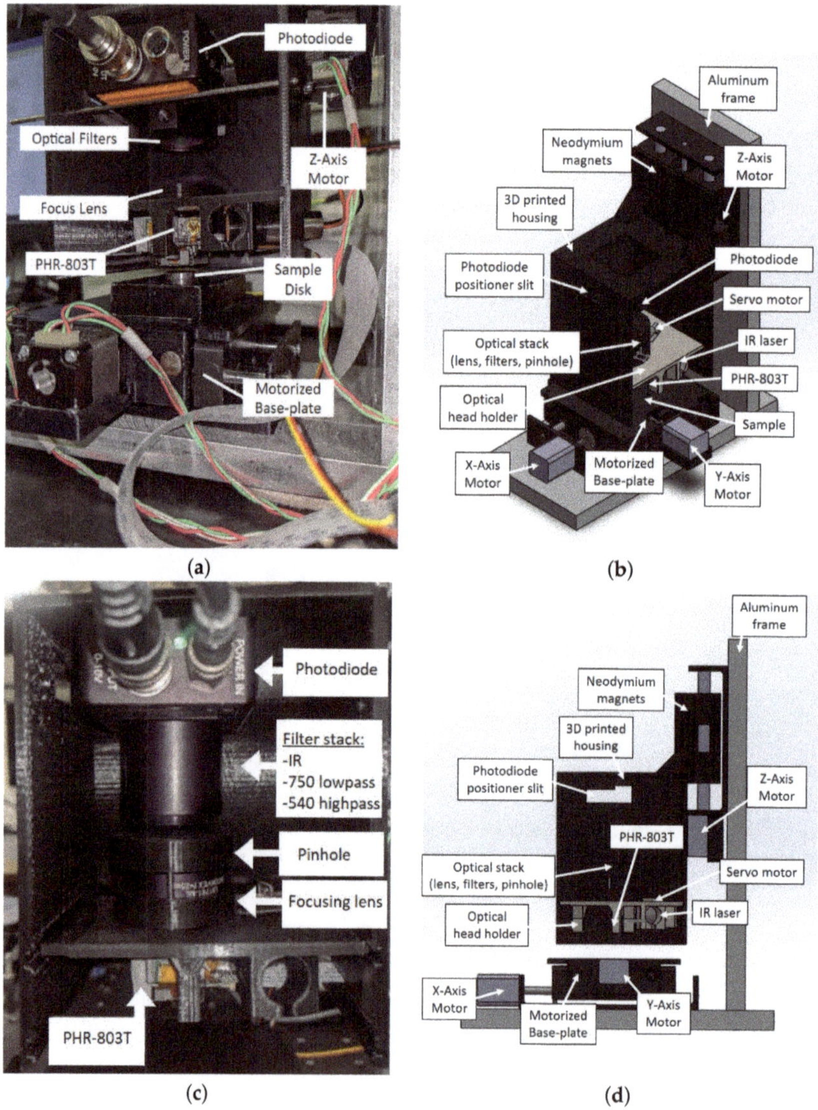

Figure 4. (**a**) Image of hardware showing optical components and motorized stages. (**b**) Schematic view of the SCOT device shown in (**a**). (**c**) Additions to the optical stack include the photodiode, filter stack, pinhole, focusing lens, and PHR mount. The numbers 750 and 450 refer to 750 nm and 450 nm as the cut-off and cut-on wavelengths, respectively. (**d**) Schematic view of the SCOT device shown in (**c**).

2.2.1. PHR-803T

The main optical component of the system is the PHR-803T, which will henceforth be referred to as the PHR. The PHR was designed to read HD-DVDs and other discs. Included in the optics of the device are three lasers: a red, a blue, and an infrared (IR). It also has its own focusing system that is capable of making minute adjustments using a small lens within a voice-coil that can be manipulated by a fast PWM signal to the PHR driver board (Figure 5a). The microscope has been designed to have manual control of this voice-coil-based focusing via manual buttons to reach an optimal intensity, because the auto focusing function is less reliable for non-mirror-like finishes. This system involves two buttons and a switch. The two buttons control the vertical actuation, and the switch changes between a "fine" and a "course" movement speed. The microscope is considered to be in focus when the output of the photodiode at the top of the optical stack reaches a maximum from the emitted blue laser.

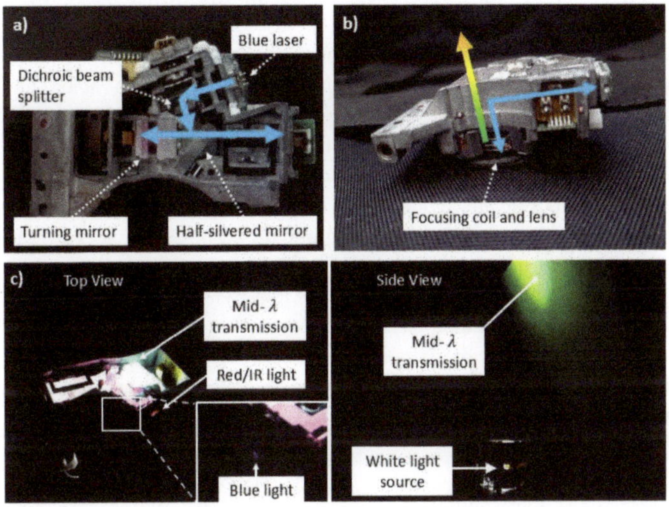

Figure 5. (**a**) Top and (**b**) side view of the PHR showing the blue laser light path and midrange visible wavelength transmission (colored green, yellow, and orange to represent the wavelengths of light transmitted to the photodiode. (**c**) When illuminated by a white light source through the focusing lens, the light is split into the red, blue, and midrange visible (mid-λ) bands. M represents a mirror, and BS represents a beam splitter.

The optics of the PHR (Figure 5c) allow red/IR (660/785 nm) and blue (405 nm) light to be transmitted within the optical head and to the sample while transmitting midrange visible wavelengths through its dichroic mirror towards the photodiode. This light is used to create the images of the microscope. The light from the blue laser is reflected through a turning mirror onto the sample. The resultant fluorescent light (in the middle of the visible range) transverses back through the focusing lens before being collected in the photodiode, which is mounted directly above the PHR and the optical stack. This can be seen in Figure 4. To locally heat the sample, the 785 nm laser in the PHR can be removed, and a more powerful external IR laser can be inserted in the 3D-printed PHR housing. Sinusoidally modulating the intensity of the IR laser with a function generator and detecting sinusoidal changes in the fluorescent signal can enable the detection of small changes in temperature, as will be shown in Section 4.3.

The benefits of using a PHR-803T confocal system include its relatively inexpensive design and the accessibility of the components that are used in its construction. The majority of its structure being 3D-printed allows for easy adjustments to the design, and the printing of these can be carried out in any environment with suitable 3D printing equipment, such as a college campus. With easily replaceable components, the quality of the results can be modulated to fit the needs of those working with the designs of the device.

2.2.2. Optical Stack

An optical stack is used to filter light and act as the confocal pinhole; Figure 4b shows the elements in the stack. To remove the blue light that is used to excite the fluorescent dye, a band pass filter (Thorlabs FESH0750, 400 nm to 740 nm passing band, Thorlabs, Newton, NJ, USA) was implemented. To reduce the possible out-of-plane light, a focusing lens and a small (~1 mm diameter), 3D-printed pinhole were added to the optical stack. All 3D-printed parts were printed using acrylonitrile butadiene styrene (ABS) on a fused deposition modeling (FDM) printer.

For the purposes of the confocal fluorescent microscope, only a single filter is needed (450 nm highpass filter, as shown in Figure 4b). Two filters are used for the ambient red light in the thermal application (IR and 750 nm lowpass filters). Any filters in use are placed in a filter mount that is connected to the photodiode surface. A pinhole is used to block light coming into the area of the photodiode at odd angles. Even with less-reflective surfaces, trace amounts of this ambient light can be observed going through the filters if the microscope is not covered, creating a need to calibrate the obtained results with the assumption that the ambient light remains static.

The focusing of the laser, performed specifically by the fine-focus voice-coil actuator as opposed to the vertical motion stepper motor, is the final stage of the focusing process and ensures that the area of laser effect on the sample matches the predetermined calculated values during readings. If a 3D image is needed, the fine-focus is able to be lowered to alternative depths of the sample (see Section 4.2.2).

2.2.3. Photodiode

The microscope uses a Thorlabs amplified photodiode (PDA36A2, Thorlabs, Newton, NJ, USA) to collect light from the microscope, which is set to a maximum output amplification (70 dB). The position of the photodiode is able to be changed to account for any error in the location of the focused fluorescent signal. This is achieved manually by use of a screw on the back of the system. The location is fixed in place at the point where the highest signal is measured. Further details of the photodiode circuit are provided in Section 2.4.3.

2.2.4. External IR "Heating" Laser

The existing IR laser in the PHR does not have sufficient power to heat the surface of sample materials (e.g., stainless steel) enough to detect heat diffusion in the samples via changes in the fluorescent intensity of deposited dyes. An external IR laser (Aziz, Wuhan, China, 780 nm 150 mW Laser Module 12 $\times$ 30 mm) was added into the system to provide heating with the requisite power. It was placed externally to the PHR optical head after the existing 785 nm laser was removed from the optical head (Figure 6b). The IR laser was housed in a cylinder that was pinned to the 3D-printed holder, and a servo motor arm was connected to the cylinder to allow the laser positions to change relative to the blue laser spot. A continuous rotation servo motor was controlled by an Arduino Mega (Arduino, Scarmagno, Italy) to adjust the position of the IR laser relative to the fluorescent emission.

IR light was used because it did not induce fluorescence and was also outside the emission spectrum of the Rhodamine B and quantum dot fluorescent materials used in this work.

Integrating the external IR laser required three key changes to the optical system that was used for basic confocal microscopy. The first inclusion was a collimator lens on the 785 nm laser, which was used to ensure that the laser beam is parallel and focused onto the sample. This better allows the PHR's built-in lens to focus the beam and more precisely target the area of interest on the sample.

The second addition is a set of filters that are mounted just below the photodiode, which is used to filter out all other wavelengths of light except for the desired emission from the fluorescent dye. The fluorescent dye has a peak emission wavelength of roughly 600 nm when excited with radiation from the 405 nm laser probe from the PHR-803T. The specific wavelength band of the filter was selected to more effectively filter out the 405 nm wavelength while still allowing the 600 nm wavelength to reach the photodiode. This ensures that only the emission of interest is collected by the detector.

Finally, a 27.5 mm focal length lens was added to focus the emitted light from the sample onto the photodiode detector. This lens is specifically designed to maximize the amount of light that reaches the detector, improving the sensitivity of the system and allowing for the detection of even smaller temperature differences (which manifested as changes in fluorescent intensity) in the sample. To further improve the optical accuracy, an additional pinhole (Thorlabs ID15, Thorlabs, Newton, NJ, USA with a minimum hole size of 1.2 mm) was used to ensure that the spatial distribution of the laser remained as a clean Gaussian beam. Because the thermal analysis occurs in the frequency domain, only relative instead of absolute changes in temperature are needed to see heat diffuse through the sample [33].

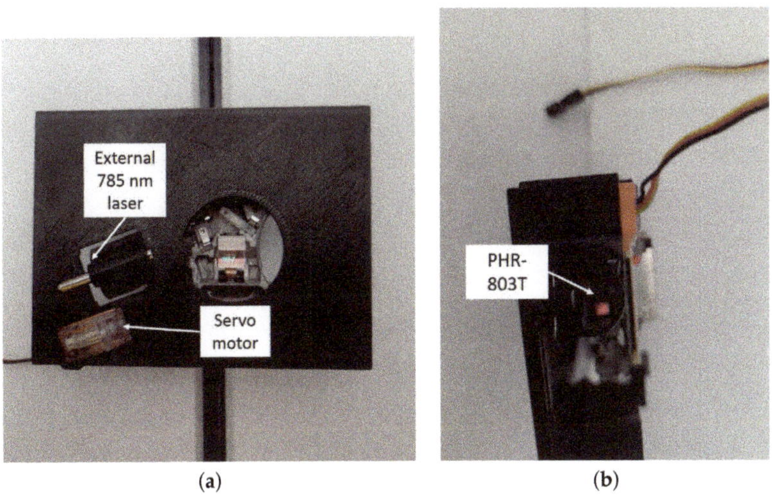

Figure 6. (**a**) Images of the additional modifications made to the PHR holder to include a higher-powered external IR heating laser and servo motor. (**b**) The 785 nm laser in the PHR was removed to allow the external laser to be directed at the sample through the PHR optics.

2.3. *Hardware—Positioning Motors*

Figure 7 shows the sample tray with its associated motor systems. The design of the position system uses motors that are mounted to the sample tray to move the "stage" in the x and y directions while the laser position remains fixed, which is easier to accomplish with a 3D-printed support structure. This approach is based on the work of Arunkarthick [34], who used a confocal microscope to create 3D images of pollen.

Three linear actuating stepper motors control the x and y location of the sample (on the sample tray), as well as the z position of the optics (for the vertical direction). NEMA 8 linear actuators with a 100 mm long lead screw and a 0.3 mm screw lead were used (Pololu Corporation, Las Vegas, NV, USA). The motors themselves have a 1.8° step angle and function at 0.5 A/Phase. These provide precision movement without having to invest in an expensive high-precision adjustable sample tray. To avoid unnecessary bending or shaking of the platform, the threaded rods of the linear actuators are centered on the tray table and run through the center of the tray table (see Figure 7). This custom stage allows the sample to be repositioned at various locations to take measurements. Section 4.1 will discuss some issues with FDM printing of the platforms and how the SCoT microscope accounts for this.

The motor control process incorporates the time that it takes to read the analog input pin with data from the photodiode into the time delay that is required for the motor to take a single step. This means that the motor is able to continuously move while the measurements are being taken, greatly decreasing the time it takes to map an image of the fluorescing sample.

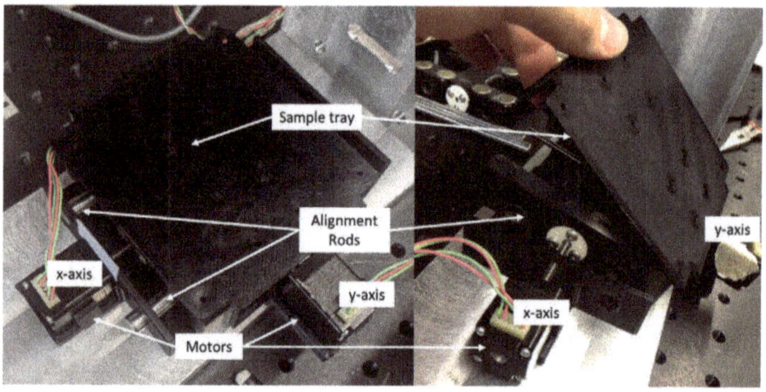

Figure 7. Image of device's motorized sample tray surface (**left**) and internal structure (**right**).

2.4. Electronics Overview

The Arduino Mega board was used as the main processing unit because it is cheap, easy to use, and easily replaceable. Outside of the Arduino, several other important circuits are used to control the device. Overall, the electronics (Figure 8) can be broken up into the following sections: the PHR-803T driver, the stepper motors, the thermal hardware, and the amplification circuit.

As shown in Figure 9, at the center of all the electronics functionality is the Arduino. It controls the flow of all information throughout the system. It communicates with nearly all other components of the device, including the blue laser control board, stepper motor driver board, laser focus system, photodiode, and MATLAB programs on the PC. After receiving the proper information from the Arduino via a mix of PWM and digital signals, the blue laser control board commands the intensity of the blue laser on the sample to remain stable. This is the source of the fluorescent signal and has limited change in function after testing has initiated.

The stepper motor driver boards (Polulu 8834, Pololu Corporation, Las Vegas, NV, USA) govern the positioning of the stepper motors. This is facilitated by the use of the full stepper motor driver PCB. This PCB simplifies the distribution of the signal from the Arduino's digital pins. It also includes voltage regulation to avoid any component burnout.

Data from the photodiode in the optical stack are passed as an analog signal to the Arduino, which converts it to a digital signal using its own internal analog-to-digital (ADC) converter (10 bit, 4.88 mV resolution). A USB cable is used for the Arduino-to-PC communication. Protocalls for this communication are governed via the MATLAB and Arduino code programming. The power for all the devices is regulated by a central power board derived from an XBox 360 disc player (Microsoft, Redmond, WA, USA) and split into 5-volt or 12-volt sources depending on the voltage demand. The only other power connection is for the photodiode, which takes a 120 VAC external wall connection.

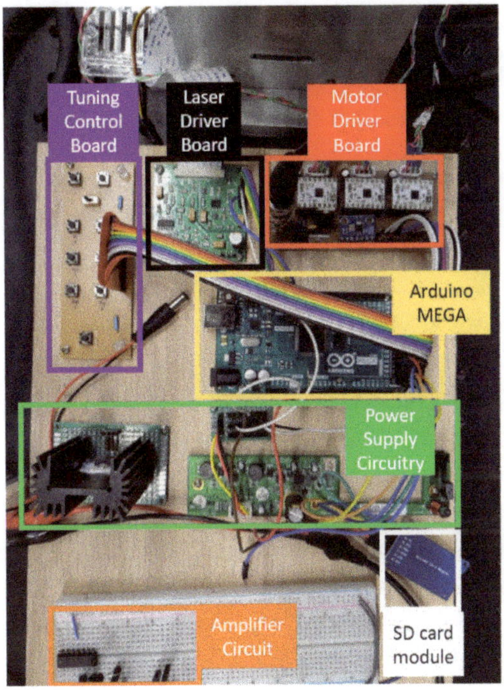

Figure 8. Image of the electronics showing the different components used in the SCoT microscope. The larger SRS 830 lock-in amplifier that is used to measure the thermally sensitive signal connects to this board via the BNC connector on the Motor Driver Board.

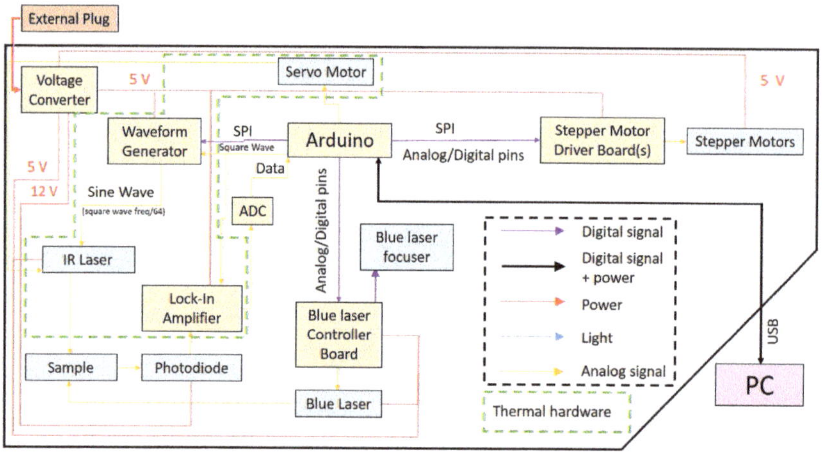

Figure 9. Block diagram of the various electronic components of the SCoT microscope. Portions of the electrical schematic in the green outlined region represent additional hardware, used to detect the thermally sensitive signal (labeled as thermal hardware).

2.4.1. Motor Control

The sample tray's horizontal motion and system's vertical motion are controlled using a system of three stepper motors. The motors are controlled using external motor driver boards that are mounted on a custom-built PCB. The motor driver board step configuration pins are set up on its lowest 32nd of a step setting. The PCB is designed as a central hub for all signal control. It is provided with general commands from the Arduino such as speed, step, and directional information. This can all be controlled by preprogramming; however, buttons to manually control each motor were also included for debugging purposes.

2.4.2. Laser Control

A few functional capabilities of the PHR, such as the laser intensity and fine-focus actuation, are only possible through a designated laser driver control board. The design for this board was developed by DiYouware, last accessed on 14 December 2023 (http://www.diyouware.com/), with some minor modifications to allow for fabrication simplicity. A 12 V output of the Xbox360 disc player power supply was connected to a 5 V voltage regulator, with the addition of a large heat sink to help dissipate the extra power that otherwise would have caused fluctuations in the laser intensity.

2.4.3. Amplification Circuit

The circuit, using a conventional setup with an LM324 amplifier (TI, Dallas, TX, USA), takes the analog signal produced by the photodiode and increases it to the measuring range of the Arduino. As the signal intensity is dependent on the setup of the system, the gains of the amplifier are tunable to either the confocal or thermal imaging configuration of the SCoT microscope. This signal is given by the photodiode and should account for a significant portion of the fluorescence that is emitted by the Rhodamine B (Millipore-Sigma, Darmstadt, Germany) or quantum dot (QD, Millipore-Sigma, Darmstadt, Germany)-coated sample, or reflected light from the PCB image. The amplifier circuit zeroes the signal to a set minimum and then amplifies it to readable levels. The amplifier gain was set using a 10–100 kΩ potentiometer. This sets the gains at about 100× based on a resistor value of 1000 Ω. The offset potentiometer is able to match an output voltage to ensure a reasonable range.

The Arduino's maximum measurable voltage is 5 V. Calibration was needed to set the photodiode output's minimum and maximum voltage range to match those of the Arduino input. This value was determined iteratively, because the output maximum and minimums are influenced by the ambient light in the room during testing, the position of the sample during testing, any minute changes in the photodiode position, and the amount of fluorescent dye on the sample.

2.4.4. Thermal Hardware

The thermal hardware consists of a servo motor, an external heating laser (Figure 6), a waveform generator to produce a sinusoidal analog signal, and a lock-in amplifier. The servo motor is directly controlled by the Arduino Mega and was included to change the relative position between the external heating laser and the fluorescent emission on the sample caused by the PHR's blue laser.

The external IR laser is used as a modulated heating source. The intensity of the IR laser is controlled with an input sine wave signal from the AD9833 function generator (Analog Devices, Wilmington, MA, USA). By modulating the heating source, the SCoT microscope is able to detect the diffusion of heat through the sample by locking it in to changes in the fluorescent intensity of the sample at the modulation frequency. Because the fluorescent intensity is a function of temperature, this allowed the relative changes in temperature to be measured. Additionally, locking in to the temperature-sensitive signal allows for small perturbations in temperature to be measured that would normally be below the noise floor of the measurement system. These variations in temperature are termed thermal waves and fall under a class of measurements called photothermal methods [35], which are often used to measure the thermal properties of materials or detect microscale defects in materials.

An SRS 830 lock-in amplifier (LIA, Stanford Research Systems, Sunnyvale, CA, USA) was used to perform the lock-in detection. The amplified output of the photodiode was recorded by the LIA as the amplitude and phase of the fluorescent light that was collected by the SCoT microscope. The diffusion of heat from the IR laser could then be observed as a decrease in the amplitude and phase as the distance between the IR and blue laser spots were changed. The lock-in amplifier requires that the temperature fluctuations reach a steady state, which takes between 2 and 40 s, based on the modulation frequency of the laser. This time is the factor that defines the scanning speed of the SCoT microscope.

3. Operation of the Device

This section will describe the basic operation of the SCoT microscope and debugging processes, as well as component replacement considerations.

3.1. Operation

The operation of the SCoT microscope consists of two fundamental procedures (Figure 10): system positioning and data acquisition. The device is first powered on by connecting to the power supply board. The Arduino is then reset to start the control program and data collection until the PC is enabled. A sample is placed on the mounting stage. The system positioning process begins with the tray table stepping through a set number of locations, performing data readings at each location as it moves. The fluorescent emission readings are taken from the amplified photodiode. The system guides the laser focus location across an initial row, steps to the next row, changes direction, and continues to collect emission data in the opposite direction. This process is repeated until the full designated collection area has been traversed. The amplified photodiode readings are written either directly to an external SD card for post-processing or transferred over a USB-to-serial connection for analysis on the PC. The benefit of the SD-card-based data collection is that it has less compatibility issues with the programs and electronics used.

To use the SCoT microscope in thermal detecting mode, the lock-in amplifier is connected to a BNC adapter that is located on the motor driver board to provide the modulated sine wave that is sent to the external heating IR laser. The output of the photodiode is also connected to the lock-in amplifier. Amplitude and phase data are transmitted to the PC, and the servo motor is used to move the IR laser to another location.

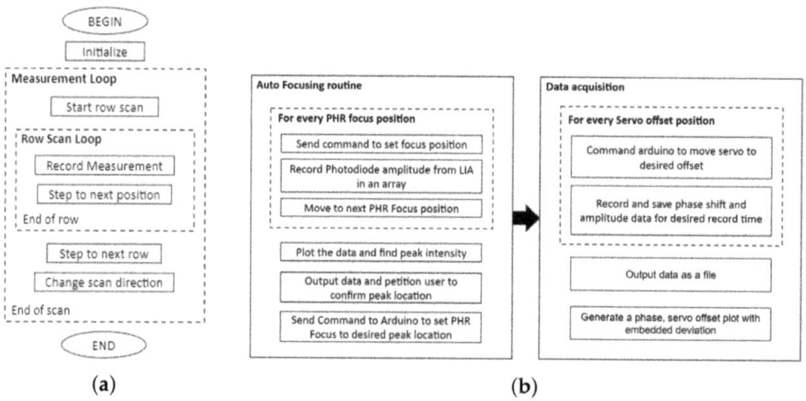

Figure 10. (**a**) Flow chart of Arduino code for operating the SCoT microscope. (**b**) Description of MATLAB software, v2019a for operating the SCoT microscope.

3.2. Debugging and Replacement Parts

During the development of the SCoT microscope, the device was dismantled and reconstructed multiple times during troubleshooting of the device's operation. This provided insights into several debugging processes when setting up the device, as well as highlighting which components need more frequent replacement.

3.2.1. Debugging

The most common issues during assembly were with the electronic components compared to the physical hardware. The general debugging process for the electronics was broken down into the following categories in the recommended order to follow when troubleshooting: (1) checking wire connections; (2) checking soldered connections; (3) checking the quality of the output data; and (4) checking the functionality of each board (power, motor control, laser focusing, Arduino Mega, etc.) and replacing if necessary. Standard test procedures were established so that the instrument had a consistent performance after component replacement.

3.2.2. Component Replacements

This section will discuss the most common components that needed to be replaced during testing and those that would be expected to need more frequent replacement when exposed to harsh conditions.

The most common component that needed to be replaced was the PHR-803t because of the blue laser diode and the IR laser. This happened because the laser would overheat when it was operated at full power for multiple days. Limiting the output of the laser and/or providing cooling helped extend its lifetime.

The second most commonly replaced components during testing were the Arduino Mega and the laser driver board. The Arduino Mega failure was often caused by a defect in the board because of the low production quality of the device. The laser driver board issues were focused mainly on soldering problems and fluctuations in laser intensity when powering both the IR laser and the PHR-803t using a 5 V source. The soldering issues were resolved by increasing the size of the PCB and using screen printing with soldering paste and surface mount electronics. The fluctuations in the laser intensity were fixed by powering the board with a 12 V source into a 5 V regulator and dissipating extra heat with a heat sink.

When exposed to harsh environments, the optical lenses will brown and need to be replaced, as will the Arduino Mega if it is not properly shielded against radiation. The 3D-printed housing, motor spindle housings, and PHR-803t holder will likely be the next most replaced components based on embrittlement or swelling. However, the stresses on the parts is low, so the swelling will likely cause the most issues with the motor spindle housings.

4. Results

This section will discuss the use of the microscope in reflection mode (without a filter) and fluorescent mode (with a filter). Both modes use the pinhole shown in the optical stack in Figure 4 to limit in-plane light. Additionally, the detection of a weak thermally sensitive signal is also presented when adding a modulated heating source by an IR laser.

4.1. Reflective Imaging

The microscope was used to image text on a PCB. During initial scanning, the device followed the "rastering" path given by Figure 11a. This had the side effect of a noticeable and consistent drift, as observed in Figure 11b, where the number "6" that was being imaged is skewed by a consistent amount. The corrected image uses a diagonal shift, as illustrated in Figure 11e. This shift is tuned to the current setup and remains constant throughout testing. Additionally, the corrected image, shown in Figure 11f, can be recreated and is comparable to the image produced by an Opti-Tekscope Digital USB Microscope Camera (Opti-Tekscope LLC, Chandler, AZ, USA).

This slight drift occurs due to marginal inconsistencies in the motorized baseplates, resulting in a change in the motion of the sample tray. Because the scanning resolution is on the order of μm, these inconsistencies result in a slight drift in the measurements. The change in the motion of the sample tray was caused by the distortion of the used 3D-printed components and imperfections in the bearing rods governing the motion of the tray. Although the use of 3D-printed parts is a root cause of this issue, one of the goals of this work was to produce a low-cost and modular device. To avoid expensive machining solutions, this issue was solved by modifying the imaging path that is taken by the microscope (Figure 11c). This greatly improved the drift issue caused by the distortion of the 3D-printed components. Figure 11d shows the improved imaging with this path, but a consistent sawtooth pattern was still observed in the image. To overcome this, a consistent shift in both the x- and y-axes was performed after a non-imaging scan, resulting in the imaging path shown in Figure 11e. The use of both of these imaging compensations resulted in the imaging of the numeral "1" in Figure 11f at a spatial resolution of 12.5 μm in the horizontal and 1.5 μm in the vertical directions. The resolution can be further improved with more expensive motor systems, and greater accuracy in the resolution could be obtained using a resolution target like 1951 USAF.

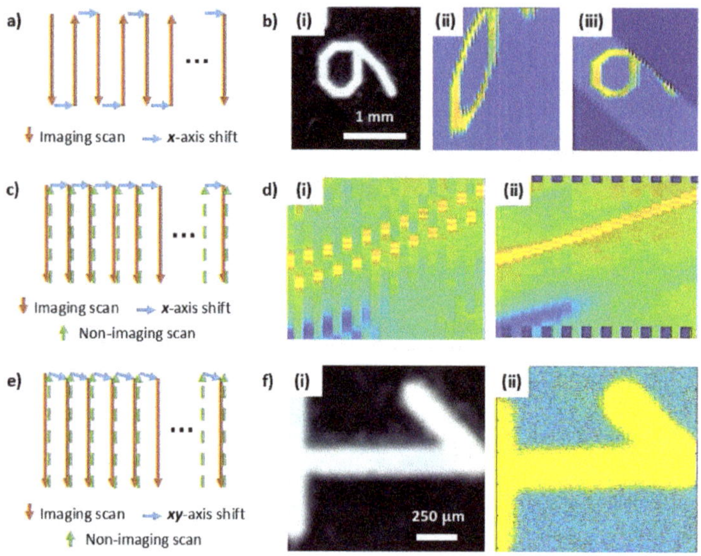

Figure 11. The path of the laser during scanning following a typical rastering pattern. (**a**) The original scanning path of the laser. (**b**) (i) Text on a PCB, imaged using a digital microscope camera. (ii) Confocal microscope image of the same sample suffering from an x-axis shift. (iii) Corrected confocal microscope image. (**c**) The necessary scanning path to compensate for the "Sawtooth" image distortion. (**d**) An example of "Sawtooth" image (i) distortion and (ii) the corrected image. (**e**) The necessary scanning path to compensate for both image drift and "Sawtooth" distortion. (**f**) (i) Text on a PCB, imaged using a digital microscope camera. (ii) Resultant image when using the correct scanning path.

4.2. Fluorescent/Confocal Imaging

This section focuses on the use of the microscope to create a simple planar image of Rhodamine B on an opaque, brass sample to test the contrast of the fluorescent image against the background. This will be followed by a series of depth images through a transparent synthetic spider silk [36] sample that is treated with quantum dots as the fluorophore. The spider silk images are compared to the results of images taken by a commercial Leica scanning confocal microscope of those same silks.

4.2.1. Imaging a Reflective Surface Coated with a Fluorescent Dye

A brass sample was coated in Rhodamine B (>95% HPLC from Millipore-Sigma, Darmstadt, Germany), as shown in Figure 12. The droplets of water containing the dyes were each applied roughly 1 month apart to test the sensitivity of the SCoT microscope to fluorescent intensity changes. The photobleaching effect of the dye is clearly seen in the colored microscopic image in Figure 12. Although this effect is not easily observed visually because the red color does not look that different, the generated image shows a significant difference in fluorescence, where the fresher, less photobleached dye provides a stronger fluorescent signal. This demonstrates the ability to differentiate between fluorescent intensities based on changes in the fluorophore.

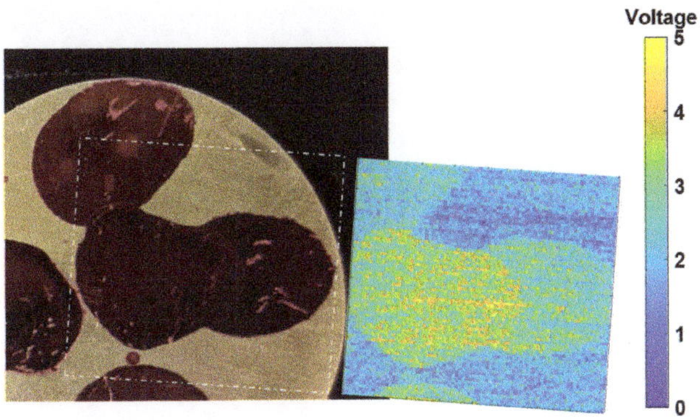

Figure 12. Image obtained using the fluorescent detection method. The image pixel resolution is 0.23 mm. The brighter yellow and orange areas highlight the unbleached section of Rhodamine B. The color bar indicates the excitation voltage generated from the photodiode used for measurement and represents the intensity of the fluorescence. While using a 1000× amplifier with an output range of 5 V, the photodiode emission range was from 0 V (dark blue) to 5 V (dark orange).

The movement of the sample tray was calculated to be approximately 1.5 µm. This was determined as an average step size when the system was jogged through a 100-step cycle. The final distance averaged to 151 µm, with an error of approximately 5 µm. The size and accuracy limitations were, respectively, limited due to the resolution of the stepper motors and the 3D-printed construction of the device. This resolution can be easily improved by decreasing the step size of these motors at the expense of speed. Improvements to the accuracy of the step size can possibly be achieved by the integration of better 3D printing methods (such as resin-based stereolithography, SLA) and higher-accuracy components into the device.

4.2.2. Multi-Planed Fluorescent Scanning

To test the confocal capabilities of the SCoT microscope, the focusing lens in the optical head was moved to allow different imaging planes to be the focus of the blue laser. The sample used for this testing was a silk thread that was mounted to a cover slip, which was previously treated with quantum dots. The synthetic silk was created from spider silk protein produced in transgenic goats that underwent the extrusion and pulling process described in Refs. [36,37]. This dye-coating process is similar to that described in our previous work [38]. The silk fiber was then imaged with the SCoT microscope, and the resulting image is shown in Figure 13a.

The axial focus of the images are rather poor quality, as each step is roughly 18 µm apart. This focus resolution can be decreased to 9 µm, but the quality of the images can only be increased by the inclusion of an improved iris that is located at the collection point to further restrict out-of-plane light. The iris will help to filter out the light from all other focus locations than the one of interest. An iris of a sufficient size would require high-resolution printing, which is achievable by a micro-3D printer [39] or the purchase of precision pinholes such as ThorLabs stainless steel foils.

Figure 13b shows the same silk fiber when it is imaged using a commercial Leica scanning confocal microscope with a much higher resolution. The images provided are roughly 4 µm apart in focus depth and show significantly better resolution in the individual images. However, the change in width of the silk is observable with both microscopes as the imaging plane moves through the fiber.

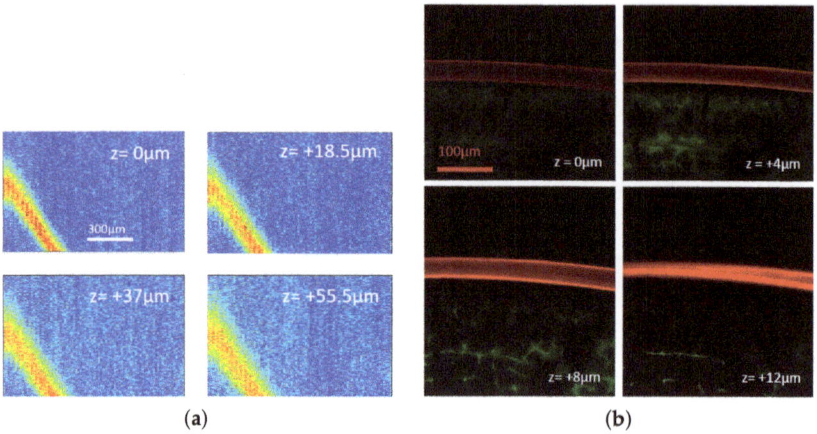

Figure 13. (**a**) Image of synthetic spider silk, obtained using the SCoT microscope. Each layer is offset by 18.5 µm. The resolution is 15 µm in the X direction and 1.5 µm in the Y direction. (**b**) Comparison image of the spider silk sample using a commercial Leica scanning confocal microscope, where the height of the microscope focus is changed in the z-direction. The offsets of each image are 4 µm apart.

4.3. Detection of Temperature-Sensitive Fluorescent Signal

This section shows the capability of the SCoT microscope to detect relative temperature changes in the sample as a function of the spacing between a heating laser and the blue laser. The photoluminescence that is emitted by a fluorescent probe (illuminated by the blue laser) is dependent on the temperature of the probe, where decreases in light intensity are associated with increases in temperature.

To allow the SCoT microscope to image temperature-dependent processes, several additions to the optical stack and electronic hardware were required. Full details were provided in the device overview (Section 2). These modifications are designed to more efficiently focus the desired light towards the photodiode and eliminate any reflected light from the IR heating laser with additional filters, as shown in Figure 14. Additionally, they provide a higher intensity of IR laser light to be transmitted to the sample surface to increase the local temperature. The data acquisition system records a batch of amplitude and phase data for each position of the servo motor moving the IR heating laser.

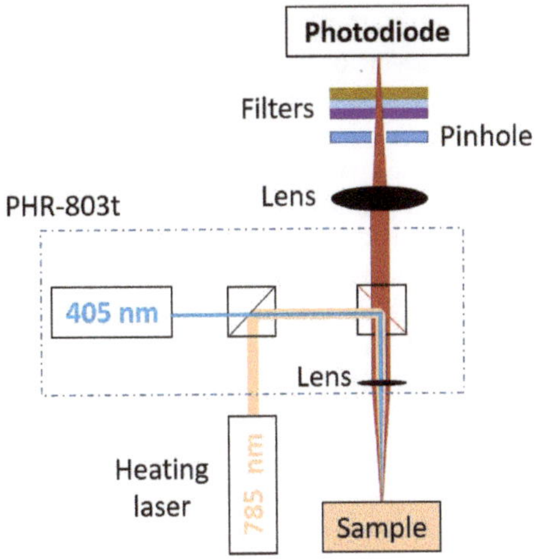

Figure 14. Schematic of the optical path of the two laser beams (blue and orange) and fluorescent luminescence (red) of the SCoT microscope in the thermal detection configuration.

To prepare a sample for measuring relative temperature changes, Rhodamine B in an ethanol solution was spin-coated onto a stainless steel 304 disc (Figure 15a). The thickness of the coating was measured using a Zeta 20 profilometer (KLA, Ann Arbor, MI, USA) as 20.7 μm thick. Stainless steel was selected as the sample material, because the current design of the SCoT microscope cannot be used with ferromagnetic materials. This is to avoid any interaction with the magnetic actuator that is located on the PHR that is used for focusing the lasers.

(a)

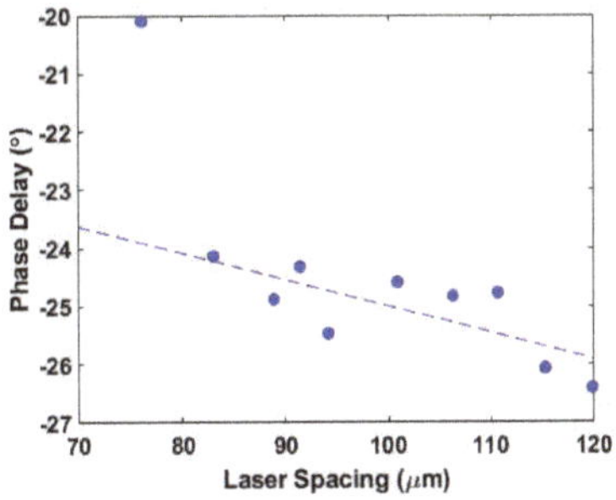

(b)

Figure 15. (**a**) A stainless steel sample with Rhodamine B film deposited by spin coating. (**b**) A graph of the phase delay vs. displacement for the measurement of a stainless steel surface coated in a layer of Rhodamine B. This phase delay is between the initial heating provided by the IR laser and the resultant temperature changes in the sample, which are measured as changes in the intensity of the fluorescent dye.

The sinusoidal modulation of the IR heating laser's intensity results in a thermal wave, which is a periodic variation in the local temperature of the material [38]. This temperature variation occurs at the same frequency as that of the modulated heating but is delayed in time, as the heat needs to diffuse from the heating spot. The use of lock-in amplification allows the temperature-sensitive fluorescent signal at the modulation frequency to be isolated and amplified, but this also results in the signal being mapped into the frequency domain. As fluorescent data are collected at increasing distances from the heating spot, the thermal wave amplitude decreases, and the time delay between the heating wave and the temperature response increases. This results in the phase delay shown in Figure 15b.

Figure 15b shows a linear trend in the phase delay when the IR and blue lasers are spaced more than 80 μm apart. Thermal wave theory predicts that at distances greater than about 5× the diameter of the laser spot size, a thermal wave has a linear slope in the phase delay between the modulated heating source and the temperature of the material away from the heating source [6]. This phase delay is large for thermally insulating materials and small for thermally conductive ones. The outlier that deviates from linearity when the laser spot spacing is about 75 μm could have been caused by the presence of a microscopic defect in the sample, such as the scratch shown in Figure 15a. Hua demonstrated that grain boundaries can create a phase jump of about 1° in the thermal wave, and larger defects are expected to create large phase delay jumps [40]. The results in Figure 15b demonstrate that the SCoT microscope is able to detect these thermal waves.

5. Conclusions

This paper presents the design and operation of a scanning confocal thermal (SCoT) microscope. Using inexpensive components, the device was able to create microscopic images using fluorescent emissions by means of the PHR-803T optical head, optical filters and lenses, positioning motors, and a 3D-printed structural frame. This was demonstrated by using the microscope in a reflective mode (imaging writing on a PCB board without fluorescent probes) and in a confocal mode (observing the photobleaching of Rhodamine B and imaging different planes of synthetic spider silk). Additional features in the design of the system include post-processing techniques and construction calibration features that are key to improving the quality of the system but are not necessary for its functionality. This research also demonstrated how the device can be used as a thermal microscope by using additional filters and a heating laser to detect thermally induced fluctuations in fluorescent dyes.

One improvement of the device could be the use of a smaller pinhole print, located at the collection sight of the laser. Based on the function of the laser, an accurately located and sized pinhole can improve the vertical resolution in 3D imaging applications. Additionally, modeling specialized components could also greatly reduce the cost of the system while maintaining the integrity and precision of the results.

Author Contributions: Conceptualization, J.L., J.R., S.H.H. and T.M.; methodology, J.L., S.H.H., R.R., I.C., S.L., J.K. and T.M.; software, J.L., R.R., I.C., J.R., S.H.H. and J.K.; validation, J.L. and J.K.; formal analysis, J.L. and J.K.; resources, T.M.; writing—original draft preparation, J.L., S.H.H., J.K., I.C., J.R., S.L. and T.M.; writing—review and editing, J.L., T.M. and R.R.; supervision, J.L. and T.M.; project administration, T.M.; funding acquisition, T.M. All authors have read and agreed to the published version of the manuscript.

Funding: We are grateful the Nuclear Regulatory Commission (Award #31310019M0006) for the support of this work.

Data Availability Statement: All code and 3D CAD model designs developed for the device are included in the following GitHub repository, last accessed 9 November 2024: https://github.com/jsloose/bluraycode.

Acknowledgments: The authors would like to acknowledge Randy Lewis and Cameron Copeland from Utah State University for access to the synthetic spider silk imaged in this paper.

Conflicts of Interest: Author T. Munro is an inventor on US patent no. US11585756B2 "Methods and systems for determining at least one thermal property of a sample", which details a non-confocal thermal microscope. The other authors declare no conflicts of interest.

Abbreviations

The following abbreviations are used in this manuscript:

ABS	Acrylonitrile butadiene styrene
ADC	Analog-to-digital converter
DIY	Do-it-yourself
FDM	Fused deposition modeling
HD-DVD	High-density digital video disc
IR	Infrared
LIA	Lock-in amplifier
PCB	Printed circuit board
PIE	Post-irradiation examination
PWM	Pulse width modulation
QD	Quantum dots
SCoT	Scanning confocal thermal
SLA	Stereolithography
UAV	Unmanned aerial vehicle

References

1. Cappia, F.; Harp, J.M.; McCoy, K. Post-irradiation examinations of UO_2 composites as part of the Accident Tolerant Fuels Campaign. *J. Nucl. Mater.* **2019**, *517*, 97–105. [CrossRef]
2. Listed, N. *International Workshop on Characterization and PIE Needs for Fundamental Understanding of Fuels Performance and Safety*; Technical Report; Idaho National Lab. (INL): Idaho Falls, ID, USA, 2011.
3. Morgan, K.N. *Window to the Hot Cell: The Challenges of Repairing a Specialized Nuclear Containment*; Technical Report; Idaho National Lab. (INL): Idaho Falls, ID, USA, 2017.
4. International Atomic Energy Agency. *Post-Irradiation Examination Techniques for Research Reactor Fuels*; Number NF-T-2.6 in Nuclear Energy Series; International Atomic Energy Agency: Vienna, Austria, 2023.
5. Degueldre, C.; Bertsch, J.; Martin, M. Post irradiation examination of nuclear fuel: Toward a complete analysis. *Prog. Nucl. Energy* **2016**, *92*, 242–253. [CrossRef]
6. Hurley, D.H.; Schley, R.S.; Khafizov, M.; Wendt, B.L. Local measurement of thermal conductivity and diffusivity. *Rev. Sci. Instrum.* **2015**, *86*, 123901. [CrossRef]
7. McKinney, C.; Hilty, F.; Murray, D.; Poudel, N.; Cappia, F.; Pavlov, T.; Aitkaliyeva, A. Three-dimensional microstructural characterization of FBR MOX fuel and the contribution of microstructural features to the thermal conductivity of the fuel. *J. Nucl. Mater.* **2022**, *572*, 154073. [CrossRef]
8. Yamamoto, T.; Odette, G.; Lucas, G.; Matsui, H. Confocal microscopy–fracture reconstruction and finite element modeling characterization of local cleavage toughness in a ferritic/martensitic steel in subsized Charpy V-notch impact tests. *J. Nucl. Mater.* **2000**, *283*, 992–996. [CrossRef]
9. Gauthier, E.; Brosset, C.; Roche, H.; Tsitrone, E.; Pégourié, B.; Martinez, A.; Languille, P.; Courtois, X.; Lallier, Y.; Salami, M. Confocal microscopy: A new tool for erosion measurements on large scale plasma facing components in tokamaks. *J. Nucl. Mater.* **2013**, *438*, S1216–S1220. [CrossRef]
10. Lee, J.; Hossain, M.S.; Taheri, M.; Jameel, A.; Lakshmipathy, M.; Taheri, H. Characterization of surface topography features for the effect of process parameters and their correlation to quality monitoring in metal additive manufacturing. *Metrology* **2022**, *2*, 73–83. [CrossRef]
11. Nwaneshiudu, A.; Kuschal, C.; Sakamoto, F.H.; Anderson, R.R.; Schwarzenberger, K.; Young, R.C. Introduction to confocal microscopy. *J. Investig. Dermatol.* **2012**, *132*, 1–5. [CrossRef]
12. Caspers, P.; Lucassen, G.; Bruining, H.; Puppels, G. Automated depth-scanning confocal Raman microspectrometer for rapid in vivo determination of water concentration profiles in human skin. *J. Raman Spectrosc.* **2000**, *31*, 813–818. [CrossRef]
13. Rana, S.; Subbaraman, H.; Fleming, A.; Kandadai, N. Numerical analysis of radiation effects on fiber optic sensors. *Sensors* **2021**, *21*, 4111. [CrossRef] [PubMed]

14. Kalk, J. *Use of Low-Cost, Disposable Components in a Remote, Hostile Environment*; Technical Report; Westinghouse Hanford Co.: Richland, WA, USA, 1988.
15. Halpern, A.R.; Lee, M.Y.; Howard, M.D.; Woodworth, M.A.; Nicovich, P.R.; Vaughan, J.C. Versatile, do-it-yourself, low-cost spinning disk confocal microscope. *Biomed. Opt. Express* **2022**, *13*, 1102–1120. [CrossRef]
16. Gong, C.; Kulkarni, N.; Zhu, W.; Nguyen, C.D.; Curiel-Lewandrowski, C.; Kang, D. Low-cost, high-speed near infrared reflectance confocal microscope. *Biomed. Opt. Express* **2019**, *10*, 3497–3505. [CrossRef] [PubMed]
17. Tsai, R.Y.; Chen, J.P.; Lee, Y.C.; Huang, C.C.; Huang, T.T.; Chiang, H.C.; Cheng, C.M.; Lo, F.H.; Chang, S.L.; Weng, K.Y.; et al. Position-addressable digital laser scanning point fluorescence microscopy with a Blu-ray disk pickup head. *Biomed. Opt. Express* **2014**, *5*, 427–438. [CrossRef]
18. Karlsson, J.; Rippe, L.; Kröll, S. A confocal optical microscope for detection of single impurities in a bulk crystal at cryogenic temperatures. *Rev. Sci. Instrum.* **2016**, *87*, 033701. [CrossRef]
19. Golparvar, A.; Panahi, A.; Khorsand, O. An Arduino-based Remote Health Monitoring and Alert System with Fingerprint Photoplethysmography Using PulseSensor. In Proceedings of the International Conference of Biophotonics and Biomedical Optics, Virtual, 17–19 November 2021; pp. 1–6.
20. Jumaah, H.J.; Kalantar, B.; Halin, A.A.; Mansor, S.; Ueda, N.; Jumaah, S.J. Development of UAV-based PM2.5 monitoring system. *Drones* **2021**, *5*, 60. [CrossRef]
21. Conceicao, C.A.; Mattiello-Francisco, F.; Batista, C.L. Dependability verification of nanosatellite embedded software supported by a reusable Test System. In Proceedings of the 2016 Seventh Latin-American Symposium on Dependable Computing (LADC), Cali, Colombia, 19–21 October 2016; IEEE: Piscataway, NJ, USA, 2016; pp. 157–163.
22. Lay, K.S.; Li, L.; Okutsu, M. High altitude balloon testing of Arduino and environmental sensors for CubeSat prototype. *HardwareX* **2022**, *12*, e00329. [CrossRef]
23. Ga, S.H.; Cha, H.J.; Kim, C.J. Adapting Internet of Things to Arduino-based Devices for Low-Cost Remote Sensing in School Science Learning Environments. *Int. J. Online Biomed. Eng. (iJOE)* **2021**, *17*, 4–18. [CrossRef]
24. Fukumoto, H.; Yamaguchi, T.; Ishibashi, M.; Furukawa, T. Developing a remote laboratory system of stepper motor for learning support. *IEEE Trans. Educ.* **2020**, *64*, 292–298. [CrossRef]
25. Chen, X.; Du, J.; Kanwal, S.; Yang, Z.J.; Zheng, L.L.; Wang, J.; Wen, J.; Zhang, D.W. A low-cost and portable fluorometer based on an optical pick-up unit for chlorophyll-a detection. *Talanta* **2024**, *269*, 125447. [CrossRef] [PubMed]
26. Hayden, S.; Munro, T. Fluorescent scanning thermal microscope based on a Blu-ray optical head to measure thermal diffusivity of radioactive samples. *Rev. Sci. Instrum.* **2019**, *90*, 024903. [CrossRef]
27. Hwu, E.E.T.; Boisen, A. Hacking CD/DVD/Blu-ray for biosensing. *ACS Sens.* **2018**, *3*, 1222–1232. [CrossRef] [PubMed]
28. Jiang, S.; Guo, C.; Wang, T.; Liu, J.; Song, P.; Zhang, T.; Wang, R.; Feng, B.; Zheng, G. Blood-coated sensor for high-throughput ptychographic cytometry on a Blu-Ray disc. *ACS Sens.* **2022**, *7*, 1058–1067. [CrossRef]
29. Kasukurti, A.; Eggleton, C.; Desai, S.; Disharoon, D.; Marr, D. A simple microfluidic dispenser for single-microparticle and cell samples. *Lab Chip* **2014**, *14*, 4673–4679. [CrossRef]
30. Unger, S.; Ito, S.; Kohl, D.; Schitter, G. Development of a compact atomic force microscope based on an optical pickup head. *IFAC-PapersOnLine* **2016**, *49*, 629–635. [CrossRef]
31. Tobón-Maya, H.; Gómez-Ramírez, A.; Buitrago-Duque, C.; Garcia-Sucerquia, J. Adapting a Blu-ray optical pickup unit as a point source for digital lensless holographic microscopy. *Appl. Opt.* **2023**, *62*, D39–D47. [CrossRef] [PubMed]
32. Diederich, B.; Lachmann, R.; Carlstedt, S.; Marsikova, B.; Wang, H.; Uwurukundo, X.; Mosig, A.S.; Heintzmann, R. A versatile and customizable low-cost 3D-printed open standard for microscopic imaging. *Nat. Commun.* **2020**, *11*, 5979. [CrossRef] [PubMed]
33. Almond, D.P.; Patel, P. *Photothermal Science and Techniques*; Springer Science & Business Media: Berlin/Heidelberg, Germany, 1996; Volume 10.
34. Arunkarthick, S.; Bijeesh, M.; Vetcha, A.S.; Rastogi, N.; Nandakumar, P.; Varier, G.K. Design and construction of a confocal laser scanning microscope for biomolecular imaging. *Curr. Sci.* **2014**, *107*, 1965–1969.
35. Balderas-López, J.; Jaime-Fonseca, M.; Abrica-González, P.; Mandelis, A. On the Importance of Using Reliability Criteria in Photothermal Experiments for Accurate Thermophysical Property Measurements. *Int. J. Thermophys.* **2024**, *45*, 56. [CrossRef]
36. Munro, T.; Putzeys, T.; Copeland, C.G.; Xing, C.; Lewis, R.V.; Ban, H.; Glorieux, C.; Wubbenhorst, M. Investigation of synthetic spider silk crystallinity and alignment via electrothermal, pyroelectric, literature XRD, and tensile techniques. *Macromol. Mater. Eng.* **2017**, *302*, 1600480. [CrossRef]
37. Copeland, C.G.; Bell, B.E.; Christensen, C.D.; Lewis, R.V. Development of a process for the spinning of synthetic spider silk. *ACS Biomater. Sci. Eng.* **2015**, *1*, 577–584. [CrossRef] [PubMed]
38. Munro, T.; Liu, L.; Ban, H.; Glorieux, C. Thermophysical properties of thin fibers via photothermal quantum dot fluorescence spectral shape-based thermometry. *Int. J. Heat Mass Transf.* **2017**, *112*, 1090–1097. [CrossRef]

39. Gong, H.; Bickham, B.P.; Woolley, A.T.; Nordin, G.P. Custom 3D printer and resin for 18 μm × 20 μm microfluidic flow channels. *Lab Chip* **2017**, *17*, 2899–2909. [CrossRef] [PubMed]
40. Hua, Z.; Spackman, J.; Ban, H. Characterization of Kapitza resistances of natural grain boundaries in cerium oxide. *Materialia* **2019**, *5*, 100230. [CrossRef]

metrology

Article

Comparison of Measurement Protocols for Internal Channels of Transparent Microfluidic Devices

Joris Kaal [1], Nicolas Feltin [2], Marc Lelong [2], Huabing Yin [3], Andrew Glidle [3], Kevin Romieu [4] and Elsa Batista [5,*]

1 CEA-Leti, Commissariat à l'Énergie Atomique et aux Énergies Alternatives, Université Grenoble Alpes, F-38000 Grenoble, France; joris.kaal@cea.fr
2 Laboratoire National de Métrologie et d'Essais-Nanometrology, CEDEX, 78197 Trappes, France; nicolas.feltin@lne.fr (N.F.); marc.lelong@lne.fr (M.L.)
3 Division of Biomedical Engineering, School of Engineering, University of Glasgow, Glasgow G12 8LT, UK; huabing.yin@glasgow.ac.uk (H.Y.); andrew.glidle@glasgow.ac.uk (A.G.)
4 CETIAT, Centre Technique des Industries Aérauliques et Thermiques, F-69603 Villeurbanne, France; kevin.romieu@cetiat.fr
5 Metrology Department, Portuguese Institute for Quality (IPQ), 2829-513 Caparica, Portugal
* Correspondence: ebatista@ipq.pt; Tel.: +351-212948167

Abstract: The microfluidic industry faces a significant challenge due to the lack of sensitive and standardized methods. One critical need is the measurement of internal channel dimensions in fully assembled chips. This study presents and compares several protocols for measuring these dimensions, including optical profilometry, optical microscopy, and tiled digital imagery. Standardized chips made from two materials commonly used in microfluidics (borosilicate glass and Cyclic Olefin Copolymer) were evaluated using each protocol. A consistency analysis using normalized error statistics identified optical profilometry as the most reliable method, offering the lowest uncertainty and the highest consistency with nominal geometry values. However, all protocols encountered difficulties with vertical depth measurements of internal structures. Future research should focus on addressing these limitations, including investigating the influence of multiple refractive surfaces on optical profilometry and exploring confocal microscopy. In conclusion, this work provides a comprehensive comparison of measurement protocols for internal microfluidic structures and offers a practical solution for applications in the microfluidic industry, while also identifying important directions for future research.

Keywords: microfluidic chips; optical measurements; channels dimensions; methods validation

1. Introduction

Microfluidics has long held the potential to disrupt a wide range of fields [1–3]. Aiming at the miniaturization of analytical and chemical methods [4], microfluidics continues to promise revolutionary advancements across many industries [5].

In recent years, the microfluidics industry has experienced remarkable growth, driven by applications such as chemical analysis, point-of-care diagnostics [6,7], and pharmaceutical research [8,9], including microphysiological systems [10,11]. The growth is projected to continue at a compound annual growth rate of 2.2% until 2028 [12].

Regardless of the application, the internal geometry of microfluidic channels is often crucial to the functionality of the device. For example, point-of-care diagnostic devices required precise dilution ratios, while microphysiological systems need physiologically relevant shear stresses [13,14], both of which impose strict geometrical constraints on chip manufacturers.

Given the importance of the internal geometry to a device's functionality, it is crucial for the industry to be able to accurately characterize the internal dimensions of a chip. Microfluidic chips are often made of multiple structured layers that are sealed together to form the final product. While measuring the dimensions of the structure before assembly is feasible (for example, using optical microscopy or stylus profilometry), once sealed, the channels are encapsulated inside the chip. This makes their characterization more difficult due to material properties and physical constraints. This issue is significant because the assembly process can change the structure of the chip compared to its pre-assembled state, leaving both the manufacturer and the user uncertain about the actual geometry and dimensions of the flow circuit in use.

The industry itself has identified the lack of sensitive and standardized testing methods as one of the major hurdles preventing microfluidics from fulfilling its promises [15,16]. To help address this challenge, this work presents multiple protocols for measuring the internal dimensions of fully assembled transparent chips. The reproducibility and precision of each protocol are analyzed and compared. Both glass and polymer chips are used as substrates to evaluate the influence of material on measurement reproducibility.

The protocols described in this study enable automated, non-destructive, reproducible characterization of the internal geometry of transparent microfluidic chips after assembly, making them suitable for industrial applications. By removing the uncertainty caused by potential deformation during assembly, these protocols ensure that users can trust the devices they are using, and manufacturers can be confident in the quality of the chips they are providing.

Here, we describe the chip designs and different measuring techniques. The different sets of results are analyzed through consistency tests between the protocols and nominal values. Finally, we examined the influence of two different materials on dimension measurements.

2. Chips Geometries

Batches of chips were designed and manufactured using two different materials: D263©bio glass [17] (a common type of borosilicate glass) and COC (Cyclic Olefin Copolymer, tradename TOPAS© [18]). The chips made from each material have different internal dimensions and designs. The choice of geometries was based on different applications for these chips within the EURAMET 20NRM02 MFMET project [19] (MFMET–Establishing Metrology Standards in Microfluidic devices [20]). These tests mainly include leakage tests [21], flow resistivity tests [22], and the dimensional measurements described here.

All designs adhere to the ISO 22916:2022 standard on interoperability requirements for dimensions, connections, and initial classification of microfluidic devices [23]. This standard has a notable influence on the chips' footprint, as well as the positions and dimensions of their connections. This allows different participants to use the same connector and be confident that the chips were compatible with each other's measurement setup. In addition, these chips are intended to serve as transfer standards for other laboratories. By adhering to ISO 22916:2022, compatibility with laboratories outside the scope of this project will also be facilitated.

2.1. Glass Transfer Standard Chips

Eight designs (footprint 15 mm × 45 mm) were developed for glass chips (see Figure 1). Each design has one or several main channels, with some connected to one or multiple "leakage channels"—these are significantly smaller in cross-section compared to the main channels, simulating a leak. All designs, except Design 08, include a reference channel (Channel 01 in Figure 1) that does not have any additional side channels. Figure 2 shows an example of Design 04 chips. Technical design drawings of these glass transfer standard chips are available in the Electronic Supplementary Information.

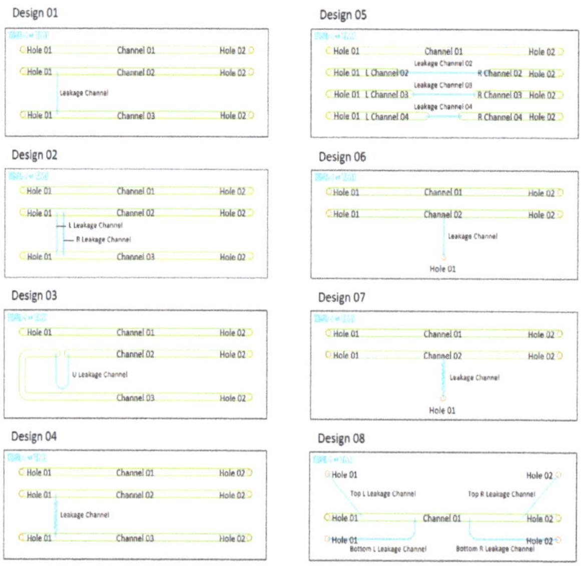

Figure 1. Different glass chip designs and their geometry nomenclature for measurements.

Figure 2. Example of a glass transfer standard chip, Design 04.

The glass chips were fabricated by IMT Masken und Teilungen AG, Greifensee, Switzerland, using D263©bio glass [17], via isotropic wet-etching techniques, employing hydrofluoric acid-based etching solutions commonly used in the semiconductor industry. The final chips consist of two halves that were individually fabricated and then bonded together. The critical dimensions of the device were verified during and after processing for quality assurance. For Designs 01 to 05, four chips were produced, while Design 06 and 07 had three chips each, and Design 08 had two. One chip from each design was reserved as a backup.

2.2. *Polymer Transfer Standard Chips*

The polymer transfer standard chip has the same footprint as a standard microscope slide and contains eight different designs on a single chip (see Figure 3). Each design consisted of two main channels with a "leakage channel". The leakage channels came in two distinct lengths: four designs had longer leakage channels, and the other four had shorter ones. The cross-section of the leakage channels is rectangular and varies between designs. Figure 4 shows an example of one of the polymer chips. Detailed designs, technical drawings, and CAD files of the polymer chip design can be found in the Electronic Supplementary Information.

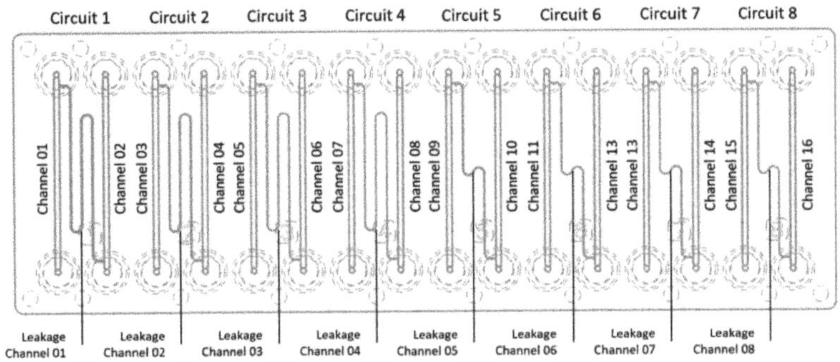

Figure 3. Polymer chip design and its geometry nomenclature for measurements.

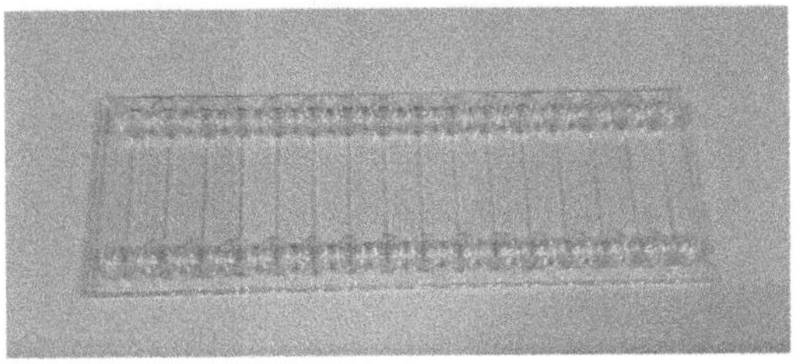

Figure 4. Example of a polymer transfer standard chip.

The polymer chips were produced by microfluidic ChipShop GmbH, Jena, Germany, using injection molding.

Once the fabrication process is complete, the top part containing the microfluidic structure is sealed onto a thin bottom slide to close the chip. The entire chip is made of COC (Cyclic Olefin Copolymer, tradename TOPAS© [18]).

3. Three Different Measurement Protocols

The different pieces of equipment used for the measurement protocols set out below are shown in Figure 5, with specifications given in Table 1.

Table 1. Specifications of the different instruments used for dimension measurements.

Instrument	Lens	Lighting	Calibration	Uncertainty Linked to Calibration
OGP SmartScope ZIP®250	×1 ×2	Substage LED profile Coaxial LED surface SmartRing™ LED ring light	Annual calibration report by OGP	In plane (XY): ±2 µm + 4 L/1000 Vertically (Z): ±2.5 µm + 5 L/1000 In-image: <1 µm

Table 1. *Cont.*

Instrument	Lens	Lighting	Calibration	Uncertainty Linked to Calibration
Olympus BX53M	×1.5 ×5 ×15	Substage tungsten bulb lighting	Test pattern (see Figure 5)	0.1%
Leica Wild M3Z	×2.56	Overhead LED ring light	Test pattern (see Figure 5)	2%
Nikon D5300	×1, f/2.8, 105 mm macro lens	Fluorescent tube lighting below sample	Test pattern (see Figure 5)	In-image: 0.45% On tiled images: 0.76%
Zeiss AxioObserver	×2.5	Transmission lighting from quartz halogen bulb	Test pattern (see Figure 5)	0.15%

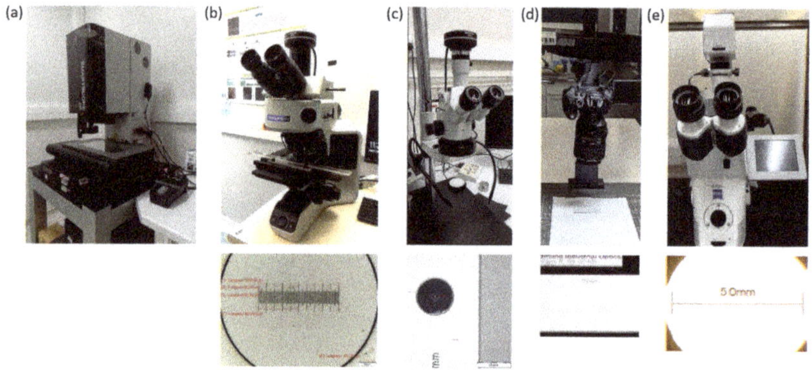

Figure 5. The different setups used for dimension measurements. (**a**) Optical profilometer OGP SmartScope ZIP®250. (**b**) Optical microscope Olympus BX53M with its calibration gauge. (**c**) Stereo binocular microscope Leica Wild M3Z with its calibration gauge. (**d**) Digital camera Nikon D5300 with its calibration gauge. (**e**) Optical microscope Zeiss AxioObserver with its calibration gauge.

Examples of the optical images obtained from each of the techniques are given in Figure 6, together with details showing which points in the images were used as reference criteria from which the measurement values were obtained.

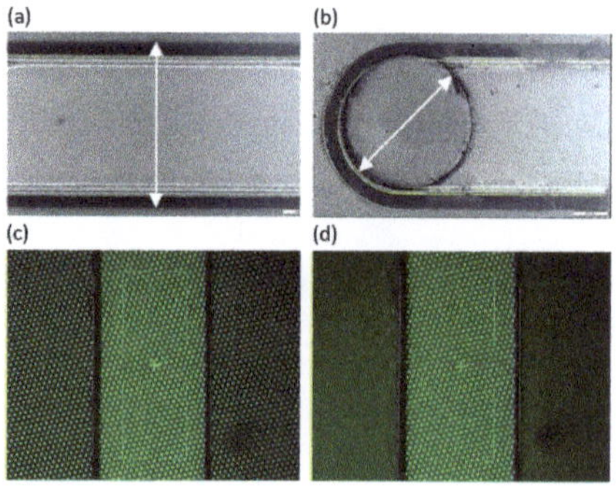

Figure 6. *Cont.*

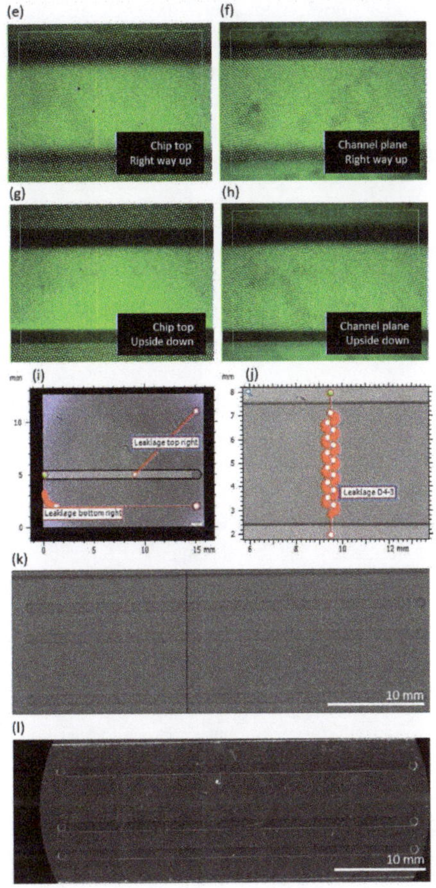

Figure 6. Definition of measurement points (images (**b–h**) from the Optical Profiler; (**i**) from the Leica Wild M3Z; (**j**) from the Olympus BX53M; (**k**) from the Nikon D5300; and (**l**) from the Zeiss AxioObserver). (**a**) The width of the channels is taken as the maximum width. (**b**) The diameter of the holes is measured by recognizing the internal hole features. (**c**) Point at the bottom Z-plane of the polymer channel. (**d**) Point at the top Z-plane of the polymer channel. (**e**) Point at the top plane of the glass chip when the chip is the right way up (see Section 3.1). (**f**) Point at the measurable channel plane of the glass chip when the chip is the right way up. (**g**) Point at the top plane of the glass chip when the chip is upside down (see Section 3.1). (**h**) Point at the measurable channel plane of the glass chip when the chip is upside down. (**i**) MountainsMap©'s "Distance between two points" and "Customized path" tools applied to Design 08. (**j**) MountainsMap©'s "Distance between two points" and "Customized path" tools applied to S-channel in design 04. (**k**) A stitched image of Design 01 created using the Nikon D5300 camera. (**l**) A stitched image of Design 04 created using the Zeiss AxioObserver with Ludl BioPoint2 stage showing the ability to discern the leakage channel (left hand side of image) when using higher NA optics.

3.1. Protocol 1: Optical Profilometry

The first protocol entails optical profilometry, a method that uses light instead of a physical probe to characterize geometries. This allows non-destructive measurements without direct contact with the object, making it particularly suitable for transparent substrates.

A SmartScope ZIP®250 (with its accompanying software, ZONE3©, both from Optical Gaging Products (OGP), part of Quality Vision International (QVI), Rochester, NY, USA) was used to perform measurements of the internal geometries. Table 1 gives details of the instrument, and the setup is shown in Figure 5a.

The instrument is annually recalibrated by OGP staff, ensuring the accuracy shown in Table 1 (Calibration report available in the Electronic Supplementary Information). It is important to note the difference in uncertainty between measurements where the stage moves a distance, L, between two measured points and static in-image measurements.

The OGP SmartScope ZIP®250 can automatically focus on a plane within a user-defined margin. The software identifies geometrical features from the focused image and measures the dimension of interest. For example, to determine the width of a channel, the profilometer finds the focus plane at the top of the channel, identifies the outermost edges, and measures the width between these edges (see Figure 6).

Depth measurements proved to be more challenging, particularly in glass compared to polymer chips. For polymer chips, the depths of all channels were measured by determining focus planes at the top and bottom of the channel using the software's "Focus" tool, which establishes a 3D point on each plane. The software then calculates the channel depth by measuring the distance in Z-axis between these two points (Figure 6).

However, depth measurements inside transparent materials using optical profilometry are subject to distortion due to the material's refractive index, which depends on both material and the wavelength of light used to determine the focus plane. The SmartScope ZIP®250 uses grid light with a wavelength range from 575 nm to 625 nm. For polymer chips, a refractive index (RI) of n_D = 1.53 for 589 nm at 25 °C (provided by microfluidic ChipShop GmbH, Germany) was used to correct for the difference between and optical path length and physical distance measurement [24]; thus, all depth measurements in polymer chips were multiplied by n_D.

For glass, the optical profilometer struggled to differentiate between the focus planes at the top and bottom of the channels. Therefore, a more complex approach was used to estimate the channel depth. The profilometer could determine the top and bottom planes of the chip and one plane of the channel (Figure 6). The assumption was made that this plane belonged to the upper channel. In this method, when the chip is right-side up, the top of the chip, the top of the channel, and the bottom of the chip are measured. When the chip is flipped upside down, the bottom of the chip, the bottom of the channel, and the top of the chip are measured. The following formula was then used to estimate the depth of the channel:

$$D = \left(\left(z_{chnl,2} - z_{top,2}\right) - \left(z_{chnl,1} - z_{top,1}\right)\right) \cdot n_D \quad (1)$$

where D is the estimated channel depth; z_(chnl,2) and z_(top,2) are the z-coordinates of the measurable channel plane and the top plane measured when the chip is upside down; z_(top,1) and z_(chnl,1) are the z-coordinates of the measurable channel plane and the top plane measured when the chip is right-side up; and n_D is the refractive index of D263©bio glass. Based on the OGP light wavelength range, a refractive index = 1.5230 for 589.2938 nm [25], provided by Schott AG, Germany, was used to correct for RI effects [17].

The length of the main channels was defined as the maximum distance between the inlet and outlet hole centers. Hole diameters were determined using the "Feature finder" tool, which measures the internal circumference of the holes (Figure 6). Leakage channel lengths were measured using start and end reference points taken from the mid-point of a line drawn across the intersection of the leakage channel with the wall of a main channel.

Measuring the lengths of more complex, non-linear channels (such as L-, U-, and S-shaped channels) posed difficulties. Despite multiple attempts using different settings and ZONE3© tools, no reproducible parameters were found.

All the above steps are programmable on the OGP SmartScope ZIP®250. This allows a specific measurement protocol—including positions, fields of view, focus zones, lighting, and image processing settings—to be stored and repeated for identical objects. Once established, the measurement program was run three times on each chip.

Using the data from each run, an average and a standard deviation (s_r) were determined. Together with the uncertainty from the instrument's calibration (u_c), noted in Table 1, the standard uncertainty (u) of the measurement was calculated using the following formula:

$$u = \sqrt{u_c^2 + s_r^2} \quad (2)$$

The calculation assumes that these are the two largest sources of uncertainty. For the purpose of this article, variability in the refractive index was not considered, which could be investigated in future research.

3.2. Protocol 2: Optical Microscopy

The second protocol uses standard optical microscopy. Depending on the size of the microfluidic geometries, two different microscopes were employed: an optical microscope (Olympus BX53M) or a stereo binocular microscope (Leica Wild M3Z) was used. Details of both instruments are provided in Table 1.

Each instrument has its own calibration gauge structure (Figure 5), ensuring that measurement results are traceable to the International System of Units (SI). The uncertainties associated with the calibration of each instrument can be found in Table 1.

The width and length of the leakage channels, the width of the main channels, and the diameters of the holes were all measured using the Olympus BX53M (with the ×5 or ×10 lens). Images were taken and analyzed using Olympus Stream Essentials 2.3.3 (Build 17023). This software has the capability to continuously capture images and automatically detect different focal planes, creating a merged image where measurements were made.

Similar to the optical profilometer in Protocol 1, the largest dimension was used to define the channel width (Figure 6). The length of the main channels was measured as the maximum distance between the inlet and outlet holes, using the Leica Wild M3Z binocular microscope. The focal plane was manually adjusted for these measurements.

For hole diameter measurements, a circle tool was used. However, identifying the correct focal plane was difficult, as multiple focal planes were closely spaced. It was hypothesized to be due to the hole-drilling process during chip manufacturing. Several measurements were performed, and an uncertainty value was assigned to take into account the various focal planes and irregularities in the structure.

The length of non-linear channels (both main and leakage channels) was measured using specific tools from the MountainsMap© version 10 software package (from Digital Surf, France). Depending on the channel shape's complexity, either the "Distance between two points" tool or the "Customized path" tool was used (Figure 6). In both cases, the length was determined along the median line of the channel width.

As with Protocol 1, each chip was measured three times, and the results were used to calculate a standard uncertainty using the same approach.

3.3. Protocol 3: Tiled Digital Imagery

The third protocol uses two different instruments, both with a wide field of view: a Nikon D5300 digital camera fitted with a 105 mm, 1×, f/2.8 macro lens; and a Zeiss AxioObserver optical microscope equipped with a Ludl BioPoint2 motorized stage, Zeiss EC Plan Neofluar 2.5×/0.085 objective, and Zeiss HRc camera. Details of both devices are included in Table 1.

Digital cameras, such as the Nikon D5300, offer portability, affordability, and high resolution. Since they can detect events within entire microfluidic devices, they have been widely used with paper–microfluidic devices for on-site diagnosis [26,27] and high-speed imaging and detection of events within microfluidic devices [28]. The Zeiss AxioObserver, similar to the microscope used in Protocol 2, provides more precise measurements.

Both instruments were calibrated using standard reference bars (Figure 6), which allowed for the determination of the resolution of the instruments and the uncertainty linked to calibration (Table 1). The calibration report is available in the Electronic Supplementary Information.

In this protocol, measurements were made using image processing. For hole diameters and channel widths, both instruments could produce results from a single image. The uncertainty in these measurements was based solely on the consistency associated with the instruments' calibration.

For measuring the lengths of the main channels, tiled images were used. The number of frames needed to cover the entire microfluidic channel depended on the field of view of the instrument. The accuracy of the measurement was affected by how well the frames were stitched together, the quality of images, and the uncertainty linked to the instrument's calibration.

The Nikon D5300 camera, with its large field of view, required only two frames to cover an entire main channel in the glass chips (see Figure 6 for an example). The images were taken with overlapping areas such that they could be stitched together in ImageJ by overlaying blemishes in successive frames. The uncertainty from stitching was 3 pixels/frame (1 pixel = 8.44 μm according to calibration). Due to the lower image quality, there was a significant uncertainty in defining the ends of the channels. This was approximately 6 pixels at each end, resulting in a total uncertainty of 15 pixels, which equals 0.31% of the total length of 39,800 μm. Furthermore, the leakage channels were not sufficiently visible in the images, making accurate measurements unreliable. Including the instrument uncertainty (0.45%; see Table 1), the potential total uncertainty for length measurements using this system was 0.76%.

The Zeiss AxioObserver, equipped with a motorized Ludl BioPoint2 stage, also used stitched images (see Figure 6 for an example). However, the precision and reproducibility of the Ludl BioPoint2 stage (<1 μm) were sufficient, so the results were highly consistent. The main advantage of this instrument was the higher numerical aperture (NA) of the 2.5× objective (NA = 0.085), which gave clearer images. This improved clarity made it easier to define channel and hole borders, resulting in a notable improvement in measurement precision. Therefore, the uncertainty in defining the channel ends was negligible, with an error of at most 1 pixel. Hence, the total uncertainty for the length measurements using the Zeiss AxioObserver was the same as its in-image uncertainty from calibration (i.e., 0.15%; see Table 1).

Both instruments were used to measure multiple glass chips, and the average of multiple measurements from each method was taken as final value. Given this combination of two different methods, the standard uncertainty definition from Equation (2) needs to be updated as follows:

$$u = \sqrt{u_{c1}^2 + u_{c2}^2 + s_r^2} \tag{3}$$

where u_{c1} is the standard uncertainty associated with the Nikon D5300 (which differs between in-image and tiled-image measurements, as shown in Table 1), u_{c2} is the uncertainty associated with the calibration of the Zeiss AxioObserver, and s_r remains the standard deviation between the two values.

3.4. Evaluation of the Measurement Results

To evaluate the consistency of the three protocols, their results are compared against a reference value. For each measurement (for example the diameter of Hole 01 in Channel 01 of Design 01), a reference value can be defined. This reference value (called RV) is determined as the mean of the measurement values from the three protocols combined, using the weighted means formula. The inverse square of the standard uncertainty (u_n) associated with the average of a protocol's measurement values (x_n) serves as its weighting factor [29]:

$$RV = \frac{x_1/u^2(x_1) + \ldots + x_n/u^2(x_n)}{1/u^2(x_1) + \ldots + 1/u^2(x_n)} \quad (4)$$

The following formula gives the standard uncertainty, u(RV), associated with the reference value [29]:

$$u(RV) = \sqrt{\frac{1}{\frac{1}{u^2(x_1)} + \ldots + \frac{1}{u^2(x_n)}}} \quad (5)$$

Once the reference value and its standard uncertainty are determined, the measurement values from each protocol can be tested for consistency with this reference value. To identify this consistency, the normalized error (E_n) is calculated [30]:

$$E_n = \frac{x_n - RV}{\sqrt{U^2(x_n) - U^2(RV)}} \quad (6)$$

where E_n is a protocol's consistency indicator for a specific measurement; x_n is the average of a protocol's measurement values; RV is the reference value of the same measurement; and U (x_n) and U (RV) are their associated expanded uncertainties, calculated as U = k × u with k = 2.

The value of E_n leads to the following conclusions:

- If $| E_n | \leq 1$, the protocol's measurement values are consistent for a certain measurement (test passed).
- If $| E_n | > 1$, the protocol's measurement values are inconsistent for a certain measurement (test failed).

This approach allows for a comparison of the protocols between each other. However, it does not necessarily indicate the accuracy of all protocols. Besides a reference value, a nominal value can also be defined for all measurements. These nominal values and their standard uncertainties are based on the design drawings with quality assurance measurements and statistical tolerances provided by IMT Masken und Teilungen AG. The nominal values represent the theoretical dimensions that the geometry should have.

For the diameters of the holes, no statistical data were available, so the nominal value from the design (i.e., 800 μm) was used. Based on IMT's experience, a standard uncertainty of 15 μm was assumed, resulting in an expanded uncertainty of 30 μm.

The depth was measured by IMT during quality assurance, with values falling within a range of (98.3 ± 0.4) μm, giving an expanded uncertainty of 0.8 μm.

The width of the main channels was estimated using the known depth, leading to a calculated nominal width of (996.6 ± 2.66) μm for this specific batch of chips.

Finally, the length of the main channels, defined as the maximum distance between the inlet and outlet holes (designed at 39,800 μm), depends on the precision of hole placement. Based on IMT's experience, a precision of 7.5 μm per hole was assumed, leading to a total standard uncertainty of 15 μm for the length of the main channels and, thus, an expanded uncertainty of 30 μm.

Using these estimations, the consistency of the measurement values of each protocol with the nominal values can be tested.

To investigate the influence of material on measurements, a straightforward approach was adopted. Protocol 1 was applied to both glass and polymer chips, and the standard uncertainty of the measurements was compared. This standard uncertainty, defined in Equation (2), consists of a standard deviation term (s_r), related to the actual measurements, and an uncertainty term (u_c), related to the calibration of the machine used. Since the calibration uncertainty for the OGP SmartScope ZIP®250 is identical for both polymer and glass measurements, it is more informative to compare the standard deviations of the actual measurements. Thus, the standard deviations from Protocol 1 for both polymer and glass measurements will be compared.

4. Results

4.1. Glass Chips

Each protocol naturally gave a set of results for the glass chips. The three complete sets of results can be found in the Electronic Supplementary Information. For analysis purposes, the results from a single chip, Design 01—series 01, and only its first channel, Channel 01, will be treated here. In this channel, the protocols performed the following measurements:

- The diameter of Hole 01;
- The diameter of Hole 02;
- The width of the channel;
- The depth of the channel;
- The length of the channel.

The subsequent figures (Figures 7–11) show the resulting values from all three protocols, their associated reference value, and the nominal value of each measurement.

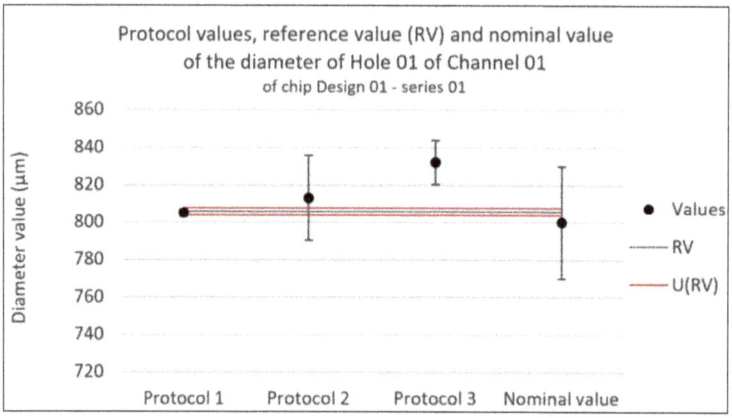

Figure 7. Consistency test for the diameter of Hole 01 in Channel 01 of chip Design 01—series 01. Error bars represent the expanded uncertainty. Likewise, U(RV) is the expanded uncertainty associated with the reference value.

To determine the consistency between the different protocols and their resulting reference value, the normalized error values (E_D) are shown in Table 2.

Table 2. Normalized error values between protocols and their resulting reference value (RV) for each measurement. Values that indicate inconsistency are marked in red.

	Diameter Hole 01	Diameter Hole 02	Width	Depth	Length
Protocol 1	−1.78	−4.44	−1.57	N/A	1.48
Protocol 2	0.33	4.14	1.65	N/A	0.32
Protocol 3	2.30	1.12	−0.40	N/A	−1.95

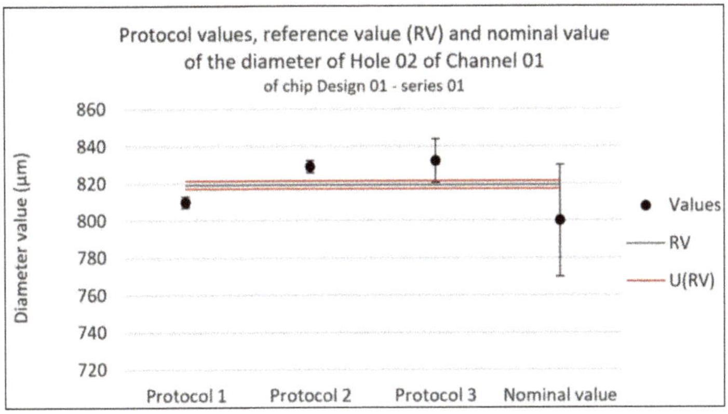

Figure 8. Consistency test for the diameter of Hole 01 in Channel 01 of chip Design 01—series 01. Error bars represent the expanded uncertainty. Likewise, U(RV) is the expanded uncertainty associated with the reference value.

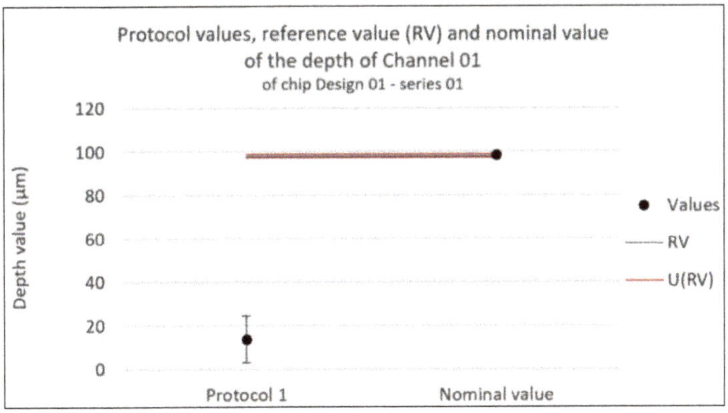

Figure 9. Consistency test for the depth of Channel 01 of chip Design 01—series 01. Error bars represent the expanded uncertainty. Likewise, U(RV) is the expanded uncertainty associated with the reference value.

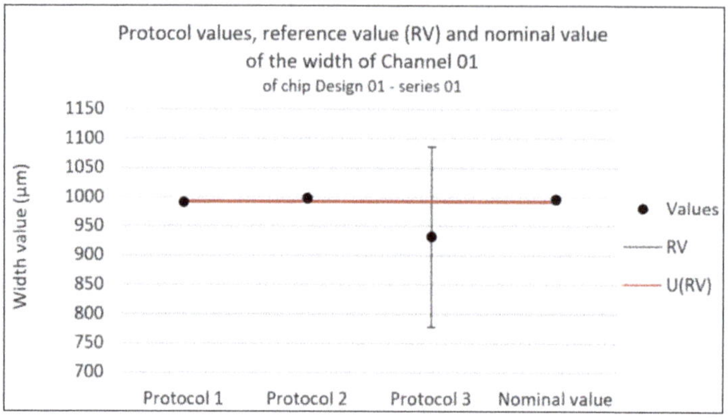

Figure 10. Consistency test for the width of Channel 01 of chip Design 01—series 01. Error bars represent the expanded uncertainty. Likewise, U(RV) is the expanded uncertainty associated with the reference value.

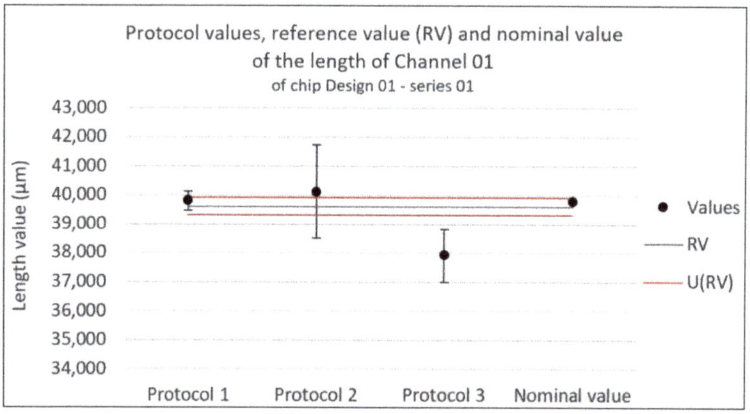

Figure 11. Consistency test for the length of Channel 01 of chip Design 01—series 01. Error bars represent the expanded uncertainty. Likewise, U(RV) is the expanded uncertainty associated with the reference value.

Given that the depth was only measured with Protocol 1, there is no reference value or normalized error for a consistency test.

Finally, the consistency between the protocols and the nominal value was determined for each measurement. The normalized errors for this consistency test are shown in Table 3.

Table 3. Normalized error values between protocols and the nominal value for each measurement. Values that indicate inconsistency are marked in red.

	Diameter Hole 01	Diameter Hole 02	Width	Depth	Length
Protocol 1	0.16	0.33	−0.93	−7.81	0.02
Protocol 2	0.35	0.96	0.23	N/A	0.20
Protocol 3	0.99	0.99	−0.42	N/A	−2.04

4.2. Polymer Chips

The full set of results from the polymer chips acquired with Protocol 1 can be found in the Electronic Supplementary Information. As an excerpt, Table 4 shows the width and depth measurements, as well as their standard deviations, for the first design of one of the COC chips. To facilitate a more meaningful comparison of these standard deviations against those from measurements made on glass chips, they are expressed in percentages.

Table 4. Measurements of the width and depth of the channels in Circuit 1 of one of the TOPAS© COC chips, as well as their associated standard deviations.

	Width		Depth	
	Average Measured	**Standard Deviation**	**Average Measured**	**Standard Deviation**
Channel 01	503.1 μm	0.1 μm (0.0%)	358.0 μm	1.7 μm (0.5%)
Leakage Channel 01	108.5 μm	0.1 μm (0.1%)	123.6 μm	1.8 μm (1.4%)
Channel 02	508.1 μm	0.1 μm (0.0%)	372.9 μm	2.7 μm (0.7%)

For comparison purposes, Table 5 provides measurements and uncertainties from Protocol 1 for the measurement directions corresponding to those of Table 4.

Table 5. Measurements of the width and depth of the channels of glass chip Design 01—series 01, as well as their associated standard deviations.

	Width		Depth	
	Average Measured	**Standard Deviation**	**Average Measured**	**Standard Deviation**
Channel 01	991.3 μm	0.2 μm (0.0%)	13.8 μm	4.6 μm (33.0%)
Channel 02	992.1 μm	0.2 μm (0.0%)	17.9 μm	1.3 μm (7.6%)
Channel 03	992.4 μm	0.2 μm (0.0%)	20.2 μm	3.3 μm (16.3%)
Leakage channel	143.0 μm	0.5 μm (0.3%)	N/A	N/A

5. Discussion

5.1. Comparison of Protocols

The normalized error values in Table 2 suggest that the protocols are often inconsistent with the reference values. On the contrary, Table 3 shows the protocols mostly consistent with the nominal values. The consistency of Protocol 1 with the nominal values slightly outperforms that of Protocol 2, which in turn slightly outperforms Protocol 3. This implies while the different protocols produce different values, they remain consistent with the nominal values and their expanded uncertainties. This also indicates the need for a more detailed exportation of the uncertainty calculations, as they are likely underestimated across all protocols.

In particular, for longer dimensions, such as the channel length, the accuracy of the optical profilometer is higher than that of the other protocols.

Several factors may explain the decreased accuracy of the length measurements in Protocol 3. The most evident reason is the extra uncertainty term introduced in the standard uncertainty definition due to the combination of two different methods (see the comparison between Equation (2) to Equation (3)). Additionally, the uncertainty of each method includes an extra factor related to image stitching, on top of the uncertainty associated with calibration. Lastly, the average and standard deviations for Protocol 3 are based on two measurement points, one from each method. Improving any of these three factors might potentially improve the consistency of this protocol with the nominal values for length.

In terms of uncertainty, Protocol 1 presents smaller values than the others in all measurement dimensions.

5.2. Close-Up on Depth Measurements

For the depth measurements shown in Figure 10, only Protocol 1 was capable of providing results, but these were inconsistent with the nominal values (see Table 3 and, additionally, Table 5). Several factors could explain this inconsistency and suggest potential improvements.

First, the measurements were corrected with the refractive index of the material. The refractive index is given for a specific wavelength (589 nm), which may not exactly match the wavelength of the SmartScope ZIP®250 used in Protocol 1. OGP indicated that the wavelength of the grid light for measurements in Z could range from 575 to 625 nm (Table 6). However, even if the wavelength is different slightly, considering the material's refractive index variations, it is unlikely to cause significant changes in the measured values [17,25].

Table 6. Refractive indices of D263©bio glass for different wavelengths spanning the SmartScope.

$n_{C'}$ (643.8469 nm) ZIP®250 focus light range.	1.5209
n_D (589.2938 nm)	1.5230
n_e (546.074 nm)	1.5255 ± 0.0015

If the value of the refractive index is not the issue, then it may be the method of applying it. The straightforward multiplication of the measured values with the refractive index to correct for deformation is regularly used for structures with a single refractive interface. However, for an internal channel with two refractive interfaces, this assumption might not hold, and further investigation is warranted, which would also take into account the NA of the imaging optic and its influence on the estimated optical path length.

Another possibility is that the optical profilometer did not accurately measure either of the two surfaces. Given the high surface quality of wet-etched channels and the proximity of its top and bottom planes, the channel itself might act as a lens. In this case, the low surface roughness, which is usually considered an advantage, might impede proper measurement. This too would be worth further investigation.

It seems unrealistic to hypothesize that the bonding process has altered the channel depth from the quality assurance value of 98.3 ± 0.4 µm to the measured values in Table 5. A destructive test could verify this; however, other tests performed on these chips within the 20NRM02 MFMET project would likely have detected such a drastic geometry change.

To suggest further improvements in depth measurement for internal microfluidic channels, an additional method was tested. The following paragraph describes preliminary results obtained during this work, which could provide an interesting avenue for future work on depth measurement protocols for internal microfluidic channels.

Leakage Channel 02 of a polymer chip was measured using a Zeiss LSM 510 confocal fluorescence microscope. The instrument operates based on a confocal principle, which eliminates out-of-focus light from focal planes (called optical sections) and collects serial optical sections. In comparison to conventional epifluorescence microscopy, confocal microscopy can produce three-dimensional images by stacking up a series of Z-images. Confocal microscopy is well suited to measure the depth of an enclosed microfluidic channel. It must be noted that a fluorophore solution was injected into the chip for these measurements.

The obtainable resolution in Z depends on the NA value and the magnification of the microscope's objectives. Two objectives were used: an ×20 NA = 0.5 objective and an ×100 NA = 1.3 objective, allowing for a resolution in Z of 2.07 µm and 0.44 µm, respectively. The higher NA value objective thus enables thinner optical slicing. With this objective, however, for optical sections further away from the base of the channel, the fluorescence intensity significantly decreases because of fluorescence self-absorption effects. This effect is clearly visible in Figure 12.

Figures 13 and 14 show the resulting Z-stacks of the confocal fluorescence measurements made with the ×20 N = 0.5 objective and the ×100 NA = 1.3 objective, respectively.

To estimate the channel height using these confocal measurements, first it is necessary to determine the sections at which the fluorescence intensity in the channel is significant compared to outside the channel. This can be performed by comparing the intensity at the center of the channel to the intensity measured outside of the channel (as shown in Figure 12).

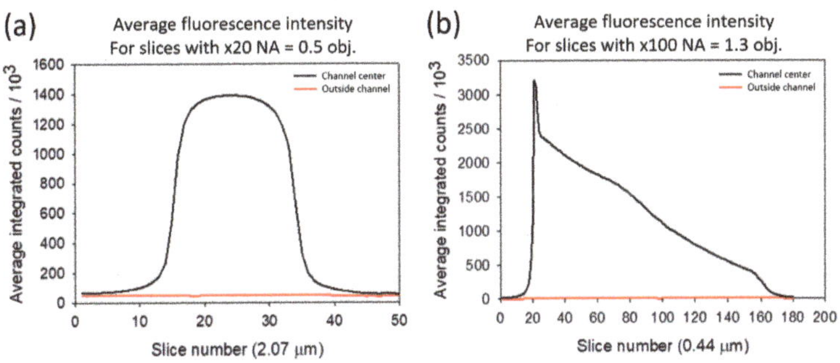

Figure 12. Average fluorescence intensity for successive optical sections (slices) measured in the center of the channel (black) and to the side of the channel (red). Base of the channel at slice 0. (**a**) Measurements from the ×20 NA = 0.5 objective, 2.07 µm sections. (**b**) Measurements from the ×100 NA = 1.3 objective, 0.44 µm sections.

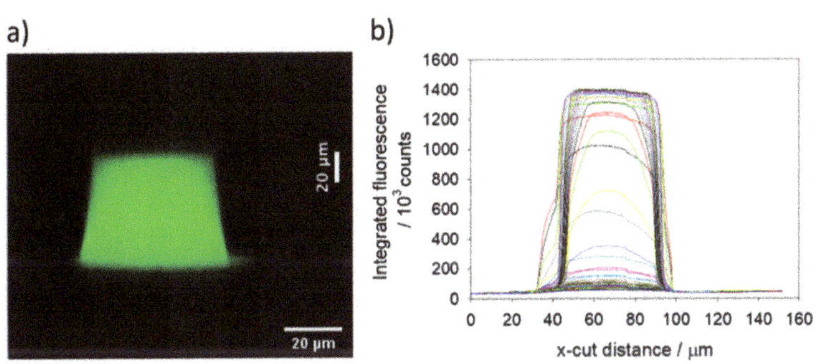

Figure 13. Integrated fluorescence intensity from Z-stack of all 50 optical sections taken with the ×20 NA = 0.5 objective. (**a**) Cross-section of channel height. (**b**) Fluorescence Intensity profile of all optical sections over an x-cut perpendicular to both the long channel axis and the channel height axis.

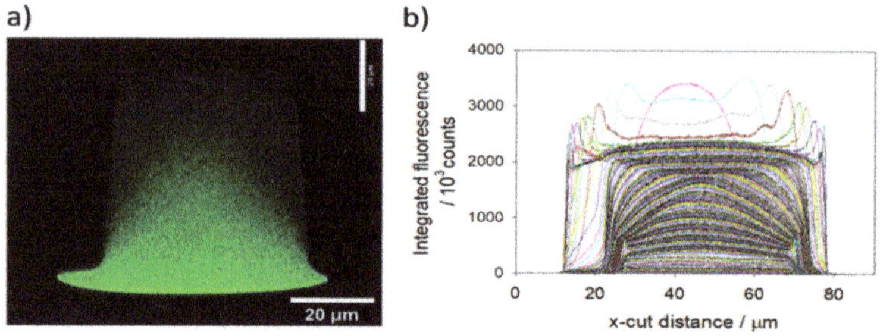

Figure 14. Integrated fluorescence intensity from Z-stack of all 180 optical sections taken with the ×100 NA = 1.3 objective. (**a**) Cross-section of channel height. (**b**) Fluorescence Intensity profile of all optical sections over an x-cut perpendicular to both the long channel axis and the channel height axis.

Secondly, a decision needs to be made about the minimum value of fluorescence intensity within an optical section corresponds to that confocal slice being substantially within the channel. This decision is necessary because the confocality is not perfect: for all practical pinhole sizes, light from a range of Z-distances will pass through. For a homogeneous fluorescence solution, such as the one in use here, a lower limit for fluorescence intensity to determine whether an optical section is substantially within the channel could, for example, be taken as 1% of that found at the channel's mid-height.

Using this 1% criteria, it is possible to estimate that 37 of the 50 optical sections from the ×20 NA = 0.5 objective are substantially within the channel. With its resolution in Z of 2.07 µm (calibrated to be accurate to 0.1 µm using an internal encoder), the channel height of the polymer device is estimated at (74.5 ± 4) µm (there will be at least on slice uncertainty at both the top and bottom of the channel).

Despite the fact that the profiles collected using the ×100 NA = 1.3 objective appear noisy (especially at sections further from the channel base), it is possible to make an accurate estimate of which slices have a fluorescence intensity above the 1% threshold. For the ×100 NA = 1.3 objective, there are 166 out of 180 optical sections above the 1% fluorescence intensity criteria, corresponding to a channel height estimate of (73.0 ± 0.8) µm.

Thus, the two measurements are consistent with each other, with the ×100 NA = 1.3 objective having greater precision.

There is a channel height discrepancy between the design specifications and the height measured by confocal microscopy. These parts are made by sealing an upper piece, which bears the imprinted channel profile, to a lower piece that is a plain (flat) plastic substrate. A significant fraction of this discrepancy in heights is most likely due to the bonding process used to seal the two pieces together. As can be seen from the fluorescence x-cut profiles of Figures 13 and 14, the measured width of the lowest 5–10 µm of the channel is significantly larger than the main part of the channel (at approximately 30 µm above the base). If this lower, wider part of the channel profile is disregarded, and the fluorescence criteria used to define the channel height is relaxed from 1% to 5% of the main channel intensity, then the measurement of upper piece channel height becomes 56 µm, significantly closer to the design specification of 50 µm.

These preliminary results hint in the direction of another interesting method worth investigating in future work for depth measurements of internal channels in transparent microfluidic devices.

5.3. The Influence of Different Materials

Following the comparison between protocols, the influence of different materials on measurements will be considered. Measurements taken on polymer and glass chips in the XY-plane will be considered separately from those taken in the Z-axis.

The standard deviations in the XY-plane (width measurements from Tables 4 and 5) are generally within the range of a few tenths of micrometers for both polymer and glass measurements. When expressed as percentages, it becomes even more evident that the standard deviation is negligible for both materials.

It would be interesting for future research to investigate whether this observation holds true for other materials commonly used in microfluidics (e.g., PP, PC, COP, and PMMA) and other measurement methods (e.g., optical or confocal microscopy). Experience suggests that the SmartScope ZIP®250's apparent indifference to material type may not necessarily extended to other techniques.

In contrast, the standard deviations of the depth measurements in TOPAS© COC are much lower than those for D263©bio glass.

During the measurements, it was noticed that the SmartScope ZIP®250 seemed to distinguish more clearly between the top and bottom planes of the internal channels in the polymer chips. For this reason, the Z-coordinates of the top and the bottom planes were subtracted directly to calculate the channel depth. As mentioned earlier, it is hypothesized that the polymer chips' higher surface roughness, which is usually a disadvantage, might have helped the optical profilometer better define a focus plane compared to the near-perfect smoothness of the wet-etched glass channels. Testing this hypothesis would be an interesting avenue for future research.

It is worth noting that, regardless of whether the standard deviation is low or high, the accuracy of depth measurements in both materials is questionable. In both TOPAS© COC and D263©bio glass, the depth measurements were inconsistent with their nominal values. In addition, although the profilometer was seemingly capable of distinguishing between the top and bottom of the internal channels in the polymer chips, it is difficult to differentiate it from the actual bottom of the chip. This might explain the overestimation of the depth of Leakage Channel 01, as shown in Table 4.

6. Conclusions

Accurately measuring internal structures after chip assembly is a well-recognized challenge in the microfluidic industry. This study, conducted as part of the EMPIR MFMET project, compared three different protocols, namely optical profilometry, optical microscopy, and tiled digital imagery, for measuring different internal microfluidic structures in chips made from D263©bio glass and TOPAS© COC.

A consistency analysis using normalized error statistics revealed Protocol 1, optical profilometry, as the preferred method due to its low uncertainty compared to the other protocols and its higher consistency with nominal geometry values.

However, challenges were encountered in measuring the depth of the internal geometries. The only protocol able to provide a measurement of the internal channel depth, optical profilometry, gave results that are highly inconsistent with their nominal values. Several avenues for future research are proposed, including a study of how to apply the refractive index for deformation compensation when dealing with multiple refraction interfaces. Another promising method is confocal fluorescence microscopy, which showed promising preliminary results.

The performance of TOPAS© COC chips was not significantly better or worse than that of D263©bio glass chips. This suggests that both materials are equally compatible with optical profilometry. However, depth measurements presented an exception, as channels with poorer surface roughness were easier to measure using the optical profilometer. Despite that, the depth measurements for the TOPAS© COC chips were also unsatisfactory. Further research comparing other common materials in microfluidics and different measurement techniques is recommended.

The results of this work directly address the current lack of accurate, robust, and validated measurement methods for internal microfluidic structures, offering a comprehensive comparison of different protocols and ultimately suggesting a preferred option for immediate application in the microfluidic industry. Additionally, this study offers valuable directions for future research, taking an important step toward overcoming a significant challenge that has hindered the microfluidic industry from reaching its full potential. The information obtained in this work also indicates the need for standardization in the field of dimensional measurements in microfluidic technology, especially after the chip's assembly. New European standardization projects will help in the development of standards for microfluidic dimension application within ISO/TC48/WG4 microfluidic devices, as foreseen in their new roadmap.

Supplementary Materials: The following supporting information can be downloaded at: https://www.mdpi.com/article/10.3390/metrology5010004/s1, Table S1: Glass Measurements Analysis; Table S2: Glass measurements for Analysis; Table S3: Glass Measurements protocol 1 CEA; Table S4: Glass Measurements protocol 2 LNE; Table S5: Glass Measurements protocol 3 UofG; Table S6: Polymer Measurements protocol 1 CEA; File S1: ChipDesign GlassTransferStandard IMT; File S2: ChipDesign PolymerTransferStandard MCS (pdf); File S3: ChipDesign PolymerTransferStandard MCS (stp); File S4: Calibration Report protocol1 CEA; File S5: Calibration Report protocol3 UofG.

Author Contributions: E.B. and K.R. were responsible for the conceptualization and supervision of the study. J.K. performed investigations of Protocol 1, defining its methodology and providing the required resources. N.F. did the same for Protocol 2, with assistance with the investigations from M.L., as did H.Y. for Protocol 3 and the confocal microscopy assisted in the investigations by A.G. Formal analysis of all results was performed by E.B. and J.K. The original draft was written by J.K., starting with input from E.B., H.Y. and N.F. for their respective parts. All authors have read and agreed to the published version of the manuscript.

Funding: This project 20NRM02 MFMET has received funding from the EMPIR programme co-financed by the Participating States and from the European Union's Horizon 2020 Research and Innovation Programme.

Data Availability Statement: The original data presented in the study are openly available on the Zenodo repository Establishing Metrology Standards in Microfluidic Devices at https://doi.org/10.5281/zenodo.11621010 (accessed on 4 December 2024).

Acknowledgments: This study is part of the work performed in the MFMET project. The authors recognize the contribution of all project participants and thank them for it. Secondly, the authors would like to express their gratitude to IMT Masken und Teilungen AG, Switzerland, and microfluidic ChipShop GmbH, Germany, for their contribution to the project, including but not limited to the development of the transfer standard chips used in this work. Finally, the authors want to thank all academic and industrial partners for continuously providing insights into microfluidic challenges and needs through discussions, workshops, or surveys conducted by The Microfluidics Association.

Conflicts of Interest: The authors declare no conflicts of interest.

References

1. Whitesides, G.M. The origins and the future of microfluidics. *Nature* **2006**, *442*, 368–373. [CrossRef] [PubMed]

2. Sackmann, E.K.; Fulton, A.L.; Beebe, D.J. The present and future role of microfluidics in biomedical research. *Nature* **2014**, *507*, 181–189. [CrossRef] [PubMed]
3. Elvira, K.S.; i Solvas, X.C.; Wootton, R.C.; Demello, A.J. The past, present and potential for microfluidic reactor technology in chemical synthesis. *Nat. Chem.* **2013**, *5*, 905–915. [CrossRef] [PubMed]
4. Berlanda, S.F.; Breitfeld, M.; Dietsche, C.L.; Dittrich, P.S. Recent Advances in Microfluidic Technology for Bioanalysis and Diagnostics. *Anal. Chem.* **2021**, *93*, 311–331. [CrossRef] [PubMed]
5. Convery, N.; Gadegaard, N. 30 years of microfluidics. *Micro Nano Eng.* **2019**, *2*, 76–91. [CrossRef]
6. Rosen, Y.; Gurman, P. MEMS and microfluidics for diagnostics devices. *Curr. Pharm. Biotechnol.* **2010**, *11*, 366–375. [CrossRef] [PubMed]
7. Behera, P.P.; Kumar, N.; Kumari, M.; Kumar, S.; Mondal, P.K.; Arun, R.K. Integrated microfluidic devices for point-of-care detection of bio-analytes and disease. *Sens. Diagn.* **2023**, *2*, 1437–1459. [CrossRef]
8. Huh, D.; Leslie, D.C.; Matthews, B.D.; Fraser, J.P.; Jurek, S.; Hamilton, G.A.; Thorneloe, K.S.; McAlexander, M.A.; Ingber, D.E. A Human Disease Model of Drug Toxicity–Induced Pulmonary Edema in a Lung-on-a-Chip Microdevice. *Sci. Transl. Med.* **2012**, *4*, 159ra147. [CrossRef] [PubMed]
9. Levner, D.; Ewart, L. Integrating Liver-Chip data into pharmaceutical decision-making processes. *Expert Opin. Drug Discov.* **2023**, *18*, 1313–1320. [CrossRef] [PubMed]
10. Quintard, C.; Tubbs, E.; Jonsson, G. A microfluidic platform integrating functional vascularized organoids-on-chip. *Nat. Commun.* **2024**, *15*, 1452. [CrossRef] [PubMed]
11. Middelkamp, H.; Weener, H.; Gensheimer, T.; van der Meer, A.D. Embedded macrophages induce intravascular coagulation in 3D blood vessel-on-chip. *Biomed. Devices* **2023**, *26*, 2. [CrossRef] [PubMed]
12. Yole Intelligence. *Status of the Microfluidics Industry 2023 Maturity of Microfluidics Devices Applications*; Yole Intelligence: Lyon, France, 2023.
13. Wang, K.; Man, K.; Liu, J.; Chen, Q.; Zhou, Y.; Yang, Y. Microphysiological Systems: Design, Fabrication, and Applications. *ACS Biomater. Sci. Eng.* **2020**, *6*, 3231–3257. [CrossRef] [PubMed]
14. Kim, H.; Lee, J.B.; Kim, K.; Sung, G.Y. Hydrophobic Sponge Structure-Based Triboelectric Nanogenerator. *J. Ind. Eng. Chem.* **2022**, *115*, 279–286. [CrossRef]
15. Gurkan, U.A.; Wood, D.K.; Carranza, D.; Herbertson, L.H.; Diamond, S.L.; Du, E.; Guha, S.; Di Paola, J.; Hines, P.C.; Papautsky, I.; et al. Next generation microfluidics: Fulfilling the promise of lab-on-a-chip technologies. *Lab Chip* **2024**, *24*, 1867–1874. [CrossRef] [PubMed]
16. van Heeren, H. Trends and Challenges in the Microfluidic Industry. 2021. Available online: https://enablingmnt.com/wp-content/uploads/2021/01/Trends-and-Challenges-in-the-Microfluidic-Industry-Henne-van-Heeren-January-2021.pdf (accessed on 4 December 2024).
17. Schott AG. D263©. Available online: https://www.schott.com/en-nl/products/d-263-P1000318/technical-details?tab=830fa6759ac84d07a3d53bfbe4535a90 (accessed on 17 April 2024).
18. TOPAS Advanced Polymers/Polyplastics, TOPAS© COC Datasheets. Available online: https://topas.com/wp-content/uploads/2023/05/TDS_6015S-04_english-units.pdf (accessed on 4 December 2024).
19. Batista, E.; Reyes, D.R. Publishable Summary Establishing Metrology Standards in Microfluidic Devices (20NRM02). 2023. Available online: https://mfmet.eu/wp-content/uploads/2023/11/20NRM02-MFMET-Publishable-Summary-M27.pdf (accessed on 4 December 2024).
20. MFMET—Establishing Metrology Standards in Microfluidic Devices. Available online: https://mfmet.eu/ (accessed on 18 April 2024).
21. Silverio, V.; Guha, S.; Keiser, A.; Natu, R.; Reyes, D.R.; van Heeren, H.; Verplanck, N.; Herbertson, L.H. Overcoming technological barriers in microfluidics: Leakage testing. *Front. Bioeng. Biotechnol.* **2022**, *10*, 958582. [CrossRef] [PubMed]
22. Copeland, M.; Ogheard, F.; Batista, E.; van Heeren, H. Whitepaper Flow Resistivity Testing. Zenodo. 2023. Available online: https://zenodo.org/records/7919134 (accessed on 4 December 2024).
23. *ISO 22916:2022*; Microfluidic Devices Interoperability Requirements for Dimensions, Connections and Initial Device Classification. International Organization for Standardization: Geneva, Switzerland, 2022.
24. microfluidic ChipShop GmbH. Material Data Sheet mcs-COC 13. 2024. Available online: https://www.microfluidic-chipshop.com/microfluidics/materials-in-microfluidics/polymers-in-microfluidics/topas/ (accessed on 4 December 2024).
25. Schott AG. TIE-29 Refractive Index and Dispersion. 2016. Available online: https://www.schott.com/shop/medias/tie-29-refractive-index-and-dispersion-eng.pdf?context=bWFzdGVyfHJvb3R8MTg4OTQ2NHxhcHBsaWNhdGlvbi9wZGZ8aDQ3L2hjYS84ODE3NDA5NTg5Mjc4LnBkZnxkMTc5MjMyYjI5YmRlZTAzZmFmYzIxZmVlNTMyMmE5NzBiNWI5OGJhODM3YWRjYmM5NmY1ZTczMjY1ZWM3NDdk (accessed on 4 December 2024).

26. Martinez, A.W.; Phillips, S.T.; Carrilho, E.; Thomas, S.W.; Sindi, H.; Whitesides, G.M. Simple telemedicine for developing regions: Camera phones and paper-based microfluidic devices for real-time, off-site diagnosis. *Anal. Chem.* **2008**, *80*, 3669–3707. [CrossRef] [PubMed]
27. Wang, B.; Li, Y.; Zhou, M. Smartphone-based platforms implementing microfluidic detection with image-based artificial intelligence. *Nat. Commun.* **2023**, *14*, 1341. [CrossRef] [PubMed]
28. Howell, J.; Hammarton, T.C.; Altmann, Y.; Jimenez, M. High-speed particle detection and tracking in microfluidic devices using event-based sensing. *Lab Chip* **2020**, *20*, 3024–3035. [CrossRef] [PubMed]
29. Cox, M.G. The evaluation of key comparison data. *Metrologia* **2002**, *39*, 589–595. [CrossRef]
30. *ISO 13528:2022*; Statistical Methods for Use in Proficiency Testing by Interlaboratory Comparison. International Organization for Standardization: Geneva, Switzerland, 2022.

metrology

Article

Polar Fitting and Hermite Interpolation for Freeform Droplet Geometry Measurement

Mike Dohmen [1,*], Andreas Heinrich [1] and Cornelius Neumann [2]

1 Aalen School of Applied Photonics (AASAP), Aalen University, 73430 Aalen, Germany; andreas.heinrich@hs-aalen.de
2 Light Technology Institute (LTI), Karlsruhe Institute of Technology (KIT), 76131 Karlsruhe, Germany; cornelius.neumann@kit.edu
* Correspondence: mike.dohmen@hs-aalen.de

Abstract: Droplet-based microlens fabrication using Ultra Violet (UV) curable polymers demands the precise measurement of three-dimensional geometries, especially for non-axisymmetric shapes influenced by electric field deformation. In this work, we present a polar coordinate-based contour fitting method combined with Hermite interpolation to reconstruct 3D droplet geometries from two orthogonal shadowgraphy images. The image segmentation process integrates superpixel clustering with active contours to extract the droplet boundary, which is then approximated using a spline-based polar fitting approach. The two resulting contours are merged using a polar Hermite interpolation algorithm, enabling the reconstruction of freeform droplet shapes. We validate the method against both synthetic Computer-Aided Design (CAD) data and precision-machined reference objects, achieving volume deviations below 1% for axisymmetric shapes and approximately 3.5% for non-axisymmetric cases. The influence of focus, calibration, and alignment errors is quantitatively assessed through Monte Carlo simulations and empirical tests. Finally, the method is applied to real electrically deformed droplets, with volume deviations remaining within the experimental uncertainty range. This demonstrates the method's robustness and suitability for metrology tasks involving complex droplet geometries.

Keywords: 3D reconstruction; contact angles; droplet deformation; image processing; optical simulations; polar fitting; polymer droplets; image segmentation; shape measurement; volume estimation; shadowgraphy

1. Introduction

Microlenses are small lenses with apertures between several micrometers and millimeters. They have emerged in recent years as important optical components in many technological areas, such as microlens arrays and optical fiber coupling, for example, in biomedical applications. There are different methods for fabricating microlenses, such as hot embossing, lithography, inkjet printing, or more recently, two-photon polymerization [1–3]. Among these, the approaches using liquid-based photopolymerization offer a significant advantage due to the inherent energy minimization properties of the liquids, making it possible to achieve smooth optical surfaces with little or no post-processing [4–6]. However, the control of the shape of the liquid droplets is still an area of active research, particularly regarding the use of electric fields. The first experiments in this field were conducted by Taylor, who discovered that the application of a high electric field on a liquid deforms the liquid and leads to electrospraying [7]. This concept has since been used in many publications to deform liquid droplets, for example, for adaptive optics [8] or for deformed and subsequently solidified aspherical lenses [9]. When the droplet is axisymmetric, the measurement of its contour is straightforward and can be achieved in several ways. An often used method is the Axisymmetric Drop Shape Analysis (ADSA), where the shape and the surface tension are related and the Laplacian equation of capillarity is used to iteratively calculate the droplet shape [10]. More recent approaches include Hou et al.'s use of two mutually perpendicular ellipses (TMPEs) to approximate the shape of an axisymmetric droplet deformed by gravity, and similarly, Tran et al. used asymmetrical ellipses to describe the contour of droplets with large contact angles [11,12]. Wang and Yu used an ellipse to approximate sessile droplets on flat and spherical surfaces [13].

For real freeform geometries, however, the droplet is not axisymmetric. For such non-axisymmetric shapes, the above methods cannot be used. There has been significant development to describe the contour of non-axisymmetric sessile droplets. Timm et al. used hydrodynamic equations to describe droplets on an angled surface [14], while El Sherbini and Jacobi applied a two-circle fitting method to droplets on inclined surfaces [15]. Bateni et al. and Quetzeri-Santiago et al. used polynomials to determine only the contact angles of sessile droplets [16,17]. Andersen and Taboryski utilized a subpixel edge detection scheme developed by Trujillo-Pino et al. to characterize the dynamic contact angles [18,19]. Stalder et al. developed a snake-based approach using b-splines and reflections of the droplet [20]. For non-axisymmetric inclined droplets, Rotenberg et al. described the shape using biquadratic spline functions [21]. All of these methods require extensive knowledge about the droplet, which limits their application to real freeform geometries. Furthermore, none of these methods provide a practical or validated way to reconstruct the full 3D geometry of electrically deformed, non-axisymmetric droplets using just two orthogonal views. This represents a critical methodological gap.

For optical components, a purely two-dimensional contour is not sufficient when the droplet is not axisymmetrical. In such cases, a three-dimensional description is required. The reconstruction of the 3D shape of sessile droplets presents additional challenges. The simplest approaches involve using the Pappus centroid theorem [22] or summed circular slices [23]. El Sherbini and Jacobi extended their two-circle method by integrating the contour over the circumference of the base [15]; however, this approach fails for droplets with freeform geometries. Ríos-López et al. demonstrated a method to reconstruct the 3D geometry of a droplet by combining side and top images [24]. Brown et al. used the finite element method to describe the 3D shape of a non-axisymmetric droplet on an inclined surface where gravity plays a significant role [25]. Other mathematical techniques include the use of Bézier curves for meniscus shapes by Lewis and Matsuura [26] and the application of cubic splines to describe the axisymmetric shape of rotating droplets by Jakhar et al. [27].

Many of these reconstruction methods originate from inkjet printing. For instance, Nguyen et al. reconstructed non-axisymmetric flying droplets using the multiplicative algebraic reconstruction technique (MART) [28]. In the same field, an effective method for analyzing flying droplets involves slicing the droplet into pixel-height disks and calculating the cumulative volume based on the assumption that flying droplets maintain circular cross-sections at each slice level [23,29,30]. This technique has also been adapted for calculating the volume of pendant drops [31]. While these methods are conceptually diverse, they share limitations: they are computationally intensive, require many viewpoints, or assume axisymmetry. None are designed for sessile, non-axisymmetric droplets imaged with only two cameras.

More recent advances in 3D reconstruction explore imaging and computational methods: Fu and Liu, as well as Masuk et al., applied the visual hull method with space carving, focusing primarily on bubble geometries [32,33].

The methods described offer a wide range of strategies for calculating both the two-dimensional contour geometry and the full three-dimensional shape and volume of droplets, whether sessile, flying, or pendant. However, these methodologies exhibit significant limitations when applied to electrically deformed, non-axisymmetric droplets, as examined in the present study. Furthermore, few studies address practical aspects such as image focus, segmentation robustness, or calibration stability, all factors that critically influence the accuracy of volume reconstruction but are often neglected.

To address this identified gap, we present the Polar-Based Contour Approximation (PBCA) method. Our approach reconstructs the 3D geometry by combining this novel contour-fitting technique with the powerful Polar-Coordinate Hermite-Interpolation-based Droplet Reconstruction (PHDR) algorithm, which was first introduced by Liu et al. for flying droplets [34]. This combination is specifically tailored to enable the 3D reconstruction of sessile, electrically deformed, non-axisymmetric droplets from only two orthogonal views.

2. Experimental Setup

The underlying aim of the experiments is to deform a UV-curable polymer droplet, which is then cured to preserve geometry and to manufacture microlenses. This experimental setup is designed to perform two primary functions. First, it must be able to generate and adjust a high-voltage electrical field. Second, the setup is required to observe and record the deformation data, including the voltage measurements. The setup is illustrated in Figure 1a. A high-voltage power supply (hivolt HAR42-4 with HA3B3-S) capable of delivering up to ±3000 V and noise of less than 20 mV_{RMS} is employed. Voltage control and data acquisition are handled by a National Instruments USB-6001 card (National Instruments, Austin, TX, USA) which has an accuracy of 26 mV and noise of 0.7 mV_{RMS}. Two orthogonal shadowgraphy sets are used for imaging the experiment, placed 90° apart. In Figure 1b, a shadowgraphy image of an experiment is shown. Each set-up includes a grayscale camera (Matrix Vision MV 1013G-1111 with 1280 × 1024 resolution and 5.3 µm pixel size, Matrix Vision GmbH (today Balluff MV GmbH), Oppenweiler, Germany) paired with a zoom lens (Thorlabs MVL6X12Z, Thorlabs GmbH, Bergkirchen, Germany). The lowest magnification setting of 1.4× provides a depth of field of 0.95 mm. This magnification is used for the conducted experiments. Illumination is provided by a white LED (Opto Engineering LTCLHP016-W LED, Opto Engineering S.r.l., Rovigo, Italy) with a diffuser that suppresses diffraction artifacts at the edges. The diffuser is made from a Leica Surgipath Apex Adhesive Slide (Leica Biosystems, Wetzlar, Germany). Figure 1c shows the complete optical setup. At the intersection of the X and Y optical axes, two motorized stages (Thorlabs PT1-Z825, Thorlabs GmbH, Bergkirchen, Germany) are positioned to focus the droplet. The Z movement of the droplet is done using a manual stage because the Z movement is only needed to move the droplet into the camera's field of view. A set of three of the same motorized stages with a resolution of 0.05 µm and repeatability under 1.5 µm is used to precisely move the anode along the X, Y, and Z axes. A tool-changing system (Schunk SHS, Schunk GmbH & Co. KG, Lauffen am Neckar, Germany) is employed for eased the swapping of the anodes. An array of precision connectors (RM 2.54 mm) serves as the anode, with a 6 mm pin or an aluminum plate as the cathode. The anode configuration is shown in Figure 1d, where the shown anode connects to the positive pole and the cathode to the negative pole of the power supply.

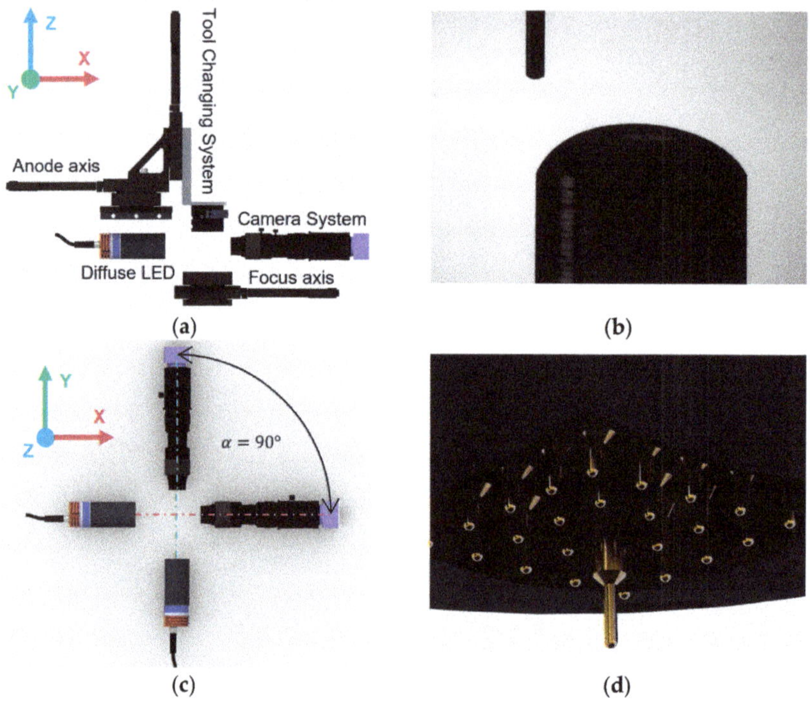

Figure 1. Overview of setup. (**a**) Sideview of setup. (**b**) Shadowgraphy image of an experiment. (**c**) Top view of the camera systems and the orientation. (**d**) Precision connector anode.

The entire setup is housed within an electrically grounded security box, maintaining a constant temperature of 17 °C with a precision of ±0.5 °C. Temperature is monitored at seven positions inside the box (using 5 PT1000 Heraeus M1020 sensors (Heraeus GmbH, Hanau, Germany) and 1 BME680 sensor (Bosch Sensortec GmbH, Reutlingen, Germany)) and at one external position (1 BME680 sensor)). The BME680 sensors also measure humidity and pressure. MATLAB R2024a is used to control the entire system.

To create ground-truth data of the droplets, the cameras need to be calibrated. The state-of-the-art method is Zhang's method. That is why both cameras are calibrated individually using MATLAB's implementation of Zhang's method for camera calibration, using a distortion target (Thorlabs R1L3S3P positive grid, Thorlabs GmbH, Bergkirchen, Germany) [35]. The object in the optical path is automatically focused using the motorized stages and the Tenengrad focus measure [19]. All images are undistorted using the camera parameters calculated from the calibration. The root means that the squared position reprojection error is 0.3 pixels, which corresponds to about 3 μm in both cameras. All experiments are conducted using this setup.

3. Image Processing and 3D Geometry Reconstruction Workflow

The complete proposed method is shown in Figure 2. First, the images are captured with both cameras as seen in Figure 2a,b. Using image segmentation and our newly proposed PBCA, the droplet contour can be extracted from both cameras, as shown in Figure 2c. Combining these contours in three-dimensional space and using a Hermite interpolation scheme, a 3D geometry can be reconstructed. In Figure 2d, the two contours in three-dimensional space is shown, and in Figure 2e, the reconstructed geometry is shown.

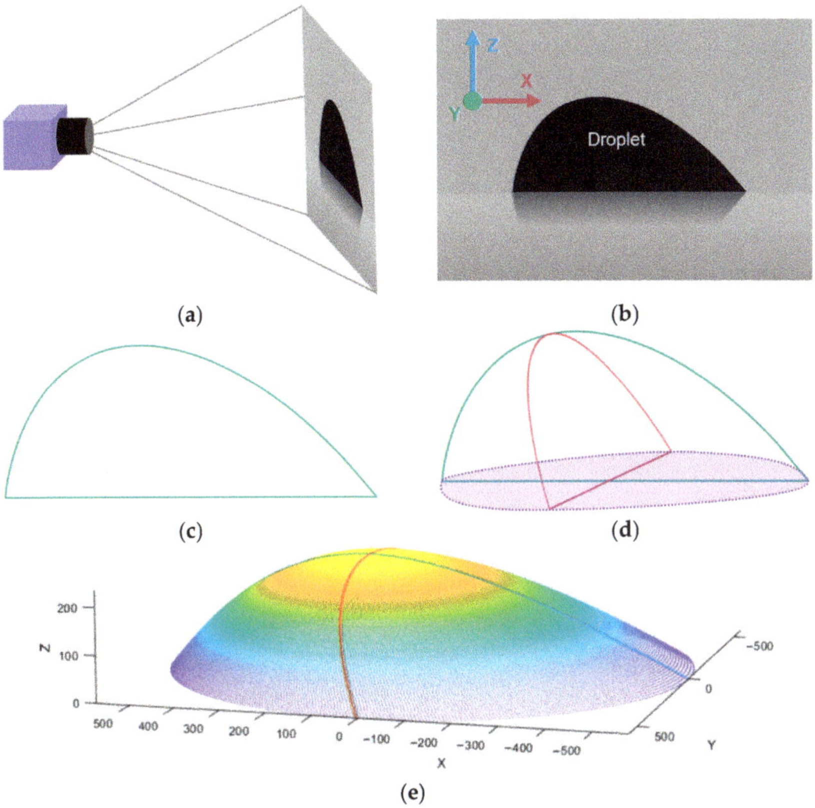

Figure 2. Reconstruction process: (**a**) Image acquisition. (**b**) Captured image. (**c**) Contour extracted fitted using PBCA. (**d**) Combined contours. (**e**) Reconstructed droplet geometry.

The components of this process are discussed in more detail in the following sections.

3.1. Segmentation of Droplet Contours via Superpixels and Active Contours

The droplet contour is segmented using a combination of conventional algorithms using MATLAB. The whole process is shown in Figure 3. The image looks like a lens with two curved sides, but in reality, the bottom half is just the reflection of the top half. Before the process, the image intensity is adjusted using 'imadjust', which enhances the contrast. After that, the input image shown in Figure 3a is segmented into so-called superpixels using the Simple Linear Iterative Clustering (SLIC) algorithm, which clusters pixels into the coherent regions seen in Figure 3b. This step makes the subsequent segmentation step more robust. The primary role of the SLIC algorithm in our workflow is to generate a robust initial mask for the subsequent active contour segmentation. Our analysis showed that a minimum of approximately 1000 superpixels is required in our setup to reliably resolve the droplet boundary and prevent it from merging with the background during the initial graph cut. The value used in all experiments is 6916, which comfortably exceeds this determined threshold [36]. Subsequently, a graph cut algorithm called Lazy Snapping is used on top of the superpixels, as seen in Figure 3c. This is an easy and robust way to get an initial mask for the next step. For the Lazy Snapping algorithm to work, it is required to define pixels as foreground and background pixels. Initially, the central pixel (x_0, z_0) of the undistorted grayscale image is the foreground pixel. Because the droplet is not always in the center of the image, a method is needed to ensure that the initial pixel is inside the droplet. This is done by searching for a pixel close to the initial pixel that has a threshold intensity of 50, which, in the images used here, has proven a good empirical threshold. This is used to initialize the foreground region for segmentation, shown as a red point in Figure 3c.

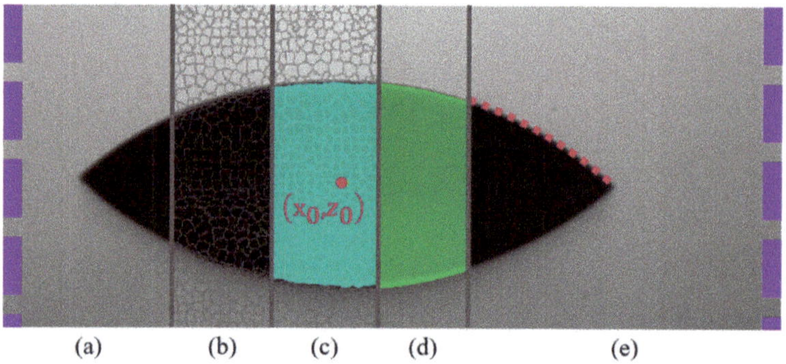

Figure 3. Sequence of the image segmentation. The red point with (x_0, z_0) is the foreground pixel, the violet lines at the left and to the right edge of the image are the background pixels. (**a**) Input image. (**b**) SLIC Superpixels. (**c**) Lazy snapping with superpixels. (**d**) Mask after active contour. (**e**) Roberts extracted pixels are shown as red dashed line.

Background pixels are defined as the rows of pixels on the left and right edges of the image, as seen at the edges in Figure 3 in violet. The resulting mask is also seen in Figure 3c. Subsequently, an active contour algorithm based on the Chan–Vese method is applied with 50 iterations to refine the droplet boundary, as shown in Figure 3d. This number of iterations was chosen as it ensures that the contour reliably converges to the droplet boundary for all observed shapes, while minimizing the unnecessary computational time. This method minimizes the energy along the contour, resulting in a binary mask that describes the shape of the drop. The segmented image is further refined by morphological closing using a 10 pixel disk, to smooth the edges, and finally use Roberts edge detector to extract the final contour points, represented as pixel coordinates (x, z) [37]. These points are shown as a red dashed line in Figure 3e and are used for a further detailed analysis of the shape of the droplet.

3.2. Polar-Based Contour Approximation

The PBCA method introduced here describes a droplet's contour by fitting it in a polar coordinate system rather than the conventional Cartesian system, akin to the representation of a signature in image processing [38]. A droplet has, because of its energy minimizing nature, a smooth surface and is generally circular in nature. The presented approach takes that into account. Another challenge in representing a smooth droplet surface from the pixelated data captured by a camera is the step-like distribution of the data. Particularly at the apex region of the droplet, the pixel representation is inadequate because it is a horizontal line due to discretization. Using our method, this straight line is transformed into a curved representation in polar coordinates, which makes approximating the points with a spline or polynomial more accurate. Figure 4 illustrates the entire methodology, and a detailed explanation is provided in the subsequent sections.

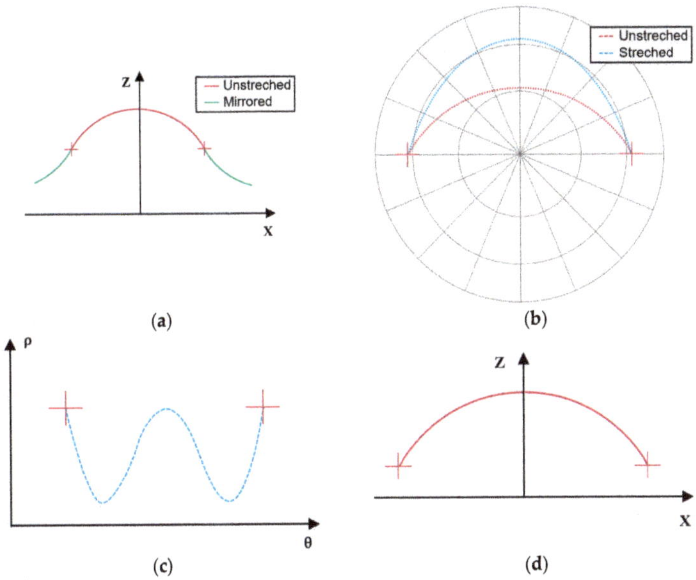

Figure 4. Aligning the centering and polar fitting of the extracted droplet contour. (**a**) Extracted contour in red and mirrored extended contour in green. (**b**) Polar plot of the contour original in red, stretched contour in blue. (**c**) Plot of the stretched contour using angular position and radial distance. (**d**) Converted back to Cartesian space and rescaled fit in Cartesian coordinates.

Converting the points into polar coordinates causes variations in their polar angles at the edges due to the tilt and their non-central positioning around zero. That can lead to significant jumps in the radial distance at 2π and 0. This is why we limit the points in polar coordinates between π and 2π. For this, the contour needs to be tilted and centered. The process begins by identifying the left (x_L, z_L) and right (x_R, z_R) contact points of the droplet along its contour. This identification occurs either by hand or algorithmically. The tilt angle β required to make the droplet leveled at these points is determined by

$$\beta = -arctan\left(\frac{z_R - z_L}{x_R - x_L}\right). \tag{1}$$

Using this angle, a rotation matrix $R(\beta)$ is used to rotate the contour points. The rotated points (x_{ut}, z_{ut}) are then shifted to center the contour around the origin with

$$\begin{bmatrix} x_{ut} \\ z_{ut} \end{bmatrix} = R(\beta) \cdot \begin{bmatrix} x \\ z \end{bmatrix} = \begin{bmatrix} \cos(\beta) & -sin(\beta) \\ \sin(\beta) & \cos(\beta) \end{bmatrix} \cdot \begin{bmatrix} x \\ z \end{bmatrix} \tag{2}$$

and then the points are centered around zero in the x direction and the z coordinates are limited to values larger than zero using

$$\begin{bmatrix} x_{al} \\ z_{al} \end{bmatrix} = \begin{bmatrix} x_{ut} \\ z_{ut} \end{bmatrix} - \begin{bmatrix} \frac{max(x_{ut})+min(x_{ut})}{2} \\ max(z_{ut}) \end{bmatrix}, \tag{3}$$

with (x_{al}, z_{al}) as aligned x and z points. Due to the discretization, the exact positions of the edge points are difficult to determine. The approach we use in PBCA is to extend the segmented contour with 10 pixels of the edge areas of the contour. This avoids approximation errors due to pixels at the contact points. This can be seen in Figure 4a, with the original contour in red with the mirrored extensions in green. Next, the aligned contour coordinates (x_{al}, z_{al}) are transformed from Cartesian to polar coordinates (θ, ρ), where θ represents the angular position and ρ represents the radial distance from the center with

$$\theta = arctan\left(\frac{z_{al}}{x_{al}}\right), \tag{4}$$

$$\rho = \sqrt{x_{al}{}^2 + z_{al}{}^2}. \tag{5}$$

One challenge presented by the transformation is the uneven distribution of points across the angle θ, dependent upon the initial point distribution in Cartesian coordinates. For a precise approximation, it is optimal when the points are uniformly distributed within the specified limits. To achieve this uniform distribution, the curve is pre-stretched prior to transformation, ensuring that the maximum height of the droplet is equivalent to half of the droplet's diameter. This ensures that the curve that is approximated is always roughly the same shape, even when the contour is not axisymmetric. This also achieves an almost equidistant distribution of the points in polar coordinates. A polar plot of the unstretched contour in red and the stretched contour in blue is shown in Figure 4b. To have a continuous contour, the coordinates are sorted by sorting the angular coordinates θ in ascending order. An unwrapped plot of θ and ρ is shown in Figure 4c. Next, a b-spline is approximated on $\rho(\theta)$ using the MATLAB implementation of least-squares b-spline approximation [39]. The knot points for the spline interpolation are selected in a two-step process. First, the minima and maxima of the curve are found. They are used as a knot with additional points between the ends. It was determined that, for the droplets utilized in the present study, employing a total knot number of 30 and a spline degree of 9 is the optimal configuration for the geometries under investigation, as it provides a good balance between overfitting to pixel noise and capturing the true contour. For the final knots, the MATLAB implementation of the "optimal" knot distribution is used [40–42]. This approximation smooths the contour while preserving its overall shape. Once the approximation process is complete, the fitted radial coordinates fit $\rho_{fit}(\theta)$ is transformed back into Cartesian coordinates using the following equations

$$x_{fit} = \rho_{fit} cos(\theta), \tag{6}$$

$$z_{fit} = \rho_{fit} sin(\theta). \tag{7}$$

After transforming, the stretching is reversed. These fitted coordinates now provide a smooth approximation of the droplet's contour, as seen in Figure 4d.

The PBCA method proves effective for the analysis of discretized irregular or complex geometries that exhibit smooth contours. The suitability of this is particularly notable in the characterization of droplet contours, as the approximated contour starts with an accurate representation of the contact point. This effectiveness was previously identified by Atefi et al., who employed the transformation from Cartesian to polar coordinates to estimate the contact angles of droplets [43]. Another inherent advantage is that PBCA does not suffer from the ambiguity that is present when a droplet has a contact angle over 90°, because in polar coordinates, the angles are unique, while in Cartesian coordinate for one x value multiple values of y are necessary to describe a droplet of that shape.

3.3. Three-Dimensional Geometry Reconstruction via Hermite Interpolation

The PBCA is used on the images of both cameras, which results in two slice representations of the droplet from two sides with an angle of 90°. The challenge presented is to reconstruct the 3D shape of the droplet using only these two slices. Each contour is represented in polar coordinates, (ρ_{fitx}, θ_x) and (ρ_{fity}, θ_y). Although both cameras are calibrated, there is still some small deviation between the maximal points of the droplet. To account for that, they must be scaled to avoid numerical errors. The scaling factor s is calculated as a factor of the maximum height with

$$s = \frac{min(\rho_{fity})}{min(\rho_{fitx})}. \tag{8}$$

A critical step in reconstruction involves the calculation of the midpoints for each contour. This is necessary to align the two slices to each other and to obtain the points in each z plane. This is done by numerical calculation of the midpoint on any given z height. The midpoints are shown in Figure 5a for the x slice and in b for the y slice. The contour lines are then combined and aligned at 90° with each other, corresponding to the orientation of the cameras. This is done using a three-dimensional rotation matrix.

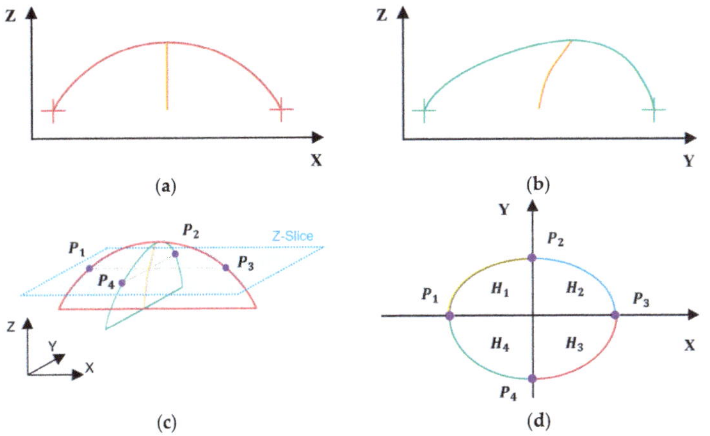

Figure 5. Middle and PHDR (**a**) Midpoint calculation of x slice. The yellow line are the midpoints at any z-height. (**b**) Midpoint calculation of y slice. The yellow line are the midpoints at any z-height (**c**) Aligned and scaled slices with points in one plane. The yellow line are the midpoints at any z-height. (**d**) Curve interpolation using PHDR, each H_i has its own color.

For the reconstruction of each z slice, two points from each x and y slice are needed at the same given z height. The aligned slices and the resulting points P_1, P_2, P_3, and P_4 can be seen in in Figure 5c. The objective is to transform these points into a slice shape that closely approximates reality. The most straightforward method for interpolation would typically involve circular or elliptical approaches. However, we employed an interpolation algorithm known as PHDR, which was first introduced by Liu et al. and has been demonstrated to be superior to circular or elliptical methods [34]. It uses a modified cubic Hermite interpolation, which considers the inherent shape of the droplets. Because the projection direction is tangential, the derivative along this direction is zero, which simplifies the Hermite formulation. The input points are transformed into polar coordinates, resulting in four radii ρ and angles θ per slice. The modified interpolation equation is

$$H_i(\theta) = \rho_i \left(1 + 2\frac{\theta - \theta_i}{\theta_j - \theta_i}\right)\left(\frac{\theta - \theta_j}{\theta_i - \theta_j}\right)^2 + \rho_j \left(1 + 2\frac{\theta - \theta_j}{\theta_i - \theta_j}\right)\left(\frac{\theta - \theta_i}{\theta_j - \theta_i}\right)^2, \quad (9)$$

where $i = 1, 2, 3, 4$ and $j = 2, 3, 4, 1$ are the indices of the points in the z plane and $H_i(\theta)$ is the reconstructed curve using PHDR. The points and the reconstructed curves are shown in Figure 5d. This is repeated for each z value, which leads to a reconstructed point cloud representation of the droplet which can be seen in Figure 2e. The optimal balance between accuracy and computation time was achieved with arc-length sampling by using a sample size of 1000.

3.4. Numerical Volume Estimation from Reconstructed Contours

The volume calculation is performed analogous to Liu et al., employing the numerical integration of the resulting contour by means of the Shoelace formula within Cartesian coordinates for each slice to determine the area A_i. Subsequently, these areas are utilized to estimate the volume between two slices through summation and multiplication, as delineated by the following formula

$$V_{3D} = \sum_{i=1}^{n-1} \Delta z \cdot A_i \quad (10)$$

with V_{3D} as the reconstructed volume, n as the number of slices, and Δz as the height between the area A_i and A_{i+1}. In conclusion, the combination of PBCA and PHDR provides a method for reconstructing 3D geometries from two shadowgraphy images.

4. Validation Experiments and Error Analysis

In this section, a series of experiments are conducted to show the effectiveness and limitations of the proposed contour approximation and the 3D reconstruction method. This is done in subsections; first, the polar PBCA interpolation method is compared to other standard methods of approximation with synthetic data. Then, the 3D reconstruction is tested with known geometries, real and synthetic, to show the effectiveness of our combined method. Furthermore, Monte Carlo simulations are used to assess the stability of the process and the effects of focus and repeated measurements. In the end, experimental research is conducted using electrically deformed droplets, which serve as a benchmark by being weighed. Then, our method allows for the calculation of the volume based on the material's density, and this is compared to the weight measurement.

4.1. Evaluation of Polar-Based Contour Approximation on Synthetic Geometries

Since there are no valid approaches for the application to represent the droplet geometry of nonaxisymmetric droplets that are produced by electrical field deformation, PBCA is compared to common methods of approximating freeform shapes that are close to the real observed data. Here, a polynomial least squares approximation of the eighth degree, a Fourier least squares approximation of the eighth degree, and a b-spline least squares approximation are used for comparison. The synthetic shapes, chosen to represent the droplet deformation observed in previous experiments, contain rounded edges, exhibit high and low contact angles, feature off-axis shapes, and have near-rectangular cross sections, reflecting the range of deformation observed. To evaluate the performance of the fit, we look at the important defining features of a non-axisymmetric droplet, such as the droplet diameter $d_{droplet}$, the contact angles θ_L and θ_R as well as the apex position defined by h_{apex} and s_{apex}. These are shown in Figure 6 on a schematic droplet.

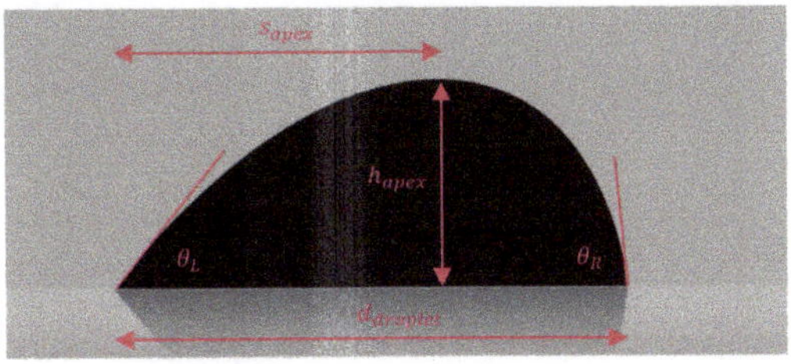

Figure 6. Defining features of a non-axisymmetric droplet.

The contact angles are calculated using a linear regression of the initial ten pixels at the edges and using the slope to calculate the contact angles trigonometrically. The apex position is calculated by finding the maximum of the droplet contour, and the diameter is the difference between the first and last contour points. The geometrical shapes consist of circle segments, hyperbolas, slanted hyperbolas, and a sigmoidal function to account for rectangular shapes observed in multiple-anode arrangements. These shapes are chosen because they all occur in the deformation of droplets. The data used to evaluate the performance of PBCA is generated using the equations for the various shapes laid out in the next few paragraphs. The shapes are sized, so that they fit into the virtual image with an image width of $w_{im} = 1280$ px and an image height $h_{im} = 1024$ px, to be of the same size as the used cameras. To discretize the data, the values of x and y are rounded. For a circle, the equations are

$$x_{circle} = r_{circle} \cdot cos(\theta_{circle}), \tag{11}$$

$$z_{circle} = r_{circle} \cdot sin(\theta_{circle}) \tag{12}$$

with (x_{circle}, z_{circle}) as circle coordinates, r_{circle} as circle radius, and θ_{circle} as the angle of the circle point. Circle segments are generated by defining the angle specific to the desired segment. For the hyperbola, the formula is

$$z_{hyp} = b \cdot \sqrt{1 + \frac{x_{hyp}^2}{a^2}}, \tag{13}$$

with z_{hyp} and x_{hyp} as hyperbola coordinates, a_{hyp} as horizontal stretch factor and b_{hyp} as vertical stretch factor. The slanted hyperbola has the same equation with a_{slhyp} and b_{slhyp}, but is tilted using a rotational matrix. The rotation is defined as 15°. The rectangular form is generated using a function with sigmoidal properties. It is defined by two hyperbolic tangent functions combined with the formula

$$z_{sig} = -0.5 \cdot \left(tanh\left(\frac{x_{sig} + c}{d_1}\right) - tanh\left(\frac{x_{sig} - c}{d_2}\right)\right) \cdot 200, \tag{14}$$

with x_{sig} and z_{sig} as rectangular coordinates, c as a distance of slope from zero an d_1 and d_2 as a parameter to control the slope. The used values for a, b, c, d_1, d_2, and r_{circle} are shown in Table 1. The curves are then scaled so that the droplet base is half the image width and the maximum height is one fifth of the image height using

$$x_{scaled} = x_{unscaled} \cdot \frac{w_{im}}{2}, \tag{15}$$

$$z_{scaled} = z_{unscaled} \cdot \frac{h_{im}}{5}, \tag{16}$$

with x_{scaled} and z_{scaled} as scaled coordinates and $x_{unscaled}$ and $z_{unscaled}$ as unscaled coordinates.

Table 1. Control variables of the curves, values are in pixels.

Line Color	r_{circle}	a_{hyp}	b_{hyp}	a_{slhyp}	b_{slhyp}	c	d_1	d_2
Blue (1)	494	50	300	50	150	50	50	25
Red (2)	319	150	300	100	150	100	50	25
Yellow (3)	533	600	300	300	150	300	50	25

This ensures similarity to the droplet contours observed in the deformation experiment. The drop image after which the curve is modeled as well as the three curves are shown in Figure 7a–d.

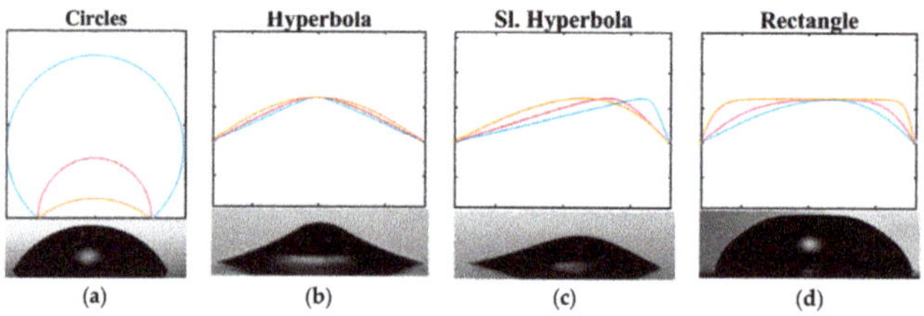

Figure 7. Used synthetic curves with the real observed experiment image. The colors correspond to the used parameters in Table 1. (**a**) Circle-shaped contour. (**b**) Hyperbola-shaped contour. (**c**) Slanted hyperbola contour. (**d**) Rectangle-shaped contour.

To compare the measurement with the ground truth data, three metrics are used. For evaluating the overall fit over the whole contour, the root mean square error (RMSE) between the approximated curve and the ground truth curve is calculated with equation

$$e_{RMSE} = \sqrt{\frac{1}{n} \cdot \sum_{i=1}^{n} (G_i - A_i)^2}, \tag{17}$$

with e_{RMSE} as the root mean square error, n as the number of points, G as the ground truth data, and A as the approximated data. To evaluate the performance over the non-axisymmetric metrics such as the contact angles and the diameter, which are in different units and magnitudes, the mean absolute percentage error (MAPE) is calculated using

$$e_{MAPE} = \frac{1}{n} \sum_{i=1}^{n} \left| \frac{G_i - A_i}{A_i} \right| \cdot 100, \tag{18}$$

with e_{MAPE} as the mean absolute percentage error. An alternative metric to compare the same is the mean normalized error (MNE).

$$e_{MNE} = \frac{1}{n} \sum_{i=1}^{n} \left| \frac{G_i - A_i}{R_i} \right|, \tag{19}$$

with e_{MNE} being the mean normalized error and R as the value range; in this case, for the angles where $R = 180°$ and for the lengths where $R = 300$ px, this corresponds to the drop base diameter. The comparison results are shown in Figure 8 as boxplots. In Appendix A.1, all measurements are shown.

In the findings across all geometries, while PBCA may not consistently be the top performer, it demonstrates the greatest reliability. Notably, the results for MAPE and MNE indicate that PBCA exhibits less variability compared to other methods. As these two metrics directly measure errors in parameters specific to droplets, such as diameter, this underscores its suitability for addressing issues related to deforming droplets. Next, the 3D reconstruction is tested.

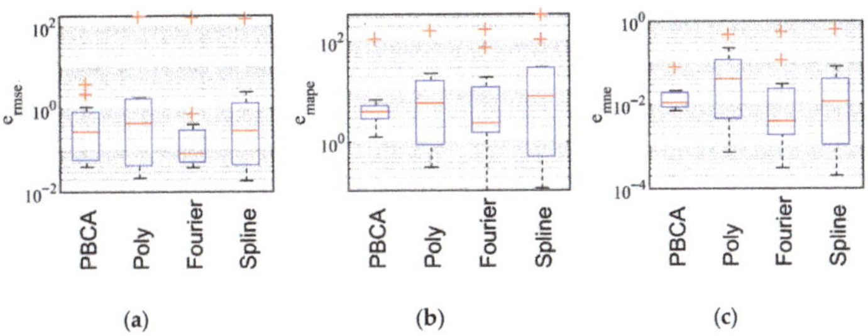

Figure 8. Boxplots of circles, hyperbola, slanted hyperbola, and rectangle measurements. The red crosses are the outliers, the red line in the blue box is the median and the blue box covers 50% of the values. (**a**) RMSE; (**b**) MAPE; and (**c**) MNE.

4.2. Accuracy of 3D Reconstruction Using Computer-Aided Design and Measured References

Initially, the approach is assessed using synthetic images that originate from 3D models generated through Computer-Aided Design (CAD) software, specifically PTC CREO PARAMETRIC 10.0.1.0. For a comparison with the reconstruction geometry, the models were converted to stereolithography (STL) files. To minimize the effect of sampling, the STLs are triangulated with the minimum possible step size of the triangulation mesh. These STL files are then imported into MATLAB, and the triangulation nodes are used as the ground truth point cloud. The images that will be used for reconstruction are generated using the CREO render feature. Subsequently, PBCA is applied with PHDR to reconstruct the 3D geometry and calculate the volume. The used geometries are like those in Figure 7 using the geometries circle, hyperbola, slanted hyperbola, and rectangle. The configurations consist of a semisphere depicted in Figure 9a, an on-axis deformed droplet shown in Figure 9b, and an off-axis deformed droplet in Figure 9c.

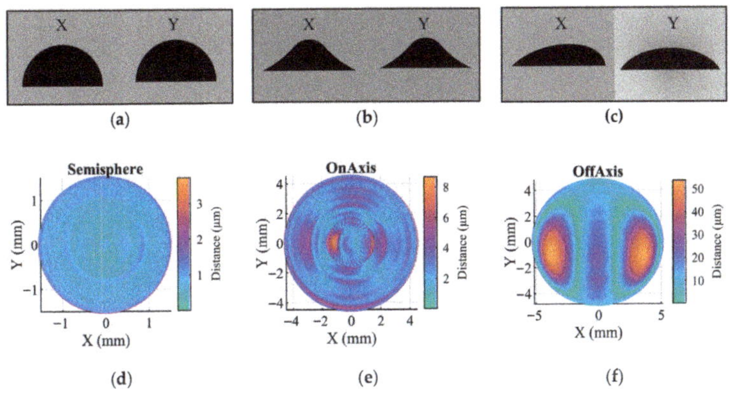

Figure 9. Synthetic CAD models resembling droplets to test the 3D reconstruction and the top view of the Euclidean distances between the ground truth and reconstructed model. (**a**) Semi sphere. (**b**) On-axis deformed. (**c**) Off-axis deformed. (**d**) Top view of semisphere. (**e**) Top view of off-axis deformation. (**f**) Top view of off-axis deformation.

To calculate the volume, the scaling factor per pixel is needed for each model, to convert the pixel values into SI units. The scaling factor is determined by counting the pixels of the base and is calculated using

$$s_{factor} = \frac{mm_{base}}{px_{base}} \tag{20}$$

with s_{factor} as a scaling factor, px_{base} as the base measurement in pixels, and mm_{base} as a base measurement in millimeters of the CAD model. For the three geometries, the reconstruction is carried out as previously described with a sampling of 1000. To align the point clouds, the STL point cloud and the reconstructed point cloud are registered using the Iterative Closest Point (ICP) algorithm [44]. Subsequently the RMSE between the ground truth geometry and the reconstructed geometry is calculated as well as the volume V_{3D} of the reconstructed model and the absolute volume difference ΔV between the ground truth and the reconstructed model. The volume is here used as a metric to evaluate how close the reconstructed and ground truth data are. These values as well as the scaling factors, base measurements, volumes, and e_{RMSE} between the points of the ground truth STL and the reconstructed geometry are shown in Appendix A.2. The volume metrics and RMSE metrics are shown in Table 2. For the rectangular structure, our algorithm does not work. For the algorithm to work, there needs to be a single maximal point with no local minima. This is not the case for the rectangular structure, thus limiting our algorithm. For the other geometries, the local Euclidean distance between the ground truth and the reconstructed geometries are shown in Figure 9d–f. What is evident in all three plots is the wavy distribution of the distance. This probably stems from spline interpolation in the polar coordinate system, as splines are oscillating around the knots. Overall, the best reconstruction is the one of the semisphere, with the maximum distance at around three microns. The on-axis deformation also has a small distance, the maximal distance being around 10 microns, but compared to the size of the whole object of 3 mm diameter, this is still quite small. The worst of the three is the geometry that is modeled on the off-axis deformation. There are two symmetric areas where the distance is around 50 microns. This is likely due to the way that the reconstruction algorithm combines the two contours. The deviation is still not large compared to the whole structure of 10 mm. In summary our approach works very well with axisymmetric geometries with a e_{RMSE} less than 3 microns and a volume deviation of well under one percent. The non-axisymmetric case is still good with an e_{RMSE} of just above 20 microns, which is a ten-fold increase compared to the axisymmetric case and a volume deviation of 3.5%.

Table 2. Metrics describing the scaling of the images and the results.

	Semisphere	On Axis	Off Axis
V_{Creo} (mm^3)	7.07	61.5	99.89
V_{3D} (mm^3)	7.08	61.46	96.58
ΔV_{abs} (mm^3)	0.01	0.04	3.31
ΔV_{rel} (%)	0.14	0.07	3.31
e_{RMSE} (µm)	1.05	3.19	21.16
Max distance (µm)	3.72	8.7	53.7

In addition to the droplet-like shapes, a more extreme geometry is tested with the algorithm, which is normally not easy to represent with any other approximation that is not defined piecewise. It is a pyramid and a crooked pyramid. The methodology is the same as for the other CREO models. In Figure 10a, the x and y view of the pyramid in CREO is shown, in Figure 10b, the crooked pyramid is shown. The Euclidean distances between the ground truth and the reconstructed models are shown in Figure 10c,d. As before, these geometries are represented rather well. A limitation that becomes obvious immediately is at the tip of the pyramids. The tip of the pyramid has no good representation, because of the continuity constraints of the spline-based polar fitting, which always leads to a smoothed corner and not a sharp corner. As with the other CREO models before, the wavy structure can be seen.

The distances are approximately 20 microns, which are relatively small when considered with the 3 mm size of the whole models. This result hints that this algorithm could also be used for other applications, such as tips, with the limitation that very sharp corners are not represented well.

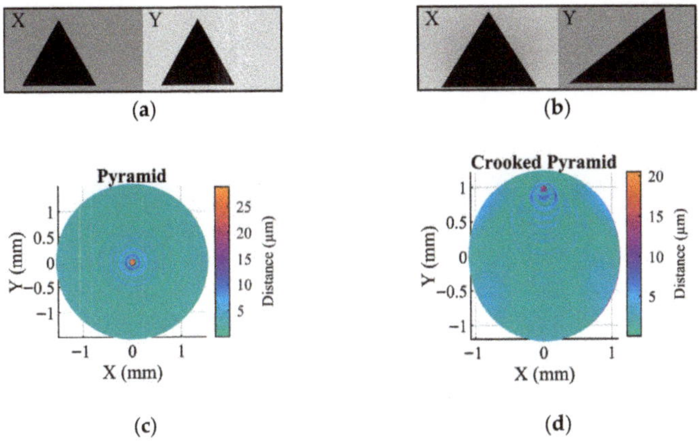

Figure 10. The synthetic CAD models of extreme geometries' reconstruction and the top view of the Euclidean distances between the ground truth and reconstructed model (**a**) Pyramid. (**b**) Crooked pyramid. (**c**) Top view of pyramid. (**d**) Top view of crooked pyramid.

In the subsequent evaluation, actual images depicting the measured geometries are utilized. Three specifically precision-machined pins with a circular section on top and a coordinate measurement machine (CMM) ball are used. The pins approximate the shape that droplets will assume on a pin with no external force, characterized by axial symmetry. Utilizing a CMM, measurements were taken for three pins. Each pin features a base with a diameter of 5 mm. The radii of their circular sections are 2.56 mm, 3.63 mm, and 6.5 mm, respectively. The probing ball of the CMM has a diameter of 3 mm. These objects were put into the shadowgraphy setup, focused, and then images were taken with the X and Y cameras. These images can be seen in Figure 11a,b,e,f.

As with the synthetic CREO data, the PBCA is applied with PHDR to reconstruct the 3D geometries. But first, the circular section must be isolated by manually finding the points where the pin and the circular section meet. This was done for all three pins. For the CMM ball, only half of the ball was used to reconstruct the geometry. This ensures that a comparable portion of the ball is used. Then, the ICP algorithm is used to align the ground truth and the reconstruction, and subsequently, the RMSE between the ground truth geometry and the reconstructed geometry is calculated as well as the volume V_{3D} and the volume difference ΔV. Furthermore, the maximal Euclidean distance between the point clouds is calculated. The measurements of the ball and the pins are shown in Table 3. The full data is shown in Appendix A.3.

In Figure 11c,d,g,h, the local Euclidian distance is shown for each object. Like the reconstruction of the synthetic CREO data, the distance also has a wavy nature as seen especially in Figure 11c,d, stemming from the knots of the spline interpolation. For the two pins with a smaller radius and the CMM ball, the deviations are rather small with a maximum distance of 14 and 10 microns, as well as a small RMSE of around 4 microns for the two pins and 2.48 microns for the CMM ball. The volume is also accurate with a deviation of less than 0.3% for the pins and the ball. The outlier here is pin 3 with a large radius of 6.5 mm. Analogous to a droplet balancing on a pin, this theoretical droplet would show very small contact angles. As illustrated in Figure 11g, the plot showing the distance of pin 3, a significant divergence appears exactly at the junction between the pin and the curved segment, which is marked with red arrows. This finding indicates a constraint in our algorithm's ability to precisely handle small contact angles.

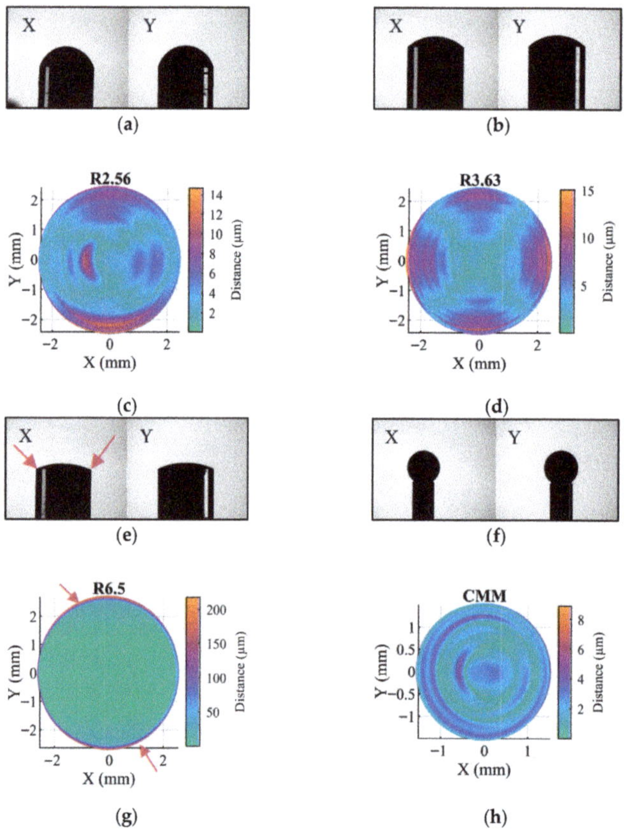

Figure 11. Real X and Y images of the precision machined pins and a CMM ball and the top view of the Euclidean distances between ground truth and reconstructed models. (**a**) Precision pin with a radius of 2.56 mm. (**b**) Precision pin with a radius of 3.63 mm. (**c**) Euclidian distance between the ground truth and the reconstructed pin with a radius of 2.56 mm. (**d**) Euclidian distance between the ground truth and the reconstructed pin with a radius of 3.63 mm. (**e**) Precision pin with a radius of 6.5 mm. The red arrows show the points with the largest deviation. (**f**) Coordinate measurement machine ball with a diameter of 3 mm. (**g**) Euclidian distance between the ground truth and the reconstructed pin with a radius of 6.5 mm. The red arrows show the points with the largest deviation. (**h**) Euclidian distance between the ground truth and the reconstructed CMM ball.

Table 3. Metrics describing the CMM ball and the pins and the results.

	Pin 1	Pin 2	Pin 3	CMM
V (mm^3)	19.21	9.21	4.59	7.07
V_{3D} (mm^3)	19.19	9.21	4.60	7.02
ΔV_{abs} (mm^3)	0.02	0	0.01	0.05
ΔV_{rel} (%)	0.1	0	0.22	0.7
e_{RMSE} (µm)	4.28	4.17	11.15	2.48
Max. distance (µm)	14.36	14.47	292.05	9.76

4.3. Focus Sensitivity and Uncertainty Analysis

In the calculations, the focus seems to have an impact on how accurate the shape and volume are calculated. To test the extent, we did two experiments to test the influence of volume, general RMSE deviation, and focus. First, we randomly moved the CMM ball along the optical axes of both cameras and took an image at each step. Second, we used our autofocus to first focus both axes and then take an image of the CMM ball and repeat this step multiple times. The first experiment quantifies how image sharpness impacts volume estimation and the second tests whether autofocus maintains high focus and reduces variability. Then, we use these images in both cases to calculate the Tenengrad focus measure to evaluate the focus in the image, and then, we use our algorithms to calculate the 3D shape and the volume. We did this with both cameras, because although they have the same components, they have a slight difference in image quality. The magnification and sharpness are slightly different, despite being the exactly the same components. The CMM ball in the first experiment in the setup with the movement direction is shown in Figure 12a. In Figure 12b,c, in blue, the calculated volumes for the moving CMM ball are shown and the red line is the Tenengrad measure. Camera X records the movement on the Y axis, and camera Y records the movement on the X axis. Additionally, the actual volume is indicated by a dashed horizontal line, and the maximum sharpness is indicated by a full vertical line. The same is depicted in Figure 12c for movement on the Y axis. The graphs clearly demonstrate that, as the image becomes more focused, the estimated volume approaches the true volume, indicating that our method is responsive to changes in focus.

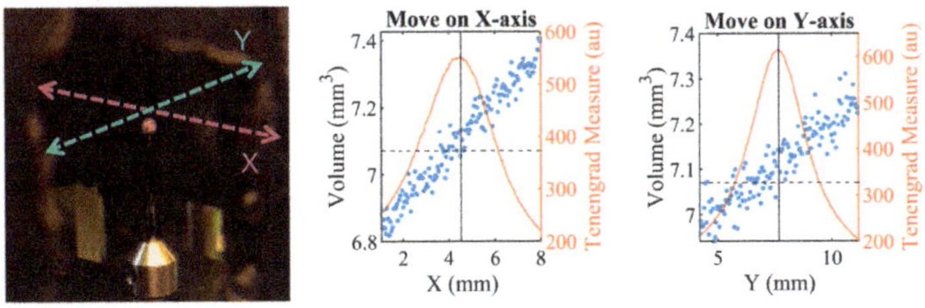

Figure 12. Experimental setup, volume, and Tenengrad measure of both cameras. The dashed horizontal line indicates the true volume of the CMM ball as a reference. (**a**) CMM ball in the setup. (**b**) Volume and Tenengrad measure for move on X axis. (**c**) Volume and Tenengrad measure for move on Y axis.

To evaluate the relationship between image sharpness and reconstruction accuracy, we computed the correlation coefficient between the Tenengrad focus measure and the RMSE of the reconstructed shape. The Pearson correlation coefficient [45] is calculated using

$$\rho_{correlation}(X_1, X_2) = \frac{Cov(X_1, X_2)}{\sqrt{Var(X_1)\,Var(X_2)}}, \tag{21}$$

with $\rho_{correlation}$ as the correlation coefficient, $Cov(X_1, X_2)$ as the covariance of X_1 and X_2 and $Var(X_1)$ and $Var(X_2)$ as the variance of X_1 and X_2, respectively. The correlation coefficient is computed by comparing the RMSE with the Tenengrad measure, illustrating how geometric deviation correlates with image sharpness. Specifically, for motion along the X axis, a negative correlation of −0.63 is observed, while for the Y axis, the correlation is more pronounced at −0.85. These values indicate a substantial reliance on geometric deviation relative to the image's focus. As seen in Figure 12b,c, the least deviation of the volume is where the image has the highest focus. This indicates not only that the volume is more correct with a more focused image, but also that the overall geometric shape is closer to the real shape with a better focus.

The thermal properties of the cameras were also examined in this experiment, as the cameras experience an increase in temperature over time despite the temperature-controlled setup. To understand the influence of the camera temperature, we tracked the camera temperature using the built-in temperature sensor of the cameras. The X camera exhibited a mean temperature of 44.49 °C, with a standard deviation of 0.16 °C and a variance of 0.02 $°C^2$. In contrast, the Y camera recorded a mean temperature of 40.61 °C, accompanied by a standard deviation of 0.30 °C and a variance of 0.09 $°C^2$. These findings indicate a discrepancy in the thermal characteristics of the two cameras. The root cause of this variation remains unidentified; nonetheless, it is likely due to differences in the cameras and their placement inside the temperature-controlled box, which exhibits slight temperature fluctuations. The correlation coefficient between temperature and the Tenengrad measure is 0.2 for the X camera and 0.16 for the Y camera, signifying a weak correlation across the temperature spectrum, suggesting that small absolute temperature fluctuations have a negligible effect on image sharpness and reconstruction quality.

We carried out the second experiment, which was mentioned earlier, to evaluate the effectiveness of our autofocus mechanism by focusing on the CMM ball through both cameras. The real volume of the ball is as before $V = 7.07$ mm^3. In this experiment, the mean volume is $V_{mean} = 7.05$ mm^3 with a standard deviation of $\sigma_V = 0.03$ mm^3 which gives a 95% coverage interval of [6.99, 7.11] mm^3. Additionally, the RMSE of the STL data and the reconstructed volume were calculated for each reconstruction, resulting in a mean RMSE of 2.7 µm with a standard deviation of 0.8 µm, suggesting the limited sensitivity in the shape reconstruction. Lastly, the correlation coefficients between the volume and the Tenengrad measure of both cameras were calculated to see whether there is any correlation left with the autofocus. The correlation coefficients are for the X camera −0.06 and for the Y camera 0.03, indicating that the autofocus compensates for focus-related variability.

In calculating the 3D volume, we presuppose a 90° angle between the two cameras, yet our setup does not allow for the precise measurement of minor deviations. Additionally, there is an imprecision in determining the contact points, which can be selected either manually or through an algorithm, specifically at the intersection of the pin and the circular section. To assess the uncertainties arising from both the camera angle and the determination of contact points, we performed a Monte Carlo simulation integrating images captured from pin 1, which possesses a radius of 2.56 mm. The contact points and the angles were varied, and subsequently, the 3D shape was reconstructed, the volume was calculated, and the RMSE between the true STL shape and the reconstructed shape was calculated after aligning using the ICP algorithm. We assumed that the true location differed from the contact points found by a normally distributed random error with a standard deviation of 2 pixels. Angle noise is also assumed to be normally distributed, with a standard deviation of 5°. We performed 10,000 simulations. In Figure 13a, the pixel noise is shown for the left and right contact points for both cameras, and in Figure 13b, the camera angles over all simulations are shown. In Figure 13c, the histogram of the simulated volumes is shown, confirming that the normal distributed input noise leads to a normal distributed volume. In Figure 13d, the boxplot of the simulated volumes is shown.

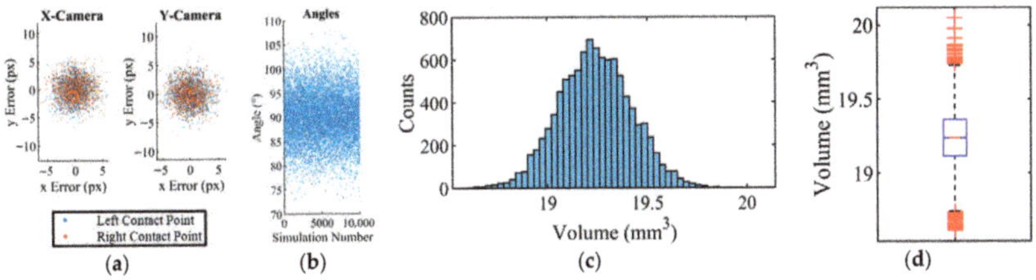

Figure 13. (**a**) Contact point random error. (**b**) Angles with random error. (**c**) Histogram of simulated volumes. (**d**) Boxplot of simulated volumes, the red crosses are the outliers, the red line in the blue box is the median and the blue box covers 50% of the values.

The mean of the volume is $V_{mean} = 19.23\ \text{mm}^3$ with a standard deviation of $\sigma_V = 0.18\ \text{mm}^3$. The 95% coverage interval is [18.88, 19.6] mm^3, and the real volume of the circular shape of the pin is $\text{V} = 19.21\ \text{mm}^3$ which lies well within the coverage interval, indicating good agreement between reconstruction and ground truth data. The coverage interval is calculated here using the standard deviation, because the simulation is based on one measurement. The standard error of the mean is 0.0018 mm^3, which indicates that the average of the Monte Carlo simulations is stable numerically. The RMSE between STL and reconstruction was also calculated each time, resulting in a mean RMSE of 4.9 µm with a standard deviation of 0.7 µm. These small RMSE values confirm that the reconstructed geometry matches the ground-truth STL closely, even with the added noise.

4.4. Real-World Application: Electrically Deformed Droplet Volumetry

As final experiment, a real deformation experiment was conducted to test the algorithm in real-world conditions with a droplet. For that, we use the full setup that is described in 2. Measuring the true shape of a deformed liquid droplet directly is challenging, so we employed an alternative method to indirectly determine the accuracy of our method. To evaluate the accuracy without measuring the real shape of the droplets, a comparing experiment was conducted.

A droplet of known density was weighed, put into the setup, and recorded while it was deformed. The previous sections showed that the reconstruction of the shape and the volume is accurate using known axisymmetric shapes, specifically a spherical cap. The initial droplet shape is a spherical cap, which has an accurate shape and volume reconstruction. In this experiment, the idea is to show how much the volume is changing while deforming, which can give an indication how good the shape of the reconstruction is. Oleic acid is chosen as the material because of its nonevaporating and non-hygroscopic properties. The material density was first measured using a Schmidt & Haensch EDM 4000+ density meter with an accuracy of $0.1\frac{\text{kg}}{\text{m}^3}$. In the experiment, the temperature was 17 °C and the density was $\rho = 893.8\frac{\text{kg}}{\text{m}^3}$. A 6 mm pin was placed inside a GRAM FV-120 analytical balance with an accuracy of 0.1 mg. These accuracies lead to an uncertainty of $\sigma_{Volume} = 0.11\ \text{mm}^3$ in the applied volume range. Afterward, a specified volume of the material is dispensed on top. The droplet is subsequently weighed and then put into the experimental setup, where it is subjected to an electric field with nonaxisymmetric deformation. The time between dispensing the oleic acid and the start of deformation is less than 5 min.

The experiment begins with a one-second interval during which no voltage is applied, followed by a one-second interval of voltage application, and concludes with another one-second interval without applied voltage. The droplet on top of the pin in the balance is shown in Figure 14a. The anode that was used for this experiment is an elongated anode, as seen in Figure 14b. As cathode the pin on which the droplet is sitting was used. This process was carried out with three volumes and different anode positions. In Figure 14c,d, the camera images of the X and Y cameras is shown.

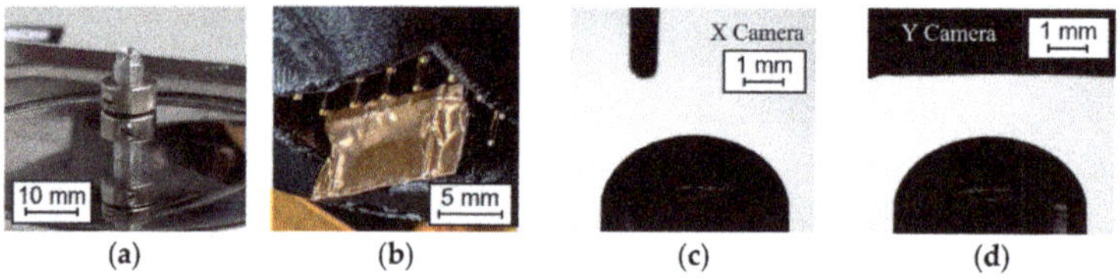

Figure 14. (**a**) Oleic acid on top of the pin inside the balance. (**b**) The anode used in the experiment. (**c**) X camera image of the undeformed droplet in the setup. (**d**) Y camera image of the undeformed droplet.

Using this process of oleic acid droplet application, weighting, and deformation, nine experiments were conducted. The applied voltages in all Experiments was 3000 V, to attain the maximum deformation. The nine experiments had different anode positions that can be seen in Appendix B.1. In all the experiments, the X view shows the thin side of the anode and the Y view shows the wide side of the anode, which is shown in Figure 14b.

These experiments were performed on three individual droplets of oleic acid, each of which was subjected to three different deformations by varying the anode position relative to the droplet. The initial weights and corresponding reference volumes of the three droplets were as follows: Droplet 1: $m_1 = 18.6$ mg ($V_1 = 20.81$ mm^3, used for Exp. 1–3); Droplet 2: $m_2 = 10.5$ mg ($V_2 = 11.75$ mm^3, used for Exp. 4–6); Droplet 3: $m_3 = 12.5$ mg ($V_3 = 13.99$ mm^3, used for Exp. 7–9).

In Figure 15, an exemplary experiment is shown. Experiment 5 is presented as a representative example of a non-axisymmetric deformation. The results for all nine experiments conducted, which show similar volumetric trends, are provided in Appendix B.2. The image number in Figure 15a is the number of images that were taken since the start of the experiment. In Figure 15b, the X-camera can be seen and the Y-camera in Figure 15c. The droplet here will deform in the direction of the anode in X.

The third experiment is empty of data and thus not shown, because during the experiment, the droplet was obscured by the anode, which eliminates the application of our algorithm. If our algorithm would reconstruct the shape perfectly, then the volume would be constant. However, the analysis of the synthetic data generated using a non-axially deformed CREO model indicates that a minor error within the low percentage range is anticipated. If we look at the volume progression during the experiment, a few things can be derived. Initially, the volume, when there is no electric-induced deformation, matches the calculated volume within the experimental measurement uncertainty, indicating the accurate reconstruction under these conditions. However, as the droplet undergoes deformation, the volume decreases, which hints at an increasing error in the reconstruction. The amount of decrease is dependent on the experiment setup, although no systematics could be derived. The only systematic is that the droplet volume reduces, hinting to an area that is not seen in the two shadowgraphy images. But, when looking at the percentage error of the volume, it ranges between 0 and 3%. Although the maximum observed volumetric change was 3%, this remains within a realistic error range for non-ideal imaging setups.

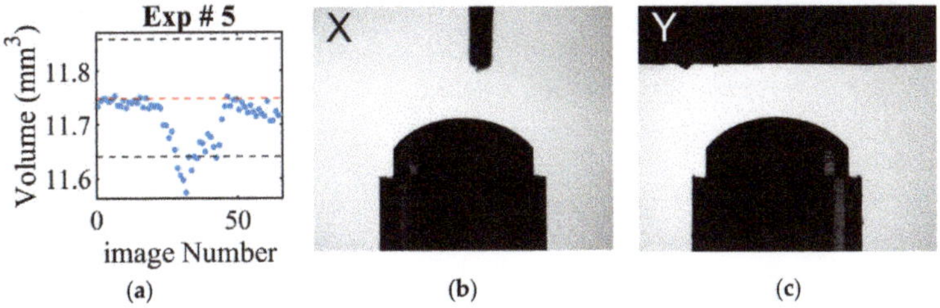

Figure 15. Reconstructed volume and experimental views for a representative non-axisymmetric deformation of Experiment 5. (**a**) Reconstructed volume over the course of the experiment. The red dashed line indicates the reference volume from weighing, while the black dashed lines show the uncertainty interval. (**b**) Shadowgraphy images from the X camera showing the droplet and anode setup prior to deformation along the X axis. (**c**) Shadowgraphy images from the Y camera showing the droplet and anode setup prior to superpixel deformation along the X axis.

This still provides good accuracy for the reconstruction of two images.

4.5. Limitations

The failure to reconstruct the droplet in experiment #3 highlights a practical limitation of the proposed two-camera shadowgraphy setup. Strong deformations that require the very close proximity of the anode can lead to the partial or full coverage of the droplet contour in one or both camera views. If the PBCA algorithm cannot capture a complete boundary, a 3D reconstruction is rendered impossible. Therefore, the method is limited to scenarios where the entire droplet contour remains visible to both cameras without being blocked by experimental hardware, such as the anode.

Our experiments also revealed the limitations inherent to the reconstruction algorithm. The spline-based nature of PBCA, as observed with the pyramid models in Figure 10, inherently smoothens sharp corners, making it less suitable for angular geometries. Furthermore, the significant deviation for Pin 3 in Figure 11g, which represents the shape of a droplet with a low contact angle, indicates reduced accuracy for flatter, less convex droplets. Finally, the algorithms' prerequisite of a single maximal point along the z axis contour prevents the reconstruction of multi-peak or rectangular objects.

While these constraints are noteworthy, they are acceptable within the context of the primary application, which is the fabrication of polymer microlenses for illumination optics. The desired lens' profiles for this purpose are typically smooth and convex. In this context, the smoothing effect of the spline-fit is not a critical drawback and can be considered beneficial as it mitigates pixel-level noise. However, for applications requiring the high-fidelity reconstruction of angular or multi-peak topographies, the proposed method would require substantial modification.

A final consideration is the transferability of the methods parameters. The values for the superpixel count, active contour iterations, and spline knots were specifically tuned to achieve optimal performance with our setup and image resolution. Consequently, the application of this method to other optical systems would necessitate a re-optimization of these parameters to ensure high accuracy.

5. Conclusions

In this work, we presented a polar coordinate-based contour approximation (PBCA) with a Hermite interpolation strategy (PHDR) for approximating the contour and reconstructing various shapes focusing on nonaxisymmetric droplets under electric field deformation. Utilizing two shadowgraphy images, the proposed framework effectively circumvents conventional assumptions regarding droplet symmetry, thus providing reliable 3D shape and volume estimations. Numerical validations against synthetic CAD models and real references confirm that our approach maintains accuracy with volume deviations typically under 3%, while still being straightforward to implement.

The study further underscores the importance of proper focus and camera calibration in minimizing measurement error; as demonstrated, slight misalignment or defocus can notably shift volume and shape reconstructions. We observed a strong correlation between the image sharpness and the reconstruction accuracy but could limit this influence by autofocusing.

However, certain limitations remain. First, extremely sharp or rectangular cross-sections like the corners of pyramids are not captured correctly, suggesting that pure polar-based fits may need extensions for highly angular geometries. Second, heavy obstructions in one camera view can degrade the reconstruction if large portions of the droplet boundary are unseen. Furthermore, shapes where there is no maximal point, like a rectangle, are also not reconstructable with this approach. Added noise to the camera angle and the contact points showed small but not significant deviations, showing the robustness of the method. Shape deviations also restrict this type of reconstruction to illumination optics only, because, for other applications, the deviations and especially the waviness is not acceptable.

Future work could incorporate multiview setups or advanced interpolation methods that better handle multipeak droplet surfaces. In practice, combining the polar-based method with real-time focus monitoring would further enhance reliability, especially in dynamic or industrial environments where droplets may shift or vibrate. With these refinements, the method promises to become an even more powerful tool for diverse metrology tasks, including adaptive optics, specialized lens fabrication, and broader microfluidic applications requiring detailed droplet shape measurements.

Author Contributions: Conceptualization, M.D. and A.H.; Data curation, M.D.; Formal analysis, M.D. and A.H.; Funding acquisition, A.H.; Investigation, M.D.; Methodology, M.D., A.H. and C.N.; Project administration, M.D. and A.H.; Resources M.D., A.H. and C.N.; Software, M.D.; Supervision, A.H. and C.N.; Validation M.D., A.H. and C.N.; Visualization, M.D.; Writing—original draft M.D.; Writing—review and editing M.D., A.H. and C.N. All authors have read and agreed to the published version of the manuscript.

Funding: This research was funded by the Deutsche Forschungsgemeinschaft (DFG) grant number HE 3533/10-1 (Project Number 440697245).

Data Availability Statement: The data presented in this study is available on request from the corresponding author.

Acknowledgments: The authors thank Sascha Wallentowitz for helping to come up with the idea of the polar approximation as well as Felix Zeller and Lutz Autschbach of Carl Zeiss Jena for manufacturing and measuring the precision machined pins.

Conflicts of Interest: The authors declare no conflicts of interest.

Abbreviations

The following abbreviations are used in this manuscript:

PBCA	Polar-Based Contour Approximation
PHDR	Polar-Coordinate Hermite-Interpolation-based Droplet Reconstruction
3D	Three-Dimensional
CAD	Computer-Aided Design
CMM	Coordinate Measuring Machine
ICP	Iterative Closest Point

LED	Light-Emitting Diode
RMSE	Root Mean Square Error
MAPE	Mean Absolute Percentage Error
MNE	Mean Normalized Error
STL	Stereolithography (file format)
DOF	Depth of Field
SLIC	Simple Linear Iterative Clustering
UV	Ultraviolet
px	Pixel

Appendix A.

Appendix A.1. Visualization of the Evaluation Metrics

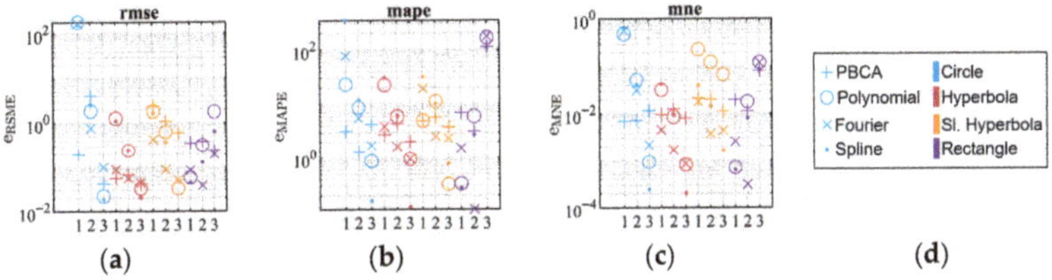

Figure A1. Detailed view of the measures. (**a**) RMSE, (**b**) MAPE and (**c**) MNE of the curves compared to the ground truth and (**d**) is the legend.

The color corresponds to the shape, where blue is the circle, red is the hyperbola, yellow is the slanted hyperbola, and purple is the rectangle. The number corresponds to the extension of the shape as described.

Appendix A.2. Detailed Results for CREO Data

All values are for the CREO data.

Table A1. Metrics more detailed describing of scaling of the images and the results.

	Semisphere	On Axis	Off Axis
px_{xbase} (px)	906	1040	1070
px_{ybase} (px)	906	1040	1138
mm_{base} (mm)	3 (X & Y)	9 (X & Y)	9.64 (X) 10.26 (Y)
$s_{xfactor}\left(\frac{\mu m}{px}\right)$	3.31	8.65	9.01
$s_{yfactor}\left(\frac{\mu m}{px}\right)$	3.31	8.65	9.02
$V_{Creo}\,(mm^3)$	7.069	61.499	99.893
V_{3D} (mm^3)	7.084	61.494	96.393
ΔV_{abs} (mm^3)	0.015	0.005	3.5
ΔV_{rel} (%)	0.212	0.008	3.631
e_{RMSE} (mm)	0.0011	0.0028	0.0224
e_{RMSE} (px)	0.33	0.324	2.486
Max distance (mm)	0.003	0.010	0.056
Max distance (px)	0.906	1.156	6.215

Appendix A.3. Detailed Results for Precision Pins and CMM Ball

All data are for the precision pins and the CMM ball.

Table A2. Metrics describing the CMM ball and the pins and the results in more detail.

	Pin 1	Pin 2	Pin 3	CMM
$r_{measured}$ (mm)	2.56	3.63	6.49	1.5
d_{base} (mm)	4.86	4.87	4.90	1.5
V (mm^3)	19.21	9.21	4.59	7.07
V_{3D} (mm^3)	19.19	9.21	4.60	7.02
ΔV_{abs} (mm^3)	0.02	0	0.01	0.05
ΔV_{rel} (%)	0.1	0	0.22	0.7
e_{RMSE} (µm)	4.28	4.17	11.15	2.48
Max Distance (µm)	14.36	14.47	292.05	9.76

Appendix B.

Appendix B.1. Images from the Start of Experiments

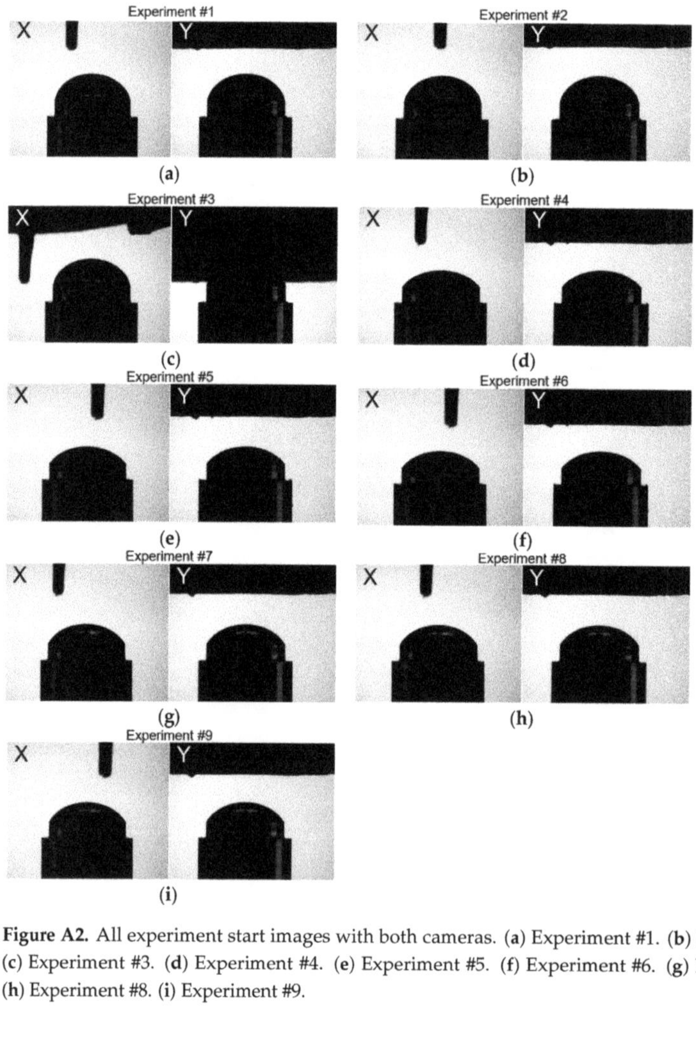

Figure A2. All experiment start images with both cameras. (**a**) Experiment #1. (**b**) Experiment #2. (**c**) Experiment #3. (**d**) Experiment #4. (**e**) Experiment #5. (**f**) Experiment #6. (**g**) Experiment #7. (**h**) Experiment #8. (**i**) Experiment #9.

Appendix B.2. Plots for All Reconstructed Volumes

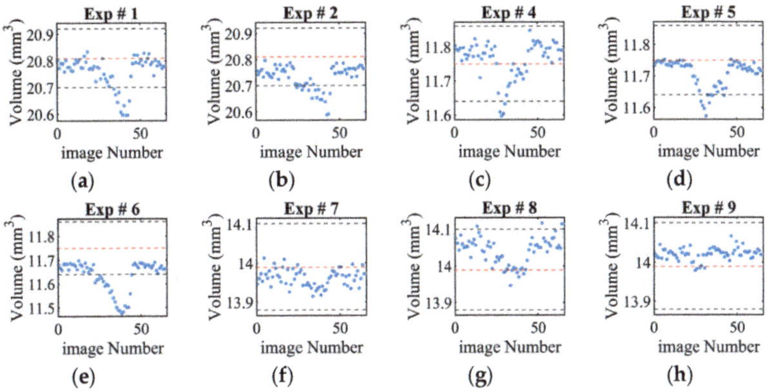

Figure A3. Reconstructed volumes of the experiments over the course of the experiments. The red dashed line indicates the reference volume from weighing, while the black dashed lines show the uncertainty interval. (**a**) Experiment #1. (**b**) Experiment #2. (**c**) Experiment #4. (**d**) Experiment #5. (**e**) Experiment #6. (**f**) Experiment #7. (**g**) Experiment #8. (**h**) Experiment #9.

References

1. Yuan, W.; Li, L.-H.; Lee, W.-B.; Chan, C.-Y. Fabrication of Microlens Array and Its Application: A Review. *Chin. J. Mech. Eng.* **2018**, *31*, 16. [CrossRef]
2. Cai, S.; Sun, Y.; Chu, H.; Yang, W.; Yu, H.; Liu, L. Microlenses Arrays: Fabrication, Materials, and Applications. *Microsc. Res. Tech.* **2021**, *84*, 2784–2806. [CrossRef]
3. Marini, M.; Nardini, A.; Vázquez, R.M.; Conci, C.; Bouzin, M.; Collini, M.; Osellame, R.; Cerullo, G.; Kariman, B.S.; Farsari, M.; et al. Microlenses Fabricated by Two-Photon Laser Polymerization for Cell Imaging with Non-Linear Excitation Microscopy. *Adv. Funct. Mater.* **2023**, *33*, 2213926. [CrossRef]
4. Frumkin, V.; Bercovici, M. Fluidic Shaping of Optical Components. *Flow* **2021**, *1*, E2. [CrossRef]
5. Elgarisi, M.; Frumkin, V.; Luria, O.; Bercovici, M. Fabrication of Freeform Optical Components by Fluidic Shaping. *Optica* **2021**, *8*, 1501–1506. [CrossRef]
6. Xu, C.; Guan, X.; Abbasi, S.A.; Xia, N.; Ngai, T.; Zhang, L.; Ho, H.-P.; Ng, S.H.C.; Yuan, W. Liquid-Shaped Microlens for Scalable Production of Ultrahigh-Resolution Optical Coherence Tomography Microendoscope. *Commun. Eng.* **2024**, *3*, 1. [CrossRef]
7. Taylor, G.I. Disintegration of Water Drops in an Electric Field. *Proc. R. Soc. Lond. Ser. A Math. Phys. Sci.* **1964**, *280*, 383–397.
8. Lima, N.C.; Mishra, K.; Mugele, F. Aberration Control in Adaptive Optics: A Numerical Study of Arbitrarily Deformable Liquid Lenses. *Opt. Express* **2017**, *25*, 6700–6711. [CrossRef] [PubMed]
9. Zhan, Z.; Wang, K. Fabrication of Aspherical Liquid Lens Controlled by Electrostatic Force. In Proceedings of the 3rd International Symposium on Advanced Optical Manufacturing and Testing Technologies: Advanced Optical Manufacturing Technologies, Chengdu, China, 8–12 November 2007; Volume 6722, pp. 1038–1044.
10. Saad, S.M.I.; Neumann, A.W. Axisymmetric Drop Shape Analysis (ADSA): An Outline. *Adv. Colloid Interface Sci.* **2016**, *238*, 62–87. [CrossRef] [PubMed]
11. Hou, B.; Wu, C.; Liu, H.; Sun, R.; Li, X.; Liu, C.; Wu, J.; Chen, M. Shape Approximation of Sessile Droplet by the Equivalence between Vertical Capillary Force and Hydrostatic Pressure. *Colloids Surf. A Physicochem. Eng. Asp.* **2023**, *656*, 130203. [CrossRef]
12. Tran, D.T.; Nguyen, N.-K.; Singha, P.; Nguyen, N.-T.; Ooi, C.H. Modelling Sessile Droplet Profile Using Asymmetrical Ellipses. *Processes* **2021**, *9*, 2081. [CrossRef]
13. Wang, X.; Yu, Y. Analysis of the Shape of Heavy Droplets on Flat and Spherical Surface. *Sci. China Phys. Mech. Astron.* **2012**, *55*, 1118–1124. [CrossRef]
14. Timm, M.L.; Dehdashti, E.; Jarrahi Darban, A.; Masoud, H. Evaporation of a Sessile Droplet on a Slope. *Sci. Rep.* **2019**, *9*, 19803. [CrossRef] [PubMed]
15. ElSherbini, A.I.; Jacobi, A.M. Liquid Drops on Vertical and Inclined Surfaces: II. A Method for Approximating Drop Shapes. *J. Colloid Interface Sci.* **2004**, *273*, 566–575. [CrossRef]

16. Bateni, A.; Susnar, S.S.; Amirfazli, A.; Neumann, A.W. A High-Accuracy Polynomial Fitting Approach to Determine Contact Angles. *Colloids Surf. A Physicochem. Eng. Asp.* **2003**, *219*, 215–231. [CrossRef]
17. Quetzeri-Santiago, M.A.; Castrejón-Pita, J.R.; Castrejón-Pita, A.A. On the Analysis of the Contact Angle for Impacting Droplets Using a Polynomial Fitting Approach. *Exp. Fluids* **2020**, *61*, 143. [CrossRef]
18. Andersen, N.K.; Taboryski, R. Drop Shape Analysis for Determination of Dynamic Contact Angles by Double Sided Elliptical Fitting Method. *Meas. Sci. Technol.* **2017**, *28*, 047003. [CrossRef]
19. Trujillo-Pino, A.; Krissian, K.; Alemán-Flores, M.; Santana-Cedrés, D. Accurate Subpixel Edge Location Based on Partial Area Effect. *Image Vis. Comput.* **2013**, *31*, 72–90. [CrossRef]
20. Stalder, A.F.; Kulik, G.; Sage, D.; Barbieri, L.; Hoffmann, P. A Snake-Based Approach to Accurate Determination of Both Contact Points and Contact Angles. *Colloids Surf. A Physicochem. Eng. Asp.* **2006**, *286*, 92–103. [CrossRef]
21. Rotenberg, Y.; Boruvka, L.; Neumann, A.W. The Shape of Nonaxisymmetric Drops on Inclined Planar Surfaces. *J. Colloid Interface Sci.* **1984**, *102*, 424–434. [CrossRef]
22. Martin, G.D.; Price, W.C.; Hutchings, I.M.; Price, W.C.; Hutchings, I.M. Measurement of Inkjet Drop Volume—The Role of Image Processing. *NIP Digit. Fabr. Conf.* **2016**, *32*, 94–102. [CrossRef]
23. Hutchings, I.; Martin, G.; Hoath, S.; Martin, G.; Hoath, S. High Speed Imaging and Analysis of Jet and Drop Formation. *J. Imaging Sci. Technol.* **2007**, *51*, 438–444. [CrossRef]
24. Ríos-López, I.; Karamaoynas, P.; Zabulis, X.; Kostoglou, M.; Karapantsios, T.D. Image Analysis of Axisymmetric Droplets in Wetting Experiments: A New Tool for the Study of 3D Droplet Geometry and Droplet Shape Reconstruction. *Colloids Surf. A Physicochem. Eng. Asp.* **2018**, *553*, 660–671. [CrossRef]
25. Brown, R.A.; Orr, F.M.; Scriven, L.E. Static Drop on an Inclined Plate: Analysis by the Finite Element Method. *J. Colloid Interface Sci.* **1980**, *73*, 76–87. [CrossRef]
26. Lewis, K.; Matsuura, T. Bézier Curve Method to Compute Various Meniscus Shapes. *ACS Omega* **2023**, *8*, 15371–15383. [CrossRef]
27. Jakhar, K.; Chattopadhyay, A.; Thakur, A.; Raj, R. Spline Based Shape Prediction and Analysis of Uniformly Rotating Sessile and Pendant Droplets. *Langmuir* **2017**, *33*, 5603–5612. [CrossRef]
28. Nguyen, X.H.; Lee, S.-H.; Ko, H.S. Comparative Study on Basis Functions for Projection Matrix of Three-Dimensional Tomographic Reconstruction for Analysis of Dropletbehavior from Electrohydrodynamic Jet. *Appl. Opt.* **2012**, *51*, 5834–5844. [CrossRef]
29. Kim, S.; Choi, J.H.; Sohn, D.K.; Ko, H.S. The Effect of Ink Supply Pressure on Piezoelectric Inkjet. *Micromachines* **2022**, *13*, 615. [CrossRef]
30. Thurow, K.; Krüger, T.; Stoll, N. An Optical Approach for the Determination of Droplet Volumes in Nanodispensing. *J. Anal. Methods Chem.* **2009**, *2009*, e198732. [CrossRef] [PubMed]
31. Portuguez, E.; Alzina, A.; Michaud, P.; Oudjedi, M.; Smith, A. Evolution of a Water Pendant Droplet: Effect of Temperature and Relative Humidity. *Nat. Sci.* **2017**, *9*, 1–20. [CrossRef]
32. Fu, Y.; Mugikura, Y.; Liu, Y. Implementation of Defocus and Space Carving Techniques in Bubbly Flow Measurement. *Meas. Sci. Technol.* **2017**, *28*, 075206. [CrossRef]
33. Masuk, A.U.M.; Salibindla, A.; Ni, R. A Robust Virtual-Camera 3D Shape Reconstruction of Deforming Bubbles/Droplets with Additional Physical Constraints. *Int. J. Multiph. Flow* **2019**, *120*, 103088. [CrossRef]
34. Liu, Q.; Chen, J.; Yang, H.; Yin, Z. Accurate Stereo-Vision-Based Flying Droplet Volume Measurement Method. *IEEE Trans. Instrum. Meas.* **2022**, *71*, 1–16. [CrossRef]
35. Zhang, Z. A Flexible New Technique for Camera Calibration. *IEEE Trans. Pattern Anal. Mach. Intell.* **2000**, *22*, 1330–1334. [CrossRef]
36. Achanta, R.; Shaji, A.; Smith, K.; Lucchi, A.; Fua, P.; Süsstrunk, S. SLIC Superpixels Compared to State-of-the-Art Superpixel Methods. *IEEE Trans. Pattern Anal. Mach. Intell.* **2012**, *34*, 2274–2282. [CrossRef]
37. Roberts, L.G. Machine Perception of Three-Dimensional Solids. Ph.D. Thesis, Massachusetts Institute of Technology, Cambridge, MA, USA, 1963.
38. Gonzalez, R.; Woods, R. *Digital Image Processing*; Springer: Berlin/Heidelberg, Germany, 2005; Available online: https://elibrary.pearson.de/book/99.150005/9781292223070 (accessed on 28 October 2024).
39. Unser, M. Splines: A Perfect Fit for Signal and Image Processing. *IEEE Signal Process. Mag.* **1999**, *16*, 22–38. [CrossRef]
40. Micchelli, C.A.; Rivlin, T.J.; Winograd, S. The Optimal Recovery of Smooth Functions. *Numer. Math.* **1976**, *26*, 191–200. [CrossRef]
41. de Boor, C. Computational Aspects of Optimal Recovery. In *Optimal Estimation in Approximation Theory*; Micchelli, C.A., Rivlin, T.J., Eds.; Springer: Boston, MA, USA, 1977; pp. 69–91. ISBN 978-1-4684-2388-4.
42. Gaffney, P.W.; Powell, M.J.D. Optimal Interpolation. In *Numerical Analysis*; Watson, G.A., Ed.; Springer: Berlin/Heidelberg, Germany, 1976; pp. 90–99.
43. Atefi, E.; Mann, J.J.A.; Tavana, H. A Robust Polynomial Fitting Approach for Contact Angle Measurements. *Langmuir* **2013**, *29*, 5677–5688. [CrossRef]

44. Pcregistericp. Available online: https://de.mathworks.com/help/vision/ref/pcregistericp.html (accessed on 5 March 2025).
45. Krystek, M. *Berechnung der Messunsicherheit: Grundlagen und Anleitung für die Praktische Anwendung; Beuth Praxis Messwesen*, 1st ed.; Beuth: Berlin, Germany, 2012; ISBN 978-3-410-20932-4.

metrology

MDPI

Article

Vision-Based Characterization of Gear Transmission Mechanisms to Improve 3D Laser Scanner Accuracy

Fernando Lopez-Medina [1,2], José A. Núñez-López [1,2,*], Oleg Sergiyenko [1], Dennis Molina-Quiroz [2], Cesar Sepulveda-Valdez [2], Jesús R. Herrera-García [2], Vera Tyrsa [2] and Ruben Alaniz-Plata [1]

1 Instituto de Ingeniería, Universidad Autónoma de Baja California, Blvd. Benito Juárez y Calle de La Normal, s/n, Col. Insurgentes Este, Mexicali C.P. 21280, Mexico; fernando.lopez.medina@uabc.edu.mx (F.L.-M.); srgnk@uabc.edu.mx (O.S.); ruben.alaniz@uabc.edu.mx (R.A.-P.)

2 Facultad de Ingeniería, Universidad Autónoma de Baja California, Blvd. Benito Juárez y Calle de La Normal, s/n, Col. Insurgentes Este, Mexicali C.P. 21280, Mexico; dennis.molina@uabc.edu.mx (D.M.-Q.); cesar.sepulveda@uabc.edu.mx (C.S.-V.); herrera.jesus27@uabc.edu.mx (J.R.H.-G.); vtyrsa@uabc.edu.mx (V.T.)

* Correspondence: jose.nunez10@uabc.edu.mx

Abstract: Some laser scanners utilize stepper motor-driven optomechanical assemblies to position the laser beam precisely during triangulation. In laser scanners such as the presented Technical Vision System (TVS), to enhance motion resolution, gear transmissions are implemented between the motor and the optical assembly. However, due to the customized nature of the mechanical design, errors in manufacturing or insufficient mechanical characterization can introduce deviations in the computed 3D coordinates. In this work, we present a novel method for estimating the degrees-per-step ratio at the output of the laser positioner's transmission mechanism using a stereovision system. Experimental results demonstrate the effectiveness of the proposed method, which reduces the need for manual metrological instruments and simplifies the calibration procedure through vision-assisted measurements. The method yielded estimated angular resolutions of approximately 0.06° and 0.07° per motor step in the horizontal and vertical axes, respectively, key parameters that define the minimal resolvable displacement of the projected beam in dynamic triangulation.

Keywords: laser scanner; vision-based calibration; stereovision; gear transmission characterization

1. Introduction

Three-dimensional scanning systems have proven to be essential tools across a wide range of applications, including obstacle detection in dynamic environments [1], industrial inspection and manufacturing tasks [2,3], and detailed 3D reconstruction for geometric analysis or autonomous navigation [4,5].

Among the most commonly used technologies are camera-based systems, which reconstruct the geometry of a scene from images using techniques such as disparity estimation, followed by epipolar triangulation for 3D reconstruction [6–8]. However, a key limitation of these passive systems is their reliance on adequate lighting conditions, which constrains their performance in dark or poorly illuminated environments [9,10]. Beyond passive stereo, photogrammetry and structured-light scanning are widely used in optical metrology: the former reconstructs geometry from multi-view images, while the latter projects coded/phase patterns to achieve high short-range accuracy. Both can be sensitive to illumination and motion [7,8]. In contrast, active laser-based scanning systems can operate reliably even in complete darkness [11,12]. One widely used solution is the LiDAR (Light Detection and Ranging) system, which applies the time-of-flight (ToF) technique by measuring the temporal delay between the emission and reception of a reflected laser pulse [4,12]. Nevertheless, ToF-based systems may suffer from limited angular accuracy, especially in compact or low-cost implementations [13–15].

An alternative approach is the Technical Vision System (TVS), which relies on the principle of dynamic triangulation [16,17]. In this system, a laser spot is projected onto the target surface, and its reflection is captured by an optical sensor. Given the precisely known emission and reception angles, the 3D coordinates of the laser spot can be computed using trigonometric relations. A complete surface scan is achieved by systematically sweeping the laser beam across the measurement field. In active triangulation systems, spatial accuracy strongly depends on the fixed angular resolution of the projected laser beam [18–21].

The TVS includes a positioning subsystem that directs the laser beam toward specific regions of interest using rotational actuators. This subsystem has been implemented using both DC motors and stepper motors, with the latter being preferred due to their ability to perform discrete angular movements, which facilitates accurate estimation of the laser position [16,17]. Although the TVS uses an 808 nm near-infrared laser, the spatial resolution of the system is primarily defined by the angular precision of the mechanical laser positioner, rather than by optical wavelength or power [9,17].

Since the triangulation process critically depends on angular accuracy, it is essential to ensure proper calibration of the mechanical components involved in laser beam steering [22]. In particular, mechanical transmissions can introduce both systematic and random errors if parameters such as the degrees-per-step ratio are not accurately known [23–26]. Many TVS prototypes are conceived as low-cost alternatives using additive manufacturing [9]. As a result, their mechanical transmissions are not standardized and often exhibit variations arising from the manufacturing and assembly processes. Therefore, experimental characterization of these components becomes necessary to ensure proper system calibration [17].

Numerous studies have focused on the fusion of heterogeneous sensors and their extrinsic calibration, which involves estimating the rigid transformation that spatially aligns the reference frames of each system, enabling coherent data integration [17,27–29]. However, very few works explore the potential of such multisensor configurations to estimate internal parameters of one of the constituent systems. In this work, we leverage the data provided by the stereovision system to characterize a key mechanical property of the Technical Vision System: the degrees-per-step ratio of the two gear transmissions responsible for controlling the orientation of the laser beam within the positioner subsystem. This approach not only enhances the accuracy of dynamic triangulation, but also enables the development of autonomous robotic systems with self-calibration capabilities, eliminating the need for external references or human intervention.

Non-contact calibration techniques based on virtual gear artefacts have been proposed for validating vision-based gear measurement systems [30]. However, these approaches remain focused on software-level verification and do not directly recover fundamental transmission parameters (such as the effective degrees-per-step ratio) in fully assembled 3D laser scanners. In contrast, our stereovision-based method performs an in situ kinematic characterization after system assembly, thereby accounting for mounting tolerances and eliminating cumulative mechanical alignment errors. To ensure accurate stereo correspondence and 3D reconstruction, the stereovision system was previously calibrated using Zhang's method [31], which provides intrinsic and extrinsic camera parameters from a planar target. This camera calibration supports the metrological reliability of the proposed angular estimation.

In this study, the main objective is to propose a method for characterizing the mechanical transmission parameters of the Technical Vision System (TVS) by leveraging a stereovision system as an auxiliary metrological reference. By segmenting the laser spot projected onto a planar surface, we developed an algorithm capable of accurately estimating the angular displacement of the beam, thereby enabling precise quantification of the degrees-per-step ratio in the gear transmission of the laser positioner subsystem. Experimental results are provided to validate the effectiveness of the proposed algorithm. The novelty of the presented method is that it provides a non-invasive and cost-effective alternative for accurate and automated characterization of the mechanical subsystem, reducing reliance on manual measurement tools or direct intervention on the laser scanner—an essential task to ensure the system's metrological reliability.

2. Materials and Methods

This study employs two 3D scanning systems: a Technical Vision System (TVS) and a two-camera module that constitutes a stereovision system. The stereovision system serves as an external reference for calibrating the gear transmission mechanism of the TVS, with the aim of improving the accuracy of its 3D measurements.

This section describes the operating principles of each system, the hardware configuration, the experimental setup, and the procedures followed during the data acquisition and calibration phases.

2.1. Stereovision System

A stereovision system consists of two cameras separated by a known horizontal baseline and aligned vertically to ensure collinearity. After performing camera calibration, which allows the estimation of the intrinsic parameters (such as focal length, principal point, and lens distortion), both cameras can capture synchronized images of the same scene.

When a 3D point is simultaneously captured by both cameras, its projections appear at different horizontal positions in each image. This difference, known as disparity, is the basis for depth estimation. This disparity, which occurs along the horizontal axis for rectified stereo pairs, can be exploited using the constraints of epipolar geometry to triangulate the 3D coordinates of the observed point.

Figure 1 illustrates the typical geometric configuration of a calibrated stereovision system under the pinhole camera model. After calibration, the coordinate system is defined at the optical center of the left camera $(0,0,0)$, while the right camera center is located at $(b,0,0)$, with b representing the baseline distance along the x-axis. A 3D point $P(x,y,z)$ is projected onto the left and right image planes as (u_l,v_l) and (u_r,v_r), respectively. The disparity between these horizontal coordinates, together with the known baseline b and focal length f, enables the estimation of the depth z via triangulation.

2.2. Technical Vision System (TVS)

The Technical Vision System (TVS) performs 3D measurements using a technique known as dynamic triangulation [16]. It is composed of two main subsystems: the positioner, which directs the laser beam, and the aperture, which serves as the optical reception module that detects the reflected signal. The geometric alignment between these subsystems is critical for ensuring metrological accuracy.

Figure 2 shows the overall configuration of the TVS and its two principal subsystems.

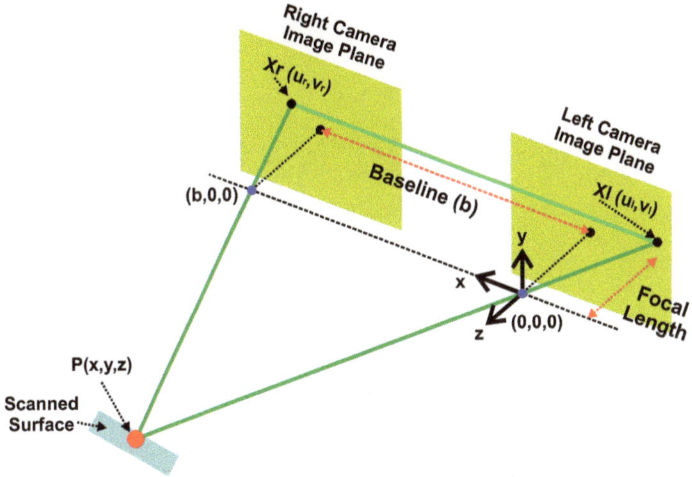

Figure 1. Geometric configuration of a calibrated stereovision system.

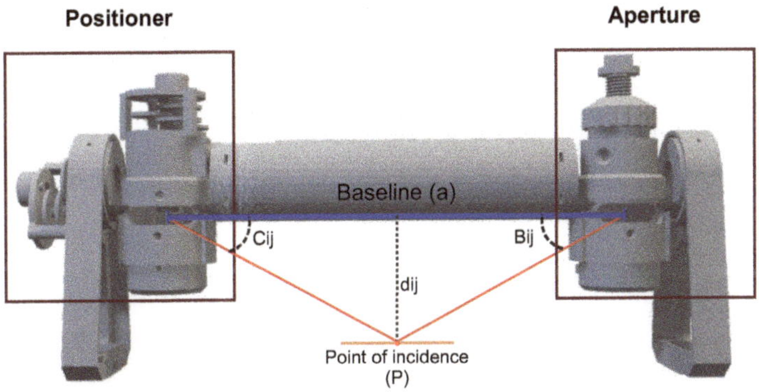

Figure 2. General configuration of the Technical Vision System (TVS).

In the positioner, the laser beam is emitted from the top and redirected by two 45° mirrors. The orientation of these mirrors is controlled by stepper motors, allowing precise redirection of the laser beam. To improve angular resolution, the motors are coupled to gear transmissions. Figure 3 details the components of the positioner.

On the other hand, the aperture subsystem is responsible for acquiring the reflected laser beam. A rotating mirror collects the incoming light and directs it toward a photodiode, which converts the optical signal into an electrical one. This signal is then digitized and processed by a microcontroller. The angular position of the rotating mirror is synchronized through an optical interrupter that detects a reference hole on an encoder disk. Figure 4 illustrates the optical acquisition subsystem, referred to as the aperture.

The 3D coordinates are computed using trigonometric relationships derived from the law of sines. The angles of emission and reception, along with the known baseline distance a, define a triangle from which the x, y, and z coordinates are computed as follows:

$$x_{ij} = a\frac{\sin B_{ij} \cdot \sin C_{ij} \cdot \cos \sum_{j=1}^{j} \beta_j}{\sin[180^\circ - (B_{ij} + C_{ij})]} \tag{1}$$

$$y_{ij} = \begin{cases} a\left(\frac{1}{2} - \frac{\sin B_{ij} \cdot \cos C_{ij}}{\sin[180^\circ - (B_{ij}+C_{ij})]}\right), & \text{if } B_{ij} \leq 90^\circ \\ -a\left(\frac{1}{2} + \frac{\sin B_{ij} \cdot \cos C_{ij}}{\sin[180^\circ - (B_{ij}+C_{ij})]}\right), & \text{if } B_{ij} > 90^\circ \end{cases} \quad (2)$$

$$z_{ij} = a\frac{\sin B_{ij} \cdot \sin C_{ij} \cdot \sin \sum_{j=1}^{j} \beta_j}{\sin[180^\circ - (B_{ij} + C_{ij})]} \quad (3)$$

A two-axis scanning motion is achieved by driving the stepper motors horizontally and vertically, while the rotating mirror in the aperture subsystem enables continuous acquisition. The resulting point cloud accurately captures the scanned surface.

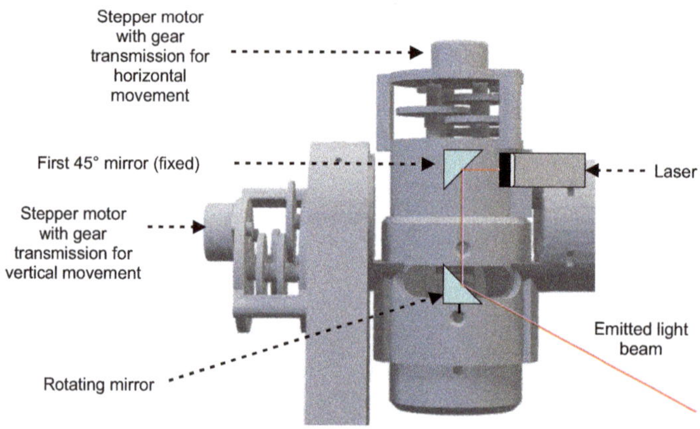

Figure 3. The positioner subsystem of the Technical Vision System (TVS).

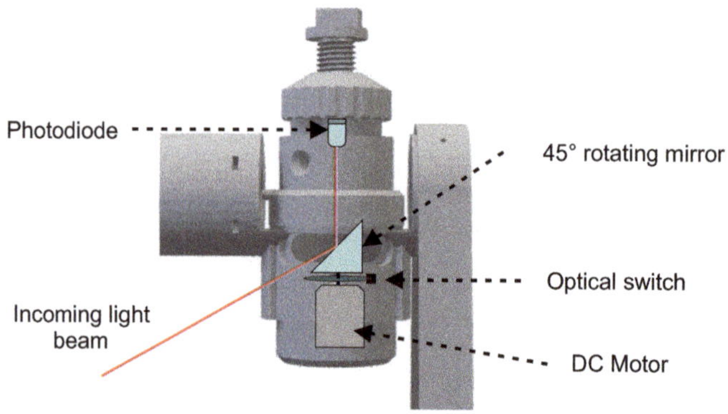

Figure 4. The aperture subsystem of the Technical Vision System (TVS).

2.3. Prototypes of Scanning Systems and Experimental Setup

The two scanning systems used in this study are shown in Figure 5. The first is a customized prototype of the Technical Vision System (TVS), which features a baseline of 20 cm and employs a near-infrared laser with a wavelength of 808 nm. The second is a low-cost commercial stereovision module (GXIVision) equipped with LSM22100 cameras. The module integrates two 1 MP CMOS sensors (1280 × 720 pixels each) with 2.4 mm M12 lenses and operates with a fixed stereo baseline of 85 mm.

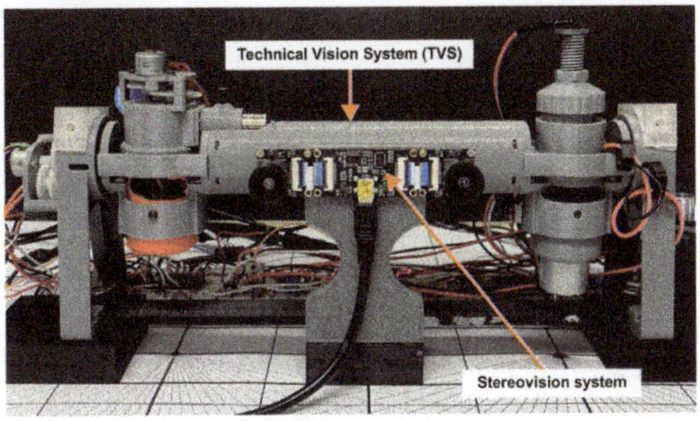

Figure 5. Prototypes of the Technical Vision System (TVS) and the stereovision system employed in the experimental procedures.

Since the stereovision system was used as a ground-truth reference for the intrinsic calibration of the TVS, it was first calibrated using Zhang's method [31]. This technique estimates both intrinsic and extrinsic parameters based on the observation of a planar checkerboard with known grid spacing. It is particularly effective when multiple images are acquired from diverse viewpoints, ensuring sufficient geometric variation.

The calibration target is shown in Figure 6. It consists of a 10×7 checkerboard, yielding 54 inner corners. A total of twenty images were captured from different positions and orientations to ensure wide field-of-view coverage and geometric richness. These images were used to minimize the reprojection error through a non-linear optimization process. Each square of the checkerboard measured 25 mm per side, which ensured an appropriate scale relative to the 1280×720-pixel resolution of the stereo cameras. This configuration provided sufficient spatial detail for reliable corner detection during calibration and guaranteed that the laser spot, whose diameter spanned several pixels, could be adequately sampled for accurate centroid estimation.

Figure 6. The checkerboard used for calibrating the stereovision system.

Once calibrated, the stereovision system was employed to capture the position of the laser spot projected by the TVS. These 3D reference measurements were used to characterize the two gear transmission mechanisms responsible for the horizontal and vertical movements of the positioner. Accurate characterization of these mechanisms is essential for precise 3D coordinate computation using the TVS.

Figure 7 shows both scanning systems and the planar target, all mounted on an optical breadboard with dimensions of 80×50 cm. The flat surface, consisting of plain white bond paper (40×40 cm), included no fiducial markers or predefined dimensions, as the proposed method relies exclusively on laser spot segmentation across the surface. Notably, the procedure does not require perfect planarity of the target surface, making it suitable for practical, unprepared environments.

Figure 7. Experimental configuration showing the Technical Vision System (TVS), the stereovision module, and the planar calibration surface mounted on an optical breadboard.

A Teensy 4.1 microcontroller was used to control the stepper motors of the Technical Vision System (TVS). Communication with the host computer (Intel Core i5-10300H, 2.50 GHz, Windows OS) was established via a serial interface. Custom Python scripts executed on the laptop were responsible for motor control, image acquisition synchronization, and 3D coordinate computation.

2.4. Novel Estimation Method for Degrees-per-Step Ratio

This section presents the methodology for estimating the relationship between the number of commanded motor steps and the resulting angular displacement of the laser beam, after transmission through the gear mechanisms coupled to the motors. The approach involves capturing the 3D coordinates of the laser impact point on a surface before and after a controlled angular shift. From these data, the beam direction is computed in each configuration, and the change in inclination is used to determine the angular resolution of the system in units of degrees-per-step.

The methodology is illustrated in Figure 8. The procedure begins by projecting the TVS laser beam onto a planar surface positioned at an arbitrary distance d_1. It is essential that the laser spot remains within the field of view (FoV) of both stereo cameras throughout the process.

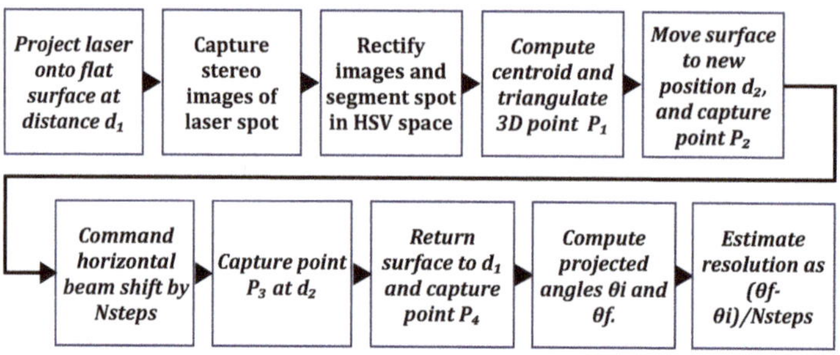

Figure 8. Flowchart of experimental procedure for degrees-per-step ratio estimation.

Next, stereo image pairs of the laser spot are captured using both cameras of the stereovision system. These images are rectified to satisfy epipolar constraints, and a region of interest is extracted and processed in the HSV color space to segment the laser spot contour. Figure 9 shows an example of the segmentation result and the identification of its centroid. Notably, the laser spot extended across multiple pixels in the images, ensuring reliable centroid estimation relative to the 1280 × 720-pixel resolution of the stereo sensors.

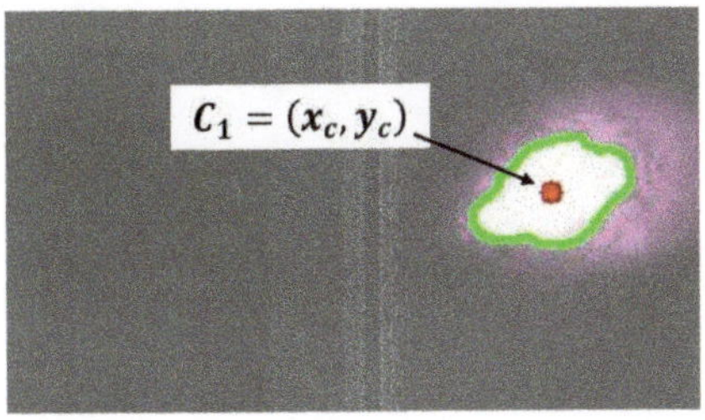

Figure 9. An example of laser spot segmentation and centroid detection. The green contour outlines the segmented region, while the red dot marks the computed centroid.

The centroid of the segmented spot, $\mathbf{C}_1 = (x_c, y_c)$, is computed from the binarized contour. This point, identified in both the left and right images, is then triangulated to obtain the 3D coordinates of the laser spot, $P_1 = (X_1, Y_1, Z_1)$, with respect to the stereo reference frame.

Next, the flat surface is moved to a new arbitrary position d_2, and the same acquisition and processing steps are repeated to obtain a second 3D point $P_2 = (X_2, Y_2, Z_2)$, corresponding to the new impact location.

Horizontal displacement of the laser beam is then performed by commanding a known number of motor steps, denoted as N_{steps}. While the surface remains fixed at d_2, a third point P_3 is acquired. The surface is then returned to its initial position d_1, and a fourth point P_4 is registered.

This sequence results in two distinct point pairs: P_1, P_2 before the beam is shifted, and P_3, P_4 afterward. Each pair defines a projected beam direction corresponding to a specific orientation of the mirror assembly driven by the stepper motor and gear transmission within the positioner subsystem of the TVS.

Figure 10 illustrates the two projected trajectories of the laser beam in the XY plane, corresponding to the beam directions before and after the commanded displacement of the mirror assembly.

Analyzing a horizontal displacement, the direction of each beam can be modeled in the XY plane, where the X-axis represents depth (i.e., distance from the stereovision system), and the Y-axis corresponds to the lateral shift of the beam. The projected angle is computed as the arctangent of the ratio between the horizontal displacement and the depth variation, as shown in Equation (4):

$$\theta_i = \tan^{-1}\left(\frac{Y_2 - Y_1}{X_2 - X_1}\right), \quad \theta_f = \tan^{-1}\left(\frac{Y_3 - Y_4}{X_3 - X_4}\right) \tag{4}$$

The angular resolution of the system, defined as the degrees-per-step ratio, is computed by dividing the difference in beam orientation angles by the number of commanded motor steps:

$$\text{Degrees-per-step ratio} = \frac{\theta_f - \theta_i}{N_{\text{steps}}} \tag{5}$$

This procedure is repeated for all four directions of motion—left, right, up, and down—to account for potential asymmetries introduced by the gear transmission, such as fabrication inconsistencies. In the case of vertical displacements, the analysis is performed in the XZ plane, where the X-axis represents depth and the Z-axis corresponds to the height of the laser spot.

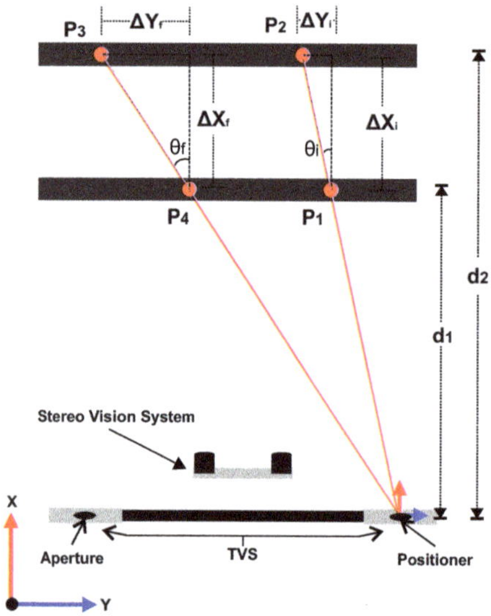

Figure 10. Angular trajectories of the laser beam projected onto the XY plane, before and after mirror actuation.

3. Results and Discussion

To implement the proposed method for characterizing the degrees-per-step ratio, a total of 24 independent experiments were conducted for each of the four movement directions of the TVS positioner: left, right, up, and down. The horizontal displacements (left and right) correspond to the Y-axis, while the vertical displacements (up and down) are associated with the Z-axis; the X-axis represents the depth direction. The aim was to experimentally evaluate the angular increment induced by each motor step, considering that it is coupled to a gear-based mechanical transmission. This entire process is performed without manual measurements, relying solely on the stereovision system as an auxiliary metrological tool.

Figure 11 illustrates the 3D coordinate measurements obtained during an experiment involving leftward displacement. Points P_1 and P_2 denote the initial position of the laser beam prior to motor actuation, whereas P_3 and P_4 correspond to its location after executing 200 motor steps. Notably, P_2 and P_3 are captured on a second position of the planar surface, which is shifted from an initial depth of approximately $d_1 = 17.5\,\text{cm}$ to $d_2 = 27.5\,\text{cm}$. The method demonstrates robustness against misalignments or placement inaccuracies of the planar target on the optical bench, as the analysis relies on stereo triangulation using 3D world-coordinate data, which contains information about the three spatial components of the laser spot and does not depend on the geometry of the optical breadboard.

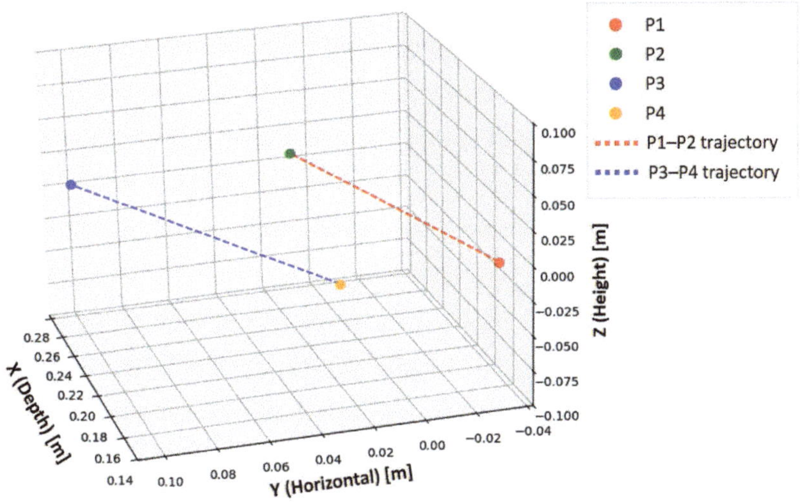

Figure 11. A 3D representation of the triangulated coordinates obtained during an experiment involving leftward laser beam displacement.

By projecting these vectors onto the XY plane, the angular inclination of each trajectory can be computed using the arctangent of the ratio between the lateral displacement and the change in depth, as expressed in Equation (6):

$$\theta_i = \tan^{-1}\left(\frac{Y_2 - Y_1}{X_2 - X_1}\right), \quad \theta_f = \tan^{-1}\left(\frac{Y_3 - Y_4}{X_3 - X_4}\right) \tag{6}$$

Figure 12 displays the projected triangles used to estimate the initial and final angles for the previously analyzed experiment.

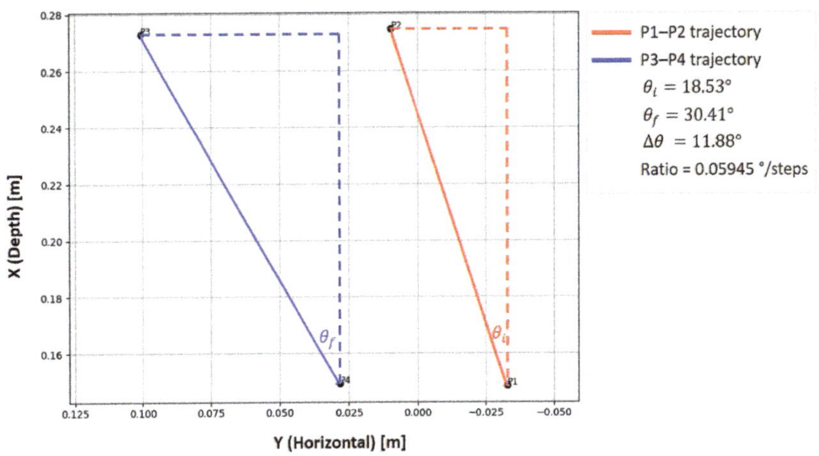

Figure 12. Estimation of the laser beam angular displacement in the XY plane, based on the projected trajectories before and after 200 motor steps.

In this particular example, the initial angle was measured as $\theta_i = 18.53°$, and the final angle as $\theta_f = 30.41°$, resulting in an angular difference of $\Delta\theta = 11.89°$. Given that

200 motor steps were applied during this experiment, the estimated ratio is presented in Equation (7):

$$\text{Degrees-per-step ratio} = \frac{\theta_f - \theta_i}{N_{\text{steps}}} = \frac{30.41^\circ - 18.53^\circ}{200} = \frac{11.89^\circ}{200} = 0.0594^\circ/\text{step} \quad (7)$$

The described procedure was repeated for the remaining three directions of motion. For rightward displacements, the same analysis in the XY plane was applied, whereas for vertical movements (upward and downward), the analysis was conducted in the XZ plane. In these cases, the depth axis was retained as the adjacent leg, and the vertical component Z was used as the opposite leg for angular estimation, which is computed according to Equation (8):

$$\theta = \tan^{-1}\left(\frac{Z_{\text{final}} - Z_{\text{initial}}}{X_{\text{final}} - X_{\text{initial}}}\right) \quad (8)$$

To assess the consistency of the results, the degrees-per-step ratio was graphically represented for each direction of motion. Figures 13–16 show the corresponding plots for the 24 experiments conducted per direction, including the overall mean and the tolerance bands corresponding to $\pm 1\sigma$, $\pm 2\sigma$, and $\pm 3\sigma$.

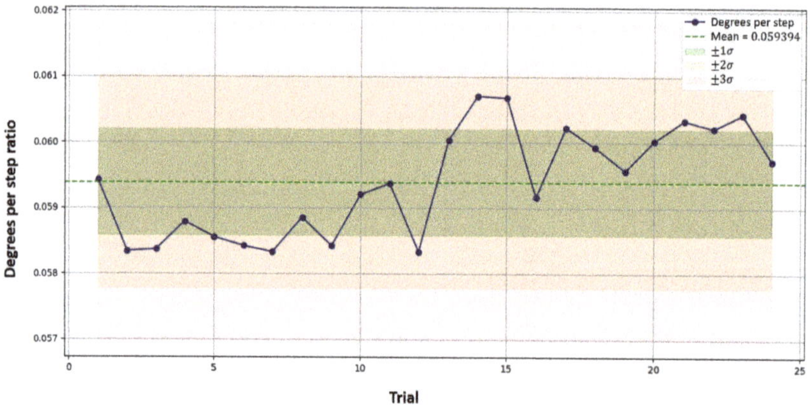

Figure 13. The statistical distribution of the degrees-per-step ratio for leftward displacements.

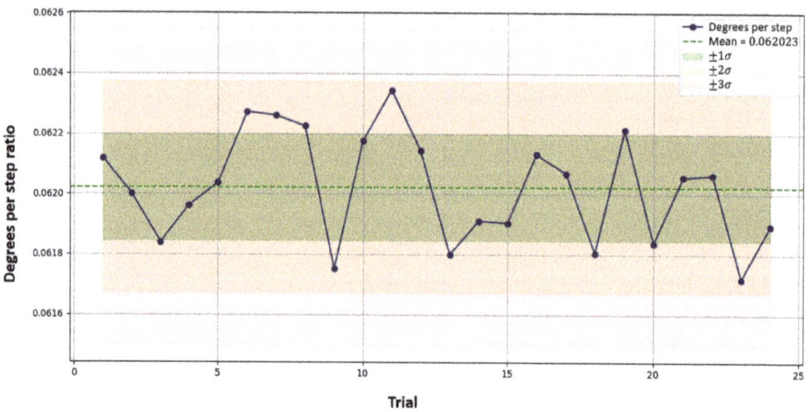

Figure 14. The statistical distribution of the degrees-per-step ratio for rightward displacements.

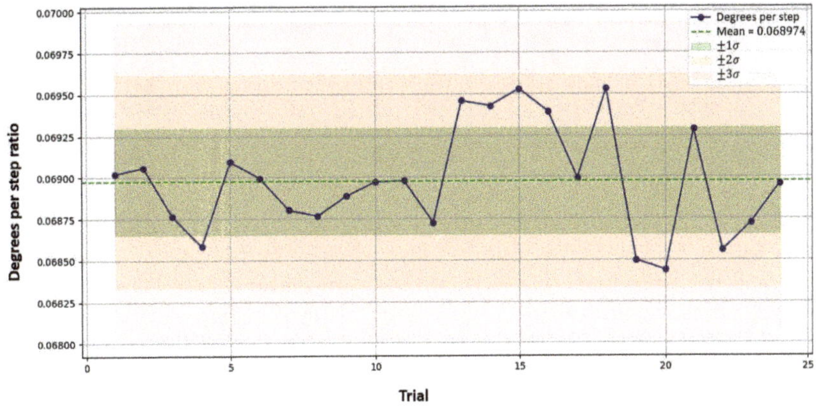

Figure 15. The statistical distribution of the degrees-per-step ratio for upward displacements.

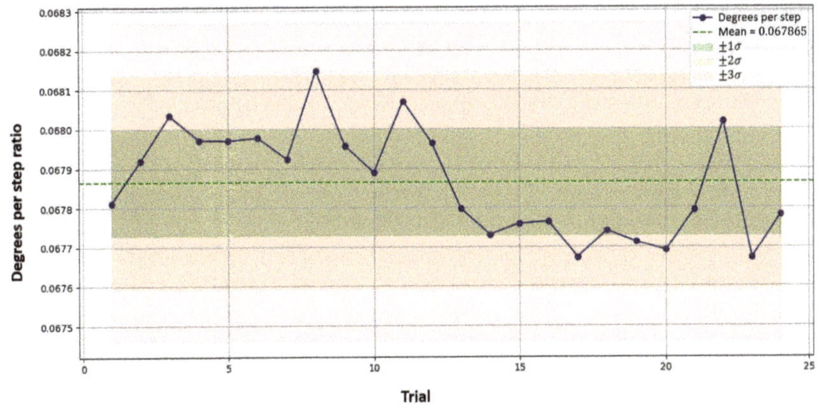

Figure 16. The statistical distribution of the degrees-per-step ratio for downward displacements.

Table 1 provides a statistical summary of the 24 experiments conducted for each direction of motion. It reports the mean and standard deviation of the degrees-per-step ratio, enabling a quantitative description of the system's behavior in each case. For the horizontal transmission, the leftward and rightward experiments yielded mean values of 0.059°/step and 0.062°/step, with standard deviations of 8.08×10^{-4}°/step and 1.76×10^{-4}°/step, respectively. The relatively small dispersion confirms the repeatability of the vision-based estimation, while the difference between leftward and rightward mean values highlights the directional anisotropy of the gear transmission. In the case of vertical motion, the upward and downward directions yielded mean values of 0.069°/step and 0.068°/step, with standard deviations below 3.2×10^{-4}°/step.

Table 1. A statistical summary of the degrees-per-step ratio for each direction of motion.

Direction	Mean [°/step]	Standard Deviation
Left (X+)	0.059394	0.000808
Right (X−)	0.062023	0.000176
Up (Z+)	0.068974	0.000319
Down (Z−)	0.067865	0.000173

Overall, the proposed method offers a non-invasive and automated solution for characterizing the laser positioner, avoiding disassembly or manual measurements. Its main limitation is the need to place a flat reference surface within the field of view, which, although practical in many setups, may constrain certain mobile or irregular scenarios.

4. Conclusions

In this work, a stereovision system previously calibrated using Zhang's method [31] was implemented as a metrological reference for the characterization of the gear-based transmission mechanisms in a Technical Vision System (TVS). This characterization is critical for accurate 3D reconstruction based on dynamic triangulation, since the identified parameter directly affects the precision of the computed 3D coordinates.

To evaluate the angular behavior of the TVS laser positioner subsystem, an experimental procedure was designed using the stereo system as an auxiliary measurement tool. This strategy enabled a high-precision estimation of the degrees-per-step ratio for the stepper motors in each motion direction of the laser positioner subsystem, including both horizontal and vertical displacements. The integration of the stereo system enhanced robustness against misplacements of the reference surface, thereby increasing the operational tolerance of the method and facilitating its use in mobile or constrained environments.

The experimental results yielded a degrees-per-step ratio of 0.059° for leftward motion, 0.062° for rightward motion, 0.069° for upward motion, and 0.068° for downward motion. These variations reveal directional anisotropy, likely caused by manufacturing tolerances or assembly misalignments in the gear transmission. Such anisotropy is particularly relevant when estimating the laser emission angle α in the dynamic triangulation method used to compute 3D coordinates with the TVS. This angle defines the laser beam's projection direction and is determined exclusively by the control commands sent to the positioner, as no feedback sensors are available to monitor its actual orientation. On the other hand, part of the observed variability may be attributed to the limited specifications of the low-cost stereo module employed in this study; nevertheless, the method proved feasible and could benefit from higher-resolution cameras in future implementations, potentially improving the segmentation reliability of the laser spot.

In addition to these experimental findings, and beyond the specific case of the TVS, the proposed vision-based characterization method for gear transmissions can be extended to other engineering systems that rely on stepper motor actuators. Potential applications include robotic platforms with hand–eye vision systems, CNC machines, and additive manufacturing equipment, where accurate motion transmission is essential and disassembly of the mechanisms is impractical. Autonomous ground vehicles equipped with 3D scanning modules for navigation, as well as agricultural robots and structural inspection systems, can also benefit from such non-invasive characterization. These examples highlight the versatility of the proposed approach as a general solution to maintain the accuracy of gear-based transmission mechanisms across diverse application domains.

Therefore, accurate and automated characterization of the mechanical subsystem is essential to ensure the metrological reliability of the TVS. The proposed method provides a non-invasive and cost-effective solution that eliminates the need for manual measurement tools or direct intervention on the laser scanner. It relies solely on two controlled displacements of a planar surface placed in front of the system, which significantly simplifies implementation and enables seamless integration into self-calibration routines. In future work, this method is envisioned to be deployed on a mobile robot platform, where the required spatial displacements can be performed autonomously by the robot itself, eliminating the need to manipulate the calibration target manually.

Author Contributions: Conceptualization, F.L.-M.; methodology, F.L.-M.; software, R.A.-P.; validation, C.S.-V. and J.R.H.-G.; formal analysis, D.M.-Q. and V.T.; investigation, J.A.N.-L. and J.R.H.-G.; resources, O.S.; data curation, C.S.-V.; writing—original draft preparation, F.L.-M.; writing—review and editing, J.A.N.-L.; visualization, D.M.-Q.; supervision, R.A.-P. and O.S.; project administration, R.A.-P.; funding acquisition, O.S. All authors have read and agreed to the published version of the manuscript.

Funding: This research received no external funding.

Data Availability Statement: The original contributions presented in the study are included in the article; further inquiries can be directed to the corresponding author.

Acknowledgments: The authors of this work would like to thank the anonymous reviewers for their valuable support.

Conflicts of Interest: The authors declare no conflicts of interest.

Abbreviations

The following abbreviations are used in this manuscript:

TVS	Technical Vision System
LiDAR	Light Detection and Ranging
3D	Three-Dimensional
ToF	Time of Flight
FoV	Field of View
HSV	Hue, Saturation, Value

References

1. Qin, H.; Bi, Y.; Feng, L.; Zhang, Y.F.; Chen, B.M. A 3D Rotating Laser-Based Navigation Solution for Micro Aerial Vehicles in Dynamic Environments. *Unmanned Syst.* **2018**, *6*, 297–305. [CrossRef]
2. Hayashi, T.; Mori, N.; Ueno, T. Non-contact imaging of subsurface defects using a scanning laser source. *Ultrasonics* **2022**, *119*, 106560. [CrossRef]
3. Stavropoulos, P. Digitization of Manufacturing Processes: From Sensing to Twining. *Technologies* **2022**, *10*, 98. [CrossRef]
4. Huang, Z.; Li, D. A 3D reconstruction method based on one-dimensional galvanometer laser scanning system. *Opt. Lasers Eng.* **2023**, *170*, 107787. [CrossRef]
5. Tran, T.Q.; Becker, A.; Grzechca, D. Environment Mapping Using Sensor Fusion of 2D Laser Scanner and 3D Ultrasonic Sensor for a Real Mobile Robot. *Sensors* **2021**, *21*, 3184. [CrossRef]
6. Lee, M.J.; Park, S.Y. Forward and Backward Propagation of Stereo Matching Cost for Incremental Refinement of Multiview Disparity Maps. *IEEE Access* **2022**, *10*, 134074–134085. [CrossRef]
7. Chiang, P.J.; Lin, C.H. Active Stereo Vision System with Rotated Structured Light Patterns and Two-Step Denoising Process for Improved Spatial Resolution. *Opt. Lasers Eng.* **2022**, *152*, 106958. [CrossRef]
8. Wu, Z.; Nan, M.; Zhang, H.; Huo, J.; Chen, S.; Chen, G.; Cheng, Z. Photogrammetric system of non-central refractive camera based on two-view 3D reconstruction. *ISPRS J. Photogramm. Remote Sens.* **2025**, *222*, 112–129. [CrossRef]
9. Lopez-Medina, F.; Alaniz-Plata, R.; Sergiyenko, O.; Núñez-López, J.A.; Sepulveda-Valdez, C.; Meza-García, D.; Villa-Manríquez, J.F.; Andrade-Collazo, H.; Flores-Fuentes, W.; Rodríguez-Quiñonez, J.C.; et al. Extrinsic Calibration Method Under Low-Light Conditions for Hybrid Vision System. In Proceedings of the 2025 International Aegean Conference on Electrical Machines and

Power Electronics (ACEMP) & 2025 International Conference on Optimization of Electrical and Electronic Equipment (OPTIM), Timisoara, Romania, 14–17 May 2025; pp. 1–7. [CrossRef]
10. Wang, W.; Luo, R.; Yang, W.; Liu, J. Unsupervised Illumination Adaptation for Low-Light Vision. *IEEE Trans. Pattern Anal. Mach. Intell.* **2024**, *46*, 5951–5966. [CrossRef]
11. Zhang, X.; Guan, Z.; Liu, X.; Zhang, Z. Digital Reconstruction Method for Low-Illumination Road Traffic Accident Scenes Using UAV and Auxiliary Equipment. *World Electr. Veh. J.* **2025**, *16*, 171. [CrossRef]
12. Wang, Z.; Wu, Y.; Li, D.; Li, G.; Zhu, P.; Zhang, Z.; Jiang, R. LiDAR-assisted image restoration for extreme low-light conditions. *Knowl.-Based Syst.* **2025**, *316*, 113382. [CrossRef]
13. Agishev, R.; Comerón, A.; Bach, J.; Rodriguez, A.; Sicard, M.; Riu, J.; Royo, S. Lidar with SiPM: Some capabilities and limitations in real environment. *Opt. Laser Technol.* **2013**, *49*, 86–90. [CrossRef]
14. Li, Y.; Ibanez-Guzman, J. Lidar for Autonomous Driving: The Principles, Challenges, and Trends for Automotive Lidar and Perception Systems. *IEEE Signal Process. Mag.* **2020**, *37*, 50–61. [CrossRef]
15. Trautmann, T.; Blechschmidt, F.; Friedrich, M.; Mendt, F. Possibilities and Limitations of Object Detection Using Lidar. In *Proceedings of the 23. Internationales Stuttgarter Symposium*; Kulzer, A.C., Reuss, H.C., Wagner, A., Eds.; Springer Vieweg: Wiesbaden, Germany , 2023; pp. 36–43. [CrossRef]
16. Sergiyenko, O.; Alaniz-Plata, R.; Flores-Fuentes, W.; Rodríguez-Quiñonez, J.C.; Miranda-Vega, J.E.; Sepulveda-Valdez, C.; Núñez-López, J.A.; Kolendovska, M.; Kartashov, V.; Tyrsa, V. Multi-view 3D data fusion and patching to reduce Shannon entropy in Robotic Vision. *Opt. Lasers Eng.* **2024**, *177*, 108132. [CrossRef]
17. Alaniz-Plata, R.; Lopez-Medina, F.; Sergiyenko, O.; Flores-Fuentes, W.; Rodríguez-Quiñonez, J.C.; Sepulveda-Valdez, C.; Núñez-López, J.A.; Meza-García, D.; Villa-Manríquez, J.F.; Andrade-Collazo, H.; et al. Extrinsic calibration of complex machine vision system for mobile robot. *Integration* **2025**, *102*, 102370. [CrossRef]
18. Surmann, H.; Nüchter, A.; Hertzberg, J. An autonomous mobile robot with a 3D laser range finder for 3D exploration and digitalization of indoor environments. *Robot. Auton. Syst.* **2003**, *45*, 181–198. [CrossRef]
19. Blais, F.o. Review of 20 years of range sensor development. *J. Electron. Imaging* **2004**, *13*, 231–243. [CrossRef]
20. Dorsch, R.G.; Häusler, G.; Herrmann, J.M. Laser triangulation: Fundamental uncertainty in distance measurement. *Appl. Opt.* **1994**, *33*, 1306–1314. [CrossRef]
21. Gerbino, S.; Del Giudice, D.M.; Staiano, G.; Lanzotti, A.; Martorelli, M. On the influence of scanning factors on the laser scanner-based 3D inspection process. *Int. J. Adv. Manuf. Technol.* **2016**, *84*, 1787–1799. [CrossRef]
22. Sergiyenko, O.; Núñez-López, J.A.; Tyrsa, V.; Alaniz-Plata, R.; Pérez-Landeros, O.M.; Selpúlveda-Valdez, C.; Flores-Fuentes, W.; Rodríguez-Quiñonez, J.C.; Murrieta-Rico, F.N.; Kartashov, V.; et al. 3D coordinate sensing with nonsmooth friction dynamical discontinuities compensation in laser scanning system. *Mechatronics* **2025**, *110*, 103382. [CrossRef]
23. Zhang, M.; Zhang, Z.; Xiong, J.; Chen, X. Accuracy Analysis of Complex Transmission System with Distributed Tooth Profile Errors. *Machines* **2024**, *12*, 459. [CrossRef]
24. Zhou, D.; Guo, Y.; Yang, J.; Zhang, Y. Study on the Parameter Influences of Gear Tooth Profile Modification and Transmission Error Analysis. *Machines* **2024**, *12*, 316. [CrossRef]
25. Theodossiades, S.; Natsiavas, S. Periodic and chaotic dynamics of motor-driven gear-pair systems with backlash. *Chaos Solitons Fractals* **2001**, *12*, 2427–2440. [CrossRef]
26. Xun, C.; Long, X.; Hua, H. Effects of random tooth profile errors on the dynamic behaviors of planetary gears. *J. Sound Vib.* **2018**, *415*, 91–110. [CrossRef]
27. Lyu, X.; Liu, S.; Qiao, R.; Jiang, S.; Wang, Y. Camera, LiDAR, and IMU Spatiotemporal Calibration: Methodological Review and Research Perspectives. *Sensors* **2025**, *25*, 5409. [CrossRef]
28. Domhof, J.; Kooij, J.F.; Gavrila, D.M. An Extrinsic Calibration Tool for Radar, Camera and Lidar. In Proceedings of the 2019 International Conference on Robotics and Automation (ICRA), Montreal, QC, Canada, 20–24 May 2019; pp. 8107–8113. [CrossRef]
29. Domhof, J.; Kooij, J.F.P.; Gavrila, D.M. A Joint Extrinsic Calibration Tool for Radar, Camera and Lidar. *IEEE Trans. Intell. Veh.* **2021**, *6*, 571–582. [CrossRef]
30. Wang, X.; Yao, T.; Shi, Z. Calibration Method Based on Virtual Gear Artefact for Computer Vision Measuring Instrument of Fine Pitch Gear. *Sensors* **2024**, *24*, 2289. [CrossRef] [PubMed]
31. Zhang, Z. A flexible new technique for camera calibration. *IEEE Trans. Pattern Anal. Mach. Intell.* **2000**, *22*, 1330–1334. [CrossRef]

metrology

MDPI

Article

Towards the Development of an Optical Quantum Frequency Standard Feasible for a Medium-Size NMI

Adriana Palos [1,2,*], Ismael Caballero [1,3], Daniel de Mercado [1], Yolanda Álvarez [1], David Peral [1] and Javier Díaz de Aguilar [1]

[1] Centro Español de Metrología, 28760 Tres Cantos, Spain; icaballeroi@cem.es or i.ciglesias@alumnos.upm.es (I.C.); dmercado@cem.es (D.d.M.); yalvarezs@cem.es (Y.Á.); dperal@cem.es (D.P.); jdiaz@cem.es (J.D.d.A.)

[2] Facultad de Ciencias Físicas, Universidad Complutense de Madrid, 28040 Madrid, Spain

[3] Escuela Técnica Superior de Ingeniería y Diseño Industrial, Universidad Politécnica de Madrid, 28012 Madrid, Spain

[*] Correspondence: apalos@cem.es or apalos@ucm.es

Abstract: Centro Español de Metrología (CEM) is developing a quantum frequency standard based on trapped calcium ions, marking its entry into the landscape of the second quantum revolution. Optical frequency standards offer unprecedented precision by referencing atomic transitions that are fundamentally stable and immune to environmental drift. However, the challenge of developing such a system from scratch is unaffordable for a medium-sized National Metrology Institute (NMI), which seems to limit the ability of an institute such as CEM to contribute to this field of research. To overcome this, CEM has adopted a hybrid strategy, combining commercially available components with custom integration to accelerate deployment. This paper defines and implements an architecture adapted to the constraints of a medium-size NMI, where the main contribution is the systematic design, selection, and interconnection of the subsystems required to realize this standard. The rationale behind the system design is presented, detailing the integration of key elements for ion trapping, laser stabilization, frequency measurement, and system control. Current progress, ongoing developments, and future research directions are outlined, establishing the foundation for spectroscopic measurements and uncertainty evaluation. The project represents a strategic step toward strengthening national capabilities in quantum metrology for a medium-sized NMI.

Keywords: calcium optical frequency standard; National Metrology Institute; set-up definition

1. Introduction

The fundamental advantage of optical quantum frequency standards is that, by working in the optical regime with different atomic or ionic species, better instability and uncertainty than those of caesium clocks can be achieved. However, the operation of these optical clocks relies on two fundamental technological advances. The first is the application of cutting-edge techniques for laser cooling, trapping, and the coherent interrogation of species that exhibit narrow optical transitions which need to be resolved. The second is the development of ultra-precise frequency metrology tools, such as frequency combs, which provide the ability to measure optical frequencies with high resolution [1]. As a consequence, advancements in these fields have led to research on and the development of optical clocks by many different groups using two leading architectures: optical lattices [2] and trapped ions [3].

At CEM, there is an awareness of the duty and responsibility NMIs have when implementing these advances, ensuring that the potential of quantum technologies is transformed into tangible benefits for science, industry, and society.

For this reason, considering the importance that optical frequency standards can have both for science and for the future redefinition, or *mise en pratique*, of the second [4], CEM is developing a standard based on ion-trapping technology. However, while keeping up to date with innovations is a major concern for the entire community, even more challenges arise when talking about medium-sized NMIs, such as CEM. Because of this, CEM has decided to approach frequency metrology from a different point of view, through the establishment of a frequency standard based on calcium ions, which will enable the use of commercially available equipment and therefore allowing an institute without a previous group working in the time and frequency domain to conduct new quantum standards research.

The research of this NMI is being developed through the MADQuantum–CM project, aimed at revolutionizing communications through the use of quantum technologies. To this end, as a network node, CEM will provide a frequency reference, which is essential for the synchronization of the nodes in the communication network [5].

2. State of the Art

Given the relevance optical clocks have, numerous developments are being made, from progress on optical lattice clocks with single species [6] to dual-mode operation [7], as well as developments in ion-trapped clocks [8].

Not only are these investigations reducing possible sources of noise, and therefore reaching uncertainties of 10^{-18} [9], they are also leading to the development of transportable clocks for comparisons between different systems [10]. Along those lines, companies all over the world are diving into the development of the state-of-the-art technology comprising optical clocks, such as ultra-stable lasers and ion traps, with the aim of developing commercially available optical clocks. It is with this technology that CEM is establishing its frequency standard.

3. Operational Principle

The isotope ^{40}Ca is the most naturally abundant form of calcium and possesses two valence electrons in the 4s orbital. Notably, it has zero nuclear spin, which eliminates hyperfine splitting and thereby simplifies its atomic energy level structure, as illustrated in Figure 1a. The relevant electronic transitions for this work span wavelengths from 375 nm to 866 nm, all of which are accessible using commercially available laser systems. Furthermore, not only are the lasers involved available but, as described in Section 4, the ion trap system itself is a commercial solution [11] developed by Alpine Quantum Technologies (AQT, Innsbruck, Austria). For this reason, ^{40}Ca ions are the ideal candidate for the realization of an optical frequency standard at CEM.

The procedure for realizing a frequency standard using a $^{40}Ca^{+}$ optical ion clock [12] begins with the generation of a low-pressure calcium vapor. This is achieved by ablating a calcium target, often referred to as a "waffle", using a 515 nm pulsed laser, Coherent Flare NX 515 (Saxonburg, PA, USA). The resulting neutral atoms are then selectively ionized through a two-step photoionization process employing 423 nm and 375 nm lasers, Toptica's MDL and iBeam smart (Munich, Germany), as illustrated in Figure 1b. The produced ions are subsequently confined in a linear Paul trap, AQT's PINE SET-UP, consisting of four electrodes and two endcaps [13]. Once trapped, the ions undergo a multi-stage cooling sequence—Doppler cooling, polarization gradient cooling, and sideband cooling—to reduce their motional energy within the trap. This cooling is facilitated by lasers at 397 nm and 729 nm, along with repumping lasers at 866 nm and 854 nm, which are included in the Toptica's MDL laser system, to prevent population-trapping in metastable D states during cooling and detection. The clock transition is driven by a highly stable 729 nm spectroscopy laser, Hz laser, whose frequency is locked using the Pound–Drever–Hall (PDH) technique [14]. State-selective detection is performed via fluorescence monitoring on the strong dipole-allowed $4S_{1/2}$–$4P_{1/2}$ transition at 397 nm. Ions in the ground state scatter photons, while those excited to the metastable $3D_{5/2}$ state remain dark, a method known as electron shelving, which enables high-fidelity quantum state discrimination. Finally, the frequency of the ultra-stable laser probing the clock transition is measured using a fiber-based optical frequency comb, FC 1500-ULN from Menlo Systems (Martinsried, Germany), ensuring the traceability of the system.

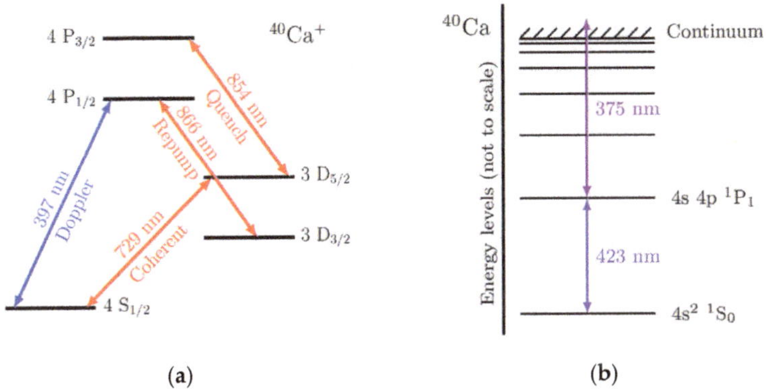

Figure 1. (**a**) Schematic diagram of the $^{40}Ca^+$ atomic structure; (**b**) schematic of the levels used in calcium to obtain photoionization.

4. Conceptual Design

As key components of the experimental setup necessary for the loading, trapping, cooling, and detection of the ions, the following elements are needed.

4.1. Ablation Laser

Although calcium ions can be generated through the use of an oven, this method has been proven to introduce contamination to the trap blades and degrade the vacuum conditions [15]. Oven-based loading typically requires a warm-up period ranging from seconds to minutes, during which the generated heat can cause residual heating of the trap and surrounding vacuum components. In addition, oxidation of the oven material can shorten its operational lifetime [16]. By contrast, laser ablation provides immediate temporal control: the production of neutral atoms can be started or stopped instantaneously. It also offers a highly localized source, faster and more precise timing of ion loading, and significantly reduced thermal load on the ion trap [17]. Although ovens are mechanically simpler and avoid the need for an ablation laser, they require continuous heating and can introduce long-term thermal stress and unwanted deposition, which is undesirable in precision systems. Consequently, ablation loading is a reliable approach for ion trap loading [18], and the preferred procedure for our system. This, combined with photoionization ensures isotope selectivity and controlled ion loading, forming an optimal strategy for precision ion trap experiments.

As outlined in Section 4.4, the PINE SET-UP is designed for the employment of an ablation laser available for the different ion species. For $^{40}Ca^+$, a single pulse at 515 nm from a passively Q-switched diode-pumped solid-state (DPSS) laser, offering a pulse duration of ~1 ns, is directed at the calcium target to produce a neutral atomic gas. The selected system for this is the Coherent Flare NX 515, a short-pulsed DPSS laser featuring a pulse width of 1.3 ns and a repetition rate of 2 kHz. The pulses are triggered via a transistor transistor logic (TTL) signal controlled through the system described in Section 4.7.

4.2. Laser System

The system is equipped with Toptica's iBeam smart, a high-performance single-mode diode laser operating at 375 nm. This free-running diode laser supports external asynchronous digital modulation, making it suitable for precision applications. As described in Section 3, isotope-selective photoionization is achieved through a two-step process: the first step employs an external cavity diode laser (ECDL) at 423 nm to enable isotope selectivity, followed by ionization using the 375 nm iBeam smart laser.

Complementing this setup is Toptica's modular, tunable single-mode diode laser system, the MDL pro, which integrates four narrow-linewidth diode lasers used in CEM's experimental platform. These include lasers at 397 nm, 423 nm, 854 nm, and 866 nm. The MDL pro system is designed for low-noise operation, providing a typical linewidth of 150 kHz over 5 μs for the cooling and ionization lasers [19], and offers remote control capabilities via the digital control unit (DLC pro), enhancing stability and flexibility.

To ensure precise frequency stabilization, a low-finesse, low-drift optical reference cavity is employed. Active stabilization is achieved via a feedback loop that precisely controls the cavity length through piezoelectric and thermal actuators, ensuring sustained resonance with a caesium reference [20]. AQT's Beech module, equipped with integrated proportional–integral (PI) controllers, can simultaneously stabilize the frequencies of up to four laser wavelengths. By utilizing external frequency shifters, the Beech module compensates for discrepancies between the target laser frequencies and the cavity's resonance modes.

The system is optimized for use with the calcium-specific wavelengths provided by the MDL pro unit, that is, 397 nm, 423 nm, 854 nm, and 866 nm. The fiber-optic connections between the lasers, reference outputs, and cavity ensure seamless integration and reliable operation, making the Beech module a natural choice for CEM's optical frequency standard.

Additionally, AQT's ROWAN module has been incorporated into the setup. This module features an acousto-optic modulator (AOM) in a double-pass configuration, enabling precise frequency shifting, pulse modulation, and dynamic control of the laser beams.

4.3. High Stability Laser

In the development of a trapped-ion optical frequency standard, the ultra-stable laser is a critical component for achieving the precision and accuracy required in high-end metrology. Its frequency is stabilized using feedback control loops, most notably the Pound–Drever–Hall (PDH) technique, which locks the laser to a resonance mode of a Fabry–Pérot optical cavity acting as a narrowband frequency filter. This locking mechanism enables extremely low linewidths [21–23] in the order of sub-hertz, essential for long-term stability. For this purpose, Toptica provides an ultra-stable clock laser system, its clock laser system, Hz Laser, specifically designed for optical clocks, offering a linewidth below 1 Hz at one-second integration time.

To maintain spectral purity during transmission, the laser beam passes through a series of Fiber Noise Cancellation (FNC) modules [24]. These modules actively compensate for phase fluctuations introduced by light propagation through the optical fiber, using AOMs and radio-frequency (RF) modulation of both frequency and amplitude. The stabilized beam is then directed into an acoustically and thermally isolated cavity setup, which enables the PDH technique to be used. Finally, the PDH error signal is processed via Toptica's Fast Analog Linewidth Control (FALC) pro and DLC pro modules, which feed back into the control loop to maintain laser stability.

4.4. Ion Trap

Building on advancements in trapped-ion quantum technologies, Alpine Quantum Technologies (AQT) developed the PINE TRAP system, based on the design of the University of Innsbruck and the Institute of Quantum Optics and Quantum Information (IQOQI). Through the meticulous selection of materials and precision fabrication techniques, the system achieves optimized thermal and electrical conductivity. As a result, it enables exceptionally low heating rates, less than one phonon per second at a trap frequency of 500 kHz, making it highly suitable for precision quantum control.

The ion trap is housed within an ultra-high-vacuum chamber, integrated into AQT's modular PINE SET-UP platform. This comprehensive setup includes not only the trap and vacuum chamber, but also an RF resonator, vacuum pump, high numerical aperture (NA) objective lens, a pump controller, multiple optical access ports for cooling, detection, ablation loading, and photoionization lasers. The modularity and compactness of the PINE TRAP system facilitate streamlined installation and operation.

In addition to these elements, the system incorporates a magnetic control architecture designed to ensure stable operation of the ions. This consists of three pairs of electromagnetic coils mounted along the principal axis of the setup. Although these coils provide controlled stabilization of the magnetic field, and given the high-sensitivity of calcium ions to magnetic fluctuations, additional shielding is required. For this purpose, a μ-metal shield is planned. Its design is currently in progress, and a study of its effect on the overall system performance will be carried out.

It is by acquiring this solution that CEM has been able to establish a foothold in the time and frequency metrology community. As a medium-sized NMI, the in-house development of a custom ion trap would have required substantial time and resources, potentially delaying progress on optical frequency standards for years. In addition, the choice of the AQT PINE TRAP was guided by its proven reliability, the availability of technical support, and its compatibility with commercially available subsystems, factors that aligned with CEM's hybrid integration strategy and ultimately made it the most suitable option for the project, balancing reliability, integration feasibility, and institutional constraints. The adoption of AQT's commercial system thus represents a strategic and efficient path toward cutting-edge timekeeping capabilities.

4.5. Frequency Comb

One of the centerpieces of an optical frequency standard is the optical frequency comb [25], which enables the down-conversion of the stabilized laser frequency, which is locked to the transition into the microwave or RF domain. This conversion allows the resulting frequencies to be distributed and processed using conventional electronic systems. The integration of the frequency comb is essential for the project in order to distribute the reference to the quantum communication network.

The frequency comb operates by circulating a single laser pulse within an optical cavity, generating a train of pulses separated by the cavity's round-trip time. The rate at which these pulses are emitted is known as the repetition rate. Each pulse is nearly identical, except for a phase shift between the carrier wave and the intensity envelope, referred to as the carrier–envelope offset (CEO) phase [26].

For this implementation, the Menlo Systems fiber-based optical frequency comb, FC 1500-ULN, is used, offering a repetition rate of 250 MHz and a CEO frequency of 20 MHz. To achieve a stabilized frequency signal, two free parameters must be stabilized: the comb spacing and the comb offset. To access the frequency offset of the FC1500 optical frequency synthesizer, the laser output is amplified in an erbium-doped fiber amplifier (EDFA), specifically P250 PM Pulse EDFA unit. Moreover, in combination with the P50 PM module, the High-Power Measuring Port (HMP) delivers a fiber-coupled, stabilized comb output.

In addition, the MVIS amplifier and control module incorporates a Second Harmonic Generation (SHG) and spectral extension into the visible range by means of a Photonic Crystal Fiber (PCF). This configuration extends the stabilized comb spectrum to the 500–1050 nm range by amplifying the light from the fiber ring, where the frequency is doubled and sent to a highly non-linear fiber for spectral broadening. To interface with the clock laser, the Beat Detection Unit (BDU), at 729 nm, generates and measures the beat signal between the comb and the external continuous wave laser through fiber-coupled optics.

As previously noted, ultra-low-noise microwave generation in the MHz and GHz range is especially needed when aiming to distribute the reference frequency. The Microwave Ultrastable RF Output module provides a commercial solution utilizing a high-sensitive photodetector and a frequency divider.

Figure 2 presents a schematic overview of the Menlo Systems's setup where the units, from top to bottom, are MVIS SHG, P250 PM Pulse EDFA with HMP, FC1500-ULN, BDU 729, and the Microwave extension package. This system comprises the optical frequency comb, a technology whose evolution over recent decades [27] has been noteworthy in advancing time precision and frequency metrology.

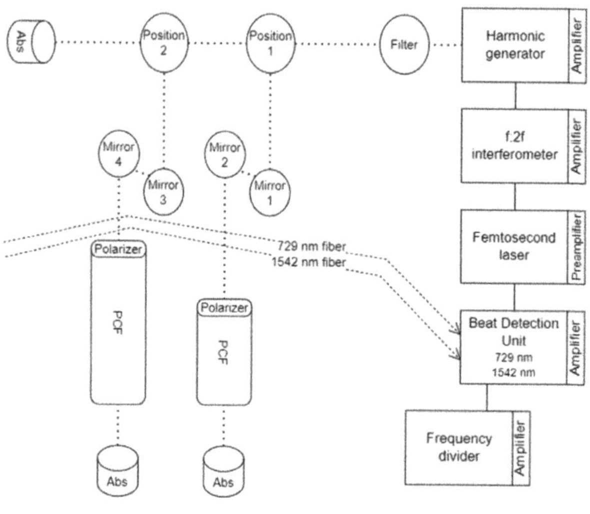

Figure 2. Schematic overview of the optical frequency comb setup.

4.6. Detection System

A robust detection system is required for a range of tasks in an optical frequency standard, including frequency monitoring, stability control, and fluorescence detection. These applications demand high sensitivity and fast frame rates to accurately capture the weak fluorescence signals emitted by trapped ions. Different tools can be used for fluorescence detection, from photomultiplier tubes (PMT) to avalanche photodiodes (APD) [28]. Among the various options, an electron-multiplying charge-coupled device (EMCCD) was selected for the present system. While PMT and APDs offer excellent time resolution and sensitivity for single-channel photon-counting, they do not provide spatial information. In contrast, the EMCCD allows us to directly image the ion fluorescence, which allows for successful ion-trapping to be confirmed. In addition, this system enables not only spatial resolution to be recorded, but also the temporal evolution of the ion position inside the trap, offering different acquisition modes [29]. At this stage of the project, the EMCCD provides evidence of ion confinement and enables the alignment and optimization of the trapping setup.

The specific model chosen is the Andor iXon Ultra 897 (Oxford Instruments, Abingdon, UK), a widely adopted solution in ion spectroscopy experiments due to its properties. This is made up of a back-illuminated 512 × 512 sensor with 16 μm × 16 μm pixel size and an electron multiplier gain up to 1000, which allows for single photon detection. Furthermore, the camera supports a frame rate of 56 fps and incorporates a thermoelectric cooling system that significantly reduces dark current, thereby minimizing thermal noise and enhancing signal fidelity.

4.7. Control System

Automatization, synchronization, and system control are some of the most critical processes in experiments with high requirements, such as those involving an optical frequency standard. Due to this, a control system which allows for high precision is needed for tasks such as laser control, frequency modulation, data acquisition, or even the execution of precise experimental sequences. For this purpose, the ARTIQ control framework [30] was adopted, in combination with various modules of the Sinara hardware.

At the core of the control architecture is the Kasli v2.0.2 FPGA carrier board from Creotech Instruments (Piaseczno, Poland), which serves as the master or main controller. Its FPGA is part of the Artiq-7 family, specially designed for high-performance applications, and includes 512 MB of DDR3 RAM. The board features 12 Eurorack Extension Module (EEM) ports, enabling seamless integration with the rest of the modules. A digital input/output extension module, specifically the DIO SMA v1.4.2, was acquired. It provides eight digital I/O channels organized into two banks with switchable directionality. The delivered outputs can supply TTL level signals into 50 Ω loads with pulse widths as short as 5 ns. This is necessary, for example, for laser pulse triggering, as stated in Section 4.1.

For RF signal generation with high-accuracy, DDS Urukul v1.5.5 modules were selected in both available models: AD9910 and AD9912. These modules are needed for the control of different optical components, such as AOMs or electro-optic modulators (EOMs). Each unit offers four independent channels which can generate frequency signals over 400 MHz, with a resolution of 0.25 Hz and 8 μHz for AD9910 and AD9912, respectively, and with power attenuation ranging from 0 dBm up to −31.5 dBm.

However, the Urukul output has limited power, which can limit the correct operation of the AOMs and EOMs. To address this, a Booster which amplifies the RF signal up to useful levels for these devices was acquired, specifically the High-Linearity Booster from Creotech Instruments. This device counts eight channels, each with up to 5 W output power and 32 dB power gain.

Finally, accurate and high-speed data acquisition is a vital aspect of system control. For this, the Sampler v2.3.1 analog-to-digital converter (ADC) module was selected. It features eight input channels with an update rate of up to 1.5 MSPS (mega-samples per second), enabling real-time monitoring and the implementation of digital feedback loops within the control system.

4.8. General Overview

The experimental platform developed at CEM for realizing a trapped-ion optical frequency standard brings together a tightly integrated set of subsystems, each tailored for precision, stability, and scalability. At its core is a modular infrastructure built around a commercial ion trap system, housed in an ultra-high-vacuum environment and supported by dedicated electronics and optics for ion generation, cooling, and interrogation.

Laser systems span a broad spectral range and serve multiple roles—from ablation loading and isotope-selective photoionization to Doppler and sideband cooling. A key element is the ultra-stable clock laser, at 729 nm, whose frequency is locked to $^{40}Ca^{+}$ narrow atomic transition, using high-finesse cavity stabilization techniques. This laser forms the basis of the optical reference and is distributed through noise-canceled fiber links to maintain coherence across the setup.

To bridge the optical and microwave domains, a fiber-based optical frequency comb enables traceable frequency measurements and supports synchronization with external systems.

Detection is carried out using high-sensitivity imaging hardware capable of resolving single-ion fluorescence, while control and timing are orchestrated through a flexible FPGA-based system that supports real-time sequencing and feedback.

The schematic in Figure 3 illustrates the interplay between these components, highlighting the layered architecture that underpins the system's performance. Together, they form a robust foundation for advanced time and frequency metrology, and position CEM to contribute to emerging quantum technologies and international standards.

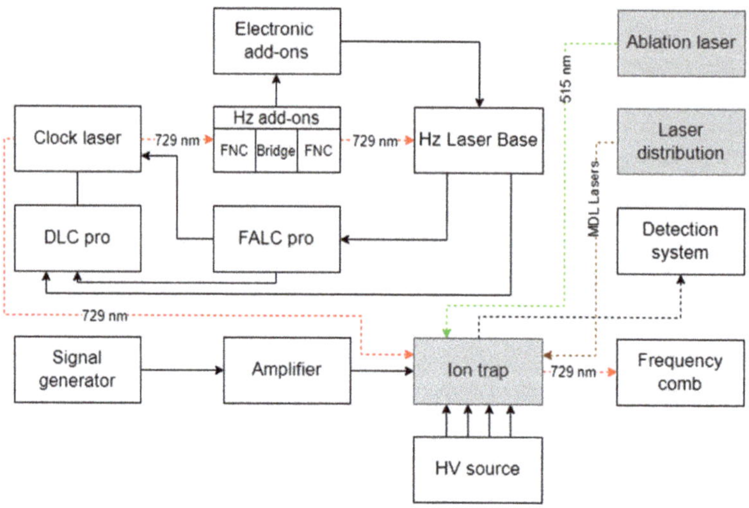

(a)

Figure 3. *Cont.*

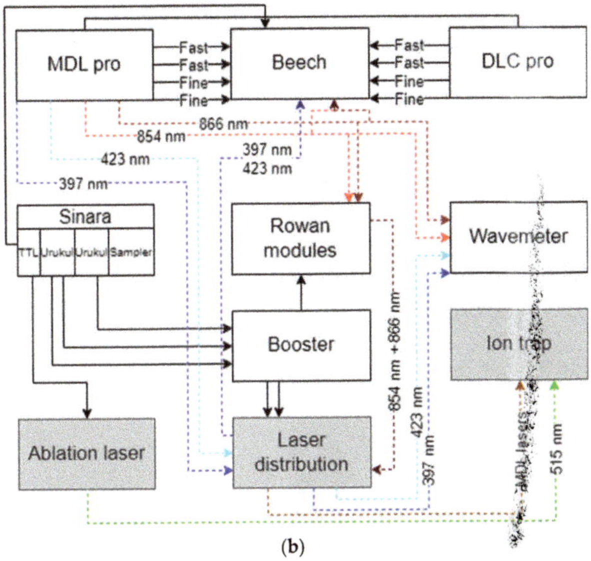

(**b**)

Figure 3. Schematic overview of the integration of all systems. (**a**) Integration of ultra-stable laser, frequency comb, and detection unit; (**b**) integration of MDL lasers and control systems.

5. Outlook

With the installation of the system completed and the first ions successfully trapped earlier this year, as illustrated in Figure 4, CEM now enters a critical phase in the development of its optical frequency standard. The immediate objective is to carry out initial spectroscopic experiments, accurately measure the clock transition of the trapped $^{40}Ca^{+}$ ions, perform Rabi and Ramsey sequences, conduct magnetic field characterization and compensation, and validate ion-trap characteristics such as heating rate. These activities form part of a broader verification and validation strategy that will progressively establish the system's uncertainty budget. Achieving this requires the full deployment of the control infrastructure, centered around the ARTIQ framework and the selected Sinara hardware modules.

The control software must be developed to handle a wide range of tasks, from basic TTL signal generation and the triggering of single laser pulses to the execution of complex pulse sequences. These capabilities will support the first experimental procedures, including ion detection, probing of the clock transition, and real-time data acquisition. In parallel, system monitoring and visualization is implemented using Grafana [31], allowing for the intuitive graphical control of laser parameters, such as laser current, temperature, applied piezo control voltage, lock status and lock slow signals of the MDL lasers, environmental conditions, such as the temperature and humidity of the laboratory, chambers and EOM temperatures, and hardware interconnections, Beech cavity transmission values and imaging, cavity pressure, ion pump current, temperature, battery voltage, and the pressure of the 729 nm high-finesse cavity.

Once the initial spectroscopy is completed, attention will shift to characterizing and quantifying systematic frequency shifts that affect the accuracy of the standard. These include Zeeman shifts due to magnetic fields, second-order Doppler shifts from residual ion motion, and excess micromotion within the trap. Special consideration will be given to the potential mitigation offered by operating at the magic wavelength [32,33], which can suppress certain systematic effects. The results of these measurements will feed directly into the evaluation of the standard's uncertainty budget.

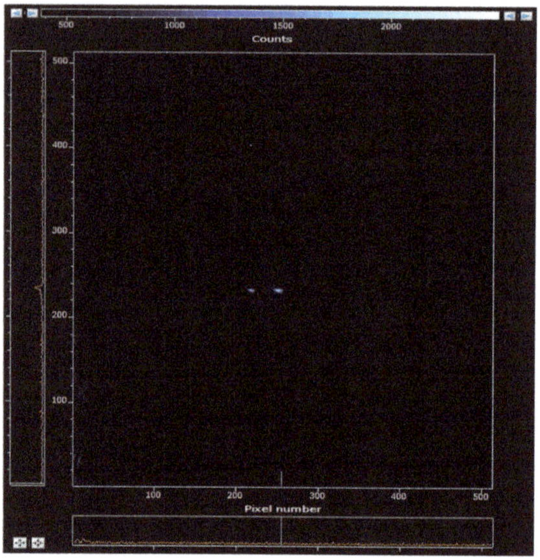

Figure 4. EMCCD camera image of the first trapped ions.

Looking ahead, CEM aims to become an active node within the MADQuantum–CM project, contributing a stable and traceable optical frequency reference to the broader quantum communication and metrology network. This long-term integration will position CEM as a key partner in advancing national and international timekeeping capabilities.

6. Conclusions

The development of a trapped-ion optical frequency standard at CEM marks a significant step toward establishing a national reference in quantum metrology. By leveraging commercially available components and a modular architecture, the system combines precision, scalability, and accessibility, making advanced timekeeping technology attainable for a medium-sized NMI. This effort is defined by the integration of subsystems into a functional architecture suited to the constraints of CEM.

With the infrastructure now in place and the first ions successfully trapped, the project is entering its experimental phase. Upcoming efforts will focus on probing the clock transition, refining control protocols, and characterizing systematic frequency shifts. These measurements will provide experimental data for the uncertainty budget and are expected to demonstrate a fractional frequency instability approaching the 10^{-16} level at the relevant averaging time. These results will validate the system's performance against international standards.

Beyond its technical milestones, this initiative positions CEM as a strategic contributor to the MADQuantum–CM network, where it will serve as a reliable frequency node supporting collaborative research in quantum communication and precision timing. The project's ultimate purpose is to provide a frequency reference for national and European quantum infrastructures, enabling comparisons via transportable optical clocks, satellite-based links, or even fiber networks. In this way, the project not only strengthens national capabilities but also reinforces Europe's broader push toward quantum-enabled infrastructure.

Author Contributions: Conceptualization, J.D.d.A. and Y.Á.; methodology, A.P. and I.C.; formal analysis, A.P.; investigation, A.P., I.C. and D.d.M.; resources, A.P. and I.C.; data curation, A.P., I.C., D.d.M. and D.P.; writing—original draft preparation, A.P.; writing—review and editing, A.P. and I.C.; visualization, Y.Á. and D.P.; supervision, J.D.d.A. and Y.Á.; project administration, J.D.d.A. and Y.Á.; funding acquisition, J.D.d.A. All authors have read and agreed to the published version of the manuscript.

Funding: This research has been conducted within the framework of the MADQuantum-CM project, supported by the Next Generation EU resilience funding and the Community of Madrid, *marco del Componente 17, Inversión 01.*

Data Availability Statement: The original contributions presented in this study are included in the article. Further inquiries can be directed to the corresponding author.

Conflicts of Interest: The authors declare no conflicts of interest.

References

1. Diddams, S.A.; Bergquist, J.C.; Jefferts, S.R.; Oates, C.W. Standards of time and frequency at the outset of the 21st century. *Science* **2004**, *306*, 1318–1324. [CrossRef] [PubMed]
2. Aeppli, A.; Kim, K.; Warffield, W.; Safronova, M.S.; Ye, J. A clock with 8×10^{-19} systematic uncertainty. *Phys. Rev. Lett.* **2024**, *133*, 023401. [CrossRef] [PubMed]
3. Spieß, L.J. An Optical Clock Based on a Highly Charged Ion. Ph.D. Thesis, University of Hannover, Hanover, Germany, 2023.
4. Margolis, H.S.; Godun, R.M.; Huntemann, N.; Le Targat, R.; Pizzocaro, M.; Zawada, M.; Abgrall, M.; Akamatsu, D.; Álvarez Martínez, H.; Amy-Klein, A.; et al. Robust Optical Clocks for International Timescales (ROCIT). *J. Phys. Conf. Ser.* **2024**, *2889*, 012022. [CrossRef]
5. Madrid Quantum. MadQCI. Available online: http://madqci.es (accessed on 25 November 2025).
6. Kobayashi, T.; Nishiyama, A.; Hosaka, K.; Akamatsu, D.; Kawasaki, A.; Wada, M.; Inaba, H.; Tanabe, T.; Yasuda, M. Improved absolute frequency measurement of 171Yb at NMIJ with uncertainty below 2×10^{-16}. *Metrologia* **2025**, *62*, 025006. [CrossRef]
7. Akamatsu, D.; Kobayashi, T.; Hisai, Y.; Tanabe, T.; Hosaka, K.; Yasuda, M.; Hong, F.-L. Dual-Mode Operation of an Optical Lattice Clock Using Strontium and Ytterbium Atoms. *IEEE Trans. Ultrason. Ferroelectr. Freq. Control* **2018**, *65*, 1069–1075. [CrossRef] [PubMed]
8. Ludlow, A.D.; Boyd, M.M.; Ye, J.; Peik, E.; Schmidt, P.O. Optical atomic clocks. *Rev. Mod. Phys.* **2015**, *87*, 673–701. [CrossRef]
9. Brewer, S.M.; Chen, J.-S.; Hankin, A.M.; Clements, E.R.; Chou, C.W.; Wineland, D.J.; Hume, D.B.; Leibrandt, D.R. An $^{27}Al^+$ quantum-logic clock with a systematic uncertainty below 10^{-18}. *Phys. Rev. Lett.* **2019**, *123*, 033201. [CrossRef] [PubMed]
10. Physikalisch-Technische Bundesanstalt. *Publishable Summary for 22IEM01 TOCK Transportable Optical Clocks for Key Comparisons*; European Metrology Partnership: Braunschweig, Germany, 2024.
11. Alpine Quantum Technologies. Pine-trap. Available online: https://www.aqt.eu/products/pine-trap/ (accessed on 25 November 2025).
12. Caballero, I.; Palos, A.; de Mercado, D.; Álvarez, Y.; Peral, D.; de Aguilar, J.D. Optical quantum frequency standard bases for MADQuantum-CM communication network. In Proceedings of the 2025 25th Anniversary International Conference on Transparent Optical Networks (ICTON), Barcelona, Spain, 6–10 July 2025.
13. Guggemos, M. Precision spectroscopy with trapped $40Ca^+$ and $27Al^+$ ions. Ph.D. Thesis, University of Innsbruck, Innsbruck, Austria, 2017.
14. Drever, R.W.P.; Hall, J.L.; Kowalski, F.V.; Hough, J.; Ford, G.M.; Munley, A.J.; Ward, H. Laser phase and frequency stabilization using an optical resonator. *Appl. Phys. B* **1983**, *31*, 97–105. [CrossRef]
15. Sheridan, K.; Lange, W.; Keller, M. All-optical ion generation for ion trap loading. *Appl. Phys. B* **2011**, *104*, 744–761. [CrossRef]
16. Battles, K.D.; McMahon, B.J.; Sawyer, B.C. Absorption spectroscopy of 40Ca atomic beams produced via pulsed laser ablation: A quantitative comparison of Ca and $CaTiO_3$ targets. *Appl. Phys. B* **2024**, *130*, 214. [CrossRef]
17. Smith, D.R.H.; Muralidharan, S.; Hablützel, R.; Croft, G.; Theophilo, K.; Owens, A.; Lekhai, Y.N.D.; Thomas, S.J.; Deans, C. A comparison of calcium sources for ion-trap loading via laser ablation. *Appl. Phys. B* **2025**, *131*, 164. [CrossRef] [PubMed]
18. Hashimoto, Y.; Matsuoka, L.; Osaki, H.; Fukushima, Y.; Hasegawa, S. Trapping Laser Ablated Ca^+ Ions in Linear Paul Trap. *Jpn. J. Appl. Phys.* **2006**, *45*, 7108. [CrossRef]
19. Roberts, M.; Taylor, P.; Gill, P. *Laser Linewidth at the Sub-Hertz Level*; NPL Report CLM 8; NPL: Teddington, UK, 1999.
20. TOPTICA Photonics. *Laser Rack Systems*; TOPTICA Photonics: Gräfelfing, Germany, 2021.
21. Takekoshi, T. Methods and Apparatuses for Laser Stabilization. U.S. Patent EP3940898B1, 21 June 2023.

22. Black, E.D. An introduction to Pound-Drever-Hall laser frequency stabilization. *Am. J. Phys.* **2001**, *69*, 79. [CrossRef]
23. Wang, W.; Subhankar, S.; Britton, J.W. A practical guide to feedback control for Pound-Drever-Hall laser linewidth narrowing. *Appl. Phys. B* **2025**, *131*, 146. [CrossRef]
24. Donley, E.A.; Heavner, T.P.; Levi, F.; Tataw, M.O.; Jefferts, S.R. Double-pass acousto-optic modulator system. *Rev. Sci. Instrum.* **2005**, *76*, 063112. [CrossRef]
25. Hänsch, T.W. Nobel lecture: Passion for precision. *Rev. Mod. Phys.* **2006**, *78*, 1297–1309. [CrossRef]
26. Heinrich, D. Ultrafast Coherent Excitation of $40Ca^+$. Ph.D. Thesis, University of Innsbruck, Innsbruck, Austria, 2020.
27. Giunta, M.; Fischer, M.; Hänsel, W.; Steinmetz, T.; Lessing, M.; Holzberger, S.; Cleff, C.; Hänsch, T.W.; Mei, M.; Holzwarth, R. 20 Years and 20 Decimal Digits: A Journey with Optical Frequency Combs. *IEEE Photonics Technol. Lett.* **2019**, *31*, 1898–1901. [CrossRef]
28. Benhelm, J.; Kirchmair, G.; Roos, C.F.; Blatt, R. Experimental quantum information processing with $43Ca^+$ ions. *Phys. Rev. A* **2008**, *77*, 062306. [CrossRef]
29. Guevara, M. Optical Clocks with Trapped Ions. Ph.D. Thesis, University of Innsbruck, Innsbruck, Austria, 2023.
30. M-Labs, ARTIQ. *Advanced Real-Time Infrastructure for Quantum Physics Web Page*; M-Labs, ARTIQ: Hong Kong, China, 2025.
31. *Grafana*, version 12.3.; GrafanaLabs: New York, NY, USA, 2025.
32. Liu, P.; Huang, Y.; Bian, W.; Shao, H.; Guan, H.; Tang, Y.-B.; Li, C.-B.; Mitroy, J.; Gao, K.-L. Measurement of Magic Wavelengths for the 40Ca+ Clock Transition. *Phy. Rev. Lett.* **2015**, *114*, 223001. [CrossRef] [PubMed]
33. Ye, J.; Kimble, H.J.; Katori, H. Quantum State Engineering and Precision Metrology using State-Insensitive Light Traps. *Science* **2008**, *320*, 1734–1738. [CrossRef] [PubMed]

metrology

MDPI

Article

Investigation and Improvement of Inconsistency in Surface-Form Measurement Results Due to Difference of Incident Direction of Measuring Light in Abramson-Type Oblique-Incident Interferometer

So Ito *, Takumi Yamagishi, Kimihisa Matsumoto and Kazuhide Kamiya

Department of Intelligent Robotics, Faculty of Information Engineering, Toyama Prefectural University, Toyama 939-0398, Japan
* Correspondence: so.ito@pu-toyama.ac.jp

Abstract: An Abramson-type oblique-incident interferometer was used for the surface-form measurement of hand-scraped marks consisting of rough surfaces. Although the Abramson interferometer could measure the rough surface of hand-scraped marks under noncontact conditions, the inconsistency in the measurement results was caused by the differences in the incident direction of the measuring light. This study investigated the inconsistency in the measurement results of the Abramson interferometer caused by the oblique incidence of the measuring light. The reproducibility of inconsistencies due to the difference in the incident direction of the measuring light was confirmed, and the relationship between the inconsistency of the measurement results and the incident angle of the measuring light was investigated. Consequently, it was confirmed that the inconsistency of the measurement results due to the difference in the incident direction of the measuring light could be reduced by decreasing the incident angle of the measuring light. To avoid the overcrowding of the interference fringes caused by the reduction in the incident angle of the measuring light, an oblique-incident interferometer with a near-infrared laser was constructed. The validity of the developed oblique-incident interferometer was evaluated by comparison with a commercially available contour measurement instrument. The surface form obtained by the developed oblique-incident interferometer was confirmed to be consistent with the envelope of the cross-sectional profile measured by the contour measurement instrument.

Keywords: oblique-incident interferometer; hand-scraped surface; near-infrared laser; surface-form measurements

1. Introduction

Hand-scraping is a finishing process to create precision flat surfaces [1]. Hand-scraping can produce a broader range of precision flat surfaces than lapping or grinding; thus, it has been applied to large high-precision workpieces, such as the sliding parts of machine tools, surface plates of precision-measuring instruments, and the matching surface of precision parts [2,3]. Hand-scraping does not require the clamping of the workpiece; therefore, high machining accuracy can be achieved without deformation. As hand-scraping can produce a highly precise large flat surface without a machine tool, it should be reviewed from the perspective of energy conservation and Sustainable Development Goals. However, developing a high-precision flat surface by hand-scraping requires skilled workmanship, and it takes a long time to acquire hand-scraping skills [4]. One reason for the difficulty in acquiring hand-scraping skills is the qualitative evaluation of scraped surfaces. In the general inspection method, the finish condition of a hand-scraped surface is evaluated based on the transfer of pigments, such as Prussian blue, coated onto the workpiece surface upon contact with the standard surface plate. Although this method can qualitatively detect convex positions on a workpiece, it cannot quantitatively estimate the height of a convex position or the fine shapes of the hand-scraped marks. Several previous studies on scraping automation proposed evaluation methods based on the observation of pigment transfer on scraped surfaces [2,5]. These methods can efficiently identify areas to be scraped by automatically determining the pigment transfer, which is visually performed by skilled technicians. However, quantitatively determining the height or surface form of scraping marks using finish evaluation methods based on pigment transfer detection is challenging. Surface profilers, or surface roughness testers, that employ tactile probes can measure the profile of hand-scraped marks consisting of a rough surface. However, measurements based on tactile probes are time-consuming because they are line measurements.

Optical measurement methods facilitate noncontact surface measurements of rough surfaces within a short duration. The measured light tended to scatter on the hand-scraped marks because of the rough surface. Optical probe methods are effective approaches for minimizing the influence of scattered light owing to rough surfaces. An evaluation system for scraping a surface using a computer numerical control machine tool and laser triangulation sensor was proposed [6]. An optical probe using a DVD pickup was developed for the rapid measurement of scraped surfaces [7]. Although these methods can measure the profiles of rough surfaces, they are time-consuming because they require individual measurements at each point. The fringe projection techniques project a pattern onto a workpiece using a laser or LED light source and observe the pattern reflected from the workpiece surface [8]. This can measure the three-dimensional form of the workpiece in a short time under noncontact conditions.

Interferometric measurement methods are effective for the rapid measurement of the surface forms. These methods allow for highly accurate measurements because they calculate the surface form based on a highly accurate reference surface and light wavelength. However, when a typical commercially available vertical incident interferometer is used, unmeasurable regions are observed during hand-scraped mark measurements owing to the scattering of the measuring light [9]. Therefore, the ingenuity of the optical system is crucial during the measurement of rough surfaces because the intensity and contrast of the interference fringes decrease. A digital signal-processing algorithm was used to analyze interference fringes to achieve fast, accurate, and repeatable three-dimensional measurements of rough surface profiles [10]. Other methods based on heterodyne interferometry have also been developed to measure the surface profile of speckle fields [11]. Although these methods can effectively measure rough-surface forms, they require specialized signal-processing algorithms and complex optical systems.

An oblique-incident interferometer based on Abramson interferometry [12] can measure the surface form using a simple optical system because a single right-angle prism acts as both a beam splitter and reference surface in the interferometer. In addition, because the oblique-incident interferometer is less susceptible to the influence of the measured light scattering, a sufficiently reflected light intensity can be obtained to generate interference fringes, even on a rough surface. Consequently, the oblique-incident interferometer enables three-dimensional surface-form measurements of hand-scraped marks [9,13]. However, inconsistencies in the surface-form measurement results due to differences in the incident direction of the measuring light were observed in the oblique-incident interferometer [9].

The reason for this inconsistency has not been experimentally elucidated. If the inconsistency in the measurement results is caused by an oblique-incident light, it may change by changing the incident angle of the measuring light. However, as explained in Section 2, when the incident angle of the measuring light decreases, the interval between the interference fringes decreases. Therefore, it is challenging to capture interference fringes using an imaging sensor, and the surface form cannot be calculated based on the interference fringes. Consequently, it is difficult for the oblique-incident interferometer used in previous studies [9,13] to reduce the incident angle of the measuring light for measuring the surface form of hand-scraped marks.

In this study, the light source of the oblique-incident interferometer was changed to a near-infrared laser, which was a longer wavelength than that in previous studies, to expand the interval of the interference fringes. Consequently, the incident angle of the measuring light could be reduced without the overcrowding of the interference fringes. This study investigated inconsistencies in the surface-form measurement results, which were obtained by the oblique-incident interferometer, by changing the incident direction and angle of the measuring light. The surface form of the same hand-scraped marks was measured by changing the incident direction and angle of the measuring light to evaluate the relationship between the inconsistency in the surface-form measurement results and the incident angle of the measuring light. The measurement position on each surface was identified using pattern matching, and the inconsistency in the measurement results was evaluated based on the cross-sectional profiles of the hand-scraped mark at the same measurement position. The inconsistency in the measurement results due to differences in the incident direction of the measuring light was investigated using the correlation coefficient and the difference between profiles acquired at the same incident angle of the measuring light. The validity of the measurement results obtained using the oblique-incident interferometer was evaluated based on comparisons with those of a commercially available optical noncontact contour profilometer.

2. Methods

Figure 1 shows the principle of Abramson interferometry used in this study [9,13]. Abramson interferometry is a type of oblique-incident interferometry that uses a right-angle prism (RAP). The *B*-*C* plane of the RAP was mounted to face the measured surface of the workpiece. A collimated laser beam was incident on the *B*-*C* plane of the RAP through the *A*-*B* plane. Part of the incident laser beam was reflected by the *B*-*C* plane and becomes the reference light for the interferometer. The other part of the incident laser beam was transmitted to the *B*-*C* plane and reflected onto the measured surface of the workpiece. The light incident on the measured surface of the workpiece is called measuring light. Angle θ, shown in Figure 1, indicates the incident angle of the measuring light with respect to the measured surface. When the measured light is reflected on the measured surface and incident on the *B*-*C* surface of the RAP, the reference and measured lights generate interference fringes on the *B*-*C* plane. Because the RAP can be used as a beam splitter and the reference surface of an interferometer, the Abramson interferometer enables the construction of a simple and compact interferometer. The distance between the measured surface and the *B*-*C* plane of the RAP, h, can be expressed by Equation (1):

$$h = \frac{1}{cos\theta} \cdot \frac{m\lambda}{2} \quad (1)$$

where m is the order of the interference fringes and λ is the wavelength of the laser beam. Therefore, the relationship between the interference fringe sensitivity, S, and the incident angle of the measuring light, θ, can be expressed by Equation (2).

$$S = \frac{\lambda}{2cos\theta} \quad (2)$$

According to Equation (2), as the incident angle θ decreases, the interference fringe sensitivity S increases. Consequently, the fringe interval decreases with decreasing incident angle θ, resulting in an overcrowding of the interference fringes. When the interference fringe interval was smaller than the resolution of the imaging sensor, the interference fringes could not be captured. However, when the fringe sensitivity remained constant, the incident angle θ could be reduced by increasing the wavelength λ of the light source. Therefore, a laser light source with a longer wavelength can simultaneously decrease the incident angle of the measured light and increase the interval between interference fringes. In previous studies [9,13], a visible-light laser with a wavelength of 632.8 nm or 635 nm was used, and the incident angle of the measuring light was set from 77° to 78°. In this study, a near-infrared laser with a wavelength of 880 nm was used. When interference fringes with the same interval as those in previous studies were generated, the incident angle of the measured light could decrease to 73.2° using a near-infrared laser source. Consequently, the reduction in the interference fringe interval caused by the reduction in the incident angle θ can be avoided, and the overcrowding of the interference fringes can be prevented.

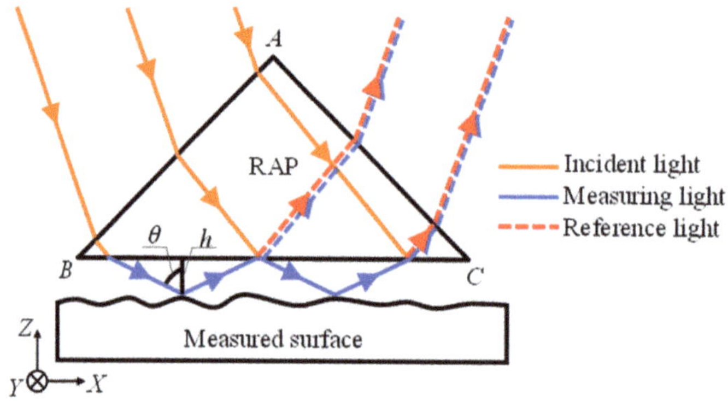

Figure 1. Principle of Abramson interferometer.

In this experiment, the surface form was calculated from the interference fringe images using the same procedure as in previous studies [9,13] to eliminate the possibility that the surface form calculation algorithm may induce changes in the measurement results. The surface forms of the measured workpiece were calculated using phase-shifting interferometry for the interference fringe images. Phase-shifting of the interference fringes was conducted based on the displacement of the distance between the measured surface of the workpiece and the *B*-*C* surface of the RAP. A five-step phase-shifting method [14,15] was used to reduce the influence of displacement errors during phase-shifting. The phase distribution, $\Psi(x, y)$, obtained by the five-step phase-shifting method, was convolved within the range of $(-\pi, \pi]$. Phase unwrapping was performed by applying the unweighted least-squares phase-unwrapping (ULSPU) method [16,17]. The ULSPU method can reduce the influence of phase singularity by minimizing the difference between the primary partial differential of the phase distribution before and after the phase connection. The surface form of the measured surface can be calculated by converting the unwrapped phase distribution, $\Psi'(x,\ y)$ into the height of the measured surface. The relationship between the unwrapped phase distribution of the interference fringes and the height of the measured surface, $h(x, y)$ can be expressed as follows:

$$\Psi'(x,y) = 2h(x,y)cos\theta \cdot \frac{2\pi}{\lambda} \quad (3)$$

3. Results

3.1. Experimental Methods

Figure 2 shows the configuration of the oblique-incident interferometer used in this study. A commercially available hand-scraped surface plate (OS-105, Ohnishi Sokutei, Higashiosaka, Japan) was used as the measurement surface. Multiple hand-scraped marks are present on the surface of the plate. The nominal flatness accuracy of the plate surface used in the study was 15 μm. A near-infrared laser with a wavelength of 880 nm (TCSQ2-08800010-4-CL, NEOARK, Hachioji, Japan) was used as the light source. The intensity of the laser light was adjusted using a neutral-density (ND) filter, and the laser beam was passed through a spatial filter (SF) consisting of a 40× objective lens and a 25 μm diameter pinhole. The laser beam was expanded into a collimated beam through the lens and incident on the *A-B* plane of the RAP (RPB-20-10H, SIGMA KOKI, Hidaka, Japan). The size of the *B-C* plane of the RAP was 40 mm × 56 mm, and the surface accuracy of the RAP was $\lambda/10$. The interference fringes generated on the *B-C* plane of the RAP were captured using an imaging sensor (EO1312LE, Edmund Optics, NJ, USA) through a tilt-shift camera lens (TS-E 90 mm F2.8L Macro, Canon, Tokyo, Japan). The number of pixels in the imaging sensor was 1280 × 1024. The tilt-shift camera lens facilitated the focusing of the entire area of the inclined plane because the *B-C* plane of the RAP and the imaging sensor satisfied the Scheimpflug principle. The size of the field of view captured by the imaging sensor was 18.1 mm × 11.7 mm; thus, the estimated lateral resolution of the interferometer was 14.1 μm × 11.4 μm. Phase-shifting of the interference fringes was achieved by moving the surface plate in the Z-direction using piezoelectric actuators (AE0203D08DF, MESS-TEK, Wako, Japan). Four piezoelectric actuators were placed under the plate on which the surface plate was mounted, expanded, and contracted in response to the driving signal from the piezoelectric drivers, controlled using a personal computer. A homemade PZT-driven Z axis positioning stage was mounted on a manual XY linear stage (LD-947-S1, Chuo Precision Industrial, Tokyo, Japan) and a manual Z axis rotation stage (KSPA-986M, SIGMA KOKI, Hidaka, Japan). The displacement of the piezoelectric actuator was monitored during the phase shift using a calibrated cantilever-type displacement sensor (TELEMICRO ESM-01, Ogasawara Precision Laboratory, Yamakita, Japan). The nominal resolution and accuracy of the displacement sensor are 10 nm and 75 nm, respectively. Red solid and dashed lines in Figure 2 indicate incident measuring light and interference light, respectively.

The incident angle of the measuring light can be changed by adjusting the height along the *Z*-direction and the angle around the *Y*-axis of Mirror 2. Because the measured light was refracted at the *A-B* and *B-C* planes of the RAP, it was not easy to precisely calculate the incident angle θ from the incident angle of the laser beam to the *A-B* plane of the RAP. In addition, it was necessary to evaluate the *Z*-directional displacement of the measured surface corresponding to the phase-shifting of the interference fringe of $\pi/2$ rad for the use of the five-step phase-shifting method. In this experiment, the surface plate was displaced in the *Z*-direction using piezoelectric actuators, while the interference fringes generated on the smooth surface of the surface plate were observed using the imaging sensor. The phase of the interference fringes was shifted to 6π rad while the Z-directional displacement of the surface plate was measured using the displacement sensor. Based on Equations (1) and (2), the interval and sensitivity of the interference fringes change with the incident angle of the measuring light. The relationship between the Z-directional displacement of a certain point on the measured surface, Δh, and the incident angle of the measuring light, θ can be expressed by Equation (4).

$$\Delta h = \frac{1}{cos\theta} \cdot \frac{\lambda}{2} \tag{4}$$

Consequently, the incident angle of the measuring light θ can be calculated from the displacement Δh, which corresponds to the phase of the interference fringe of 2π. The incidence angle θ was calculated from the interference fringe phase-shifting on a smooth surface, which was the dark area shown in Figure 3a, and the displacement of the PZT-driven Z-stage.

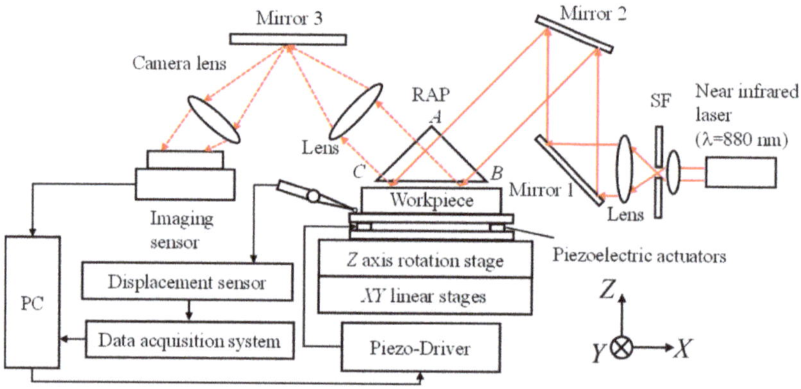

Figure 2. Experimental configuration of oblique-incident interferometer.

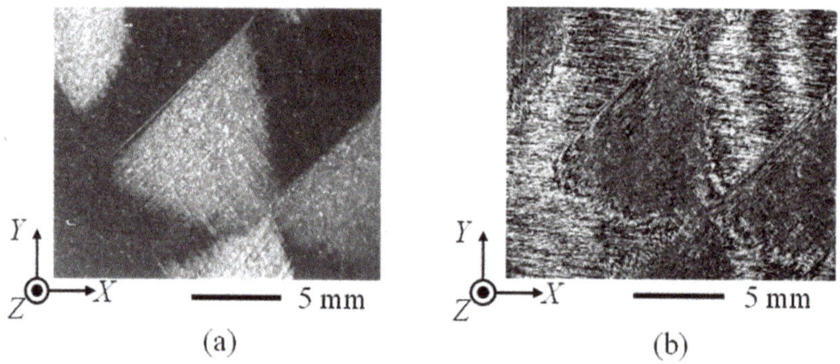

Figure 3. Observation of the hand-scraped marks. (**a**) Hand-scraped marks observed under incoherent light. The dark area is a ground smooth surface. (**b**) Interference fringes on the hand-scraped marks.

3.2. Experimental Results and Discussions

The reproducibility of the surface-form measurements using the oblique-incident interferometer was investigated by measuring the same hand-scraped marks while changing the direction and angle of incidence of the measuring light. Figure 3 shows the hand-scraped marks observed using the developed oblique-incident interferometer. Figure 3a shows the hand-scraped marks observed under incoherent light. The hand-scraped marks appeared brighter than the smooth surface because the incident light was scattered on the rough surface created by hand-scraping. Figure 3b shows an example of interference fringes on a hand-scraped surface irradiated by a near-infrared laser. The incident angle of the measuring light was 76.0°. The incident direction of the measuring light was changed by rotating the surface plate by 180° around the Z-axis. Because the surface form of the hand-scraped marks was rotated around the Z-axis after the rotation of the surface plate, the surface form data were rotated around the Z-axis so that they were the same as before the rotation. The rotational alignment of the workpiece was adjusted to within 0.1° using the Z axis rotation stage and the images captured by the imaging sensor under incoherent light. The rotational error of the workpiece corresponded to an alignment error of ±1 pixel of at most.

Figure 4 shows the surface forms of the hand-scraped marks calculated from the interference fringes generated when the incident angle of the measured light was set to approximately 77°. The incident angle of the measured light was the maximum angle achievable with the constructed oblique-incident interferometer. At larger incident angles, it was difficult to illuminate the entire measurement surface because of the interference between the laser beam and optical components. The arrowheads in Figure 4 indicate the incident direction of the measured light. It can be observed that the hand-scraped marks are lower than the surrounding smooth surface. The incident angle of the measuring light and the Z-directional displacement per step of the phase-shifting shown in Figure 4a were set to 77.4° and 0.51 μm, respectively. Figure 4b shows the surface form of the same hand-scraped marks measured by changing the incident direction of the measuring light. In the case of measurement results presented in Figure 4b, the incident angle of the measuring light and the Z-directional displacement per one step of the phase-shifting were set to be 76.0° and 0.46 μm. Although Figure 4 shows the measurement results of the same hand-scraped marks, the right side of the hand-scraped mark in Figure 4a is slightly deeper. However, the left side of the hand-scraping mark is somewhat deeper, as shown in Figure 4b. Even when a near-infrared laser source was used, inconsistencies in the surface-form measurement results due to the incident direction of the measuring light were confirmed, as in a previous study [8].

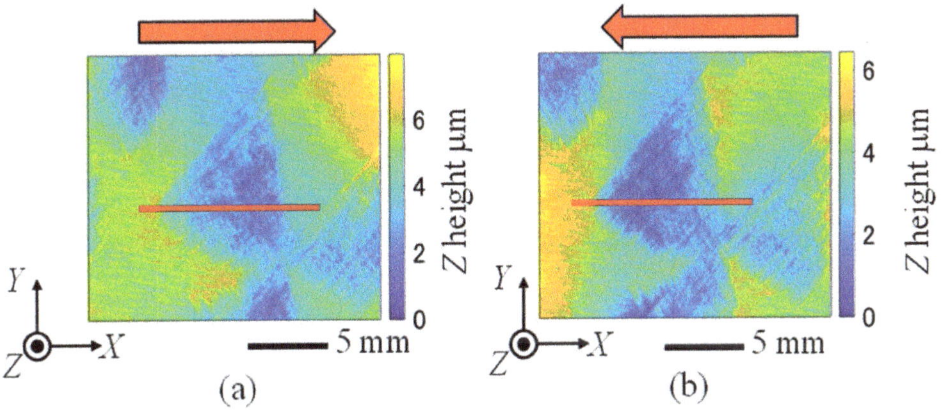

Figure 4. Surface form obtained with incident angle of approximately 77°. (**a**) Incident angle of 77.4°. (**b**) Incident angle of 76.0°.

Figure 5 shows the surface forms of the hand-scraped marks measured at smaller incident angles of the measuring light. The incident angle of the measuring light was set to approximately 70°, which was the minimum incident angle in the oblique-incident interferometer used in this experiment. When the incident angle was smaller than 70°, phase-shifting of the interference fringes could not be detected because of the increase in the scattered light intensity on the rough surface of the hand-scraped marks. In addition to Figure 4, the arrowheads in Figure 5 indicate the direction of the incident light. In Figure 5a, the incident angle of the measuring light and the Z-directional displacement per step of the phase-shifting were set to 70.1° and 0.32 μm, respectively. Similarly, in Figure 5b, the incident angle of the measuring light and the Z-directional displacement per step of the phase-shifting were set to 70.5° and 0.33 μm, respectively.

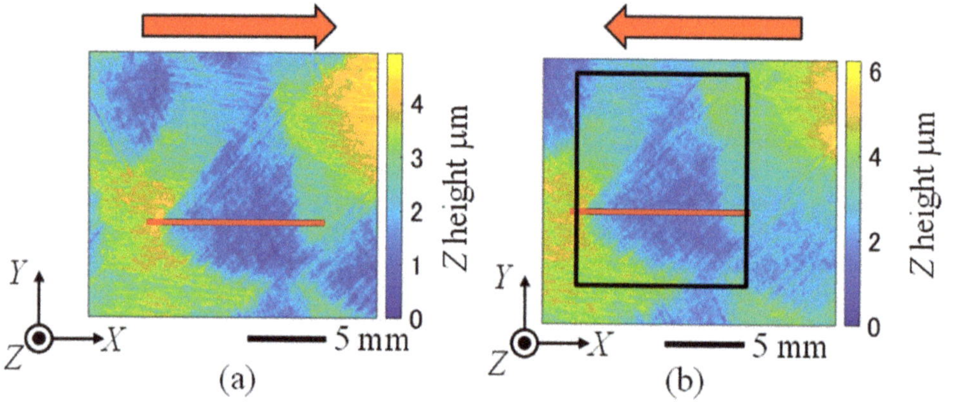

Figure 5. Surface form obtained with incident angle of approximately 70°. (**a**) Incident angle of 70.1°. (**b**) Incident angle of 70.5°.

To investigate the effects of the incident angles of the measuring light, the cross-sectional profiles of the same position on the hand-scraped marks were compared. The measurement position on each surface form was identified pixel-by-pixel by pattern matching, using the area surrounded by the black frame indicated in Figure 5b as a template. As for the pattern matching, the method from previous research shown in Reference 13 was applied. Template matching using the normxcorr2 function in MATLAB 2023a was used. The template area was set to include the entire the hand-scraped mark near the center of Figure 3a because it includes the lowest position of the hand-scraped mark. The red lines in Figures 4 and 5 represent the same positions on the same hand-scraped mark identified by pattern matching. Figure 6 shows the cross-sectional profiles represented by the red lines in Figures 4 and 5. The number of measurement points for each profile was 786. The correlation coefficients between the template of the pattern matching and identified locations extracted from Figure 4a,b were evaluated as 0.80 and 0.77, respectively. Similarly, the correlation coefficient between the template location and the identified location extracted from Figure 5a was 0.94. The correlation coefficients were larger than 0.7, and each location indicated a strong correlation with the template of pattern matching. Therefore, the profiles shown in Figure 6 are considered to be at the same position on the surface plate. As shown in Figure 6a, when the incident angle of the measured light was approximately 77°, a significant difference in the cross-sectional profiles was observed. The correlation coefficient between the two profiles, shown in Figure 6a, was estimated to be 0.78. However, when the incident angle of the measuring light was approximately 70°, the two profiles shown in Figure 6b exhibited good agreement. The correlation coefficient between the two profiles, shown in Figure 6b, was estimated to be 0.96. Figure 7 shows the absolute values of the differences between the two cross-sectional profiles shown in Figure 6a,b. The green plots in Figure 7 indicate the difference in the cross-sectional profiles when the incident angle of the measuring light is approximately 77°, and the average and the maximum difference are 0.71 μm and 1.91 μm, respectively. In contrast, the yellow plots in Figure 7 represent the difference between the cross-sectional profiles when the incident angle of the measuring light is approximately 70°, and the average and the maximum difference are 0.20 μm and 0.75 μm, respectively. It can be observed that the discrepancy in the measurement results due to the incidence direction is significantly reduced by decreasing the incidence angle of the measurement light.

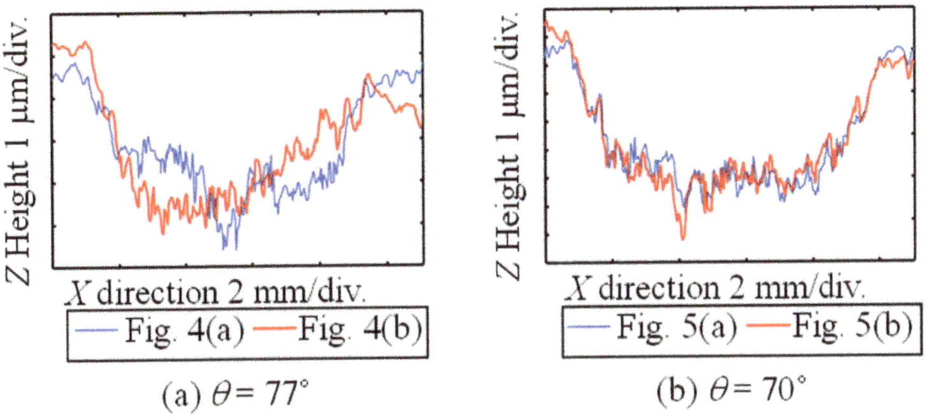

Figure 6. Cross-sectional profiles indicated by red lines in Figures 4 and 5. (**a**) Cross-sectional profiles in Figure 4. Incident angle of approximately 77°. (**b**) Cross-sectional profiles in Figure 5. Incident angle of approximately 70°.

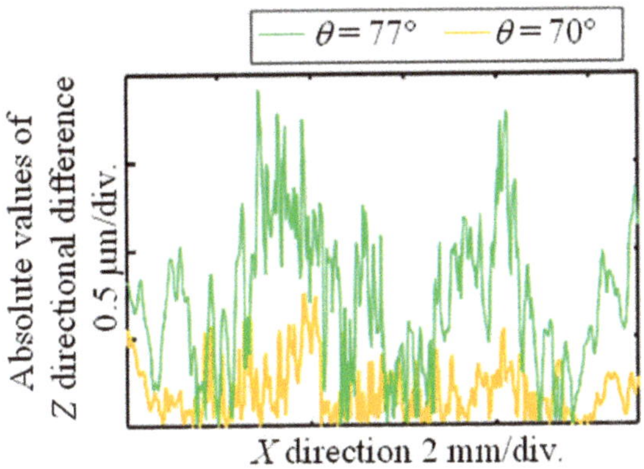

Figure 7. Absolute values of the difference in the cross-sectional profiles shown in Figure 6.

The cross-sectional profile of the same hand-scraped mark was measured using a commercially available noncontact contour-measuring instrument (Mitaka Koki, NH-3s) to confirm the validity of the surface-form measurement using the developed oblique-incident interferometer. Figure 8 shows a comparison of the cross-sectional surface profiles. The orange line represents the average cross-sectional profile shown in Figure 6b, measured using the developed oblique-incident interferometer with an incident angle of 70°. The black line represents the surface profile obtained using NH-3s. The green line represents the peak envelope of the surface profile obtained by NH-3s. The envelope was calculated using the envelope function in MATLAB 2023a. The number of samples in the envelope calculation was set to 30, which is the condition where the difference between the envelope and the oblique incidence interferometer profile was the smallest. The surface form was measured using a point autofocus probe [18] with a 100× objective lens (numerical aperture: 0.80). The number of measurement points and measurement intervals of the NH-3s were set to 1108 and 10 μm, respectively. The measurement interval of the NH-3s was almost the same as the lateral resolution of the oblique-incident interferometer. The root-mean-square heights P_q of the surface profiles measured using the oblique-incident interferometer and NH-3s were 0.93 μm and 2.71 μm, respectively. The maximum difference between the cross-sectional profile obtained by the oblique-incident interferometer and the envelope was evaluated to be 3.6 μm. NH-3s could measure finer and deeper groove shapes on the hand-scraped surface than the oblique-incident interferometer. These differences are attributed to the difference in the lateral resolution and incident angle of the measuring light between the oblique-incident interferometer and the NH-3s. The lateral resolution of the oblique-incident interferometer was determined from the field of view of the oblique-incident interferometer and the number of pixels of the imaging sensor, which was determined to be 14.1 μm × 11.4 μm. The laser spot diameter of the NH-3s in this experiment was 1 μm, which corresponded to the lateral resolution of the NH-3s. Since the laser spot diameter of the NH-3s was smaller than the lateral resolution of the oblique-incident interferometer, it was possible to measure finer grooves on the hand-scraped marks. Furthermore, the incident angle of the measuring light of the NH-3s is 53°, which is smaller than that of the oblique-incident interferometer. Consequently, the measured light of the NH-3s can reach deeper into the grooves than the oblique-incidence interferometer, facilitating measurements inside the deep grooves. However, the cross-sectional profile obtained using the oblique incidence interferometer was almost the same as the envelope of the surface-shaped profile measured using the NH-3s. Therefore, it is assumed that the developed oblique-incident interferometer can adequately measure the surface of hand-scraped marks to a depth of several micrometers. It was confirmed that the inconsistencies in the measurement results of the surface form of the hand-scraped marks using the oblique-incident interferometer could be improved by reducing the incident angle of the measuring light. As shown in the measurement results using NH-3s in Figure 8, the hand-scraped marks are several μm deep, and their surfaces consist of steep undulations. In the surface-form measurement using the oblique-incident interferometer, it was assumed that the measurement results changed depending on the incident direction of the measuring light because part of the measuring light was blocked by depressions and steep undulations of the hand-scraped marks. It is believed that a reduction in the incident angle of the measuring light reduces the partial blocking of the measuring light near the surface, thereby improving the inconsistency in the measurement results.

Although the horizontal resolution of the oblique-incident interferometer was inferior to that of the NH-3s used in this study, it had an advantage in terms of measurement time. NH-3s is a line measurement, and the measurement time for one line, as shown in Figure 8, is approximately 5 min. In contrast, the developed oblique-incidence interferometer is a surface measurement, and the measurement time for each surface form was shorter than 1 min. This is expected to achieve the rapid measurement of hand-scraped surfaces in the range of tens to hundreds of square millimeters.

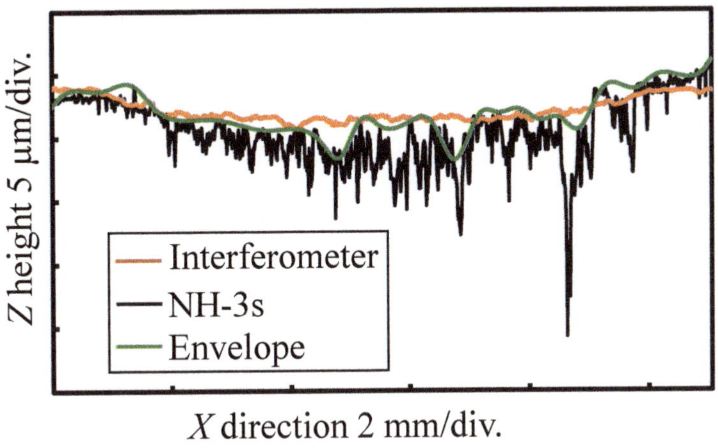

Figure 8. Comparison of the cross-sectional profiles.

The surface-form measurement using the oblique-incident interferometer consists in area scanning. In this method, discontinuities in the phase of the interference fringes make it difficult to calculate the surface form. On the other hand, since measurements are taken simultaneously in all measurement directions, errors due to drift, creep, and so on during the measurement are very small. The commercially available profiler (NH-3s) performs point scanning, which means that profiles can be obtained even if there are partially unmeasurable areas. The profile acquired in the probe scanning direction as shown in Figure 8 shows high measurement accuracy. However, the profile in the direction perpendicular to the probe scanning direction in two-dimensional measurement is significantly affected by measurement errors due to drift, creep, and so on. Therefore, the proposed method using the oblique-incident interferometer is expected to be effective for the wide-area scan measurement of hand-scraped surfaces. Furthermore, the developed oblique-incident interferometer may be applicable to other rough surfaces as long as the intensity of the specular reflected light is sufficient to detect the interference fringes.

On the other hand, although this study qualitatively clarified the inconsistencies in the measurement results of the oblique-incident interferometer, it has not yet elucidated the cause. In particular, the quantitative relationship between the measurement accuracy and the angle of incidence of the measurement light, surface roughness, shape, and so on has not yet been clarified. In order to analyze these phenomena, the introduction of ray-tracking simulations is planned as a future direction of this study. The reflection of the measuring light on the microtopography of the workpiece surface or phase difference with the reference light will be simulated, and the relationship between the incident angle of the measuring light, the workpiece surface microtopography, and the interference fringe phase distribution will be clarified.

4. Conclusions

This study investigated the inconsistency in the surface-form measurement results, which were obtained by the Abramson-type oblique-incident interferometer, by changing the incident direction and angle of the measuring light. An oblique-incident interferometer with a near-infrared laser was developed to expand the interval of the interference fringes. The expansion of the interference fringe interval prevented the overcrowding of the interference fringes on the rough surface by hand-scraping and enabled a reduction in the angle of incident angle of the measuring light. The inconsistency in the measurement results due to the difference in the incident direction of the measuring light was also confirmed by the measurement using the oblique-incident interferometer with a near-infrared laser. Therefore, it was confirmed that the cause of the inconsistency was the oblique incidence of the measuring light. The relationship between the incident angle of the measuring light of the oblique-incident interferometer and the inconsistency in the measurement results of the hand-scraping surface form was investigated. The forms of the same hand-scraped surface were measured at the maximum and minimum incident angles of the measuring light, which could be realized using the developed oblique-incident interferometer. It was confirmed that the inconsistency in the measurement results due to the incident direction of the measuring light could be improved by reducing the incident angle of the measuring light. The validity of the measurement results obtained using the oblique-incident interferometer was evaluated by comparison with the results obtained using a commercially available noncontact contour measurement instrument. The cross-sectional profile of the surface form measured by the oblique-incident interferometer was in agreement with the envelope of the contour form measured by the noncontact contour measurement instrument, confirming the validity of the oblique-incident interferometer.

The method proposed in this study enables the area scanning of rough surface forms in a short time. Attempts to expand the measurement range of oblique incidence interferometers by stitching surface profile data have already been reported [13]. The oblique incidence interferometer developed in this study may be applicable to other rough surface profile measurements, especially for on-machine or in-process measurements, and is expected to be applied to quality control and automated measurements.

Author Contributions: Conceptualization, S.I. and K.K.; methodology, S.I. and T.Y.; software, T.Y.; validation, S.I. and T.Y.; investigation, T.Y.; resources, K.M.; writing—original draft preparation, S.I.; writing—review and editing, S.I.; visualization, T.Y.; project administration, S.I.; funding acquisition, S.I. All authors have read and agreed to the published version of the manuscript.

Funding: This research was supported by the Japan Society for the Promotion of Science (JSPS), KAKENHI (Grant Number: 23K03606).

Data Availability Statement: Data is contained within the article.

Conflicts of Interest: The authors declare no conflicts of interest.

References

1. Moore, W.R. *Foundations of Mechanical Accuracy*; The Moore Tool Company: Bridgeport, CT, USA, 1970; pp. 16–90, ISBN 9780262130806.
2. Oßwald, K.; Lochmahr, I.; Bagci, Y.; Saile, P. Investigation into hand scraping: A microanalysis. *J. Manuf. Mater. Process.* **2018**, *2*, 76. [CrossRef]
3. Tsutsumi, H.; Kyusojin, A.; Fukuda, K. Tribology characteristics estimation of slide-way surfaces finished by scraping. *Trans. JSME Ser. C* **2006**, *72*, 3009–3015. [CrossRef]
4. Ito, Y. *Thought-Evoking Approaches in Engineering Problems*; Springer: Berlin/Heidelberg, Germany, 2014; pp. 277–295, ISBN 3319041193.
5. Tsutsumi, H.; Yamada, R.; Kyusojin, A.; Nakamura, T. Development of an Automatic Scraping Machine with Recognition for Bearing of Scraped Surfaces (3rd report). *J. Jpn. Soc. Precis. Eng.* **2005**, *71*, 358–362. [CrossRef]
6. Hsieh, T.H.; Jywe, W.Y.; Huang, H.L.; Chen, S.L. Development of a laser-based measurement system for evaluation of the scraping workpiece quality. *Opt. Lasers Eng.* **2011**, *49*, 1045–1053. [CrossRef]
7. Fan, K.C.; Torng, J.; Jywe, W.; Chou, R.C.; Ye, J.K. 3-D measurement and evaluation of surface texture produced by scraping process. *Measurement* **2012**, *45*, 384–392. [CrossRef]
8. Feng, X.; Du, Z.; Yang, J. Non-scanning techniques. In *Advanced in Optical Surface Texture Metrology*; Leach, R., Ed.; IOP ebooks: Bristol, UK, 2020; pp. 5-1–5-22, ISBN 978-0-7503-2526-4.

9. Caber, P.J. Interferometric profiler for rough surfaces. *Appl. Opt.* **1993**, *32*, 3438–3441. [CrossRef] [PubMed]
10. Fercher, A.F.; Hu, H.Z.; Vry, U. Rough surface interferometry with a two-wavelength heterodyne speckle interferometer. *Appl. Opt.* **1985**, *24*, 2181. [CrossRef] [PubMed]
11. Ito, S.; Kameoka, D.; Matsumoto, K.; Kamiya, K. Design and development of oblique-incident interferometer for form measurement of hand-scraped surfaces. *Nanomanuf. Metrol.* **2021**, *4*, 69–76. [CrossRef]
12. Abramson, N. The interferoscope: A new type of interferometer with variable fringe separation. *Optik* **1969**, *30*, 56–71.
13. Aruga, M.; Ito, S.; Tsugawa, F.; Matsumoto, K.; Kamiya, K. Expansion of measurement area of hand-scraped surface using stitching method for oblique-incident interferometer. *J. Adv. Mech. Des. Syst. Manuf.* **2023**, *17*, JAMDSM0010. [CrossRef]
14. Hariharan, P.; Roy, M. A geometric-phase interferometer. *J. Mod. Opt.* **1992**, *39*, 1811–1815. [CrossRef]
15. Malacara, M. Optical Shop Testing. In *Wiley Series in Pure and Applied Optics*; Wiley: Hoboken, NJ, USA, 2007; ISBN 9780471484042.
16. Ghiglia, D.C.; Romero, L.A. Robust two-dimensional weighted and unweighted phase unwrapping that uses fast transforms and iterative methods. *J. Opt. Soc. Am. A* **1994**, *11*, 107–111. [CrossRef]
17. Ghiglia, D.C.; Pritt, M.D. *Two-Dimensional Phase Unwrapping, Theory, Algorithms, and Software*; Wiley: Hoboken, NJ, USA, 1998; pp. 188–190, ISBN 9780471249351.
18. *ISO 25178-605:2025*; Geometrical Product Specifications (GPS)—Surface Texture: Areal. Nominal Characteristics Non-Contact (Point Autofocus Probe) Instruments. International Organization for Standardization: Geneva, Switzerland, 2025; p. 605.

metrology

MDPI

Article

Effect of Dispersed Particle Concentration on Photoacoustic Flowmetry Using Low-Frequency Transducers

Haruka Tsuboi, Taichi Kaizuka and Katsuaki Shirai *

Department of Mechanical Engineering, Graduate School, Shibaura Institute of Technology, 3-7-5 Toyosu, Koto-City, Tokyo 135-8548, Japan
* Correspondence: kshirai@shibaura-it.ac.jp

Abstract

Photoacoustic (PA) velocimetry offers a promising solution to the limitations of conventional techniques for measuring blood flow velocity. Given its moderate penetration depth and high spatial resolution, PA imaging is considered suitable for measuring low-velocity blood flow in capillaries located at moderate depths. High-resolution measurements based on PA signals from individual blood cells can be achieved using a high-frequency transducer. However, high-frequency signals attenuate rapidly within biological tissue, restricting the measurable depth. Consequently, low-frequency transducers are required for deeper measurements. To date, PA flow velocimetry employing low-frequency transducers remains insufficiently explored. In this study, we investigated the effect of the concentration of particles that mimic blood cells within vessels under low-concentration conditions. The performance of flow velocity measurement was evaluated using an ultrasonic transducer (UST) with a center frequency of 10 MHz. The volume fraction of particles in the solution was systematically varied, and the spatially averaged flow velocity was assessed using two different distinct analysis methods. One method employed a time-shift approach based on cross-correlation analysis. Flow velocity was estimated from PA signal redpairs generated by particles dispersed in the fluid, using consecutive pulsed laser irradiations at fixed time intervals. The other method employed a pulsed Doppler method in the frequency domain, widely applied in ultrasound Doppler measurements. In this method, flow velocity redwas estimated from the Doppler-shifted frequency between the transmitted and received signals of the UST. For the initial analysis, numerical simulations were performed, followed by experiments based on displacement measurements equivalent to velocity measurements. The target was a capillary tube filled with an aqueous solution containing particles at different concentration levels. The time–domain method tended to underestimate flow velocity as particle concentration increased, whereas the pulsed Doppler method yielded estimates consistent with theoretical values, demonstrating its potential for measurements at high concentrations.

Keywords: photo-acoustics; particle concentration; velocimetry; pulsed Doppler; cross-correlation; spatial resolution; measurement uncertainty

1. Introduction

Blood flow measurement is essential for detecting abnormalities in the human body. In patients with diabetes, the amount of low-density lipoprotein cholesterol in the blood increases, accumulating beneath the endothelial cells of blood vessels and forming substances known as plaques. These substances accumulate, and can lead to peripheral artery disease, thereby resulting in abnormal blood flow. In cases of peripheral artery disease, small vessels in the feet tend to become clogged, which can eventually lead to difficulty in walking [1]. Therefore, detecting abnormalities in the body before they progress into serious diseases through blood flow measurement is highly effective.

Existing diagnostic methods for blood flows include ultrasound Doppler and laser Doppler methods. In the ultrasound Doppler method, the blood velocities are estimated by measuring the frequency shifts between the transmitted and received waves [2,3]. Although it enables deep tissue measurement because of the low scattering of sound waves in the body, it has low spatial resolution because it is difficult to distinguish between the reflected waves from the target and those from surrounding tissues. The laser Doppler method [4,5] estimates flow velocities from Doppler shifts of the frequencies of the scattering light caused by the particles' motions through the region where a pair of laser beams are focused. This method offers a high spatial resolution due to significant differences in the optical absorption characteristics of tissues. However, the strong scattering of light within the body limits measurements to shallow depths near the skin surface. In this study, we focus on blood flow measurement using PA technology [6]. Photoacoustics enables the measurement of microvessels at moderate depths that can not be measured using conventional methods, with the advantage of differences in optical absorption contrast of tissues and the deep penetration of ultrasound [7]. Table 1 lists a comparison of the resolution and measurement depth of ultrasound Doppler, laser Doppler, and PA flowmetry (PAF) [8]. PAF includes optical resolution (OR) and acoustic resolution (AR). In OR-PAF, successful measurements were confirmed using animal blood; however, it requires focused light inside the tissue, and thus the measurement depth is limited to near the skin surface, which restricts utilizing the potential of photoacoustics to measure at moderate depths [9]. AR-PAF enables deep-tissue measurements by diffusing laser light and acquiring localized PA signals using a focused probe. Brunker and Beard reported OR-PAF measurements using particle suspension [10]; however, these were limited to concentrations one order of magnitude lower than the actual blood volume ratio, and measurements at the high concentrations required for actual blood have not been achieved. In addition, for the spatial resolution, OR-PAF requires the ability to distinguish individual particles, meaning that the spatial resolution of PA ultrasound must be smaller than the inter-particle distance by principle. This necessitates a receiver element with a frequency bandwidth exceeding tens of MHz [11]. On the other hand, high-frequency ultrasound attenuates easily within the body and is unsuitable for deep measurements, which makes low-frequency measurements necessary [12]. Recently, flowmetry based on a series of reconstructed three-dimensional images redhas been implemented in three-dimensional PA tomography [13,14]. In their measurements, the magnitude and direction of blood flow velocities were estimated based on the image processing of the reconstructed volume fields of the blood vessels. However, their processing is based on the reconstructed images that suffer from the imperfect reconstruction of the blood vessels [15]. Flowmetry based on a physical principle is expected.

Table 1. Comparison of measurement performance of existing techniques for blood flow velocity.

	Resolution	**Measurement Depth**
Ultrasound Doppler	Several hundred micrometers	Several hundred millimeters
Laser Doppler	Several micrometers	Several millimeters
redPhotoacoustic	Tens to hundreds micrometers	A few to several tens redof millimeters

In this study, flow velocity measurements are conducted using a low-frequency ultrasound transducer (UST). The volume ratio of the particles to the solution is varied to 1%, 5%, 10% for investigating how the volume ratio affects the accuracy of the low-frequency UST. In addition, time–domain analysis using the time-shift method and frequency–domain analysis using the pulsed wave (PW) Doppler method are performed to compare the results.

The rest of this manuscript is organized as follows. In Section 2, we explain the principles of measurement methods with the limit of measurement uncertainty. In Section 3, we describe the methods and conditions used in both numerical analysis and experiments. In Section 4, we present the results of the numerical analysis and measurements in the experiments. The results are discussed concerning the volume fraction of particles (VFPs) and different measurement methods: time-shift method and PW Doppler method. In Section 5, we present the conclusions of this study.

2. Principle

2.1. Time-Shift Method

The velocity of an absorbing object is obtained as the displacement of the object divided by a time difference of the pulsed irradiation of light [10]. The displacement is measured as a product of the sound speed multiplied by the time difference of the arrival time of a pair of PA waves detected by a UST. The time difference arises because of object movement; otherwise, it remains zero. The sign of the time difference indicates the direction of object motion. For calculating the time difference of arrival times, a cross-correlation (CC) analysis is used for signal processing. The CC of a pair of PA waves enables evaluating the time difference, assuming the object velocity is unchanged during the emission of the signal pair. The measurement performance of the time-shift method has been redextensively investigated in a previous study [16].

We consider a pair of continuous PA signals in the time domain, $x(t)$ and $y(t)$. If the CC function is denoted as $R(red\tau)$, and time-shift is τ, then $R(\tau)$ can be expressed as

$$R(\tau) = \int_{-\infty}^{\infty} x(t)y(t-\tau)dt. \tag{1}$$

Next, we consider the discrete case. Let us take two discrete data sets $x[j]$ and $y[j]$, with j being their index. If the CC function in the discrete case is denoted as $r[k]$ with k being the shift index, and then, $r[k]$ can be expressed as

$$r[k] = \sum_{j=-\infty}^{\infty} x[j]y[j-k]. \tag{2}$$

The CC function shifts when there is a phase difference between the signals before and after the object movement. This shift enables us to determine the shift amount n at which the correlation value between the signals before and after movement is maximized. The product of this value and the time resolution of the oscilloscope dt corresponds to the difference in signal arrival time. Therefore, the time difference t_p can be obtained as

$$t_p = n\, \mathrm{d}t. \tag{3}$$

We set the time interval of successive pulse irradiations Δt, the particle displacement during the time interval L, speed of sound c, time difference in the arrival of the signal t_p, resolution of the time dt, and amount of data shift n. The data shift n is defined as the value at which the CC between the two signals reaches its maximum. Then the velocity v can be expressed as follows.

$$v = \frac{L}{\Delta t} = \frac{cndt}{\Delta t \cos\theta}. \quad (4)$$

2.2. Pulsed-Wave Doppler Method

The PW Doppler method is a technique used in ultrasound Doppler measurements. In ultrasound Doppler, an ultrasound wave is transmitted toward the target, and the reflected wave from the target is received. The frequency spectrum of the reflected wave shifts from that of the transmitted wave (Doppler shift when the target is in motion) [12]. The flow velocity is measured based on this Doppler frequency. We verify this method using PA waves. When pulsed lasers are sequentially irradiated with a time shift onto light-absorbing particles dispersed in a fluid, the generated PA signals exhibit a phase shift because of the Doppler effect caused by particle motion. The Doppler frequency can be determined, from this phase difference and the flow velocity v can be calculated. The theoretical expression for the PW method is

$$v = \frac{f_d c}{f_{pho} \cos\theta}. \quad (5)$$

Here, f_d, c, f_{pho} and θ represents the Doppler frequency, speed of sound, frequency of the PA wave, and angle between the target and the probe axis of the UST, respectively. Figure 1a shows a sine wave with a phase shift of $-\pi/8$ from the original wave. When the phase shift is small, the value of the convolution integral at the zero shift approaches 1. Figure 1b shows a sine wave with a phase shift of $-\pi$, which results in an inverse phase compared to the original wave, yielding an integral value of -1. Figure 1c shows a sine wave with a phase shift of $-15\pi/8$, and the corresponding integral value becomes 0. By shifting the phase in steps of $-\pi/8$ and calculating the convolution integral value at each zero shift, the integral value first decreases and then increases again. This behavior is plotted in Figure 1d. The resulting waveform in Figure 1d has a period T_d, which corresponds to the time it takes for the PA wave to shift by one wavelength. The Doppler frequency can be obtained by taking the inverse of this period. Since PA waves are broadband, it is difficult to determine their frequency precisely. Therefore, the PA signal is processed with a fast Fourier transform (FFT), and a bandpass filter is applied around the frequency peak to approximate a redsingle-wavelength signal, determining the PA frequency f_{pho}. Moreover, filtering helps approximate a single-wavelength signal and facilitates the observation of waveforms such as those shown in Figure 1 because actual PA signals include multiple frequency components.

2.3. Directional Characteristics of UST

An UST exhibits either directional or omnidirectional characteristics. A fully directional UST has an extremely narrow, cylindrical measurement volume. In this case, more than one absorber does not exist at the same distance from the transducer, and thus, the PA signals are not spatially averaged. An omnidirectional UST spatially averages PA signals generated from absorbers located at the same distance from the transducer. Variations between adjacent particles are smoothed out when the distance between particles is smaller than the spatial resolution, thereby resulting in spatial averaging. A focused UST may exhibit intermediate characteristics between the directional and omnidirectional types because it forms a narrow cylindrical measurement volume at the focal point. The directional and omnidirectional characteristics of USTs were investigated using k-Wave: a redMATLAB® R2023b Toolbox for the time–domain simulation of acoustic wave fields [17].

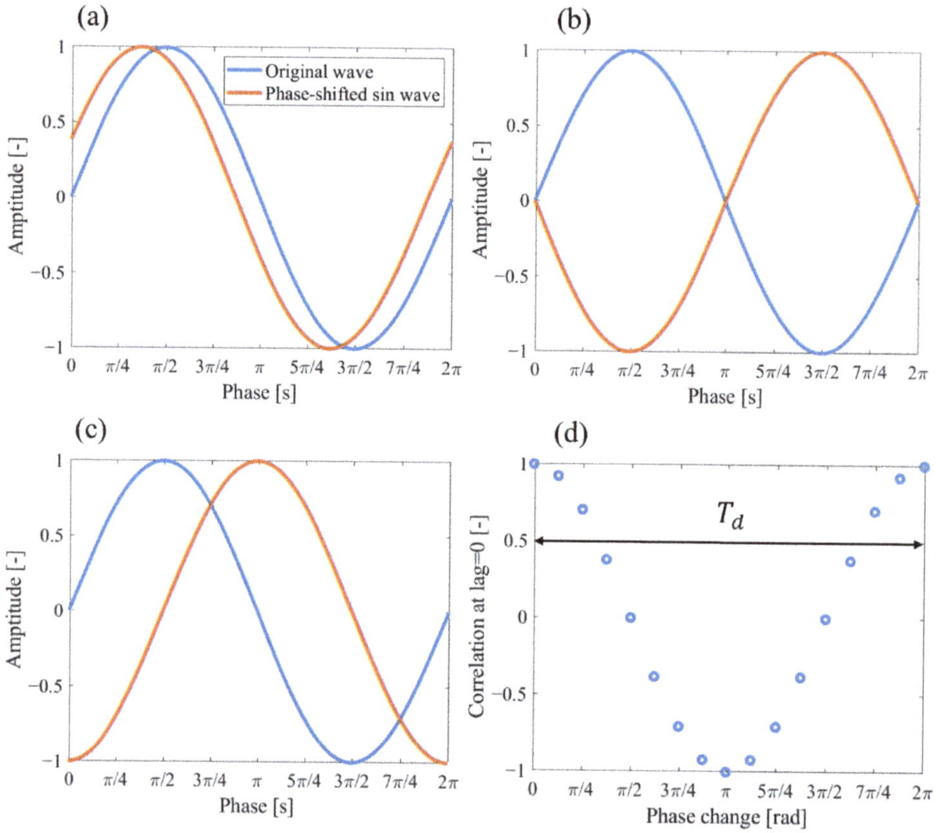

Figure 1. Theoretical diagram of Doppler frequency analysis using the PW Doppler method: (**a**) time signal with a phase shift of $-\pi/8$, (**b**) time signal with a phase shift of $-\pi$, (**c**) time signal with a phase shift of $-3\pi/2$, and (**d**) variation of correlation values with a phase change.

2.4. Uncertainty Limit

The measurement uncertainty of the flowmetry includes a statistical part contributed by randomly changing samples and a biased one intrinsic in the method or instrument. The statistical part can be reduced by acquiring a greater quantity of samples, whereas the biased part remains constant. One can recall the concept of the Cramér-Rao Lower Bound (CRLB) in the statistical signal processing to estimate the uncertainty limit [18]. Although the lower limit by the CRLB originates from the statistical process, it contributes to the uncertainty as a bias. The CRLB provides a base value of uncertainty at a given condition of the signal-to-noise ratio (SNR). In the time-shift method, the deviation $\Delta\tau$ of time shift τ caused by electronic noise and uncorrelated physical processes is referred to as a jitter error. The lower bound of the jitter error based on the CRLB under a given SNR condition was derived by [19] as

$$\sigma(\Delta\tau - \hat{\Delta\tau}) \geq \sqrt{\frac{3}{2f_0^3\pi^2T(B^3+12B)}\left\{\frac{1}{\rho^2(1+\mathrm{SNR}^{-2})^2-1}\right\}}, \tag{6}$$

where σ, f_0, T, B, redand ρ redrepresent the jitter error, center frequency, time window length, fractional bandwidth, normalized CC coefficient, and signal-to-noise ratio, respectively. Based on the experimental conditions, the center frequency f_0 was set to 10 MHz, time window T to 3 μs, and fractional bandwidth B to 1.2. The normalized cross-correlation coefficient ρ strongly depends on the SNR, and therefore the CRLB was calculated by varying ρ between 0.8 and 1.

3. Methods and Conditions

The UST used in this study had a focal diameter of 2 mm with the performance regarded as intermediate between directional and omnidirectional USTs described in Section 2.3. The characteristics of both directional and omnidirectional USTs were investigated using numerical analysis.

3.1. Numerical Analysis

3.1.1. Directionality of UST

The characteristics of a fully directional UST were investigated using numerical analysis. A computational grid of 150 × 150 × 150 points with a spacing of 15 μm was generated. An omnidirectional sensor was placed at the position (20, 75, 75). The sensor characteristics were set with a center frequency of 10 MHz and a frequency range from 3.8 MHz to 16.2 MHz. A spherical initial pressure source simulating a particle was placed along a single direction, coaxial with the sensor to reproduce the characteristics of a directional UST. The center of the sphere was positioned along the line from (50, 75, 75) to (150, 75, 75), and a spherical initial pressure with a diameter of 50 μm was generated for each center coordinate. The number of particles N was varied from 1 to 100, and a numerical simulation was performed for each case.

3.1.2. Non-Directionality of UST

The characteristics of a nondirectional UST were investigated using numerical analysis. A computational grid of 150 × 150 × 150 points with a spacing of 15 μm was generated. An omnidirectional sensor was placed at the position (20, 75, 75). The sensor characteristics were set with a center frequency of 10 MHz and a frequency range from 3.8 MHz to 16.2 MHz. Particles were randomly distributed according to each VFP within the coordinate range from (25, 25, 25) to (125, 125, 125) to reproduce the features of an omnidirectional sensor. Spherical initial pressures with a diameter of 50 μm were generated at each particle position. The VFP was varied from 0.01% to 40%, and a numerical simulation was performed for each case. The Wigner–Seitz radius was computed to compare the weighted average of frequency spectrum (WAFS) with the inter-particle distance. Assuming the effective volume occupied by a single particle as a sphere, the total solution volume V was divided by the number of particles N, and the radius of this sphere was referred to as the Wigner–Seitz radius r_s.

$$r_s = \left(\frac{3V}{4\pi N} \right)^{\frac{1}{3}}. \tag{7}$$

Using the Wigner–Seitz radius r_s and particle radius r, the inter-particle distance g was calculated under the assumption that the particles were uniformly arranged.

$$g = 2(r_s - r). \tag{8}$$

3.2. Experimental Apparatus

The experimental setup for the time-shift method is shown in Figure 2. A particle suspension prepared by mixing black particles with a solution was used as the measurement target. The suspension was injected into a silicone tube with outer and inner diameters of 1.5 mm and 1.0 mm, respectively. We used black paramagnetic polyethylene particles with a specific gravity of 1.2 and a particle diameter in a range of 53–63 μm (redCospheric: Santa Barbara, California, USA, BKPMS-1.2 53–63 μm). The solution was prepared by mixing water and glycerol at a mass ratio of 1:4.2 to prevent the particles from settling; this resulted in a specific gravity of 1.2. An Nd:YAG pulsed laser with a wavelength of 532 nm and a pulse duration of 5–9 ns (redRayture Systems: Shinjuku, Tokyo, Japan, GAIA Dual) was used as the irradiation source. Although the maximum repetition rate of a single laser was around 20 Hz, two lasers were used in combination, and the pulse interval was controlled using a function generator (redRigol Technologies: Suzhou, China, DG1022Z) and a delay generator (Quantum Composers: Bozeman, Montana, USA, 9618). A focused UST (redEvident Scientific: Shinjuku, Tokyo, Japan, V311-SU) with a center frequency of 10 MHz, a focal length of 30 mm, and a focal diameter of 2 mm was used. The UST was connected to an amplifier to amplify the signal, which was then recorded using an oscilloscope (redRohde & Schwarz: Munich, Bavaria, Germany, RTM3004). The timing of the laser irradiation was detected using a photodetector (redThorlabs: Newton, New Jersey, USA, DET10A2).

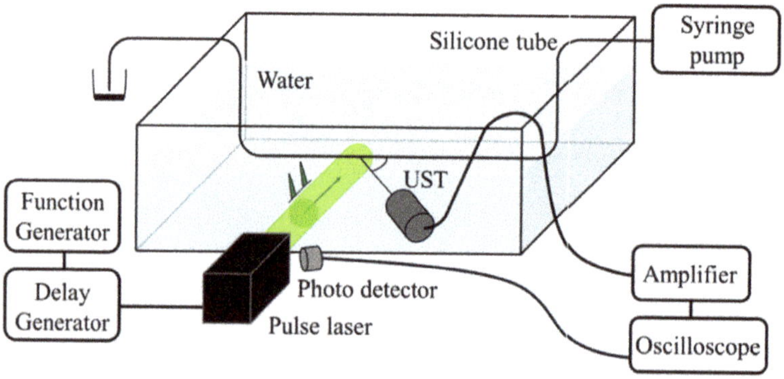

Figure 2. Experimental setup at the time-shift method: Black polyethylene particles were used as the light-absorbing particles, and a pulsed laser with a 532 nm wave length was irradiated. The time interval of the irradiation was set to 500 μs, and the actual timing was monitored with a photodetector. The generated photoacoustic waves were acquired using an UST with a center frequency of 10 MHz.

3.3. *Time-Shift Method*

A pulse signal with a frequency of 15 Hz was sent from the function generator to the delay generator, and the laser excitation and irradiation timing were set with reference to the first pulse signal. The laser irradiation interval was set to 500 μs. Each pulse emission timing was detected by a photodetector (response time: 1 ns). The VFP in the solution was set to 1%, 5%, 10%. The average flow velocity inside the tube, based on the flow rate setting of the syringe pump, ranged from 20 mm/s to 90 mm/s, and ten pairs of PA signals were acquired at 10 mm/s intervals. The photodetector and PA signals were interpolated 100 times using spline interpolation. The irradiation timing was determined by calculating the time derivative of the photodetector signal using the central difference scheme and identifying its maximum value. Based on this reference, the PA signals were extracted using an arbitrary number of data points. The data shift between the two PA signals was obtained via CC analysis. The measured flow velocity v_m corresponding to each preset flow velocity v_t was calculated from this data shift using Equation (4). The measured velocities were averaged over ten trials for each flow rate condition. The bias between the measured and preset velocities for each volume ratio was calculated using

$$Bias = \frac{v_m - v_t}{v_t} \times 100. \quad (9)$$

3.4. PW Doppler Method

The experimental configuration for the PW Doppler method is schematically shown in Figure 3. The displacement was estimated using the PW Doppler method. The flow tube into which the solution was injected was fixed using a device fabricated with a 3D printer. The setup was mounted on a redlinear translation stage (Thorlabs XR25P/M), which enabled movement in 10 μm increments. Agar (mixture mainly composed of agarose and agaropectin [20]) was added to the solution at a mass ratio of 10% to suppress particle movement within the flow tube. A photograph of the experimental setup was captured, and the angle between the flow tube and probe was measured using the software tool ImageJ 1.54d. The fixed flow tube was moved in steps of 10 μm, 20 μm, 30 μm, 40 μm, and 50 μm, and the signals were acquired ten times at each displacement. The displacement was calculated from the signal at 0 μm and the signals at each displacement; these values were compared with the actual displacements.

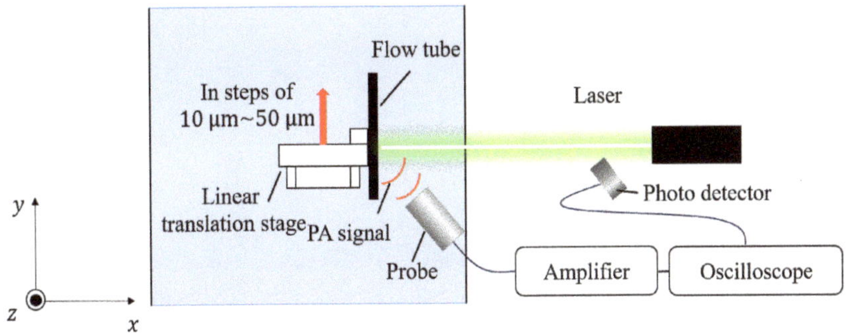

Figure 3. Experimental configuration at the PW Doppler measurement: Black polyethylene particles were used as light-absorbing particles, and a nano-second pulsed laser was irradiated. A particle suspension solidified with agar was placed in the flow tube, and it was displaced at equal intervals using a redlinear translation stage.

4. Results and Discussion

4.1. Numerical Analysis

4.1.1. Effect of Directional UST

Representative results of the numerical analysis redfor the directional UST are shown in Figure 4. The first column shows initial pressure distributions; the second column, acquired signals; and the third column, frequency spectra of the signals. Changes were observed in the frequency spectra with the VFP. We calculated the WAFS for each case to evaluate the variation. The results are shown in Figure 5, where the horizontal axis indicates the inter-particle distance for each number of particles, and the vertical axis shows the WAFS. When the inter-particle distance was longer than 50 μm, signals did not overlap, and the WAFS remained nearly constant. The low-frequency components decreased as the signals began to overlap, and the WAFS shifted toward higher frequencies. The WAFS dropped sharply, when the inter-particle distance fell below 0 μm. In other words, when the distribution changed from heterogeneous to homogeneous, the WAFS shifted toward the lower-frequency range. The center frequency of the UST was 10 MHz, which redcorresponded to a spatial resolution of around 75 μm. Even when compared to this value, the WAFS did not shift to lower frequencies below the spatial resolution. This implies that UST can individually identify particles within a heterogeneous target if the UST has perfect directivity, regardless of the axial spatial resolution.

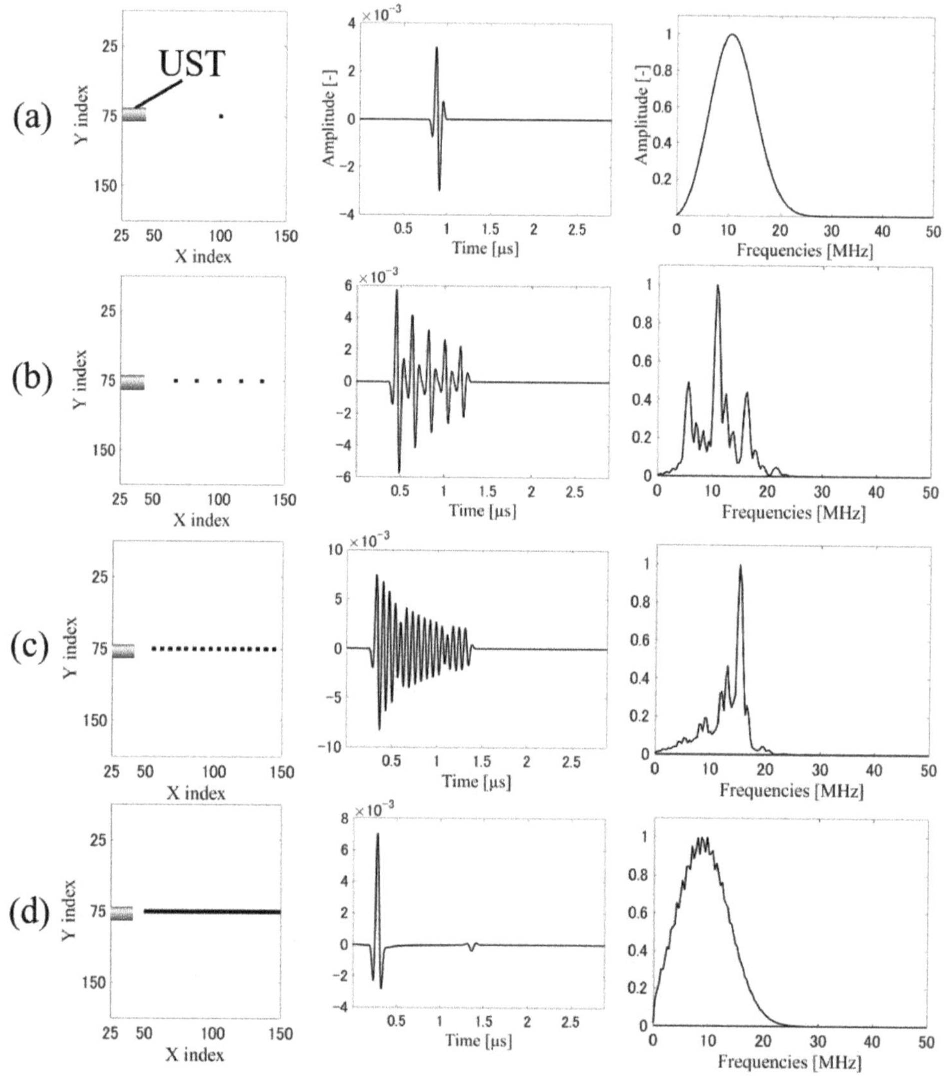

Figure 4. Simulation of directional UST: A 150 × 150 × 150 grid with a spacing of 15 μm was generated, and an omnidirectional sensor with a center frequency of 10 MHz and a frequency range from 3.8 MHz to 16.2 MHz was placed at (25, 75, 75). (**a**) Simulation results with a single particle: The spectrum peak spreads around 11 MHz in accordance with the characteristics of the sensor. (**b**) Simulation results with five particles: With the increase of inter-particle distance, the signals hardly overlap. Further the spectrum spreads around 10 MHz, following the characteristics of the sensor. (**c**) Simulation results with 16 particles: The signals overlap, which lead to a reduction in low-frequency components. (**d**) Simulation results with 100 particles: The particles overlap and form a cylindrical initial pressure distribution. The signals overlap, and the spectrum shifts toward the lower frequency range compared to (**a**).

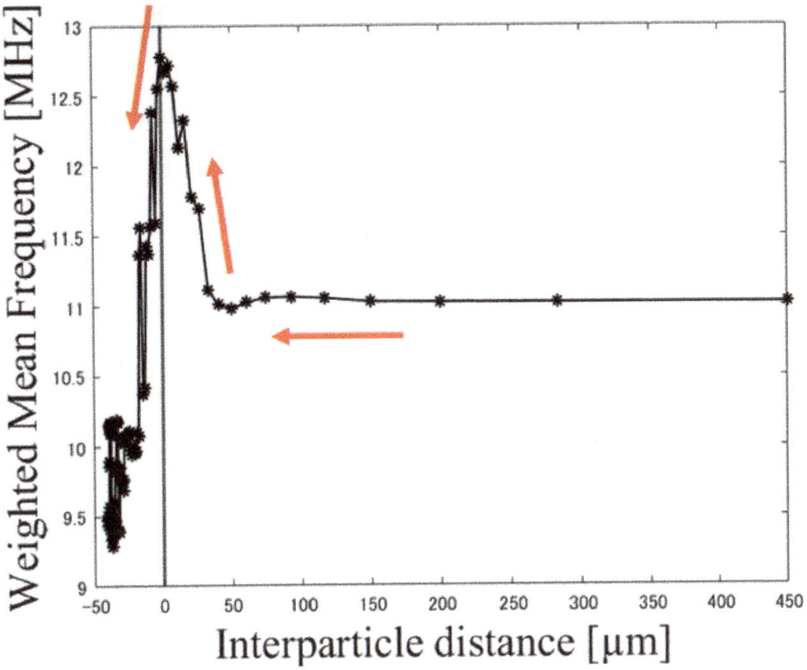

Figure 5. Relationship between inter-particle distance and weighted-averaged frequency spectrum (WAFS) in directional UST. The horizontal axis represents the particle spacing, and the vertical axis shows the WAFS of the frequency spectrum obtained from the simulation results. Up to around 50 µm, the WAFS remains nearly unchanged where the signals do not overlap. The low-frequency components decrease as the signals begin to overlap causing the WAFS to increase. When the particle spacing falls below 0 µm, which results in overlapping particles, a downshift occurs toward lower frequencies occurs. This continues until the particles completely overlap, forming a cylindrical initial pressure distribution.

4.1.2. Effect of Non-Directional UST

Representative results of the numerical analysis redfor the non-directional UST are shown in Figure 6. The first column shows the initial pressure distributions; the second column, acquired signals; and the third column, frequency spectra of the signals. Figure 7 shows the inter-particle distance and spatial resolution for each VFP. Figure 8 presents a comparison between the inter-particle distance and WAFS. By comparing Figures 7 and 8, it can be observed that the WAFS remains nearly constant when the inter-particle distance is well above the lateral spatial resolution (i.e., below 1% VFP). When the inter-particle distance approaches or falls below the spatial resolution (i.e., above 5% VFP), the WAFS shifts toward lower frequencies. This shift can be attributed to spatial averaging, which smooths out the variations between particles. Thus, under these conditions, the omnidirectional UST exhibits spatial averaging above 5% VFP, which treats particles within a heterogeneous target as a uniform medium.

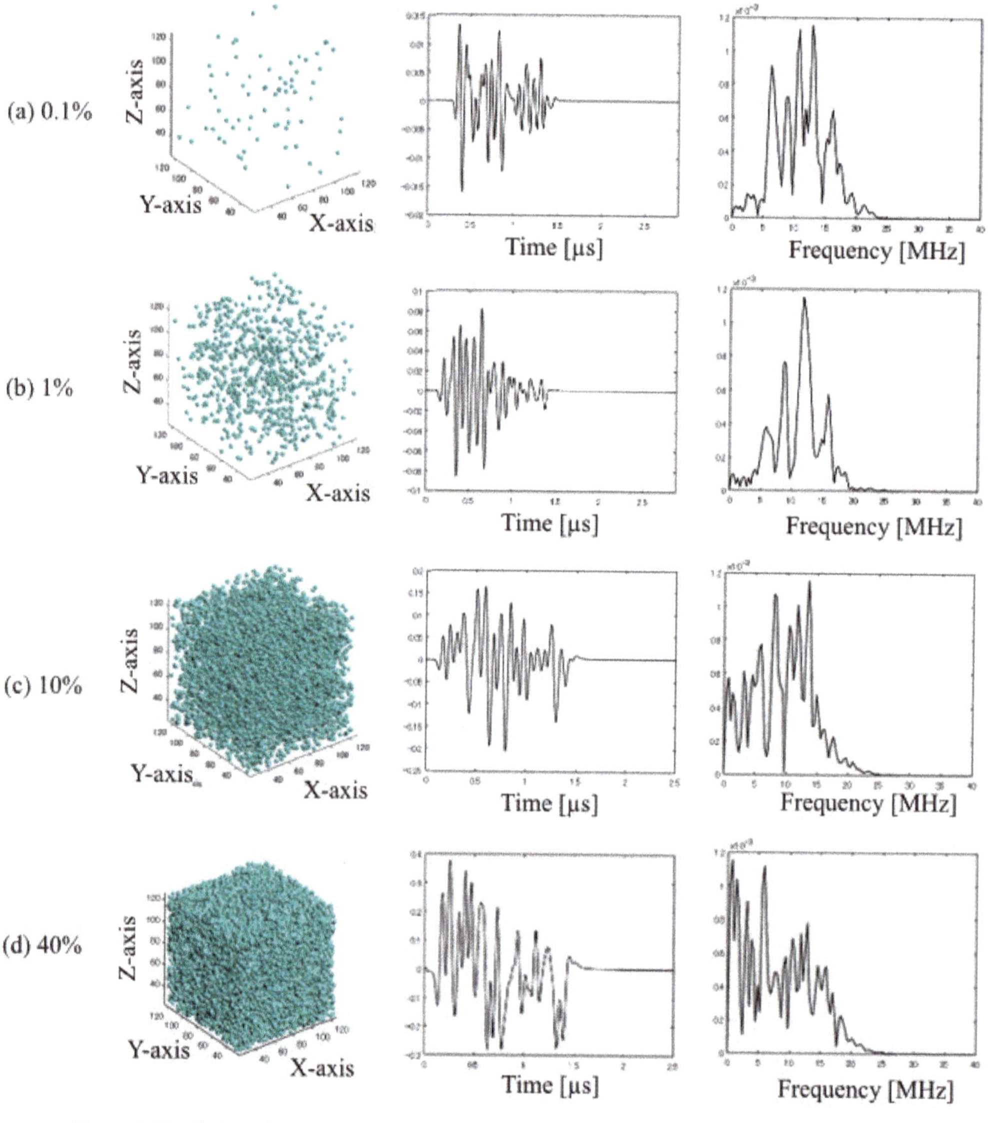

Figure 6. Simulation of omnidirectional UST. A 150 × 150 × 150 grid with a spacing of 15 μm was generated, and an omnidirectional sensor with a center frequency of 10 MHz and a frequency range from 3.8 MHz to 16.2 MHz was placed at (20, 75, 75). At 1% VFP, where the particle spacing is below the spatial resolution, the frequency spectrum follows the characteristics of the sensor and is distributed around 11 MHz. At 10% VFP, where the particle spacing is also below the spatial resolution, it increases the low-frequency components of the frequency spectrum. At 40% VFP, the low-frequency components further increase.

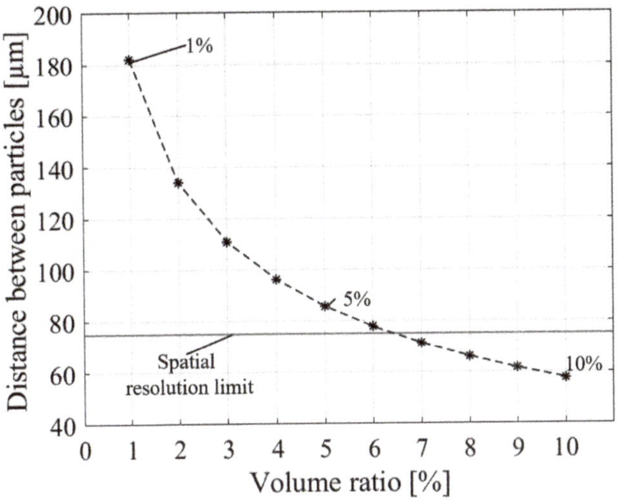

Figure 7. Particle spacing at each volume fraction of particles. The horizontal axis represents the VFP, and the vertical axis represents the particle spacing. Comparing the spatial resolution of 75 µm red (illustrated as horizontal line) with the particle spacing , at 1% VFP, the particle spacing is well above the spatial resolution, whereas at 10% VFP, it falls below the redresolution.

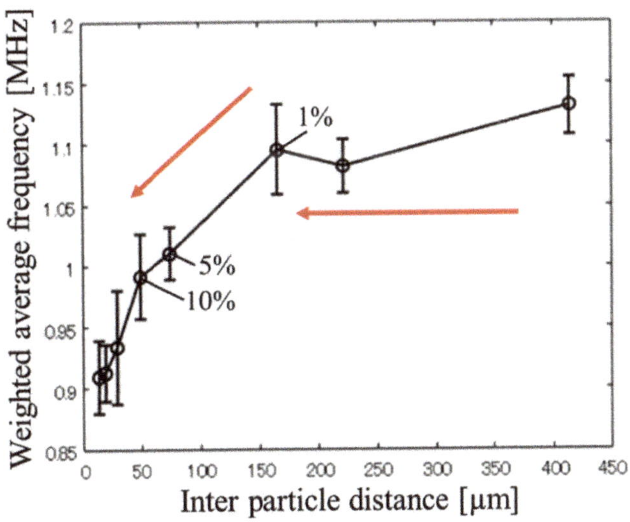

Figure 8. Relationship between particle spacing and spectrum in omnidirectional UST. The horizontal axis represents the inter-particle distance, and the vertical axis represents the WAFS of the frequency spectrum. For particle spacings below 1% VFP, which are well below the spatial resolution, the WAFS shows little change. The frequency spectrum shifts toward the lower frequencies when the particle spacing approaches or falls below the spatial resolution.

4.2. Measurements Based on the Time-Shift Method

4.2.1. Effect of VFP on Measurement

Figure 9 shows the measurement results of the flow velocities at 1% VPF. The mean bias is 5.7%, and the measured flow velocity changes linearly with the theoretical values. The uncertainty is 13 mm/s, which corresponds to a time delay of 3 ns. Here, the average SNR of the signal is 28 dB, and the normalized CC coefficient is 0.9. The CRLB was calculated by substituting these values into Equation (6). Under the experimental conditions, the CRLB was estimated to be ~1 ns, which is on the same order as the uncertainty in the experimentally obtained time shift. This implies that the uncertainty in the measurement is reasonable and likely caused by factors such as electronic noise and uncorrelated physical processes.

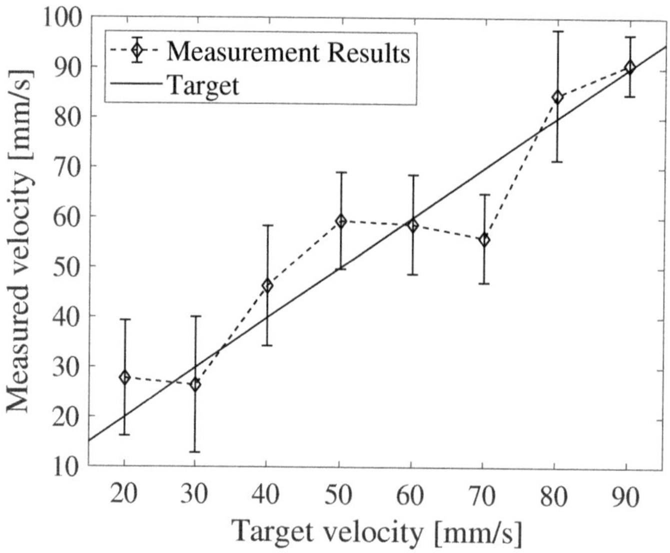

Figure 9. Flow velocity measurement results at 1% VFP. The average bias was 5.7%, and the measurement results varied linearly by the theoretical values.

The sound speed in the solution without particles was 1500 m/s at the experiment [21]. Under the same temperature, the sound speeds at each particle concentration were estimated based on existing models [22,23]. In general, the sound speed increases when solid particles are suspended in a liquid. The estimated sound speeds were 1505 m/s, 1528 m/s, and 1551 m/s for the concentrations of 1%, 5%, and 10%, respectively [21]. Figure 10 shows the measurement results when the variation of VPF. The target velocities were plotted in the graph for the individual VFPs taking into account of the viscosity increases with an assumption of Newtonian fluid with particle suspensions [24]. The average bias was 5.7% at 1% VFP, −42% at 5% VFP, and −68% at 10% VFP. Figure 11 shows representative frequency spectra for 1% VFP and 10% VFP. The measurement results show that increasing the VFP underestimates the flow velocity. Two factors can be considered in this regard: (1) the effect of the light penetration depth. Increasing the VFP increases the amount of light absorption, which limits light absorption to the low-speed region of the flow inside the tube, possibly leading to an underestimation of the flow velocity. (2) The other is the effect of the UST characteristics. The USTs have a narrow cylindrical measurement area at the focal volume, potentially exhibiting intermediate characteristics between directional and non-directional USTs. As shown in Section 4.1.1, directional USTs can individually identify particles in non-uniform media regardless of the lateral spatial resolution. The omnidirectional UST may not be able to individually identify particles when the inter-particle distance is below the spatial resolution, thereby resulting in spatial averaging because of the dominance of low-frequency components in the frequency spectrum. If the UST used in this experiment is omnidirectional, it may not individually identify particles or observe particle movement, potentially leading to an underestimation of flow velocity.

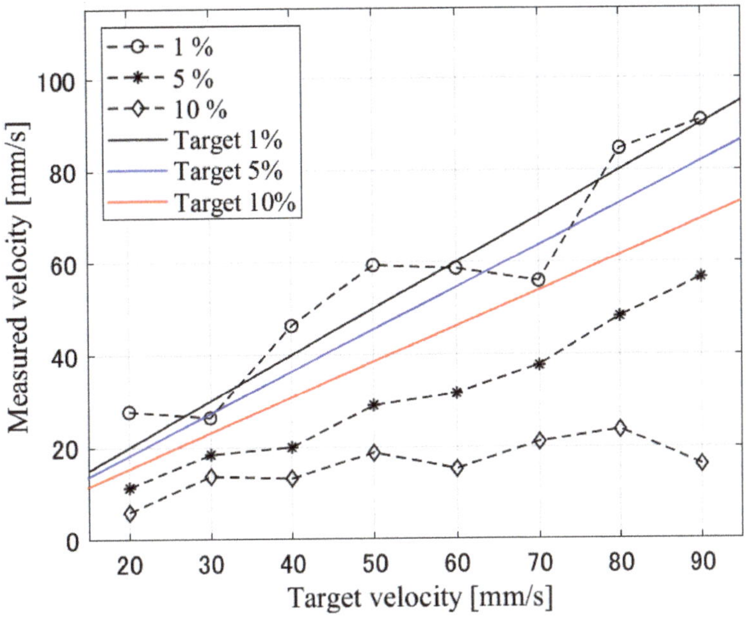

Figure 10. Measurement result of the flow velocity in the tube with different concentrations of the particles at 1% VFP, 5% VFP, and 10% VFP. The results are compared to the redcorresponding theoretically-expected value as the bulk mean velocity of the fully-developed laminar flow of Newtonian fluid based on the volumetric flowrate of the syringe pump. The results shows a tendency to underestimate with an increase in the VFP, and bias of 5.7% for 1% VFP, −36% for 5% VFP, and −65% for 10% VFP.

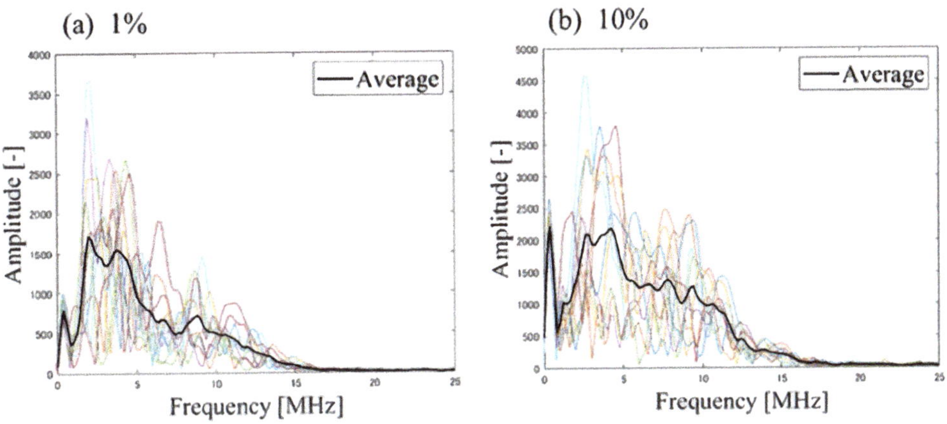

Figure 11. Comparison of frequency spectra of photoacoustic signals with different concentrations at (**a**) 1% VFP, (**b**) 10% VFP. At 10% VFP, low-frequency components are more dominant compared at 1% VFP.

4.2.2. Light Penetration Depth

Increasing the VFP increases the amount of light absorbed per unit volume, limiting light irradiation to the vicinity of the tube wall. When the flow inside the tube follows the velocity distribution of a fully-developed laminar flow (Hagen–Poiseuille flow) of a Newtonian fluid, the flow velocity will be underestimated if light irradiation is limited to the vicinity of the wall. The light absorption coefficient at each VFP was calculated using Lambert-Beer's law to investigate the effect of the light penetration depth [25].

Table 2 presents the absorption coefficients and attenuation ratios of the light energy before and after transmission through a 1 mm-thick glass cuvette for each VFP. The light energy was corrected based on the measurement results at VFP 0%. The absorption coefficients were calculated using the redLambert-Beer's law. The light attenuation ratios across the cross-sectional area of the flow tube were calculated using these values. The results are shown in Figure 12. The computational grid was set to 100 × 100 with an interval of 0.01 mm, and a circle with a radius of 0.5 mm was used as the cross-section of the flow tube. Assuming that light was irradiated from the positive X direction, the distance between each coordinate and the wall surface in the positive X direction was taken as the light path, and the light attenuation ratio was calculated using Lambert-Beer's law. Light is sufficiently irradiated near the wall surface in the positive X direction and attenuates as it progresses in the negative X direction. This was calculated based on the light absorption coefficient at each VFP. The light attenuation became more pronounced with an increase in VFP. The weighted flow velocity v_ω was calculated from the following equation, using this light attenuation ratio as the weight.

$$v_\omega(x,y) = \omega(x,y) \times v_{max}\left(1 - \frac{x^2 + y^2}{R^2}\right). \tag{10}$$

Table 2. Absorption coefficients and attenuation ratios at each VFP.

	Absorption Coefficient [mm^{-1}]	Attenuation Ratio
1% VFP	0.42	0.66
5% VFP	0.87	0.42
10% VFP	2.0	0.14

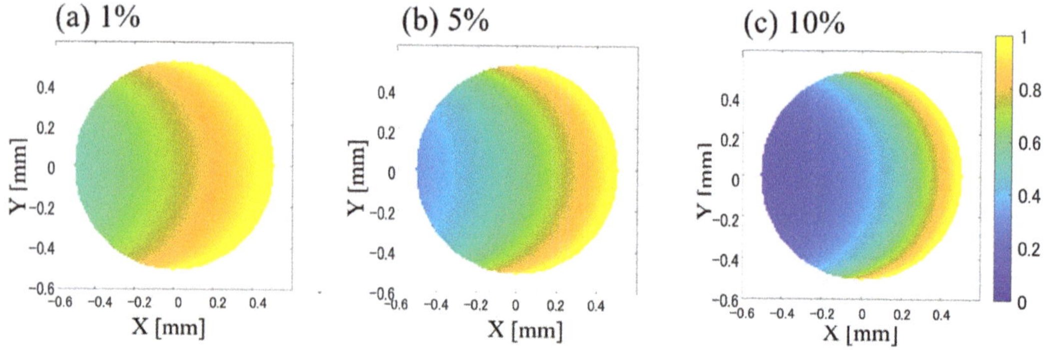

Figure 12. Light attenuation ratio across the cross-section of the flow tube. The light attenuation ratio in the cross-sectional area of the flow was calculated using the light absorption coefficient for each VFP. When the incident light is irradiated from the positive X-direction, the attenuation is smaller near the wall in the positive X-direction and increases toward the center. Higher VFP results in more pronounced light attenuation.

We calculated the weighted average flow velocity for each velocity range. The spatial distributions of the flow velocities were calculated for the cross-sectional area inside the tube. The results are shown in Figure 13. The redunderestimation rate was −3.2% at 5% VFP and −9.1% at 10% VFP, which is smaller than the redunderestimation rate of flow velocity measurements. Therefore, light penetration depth has a minor effect on the underestimation.

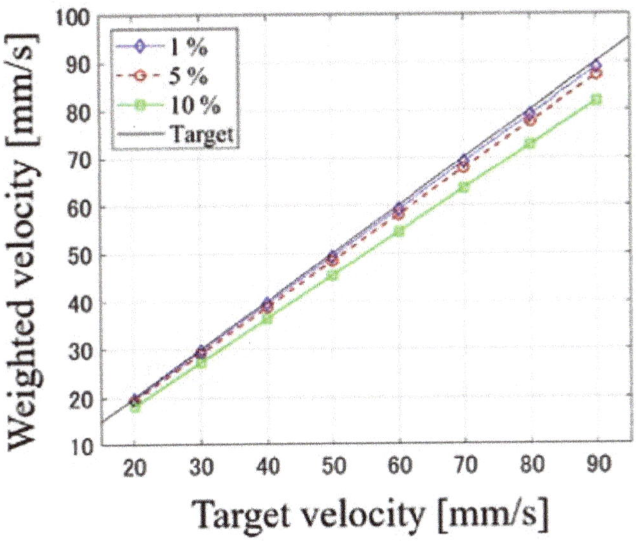

Figure 13. Weight-averaged flow velocity. The weight-averaged flow velocity was calculated using the light attenuation ratio across the cross-sectional area of the flow, weighted by the light absorption coefficient for each VFP. For all the VFP, the flow velocity changes linearly with the target.

4.2.3. Effect of UST Properties

Spatial averaging occurs in an omnidirectional UST when the inter-particle distance falls below the lateral spatial resolution, and low-frequency components become dominant. Figure 7 shows that the particle spacing is well above the spatial resolution at 1% VFP; however, it falls below it at 10% VFP. In addition, as shown in Figure 11, at 10% VFP, low-frequency components become dominant compared to those at 1% VFP. Under the experimental conditions of this study, increasing VFP causes the inter-particle distance to fall below the spatial resolution, which leads to spatial averaging. The spatial averaging prevents the identification of individual particles, thereby hindering the observation of particle movements and leading to an underestimation of flow velocity. This is likely because the focal diameter (2 mm) of the UST at the experiment was 40 times larger than the particle diameter (50 μm), leading to the omnidirectional effect becoming dominant.

4.2.4. Effect of Spatial Resolution

Directional UST can identify individual particles within an inhomogeneous target regardless of the axial spatial resolution. This suggests the possibility of improving the measurement performance at a high VFP by reducing the focal diameter and narrowing the measurement area. We describe the experimental results obtained using another UST with a smaller focal diameter (Japan Probe, B10K20I R30). We used a UST with a center frequency of 10 MHz and a focal diameter of 2.0 mm (hereafter UST (2.0 mm)), and another UST with a center frequency of 10 MHz and a focus diameter of 0.5 mm (hereafter UST (0.5 mm)). The experiment using the UST (0.5 mm) was conducted under the same conditions as that using the UST (2.0 mm). The particle concentration was set to 5% VFP and 10% VFP, and the measurement performance was compared. Figure 14 shows the measurement results of the flow velocity at 5% VFP and 10% VFP. At 5% VFP, the UST (2.0 mm) underestimated the flow velocity by 36%, whereas the UST (0.5 mm) underestimated it by 6.9%. At VFP 10%, the UST (2.0 mm) underestimated the flow velocity by 65%, whereas the UST (0.5 mm) underestimated it by 24%. Narrowing the measurement area reduced the degree of underestimation. This can be attributed to the increased effect of the directionality of a UST and the reduced influence of spatial averaging. However, given the 32% underestimation at 10% VFP, measurement at 40% VFP close to whole blood, would be difficult even with the UST (0.5 mm). Therefore, verification with a UST having an even smaller measurement area is desired to measure particle phantoms close to whole blood in the low-frequency range.

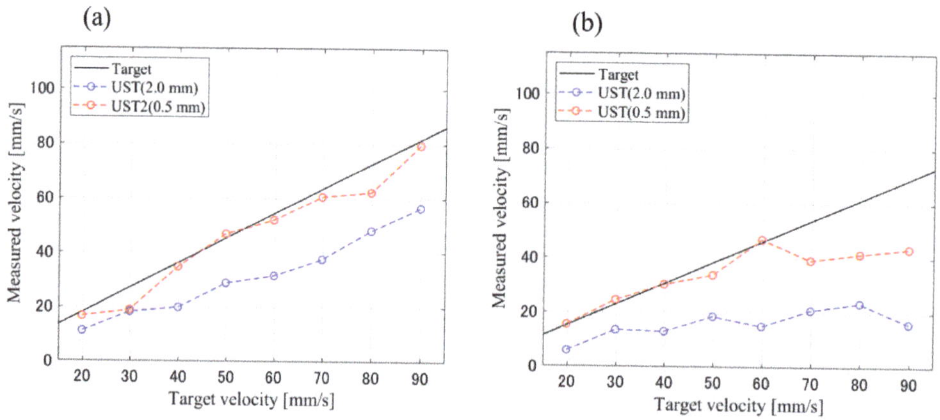

Figure 14. Comparison of the flow velocities measured with the two probes with different focal diameters for the different concentrations at (**a**) 5% VFP, (**b**) 10% VFP. One UST was with a focus diameter of 2.0 mm (UST (2.0 mm)), and the other with 0.5 mm (UST (0.5 mm)). The degree of the underestimate was consistently smaller for the UST (2.0 mm) compared to that for the UST (0.5 mm).

4.3. Measurements Based on the PW Method

Figure 15a shows the waveform obtained by interpolating the signal with zero displacement 1000 times using spline interpolation. The frequency spectrum is shown in Figure 15b. The weighted average frequency was 9.7 MHz. A bandpass filter was applied by setting the transmission frequency range to ±2.5 MHz around the weighted average frequency. Figure 15c shows the bandpass filtered PA signals. The application of the filter made the PA signal closer to a single wavelength. Figure 15d presents the frequency spectrum of the filtered signal. The weighted average frequency of the bandpass filtered signal was 7.6 MHz, which was defined as the frequency of the PA wave f_{pho}. Figure 16a shows a plot with the horizontal axis representing the time interval when the pulsed laser irradiation was applied at 20 Hz, and the vertical axis representing the normalized convolution integral values for each displacement. Figure 16b shows the result of applying spline interpolation 1000 times to Figure 16a. The angle between the flow tube and probe is $\theta = 49°$. The flow velocity v can be expressed using the PA wave frequency, Doppler frequency, and angle between the flow tube and the probe. Figure 15a shows the waveform extracted by averaging the signal with zero displacement ten times and interpolating it 1000 times using a spline interpolation. The frequency spectrum is shown in Figure 15b. The weighted average frequency was 9.7 MHz. A bandpass filter was applied by setting the transmitting frequency range to ±2.5 MHz around the weighted average frequency. Figure 15c shows the PA signal after the filtering. The application of the bandpass filter resulted in the PA signal approaching a single wavelength. Figure 15d presents the frequency spectrum after the filtering. The weighted average frequency after the filtering was 7.6 MHz, which was defined as the frequency of the PA wave f_{pho}. Figure 16a shows a plot with the horizontal axis representing the time interval when the pulsed laser irradiation was applied at 20 Hz, and the vertical axis representing the integral values of the normalized convolution for each displacement. Figure 16b shows the result of applying spline interpolation 1000 times to Figure 16a. Assuming that the particle moves 10 μm during a single pulsed irradiation, the estimated velocity is 0.2 mm/s. If the particle moves 20 μm and 30 μm, the estimated velocities are 0.4 mm/s and 0.6 mm/s, respectively. These values are used as the theoretical flow velocities. From Figure 16, the times at which the CC value reached 0.5 or 0 were obtained. These times correspond to 1/8 or 1/4 of the wave period, and their eightfold or fourfold reciprocals were defined as the Doppler frequency. The angle between the flow tube and probe is $\theta = 49°$. The flow velocity v can be expressed using the PA wave frequency, Doppler frequency, and angle between the flow tube and the probe as

$$v = \frac{f_d c}{f_{pho} \cos\theta} = \frac{0.28 \times 1500 \times 10^3}{4.79 \times 10^3 \times \cos 49°} = 0.12\ [\text{mm/s}]. \quad (11)$$

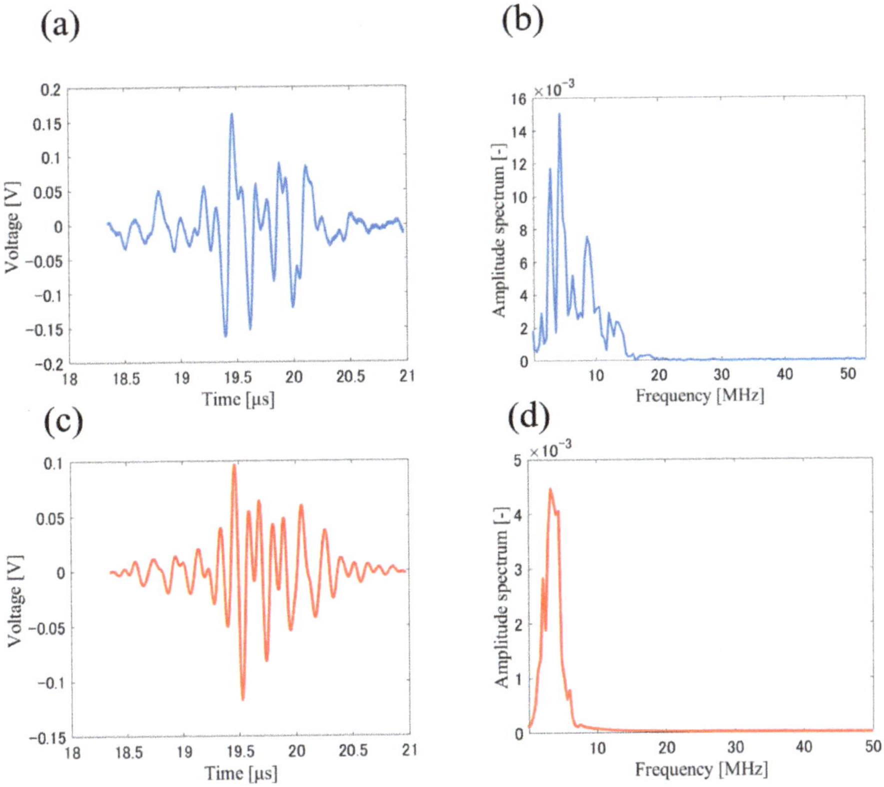

Figure 15. Typical time signals and their frequency spectra obtained in the experiment, (**a**) extracted time signal, (**b**) frequency spectrum of the time signal shown in (**a**), (**c**) bandpass filtered time signal shown in (**a**), (**d**) frequency spectrum of the bandpass filtered time signal shown in (**c**).

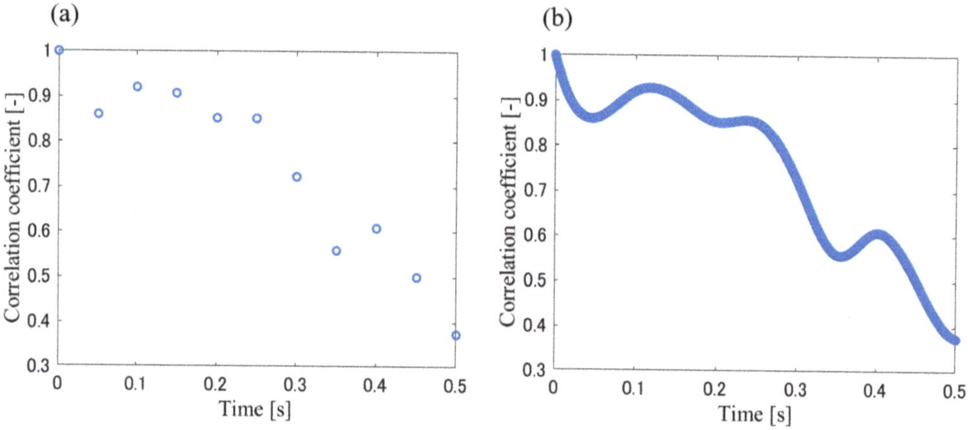

Figure 16. Comparison of the normalized cross-correlation distributions, (**a**) before the interpolation, (**b**) after the interpolation.

This corresponds to the result for a theoretical flow velocity of 0.2 mm/s. The measured results obtained using the time-shift method are compared with the theoretical values. The measurement results are shown in Figure 17. Each estimated flow velocity was measured ten times, and the average value was plotted. The standard deviations were shown as error bars. From the comparison in Figure 17, the time-shift method showed a bias from −9% to −33% compared to the theoretical flow velocity, while the PW Doppler method exhibited a bias ranging from −0.085% to −35%. Both the time-shift method and the PW Doppler method generally followed the theoretical values.

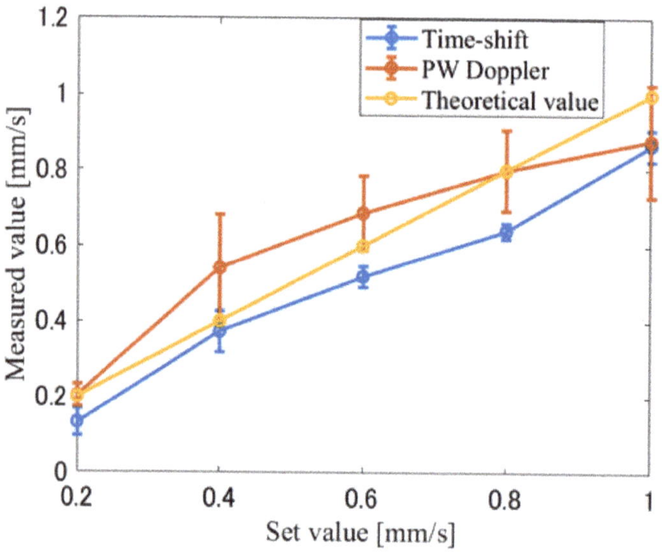

Figure 17. Comparison of the measurement results of the time-shift and PW Doppler methods with the theoretical values. The results of both methods are consistent with the theoretical values. The time-shift method shows a bias from −9% to −33%, whereas the PW Doppler method shows a bias from −0.085% to −35%.

5. Conclusions

We investigated the performance of the PA measurement of flow velocity at the different VFPs using an ultrasound transducer in the low-frequency range. The target VFPs were set to 1% VFP, 5% VFP, and 10% VFP dispersed in fluid flow in a silicone tube. The numerical analysis was performed on the directional and non-directional characteristics of a UST. In the experiment, the measurement of the flow velocities was conducted with the set velocities ranging from 20 mm/s to 90 mm/s. The two different methods were employed for the velocity measurements. The time-shift method is based on the CC of a pair of PA signals, whereas the PW Doppler method relies on the Doppler frequency shift of the PA signals. The following conclusions are drawn:

- The directivity characteristics of USTs was revealed with the numerical analysis. For a directional UST, the WAFS of the PA signal did not shift into the low-frequency direction if the inter-particle distance did not move toward lower frequencies. In other words, directivity USTs can discriminate individual particles in a heterogeneous target, regardless of the axial spatial resolution. On the other hand, for an omnidirectional UST, the WAFS of the PA signal shifted toward lower frequencies when the inter-particle distance was smaller than the lateral spatial resolution. This is considered to be due to spatial averaging and smoothing of variations between adjacent particles.
- From the results at 1% VFP, the time delay was 3 ns. The time delay was consistent in the order with the value of 1 ns predicted from the CRLB, indicating the lower bound of the jitter. The jitter includes factors such as electronic noise and uncorrelated physical processes.
- In the flow velocities measured at the different VFPs, the bias against the set velocity was 5.7% at 1% VFP, −36% at 5% VFP, and −65% at 10% VFP for the time-shift method. There was a tendency to underestimate the flow velocity with an increase in the VFP. The underestimation was not attributed to the penetration depth of the incident light based on the simulation of the attenuation of the irradiated light in the tube. The effect of light attenuation is minimal because the weight-averaged flow velocity exhibited linear variation with the VFP.
- On the effect of UST characteristics on the measurement, the inter-particle distance was smaller than the spatial resolution at 10% VFP, which resulted in the dominance of low-frequency components. With the increase of the VFP, the spatial averaging hindered the ability to distinguish individual particles, leading to an underestimation of the flow velocity for the time-shift method. Hence, an omnidirectionality of the UST was predominant in the high VFP conditions.
- In the measurement with a UST (2.0 mm), the bias relative to the set flow velocities was −36% at 5% VFP and −65% at 10% VFP for the time shift method. The reduction in the degree of underestimation was confirmed when using a focused UST (0.5 mm), as the stronger influence of the UST's directionality led to a smaller measurement volume. Biases of −6.9% at 5% VFP and −24% at a 10% VFP were obtained.
- In the displacement measurement experiment, both the time-shift method and the PW Doppler method generally agreed with the theoretical values.

These conclusions revealed that PAF using a 10 MHz UST can be performed with a focal diameter of around 2 mm at up to 1% VFP. However, at concentrations of 5% VFP or higher, the measurement performance deteriorated rapidly because of the effect of the omnidirectionality of a UST. Nevertheless, in the displacement measurement using the PW Doppler method, the results generally followed the theoretical values. The concentration of the particle suspension remained lower than that of actual blood. Therefore, future work should involve flow velocity measurements at concentrations closer to that of blood to investigate the effect of higher particle concentrations on measurement accuracy in realistic environments.

Author Contributions: Conceptualization, H.T. and K.S.; Methodology, H.T., T.K. and K.S.; Validation, H.T. and T.K.; Numerical analysis, T.K.; Experiments, H.T. and T.K.; Writing—Original draft, H.T. and K.S.; Writing—Review and editing, K.S.; Supervision, K.S.; Funding acquisition, K.S. All authors have read and agreed to the published version of the manuscript.

Funding: The redpresent study was entirely supported by the internal funding of the SIT.

Data Availability Statement: The data that support the findings of the present study are available upon reasonable request from the authors.

Conflicts of Interest: The author declare no financial or personal interests related to the results of the present study.

Abbreviations

The following abbreviations are used in this manuscript:

AR	Acoustic resolution
CC	Cross-correlation
CRLB	Cramér-Rao lower bound
FFT	Fast Fourier transform
OR	Optical resolution
PAF	Photoacoustic flowmetry
PA	Photo-acoustic
PD	Photo detector
PW	Pulsed wave
SNR	Signal-to-noise ratio
UST	UltraSound transducer
VFP	Volume fraction of particles
WAFS	Weight-averaged frequency spectrum
YAG	Yttrium aluminum garnet

References

1. Singh, M.S.; Jiang, H. Estimating both direction and magnitude of flow velocity using photoacoustic microscopy. *Appl. Phys. Lett.* **2014**, *104*, 253701. [CrossRef]
2. Satomura, S. Ultrasonic Doppler method for the inspection of cardiac functions. *J. Acoust. Soc. Am.* **1957**, *29*, 1181–1185. [CrossRef]
3. Szabo, T.L. *Diagnostic Ultrasound Imaging: Inside Out*, 2nd ed.; Academic Press: Oxford, UK, 2013.
4. Micheels, J.; Alsbjorn, B.; Sorensen, B. Laser Doppler flowmetry. A new non-invasive measurement of microcirculation in intensive care? *Resuscitation* **1984**, *12*, 31–39. [CrossRef]
5. Rajan, V.; Varghese, B.; van Leeuwen, T.G.; Steenbergen, W. Review of methodological developments in laser Doppler flowmetry. *Lasers Med. Sci.* **2009**, *24*, 269–283. [CrossRef]
6. Manohar, S.; Razansky, D. Photoacoustics: A historical review. *Adv. Opt. Photonics* **2016**, *8*, 586–617. [CrossRef]
7. Wang, L.H. *Photoacoustic Imaging and Spectroscopy*; CRC Press: Boca Raton, FL, USA, 2009.
8. Shiina, T. Novel Medical Imaging Technology by Integration of Optics and Ultrasound. *J. Jpn. Soc. Laser Surg. Med.* **2013**, *33*, 367–373. [CrossRef]
9. van den Berg, P.J.; Daoudi, K.; Steenbergen, W. Review of photoacoustic flow imaging: Its current state and its promises. *Photoacoustics* **2015**, *3*, 89–99. [CrossRef] [PubMed]
10. Brunker, J.; Beards, P. Velocity measurements in whole blood using acoustic resolution photoacoustic Doppler. *Biomed. Opt. Express* **2016**, *7*, 2789–2806. [CrossRef] [PubMed]
11. Bauer-Marschallinger, J.; Berer, T.; Grun, H.; Roitner, H.; Reitinger, B.; Burgholzer, P. Broadband high-frequency measurement of ultrasonic attenuation of tissues and liquids. *IEEE Trans. Ultrason. Ferroelectr. Freq. Control* **2012**, *59*, 2631–2645. [CrossRef]
12. Ito, M.; Motizuki, T. *Ultrasound Diagnostic Equipment*; Corona Publishing: redBunkyo, Tokyo, Japan, 2002; pp. 120–154.

13. Godefroy, G.; Arnal, B.; Bossy, E. Full-visibility 3D imaging of oxygenation and blood flow by simultaneous multispectral photoacoustic fluctuation imaging (MS-PAFI) and ultrasound Doppler. *Sci. Rep.* **2023**, *13*, 2961. [CrossRef]
14. Zhang, Y.; Olick-Gibson, J.; Khadria, A.; Wang, L.V. Photoacoustic vector tomography for deep haemodynamic imaging. *Nat. Biomed. Eng.* **2024**, *8*, 701–711. [CrossRef]
15. Rietberg, M.T.; Gröhl, J.; Else, T.R.; Bohndiek, S.E.; Manohar, S.; Cox, B.T. Artifacts in photoacoustic imaging: Origins and mitigations. *Photacoustics* **2025**, *45*, 100745. [CrossRef] [PubMed]
16. Fujinami, K.; Shirai, K. Performance evaluation of cross-correlation based photoacoustic measurement of a single object with sinusoidal linear motion. *Appl. Sci.* **2023**, *13*, 13202. [CrossRef]
17. Treeby, B.E.; Cox, B.T. k-Wave: MATLAB toolbox for the simulation and reconstruction of photoacoustic wave fields. *J. Biomed. Opt.* **2010**, *15*, 021314. [CrossRef] [PubMed]
18. Kay, S.M. *Fundamentals of Statistical Processing, Volume I: Estimation Theory*; Prentice-Hall: Hoboken, NJ, USA, 1993.
19. Walker, W.F.; Trahey, G.E. A fundamental limit on delay estimation using partially correlated speckle signals. *IEEE Trans. Ultrason. Ferroelectr. Freq. Control* **1995**, *42*, 301–308. [CrossRef]
20. Wang, C.; Long, J.; Li, X.; Zhou, X.; Chen, L.; Qiu, C.; Jin, Z. Preparation of agar polysaccharides and biological activities and relationships of agar-derived oligosaccharides and monosaccharides: A review. *Int. J. Biol. Macromol.* **2025**, *295*, 139552. [CrossRef]
21. Greenspan, M.; Tschiegg, C.E. Speed of Sound in Water by a Direct Method. *J. Res. Natl. Bur. Stand.* **1957**, *59*, 249–254. [CrossRef]
22. Epstein, P.S.; Carhart, R.R. The absorption of sound in suspensions and emulsions. I. Water fog in air. *J. Acoust. Soc. Am.* **1953**, *25*, 553–565. [CrossRef]
23. Allegra, J.R.; Hawley, S.A. Attenuation of sound in suspensions and emulsions: Theory and experiments. *J. Acoust. Soc. Am.* **1972**, *51*, 1545–1564. [CrossRef]
24. Krieger, I.M.; Dougherty, T.J. A mechanism for non-Newtonian flow in suspensions of rigid spheres. *Trans. Soc. Rheol.* **1959**, *3*, 137–152. [CrossRef]
25. Mayerhofer, T.G.; Pahlow, S.; Popp, J. The Bouguer-Beer-Lambert law: Shining light on the obscure. *ChemPhysChem* **2020**, *21*, 2029–2046. [CrossRef] [PubMed]

MDPI AG
Grosspeteranlage 5
4052 Basel
Switzerland
Tel.: +41 61 683 77 34

Metrology Editorial Office
E-mail: metrology@mdpi.com
www.mdpi.com/journal/metrology

www.ingramcontent.com/pod-product-compliance
Lightning Source LLC
Chambersburg PA
CBHW061822210926
51850CB00006B/775
* 9 7 8 3 7 2 5 8 7 0 5 0 9 *